THE SOVIET UNION
AND EASTERN EUROPE

A HANDBOOK

HANDBOOKS TO THE MODERN WORLD
  General Editor: Andrew C. Kimmens

WESTERN EUROPE
THE SOVIET UNION AND EASTERN EUROPE
THE MIDDLE EAST
AFRICA
ASIA
LATIN AMERICA AND THE CARIBBEAN
AUSTRALIA, NEW ZEALAND AND THE SOUTH PACIFIC
THE UNITED STATES AND CANADA

THE SOVIET UNION AND EASTERN EUROPE

Edited by
GEORGE SCHÖPFLIN

106371

Facts On File Publications
New York, New York • Oxford, England

First published in Great Britain in 1970 by Anthony Blond Ltd.
This completly revised and updated edition published in the
United States in 1986 by Facts on File Publications, 460 Park Avenue South,
New York, N.Y. 10016, in association with Muller, Blond & White,
55 Great Ormond Street, London WC1N 3HZ.

ISBN 0-8160-1260-1

10 9 8 7 6 5 4 3 2 1

Printed in Great Britain at The Bath Press, Avon

CONTRIBUTORS

TERENCE ARMSTRONG is emeritus reader in Arctic studies at the Scott Polar Research Institute, Cambridge. He has traveled widely in the Arctic, has visited northern Siberia several times and is the author of *The Northern Sea Route*, *The Russians in the Arctic* and *Russian Settlement in the North*.

J. F. BROWN formerly director of research and then director, Radio Free Europe, resigned in 1983 and now lives in Oxford. He is the author of *The New Eastern Europe: the Khrushchev Era and After*, *Bulgaria under Communist Rule* and numerous articles and chapters in books on Eastern European affairs. He is writing a history of Eastern Europe since the invasion of Czechoslovakia.

ABRAHAM BRUMBERG is a former editor of the journal *Problems of Communism*. He has edited *Russia under Khrushchev* and *In Quest of Justice—Protest and Dissent in the Soviet Union Today*. He is also a contributing editor of the *New Republic*.

WILLIAM E. BUTLER studied law at Harvard University and holds doctorates in international law from Johns Hopkins University and the University of London. He is currently professor of comparative law at the University of London and directs the Centre for the Study of Socialist Legal Systems at University College, London. He has published books and articles on both the international and municipal aspects of socialist legal systems, including those in the Soviet Union, Eastern Europe, China and Mongolia.

WALTER D. CONNOR is professor of political science, Boston University, and fellow of the Russian Research Center at Harvard University. From 1976 to 1984 he directed Soviet and Eastern European studies at the Foreign Service Institute of the U.S. Department of State. He is the author of, among other books and articles, *Socialism, Politics and Equality*.

K. F. CVIIĆ is a broadcaster and journalist on the affairs of Yugoslavia, where he was born. He has lived in Britain since 1954, has worked on the staff of *The Economist* and is currently editor of *The World Today*.

JUDY DEMPSEY is Eastern European correspondent of the *Irish Times* and has broadcast extensively on the region for the British Broadcasting Corporation. She is a regular visitor to the area.

DAVID A. DYKER is lecturer in economics, School of European Studies, University of Sussex. He has published widely on the Soviet Union and Eastern Europe.

IAIN ELLIOT is senior lecturer in Soviet studies at Brighton Polytechnic. He is also a part-time editorial writer for *The Times*, as well as editor of *Soviet Analyst*.

JOHN ERICKSON is director of defense studies at the University of Edinburgh. His publications include *The Road to Stalingrad* and *The Road to Berlin*.

PETER FRANK is senior lecturer in Soviet politics in the department of Government at the University of Essex.

GEORGE GÖMÖRI was born in Budapest and left Hungary in 1956, completing his studies at St. Antony's College, Oxford. He is the author of *Polish and Hungarian Poetry 1945 to 1956* (1966) and coeditor (with Richard Burns) of the multilingual verse anthology *Homage to Mandelstam* (1981). He is currently lecturer in Slavonic studies at the University of Cambridge.

PHILIP HANSON is reader in Soviet economics at the University of Birmingham. His publications include *Trade and Technology in Soviet–Western Relations*.

NEIL HYAMS, a close observer of Soviet affairs for many years, has a particular interest in questions of nationalism. He has written under various pseudonyms.

EVERETT M. JACOBS, senior lecturer in the Division of Economic Studies, University of Sheffield, has written numerous articles on aspects of Soviet and Eastern European agriculture and Soviet local politics and government. He was editor of *Soviet Local Politics and Government* (1983).

JOHN KEEP, professor of Russian history at the University of Toronto, has written *The Rise of Social Democracy in Russia* (1963), *The Russian Revolution: A Study in Mass Mobilization* (1976), *The Debate on Soviet Power* (1979) and is the author of a number of articles on Soviet history and politics.

DAVID KIRBY is reader in history at the School of Slavonic and East European Studies, University of London. His publications include *Finland in the Twentieth Century*. He is currently working on the European labor movement during World War I.

GEORGE KOLANKIEWICZ is lecturer in sociology at the University of Essex and the author of numerous articles on Polish affairs. His publications include *Social Groups in Polish Society* (with David Lane). He is currently working on *The Politics of Reform in Poland*.

VLADIMIR V. KUSIN is deputy director, Radio Free Europe Research and Analysis Department, Munich. He is the author of several books and many articles on Czechoslovakia in particular and on Eastern Europe in general.

MALCOLM MACKINTOSH is a specialist on Soviet foreign policy and strategic questions. His publications include *Strategy and Tactics of Soviet Foreign Policy* and *Juggernaut: A History of the Soviet Armed Forces*.

MERVYN MATTHEWS is reader in the University of Surrey's linguistic and regional studies department. His publications include *Soviet Education, Class and Society in Soviet Russia* and *Privilege in the Soviet Union.*

MARTIN MCCAULEY is lecturer in Russian and Soviet institutions at the School of Slavonic and East European Studies, University of London. His books include *Marxism–Leninism in the German Democratic Republic: The Socialist Unity Party (SED)* and *The German Democratic Republic since 1945* (1983).

GARY MEAD is a researcher with Granada Television, who has written extensively on Polish affairs since 1980.

ALEX PRAVDA is lecturer in politics at the University of Reading. He has published widely on Eastern European politics and in particular on the working class in the Soviet Union and Eastern Europe. He was a contributor to R. L. Tőkés, ed., *Opposition in Eastern Europe* and to J. Triska and C. Gati, eds., *Blue-Collar Workers in Eastern Europe*, and was coeditor of *Trade Unions in Communist States.* He is currently completing a comparative study of workers and political change in the Soviet Union and Eastern Europe.

PETER REDDAWAY is senior lecturer in political science at the London School of Economics and Political Science. He has written extensively on opposition and dissent in the Soviet Union.

GEORGE SCHÖPFLIN is joint lecturer on Eastern European political institutions at the London School of Economics and Political Science and the School of Slavonic and East European Studies, University of London. He is the author of numerous studies on political institutions in Hungary and other Eastern European countries.

FRANCIS SETON, Official Fellow emeritus of Nuffield College, Oxford, has written numerous articles on the economies of the Soviet Union and Eastern Europe.

MICHAEL SHAFIR, who was born in Romania, is lecturer in political science at the University of Tel Aviv. His publications include *Romania—Political Stagnation or Simulated Change.*

VLADIMIR SOBELL is an analyst in the research department of Radio Free Europe.

GEOFFREY STERN is lecturer in international relations at the London School of Economics and Political Science and a regular broadcaster on communist affairs. His publications include *Fifty Years of Communism.*

VICTOR SWOBODA was until recently for many years senior lecturer in Russian and Ukrainian at the School of Slavonic and East European Studies of the University of London. He edited Taras Shevchenko's selected poetry, *Song out of Darkness* (1961), and has written on Soviet nationalities for the Open University and the journal *Conflict Studies*; he is currently writing a historical study of the Soviet nationalities.

DAVID TURNOCK is reader in the department of geography at the University of Leicester.

MARCUS WHEELER has since 1968 been professor of Slavonic studies at the Queen's University, Belfast.

CONTENTS

EASTERN EUROPE

Part Three: ECONOMIC

Part Four: SOCIAL

MAPS

CONTENTS

PREFACE

THE fate of the Soviet Union and Eastern Europe since World War II, the subject of this Handbook, has aroused endless debate and discussion among Western analysts of the area and among those who actually live there. There is hardly a single aspect of the history, politics, economics, social development or geography of communist-ruled Europe that is not contested. The inner meaning of this is that Western Europeans retain more than a passing interest in Soviet and Eastern European affairs; that there is major political disagreement—a contest over power—concerning the area; that politically determined criteria are regularly used to settle and to attack issues that academics, journalists, businesspeople and others would prefer to keep out of the political arena; and that therefore the contents of this Handbook will certainly prove unacceptable to some people. This is not only unavoidable, it is probably intellectually healthy as well. It shows that the study of communist politics retains its vitality. It should also be evident from the foregoing that the Handbook does not aspire to infallibility. Its contents have been put together from the standpoint of sympathetic but critical detachment. In general, the contributors analyze rather than prescribe, but it would be absurd to pretend that what they have written does not bear the marks of the culture in which they live. That culture is not the same as the culture found in the Soviet Union and Eastern Europe.

"The purpose of this volume is to provide both basic information and comment about the Soviet Union and the communist-ruled part of Europe." This statement of purpose, made in the Preface to the first edition of the Handbook in 1969, still stands unmodified. Some things have changed, however. A great deal more is known about the Soviet Union and Eastern Europe, and how the political systems there operate. We understand much better the nature of Soviet-type politics and Eastern-bloc political power, and how this power is used than was the case a decade and a half ago. I have tried to compile the second edition with this in mind, and I hope that the deepening of understanding is reflected in the contributions, with no loss of the information that a reference work of this kind is expected to provide.

My thanks go to all the contributors, both those who revised and rewrote what they had written for the first edition and those who contributed for the first time to the second. I am grateful to Margaret Budy, who gave me extensive help with putting the volume together and support during its compilation; to Penny Southgate, for having helped with some of the typing; to William Forwood, John Williams and George Kurian, for preparing and updating the sections on Basic Information and Comparative Statistics; to F. H. C. Tatham, for the index; and to Andrew C. Kimmens, general editor of the series Handbooks to the Modern World, who persuaded me to undertake the editing of the Handbook the second time around and saw to it that I did not flag.

GEORGE SCHÖPFLIN.

PRONUNCIATION GUIDE

CZECH AND SLOVAK
ä is a long sound between *e* as in let and *a* as in cat
c English *ts* in le*ts*
č English *ch* in *ch*urch
ch as in lo*ch*
ď English *d* in *d*uke
g as in *g*ave
j English *y*et
ľ English *l* in al*l*ure
ň English *n* in te*n*ure
ř approximately as *rsh* or *rzh*
š English *sh* in *sh*ow
ť English *t* in *t*une
ů English *oo* in b*oo*t
ž English *s* in plea*s*ure, usually indicated by *zh*
y English *i* in h*i*t
ě English *ye* in yell

An acute accent on a vowel indicates length, thus *i* is pronounced as in h*i*t while *í* is as in b*ee*t; the stress is invariably on the first syllable.
ě, ř and ů are found only in Czech; ä only in Slovak.

POLISH
ą French *on* as in b*on*
ę varies between English en or em and French *en* as in *en*terrer
ó English *oo* as in b*oo*t but somewhat shorter
y as in Czech
sz as Czech š
cz as Czech č
ń as Czech ň
rz and ż as Czech ž
ł English *w* in *w*ait
ś English *s* in *s*ue
ć as Czech ť
c and j as in Czech
w as English *v* in *v*ictory

The stress in Polish is usually on the penultimate syllable.

xv

HUNGARIAN
a is appx. English *o* in h*o*t
á is appx. English *i* in f*i*ve but without the "y" sound
c and j as in Czech
cs as Czech č
g as in Czech
gy as Czech ď
ly as j in Czech
ny as Czech ň
ö as in German
ő is the lengthened form of ö
s as Czech š
sz English *s* in *s*it
ty as Czech ť
ü as in German
ű is the lengthened form of ü
zs as Czech ž

Acute accent and stress are as in Czech.

SERBO-CROAT
c, č, j, š and ž as in Czech
ć as in Polish

ROMANIAN
ă English *er* in weath*er*
â, î English *e* in garm*e*nt
ş as Czech š
ţ as Czech c
j as Czech ž
c before o, a, u is pronounced as k; before e and i as Czech č; when ce
    and ci come before a, o, u the e or i is not pronounced.
ch before e and i as k
oa, ua English *wa* in *wa*s
g before a, o, u as g in Czech; before e and i, as English g in general;
    gh as g in Czech, the h is not pronounced.

The stress in Romanian varies. In general, these rules apply: words ending
in a consonant are stressed on the last syllable; words ending in a vowel
on the penultimate syllable, but there are many exceptions.

ALBANIAN
c as in Czech
ç as *ch* in English *ch*urch
dh as *th* in English *th*is
ë as *e* in English t*e*rm
gj as Czech ď
j as in Czech
l as Czech í

ll as Polish ł
nj as Czech ň
q as the initial sound in the English *q*ueue, something like ky
rr a trilled r
sh as in English
th as *th* in English *th*in
x as *dz* in English a*dz*e
xh as *j* in English *j*oin
y as ü in Hungarian
zh as ž in Czech

Stress is on the penultimate syllable, unless otherwise marked by an acute accent.

INTRODUCTION

THE SOVIET UNION AND EASTERN EUROPE: PATTERNS OF POLITICAL DEVELOPMENT

GEORGE SCHÖPFLIN

THE variant of communism that Eastern Europe received readymade from the Soviet Union after 1945 was Stalinism. There is endless discussion about whether Stalinism is a perversion of Marx, or whether it is the natural outcome of Marx and Lenin. For the present purposes, it will be taken as central that Stalinism was the political ideology and political system developed after the 1930s and brought to Eastern Europe as "communism" in the 1940s, and that this Stalinism constituted the political reality with which Eastern Europeans had to live. What has happened in both the Soviet Union and Eastern Europe has been the slow adaptation of the original Stalinist model, with very different outcomes, in different countries.

At times, as in Hungary in 1956, Czechoslovakia in 1968 or Poland in 1980–81, attempts to transform the model went too far for the Soviet Union to tolerate, and it intervened directly or indirectly to reimpose something more like an acceptable variant of the system. In this sense, the tension in communist countries derives from the degree to which the communist system is or is not in harmony with what the populations want. The answers given to the questions raised by this inner tension have varied greatly.

STALINISM

Stalinism, put very simply, was a model of politics by which one man sought to concentrate all power in his hands and to use that power to achieve a set of relatively straightforward economic goals, such as industrialization, over a vast geographical area inhabited by very different peoples with very different values. Consequently, Stalinism had to destroy all competing and preexisting values and to simplify its objectives to a few, relatively straightforward propositions in order to make them applicable everywhere. The essence of Stalinism in politics was the concentration of power. Stalin controlled

3

both the ideology of the party and the institutions of the party as well; the Communist party of the Soviet Union (CPSU) controlled the Eastern European communist parties; all the Communist parties controlled the institutions of the state (government, local administration, parliament, judiciary) and of society (trade unions, press, culture, etc.). To ensure that this system functioned, terror was used.

At the level of rhetoric, the unprecedented concentration of power was justified in the name of the perfect society, the Marxist utopia of full communism, toward which all these countries were supposedly moving. This had the added advantage, from the standpoint of those who held the power, that in logic perfection could not be questioned. Once one accepted that the perfect society was being built, then it followed logically that there could be no opposition to it—how can anyone oppose perfection? This made it even easier to justify the use of terror against the system's opponents, real or putative.

The aims of Stalinism were not, however, distilled from the precepts of Marx and Lenin, but were in reality derived from the temporary, contingent needs of the Soviet Union during the 1930s. Above all there was the need to build up Soviet power through industrialization and to create a military base thereby. In the relatively backward conditions of postrevolutionary Russia, Stalin sought to achieve this aim by concentrating power in the hands of the party and to use this power to force the population to undergo the travails of modernization.

The process that took two generations for England to go through—the Industrial Revolution—was squeezed into a decade for the Soviet Union. Inevitably, this cutting of corners, this forced march through history, was costly. It was certainly costly in human terms, because the only way in which the bulk of the Soviet population could be constrained to endure the massive changes of attitudes, values and ways of life required by industrialization was through force. Hence the need for terror. But this was not the only cost. What Stalin did to justify his program of accelerated industrialization was to claim that his targets and objectives constituted the eternal truths of Marxism-Leninism.

This left the entire Marxist tradition saddled with the legacy of Russian backwardness and Stalin's time-bound method of overcoming it. At a deeper level, Stalin's redefinition of what actually constituted modernity was a serious oversimplification of the process. For Stalin, modernity was boiled down to a few, easily understood aims, like creating a heavy metallurgical industry (steel above all), upping the output of the extractive industries (such as energy) and extending an administrative system to oversee these. The militarized work methods relying on enforced discipline, the emphasis on crudely quantitative targets that ignored quality, and the elimination of individual initiative and innovation (still characteristic of the Soviet system) were the unavoidable corollaries of Stalin's model of modernization. Whenever the Stalinist model ran into a problem, it tended to come up with the same answer—throw more resources at it. In the Soviet Union, after the revolution, this was not a wholly irrational approach. Labor and raw materials were, indeed, plentiful; their ever-increasing deployment, however wasteful, offered a straightforward, simple solution. But this was a very different approach from that which had evolved in the West, where, in essence, modernity involves ever-greater complexity, the widening of choice and continuous change. Stalin's conception of modernity was much more static—as if to say, in effect, that that which was created under him represented the final result of socialism and could never be questioned.

This was the ideological, political and economic system that Stalin exported to Eastern Europe after 1945. It was breathtaking in its claim to totality. It attempted to exercise control over eight very different countries and to do so in an identical way. What is more, Eastern Europe—at any rate many areas of Eastern Europe—was more developed than Russia had been in 1917, so that Stalin's ways of overcoming backwardness were not just inappropriate to them but actually counterproductive. The kernel of the problem was that much of Eastern Europe was already embarked on a process of modernization before 1945. This may not have been modernization identical with that in the West, but growing social and economic complexity, increasing choice and accelerating change were, in fact, being experienced by Eastern Europeans.

Indeed, a strong argument can be made for the proposition that the widespread expectation of radical political change in 1945, which the communists were able to use to their advantage, was essentially about the transformation of political institutions to correspond to the expectations created by these changes. Consequently, the imposition of Stalin's time-bound model on Eastern Europe had an entirely different outcome from its effect on the Soviet Union. In countries where the level of development was low (much of the Balkans, for example), the Soviet model could produce some positive results. But where there already existed pockets of industrialization (in Poland and Hungary), let alone in countries that were industrialized (East Germany and the Czech lands), the results were strongly negative—politically, economically and in human terms. The Stalinist experience, in this sense, was largely unnecessary.

The institutions of Stalinism pivoted around the Communist party, which aimed at, and to a considerable extent succeeded in, penetrating society. The party attempted to control everything that happened. Unsanctioned activity was regarded as politically suspect. In this way, everything was politicized and everything that did not happen as the party wanted it to was treated as deliberate opposition to its will. There was no middle ground. Chance and accident were excluded and the system was ruled by a clear-cut set of black-and-white criteria. In this system there was no room for any autonomous, unsupervised activity, such as press freedom, trade unions, charitable organizations, and the like. In Czechoslovakia, it emerged during the Prague Spring of 1968, even angling clubs were subordinated to the party—as if there were a Marxist-Leninist way of catching fish. From the standpoint of political complexity and change, Stalinism represented a huge step backward.

At the same time, there was no letup in the mobilization of energies, the enforced activism, the ritual participation in parades, the compulsory attendance at Marxism-Leninism classes, the adoration of Stalin, the imposition of ever-higher work norms, the Stakhanovite campaigns, and so on. Stalinism brought with it the language of Marxism-Leninism too, as a way of making certain that alternative ideas would not find public expression. The result was overheating on a massive scale. It emerged that there were human limits to how far mobilization, even when backed up by an efficient terror machine, could be stretched.

DE-STALINIZATION

When Stalin died in 1953, his successors were in an entirely novel situation. There were no blueprints for where they should now go, in what way these societies should now be governed. It was recognized that some changes were essential, but exactly which ones was a matter of debate. The post-Stalin leadership was, in any case, disunited on future development and, furthermore, tended to assume that what was appropriate for the Soviet Union would be suitable for Eastern Europe too. By and large, this was an error. The Soviet Union, with its different traditions and historic readiness to accept a relatively high degree of state control, could be satisfied with the ending of the worst features of the terror. The gulags were emptied; the excessively heightened, forced industrialization was cut back; some greater attention was devoted to the consumer; and the leadership embarked on a slow shift toward a more routinized system of governance. This definition of change proved to be sufficient to avoid a major upheaval in the Soviet Union. The population, still shell-shocked by two decades of terror and the devastation of the war, accepted the concessions and did not look for much more, at any rate not for the time being.

Interestingly, the reaction of the Eastern European populations was not altogether dissimilar. The great majority, traumatized by the Stalin years or, alternatively, beneficiaries of the new order, accepted the status quo. Only in three cases were there major upheavals. The East Berlin eruption of 1953 was triggered off by bad crisis management—the decision to intensify work norms at a time when the population sensed uncertainty in the leadership. Opposition was aroused at a point when expectations had already increased. This uprising was quickly put down by force, something made easier because, on the whole, the East German leadership remained united and the workers were not joined by the intelligentsia.

This pointed toward the crucial features that differentiated East Germany from Poland and Hungary. In the latter two countries the leadership was deeply divided, so much so that different sections of the party began to muster their strength and gather support. Essentially, a gap opened in the monolithic structure of Stalinist power, and the people's real aspirations made themselves apparent through that gap. Intellectuals played a vital role in this, expressing, channeling and integrating popular feelings. Once their grievances were given voice, individuals discovered they were no longer alone, atomized. The possibility of united action, not controlled from above, had returned to the political stage.

In Poland, the party leadership barely kept control of the surging political forces that were threatening to sweep away the Marxist-Leninist structures.

6

In Hungary, on the other hand, the leadership did lose control, and popular aspirations matured into revolution—the demand for a thoroughgoing transformation of the political order—which saw the disappearance of the established communist order. It took the Red Army to subdue the Hungarian revolution. The effect of the Polish and Hungarian upheavals was to anchor conservatism in the system, both in the Soviet Union and in Eastern Europe. Those opposed to reform could point to what had happened as a justification for caution. Reformers saw, or thought they saw, that one particular avenue of reform was closed. The limits of reform were, therefore, tighter than they had been before.

Yet the need for something new had not vanished from the political agenda; Nikita Khrushchev recognized this; however awkwardly, he sought to find a new relationship between rulers and ruled. The essence of his concept of politics was that after so many years of Soviet power, the population had accepted socialism and thus coercive methods of rule were unnecessary. The party could trust the people, so the excessive supervision of society could therefore be dismantled. The problem with this vision of Soviet rule was that it ignored the vested interests that the bureaucracy had every intention of protecting. Khrushchev tried repeatedly to shake the bureaucracy out of its torpor, to introduce more innovation and to make the system more efficient, but he ran into the immovable unwillingness of the apparat. Neither his secret speech of 1956 nor his return to denouncing Stalin at the 22nd Congress of the CPSU in 1961 was received with unreserved joy. What is more, his attempts to introduce change turned his power base against him. One by one, the various Soviet bureaucracies—the party, the state administration, the managers, the agricultural specialists, the armed forces and the technical intelligentsia—concluded that they would be better off without him. In the end, he was removed by a coup in the Central Committee in 1964.

HOW AND WHAT TO REFORM?

The removal of Khrushchev did not immediately affect the reform programs that had been launched in Eastern Europe. The second de-Stalinization of 1961 was used by those who wanted to improve the system within the broad limits of Soviet-type socialism—keeping the existing ideological framework, preserving the leading role (political monopoly) of the party over politics, maintaining the Warsaw Pact and COMECON (CMEA) and permitting controlled decentralization of power. The central theoretical change effected by Khrushchev and justly attributable to his influence was that Communist parties would no longer rule monolithically. This meant that, unlike under Stalin, there could be some middle ground. The party would retain its control of most activity, but there could be some autonomous activity by individuals. This raised some very difficult questions: How far could power be devolved and decentralized? What was to be the party's leading role in practice? Was the party to formulate strategies for the future, or was it to exercise day-to-day control over the execution of policy? How much room for maneuver should be granted to groups not fully supervised by the party? What kinds of differentials should be acceptable, and what sort of political expression should these differences ("nonantagonistic contradictions") be given in politics? None of these questions had easy answers.

The various national parties came up with different answers. In the Soviet Union, the answers turned out to be highly conservative. The post-Khrushchev leadership of Brezhnev and Kosygin owed its power to a strategy of minimal disturbance of the bureaucracy. The very modest economic reforms introduced in the mid-1960s and associated with the economist Yevsei Liberman ran into the sand fairly rapidly.

In Eastern Europe, on the other hand, more thoroughgoing reforms were attempted, the one that eventually emerged as the Prague Spring of 1968 being the most far-reaching. Essentially, there were three broad categories of countries: those that held some promise of political as well as economic change; those that were restricted to economic changes only; and, of course, those where nothing changed at all. Czechoslovakia evidently fell into the category where serious political reform was promised; so to a lesser extent did Hungary and Bulgaria. Common to all three countries was the elimination of the compulsory nature of central-plan instructions. In all three, reforms were to a greater or lesser extent watered down—in Czechoslovakia after the invasion, in Hungary during the 1970s and in Bulgaria even before the reform was introduced. East Germany introduced a reform restricted to economic planning that was not unsuccessful for a while. Poland, after enjoying a very liberal relationship between rulers and ruled for a brief period, stagnated during the 1960s.

Romania underwent only simulated change, smoke without fire. Yugoslavia and Albania were, of course, entirely outside the Soviet sphere and pursued separate courses. The Albanians remained wedded to Stalinism mixed with nationalism, while the Yugoslavs saw a remarkable period of very liberal reforms in the 1960s, which were withdrawn in the 1970s. In the end, all that was left of the 1960s quest for reform was that (1) some areas of what people did were no longer subject to political control, for example in consumption; and (2) the party accepted the futility of trying to build socialism on its own, recognizing that the cooperation of the technical intelligentsia was necessary to this end. This was the foundation for the technocratic approach to government of the 1970s.

SEEDS OF STAGNATION: THE 1970s TO THE 1980s

The Brezhnev years were characterized by caution and a commitment to only minimal change. Greater attention was paid to the consumer, and the secret police were more circumspect in their activities; but the Brezhnev vision of the future appeared to be based on a very slow but inexorable process of integrating all elements of conflict into a single homogeneous whole under the aegis of the party. Initiatives from below were discouraged; the system was hierarchical and cumbersome. And an ever-increasing slice of the national cake was being eaten up by the armed forces. This gradualist, conservative approach was, as so often before, projected onto Eastern Europe. After the debacle of Czechoslovakia, there could be no question of political reform to introduce genuine popular participation. Yet the need for some element of greater dynamism was accepted, and this turned out to be a greater openness toward the West for the purpose of gaining access to Western credit and Western technology. Here again, a solution appearing to suit Soviet needs was more or less unthinkingly applied to Eastern Europe, inevitably with different outcomes.

Poland turned out to be a prime example of how this strategy failed. The Polish leadership took on massive Western credits with the aim of effecting economic modernization. This came unstuck partly because, after the 1973 and the 1979 oil shocks, the terms of trade shifted radically against Eastern Europe (so poor in raw materials), but even more because the system proved incapable of absorbing and using Western technology efficiently. In Poland's case, a major crisis ensued, one that shook the system to its foundations. But none of the Eastern European countries was left unaffected. They had all been exposed to Western technology and Western ideas, and found them more attractive than what the Soviet Union had to offer. More importantly in the short term, several of these countries were deeply in debt to the West and found themselves obliged to repay vast sums of money over very short periods of time. This bunching of the debt during the early 1980s hit Eastern Europe with especial severity.

The outlook in the mid-1980s was bleak, with cutbacks in consumption, diminished investment, a narrowing of horizons and a general reluctance to contemplate the kind of reform that would create greater harmony between popular expectations and political institutions. Neither the Soviet nor any of the Eastern European elites had any commitment to political reform radical enough to diminish its own powers. They were comfortable with things as they were, preferring to define "reform" only as a means of improving the existing system, not as introducing democratization. The most significant issue under discussion was not primarily political at all, but concerned how far individual initiative should be permitted in the economy. Hungary accepted that in agriculture, the service sector and even in parts of industry, entrepreneurial skills and the profit motive could be useful in mobilizing energies and maintaining income levels at a time of austerity. The fact that this provided an acceptable level of services and ensured a steady supply of consumer goods was additionally useful in satisfying urban expectations, while at the same time the incomes of significant sections of the population were protected from excessive deterioration. People accepted growing income differentials as the necessary price for this. Several other Eastern European countries used this device, though none of them went as far as Hungary in giving it official toleration, others preferring to keep it more informal or less legal.

ROOTS OF THE SYSTEM

As the Soviet Union and Eastern Europe have undergone a growing conservatism over the last two or three decades, the official ideology of Marxism-Leninism has also found itself with a different function. It would probably be hard to find anyone in Eastern Europe today who genuinely believes in the formulations of Marxism-Leninism as officially laid down. Even in the Soviet Union, true believers are becoming fewer than they once were. This does not mean that the elites and the people have abandoned all collectivist and egalitarian aspirations and have embraced capitalism. But official ideology no longer plays much of a role as a guide to action, as the doctrinal verity leading these societies toward secular utopia. The real ideology of these states lies elsewhere; it is an eclectic mixture of economic criteria, nationalism and, above all, the firm maintenance of the power of the elite. The language of Marxism-Leninism is kept in order to symbolize the claim to rule by virtue of the original revolution and to prevent the public expression of competing ideas.

This does raise the question of the real nature of Soviet-type systems— assuming that they are not Marxist-Leninist in the strict sense of the word, conforming to what is actually stated by the doctrine. Soviet and Eastern European specialists are inclined to give different answers to this question. They often explain the Soviet Union as a political system in which the elite does have an objective, which includes the economic betterment of the ruled and in which there is slow evolution toward a more participatory system. The Soviet-type system in Eastern Europe, on the other hand, is regarded as dependent on Soviet power and thus alien; very weak in terms of domestic legitimacy and thus liable to regular destabilization; suffering a qualitative gap between the system and popular aspirations; and very largely dedicated to the maintenance of the power of the elite over all other considerations. Whereas in the USSR there does appear to be some move towards political evolution, however gradual and painful, this is generally too slow for Eastern Europe. In this respect, the mismatch is far greater in Eastern Europe than in the Soviet Union.

Still, it would be a gross oversimplification to argue that what keeps these systems in being is just the crude exercise of power. Even where they are relatively weak, as in Poland, they do have some domestic sources of support. Obviously, the elite (which includes entire families) has a vested interest in the survival of the system. But other groups are in an analogous position. Workers in outdated industries, for example, often enjoying preferential wages, prefer to maintain this state of affairs because they know (and they are right) that economic reform would be to their disadvantage. There are also the natural authoritarians who are found everywhere, for whom a hierarchical system of subordination and obedience is the most comfortable one. Even the political neutrals, who will invariably give the government the benefit of the doubt regardless of what it actually does should be counted in this category. Furthermore, whenever a particular regime satisfies some of the expectations of the population—by meeting some of its national aspirations, for example—it can expect a measure of at least conditional support. It is only when these resources are exhausted that the system has to resort to coercion.

SOCIAL DECAY

One of the more striking aspects of political development since Stalin's time has been the gradual, barely perceptible transformation of the role of the party. Having once sought to control everything under the doctrine of monolithism, Soviet-type parties (Albania excepted) nowadays appear to accept that a variety of activities and initiatives will take place outside the party's control or be only partially affected by it. This, in turn, has led to a situation where groups not technically within the party have begun to exercise influence in combination with it—such groups as local or regional coteries, or representatives of such functional interests as health, transport, economics or ethnic groups. The local level of the party has now begun to gain a measure of autonomy at the expense of the center. In particular, the center is finding it increasingly costly to impose its will on the regions over routine questions and to some extent in personnel matters. It can still do so where a really major matter is at stake, but much of the day-to-day wielding of power has effectively been taken away from the center. This constitutes a significant deviation from the strict norms of democratic centralism, the Leninist form of party organization by which these systems are supposedly ruled.

Just as the party has begun to go soft at the edges, there is growing evidence that the effectiveness of the system as a whole has also started to decline. In a word, the Soviet-type of state has also been growing soft and appears less and less capable of doing what it claims to be doing. Its instructions are directly flouted, or are not carried out because of inertia or corruption; its prescribed routines are distorted in the interests of one group or another. This means that sections of the population are only marginally affected by what the state does and their loyalty to it becomes questionable.

The welfare state, by which much of the relationship between rulers and ruled is supposed to be secured, is frequently unable to deliver on its promises. So, for example, the health-care system is close to a public scandal in much of Eastern Europe, with medical attention a commercial commodity and staffs charging high fees for medical care. Although the deleterious effects of pollution on the health of the population is officially acknowledged, there is little that the state can or will do to curb polluters. The result of this inertia has been an accelerating deterioration of the environment. In Poland, for example, water pollution was so far advanced that in 1977 only 9.7 percent of waters were classified as fit for human consumption; nearly three-fifths were classified as unfit for even industrial or agricultural use in 1980. Such examples could be multiplied in all the countries of Eastern Europe. Whether directly related or not, communal and personal well-being declined sharply. All these countries suffered from very high levels of alcohol consumption, particularly among males between 25 and 50 years of age. In the Soviet Union, life expectancy for adult males actually fell from 66 years in 1964 to 61.9 years in 1980. In the 1970s, Soviet infant mortality rates began to rise, after which such statistics were no longer made public. Hungary has for decades been the world leader in numbers of suicides with the rate at 43 per 100,000 in 1982. In Czechoslovakia and Poland there were reports—no official figures—of an increase in drug addiction, especially glue-sniffing. Taken together, all these indicators suggested an alarming and accelerating process of social decay over which the state had little or no control. The one area where control was firmly retained, however, was over political opposition.

The 1970s saw the emergence of political movements outside the control of the party, organized in form and with direct political objectives. Democratic opposition movements, prominent in the Soviet Union, Poland,

11

Czechoslovakia and Hungary, had one overriding aim: to persuade Communist parties and governments to abide by their own legality. If Soviet-type constitutions contained provisions guaranteeing freedom of speech, assembly, worship, organization and expression, these guarantees should simply be respected. Naturally, any move in this direction would completely undermine the parties' basis of power and would radically transform relations between rulers and ruled. In this sense, the inner message of the opposition was that socialism as a doctrine had to go beyond state control of resources; it had to introduce genuine democracy as well. Only in Poland did the democratic opposition play a political role overtly, and that took place in the very special conditions of the Solidarity period. Democratic oppositions were otherwise, for all practical purposes, restricted by repression to merely ensuring their own survival and acting as alternative channels of information. But in that they articulated distinctive visions of the future and formulated competing strategies of development, their role in the political system was authentic and significant.

SOVIET CONSTRAINT

There was universal agreement that the will of the Soviet Union, its readiness to change and to accept change in Eastern Europe, constituted the outer limit to reform. Soviet power was rooted in Eastern Europe not merely through such agencies of direct power as the Red Army, the KGB, the Warsaw Pact and CMEA, but also indirectly. The creation of Eastern European parties owing their survival to the Soviet Union was central in this respect. This establishment of a shared interest was the pivot around which much of the structure of Soviet power revolved. Both sides, therefore, had an interest in sustaining at least the outer facade of ideology; both had an interest in preventing economic reform going too far in the direction of marketization; and both would act to suppress political challenges.

The Soviet Union retained its power over Eastern Europe for many reasons—prestige; the so-called blood-price (these areas had been liberated at the cost of Soviet lives); the imperatives of ideology (without Eastern Europe, Soviet claims to possess a global ideology would be undermined); economic advantage; security against the West; domestic legitimacy (the Soviet population supported the exercise of power over Eastern Europe); and simply power itself (which no one likes to give away). These factors in combination stood in the way of any serious deconcentration of Soviet power over Eastern Europe. They were summed up in the idea of "the Finlandization of Eastern Europe," popular with the opposition in Poland during the 1970s.

With the succession of Gorbachev to lead the CPSU in 1985, there were expectations that the sclerosis of the late Brezhnev years would finally be over and that the Soviet Union would gradually move toward some kind of reform. Few people expected that any reform introduced in Gorbachev's USSR—a significant indicator of the possibilities of reform in Eastern Europe—would go far enough to meet the more thoroughgoing needs of the area. At most, the chances were that the Soviet Union would assume, as it had so often before, that whatever reform was appropriate for itself would be sufficient for Eastern Europe too.

BASIC INFORMATION

ALBANIA

GEOGRAPHY

Features: Albania, the smallest country in Eastern Europe and approximately the size of Belgium, is situated on the Adriatic coast of the Balkan Peninsula and is bounded to the north and east by Yugoslavia and to the south by Greece. Three-quarters of the territory is mountainous and there are elevations of over 8,000 ft/2,400 m. in the North Albanian Alps, the Korab Mountains and the Morava and Gramoz Ranges, all of which constitute a part of the Dinaric mountain system. Much of the marshy coastal plain is lacustrine in origin.

Animal grazing on the lower slopes has reduced the once prevalent forest (oak, beech, chestnut, pine), and sheep rearing and the cultivation of maize, tobacco, wheat, sugar beets and wine represent the chief economic activities of this predominantly agricultural country. There is a limited production of brown coal, chrome, oil and other minerals. The principal centers of settlement and industry are widely dispersed, but Albania's terrain inhibits both internal and external communication.

Area: 10,600 sq. miles/28,700 sq. km.

Mean max. and min. temperatures: Durrës (41° N, 19° E; 25 ft/8 m.) 79°F/26°C (July) 47°F/8°C (Jan.); Shkodër (42° N, 19° E; 30 ft/9 m.) 77°F/25°C (July) 39°F/4°C (Jan.).

Relative humidity: Durrës 81%; Shkodër 82%.

Mean annual rainfall: Durrës 43 in./1,090 mm.; Shkodër 57 in./1,450 mm.

POPULATION

Total population (1983 est.): 2,840,000.

Chief towns and populations: (1981 est.) TIRANA (220,000); Durrës (It. Durazzo) (70,000); Shkodër (It. Scutari) (65,000); Elbasan (60,000); Vlorë (It. Valona) (58,000).

Ethnic composition: Gegs (in North Albania) comprise 65% and Tosks (in South Albania) 33% of the population. The largest non-Albanian minority are Greeks (0.5%).

Language: Albanian, the official language adopted in 1909, is based on the northern (Geg) and southern (Tosk) dialects of the country.

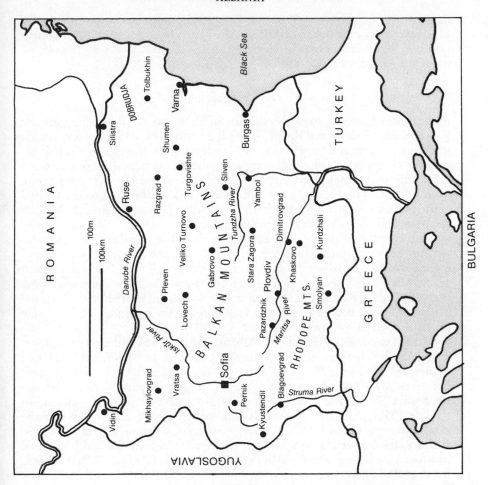

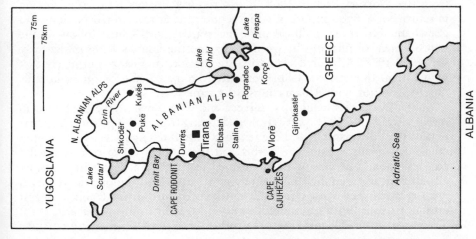

15

Religion: In the early 1960s about 65% of the population was nominally Muslim (Sunni and Bektashi), 25% Albanian Orthodox and 10% Roman Catholic, but public worship has been practically abolished with the official closure of churches and mosques.

RECENT HISTORY

Albania was liberated from the Italians in 1944 and the following year the Western allies recognized the provisional government under the communist secretary-general, Enver Hoxha, on condition that it hold free elections. Amid a savage purge of anticommunists, the subsequent elections resulted in a communist-dominated assembly. Britain and the United States broke relations with Hoxha, and their veto of Albania's admission to the United Nations was not lifted till 1955. In 1946 Albania was declared a People's Republic and King Zog was formally deposed.

Until 1948 the Albanian communists were largely controlled from Yugoslavia and the two countries formed a monetary and customs union. But following the Soviet-Yugoslav schism, Albania aligned itself with the Soviet Union against the Titoist deviationists and executed pro-Yugoslav members of the party, including Koci Xoxe, chief of the secret police. By 1950 the Albanian-Yugoslav Treaty had been abrogated, diplomatic links severed and Yugoslav officials replaced by Soviet officials.

Of all Eastern European states, Albania has most resisted internal change, and old Stalinists still constitute today's leadership. In 1956 Albania acceded to membership in the Warsaw Pact and was visited in 1959 by Khrushchev, but destalinization in Soviet bloc countries and the rapprochement between the Soviet Union and Yugoslavia drew a negative response in Tirana. In the late 1950s, Albania increasingly aligned itself with China and after the 22nd Congress of the CPSU in 1961, at which Chou En-lai alone defended Albania, the Soviet Union withdrew economic and technical aid, evacuated its submarine base at Vlorë and broke off diplomatic relations. While Albania has ceased to be an effective member of COMECON and formally withdrew from the Warsaw Pact in 1968, it has received material aid from Peking in return for active support of Chinese interests at the United Nations and elsewhere. However, political differences arose with China following the improvement of relations between China and the United States in the early 1970s. In 1978, Albania declared its full support of Vietnam in its conflict with China. In response, China formally terminated all economic and military cooperation with Albania during the same year.

Contacts with its neighbors, Greece and Yugoslavia, have fluctuated in recent years. Until 1971, party rivalries deriving from Tito's postwar domination of the Albanian CP and the tensions between Yugoslavia's 1.6 million ethnic Albanians in southern Serbia and the Serbian majority precluded a reconciliation. The Greeks had remained technically at war with Albania, claiming nearly one-half of its territory. In 1971, diplomatic relations were reestablished with Greece. Yugoslavia is currently Albania's biggest trading partner, with a planned increase in trade turnover of 8% in 1985. The status of the Albanian minority in Serbia, however, remains a sensitive issue. Trade with Greece in 1985 is expected to double, and recently the border crossing with Greece at Karkavija, closed since the 1940s, was re-opened.

Foreign relations with other nations have not been smooth because of Albania's extreme mistrust of foreign powers, although currently it has diplomatic relations with more than 100 countries—including France, Italy, and Austria—and trade relations with approximately 50. During the 1980s, Albanian foreign policy has been to encourage contacts with several European countries while firmly rejecting any overtures from the United States and the USSR—the two countries Albania mistrusts the most.

Internally, Stalinism continues to prevail in the regime's strictly orthodox administration of the economy, the secret police and culture. China's Great Proletarian Cultural Revolution scarcely affected Albania, but in 1966 a campaign of Great Revolutionary Action was introduced to streamline administrative efficiency. Extensive reshuffling of the Albanian leadership occurred during the early 1980s. In 1981 Mehmet Shehu, chairman of the Council of Ministers since 1954, was officially reported to have committed suicide. Other sources suggested his involvement in a leadership struggle with Party Secretary Enver Hoxha, leading to his execution. Ten months later Hoxha attacked Shehu, describing him as one of Albania's most dangerous traitors and enemies. In the ensuing major cabinet reorganization, all Shehu supporters were demoted. In 1982, Ramiz Alia replaced Haxhi Lleshi as the country's nominal president. Alia became Albania's first new leader in four decades following the death of Hoxha in 1985. As Alia was apparently Hoxha's choice as successor, any significant softening of repression appears unlikely.

Defense (1983): Military service is compulsory, for two years in the army and three years in the navy and air force. The rank system was abolished in 1966 (on the Chinese model) and political commissars reintroduced. Strength is estimated at: army 30,000, navy 3,200, air force 7,200, paramilitary forces 13,000. Albania formally withdrew from the Warsaw Pact in 1968 after six years of inactive membership. Naval and military agreements had been reached with China in the early 1960s, but were terminated in 1978.

ECONOMY

Background: Recent statistical information on the Albanian economy is sparse; yet available data indicate that it has achieved above-average per capita growth rates since 1960, more than 4% annually. Significant mineral resources and strong central direction have offset increasing political and economic isolation, lack of foreign aid since 1978, and periodic earthquakes and torrential rains. A backward agricultural country before World War II, Albania has since the break with the Soviet Union in 1961 steadily pursued an industrialization policy with Chinese technical and financial assistance. The fifth five-year plan (1971–75) aimed to develop production through extensive capital investments and large industrial building projects. During the sixth five-year plan (1976–80), the annual growth in net material product

17

(NMP) averaged 5%. Industrial output increased by an average annual rate of 6.8%. Agricultural production rose by 21.4% over the previous five-year period. Exports increased by 33%. The seventh five-year plan (1981–85) envisages an increase of 35% to 37% in NMP. Industrial production is expected to rise by 36% to 38%, agricultural output by 30% to 32%, exports by 58% to 60%, and imports by 56% to 58%. In 1982 the general social product went up by 4.4% and NMP increased by 4.5% over 1981. Industrial production went up by 4.7%, and agricultural production by 5%. In 1983 industrial output rose by 3% and agricultural output by 9%. Priority is being given to the development of the power industries. The Chinese financed and equipped new power stations, a radio station, engineering works and a large copper wire factory at Shkodër. Elbasan is now the chief industrial town.

Agriculture still employs about two-thirds of the labor force although its contribution to the NMP is less than that of industry. The country became self-sufficient in bread grains in 1976.

Agriculture is almost entirely socialized, with 80.5% of the cultivated area in the hands of collective farms and 18.1% as state farms. Main crops are maize, sugar beets, wheat and potatoes. A large-scale land reclamation scheme is under way together with mechanization and increased use of fertilizers.

Industry is dominated by mining. Twenty-three minerals are produced commercially, including chrome, copper, iron and steel, tungsten, cobalt and nickel. The country is also relatively self-sufficient in energy and remains an energy exporter, with net foreign sales of crude oil, petroleum products and hydroelectric power more than covering the small imports of coal. Albania has also managed to outperform Greece and Yugoslavia in electrifying all towns and villages by 1970.

As with other centralized command market economies, economic performance is plagued by mismanagement, production bottlenecks, poor planning, overproduction in some areas and underproduction in others, rigid pricing, and the lack of a corps of trained professionals and managers.

Foreign trade: The forced industrialization of Albania under the Hoxha regime has changed the direction and content of foreign trade. Minerals and semifinished goods overtook agricultural and livestock products in the mid-1960s, while the trading partners changed according to the diplomatic alignments in force. China was the principal trading partner after Albania's break with the Soviet Union and Yugoslavia, but since 1975 nearly 35% of the trade has been with the West. Trade relations with Yugoslavia have been resumed but on a more modest scale. Albanian trade is generally in the form of bilateral barter in order to avoid deficits and borrowing abroad. Because the lek is not convertible, most payments are made in foreign currencies. Trade agreements have been concluded with Yugoslavia, Sweden, Romania, East Germany, Italy, Turkey and Czechoslovakia, as well as with Japan, Mexico and the Philippines. Trade with the United States, which does not have diplomatic relations with Tirana, takes place through third countries. Chrome, of which Albania is the world's third largest producer, figures prominently in trade with foreign countries. In 1982, merchandise exports amounted to $267 million and merchandise imports to $246 million, leaving a small trade surplus of $21 million. Nearly 93% of merchandise exports goes to Eastern European markets, 1% to industrial market economies and 6% to developing countries.

Employment: The labor force of the economy's socialized sector is estimated at 584,000, of which 21.9% are employed in agriculture and 37.8% in industry. Population is growing at the fastest rate of any European country (about 3% a year) and the new demands for industrial labor should be satisfied. The estimated average annual growth rate of the labor force for the years 1980–2000 is 2.4%.

Consumption: Standards of living have risen substantially in recent years, with a steady growth in retail trade turnover. Supplies of consumer goods, especially in textiles, foodstuffs and footwear have improved. However, per capita consumption of energy, ownership of consumer durables and availability of social services are the lowest in Eastern Europe.

SOCIAL WELFARE

The current state Social Insurance Law came into force in 1967. Social insurance is noncontributory for all workers except lawyers and members of craft guilds and fishing cooperatives who are eligible for all benefits but on a contributory basis. All social security benefits are tax free. Income tax has been abolished. Government expenditure is met by surpluses earned by state enterprises.

Health services: Notable improvements in Albania's health services have been made in recent years and the former chronic incidence of malaria, TB, trachoma and other endemic diseases has been radically reduced. Infant mortality, however, was still an exceptionally high 86.8 per 1,000 live births as late as 1971. The life expectancy for males is 64.9 years and for females 67 years. There are now hospitals, clinics and maternity homes throughout the country. As of 1977, there were 62.4 hospital beds per 10,000 population and 10.1 doctors per 10,000 population. Free medical services are granted to all citizens. As sickness benefit most workers are entitled to 85% of average earnings if service has exceeded 10 years (70% if less) while miners are entitled to 95% in the case of more than five years service (80% if less). In the case of occupational disease or injury, the worker receives 95% of earnings (miners 100%) regardless of service record. A worker permanently disabled as a result of a work injury is entitled to 80% of average earnings for the last year of work. The pension for partial disability is 50% of earnings. Various bonuses are granted to special categories of invalid pensioner (e.g., a monthly supplement of 100 leks to the permanently incapacitated veteran of the War of National Liberation). During the 180-day maternity leave, the expectant mother is entitled to 95% of earnings if she has worked over five years, 75% if under five years. A worker, pensioner or student receives a bonus of 280 leks on the live birth of a child.

19

Pensions and other benefits: All employment since 1912 (save high-ranking administrative posts under former governments) counts as employment qualifying the worker for pensions. Also counted is work abroad of a "progressive" kind and political exile or imprisonment during the Zog era. Time spent in the people's armed forces is counted as double time. Pensions and benefits are calculated on the basis of average monthly earnings, during the preceding year (or, at applicant's request, during any three-year period within the previous 10 years). For old-age benefits the pensionable age varies according to three categories of employment and length of service, but as a rule the age is 60 for men, 55 for women, and the pension calculated at 70% of earnings at the time of retirement (within the limits of 350 to 900 leks monthly). Women raising six or more children are eligible for retirement at age 50. The pension is not paid to citizens abroad unless authorized. Partial old-age pensions (at not less than half the full retirement benefit) and special merit pensions may be awarded to distinguished men retiring at 55 and women at 50, and to their dependents. Family pensions payable to nonworking dependents of a worker who dies in (or within two years of) employment, range from 65% of earnings for families comprising three or more dependents, to 40% of earnings to one dependent. The orphan is entitled to a family pension computed on the basis of both parents' earnings. A worker attending a sick spouse or dependent is entitled to a compassionate leave benefit of 60% of earnings for up to three days (or 10 days in each three months if the invalid is under seven years of age). A funeral allowance of 300 leks is paid to the family in the case of death of a worker or pensioner or of a dependent/spouse of his/hers.

Housing: Between 1976 and 1978, housing construction made up 3.9% of the total investment of the state sector. During the same period, 32,805 houses and apartments were built, 14,662 by the state and 18,143 by the people. Of the latter, 17,444 were built by people in villages. State credits are available to cooperatives and to individuals, and Albania claims to have the world's lowest rents.

EDUCATION

All educational institutions are ultimately supervised by the Ministry of Education and Culture, with the exception of the Higher Institute of Agriculture which comes under the Ministry of Agronomy. The executive committees of district people's councils provide administration at primary and secondary levels. Schooling is officially compulsory for children aged seven to 15. The system has been greatly expanded since World War II. The illiteracy rate is currently about 25%. In 1971, 11% of the annual budget was allotted to education. Since 1979 a number of Albanian students have been permitted to attend training courses in the West. Education is free.

Primary education: This consists of compulsory seven-year school leading to the seven-year school leaving certificate.

Secondary and vocational education: This consists of three main divisions: (a) the three- to four-year general secondary school, which forms the secondary extension of an 11-year course and mixes academic studies with polytechnical training; (b) the three- to four-year vocational school, which emphasizes practical and specialized instruction; (c) the lower vocational schools, which train workers in the fields of agriculture and industry. All secondary school graduates are required to spend a year working in factories or on collective farms.

University and higher education: Albania's only university, at Tirana, was founded in 1957, and has seven faculties plus two associated institutes (of historical research and ethnology). There are in addition higher institutes of agriculture, fine arts, drama and music (Tirana), of zootechnics (Shkodër) and two teacher-training colleges (Tirana, Shkodër). The students at the university and higher institutes (excepting the two-year teacher-training colleges) take four or five years to obtain their diplomas. Students spend seven months of every year at the institute, two months in production or construction work, one month in physical culture and military training, and two months on vacation. Written examinations in the area of specialization are complemented by oral tests in general subjects.

Educational Institutions (1979)

	Institutions	Teachers	Students
11-year/general secondary	n.a.	26,857[1]	586,365
Other secondary	n.a.	n.a.	126,559
Higher[1,2]	n.a.	1,015	14,695

[1] Including evening and correspondence courses.
[2] 1977 figures.

Adult education: Basic and remedial courses for workers are provided at primary and secondary levels; the higher institutions organize evening and correspondence courses for those who have completed secondary school and are employed. In the latter case, curricula are as for day students but require an extra year of study. Paid study leave is granted annually to all extramural students at the higher level.

MASS MEDIA

The press (1984): (Tirana).[1]

Dailies: Zëri i Popullit, Labor Party, 105,000; *Bashkimi*, Democratic Front, 30,000.

Periodicals: Zëri i Rinisë (biweekly), Youth Union; *Ylli* (m), illustrated; *Drita* (w), literary/art; *10 Korriku* (w), military; *Hosteni* (irreg.), satirical; *Probleme Ekonomike* (irreg.), economic; *Kultura Popullore* (irreg.), cultural; *Nendori* (m), literary; *Shqiptarja e Re*, women's; *Llaiko*, Democratic Front, in Greek; *Shqipëria e Re* (f), Committee for Foreign Cultural Relations,

[1]Circulation figures generally unavailable.

21

in Chinese, French, English, Russian; *New Albania* and *Bulletin d'Informa-tion* (irreg.), govt. and Labor Party.

Broadcasting: The state-controlled radio broadcasts daily from Tirana for 18 hours. There are regional stations in Stalin (Berat), Gjirokastër, Korçë, Kukës, Rogozhina, Sarandë, and Shkodër. In addition, overseas broadcasts are made daily in 20 foreign languages and in Albanian for the Albanian minority in southern Yugoslavia. There are television stations at Tirana, Berat, Kukës and Pogradec. Programs are broadcast in black and white only.

CONSTITUTIONAL SYSTEM

Constitution: The 1946 Stalinist constitution was superseded in 1976 by a new constitution that did not materially alter the system of government. Under the new constitution, the former People's Republic was redesignated as the People's Socialist Republic, and the Albanian Party of Labor (APL) was identified as the sole directing political power in state and society. The organs of government are the unicameral National Assembly of 250 members, the Council of Ministers, Politburo and the Central Committee of the APL.

Legislature: The unicameral National Assembly, which sits at least twice a year, is the highest legislative organ and consists of 250 deputies elected for four years by all citizens over 18 years of age. In the 1982 elections, practically 100% of the electorate voted for the single-state candidates nomi-nated by the Albanian Democratic Front. The Assembly appoints the nomi-nally subordinate Presidium, or collective presidency, comprising a president, three vice presidents, a secretary and 10 members. This includes (1985) two members of the party's Politburo. It convenes the National Assembly and exercises the functions of the latter between sessions, repre-sents the state in international affairs, interprets the law, issues decrees, ratifies treaties, grants pardons, awards honors, appoints diplomats, may declare war and hold referenda.

Executive: Highest executive authority is vested in the Council of Ministers which is elected by the National Assembly and theoretically responsible to it. Its members comprise (1985) a chairman, two deputy chairmen, 15 ministers and the chairman of the State Planning Commission. Seven of these, including the chairman and the two deputy chairmen, hold concurrent membership in the party's Politburo. The Council directs state admini-stration, may rule by decree and generally exercises considerable legislative power.

Local government: Albania is divided into 26 districts (*rrethe*) subdivided into 140 communities (*lokaliteteve*). Each unit is administered by a people's council, directly elected in the districts for a three-year term and in the communities for two years. These appoint executive committees from among the council membership.

Judiciary: Civil and criminal justice is administered through the Supreme Court (whose judges are elected for four years by the National Assembly) and through the people's courts of districts and communities (whose judges and magistrates are locally elected for a three-year term and may be recalled). The lower courts are tribunals of first and second instance. The procurator-general and deputies, appointed by the National Assembly, heads a separate body charged with supervision of administrative legality and with criminal prosecution.

Basic rights: These include social services and qualified freedom of speech, press, assembly, worship and artistic and scientific endeavor.

Party: Albania's sole party, the Labor (Communist) party, has 122,600 members (1981). It controls the entire functioning of government, and all the country's leaders are members. The party congress, convened every five years, elects the Central Committee (81 full members and 40 candidate members were elected in November 1981), which in turn elects the Politburo.

Leading government and party figures: Ramiz Alia (titular president and head of state), Adil Çarçani (prime minister), Rita Marko (vice president), Reis Malile (foreign minister), Prokop Murra (defense minister), Manush Myftiu (deputy prime minister), Besnik Bekteshi (deputy prime minister), Shane Korbesi (foreign trade minister), Qirjako Mihali (deputy prime minister), Niko Gjyzari (finance minister).

BIOGRAPHICAL SKETCH

Ramiz Alia. Alia succeeded Enver Hoxha as chairman of the Albanian Communist party in 1985, after increasingly taking control of Albanian affairs during the 1980s. He was born to a poor Muslim family in 1925. After a spell in the Italian-inspired Fascist youth organization Lictor, he joined the Communist party in 1942 and two years later fought as a partisan, ending the war as a lieutenant colonel and political commissar. Much of Alia's immediate postwar career was in the youth movement. In 1955 he was minister of education, was made a candidate member of the Politburo in 1956 and moved to the Central Committee's agitprop department in 1958. In 1960 he joined the Secretariat, succeeding the disgraced Liri Belishova; a few months later he entered the Politburo as a full member. His subsequent career was as a close associate of Hoxha. He was in charge of ideological policy, titular head of state and member of the Secretariat. There were some indications that Alia was not as insistent as Hoxha had been on the total isolation of Albania.

BULGARIA

Features: Bulgaria, one of the smaller of the communist countries, occupies the northeastern part of the Balkan Peninsula and is divided in two by the Balkan Mountains (*Stara Planina*) which extend on an east–west axis to the Sofia depression. The highest relief, however, comprises the Rila Range (Mt. Musala 9,590 ft/2,920 m.) with its southern continuation, the Pirin Mountains and its southeastern spur, the Rhodopes. Neighboring states are Romania, Yugoslavia, Greece and Turkey.

The Danubian Plain, or Bulgarian Plateau, stretches northward to the Danube, which forms a political frontier with Romania, and is dissected by loess-covered valleys. The Iskăr Valley in the west and Shipka Pass in the east provide the traditional crossing of the Balkan Mountains to the broad Maritsa Valley in southern Bulgaria. The climate is of the transitional continental-Mediterranean type.

Of the total land area, 41% is agricultural, 33% is forest and 26% unproductive. The two plains, north and south of the Balkan Range respectively, are extremely fertile. Wheat and maize (especially in the Danubian Plain) and tobacco, fruit and wines (notably in the Maritsa Valley) are the chief crops, but there is considerable cultivation of rye, barley, oats, vegetables and cotton. Wool, dairy and meat production are well distributed.

Lignite and some reserves of bituminous coal are mined in the Tvurditsa and Dimitrovgrad regions; oilfields have been found on the northeastern coast.

The Sofia depression in the west forms the population, communications and manufacturing hub of the country, but Plovdiv, Pernik, Pleven and the port cities of Burgas and Ruse are industrially important. Tourism is being rapidly developed on Bulgaria's 150 miles/250 km. of Black Sea coast, notably along the Dobrudjan shore around Varna.

Area: 42,800 sq. miles/111,000 sq. km.

Mean max. and min. temperatures: Sofia (43° N, 23° E; 1,805 ft/550 m.) 69°F/21°C (July) 28°F/−2°C (Jan.); Varna (43° N, 28° E; 115 ft/35 m.) 74°F/23°C (July) 34°F/1°C (Jan.).

Relative humidity: Sofia 82%; Varna 83%.

Mean annual rainfall: Sofia 25 in./635 mm.; Varna 19 in./485 mm.

POPULATION

Total population (1983 est.): 8,940,000.

Chief towns and populations (1981 est.): SOFIA (1,070,358); Plovdiv (358,176); Varna (293,950); Ruse (176,013); Burgas (173,078).

Ethnic composition: 85.3% of the population is Bulgarian, 8.5% Turkish, 6.2% others (including Gypsies, Macedonians, Armenians and Russians).

Language: The official language is Bulgarian.

Religion: About 85% are nominally Bulgarian Orthodox, 13% Muslim (of whom 10% are Turkish and 3% Bulgarian-speaking Pomaks). There are small numbers of Roman Catholics and Protestants.

RECENT HISTORY

Although Bulgaria had been at war with Britain and the United States since 1941, it retained diplomatic relations with the Soviet Union until the latter declared war on Bulgaria (September 8, 1944). At the very moment when a new pro-Allied coalition under the Agrarian Party's Konstantin Muraviev was framing a democratic program that would have reversed Bulgaria's Axis alignments, a Soviet-supported grouping of communists and other left-wing parties, the Fatherland Front, was installed as a government under Kimon Georgiev (September 9, 1944). Henceforth, the Bulgarian forces operated against Germany under Soviet command and several key government positions became a communist monopoly. Special committees and a people's militia (under Anton Yugov) conducted the most ruthless purge of opponents, including several thousand executions. In consequence, the communists and their allies within the Front obtained a majority in the 1946 general elections, although the surviving opposition managed still to win 30% of the vote. King Simeon II having been deposed and exiled, the government of the new people's republic was placed in the hands of Georgi Dimitrov, a former secretary-general of the Comintern.

In 1947, the opposition Agrarian Union was in effect dissolved and its leader, Nikola Petkov, executed. In 1948 the smaller parties were either abolished or merged in the Fatherland Front with the Bulgarian Communist party and the Agricultural People's Union. For 14 years Bulgaria was ruled by Stalinists, and the tradition of a Russo–Bulgarian connection based on linguistic, cultural and historical affinities was reinforced by the closest party link.

Dimitrov died in 1949 and his brother-in-law, the party secretary-general, Vălko Chervenkov, became prime minister until succeeded in 1956 by Yugov who, two years later, attempted an unsuccessful rapid industrialization program coterminous with China's Great Leap Forward. Both Chervenkov and Yugov were expelled from the party's Central Committee in 1962 when Todor Zhivkov, chief architect of Bulgarian destalinization and party first secretary since 1954, became prime minister; several hundred political prisoners were released. Zhivkov, a protégé of Khrushchev, has since had to contend with a number of party dissensions, including, in 1965, an alleged army conspiracy. But in the 1966 general elections, the unopposed communist candidates and their allies were predictably returned to power under his continuing government and party leadership.

In 1971 a new constitution was adopted. Zhivkov resigned from his position as prime minister in order to become the first president of the newly formed State Council. This body was established to replace the Presidium of the National Assembly. Zhivkov was reelected to this post in 1976 and again in 1981. Factional struggles and frequent personnel changes have characterized the Bulgarian leadership since the early 1970s. The Politburo experienced a radical reshuffling in 1974 and again in 1977, along with the Secretariat. Immediately following the 12th Party Congress of 1981, an extensive reorganization of the Council of Ministers took place. In 1984, the government announced the dismissal of five top-level officials. Throughout, however, Zhivkov has remained firmly in charge.

Open dissent is relatively rare in Bulgaria, the standards of "socialist realism" in the arts and the media being strictly enforced. Brief incidents have occurred, such as the open support by some 40 Bulgarian dissidents for the Charter 77 human rights activists in Czechoslovakia in 1977, but they have been quickly suppressed.

In its foreign policy, Bulgaria has been a consistently strong supporter of Soviet policies in COMECON and the Warsaw Pact. Bulgarian troops participated in the 1968 Soviet invasion of Czechoslovakia. In 1984, Bulgaria was the first Soviet-bloc nation to join the USSR in its boycott of the 1984 Olympic Games. On a visit to Moscow in 1977, Zhivkov was awarded the title of "Hero of the Soviet Union." Relations with Bulgaria's neighbors have generally improved under Zhivkov's rule; however, various thorny issues exist, each currently creating some tension: the dispute with Yugoslavia on the so-called "Macedonian question"; the dispute with Turkey regarding Bulgarian attempts to "Bulgarize" Turkish last names; and the dispute with Greece over Bulgaria's diversion of the Nestos river, which empties into Greece. Relations with Western states have also steadily improved, Bulgaria being particularly interested in obtaining advanced technology; but significant setbacks have occurred in recent years. Ties with Italy and subsequently the United States became strained following the 1982 papal assassination attempt by Mehmet Ali Ağca, who claimed Bulgarian involvement in the attempt. In 1984 Zhivkov, apparently under pressure from Moscow, canceled his scheduled trip to West Germany.

Defense (1983): Military service is compulsory for two years in the army and air force and three years in the navy. Strengths of the defense forces: army 120,000, navy 8,500, air force 33,800. Paramilitary forces number 22,500, people's militia 150,000. The 1980 defense expenditure was $1.2 billion, representing 3.2% of GNP. Bulgaria is a member of the Warsaw Pact and there are no Soviet divisions on Bulgarian territory.

ECONOMY

Background: Bulgaria emerged from World War II as one of the poorest of Balkan economies, with the lowest per capita income and over 80% of its labor force in agriculture. During the next 30 years, a policy of rapid industrialization launched by the communist leadership reduced agricultural contribution to GNP to 20% and generated the highest per capita growth rate in the region during 1960–79: 5.6% annually. Bulgaria achieved this without any bilateral aid from the West or from such international organizations as the World Bank or IMF, although it received substantial and generous Soviet aid in the form of loans and credits as well as trade agreements guaranteeing favorable prices for Bulgarian exports to the Soviet Union.

Since 1964, when the Politburo launched a decentralization program, official economic policy has experimented with various innovative forms of control. In the late 1960s, related industries were consolidated into 97 large state economic associations (SEAs), later reduced to 64. Other structures were introduced in 1974. The national economic complexes were established as umbrella bodies encompassing smaller units with some measure of autonomy. In 1979 the New Economic Mechanism (NEM) was adopted, by means of which centralized planning was reduced in favor of state enterprises enjoying accountability. In the agricultural sector, this led to the abolition of the Ministry of Agriculture and its replacement by the National Agro-Industrial Union. By 1980, the NEM had been extended to all sectors of the economy.

Consolidation and vertical integration have been the hallmarks of agricultural reform. Groups of farms have been merged into agro-industrial complexes (AICs), and the more than 160 AICs have been organized into 28 unions following territorial boundaries and 13 units following product categories. More recently, the role of private agriculture has increased significantly, accounting for 27% of Bulgaria's total agricultural output in 1982.

Unofficial World Bank estimates place the share of the industrial sector at more than 60% of GDP. The development plans have tended to emphasize industrial complexes linking mining and manufacturing. However, much of the iron ore, natural gas and petroleum have to be imported from the Soviet Union. Following the seventh five-year plan (1976–80), heavy industry contributes more than half of all industrial output. The manufacture of consumer goods also rose substantially during the plan period.

Since 1977 there have been indications of a decline in the growth rate, due mainly to higher prices of raw materials. The current five-year plan (1981–85) calls for an average growth in real income of 3%, and priority is to be given to the development of heavy industry. Because of the persistence of the problems that plagued the previous five-year period, it is unlikely this goal will be met in full. Official Bulgarian sources claim, however, that economic growth averaged 4.1% during the 1982–84 period. In addition, significant progress has been made in electric power generation, and by 1990 nuclear energy is expected to provide 40% of the nation's energy needs.

Foreign trade: External trade is a state monopoly under the direction of the Ministry of Foreign Trade and the Bulgarian Foreign Trade Bank. Most international commercial transactions are conducted by a foreign trade organization for each industry.

Foreign trade is conducted principally with other communist countries, between 55% and 60% of it with the Soviet Union and 20% with Eastern Europe. A substantial share of the foreign exports goes to developing countries with which the Soviet Union maintains friendly relations: South Yemen, Ethiopia, Iran, Libya, Iraq and Mozambique. Machinery and equipment make up the bulk of exports, but because these products are not competitive in the international markets, agricultural exports yield most of the Western currency earnings. In a search to expand its contacts, Bulgaria has obtained contracts to build ships for Dutch and West German firms. The balance of trade was in surplus until 1981. In 1982, merchandise exports amounted to $1.969 billion and merchandise imports to $2.281 billion, leaving a deficit of $312 million. The average annual growth rate was 11.4% for exports and 7.8% for imports from 1970 to 1982. The principal exports were machinery, vehicles and equipment (45%); raw materials and foodstuffs (26%); fuels and mineral raw materials (13%); and industrial consumer goods (10%). The principal imports were fuels and mineral raw materials (41%); machinery, vehicles and equipment (37%); raw materials and foodstuffs (10%); and chemicals, fertilizers and rubber (7%).

Employment: Of the total labor force of 4.1 million (1982), 22.8% is employed in the agricultural sector and 34.5% in industry. The annual growth rate of the labor force from 1980 to 2000 is projected at 0.2%. Labor shortages are likely to pose serious problems to Bulgaria's economic planners in the next decade.

Prices and wages: In the decade after 1972, the average gross monthly wage grew from 125 to 197 leva, and the average worker's real income increased by 4% annually. Increases in the minimum monthly wage and entry-level wages are expected to increase by the end of the current five-year plan (1981–85). In future years, real income is expected to grow by 3% annually. Prices generally remain stable, although a severe drought in 1983 was used to justify large price increases in citrus fruits, pork, poultry and ground meat.

Consumption: Recent advances in both industry and agriculture have led to improvements in living standards, although they are still low in comparison with other Eastern European countries. Average annual per capita consumption of meat, milk, eggs and fruits increased substantially during the 1972–82 period. Consumer durables are now more freely available, with significant annual advances in the supply of television sets, refrigerators, washing machines and cars.

SOCIAL WELFARE

The Central Council of Trade Unions directs all social security save health services (see below) and pensions, which come within the jurisdiction of the Ministry of Finance. All contributions are paid by the employer enterprise, institution or organization, except for the liberal professions, and their payment is included in the state budget.

The following data refer to 1984–85 unless otherwise stated.

Health Services: Public health is supervised by the Ministry of Public Health, financed from state budget allocations and administered by the district people's councils through their departments of public health. Free health facilities are available to all citizens; patients pay only for medicine acquired in cases of outpatient treatment. After three months of service a worker is entitled to paid sick leave. Compensation for accidents at work is paid immediately. For temporary disablement, indemnities range between 70% and 90% of the worker's wage, depending upon length of service. Disablement benefits depend on the degrees of disablement and income and range between 35% and 100% of the worker's wage. Working women are entitled to leave at full pay before and after childbirth, ranging from 165 to 225 days.

In 1982 there were some 80,000 hospital beds, or 10.7 per 1,000 population, and 22,086 physicians, or 2.4 per 1,000 population. Outpatient aid and consultation are provided by polyclinics attached to city hospitals or organized on a regional basis in the countryside. In addition, a separate network of polyclinics and hospitals serves workers in industrial, mining, transport and building enterprises. Formerly endemic diseases such as malaria, typhoid and infantile paralysis have been practically eradicated. As of 1974, the maternal mortality rate stood at 20.1 per 100,000 live births, while the infant mortality rate as of 1980 was 20.2 per 1,000 live births. The average life expectancy as of 1980 is 69.3 years for males and 74.9 years for females.

Pensions and other benefits: Pension rates are determined on the basis of the remuneration received during three successive years in the last 15 years of service. Old-age pensions are granted according to the category of work. Workers in the first category, which includes the hardest jobs, are pensioned off after 15 years of service and at the age of 45 for women and 50 for men; those of the second category after 20 years of service and at the age of 50 for women and 55 for men; those of the third category after 20 years of service and at the age of 55 for women, and after 25 years of service and at the age of 60 for men. The rate of pensions ranges from 55% to 80% of wages and may be increased by 12% for years of service beyond the statutory work span. Dependents of a deceased insured worker are entitled to life insurance payment and a pension. The latter is paid to the amount of 50% for one dependent, to 75% for two dependents and to 100% for three or more dependents. Students are entitled to the whole or a part of the pension of the deceased until they reach 25 years of age if female, 27 years of age if male. Insured cooperative farm workers are also entitled to pensions, at the age of 55 for women and 60 for men, if they have been employed for 25 years in agriculture. The monthly pension ranges from 30 to 55 leva. The pensions for permanent disability are 55, 45 and 35 leva per month for the three categories. Disablement pensions for general loss of health range from 30 to 50 leva per month. Farmers' pensions are financed by state-made contributions amounting to 6.2% of the cooperative farm's income and by additional taxes levied on the sales of alcohol and tobacco.

There also exist two further types of pension: pensions for special merits (granted to distinguished persons who have made "an exceptional contribution" to national life) and national pensions (granted to "fighters against

29

fascism, reaction and capitalism"). Family allowances as well as lump-sum payments are granted at childbirth; these increase with the number of children, ranging from 100 to 500 leva. At the death of the insured, his/her family is entitled to a lump-sum payment of 80 leva.

Housing: In general, state plans for housing construction are underfulfilled year after year. Only 352,000 housing units of the planned 420,000 were actually built during the 1976–80 five-year plan. As a rule, housing construction is financed and directed by the state building organizations and individual industrial enterprises, but a cooperative system is also maintained; this allows citizens to acquire tenancy of individual apartments in houses containing up to four units. In addition, a recent decree issued by the Central Committee and the Central Council of Trade Unions permits enterprises to build housing with their own funds, using the labor of their employees. It is hoped that this will increase overall housing construction.

In the larger cities such as Sofia and Plovdiv, much of the old Turkish housing has been cleared in favor of planned housing projects. High-rise housing is increasingly in evidence, especially in towns and along the holiday coast.

EDUCATION

The fast expanding education system, which is free and coeducational, is generally the responsibility of the Ministry of Public Education, while immediate supervision is exercised by the district public education departments comprising two sectors, dealing with organization and pedagogical guidance respectively. Since 1964, however, 80% of the vocational and technical secondary schools have been subordinated to the economic ministries. The performance and conduct of pupils are reviewed by the individual teacher's council, but there is stress on student participation in the life, order and extracurricular activity of the school. Supplementary instruction is provided by the Dimitrov Pioneer-Children's Organization Septemvriiche and the Dimitrov Young Communist League. Education is compulsory from seven to 16. The illiteracy rate is currently estimated at less than 5%.

Primary and general secondary education: Preschool kindergarten (*detska gradina*) is mainly of an all-day type, but some operate seasonally in case of parental absence and may offer boarding facilities. Primary and general secondary education provide, wherever possible, a unified 12-year system in which the compulsory basic four-year course at primary school (*osnovno uchilishte*) leads to a subsequent four years of compulsory secondary education. About one-third of pupils continue to the general secondary school (*gimnazia*). Matriculation for higher education takes place on the basis of final examination in the fourth year of gymnasium. The 1959 Statute for a Closer Link between School and Life (on the Soviet model of 1958) stressed the connection between study and production training, and all primary and secondary education has since included elements of polytechnical instruction. Even in the gymnasia there is heavy emphasis on scientific subjects and on practical experience of "labor training" in the workshop, farm, factory

30

and enterprise. Grades 9 to 11 are given a preponderantly polytechnical curriculum, and in grades 11 to 12 an "elements of communism" course is obligatory. There is compulsory physical education.

Vocational and technical secondary education: 63% of all secondary pupils in 1982 were enrolled in vocational-technical schools (*sredno politekhnichesky uchilishta*) and "technicums" (*teknikumi*), which follow on the 8th grade. The first of these train skilled workers by means of a two-year course, and the latter combine skilled training with three and a half to four and a half years of academic/polytechnical study. There are also special polytechnical language gymnasia where instruction is in Russian, English, French or German and the curriculum includes foreign trade, secretarial skills and tourist guidance.

Special education: There are free special schools for the mentally and physically handicapped at the kindergarten, primary and secondary levels.

University and higher education: All institutions of higher learning, with the exception of those in medicine and fine arts, which come under their appropriate ministries, are supervised by the Ministry of Public Education. Admission of students is on the basis of entrance examinations in two subjects related to the field of specialization. Courses last from four to six years and include, in addition to the main subject, ideology and politics, foreign languages and physical education. Besides Sofia University there are 28 higher institutes in the country and separate academies of music, art, drama and ballet, each in Sofia.

Educational Institutions (1982)

	Institutions	Staff	Students
Primary/general secondary	3,541	68,695	1,170,434
Other secondary	645	19,363	234,350
Higher	29	13,254	83,633

Adult education: Evening and correspondence courses are popular with working people. Two-year "semiuniversity" courses are offered in practical subjects such as library science, postal communications, etc.

MASS MEDIA

The Press (1984):
Dailies: (Sofia) *Rabotnichesko Delo*, CP, 850,000; *Otechestven Front*, Fatherland Front, 280,000; *Narodna Mladezh*, youth, 250,000; *Trud*, trade union, 250,000; *Zemedelsko Zname*, Agrarian People's Party, 165,000; *Kooperativno Selo*, agric., 130,000; *Vecherni Novini* (e), CP, 125,000; (Plovdiv) *Otechestven Glas*, CP and Fatherland Front, 65,000; *Narodna Armia*, military, 55,000.

Periodicals: (Sofia) *Zhenata Knes* (m), women's, 580,000; *Radio-Televizionen Pregled* (w), radio, 310,000; *Septemvriiche* (w), youth, 300,000; *Stărshel* (w), satirical, 280,000; *Naroden Sport* (3 per week), 270,000; *Bulgaria* (m), illus., in Russian, German and Spanish, 157,000; *Bălgarosăvetska Druzhba* (m), Soviet friendship, 68,000; *Dărzhaven Vestnik* (bw), Nat. Assembly, 64,000; *Lov i Riholov* (m), hunting/fishing, 60,000; *Narodna Kultura* (w), cult., 50,000; *Literaturen Front* (w), lit., 40,000; *Nasha Rodina* (m), socio-polit., 35,500; *Novo Vreme* (m), CP, 32,000; *Slavyani* (m), Slav Committee, 20,000; *Septemvri* (m), lit., 15,000; *Bulgaria Today* (m), in French, English and Italian, 25,000; *Studenska Tribuna* (w), student; *Eiliulcu Çocuk* (w), Turkish; *Erevan* (bw), Armenian; *Evreiski Vesti* (bw), Jewish; *Lefteria* (w), Greek; *Nov Put* (m), Gypsy; *Yeni Yaşik* (3 per week), Turkish.

Broadcasting: This is controlled by the government Committee for Culture. There are 10 radio stations—five in Sofia and local stations in Blagoevgrad, Plovdiv, Shumen, Stara Zagora and Varna. Foreign broadcasts are made in 12 languages, including Turkish, Greek, French, English, Albanian and Arabic. Bulgarian television broadcasts daily. Color television was introduced in 1977.

CONSTITUTIONAL SYSTEM

Constitution: The 1971 constitution replaced the constitution of 1946. It defines Bulgaria as a socialist state and declares the Communist party to be "the leading force in society and the state."

Legislature: The supreme legislative body is nominally the unicameral National Assembly (*Narodno Săbranie*) elected for a five-year term by universal suffrage (19 years and over) from single-member districts. In the 1981 general elections, in which nearly 100% of the electorate participated, 99% of the votes were cast for the 400 single-slate nominees of the Fatherland Front. Meeting at least three times a year, the Assembly enacts laws, determines the budget, approves the economic plan, may declare war and grant amnesty, and elects the State Council, the Council of Ministers and the Supreme Court. The State Council, whose president is the head of state, is the most important permanent organ of state power. In addition to the president, it comprises a first vice president, four vice presidents, a secretary, and 22 members. Its responsibilities include: the conduct of foreign affairs, the issuing of decrees, the convening of the National Assembly, the decision on the general election date and the supervision of ministerial activities.

Executive: The Council of Ministers (*Ministerski Săvet*) is the supreme organ of government and consists of a chairman, deputy chairmen, ministers and the chairmen of key committees such as State Planning. Currently (1985), several members, including both the chairman and the first deputy chairman, are members of the Politburo. The Council of Ministers controls state administration and ensures the execution of the economic plan and the observance of laws.

Local government: This is exercised by the people's council (*narodni săvet*) at the levels of region (*okrăg*) and urban or rural municipality (*grad* and *selo*). Members of the people's council are directly elected for a two and a half year term, and in turn appoint a standing committee (*postoyanen komitet*) as the executive branch. The 30 political subdivisions, composed of

27 regions and three municipalities, correspond to the economic subdivisions. People's councils report annually to their electors.

Judiciary: Civil and criminal justice is administered through the Supreme Court (*Vărkhoven Săd*), 28 regional courts and 103 people's courts. The Supreme Court, whose judges are elected by the National Assembly for five years, supervises the judiciary and acts as the highest court of appeal, while the lower courts, composed of a directly elected judge and two lay assessors (*zasedateli*), exercise original jurisdiction. The judiciary is deemed independent of government. There are also special courts such as military tribunals. A chief procurator (*glaven prokuror*), elected for five years by the National Assembly and responsible to it, personally appoints and removes subordinates. Procurators supervise the observance of legality by public bodies and citizens and prosecute in criminal cases. Citizens have the right to choose their own legal representatives and state enterprises may employ their own legal adviser. In 1961, on the Soviet model, comrades' courts (*drugari sădy*) were established to deal with minor offences in institutions and enterprises. Capital punishment is maintained.

Basic rights: These include equality, a broad scope of social services, cultural and educational rights for national minorities, and qualified freedom of speech, press, assembly and religion.

Party: There are nominally two political parties, the Communist party (BCP) and Agrarian People's Union (APU), which collaborate in the Fatherland Front (*Otechestven Front*), a mass organization with a membership (1984) of 4,388,000, and which alone nominates candidates. There is no parliamentary opposition. The BCP numbers (1981) 826,000, and the APU 120,000. There are two mass social and political youth organizations—the Dimitrov Pioneer-Children's Organization Septemvriiche and the Dimitrov Young Communist League.

Leading government and party figures: Todor Zhivkov (president of the State Council, general secretary of the BCP), Grisha Filipov (chairman of the Council of Ministers), Chudomir Alexandrov (first deputy chairman of the Council of Ministers), Stanish Bonev (deputy chairman of the Council of Ministers, chairman of the State Planning Committee), Petur Mladenov (foreign minister), Dimitur Stoyanov (interior minister), General Dobri Dzhurov (defense minister), Khristo Khristov (foreign trade minister).

BIOGRAPHICAL SKETCHES

Chudomir Alexandrov. Alexandrov, born in 1936, emerged as one of the most prominent politicians of the younger generation when, in January 1984, he was promoted to full membership in the Politburo. He trained as an engineer and worked in the Central Committee organizational department (1977–79) before taking on the first secretaryship of the Stara Zagora party organization, at which point he was moved to the equivalent post in the capital, Sofia. Promoted to the Central Committee Secretariat in 1981, his elevation to the Politburo confirmed his preeminent status.

Grisha Filipov. Filipov, prime minister of Bulgaria from 1981, was born in the Soviet Union in 1919 and lived there until 1936; he was reputed to speak Bulgarian with a Russian accent and was generally regarded as markedly pro-Soviet. He spent 1948 to 1951 in the Soviet Union as a student of industrial and trade economics. From 1951 to 1958 he worked for the State Planning Committee, in 1958–62 headed a Central Committee department, then returned to the State Planning Committee (until 1971). He was a member of the Central Committee Secretariat and the Politburo from 1974. Although Filipov was regarded as Moscow's man in Bulgaria, this apparently did not mean that he was wholly inflexible; it was during his tenure of office that the Bulgarian economic reform of 1982 was introduced.

Todor Zhivkov. Zhivkov, party leader since 1954 and the longest-serving party boss in the Warsaw Pact, was born in 1911. He joined the Communist party in 1932 and fought with the partisans during the war. He became a candidate member of the Central Committee in 1945 and a full member in 1948. In 1948–49 he headed the Sofia party organization; in 1950 he was made a member of the Central Committee Secretariat—he was evidently regarded as reliable by Bulgaria's Stalinist leader, Vulko Chervenkov. In 1951 he was taken into the Politburo. Three years later, when under Soviet pressure Chervenkov acquiesced in splitting the offices of party leader and prime minister (he had held both until then) and took the latter post, he made Zhivkov party leader. Presumably Chervenkov thought he could continue to dominate Bulgarian politics through Zhivkov, whom he regarded as under his patronage. In the event, it took Zhivkov until 1962 finally to remove Chervenkov (together with another rival, Anton Yugov), and even at that he needed express Soviet support. Thereafter, Zhivkov built up his power slowly. His particular pattern of rule was to elevate relatively youthful functionaries to high office, then purge them after a few years. In the 1970s, however, he began to groom his daughter, Lyudmila Zhivkova, as possible successor. Her death in 1981 at the age of 38 was a major setback. Zhivkov presided over the gradual development of Bulgaria from a predominantly agrarian economy to a mixed agrarian-industrial structure with a corresponding increase of prosperity. Although there was never any doubt concerning Zhivkov's loyalty to the Soviet Union, the suggestions made in the 1970s that Bulgaria join the USSR as another federal republic were dropped in the 1980s. In any case, Zhivkov was no enemy of Bulgarian nationalism, which he promoted strongly during the 1970s and after. Perhaps his most signal contribution to Bulgarian politics was to provide the country with more than two decades of stability. Given the country's long history of upheavals, this was something of an achievement.

Yordan Yotov. Yotov, editor of the party newspaper *Rabotnichesko Delo* and from January 1984 a member of the Politburo, was born in 1920. He came from the same region as the party leader, Zhivkov, and fought in the Chavdar partisan brigade. For several years he was a professor of party history, then in 1977 was made editor in chief of the party daily; a year later he joined the Central Committee. Yotov was seen as a reliable ally of the party leader, with special responsibility for propaganda.

CZECHOSLOVAKIA

Features: Czechoslovakia is a medium-sized, landlocked state composed of the Czech lands of Bohemia and Moravia in the west and of Slovakia in the east. It is contiguous with Poland, East and West Germany, Austria, Hungary and, since World War II, the Soviet Union (which annexed Sub-Carpathian Ruthenia). Bohemia comprises a mountain-girt plateau (av. height: 1,600 ft/500 m.) diminishing toward the north where it is dissected by the Labe (Ger. Elbe) river and its tributaries, on one of which, the Vltava (Moldau), stands Prague. The lower slopes and the low-lying plain of the Labe are fertile. In the west, the frontiers with West and East Germany comprise the Český Les (Böhmer Wald) and Krušné Hory (Erzgebirge) respectively. In the northeast, the Krkonoše Hory (Riesengebirge) form the highest range of the Sudetes (Mt. Sněžka: 5,259 ft/1,603 m.) and, in common with the Sudetes (Sudeten) of Moravia and the Carpathians of Slovakia, constitute a political boundary with Poland. Moravia, which includes a small part of Silesia, is a mainly lowland region under 1,000 ft/300 m.; it is a water divide and a traditional crossing between northern and southern Europe. Slovakia, covering half the land area of the country, is two-thirds mountainous, with parallel ranges of the Carpathians culminating in the High Tatra (Mt. Gerlachovká: 8,737 ft/2,663 m.). In Slovakia, fertile plains are confined to the Danubian Basin in the extreme southwest and the basin of the Uh river in the southeast. The climate of Czechoslovakia represents a transition from the maritime to the continental types.

Although the country is generally poor in minerals, it is one of the most industrialized in Eastern Europe. The chief mineral resources are brown coal and lignite (centered on Ostrava and Kladno), iron ore, uranium ore and magnesite. Heavy industry has been traditionally based in Bohemia and Moravia, in Prague, Plzeň (Pilsen), Brno (Brünn) and Ostrava. The industrialization of Slovakia has received priority since the 1960s.

About 40% of the total area is cultivated, 30% is forest and a further 16% is pasture. Intensive agriculture (maize, wheat, beets, fruit, potatoes, fodder crops) is practiced in the fertile plains of the chief rivers, e.g. Danube, Morava, Vltava, Labe, Váh, Hron and Hornád. There are timber industries, but the hydroelectric potential (outstanding in Slovakia) is still largely untapped. Czechoslovakia's road and railway networks are dense, and the Danube and lower reaches of the Vltava and Labe are navigable.

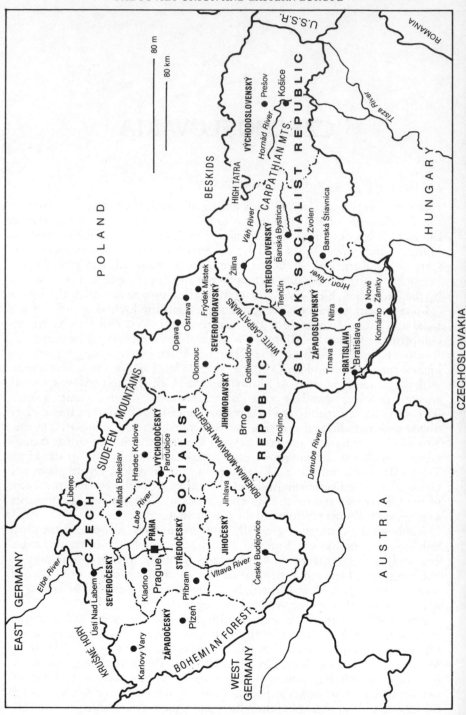

Area: 49,400 sq. miles/127,900 sq. km. (Bohemia and Moravia 78,900 sq. km.; Slovakia 49,000 sq. km.).

Mean max. and min. temperatures: Prague (50° N, 14° E; 660 ft/201 m.) 66°F/19°C (July) 30°F/−1°C (Jan); Zvolen (48° N, 19° E; 980 ft/299 m.) 69°F/21°C (July) 29°F/−2°C (Jan.).

Relative humidity: Prague 82%; Zvolen 87%.

Mean annual rainfall: Prague 19 in./485 mm.; Zvolen 30 in./760 mm.

POPULATION

Total population (1983 est.): 15,410,000. Czech regions (Bohemia and Moravia): 10,320,000; Slovakia: 5,090,000.

Chief towns and populations (1983 est.): State capital and capital of the Czech Socialist Republic, PRAGUE, 1,185,000. Capital of Slovakia, Bratislava (Pressburg), 395,000. Other major towns: Brno (Brünn) 378,000, Ostrava 323,000, Plzeň (Pilsen) 173,000, Košice (Kaschau) 210,000.

Ethnic composition: Czechs number 64.3%, Slovaks 30%, Magyars 4%, Germans 0.6%, Poles 0.5%, Ukrainians 0.2%.

Language: Czech and Slovak are the official languages and are mutually understandable.

Religion: 70% of the population is nominally Roman Catholic, 20% Protestant (mainly Reformed and Lutheran), 8% Czechoslovak Catholic, 2% Greek Orthodox.

RECENT HISTORY

Czechoslovakia was not only the most industrialized country of Eastern Europe before World War II, it could also claim the longest tradition of parliamentary democracy. Betrayed by the West at Munich and subsequently dismembered by Germany, Hungary and Poland, it was liberated in 1945 by Soviet and American armies. The eastern province of Carpatho-Ruthenia was annexed by the Soviet Union while the Sudetenland, Těšín (Teschen) and the lost territories of southern Slovakia were restored to Czechoslovakia and a large proportion of the German and some of the Hungarian minorities expelled. President Beneš and many others believed that close relations with the Soviet Union were a guarantee of the nation's independence, and the 1946 elections returned the communists as the strongest single party (38% of the vote). Its chairman, Klement Gottwald, became prime minister of the new National Front government. In 1948, 12 noncommunist ministers tendered their resignation in protest against communist infiltration of the police, and in the subsequent elections the communists and their allies, who were unopposed, gained an 89% majority. The ailing Beneš himself resigned in June 1948 and was succeeded by Gottwald.

There ensued over a decade of totalitarian rule by a strictly Stalinist party. With noncommunist leaders exiled or imprisoned, massive purges and show trials of party deviationists took place in the early 1950s, culminating (1952) in the show trial of Rudolf Slánský, the party secretary-general. Under Soviet pressure, the economy from 1949 onward was overwhelmingly geared to heavy industry, and riots at Plzeň in 1953 were suppressed. On the death in the same year of Gottwald, Antonín Zápotocký became president and Viliám Široký prime minister. Khrushchev's secret speech at the 20th Congress of the CPSU in 1956 had no immediate repercussions in Czechoslovakia, unlike in Poland and Hungary, and a genuine opposition to the old Stalinist leadership was not felt until the 1960s. In 1957, Party First Secretary Antonín Novotný succeeded to the presidency, and was reelected in 1964. At the end of the second five-year plan in 1960, Czechoslovakia was proclaimed the first socialist republic in Eastern Europe, and in 1963 the Czechoslovak-Soviet Treaty of Alliance was reaffirmed for a 20-year period.

A modest program of destalinization was begun in the early 1960s. In 1963, prominent communists purged during the 1950s, including Vladimir Clementis and Slánský, were posthumously rehabilitated, while Prime Minister Široký was dismissed. Archbishop Beran and other ecclesiastics were freed. Under the new prime minister, Jozef Lenárt, Czechoslovakia also embarked on a new economic course, associated with Professor Ota Šik's radical system of management. Thus, until 1968, Novotný's orthodox leadership paradoxically presided over Czechoslovakia's New Economic Model and probably the most lively cultural ferment in Eastern Europe.

In January 1968, Alexander Dubček, Slovak party leader, replaced Novotný as first secretary of the Czechoslovak Communist party, and it was not long before the latter lost the presidency as well, to General Svoboda who, as a war hero, was equally respected by the reformers and by the Soviet leadership. Amid a spate of suicides and defections (Gen. Šejna, political chief of the army, escaped ironically to the United States), the remaining old guard was removed and its policies discredited. The "action program" of the new party and state leaders heralded seven months of political and economic reform, cultural efflorescence and personal freedom unknown in the country since 1948. The rehabilitation of party and nonparty persons who had suffered during the Stalinist era, the reorganization of the Czechoslovak Communist party and revitalization of other political parties, provisions for a Czecho-Slovak federation, and the lifting of press censorship and of the ban on foreign travel were among the most remarkable of the innovations.

While a new Czechoslovakia was taking shape, its leaders took pains to stress their continued adherence to socialism and to membership of the Warsaw Pact and COMECON in particular. Support for Czechoslovakia's reforms and its position vis-à-vis the Soviet Union was soon received not only from most of the non-Soviet world but also from the Yugoslav, Romanian and major Western Communist parties; the stream of summer visitors included Tito and Ceauşescu, who were accorded a tumultuous welcome. Meanwhile, the remaining states of the Soviet bloc grew increasingly alarmed at this specter of liberal socialism and, in meetings with Dubček at Dresden,

38

Warsaw and Prague, exerted diplomatic and economic pressures. Stalemate led to military pressures, and Soviet and Polish troops assigned to Warsaw Pact exercises were not withdrawn from Czechoslovak soil. Moscow, East Berlin and Warsaw alleged West German "penetration" of Czechoslovakia.

On July 18 the Soviet Union, Poland, East Germany, Bulgaria and Hungary dispatched the so-called Warsaw Letter to Prague, stating that "a determined struggle for the preservation of the socialist system in Czechoslovakia is not only your task but ours as well." The Presidium of the Czechoslovak Communist party and the Politburo of the CPSU met *in plenum* at Cierna in Slovakia at the end of July, but neither this confrontation nor the subsequent meeting of the Czechoslovak leaders with the combined hierarchs of the Warsaw "Five" at Bratislava satisfied the latter (in particular Ulbricht, Gomułka and Shelest, the Ukrainian party secretary). After a massive buildup in the frontier zones, the Soviet Union and its allies invaded Czechoslovakia without warning (August 21) and Dubček and others were temporarily arrested. Svoboda's mission to Moscow and the ensuing negotiations led to a repeal of the more liberal reforms and to an uneasy modus vivendi.

At the beginning of 1969, a new federal constitution went into effect, setting up a Czech Socialist Republic and a Slovak Socialist Republic, with a federal government to be responsible for foreign affairs, defense and foreign trade. In April, Gustáv Husák replaced Dubček as party secretary. Husák, a conservative, did little to resist pressure for the strictest control, and he presided over a severe purge of some 400,000 Communist party members; the imposition of rigid censorship on education, the arts, and the media; an intense campaign of antireligious propaganda; and the enactment, in 1973, of a harsh penal code. President Ludvík Svoboda was reelected to a second five-year term in 1973, but fell ill and was replaced by Husák in 1975. Husák was reelected party leader in 1976 and again in 1981, and was reelected president in 1980. The salient features of Husák's regime have been economic orthodoxy and loyalty to Moscow.

The leading Czech dissident group, Charter 77, was formed in 1977 to monitor government adherence to the U.N. Declaration of Human Rights, the Helsinki Accord and U.N. covenants on civil, political, economic, social and cultural rights. The group's initial manifesto was signed by 242 members, but its membership is reported to be over 1,000, including many currently in jail.

The foreign policy of Czechoslovakia centers on its close relationship with the Soviet Union. In 1984, the government agreed to deploy new Soviet nuclear missiles on its territory. Relations with its Eastern European neighbors are generally smooth, although the Polish crisis of the early 1980s was a cause of serious concern to the Czechoslovak leadership. The Husák government has been generally successful in improving relations with Western European and Third World nations. Relations with West Germany were established in 1973. The long-standing dispute with Great Britain and the United States over the return of Czech gold confiscated by Germany during World War II was settled in 1981. The attempted suppression of the Charter 77 movement, however, has strained relations with Western countries in recent years.

Defense (1984): Military service is compulsory, for two years in the army and three years in the air force, and is followed by first reserve status till the age of 40, second reserve status till the age of 50. Strength is estimated at: army 198,000, air force 59,250, border troops 11,000. The People's Militia comprises 120,000 part-time personnel. 1980 defense expenditure was $2.75 billion, representing 3.1% of GNP. The country is a member of the Warsaw Pact and until August 1968 was free of foreign troops. Since Soviet intervention, however, five Soviet divisions have been stationed on Czechoslovak soil.

ECONOMY

Background: The two salient characteristics of the Czechoslovak economy are its central planning and its dependence on the Soviet Union and CMEA. In COMECON it ranks second only to East Germany in industrialization and per capita income, but its per capita growth rate has been slower than that of most others and about equal to that of the Soviet Union.

The degree of centralization has varied with the ideological rigor of the leadership. During the Stalinist period it was absolute, but the end of that era witnessed a slow process of relaxation of controls coinciding with a thaw in the political system during the late 1960s. The process was reversed following the fall of Dubček and the invasion of the country by Soviet troops. Other difficulties set in to slow growth—poor harvests, the energy crisis and chronic labor shortages. Western estimates of GNP show average annual GNP growth rates declined from 3.5% for 1965–70 to 2.1% for 1975–80. While output exceeded the goals set in the fifth five-year plan (1971–75), even the more modest goals of the sixth five-year plan (1975–80) were not met and had to be revised downward in 1978. These difficulties were acknowledged in the seventh five-year plan (1981–85), the overall goals of which were not only below those of the previous plan but well below previous achievements. Average annual increases in the NMP were set at 2.7% to 3.0%. There was also a move towards more flexible economic organization coupled with a warning that this did not signal a return to free-market principles. Since the stagnation of 1981–82, a slight recovery has taken place. In 1984 the economy grew by 3.2%, according to government figures.

After the Prague Spring, the radical economic reforms of the 1960s were dismantled and a highly conservative, centralized planning mechanism was reintroduced. It was only in the early 1980s, with a deteriorating growth rate and an actual negative figure in 1982, that the Czechoslovak authorities accepted the need for minimal changes. These changes, generally known as "the set of measures," were similarly conservative in design and sought to reinvigorate the economy by rather centralized instruments, emphasizing greater discipline and moral, as distinct from material, incentives. However, there was growing concern that the leadership's economic policy was paying insufficient attention to questions of raising labor productivity, higher technological content of manufactures and capital rejuvenation.

Agriculture has suffered from a persistent decline in the rural labor force and some neglect in terms of investments in machinery and fertilizers. Main crops are sugar beets, wheat, barley and potatoes. In 1979, the agricultural sector employed 14% of the labor force and produced 7% of the NMP (or 17% of the GNP). On the other hand, industry employed nearly half the labor force and produced 48% of the GNP. Agricultural land is almost entirely collectivized, with 90% of it in state farms, cooperative farms and state enterprises, and only 7% in private holdings. Engineering is the major branch of industry, accounting for one-third of industrial output.

Foreign trade: Foreign trade accounts for a third of Czechoslovakia's national income. Although about two-thirds of trade is with other CMEA members, trade with the West and with developing countries has become increasingly important. Most exchanges with the non-CMEA world are barter arrangements, while even trade with CMEA countries is balanced on a bilateral basis. Nevertheless, recent years have left substantial trade deficits because protectionist pressures have hurt such staple exports as shoes, steel and textiles, and because most raw-material imports have to be paid for in hard currencies.

In 1982, merchandise exports amounted to $15.637 billion and merchandise imports to $15.403 billion, leaving a surplus of $234 million. The annual average growth rate was 6.1% for exports and 4.3% for imports during 1970–82. The percentage share of merchandise exports was 5% for fuels, minerals and metals; 8% for other primary commodities; 6% for textiles and clothing; 52% for machinery and transport equipment; and 29% for other manufactured commodities. The percentage share of merchandise imports was 10% for food; 23% for fuels; 14% for other primary commodities; 35% for machinery and transport equipment; and 18% for other manufactures. The principal export partners are Soviet Union (36%), East Germany (10%), Poland (8%), West Germany (6%) and Hungary (6%). The principal import partners are Soviet Union (36%), East Germany (10%), Poland (8%), West Germany (6%) and Hungary (6%).

Employment: The employed civilian labor force was estimated in 1982 at 7.4 million, of which 14% were employed in agriculture and 37.7% in industry. Currently, shortages of manpower with special skills and a surplus of workers who cannot find employment in the fields in which they have been trained, present two of Czechoslovakia's most pressing problems. The anticipated annual growth rate of the labor force from 1980 to 2000 is projected at 0.6%.

Prices and wages: Nominal wages have risen sharply since the reforms started. Prices have also shown a strong upward tendency, resulting in little improvement in real incomes. In 1982, the government announced sharp price increases, including an average 41% increase in the cost of meat, 40% in the cost of tobacco products and 25% in the cost of domestic vodka.

Consumption: Standards of living are quite high on average in comparison with other Eastern European countries, but there are substantial differences between regions and between town and country. Consumer goods are becoming more freely available, but are often of poor quality and are frequently ill-matched to demand.

41

SOCIAL WELFARE

Social insurance (1981) in Czechoslovakia was financed from state funds, administered locally by the national committees and (with the exception of health services) supervised by the Ministry of Social Security.

Health services: Health care is supervised by the Ministry of Health (which is directly responsible for research institutes, spas and special clinics) and by regional national health institutes responsible to regional national committees. Direct administration is the function of district national health institutes (responsible to district national committees) comprising at least one hospital plus polyclinics, specialist clinics, pharmacies, etc. In 1982, there were 33.1 doctors per 10,000 population and 339.3 hospital beds per 10,000 population. The maternal mortality rate was 12.8 per 100,000 live births in 1977, and the infant mortality rate in 1981 was 16.8 per 1,000 live births. The average life expectancy for males is 67 years and for females 74 years. Free health facilities are available to all employees, apprentices, students, self-employed artists, members of producer cooperatives and, with some modifications, to members of farming cooperatives, together with their families. Sickness benefits for employees comprise 50% to 70% of average net earnings for the first three days of incapacity and 60% to 90% thereafter, the sum payable depending on length of service. Workers attending a sick member of the family are entitled to three to six days of special financial aid on a par with sickness benefits. During the 26-week maternity leave (35 weeks for a single mother) a mother is entitled to 90% of her average earnings. On giving birth, the working woman (or wife of a worker) receives a bonus of 2,000 crowns.

Pensions and other benefits: Retirement pensions, covering all wage earners, are tied to average income on a percentage scale according to length and type of employment. The three categories of occupation include (1) miners and air crews, (2) persons working in hard conditions and (3) others. Given the prerequisite minimum of 25 years of employment, men are pensionable at 60, women at from 53 to 57 according to the number of children reared. Minimum retirement pension amounts to between 50% and 60% of average earnings during the preceding five or 10 years (whichever is more favorable). The maximum full pension is 3,060 crowns per month and the minimum is 880, with higher rates for the first two occupation categories. Disability pensions amount to a minimum 50% of earnings—or minimum 60% in case of work injury. Widows' pensions (amounting to 60% of pension due to the employee at the time of decease) are available for the first year of widowhood (longer for crippled women and mothers of dependent children). Orphans' pensions are between 30% and 50% of the late employee's pension. Workers in farming cooperatives (and their families) are also entitled to retirement, disability, widows' and orphans' pensions, which are computed on the basis of length of service and average earnings. Pensions of private farmers depend on their contributions. Family allowances, available for children till leaving school and for students under 25, are proportionate to a worker's earnings. In addition, the family receives a monthly allowance for each child, ranging from 180 to 540 crowns depending on the number of children. Large families can also claim tax deductions, reduced nursery fees and lower rents. On the death of a worker, the family is granted 1,000 crowns for funeral expenses; if a member of the family dies, the employee receives 200 to 800 crowns.

Housing: In Czechoslovakia, housing compares favorably with the rest of Eastern Europe. As of 1982, more than 5 million dwellings existed, with an average of 3.8 rooms per dwelling. During the early 1980s, construction of new dwellings averaged more than 100,000 per year. Construction is financed by the state, cooperatives or individuals. State construction is geared to the needs of poorer families, dwellings being allocated by national committees on the basis of a waiting list. Cooperative housing construction is financed by members of housing and building cooperatives, which are founded by employees of individual enterprises, or by inhabitants of larger towns. The state provides a subsidy to the cooperatives and the state bank grants credit. Direct membership shares cover about 40% of the construction cost in towns, the remainder being met equally by credit and state subsidies. For working members of enterprise cooperatives, the debt deriving from credits is gradually written off. Private housing is financed by owners from personal means or with a 20 to 30 year state loan. Units administered by the national committees are divided into four rent categories, in each of which rent is computed on the basis of floor space plus equipment. In cooperative units, the relatively lower rent is on the basis of actual amortization of credit and the cost of maintenance, repairs and administration. Tenants in private housing negotiate rent separately with the owner.

EDUCATION

The unified system of Czechoslovak education comes under the authority of the Ministry of Education and Culture. Immediate supervision and control of primary and secondary schools is exercised by the local national committees, each of which must, nonetheless, comply with ministerial directives. Tuition is free at all levels, books and materials free up to secondary schooling. The language of instruction is Czech or Slovak, but in primary and secondary schools established for Hungarian, German, Ukrainian and Polish minorities, pupils are taught in their native tongue and Czech or Slovak is a compulsory subject. Illiteracy is negligible.

Primary education: Basic general education, which is compulsory, is provided by the nine-year school (*základní devítiletá škola*) for all children aged six to 16. Study is for six days a week and follows the same curriculum. Special emphasis is placed on the study of the native tongue, on basic natural and social sciences, and on mathematics. Timetables include practical lessons in workshops and in factories or on farms. Study groups are maintained to help weaker pupils. For children with fully employed parents there are after-school-hours facilities. Extracurricular activities, often sponsored by the Union of Youth organizations, are encouraged. Attached to schools are parents' associations, which provide contact between parents and teachers.

Secondary education: The nine-year school is followed by one of three types of secondary school: (a) the four-year general secondary school (*střední vseobecně vzdělávací škola*), which concentrates mainly on preparing pupils for university education but includes a polytechnical syllabus; (b) the four-year vocational secondary school (*střední odborná škola*), which combines vocational secondary training with a wide range of academic subjects and which feeds the higher technical schools; (c) the two- to four-year apprentice-training center (*odborné učiliště*), which leads directly into either the three-year workers' secondary school (*střední škola pro pracující*) or five-year vocational technical and training schools for workers (*podnikový institut* or *podniková technická škola*)—the latter being geared to higher technical positions and the former to general positions, or, in some cases, to further higher education. Matriculating pupils from all three main categories are, however, eligible for higher education. In the third category, apprentice training is run by the enterprises and trade unions concerned, together with the national committees.

Special education is available, with free tuition and treatment where necessary, for handicapped children at all levels.

Universities and higher education comprise six full universities (the Charles at Prague; Comenius at Bratislava; Purkyňová at Brno; Palacký at Olomouc; Pavla Jozefa Šafárika at Košice, founded in 1959; the 17 November University at Prague, founded in 1961, and offering foreign students courses conducted in Czech, Slovak, English and French), 16 technical universities and higher colleges (including the Prague School of Economics; Bratislava School of Economics; Prague, Brno and Slovak technical universities; universities of agriculture at Prague, Brno and Nitra, etc.), nine academies of music, drama and art (Prague, Bratislava and Brno) and several teacher-training colleges. The medical faculties are incorporated in the universities. Courses of higher education last five years except in teacher-training colleges and most art academies (four years), and for medicine, architecture and theatre science (six years). All higher studies are completed with examinations. First degrees granted are either *promovaný* (graduated) in the humanities and pure sciences, or *inženýr* (engineer). There are two higher degrees.

Educational Institutions (1982–83)

	Institutions	Staff	Students
Primary/general secondary	6,852	99,716	2,138,088
Other secondary	2,505	n.a.	731,885
Higher	36	21,146	191,928

Adult education: Secondary schools for workers offer evening and day courses. Curricula include most of the subjects taught in secondary schools and polytechnical training. Courses at university level usually last a year longer than normal courses.

MASS MEDIA

The Press (1981):
Dailies: *Rudé Právo*, Prague and Bratislava (Czech and Slovak editions), Communist, 950,000; *Práce*, Prague, trade union, 317,000; *Pravdá* (s),

Bratislava, Slovak CP, 330,000; *Mladá Fronta*, Prague, youth, 239,000; *Zemědělské noviny*, Prague, agricultural/forestry, 342,000; *Československý sport*, Prague, sport, 185,000; *Smena*, Bratislava, youth, 129,000; *Svobodné slovo*, Prague, Socialist, 228,000; *Lidová Demokracie*, Prague, Catholic, 217,000; *Rovnost*, Brno, CP, 115,000; *Práca*, Bratislava, Slovak trade union, 230,000; *Večerní Praha* (e), Prague, CP, 120,000; *Új Szó*, Bratislava, Hungarian, 85,000; *Nová Svoboda*, Ostrava, CP, 198,000; *Pravda*, Plzeň, CP, 72,000.

Periodicals: (Prague) *Vlasta* (w), women's illus., 740,000; *Mladý Svét* (w), youth illus., 420,000; *Svět socialismu* (w), Soviet friendship, 105,000; *Květy* (w), illus., 360,000; *Literární měsíčník* (m), Writers' Union political/cultural, 15,000; *Odborár* (f), trade union, 160,000; *Svět v obrazech* (w), illus., 120,000; *Technický týdenik* (w), technical, 33,000; *Kulturní práce* (m), trade union cultural, 14,500; *Dikobraz* (w), satirical, 525,000; *Světova literatura* (f), for. lit., 12,000; *Kino* (f), film, 150,000; *Katolické noviny* (w), Catholic, 130,000; (Bratislava) *Život* (w), Slovak illus., 180,000; *Nové Slovo* (formerly *Predvoj*) (w), Slovak CP, 50,000; *Slovenské Pohľady* (m), Slovak lit., 6,000; *Roháč*, Slovak satirical, 120,000; *Slovenka* (w), women's, 220,000.

Broadcasting: The state-run Czechoslovak Radio, based in Prague and Bratislava, maintains a national service and is comprised of five national networks. Various local stations broadcast from around the country. Foreign broadcasts are made in 12 languages including English, French, Italian and Ukrainian. Czechoslovak Television, with studios in Prague, Bratislava, Brno, Ostrava and Košice, broadcasts daily for morning and evening periods.

CONSTITUTIONAL SYSTEM

Constitution: The Czechoslovak Socialist Republic, whose second communist constitution, of the Soviet type, was adopted in 1960 and amended in 1968, 1971 and 1975, is a federal state of two nations possessing equal rights, the Czechs and the Slovaks. The status of "Socialist Republic" presupposes the completion of a period of "socialist construction."

Legislative: The bicameral Federal Assembly sits in Prague. The two chambers of the Federal Assembly are the House of the People, with 200 deputies, and the House of Nationalities, composed of 75 Czech and 75 Slovak deputies. All assembly members are elected to five-year terms. The two houses have equal powers, and legislation must be approved by both. For most important matters, there must be a majority of both Czechs and Slovaks separately in the House of Nationalities, a provision intended as a safeguard for Slovak interests. A permanent body, the Presidium of the Federal Assembly, composed of 20 Czech and 20 Slovak deputies, carries out the functions of the Federal Assembly when it is not sitting. Constitutional amendment and the election of the president of the Republic require a majority of three-fifths in the House of the People and three-fifths of Czechs and Slovaks separately in the House of Nationalities. The competence of the Federal Assembly is over federal matters, and these are constitutionally defined as being those specifically delegated by the Czech and Slovak republics. The following are within the exclusive jurisdiction of the federal authorities: foreign policy, national defense, material resources of the federation and protection of the federal constitution. In fairly wide areas, jurisdiction is divided between the federal and republican authorities. The legislature of the *Czech Socialist Republic* is the Czech National Council with 200 members and of the *Slovak Socialist Republic* it is the Slovak National Council with 150 members. The Slovak National Council, in common with all Slovak republican organs, sits in Bratislava.

Executives: At the federal level, executive power is vested in the federal government, which is answerable to the Federal Assembly (in theory). The government is headed by a president who is elected by the Federal Assembly to a five-year term. The president, with the approval of the Federal Assembly, appoints the federal government, currently composed of a prime minister, 10 deputy prime ministers and 16 ministers. At the republican level, administration is exercised by the governments of the Czech and Slovak republics.

Local government: Czechoslovakia is divided into 12 regions (*kraje*) and over 100 districts (*okresy*). Local government is vested in the national committee (*národní výbor*) at regional, district, municipal and local levels, while Prague has its central national committee and 10 city district national committees. Candidates proposed by the National Front are elected directly for a five-year term. The national committees comprise a membership of 15 to 25 at local, 60 to 120 at district and 80 to 150 at regional or Prague central levels. Members elect councils whose function is to direct and coordinate the activities of the national committee.

Judiciary: There is a Constitutional Court to decide potential legislative conflict between the federal and republican assemblies and (in theory) to safeguard the right of the individual, as constitutionally guaranteed. There is, however, no right of individual recourse to the Constitutional Court. Otherwise, justice is administered through a Supreme Court (*Nejvyšší Soud*) and regional, district, military and local people's courts. Judges of the Supreme Court are elected by the Federal Assembly, of regional courts by regional national committees, of district and people's courts by citizens. The judiciary is independent. Supervision of the observance of laws by public bodies and by individual citizens rests with the procuracy (*prokuratura*). The procurator-general is appointed or removed by the president of the republic and is responsible to the Federal Assembly.

Party: Five political parties and several nonpolitical organizations form the National Front (*Národní Fronta*), but this is dominated by the Communist party and its allies, the remaining Socialist party (middle-class intelligentsia), People's party (Catholics), the Slovak Revival party and Slovak Freedom party (both comprising former Democrats). In Slovakia, the Communist party of Slovakia is predominant. The Czechoslovak Communist party is constitutionally designated as the guiding force in society and the state, and has a membership of 1,600,000. The structure of the Czechoslovak Communist party follows that of the Soviet Communist party, with supreme authority theoretically resting in the periodic party congress. The congress elects a Central Committee with a Presidium and Secretariat that are in practice the real policy making units.

Leading political figures: Gustáv Husák (president of the republic, general secretary of the Czechoslovak Communist party), Ľubomir Štrougal (prime minister), Bohuslav Chnoupek (foreign minister), Col.-Gen. Milan Vaclavik (defense minister), Leopold Ler (finance minister), Bohumil Urban (foreign trade minister), Vratislav Vajnar (interior minister), Josef Korčak (deputy prime minister, Czech Republic prime minister), Peter Colotka (deputy prime minister, Slovak Republic prime minister).

BIOGRAPHICAL SKETCHES

Vasil Biľak. Biľak, a Ukrainian from Slovakia and Central Committee secretary in charge of ideology and international questions, was born in 1917 to a family of poor peasants. He took part in the Slovak national uprising of 1944, joined the party in 1945, worked at a variety of junior posts in party administration and became party head in the Prešov region of eastern Slovakia, where the bulk of the Ukrainian minority is to be found. In 1962 he was promoted to the Presidium and Secretariat of the Slovak party and to the Czechoslovak party's Central Committee at the same time. In 1964 he was chairman of the influential Ideological Committee of the Slovak party and became very close to Dubček, whom he succeeded as Slovak party head in 1968. During the 1968 reforms, Biľak played an equivocal role, and in consequence, Husák managed to have him removed from the Slovak post. Biľak, however, had powerful backers in Moscow; in 1969 he took over as secretary in charge of ideology and held the post thereafter. From that time on, he was one of the most forceful and intransigent advocates of the ultraorthodox line in Czechoslovak politics.

Gustáv Husák. Husák, a Slovak, party leader after 1969 and president from 1975, was born in 1913 near Bratislava. A member of the Communist party before the war, he was one of the leaders of the Slovak national uprising of 1944. In 1946–50 he was chairman of the Board of Commissioners of Slovakia, the de facto Slovak government, so that he played a major role in promoting the communist takeover in Slovakia. In 1950, together with several other prominent Slovak political figures, he was purged as a "bourgeois nationalist"; despite expressing self-criticism, he was arrested in 1951 and given a life sentence in 1954. He was released only in 1960, won readmission to the party in 1963 and was fully rehabilitated later that year. In 1968 he used the more open political situation to his own advantage, appearing as a strong supporter of the reform whereas in reality he was primarily an opponent of Novotný, then party leader. Husák was made deputy prime minister and supervised the federalization of the country. After the Soviet-led invasion, he succeeded in ousting Biľak from the leadership of the Slovak party, impressing the Kremlin with his readiness to support Soviet policies,

47

notably during negotiations on the Moscow protocols intended to legalize the invasion. His reward was the succession to Dubček in April 1969, at which point he gave up the leadership of the Slovak party. In the early 1970s he presided over a massive purge of real and alleged supporters of the 1968 reforms, a purge involving half a million people. Thereafter he achieved his greatest success, maintaining the same system, intact and unchanging for a decade and a half.

Miloš Jakeš. Jakeš, a Czech and a full member of the Presidium and of the Central Committee Secretariat, was born in 1922. In the 1960s he served in the interior ministry, and at the moment of the Soviet-led invasion lined up with the handful of those supporting the Soviet action. Jakeš concerned himself with economic activities in the 1970s and was generally regarded as a relatively hard-line figure, with considerable influence in the party.

Jozef Lenárt. Lenárt, a Slovak and head of the Slovak party, was born in 1923. In 1944 he took part in the Slovak national uprising, then worked in various party and state posts until 1953, when he was sent to Moscow for three years to study at the Higher Party School. After his return, his rise in the Slovak hierarchy was rapid. In 1958 he joined the Secretariat of the Slovak party Central Committee; in 1962 he took over as chairman of the Slovak National Council (the Slovak government). This gave him a seat on the Czechoslovak party's Presidium. A year later he became prime minister of Czechoslovakia, an office he held until 1968. He was ambivalent on the reforms, and so suffered demotion to candidate membership in the Presidium; at the same time, he was given charge of international policy in the Secretariat. He retained his posts after the invasion, and in 1970, no doubt because he was regarded as trustworthy by Husák, was made head of the Slovak party. Lenárt's career was somewhat unusual in communist terms—very few politicians have succeeded in making the kind of comeback he did. This may be explained largely by his caution and colorlessness.

Jaromír Obzina. Obzina, a Czech and the federal interior minister, was born in 1929. After the war he served in various regional party posts, then in 1951 studied in Moscow at the Higher Party School, returning in 1957. Thereafter he held political-military posts, notably at the Military Technical Academy in Brno. He was transferred to the Central Committee apparatus in 1965, played no role in the reforms of 1968, then served in the education and science department of the Central Committee (1969–73), ending up as its head. He took over as interior minister in 1973. Obzina was evidently one of the architects of the hard-line measures taken against the Charter 77 opposition.

Ľubomir Štrougal. Štrougal, a Czech and prime minister of Czechoslovakia, was born in 1924, the son of a railway worker. His most striking political characteristic was an ability to survive all major political upheavals, remaining at the top and even enjoying a measure of popularity. He joined the party in 1945 and worked in its apparatus until 1949, studying law at the same time. He joined the Central Committee in 1958, was made minister of agriculture (1959–61), then took over the sensitive post of interior minister from the purged Rudolf Barák, a rival of Novotný. A protégé of the party leader, Štrougal was made Central Committee secretary in 1965 (in charge of agriculture). Despite his association with Novotný, Štrougal decided to back the Dubček reform movement, and was made deputy prime minister in April 1968. At this point he was seen as a supporter of market-oriented economic reform. After the Soviet-led invasion, Štrougal emerged as a supporter of the contrary course and became a protagonist of normalization. He was a full member of the Presidium from November 1968, and was promoted to the prime ministry in 1970. Štrougal enjoyed a somewhat undeserved reputation as a reformer during the Husák years; in reality, he presided over the economic stagnation of the 1970s, and there was little direct evidence to suggest that he had any commitment to genuine reform. Where he did differ from his colleagues was in his style, which was more direct and down to earth than that of most Czechoslovak politicians.

EAST GERMANY

EAST GERMANY

Features: East Germany, the German Democratic Republic, bounded by West Germany, Czechoslovakia, Poland and the Baltic Sea, has under half the size and one-third the population of West Germany. Formed from the postwar Soviet zone of occupation plus East Berlin, it covers much of the traditional German provinces of Brandenburg, Mecklenburg, Saxony, Saxony-Anhalt and Thuringia. Two-thirds of the territory comprise part of the glaciated North European Plain, 200 miles (124 km.) broad at the Oder-Neisse frontier. This is characterized by low morainic ridges, marsh, numerous lakes, sand, clay and gravel heathland and north-flowing rivers rising in the upland third of the country. In the southwest, a section of the German Central Uplands (*Mittelgebirge*) reaches altitudes of 3,500 ft/1,000 m. in the Thuringer Wald and Harz Mountains (Brocken 3,747 ft/1,142 m.), while in the south the Erzgebirge, serving as political frontier with Czechoslovakia, contain the state's highest peak, Fichtelberg (4,078 ft/1,214 m.). The Elbe River drains most of the area and is separated from the Oder Basin by the Lausitz and Fläming heathlands. The Baltic coast is fringed with sandy islands, notably Rügen. The climate is continental with strong maritime influences.

Although lagging behind western parts of Germany, the prewar territory was industrialized in relation to most of Eastern Europe. Generally poor in minerals, East Germany contains major lignite deposits, considerable potash and rock salt and small quantities of iron, copper and tin, and it is now one of the foremost industrial states of Europe. Industry is associated with the lignite- and chemical-producing regions of Saxony and the Middle Elbe, and with East Berlin, lignite being the major energy source. Forestry is concentrated in the mountain areas of the south. East Germany is not agriculturally self-sufficient, but there is large-scale cultivation of rye, wheat, barley, sugar beets, potatoes and vegetables, and widespread animal husbandry.

Roads and railways, radiating from Berlin and Leipzig, and extensive inland waterways form the densest communications network in Eastern Europe, though Berlin's economic advantages as a prewar transportation hub are nullified by partition. Four highways and four railways between West Berlin and West Germany constitute corridors across East Germany. Rostock is the only major port.

Area (incl. E. Berlin): 41,500 sq. miles/108,200 sq. km. (East Berlin 150 sq. miles/400 sq. km.).

Mean max. and min. temperatures: E. Berlin (53° N, 13° E; 190 ft/58 m.) 65°F/18°C (July) 30°F/−1°C (Jan.) Leipzig (51° N, 12° E; 410 ft/125 m.) 65°F/18°C (July) 31°F/−1°C (Jan.).

Relative humidity: E. Berlin 86%; Leipzig 85%.

Mean annual rainfall: E. Berlin 23 in./595 mm.; Leipzig 24 in./610 mm.

POPULATION

Total population (1983): 16,700,000, including East Berlin.

Chief towns and populations (1981): EAST BERLIN (1,157,600), Leipzig (561,900), Dresden (516,600), Karl-Marx-Stadt (317,700), Magdeburg (289,300), Halle (232,400), Rostock (234,500), Erfurt (212,000).

Ethnic composition: There is a Sorb minority of about 30,000.

Language: The official language is German.

Religion: About 47% of the population is Protestant (mainly Evangelical) and 7% Roman Catholic.

RECENT HISTORY

Following the unconditional surrender of Germany in 1945, the Tripartite Conference at Potsdam divided the central and western parts of the country into four zones of occupation, British, American, French and Soviet, providing for a four-power administration of Berlin. The Soviet zone included the *Länder* of Mecklenburg, Saxony-Anhalt, Brandenburg, Saxony and Thuringia (replaced in 1952 by 14 *Bezirke* or regions, named for their capital cities). Germany's present frontiers are in effect based upon a provisional allied demarcation.

In 1946 the Soviet Union laid the foundations of a communist administration in the Soviet zone of occupation lying to the west of the river Oder and Neisse and, under Soviet aegis, a communist-dominated Socialist Unity party (SED) was founded. In 1948 the Soviet Union blockaded Berlin from the west, and in the subsequent 15-month siege only a massive Anglo-American airlift could prevent further Soviet encroachments on West Berlin. With the virtual breakdown of the Berlin Inter-Allied Control Commission, Allied condominium of Germany ceased. Five months after the German Federal Republic had been established in the West, a Soviet-style constitution (October 1949) proclaimed the German Democratic Republic (DDR) in the East. The new state remained unrecognized outside the communist world. Wilhelm Pieck was appointed as president and Otto Grotewohl as chancellor, while the secretary-general of the SED, Walter Ulbricht, became the latter's deputy. By 1950 the People's Chamber (*Volkskammer*) contained only SED members and their allies. A Stalinist system of terror and the Soviet military

52

presence reinforced the communists' totalitarian rule. General rioting in several cities in 1953 was suppressed with Soviet army intervention and followed by ruthless reprisals but, despite some modest attempts at internal liberalization, a stream of refugees, including thousands of young and skilled workers, flowed westward during the 1950s. In 1955 the Soviet Union accorded East Germany full sovereignty.

President Pieck died in 1960 and the SED secretary, Ulbricht, was appointed chairman of the State Council, thus heading both party and government. For a while in 1961, at the height of the Cold War, it appeared that the Soviet Union, hinting at the conclusion of a separate peace with East Germany, was ready to relinquish direct control of West Berlin's corridors to the Federal Republic, and in that year the Berlin Wall was built with the purpose of stopping East German migration and of further isolating West Berlin.

The building of the Berlin Wall served in many ways to transform the internal situation by forcing the population of the state to come to terms with its existence. On this basis, Ulbricht could begin the process of creating a more stable and in many ways more self-confident regime. The introduction of the New Economic System in the 1960s and the integration of the technocratic elite achieved thereby provided the foundations for a significant economic takeoff. These internal changes were confined to economics. Political controls remained strict; in international affairs, the GDR followed the Soviet line very closely.

With the advent to power in 1963 of the liberal wing of the SED, a two-year period of internal liberalization, including dynamic economic reforms, and of conciliatory overtures toward West Germany was inaugurated, but after the removal of Khrushchev in 1964, the conservative faction led by Erich Honecker recaptured power at the 11th SED Plenum (1965). The liberal intelligentsia was drastically purged and there was a reversion to orthodoxy at home and a brake on détente with the West. In 1968, East Germany played a notably assertive role in the Soviet military intervention in Czechoslovakia.

Only recently has the DDR emerged on the world diplomatic scene, following two decades of isolation from the noncommunist world. This has been due largely to superpower détente and changing relationships in Europe during the early 1970s. The adoption then of a new policy toward Eastern Europe (*Ostpolitik*) by the government of the Federal Republic of Germany (FRG) resulted in talks being held for the first time since 1945 between representatives of the two German states. In August 1970, the FRG signed a treaty with the Soviet Union renouncing the use of force and accepting all postwar European boundaries. The four occupying powers of Berlin concluded the Quadripartite Agreement in 1971, which clarified the details of access rights to West Berlin and allowed West Berliners to visit the DDR. In 1972, a Basic Treaty was signed between the DDR and the FRG, officially recognizing the postwar borders of the two German states and acknowledging each other's internal and external sovereignty. As a result of these various agreements, many Western countries established diplomatic relations with the DDR. The DDR became a full member of the United Nations in 1973.

In 1974, a further agreement was signed between the two Germanies to establish permanent representative missions in Bonn and East Berlin.

In 1971, Erich Honecker replaced Ulbricht as SED leader. Upon Ulbricht's death in 1973, Willi Stoph became chairman of the State Council. Honecker replaced Stoph in 1976, thus becoming the leader of both the party and the state. Stoph was reappointed chairman of the Council of Ministers, a position he had held from 1964 to 1973. The leadership has since maintained a high degree of stability.

The recent buildup of nuclear weapons by the two superpowers on European soil has sparked a widespread popular peace movement in the DDR. The movement is linked closely with the Protestant church and has been a constant source of irritation for the government. The applications of an estimated 400,000 East Germans to emigrate to the West also pose a serious problem for the regime. In 1984, at least 50 people who had applied to emigrate were arrested, in order to discourage further emigration applications.

Since the mid-1970s, relations between the DDR and the FRG have been in flux. In 1981, the first official meeting of the two leaders in 11 years took place, resulting in the easing of travel restrictions and discussion of new trade agreements. In 1983, however, a deterioration in relations occurred as a result of the death of three West Germans at a border checkpoint, and Honecker's scheduled trip to the FRG was canceled. Since the deployment of U.S. missiles in West Germany in 1983, however, both states have made attempts to improve relations in order to reduce tensions. In late 1984, Honecker's scheduled trip to the FRG—it was to have been the first by an East German leader—was postponed, apparently due to Soviet pressure.

The DDR is a member of COMECON. Its reaction to the Polish crisis of the early 1980s was condemnation of the Solidarity movement and approval of martial law. In 1984, the DDR agreed to accept the deployment of new Soviet medium-range nuclear missiles on its territory.

Defense (1983): Military service is compulsory and lasts 18 months. Strength is estimated at: army 116,000, navy 14,000, air force 37,000. Paramilitary forces include 70,000 security and frontier troops and 450,000 armed workers (*Betriebskampfgrupfen*). The estimate of 1980 defense expenditure was $6.02 billion, representing 5.0% of GNP. East Germany is a member of the Warsaw Pact, and Soviet troops maintain permanent positions on its soil.

ECONOMY

Background: The most industrialized country in Eastern Europe with a per capita GNP that is not only the highest in the communist world but also higher than that of Britain and Italy, East Germany has been the economic bellwether of COMECON countries. It also has a rather conservative communist leadership, with a deep distrust of West German penetration of its economy. As a result its centralized planning and industrial structures have grown more, not less, rigid over the years, even at the expense of growth and expansion. All industry is state-owned; the last private enterprises were absorbed in 1972. Agriculture is also fully collectivized, apart from small private plots. The economy has suffered severe constraints in other directions. There is an acute labor shortage, the result of declining birthrates; unlike West Germany, East Germany has not been able to make up this shortage through immigrant guestworkers. Although war-reparation payments to the Soviet Union ceased in 1953, the Soviets continued to milk East Germany thoughout the Ulbricht and Honecker regimes. There is also a serious lack of natural resources, particularly of energy, and about two-fifths of the country's energy needs must be met by imports. Notwithstanding these drawbacks, East German industry has made impressive strides, providing 61% of NMP. The manufactures are diversified and include metals, machinery, machine tools, chemicals, rubber, electronics, consumer durables, textiles, buses, locomotives, bicycles and construction materials.

Although agricultural contribution to the NMP has decreased, nearly 70% of domestic food requirements are produced locally. Unlike some other Eastern-bloc countries, collectivization has been a relative success, and farm productivity is well rewarded in low taxes, high salaries, fringe benefits and subsidized housing.

The 1975–80 five-year plan was relatively successful, with an actual growth rate of 4.3%. The five-year plan for 1980–85 projected an annual growth rate of 5% in national income, industrial production and labor productivity, and 6% in foreign trade. Political developments, especially those in Poland, may have modified these projections.

In 1983, the economy grew by 4.3%, fulfilling the planned target of 4.2%, and achieved the highest growth rate among COMECON members except for Bulgaria. Industrial production rose 4.6% (4.5% targeted) and net output rose by 6.6%.

Foreign trade: Within COMECON, East Germany's primary trading partners, trade deficits or surpluses are irrelevant, because exports and imports are based on long-term balanced contracts, and imbalances can be corrected through increased shipments in the required direction. East Germany's ties to West Germany are also reflected in trade. The Federal Republic treats this trade as intranational and extends an annual interest-free swing credit of several hundred million dollars to its neighbor. West Germany also provides some access to the EC. Merchandise trade between the two countries has therefore been growing despite political distrust; the trade balance is in favor of East Germany. East Germany has recently expanded its trade contacts to include not only such industrialized countries as Britain, Sweden and France, but also many Third World countries, including India, Nicaragua, Morocco and Thailand.

The categories and quantities of imports are strictly regulated and are generally limited to goods not produced within COMECON. All trade is conducted directly through foreign trade organizations rather than individual enterprises, although the latter may use a portion of their foreign-currency earnings independently to bolster exports.

In 1982, merchandise exports amounted to $21.743 billion and merchandise imports to $20.196 billion, leaving a surplus of $1.547 billion. The principal exports are machinery, equipment and transport vehicles (56%);

durable consumer goods (15%); fuels, minerals and metals (12%); and chemicals and building materials (11%). The principal imports are machinery, equipment and transport vehicles (33%); fuels, minerals and metals (33%); other raw materials, semimanufactured goods and food (19%); and chemical products and building materials (9%). The principal export partners are the Soviet Union (35%), Czechoslovakia (10%), Poland (9%) and West Germany (7%). The principal import partners are the Soviet Union (35%), West Germany (8%), Czechoslovakia (8%) and Poland (7%).

Employment: East Germany has had an almost static labor force for many years, increased industrial employment being almost wholly at the expense of agriculture. Consequently, much stress has been placed on labor productivity. Multiple shift working is widely practiced. The total labor force was estimated in 1981 at 8,296,000, of which 10.7% was employed in agriculture and 41.2% in industry.

Prices and wages: Real wages have risen by about 3% per annum between 1978 and 1982. Retail prices have been stable throughout the 1970s and into the 1980s.

Consumption: Standards of living in East Germany now compare favorably with those of Western Europe, although difficulties have been experienced in matching consumer goods production and demands. As of 1982, 40% of all East German households owned cars, 90% owned refrigerators, 93% had television sets and 84% had washing machines. Housing was given high priority, with a move toward larger units.

SOCIAL WELFARE

A unified social insurance system has since 1951 been operated by the Confederation of the Free German Trade Union to cover all workers except collective farmers, private craftsmen, owners of private enterprises and certain other classes, who are insured under the German Insurance Institution. The latter is also responsible for voluntary property and personal insurance. Social insurance is supervised by the Central Social Insurance Board and administered locally by enterprises. Workers make a compulsory contribution of 10% of gross earnings or a monthly maximum of 60 marks; employers contribute 12.5% (mining enterprises 22.5%) of gross earnings and an amount for accidents proportionate to danger; the state contributes the balance. In 1982, total expenditure on social insurance was almost 26 billion marks. University, college and trade school students, workers in cooperatives, and family labor contribute according to special rates. Pensioners are insured without contributions. A five-day working week is now constitutionally enforced. Annual paid vacation leave for workers is from 18 to 24 days.

Health services: Free health services, available to all insured and their dependents, include hospitalization, medical and dental treatment, artificial aids and spa therapy. There are no prescription charges. Recent expansion of health services has strengthened the role of industrial and enterprise clinics and of rural outpatient dispensaries. As of 1978, there were 106.3 hospital beds per 10,000 population, and as of 1980 20.2 doctors per 10,000 population. The maternal mortality rate in 1978 was 18.5 per 100,000 live births. The infant mortality rate was 12.3 per 1,000 live births in 1981. As of 1979, the average life expectancy for the East German male was 68 years and for the female 74 years. The insured has the right to choose a doctor, on whose panel he or she remains for a minimum of three months. Sick workers receive wage equalization payments from their place of employment totaling 90% of their net earnings for the first six weeks of illness and up to 90% thereafter, according to the number of dependents and the earnings category. Special schemes exist for sick miners, railway and postal employees, workers in cooperatives, self-employed persons and TB patients. The temporary disability pension granted in the case of occupational injury or disease is 100% of net earnings. A grant of $66\frac{2}{3}\%$ of earnings is given if permanent disability results from a work injury. Maternity benefit for working women is 100% of earnings, payable for six weeks before and 20 weeks after confinement.

Pensions and other benefits: Given at least 15 years of prior insurance, men are pensionable at 65, women at 60 and those continuing in employment are granted both full pay and pension. Workers in certain vocations and victims of Nazism are pensionable at an earlier age. The monthly minimum pension is fixed at 270 marks. The People's Solidarity and other mass organizations provide, free of charge, additional assistance to the aged. There is a state grant for every child born, consisting of 1,000 marks. A state children's allowance of 20 marks a month is paid for the first and second child, 50 marks a month for the third child, 60 for the fourth child and 70 for each additional child.

Housing: The ravages of World War II, in particular as a result of Allied bombing, created grave housing problems above all in the cities. In recent years construction of new dwellings has been on the rise. Over 125,000 new units were built in 1982. In the same year, East Germany was the only Eastern European state to have inside running water and a bathroom in 100% of its dwellings. The state sector of housing is predominant; new state housing is allocated by the housing offices of local councils, operating in conjunction with housing commissions comprising three to five local citizens. Distribution of enterprise dwellings is influenced by enterprise management and trade unions. Large annual subsidies by the state have been necessary to meet construction costs of new housing and, as a result, a new rent tariff for state housing was introduced in 1966. Rent for new units let after this date is based on individual costs of construction, equipment and maintenance. Cooperative dwelling units are built by the Workers' Housing Construction Cooperatives (AWGs) formed by workers in industry, trade, state administration, mass organizations and higher educational institutions. The AWGs are financed by interest-free state loans (of up to 85% of building costs); by the shares of members, which are proportionate to size of the housing unit; by workers' (optional) assistance in the construction or maintenance of the housing complex; and by contributions from the cultural and social funds of the particular enterprise. The AWG system of allocation entitles one person to a one-room apartment (excluding bathroom, kitchen, etc.), two or three persons to two rooms, three or four persons to three rooms and four or five persons to three or four rooms. Cooperative rents are lower than state rents. The private sector includes mainly rural housing stock. East German construction usually takes the form of prefabricated high-rise multiple units; large-scale townships include the Black Pump complex (at Hoyerswerda-Neustadt), Schwedt, Eisenhüttenstadt, Leuna II (at Halle) and Guben. Wartime damage to historically outstanding areas such as Görlitz (in Dresden) has been made good.

EDUCATION

The Ministry of National Education is broadly responsible for education at all levels; immediate control is exercised by local organizations of government and the school boards, representing staff and general public. The entire system is highly centralized. The illiteracy rate is 1%.

Primary and secondary education: In 1975, the replacement of elementary and secondary schools by comprehensive schools, begun in 1959, was completed. After the municipally or industrially run optional kindergarten, there is free and obligatory education for all children aged six to 16. Upon completion of study at the 10-year comprehensive school, the student has three options: (a) he/she may apply to stay in the comprehensive school for a further two years to take the advanced-level examination (*Abitur*), necessary for admission to establishments of higher education; (b) he/she may serve a two-year technical apprenticeship, thus qualifying for enrollment at a three-year polytechnical school preparing the student for specialized jobs; or (c) he/she may serve a three-year vocational apprenticeship, offering a mixture of academic and polytechnical training, leading to enrollment in a university or college.

University and higher education: Higher education is provided at Humboldt University, Berlin; the five other universities of Leipzig, Rostock, Greifswald, Jena and Halle; three universities of technology (*Technische Universitäten* and *Hochschulen*) at Dresden, Magdeburg and Leuna-Merseburg; higher institutes (*Hochschulen* and *Hochschulinstitute*) for specialized study in medicine, economics, art, architecture, political science, agronomy, forestry, sport, etc.; and technical colleges (*Fachschulen*). Many of these, including the eight teacher training colleges, have been founded since World War II. All establishments of higher education are legally government institutions and are centrally administered. In the more specialized *Hochschulen* and *Fachschulen*, departments rather than faculties are the usual division. Student affairs are supervised by the Free German Youth movement (*Freie Deutsche Jugend*), which embraces the majority of students. The great majority of students receive either full or partial tuition assistance. In addition, a monthly bonus may be awarded for outstanding performance; this is commensurate with the equivalent income from a job.

Educational Institutions (1981)

	Institutions	Staff	Students
Comprehensive (primary/secondary)	5,127	n.a.	2,106,463
Extended comprehensive	276	n.a.	46,051
Technical schools	240	n.a.	173,411
Vocational schools	973	n.a.	448,386
Higher	54	n.a.	130,633

Adult education: Four "faculties" provide basic and remedial secondary education (leading to matriculation), and there are extramural courses at university level.

MASS MEDIA

The Press (1984):

Dailies: Neues Deutschland, Berlin, SED, 1,094,327; Berliner Zeitung, Berlin, SED, 353,421; Berliner Zeitung am Abend, Berlin, SED, 197,931; Tribüne, Berlin, trade union, 407,000; Sächsisches Tagesblatt, Dresden, LDPD, 66,430; Liberal-Demokratische Zeitung, Halle, LDPD, 56,500; Der Morgen, Berlin, LDPD, 51,840; National-Zeitung, Berlin, NDPD, 55,038; Neue Zeit, Berlin, CDU, 91,643; Sächsische Neueste Nachrichten, Dresden, NDP, 29,623; Der Neuer Weg, Halle, CDU, 36,745; Thüringische Landeszeitung, Weimar, LDPD, 59,000; Thüringer Neueste Nachrichten, Weimar, NDP, 30,625; Der Demokrat, Rostock, CDU, 18,393; Märkische Union, Dresden, CDU, 3,964; Mitteldeutsche Neueste Nachrichten, Leipzig, NDPD, 19,561; Thüringer Tagesblatt, Weimar, CDU, 30,340; Norddeutsche Zeitung, Schwerin, LDPD, 21,997; Norddeutsche Neueste Nachrichten, Rostock, NDP, 33,013; and the following SED organs: Freiheit, Halle, 547,146; Märkische Volksstimme, Potsdam, 301,320; Leipziger Volkszeitung, Leipzig, 465,000; Neuer Tag, Frankfurt/Ode, 180,728; Das Volk, Erfurt, 370,029; Volksstimme, Magdeburg, 423,378.

Periodicals: Neue Berliner Illustrierte (w), Berlin, illus., 747,317; Für Dich (w), Berlin, women's, 936,044; Sonntag (w), Berlin, cult., 20,000; Eulenspiegel (w), Berlin, satirical, 457,604; Die Weltbühne (w), Berlin, internat. affairs, 30,000; Sibylle (f), Leipzig, fashion; Pramo (m), Leipzig, fashion, 753,100; Neue Deutsche Literatur (m), Berlin, lit.; Einheit, Berlin, SED theory, 250,000.

Censorship of publications: Acquisition of licenses and newsprint is strictly regulated by the ministerially supervised Presseamt (Press Office), and since 1953 the Allgemeines Deutsches Nachrichtenbüro (ADN) news agency has been a state monopoly.

Broadcasting: The Staatliches Komitee für Rundfunk beim Ministerrat der DDR (State Committee for Radio Broadcasting) maintains three domestic networks: Berliner Rundfunk (broadcasts 142 hours a week), Radio DDR (168 hours a week on Program 1; 104 hours a week on Program 2; and 329 hours a week on regional programs) and Stimme der DDR (168 hours a week). Radio Berlin International broadcasts in 11 languages, including

English, Arabic, Hindi and Swahili. Radio Volga, based in Potsdam, broadcasts 18 hours a day with its own Russian-language programs and relays from Radio Moscow for Soviet forces in East Germany. Television broadcasts are made daily over the network Fernsehen der DDR. In 1980, Program 1 broadcast 94 hours a week (84 in color) and Program 2 broadcast 54 hours a week (43 in color). About 80% of East Germans live in areas where they can receive television programs from West Germany.

CONSTITUTIONAL SYSTEM

Constitution: The East German state, which was established in 1949 on part of Germany's Soviet-occupied territory, adopted in October 1949 a constitution superficially based upon the Weimar Constitution of 1919. East Germany was declared an indivisible German Democratic Republic (GDR). A new constitution was introduced in 1968, and was most recently amended in 1974. It establishes the DDR as "a socialist state of workers and farmers" and states that the DDR is an "inseparable part of the socialist community of states." A passage stating that East Germany had the responsibility to "point the way to peace and socialism for the whole German nation" was deleted in 1973.

Legislature: The highest legislative organ is in theory the unicameral *Volkskammer* (parliament) elected for five years by universal franchise (18 years and over). It has 500 deputies representing 67 multimember constituencies comprising from 130,000 to 240,000 electors. Its main functions include initiation and approval of legislation, approval of budget and the economic plan, ratification and abrogation of treaties, and election and dismissal of the State Council, Supreme Court judges and the procurator-general. In the 1981 elections, the candidates sponsored by the National Front, a mass organization, received over 99% of the vote, in which 99% of the electorate participated. The presidency was abolished in 1960 on the death of President Pieck and replaced by a collective presidency, the State Council. Elected by the *Volkskammer* for four years and officially responsible to it, the State Council consits of a chairman (who currently is also party leader), seven vice chairmen, 17 members and a secretary. It appoints diplomats, ratifies treaties, confers honors, grants pardon, convenes the *Volkskammer* and may decide to hold a referendum. It can issue statutory decrees and interpret existing laws, is responsible for national defense and security and may order mobilization.

Executive: Since 1952, the more senior ministers have formed a Presidium within the Council of Ministers and this has largely superseded the ministerial body itself as the highest executive cabinet. The Presidium, which supervises all ministries, includes the heads of key ministries and commissions such as Finance and State Planning, but excludes, among others, the ministers of defense and foreign affairs. Members of the Council of Ministers represent theoretically separate parties, but the Socialist Unity party predominates. Ministers are nominated by the State Council and approved by the *Volkskammer*.

Local government: In 1952, the five traditional *Länder* were replaced by 14 *Bezirke* (regions), each of which has its own Assembly (*Bezirkstag*) and Council (*Bezirksrat*). Berlin has separate administration. Each *Bezirk* is subdivided into 15 or 16 districts (*Kreise*), which in turn contain some 50 communes (*Gemeinden*) each.

Judiciary: In 1952, the sytem of courts was reorganized in accordance with the new territorial pattern. This provided for three kinds of court, the Supreme Court (*Oberster Gericht*), regional court (*Bezirksgericht*) and district court (*Kreisgericht*). The chief function of the Supreme Court, whose judges are appointed by the *Volkskammer*, is as the high court of appeal. First instance civil and criminal cases are heard at the regional and district levels by one professional judge and two lay assessors (*Schöffen*). Judges, who serve for four years, are officially independent and subject only to the constitution and law. The Soviet-style procurator-general (*Generalstaatsanwalt*) heads a body of procurators separate from the judiciary, which both ensures observance of legality and prosecutes in criminal cases. Capital punishment is maintained.

Basic rights: These include equality; a wide range of social services; freedom of worship and conscience, of speech and assembly; and the right to emigrate. Press censorship is constitutionally forbidden.

Party: Of the National Front bloc, which issues a joint program before general elections, the Socialist Unity party (*Sozialistische Einheitspartei Deutschlands*, SED), heir to the former Communist and Social Democratic parties, is predominant, with key positions in government and a current membership of 2,202,277. The SED is allocated 127 of the 500 seats in the *Volkskammer*. Most of the other parties are formally in league with the SED and include the Liberal Democrats (LDPD), National Democrats (NDPD), Christian Democrats (CDU) and Democratic Farmers' Party (DBD). There is no parliamentary opposition.

Leading government and party figures: Erich Honecker (chairman of the State Council, general secretary of the SED), Willi Stoph (prime minister, vice chairman of the State Council), Oskar Fischer (foreign minister), Ernst Höfner (finance minister), Horst Sölle (foreign trade minister), Col.-Gen. Friedrich Dickel (interior minister, chief of People's Police), Gerhard Schürer (deputy prime minister, chairman of the State Planning Commission).

BIOGRAPHICAL SKETCHES

Erich Honecker. Honecker, secretary-general of the Socialist Unity party, was born in 1912 in the Saar. He became a member of the German Communist party (KPD) in 1929, was arrested under Hitler in 1935, sentenced to 10 years in prison in 1937 and released only at the end of the war. His career was in the party's youth organization, the *Freie Deutsche Jugend* (FDJ), having been its first secretary from 1946 to 1955. He joined the Central Committee in 1946 and the Politburo as candidate member in 1950, then as full member from 1958. He succeeded Walter Ulbricht as party leader

61

in 1971, the latter having been removed under Soviet pressure. Honecker's policy was essentially aimed at strengthening East Germany economically, but preventing the emergence of any intellectual currents that might challenge the party's position. In no sense a liberal, he presided over East Germany's transformation into a major industrial and military power, second only to the Soviet Union in the Warsaw Pact. In international affairs, he enjoyed some success in putting East Germany on the world stage as an independent state. By the early 1980s he was cautiously exercising some of this independence, even in relation to the Soviet Union. East Germany's relations with West Germany, during his tenure, switched from thoroughgoing delimitation (*Abgrenzung*) to a somewhat less rigid relationship, in which West German economic support proved to be of considerable help in allowing East Germany to weather the deterioration of the world economic climate.

Egon Krenz. Krenz rose steadily in the East German hierarchy, and by 1984 he was regarded as one of the leading contenders for the succession to Erich Honecker. Born in 1937, Krenz's career was primarily in the party's youth movement, the FDJ. In November 1983 he was promoted to the Central Committee Secretariat and was elevated to full membership in the Politburo, the institutional springboard for any claim to the succession. Krenz was born into a working-class family—his father was a tailor—and he himself was trained as a teacher, although there is no evidence that he ever actually faced a class. Instead, his entire career was spent in the FDJ as an administrator. Between 1964 and 1967 he was in Moscow at the Soviet party's Central Committee College. On his return to East Germany, he took over as head of the FDJ agitprop department. He became chairman of the FDJ in 1974 and candidate member of the Politburo in 1976.

Konrad Naumann. Naumann was born in 1928 in Leipzig and moved up the hierarchy through the FDJ. He was made a candidate member of the Politburo in 1973 and a full member three years later; in 1984 he was elevated to a Central Committee secretaryship. His power base, however, was the East Berlin party organization; he was second secretary in 1967–71, then first secretary from 1971. The combination put him in a strong position to bid for the succession.

HUNGARY

GEOGRAPHY

Features: Hungary is one of the smaller countries of Eastern Europe, is landlocked and is bordered by Austria on the west, Czechoslovakia on the north, Romania on the southeast, Yugoslavia on the south and southwest and, since World War II, by the Soviet Union on the northeast. Only 2% of the total area exceeds 1,500 ft (400 m.), and this falls entirely within the drainage basin of the Danube. A chain of mountains running southwest to northeast and reaching elevations of over 3,000 ft (1,000 m.) in the Mátra, Bükk and Hegyalja ranges, links the Alpine and Carpathian systems. Three-quarters of the country, however, comprises the very fertile loess-covered and alluvial Hungarian or Pannonian Plain (*Nagyalföld*) dissected by the rivers Danube and Tisza. The largest lake in Central Europe, Balaton, is located in a tectonic basin of the upland region of Transdanubia. The climate is continental.

Hungary has always been preponderantly agrarian and the plains still lend themselves to the intensive cultivation of maize, wheat, beets, paprika, sunflowers and fodder crops. The upland regions support wine and timber industries, and there is widely distributed fruit cultivation. The once great deciduous forests are now depleted. Minerals include bituminous coal (in the vicinity of Pécs and Miskolc), lignite, ferrous metals, bauxite (largest deposits in Europe), uranium, petroleum and natural gas.

The chief centers of the important engineering, vehicle and chemical industries—Budapest, Veszprém, Miskolc, Debrecen, Szeged and Pécs—are dispersed but enjoy easy intercommunication. The Danube and Lake Balaton are navigable.

Area: 35,900 sq. miles/93,000 sq. km.

Mean max. and min. temperatures: Budapest (47° N, 19° E; 395 ft/120 m.) 71°F/22°C (July) 30°F/−1°C (Jan.); Debrecen (47° N, 22° E; 430 ft/131 m.) 69°F/21°C (July) 27°F/−3°C (Jan.)

Relative humidity: Budapest 80%; Debrecen 85%.

Mean annual rainfall: Budapest 24 in./610 mm.; Debrecen 23 in./595 mm.

POPULATION

Total population (1983 est.): 10,690,000.

Chief towns and populations (1983 est.): BUDAPEST (2,064,307), Miskolc (211,200), Debrecen (204,891), Szeged (174,836), Pécs (173,396).

Ethnic composition: Hungarians (Magyars) constitute 95% of the population but there are small German, Slovak, South Slav and Romanian minorities.

Language: Hungarian.

Religion: 67.5% of the population is nominally Roman Catholic, 25% Protestant (mostly Calvinist and Lutheran), and there are small Jewish and Eastern Orthodox communities.

RECENT HISTORY

Having been occupied by German forces as late as 1944, Hungary was soon thereafter invaded and occupied by Soviet troops; in early 1945 an armistice was signed in Moscow between the Allies and Hungary. In November, free elections returned an overwhelming anticommunist majority, and the Smallholders' party emerged as the largest unit in a coalition which, however, was obliged to fill key posts with communists. In 1946, a republic was declared with Zoltán Tildy as president and Ferenc Nagy (president of the Smallholders) as prime minister. By 1947, leading Smallholders and other noncommunists were purged, many arrested or exiled, new elections were called and the Social Democratic party was forced in 1948 to merge with the communists in the new Hungarian Working People's party. The 1949 Soviet-type constitution declared Hungary a people's democracy and, in effect, a one-party state. There followed, until 1953, a period of Stalinist terror and coercion enforced by the Mátyás Rákosi leadership. From 1952 to 1953, Rákosi combined both top party and government posts. The ferocious purge affected not only noncommunist politicians and Catholic and Protestant churchmen, but also party dissidents like János Kádár and Gyula Kállai, who were imprisoned, and László Rajk, who was executed as a "Titoist."

After Stalin's death in 1953, Rákosi retained the party secretaryship, but the appointment of Imre Nagy as new prime minister (till 1955) led to some relaxation, notably the release of a number of political internees and the partial decollectivization of agriculture. The great revulsion against the Rákosi dictatorship reached its apogee, however, only in 1956, first in July, when Rákosi was ousted from the party secretaryship (following a ferment among writers and the Petőfi circle of intellectuals) and then monumentally in October when a full-blown democratic and anticommunist revolution took place. On October 23 a student demonstration in Budapest, calling for free elections and national independence, was fast joined by other sectors of society, and by October 30 a new government under Imre Nagy promised a multiparty democracy and the negotiated removal of Soviet troops. On November 1 Hungary withdrew from the Warsaw Pact and requested U.N. and Western protection of the country's neutrality. There was no response from the West, and, two days later, one of Nagy's ministers, János Kádár, formed an alternative government, seeking Soviet support. Soviet forces entered Budapest and suppressed the uprising; Nagy and other ministers were abducted and later executed.

Disenchantment with the West and a massive retaliatory offensive on the part of the Kádár administration contributed to the anarchy and economic paralysis that beset Hungary for several years after 1956. Political apathy was to help rather than hinder the government; the party was reorganized and renamed the Hungarian Socialist Workers' party, and in 1961 Kádár initiated a New Course of liberalization and modernization. Old Stalinists were dropped in 1962, and in 1963 a general amnesty affecting most detainees and refugees was declared. In 1965, Gyula Kállai became prime minister, Kádár continuing as party first secretary.

Despite, or because of, the shadow of 1956, the reforms of the past two decades have created a greater freedom. In 1968, economic reforms were introduced that have brought a considerable increase in the standard of living, although recently there has been noted an increase in corruption and the failure of living standards to continue improving. Modest social and political reforms have also been introduced, such as the law passed in 1983 making it mandatory for there to be at least two candidates for each parliamentary and local contest in general elections.

The Hungarian government has proved relatively liberal in its tolerance of dissent. The jamming of Western radio broadcasts has not occurred since 1964, Western magazines and newspapers are available, and travel to and from the West has been relatively free. In 1977, some 34 intellectuals publicly expressed their solidarity with the signers of the Czechoslovak Charter 77 on human rights and were not reprimanded. Hungary did, however, join the Soviet Union in its invasion of Czechoslovakia in 1968, and in recent years there have been severe crackdowns on the publication of samizdat literature and on those who sympathize with the Polish Solidarity movement. Church-state relations remained stable during the early 1980s.

The Kádár regime has now lasted for three decades since the 1956 revolution, but while Kádár himself is a stabilizing force, the 1980s have seen extensive reshuffling of top party and government posts. As a result, there is no obvious successor to the 73-year-old leader.

Hungary is a member of COMECON, and its policy echoes the Soviet approach to most questions. The fate of the Hungarian minority in Romania is a constant source of friction. Relations with China and the West, particularly Austria, France and the Federal Republic of Germany, are improving steadily. An enormous debt to Western countries of about $8 billion encouraged Hungary in 1982 to become the only Eastern-bloc country other than Romania to join the World Bank and the IMF.

Defense (1983): Military service is compulsory, for 18 to 24 months. Strength is estimated at: army 84,000, air force 21,000. Paramilitary forces comprise 15,000 border guards plus a workers' militia of more than 60,000. 1980 defense expenditure was $1.1 billion, representing 2.4% of GNP. Hungary adheres to the Warsaw Pact, and in 1969 joined the Geneva Disarmament Commission.

ECONOMY

Background: The Hungarian economy is unique in the Soviet bloc because it does not have a command or centralized system shaped by quantitative planning, although there is near total state ownership of all productive facilities and resources. Market forces have a more significant impact on economic decisions than in other socialist countries. Centralized control operates effectively over international economic relations, while the market system operates within the enterprise level.

Hungary's New Economic Mechanism was introduced in January 1968 following almost three years' preparation. The aim of the reform was to restructure the economy for more effective participation in trade, especially with the West. New wholesale prices were implemented to eliminate most subsidies, except for basic raw materials, and at the same time, capital and supply allocation was decentralized. Eventually, only 20% of investment finance will flow from the state budget; much of the remainder will be in the form of bank credits. Capital interest charges were extended and profitability became the chief success indicator. Enterprises are free to set output targets and the volume of employment, and to extend direct contracts with other units. The state sets overall guidelines and exerts control through the manipulation of credit, the centrally controlled prices and profit and turnover taxes. In the early stages, the state retains control of wages. Periodically, unforeseen international crises (such as the oil price rises) or domestic circumstances (such as poor weather) may necessitate a return to centralized control, but this has generally proved temporary.

The operation of market forces has resulted over the years in a second, "underground," economy that has been largely tolerated by the government. As many as two out of three workers produce goods and services through self-employment or private jobs. Productivity is much lower in the official sector than in the second sector because of reduced incentives in the former. In 1979, the government acknowledged this problem by tying wages to productivity, closing unprofitable enterprises and removing subsidies. Hungary has been bolder than other Eastern European states in raising prices of consumer goods and laying off workers, because market forces act as a buffer and because the slow rate of growth in the labor force makes it easy for workers to find new employment.

Under Kádár, the government has also developed important commercial and financial relations with the West. In 1979, the National Bank of Hungary joined a consortium of six foreign banks to form an East–West trade bank. The Central European International Bank, located in Budapest, has a minority Hungarian participation and is actively involved in promoting a number of development projects in the Danubian region.

The share of agriculture in the NMP has fallen to 15%, but improved productivity has kept Hungary generally self-sufficient in food, and even an exporter of grain, meat products, live animals, wines, fruits and vegetables. Although deficient in petroleum and natural gas, Hungary has an expanding industrial base led by aluminum products, transport vehicles, machinery and machine tools. During 1965–80, industry grew on the whole by 3%.

The overall results of the fifth five-year plan (1976–80) fell below their targets, with the average annual increase of the national income remaining at 2.7% as against a projected 5.5%, and the annual average gain in per capita income at 1.6% as against a projected 3.5% target. Only agriculture exceeded its planned growth rate by achieving 2.9% as against a projected

2.7%. As a result, the sixth five-year plan (1981–85) incorporated less ambitious goals, including an overall growth of 2.7% to 3.2%.

Foreign trade: Hungarian trade with the West now forms about half of the total. Hungary joined GATT in 1973, and in 1978 began to benefit from a U.S.–Hungarian trade agreement, involving reciprocal most-favored-nation tariff treatment. Under the agreement, Hungary receives credit from the U.S. Export–Import Bank and the Commodity Credit Corporation. Exports and imports account for one-fifth of the GNP.

In 1982, merchandise exports amounted to $8.767 billion and imports to $8.814 billion, leaving a small trade deficit of $47 million. The average annual growth rate was 7.4% for exports and 5.0% for imports during 1970–82. The percentage share of merchandise exports was 8% for fuels, minerals and metals; 27% for other primary commodities; 7% for textiles and clothing; 31% for machinery and transport equipment; and 27% for other manufactures. The percentage share of merchandise imports was 9% for food, 17% for fuels, 11% for other primary commodities, 28% for machinery and transport equipment and 35% for other manufactures. The principal export partners are the Soviet Union (28%), West Germany (9%), East Germany (8%), Czechoslovakia (7%), Italy (5%) and Poland (5%). The principal import partners are the Soviet Union (29%), West Germany (12%), East Germany (7%), Czechoslovakia (5%) and Austria (5%).

Employment: In 1982, the total labor force was estimated at 4,997,000, of which 22.9% was employed in agriculture and 32.1% in industry. The five-day work week was adopted in 1981. In 1983, a new program came into effect providing a state subsidy for retraining redundant and otherwise unemployable workers. In 1984, greater wage differentials were introduced to encourage promotion and harder work.

Prices and wages: Retail prices have risen periodically since the reform began, most recently in January 1985 when price increases were announced on food, transport and heating fuel. In 1983, Hungary's inflation rate was 7.3%

The average monthly wages of workers in the state and cooperative sectors of the economy rose from 1,553 forints in 1960 to 2,152 forints in 1970, 2,821 forints in 1975, 3,987 forints in 1980 and 4,748 forints in 1983. The highest wage rate is in construction, where a worker receives an average of 5,071 forints per month.

Consumption: Living standards improved substantially during the 1970s, especially in the countryside, but have stagnated in recent years. Retail trade turnover rose by 12% in 1981 and 1982, and by 11.7% in 1983.

SOCIAL WELFARE

The national insurance scheme, amended most recently in 1975, is largely noncontributory, and is supervised by the General Directorate of Social Insurance of the Central Trade Union Council. Local administration is through the trade union committees based in principal county towns. In 1982, the state budget allotted 25.4 billion forints, or 5.1%, to health and social welfare.

Health services: Employees contribute between 3% and 10% of earnings, depending on salary. Employers contribute 10% of payroll if the government is the employer, 17% if agricultural cooperative and 24% if other. Sick pay for workers with over two years of service amounts to 75% of net earnings, 65% for workers with shorter service, payable from first day of incapacity for up to one year, or for length of continuous employment immediately before illness if less than one year. Sick pay is granted for two years in the case of TB. Medical benefits for dependents are the same as for the workers. Continued or permanent disability entitles the invalid to a disability pension. Workers temporarily disabled as a result of occupational injury receive 100% of average earnings payable until recovery or payment of pension. Those permanently disabled as a result of work injury receive a pension of 65% to 70% of average earnings during the previous year. Women employed for at least nine months during the previous two years are eligible to receive a maternity benefit of 100% of earnings, payable for up to four weeks before and 16 weeks after childbirth. In addition, the mother obtains a lump sum of up to 2,500 forints for each birth if she has attended the requisite number of prenatal consultations. For extended infant-care benefits, the mother must have been employed at least 12 of the 18 previous months. The dependent wife of an insured worker receives the same maternity grant as an employed woman. Patients pay 15% of the cost of medicines and appliances. Certain drugs like protective vaccines, TB therapeutics and life-saving medicaments are always free. Dental treatment, including extraction, is free for workers and their families. Travel expenses in connection with all socially covered therapy is free. In 1981, there were 91.7 hospital beds and 25.6 doctors per 10,000 population. The maternal mortality rate was 17.5 per 100,000 live births. The infant mortality rate was 20.6 per 1,000 live births in 1983. The average life expectancy as of 1981 for the Hungarian male was 66 years and 73.4 years for the female.

Pensions and other benefits: The source of funding for retirement pensions is the same as that for health services. Men are pensionable at 60, women at 55. Retirement pensions are generally fixed at 33% of average earnings during the best three of the previous five years. There is an increment of pension for manual workers. The minimum monthly pension has been set at 1,800 forints. Employees, members of handicraft and agricultural cooperatives, apprentices in skilled labor and pensioners with two or more children are eligible for family allowances, which are set at a monthly 980 forints for a second child, 660 forints for a third and fourth child, 630 for a fifth and 610 for each other child. A single person receives 490 forints a month for a first child and 660 for a second. Widows and orphans receive percentages of the deceased worker's pension. A funeral grant of 800 forints is available to the family of the deceased. An unemployment benefit of 30% of earnings for up to six months is provided to members of trade unions who pass a means test, are involuntarily unemployed and have not refused a suitable offer.

Housing: As of 1982, there were over 3,700,000 occupied dwellings, with an average of 3.4 rooms per dwelling. Housing falls into public and private sectors. State-built dwellings comprise cooperatives and freehold apartments both of which as a rule form multiple units on housing estates. Cooperative units are geared to large low-income families and their purchase price is fixed at about 80% of construction cost, towards which the new owner makes a 15% to 30% down-payment, the balance payable over 30 years. The construction of freehold apartments is state-financed through the National Savings Bank (OTP) the price being determined by actual building costs, although the amount of the cash deposit is not influenced by the size of the family as in the case of cooperative dwellings. The private sector accounts for 40% of housing construction; state building loans, amounting to around 75% of total cost and repayable over 20 years at 2% interest, are available. Private housing is prevalent in rural and outer suburban areas. 99% of dwellings had inside running water and 98.8% had a bathroom by 1982.

EDUCATION

Lower and higher education come under the general control of the Ministry of Education, with the exception of all higher industrial and agricultural schools, and several commercial secondary schools, which are administered by the various industrial authorities or the Ministry of Agriculture. The Ministry of Health is responsible for the medical schools. More immediate control over the general primary and secondary schools in Budapest is exerted by the district, city and borough councils. In the small number of sectarian Catholic, Reformed, Lutheran and Jewish secondary schools, which are staffed and administered by their respective denominations, the state curricular system is slightly modified. Primary education, which is free, is compulsory between the ages of six and 14. Those unable to complete the eight grades at 14 must attend school for an additional two years (*továbbképző iskola*). At higher levels tuition is free and over 80% of students obtain academic awards or else "social scholarships," by means of which the student is subsequently under contract to the donor institution, enterprise or organization for the same number of years as their period of study. The illiteracy rate is about 2%.

Primary education: After voluntary kindergarten, most six-year old children enter the general primary school (*általános iskola*), composed of four lower and four upper grades, and those successfully passing through the final grades can continue to any type of secondary school. In 1962, a revised curriculum put emphasis on practical aspects of "modern" and "socialist" education. Upper grade primary pupils must take two hours weekly of polytechnical instruction, and one foreign language (Russian). There are also over 100 music primary schools and 150 primary schools with special language divisions in which Russian, English, French or German are given particular stress from the third lower grade onward. For children whose parents work, the schools provide after-school-hours facilities. Extracurricular activities, especially those of the Young Pioneers, are promoted.

Secondary education: There are three main types of secondary school, the gymnasium (*általános gimnázium*), the technical school (*technikum*) and the skilled-worker training school (*ipari tanulók gyakorló iskolái*). In the gymnasium, a four-year course of study, the traditional academic orientation has been modified by the gradual introduction of the "education for work" course and the so-called five plus one system, in which the regular five-day school week is supplemented by a sixth day spent in a factory or enterprise, or on a farm. All gymnasia follow the same general syllabus, but there is specialization in the upper grades. Two foreign languages are compulsory and a third, as is also religion, is optional. The secondary technical schools, also a four-year course of study, offer full vocational training together with a general education. Emphasis is placed on practical work. The skilled-worker training schools, introduced in 1969, are attached to factories, agricultural co-operatives, etc., generally last for three years and lead to full trade qualifications in one of 186 trades. Matriculation is by written and oral examination or, in the case of the skilled-worker training schools, by a practical examination.

Special education is available to the physically and mentally handicapped; tuition, board and treatment are free.

Universities and higher education: There are nine main universities in Hungary, including four full universities, at Budapest, Szeged, Debrecen and Pécs, and four separate medical schools in the same cities, as well as the Karl Marx University of Economics in Budapest. There are three technical universities, in Budapest, Miskolc and Veszprém, and the universities of Building and Transport Engineering (Budapest), Agronomics (Gödöllő), Forestry (Sopron) and Veterinary Science (Budapest). There are four teacher training colleges (Pécs, Szeged, Eger, Nyíregyháza) and one school each of drama, music, fine arts and applied arts (all in Budapest). Other special institutions include one Reformed and one Lutheran Academy and a Jewish Seminary, in Budapest, each of which is autonomous. University courses last from five to six years; technical and agricultural colleges two to three years; teacher training colleges two to four years.

Educational Institutions (1982–83)

	Institutions	Staff	Students
Primary	3,567	80,798	1,244,094
Secondary	539	16,357	319,227
Higher	56	14,011	100,564

Adult education has since 1945 allowed working people to complete their primary, secondary and higher education through evening or correspondence courses at the Workers' General School and the Workers' Secondary School. In the correspondence courses, standards are less strict, study plans more flexible and consultation occasional, but regular curricula are maintained.

MASS MEDIA

The Press (1984):

Dailies: (Budapest) *Népszabadság*, HSWP, 727,000; *Népszava*, trade union, 295,000; *Esti Hírlap* (e), 240,000; *Népsport*, sport, 242,000; *Magyar Nemzet*, Patriotic People's Front, 119,000; *Magyar Hírlap*, 57,000.

Weeklies: (Budapest) *Rádió és Televízió Újság*, radio/TV, 1,330,000; *Ludas Matyi*, satirical, 400,000; *Nők Lapja*, women's, 1,019,000; *Szabad Föld*, rural polit., 510,000; *Ország-Világ*, illus., 230,000; *Magyar Ifjúság*, youth, 262,000; *Képes Újság*, illus., 551,000; *Élet és Tudomány*, pop. science, 104,000; *Film, Színház, Muzsika*, music/theater, 80,000; *Hétfői Hírek*, polit., 289,000; *Magyarország*, foreign sociopolit., 215,000; *Élet és Irodalom*, literary, 53,000; *Figyelő*, polit./econ., 24,000; *Új Ember*, Catholic, 90,000; *Evangélikus Élet*, Lutheran, 10,000; *Ludové Noviny*, Slovak; *Neue Zeitung*, German; *Narodne Novine*, Serbo-Croat.

Biweeklies: (Budapest) *Magyar Mezőgazdaság*, agric., 24,000; *Szövetkezet*, cooperatives; *Foaia Noastră*, Rumanian; *Új Élet*, Jewish.

Monthlies: (Budapest) *Kortárs*, literary, 15,000; *Nagyvilág*, literary, 15,000; *Nemzetközi Szemle*, internat. review, 32,000; *Társadalmi Szemle*, polit., 95,000; *Magyar Tudomány*, science; *Közgazdasági Szemle*, econ., 15,000; *Népfront*, Patriotic People's Front.

Broadcasting: The state Hungarian Radio operates three domestic services, the Kossuth program (continuous daily, with light material) and the Petőfi program (intermittent daily, with serious material), and Radio 3, all based in Budapest. Foreign broadcasts are made in six languages. Hungarian television operates on two channels. The first broadcasts about 66 hours a week, and the second about 20 hours a week, mostly in color.

CONSTITUTIONAL SYSTEM

Constitution: The Hungarian People's Republic was established under the constitution of 1949. The constitution was most recently amended in 1972. It provides for a socialist economy with central planning, but does not forbid private property and enterprise by individuals, as long as it is not used against the public interest.

Legislature: The unicameral Parliament (*Országgyűlés*) is the highest legislative organ, theoretically exercising all rights deriving from the sovereignty of the people. It decides on the organization, general course and conditions of government, and upon the state budget and economic plan. It elects the Presidential Council, Council of Ministers, Supreme Court and procurator-general, can declare war, conclude peace and exercise the prerogative of amnesty. Parliament is elected for five years by universal franchise (18 years and over). Its 352 deputies are elected from single-member districts. 99% of the electorate participated in the 1980 elections. In 1983, Parliament adopted a new law making mandatory a choice of candidates in all parliamentary and local council elections. Parliament decides by a simple majority, but changes in the constitution require the approval of a two-thirds majority. The right of legislation is vested in Parliament, but legislation may be initiated by the Presidential Council, Council of Ministers or any deputy. A newly elected Parliament must be convened by the Presidential Council (*Elnöki Tanács*) within one month of elections. In turn, Parliament at its first sitting elects from its members the Presidential Council (i.e., collective presidency) consisting of a president, two vice presidents, a secretary and 17 members. This is empowered to call elections, conclude and ratify international treaties, appoint and recall diplomats, appoint higher officers of the civil service and armed forces, hold plebiscites on matters of national importance, supervise the local organs of state power, and annul or modify any legislation enacted by central or local authority if this be deemed unconstitutional or detrimental to the interests of the working people. When Parliament is not sitting, the Presidential Council exercises full legislative functions.

Executive: The supreme organ of state administration is the Council of Ministers (*Minisztertanács*) (i.e., government), elected and removed by Parliament on the initiative of the Presidential Council and officially responsible to Parliament. Its members comprise a chairman (i.e., prime minister), vice chairmen, 13 ministers and the president of the National Planning Office. Central bureaus such as the Information Office and Bureau of Statistics come under their direct control. The Council of Ministers is closely associated with the upper hierarchies of the party and exercises considerable legislative as well as executive authority. It supervises ministerial functions, ensures law enforcement and the fulfillment of national economic plans, may issue decrees with the force of law and exercise direct control over any branch of the state administration. Its members participate in Parliament but are ineligible for election to the Presidential Council.

Local government: Hungary is divided into 19 counties, five muncipalities with the status of counties and the capital, Budapest. These are subdivided into districts, towns and precincts. County councils are subordinate to the Council of Ministers, district councils to county councils, etc. All local councils, which function for five-year terms, elect from their membership executive committees presided over by a chairman.

Judiciary: Modeled on Soviet practice, justice is administered through a Supreme Court, county courts (in Budapest the Municipal Court is equivalent) and district courts. The president and judges of the Supreme Court (*Legfelsőbb Biróság*) are elected for an indefinite period by Parliament. Courts of first instance comprise one professional judge and two lay assessors, while the three-member courts of appeal consist exclusively of professional judges. Special courts are provided for by the constitution. The procurator-general (*Legfőbb Államügyész*), whose office was instituted in 1953, heads a theoretically independent body of prosecutors on the county, municipal, district and town levels. Their task is to safeguard observance of legality and to prosecute in criminal cases. Capital punishment is maintained.

Basic rights: These include a wide range of social services; freedom of the press, of assembly, of speech, of worship and conscience, and scientific and artistic activity compatible with working people's interests; equality; and the right of national minorities to their own cultural life.

Party: Hungary is a one-party state and there is no parliamentary opposition. The Hungarian Socialist Workers' party (*Magyar Szocialista Munkáspárt*) is successor to the pre-1956 Working People's party, which had incorporated the Communist and Social Democratic parties. Its basic structure is patterned on that of the Soviet Communist party. The party congress meets every four years. It elects a Central Committee, which in turn elects a

Politburo and Secretariat. The Patriotic People's Front (*Hazafias Népfront*), consisting of party and nonparty members, recommends candidates for national and local elections. HSWP membership numbers some 852,000 (1983), while the Communist Youth Union (*Kommunista Ifjúsági Szövetség*) numbers 910,000 (1982).

Leading government and party figures: János Kádár (first secretary of the Hungarian Socialist Workers party), Pál Losonczi (president of the Presidential Council), György Lázár (prime minister), Lajos Faluvégi (deputy prime minister, president of the National Planning Office), Peter Várkonyi (foreign affairs minister), István Hetényi (finance minister), Col.-Gen. István Horváth (interior minister), Peter Veress (foreign trade minister).

BIOGRAPHICAL SKETCHES

György Aczél. Aczél, secretary of the Central Committee and member of the Politburo, was born in 1917. He was generally seen as Hungary's cultural czar, the man responsible for the subtle, occasionally manipulative relationship between the party and the intellectuals. He began as an unskilled construction worker and later acted on the stage. He joined the illegal party in 1935, made a career in its administration and was arrested during the purges of 1949, to be released in 1955. After 1956 he rallied to Kádár; in effect, he was the formulator of the cultural policy of Kádárism thereafter. He suffered an occasional setback to his career, such as losing his place on the Secretariat in 1975, but he managed to bounce back later.

Károly Grósz. Grósz, born in 1932, was originally a printer, but later qualified as a teacher. His career was made entirely in the party administration. He was, at various times, editor of the party newspaper in his native Borsod county, which includes the heavily industrial town of Miskolc; first secretary, in 1973–74, of the Fejér county party organization; and, in 1979–84, first secretary of the Borsod county party organization. He also worked in the party center, as head of the Central Committee agitprop department in 1974–79. In 1984 he was promoted to head the Budapest party organization. He was regarded as a spokesman for heavy-industrial workers and as no friend of market-oriented reform.

János Kádár. Kádár, born in 1912, was leader of the Hungarian Socialist Workers' party from 1956, when it was founded. His earlier career led him into the illegal Communist party in 1932; he joined its Central Committee in 1942 and was one of those responsible for the decision to dissolve it in 1943, apparently as a result of misinterpreting the significance of the Comintern's dissolution. After the war he successively took part in reorganizing the Budapest police and running the Budapest party. He became a member of the party's Political Committee in 1948 and of its eight-man Secretariat; in the same year he became interior minister, a post he held until 1950. During his tenure, his former associate László Rajk was tortured, tried and executed at the behest of Mátyás Rákosi, then party leader. Kádár's own role in the Rajk affair is still not fully clear, but it is generally accepted that he was in no sense an active participant. Arrested himself in 1951, he too was tortured and sentenced to life imprisonment, but was released in 1954. He returned to the Central Committee and the Politburo in July 1956, at the time of Rákosi's downfall. When Rákosi's successor as party leader, Ernő Gerő, was removed from this post in the midst of the revolution, Kádár succeeded. In this capacity he oversaw the crushing of the revolution, the renewed terror of the late 1950s and the execution of Imre Nagy, leader of the revolution, in 1958. During the early 1960s, however, Kádár launched his alliance policy, accepting that nonmembers of the party had a useful role to play and that party loyalty could not be the sole criterion of advancement. Thereafter he presided over and guided the affairs of Hungary as unchallenged party leader. While no Stalinist, Kádár's conception of reform was cautious and minimal. His tenure of office was one of the longest in modern Hungarian history.

György Lázár. Lázár, prime minister from 1975, was born in 1924 and had a background in technical planning, having served at the National Planning Office from 1948. In 1970 he was appointed labor minister and joined the Central Committee; in 1973 he was promoted to deputy prime minister and made chairman of the State Planning Committee and the National Planning Committee. In March 1975 he was elected to the Politburo, and in May of that year replaced Jenő Fock as prime minister. During his tenure of office, Lázár was regarded as a relatively colorless figure, more concerned with executing policy than with initiating it.

László Maróthy. Maróthy, born in 1942, belonged very much to the younger generation of politicians. Having taken a degree in agricultural engineering, his career was made in the communist youth movement (KISz), ending up as its first secretary in 1973; he joined the Central Committee in the same year. In 1975 he was elected to the Politburo as its youngest member, and in 1980 was made first secretary of the influential Budapest party organization. He was moved from this post in 1984 to become deputy prime minister.

Mátyás Szűrös. Szűrös, born in 1933, was Central Committee secretary in charge of foreign affairs and was regarded as a highly influential figure. From 1965 to 1975 he worked in the foreign affairs department of the Central Committee, becoming its deputy head. In 1975 he became Hungary's ambassador to East Germany, and on completing this assignment in 1978, was appointed to the crucial post of Hungarian ambassador to Moscow.

He was promoted to head the foreign affairs department of the Central Committee in June 1982; 13 months later he was taken into the Secretariat. Szűrös was widely seen as one of the architects of Hungary's active and cautiously independent foreign policy in the mid-1980s, and he drew attention to himself by writing a number of articles stressing the significance of the national interest.

POLAND

GEOGRAPHY

Features: Poland lies in the geographical center of the European continent and is the largest country in Eastern Europe after the Soviet Union. The Oder (Pol. Odra) and Neisse (Pol. Nysa) rivers in the west, the Bug River in the east, the Sudetes Range in the southwest and the Carpathians in the southeast constitute the nation's postwar political boundaries, while in the north there are 320 miles (520 km.) of Baltic seacoast. As a result of World War II, Poland lost nearly half its prewar territory to the Soviet Union but acquired from Germany parts of east Prussia and Brandenburg, much of Pomerania and Silesia, and also the free city of Gdańsk (Ger. Danzig). Poland's present neighbors are thus East Germany, Czechoslovakia and the Soviet Union.

Of present Polish territory, one-half is drained by the Vistula and tributaries, and one-third by the Oder, which, entering Poland by the Moravian Gate, divides the Sudetes on the west (max. height 5,000 ft/1,500 m.) from the alpine-featured High Tatra section of the Carpathians on the east (max. height 8,200 ft/2,500 m.). The upper basins of the Oder and Vistula are separated by the Little Polish (*Małopolska*) Tableland (1,600 ft/500 m.). The fertile loess-covered Silesian lowlands, centering on Katowice, together with the upper basin of the Vistula, contain some of the world's richest coal, copper and sulfur deposits, and also natural gas. Two-thirds of the country, comprising part of the North European Plain, is glaciated lowland, agricultural and forested. In the north, the plains of Pomerania and Mazovia, west and east of the Vistula respectively, are of sand, clay and gravel composition and are characterized by numerous lakes, marsh, forest and morainic ridges giving way on the Baltic coast to lagoon-and-bar formations. The continental climate of the country is subject to maritime influences in the west.

Poland is one of the more industrialized countries of Eastern Europe. Its industrial heartland is based on the bituminous coalfields of Silesia. The chief manufacturing centers for metallurgical, chemical, textile, cement and food industries are Warsaw, Cracow, Wrocław (Ger. Breslau), Łódź, Poznań (Posen) and Gdańsk. There is lignite mining near Łódź and shipbuilding at Gdańsk and Gdynia, which, together with Szczecin (Stettin), are major ports. More than half the land is agricultural, the main crops being rye, wheat, oats, barley and potatoes. Fruit cultivation and forestry are important. Some hydroelectric power is harnessed, especially in the upper Oder region.

Area: 120,400 sq. miles/312,700 sq. km.

POLAND

Mean max. and min. temperatures: Warsaw (52° N, 21° E; 395 ft/120 m.) 65°F/18°C (July) 25°F/−4°C (Jan.) Cracow (50° N, 20° E; 720 ft/219 m.) 67°F/19°C (July) 27°F/−3°C (Jan.) Gdańsk (54° N, 18° E; 35 ft/10 m.) 63°F/17°C (July) 29°F/−2°C (Jan.).

Relative humidity: Warsaw 86%; Cracow 87%; Gdańsk 80%.

Mean annual rainfall: Warsaw 22 in./560 mm.; Cracow 29 in./745 mm.; Gdańsk 21 in./545 mm.

POPULATION

Total population (1983 est.): 36,570,000.

Chief towns and populations (1983 est.): WARSAW (1,628,900), Łódź (845,700), Cracow (730,900), Wrocław (Ger. Breslau) (627,100), Poznań

(Posen) (563,000), Gdańsk, (Danzig) (462,900), Szczecin (Stettin) (390,500), Katowice (366,100), Bydgoszcz (356,500), Lublin (314,700).

Ethnic composition: Less than 2% of the population is non-Polish, the largest minorities being Ukrainians and Belorussians.

Language: The official language is Polish.

Religion: About 95% of the population is nominally Roman Catholic. Of the 13 other religious denominations, the Polish Orthodox church is the largest.

RECENT HISTORY

In 1945, the Moscow-oriented Polish provisional government established in Lublin was supplemented by members of the London-based government-in-exile and recognized by the Western allies, but opponents of the communists and their allies were soon liable to fierce persecution, arrest, deportation to the Soviet Union, and extermination. Most of Poland to the east of the Curzon Line had been occupied by Soviet troops since the 1939 Ribbentrop-Molotov Pact, while the liberation of the German-occupied regions now placed the rest of the country under Soviet control. The Teheran Conference (1943) had confirmed the Soviet annexation of 1939, and at Potsdam in 1945 the Great Powers sanctioned Polish suzerainty over former German territories east of the rivers Oder and Neisse and over the larger part of east Prussia including Gdańsk.

After the 1947 elections, at which the Peasant party opposition under Stanisław Mikołajczyk was subjected to coercion and police intimidation, the communist leadership inaugurated a decade of totalitarian rule based upon the closest dependence on Moscow and a Stalinist system of terror. In 1947, Bolesław Bierut, a Pole with Soviet citizenship, was elected the country's president and Mikołajczyk and other anticommunists fled to the West. In 1948, Władysław Gomułka, secretary-general of the Polish Workers' (Communist) party and deputy prime minister, was purged as a Titoist. The campaign against the Roman Catholic church was intensified and by 1953, when the primate of Poland, Cardinal Wyszyński, was arrested, several hundred clergy had already been imprisoned. In 1948 the Polish Workers' party and Socialists were merged in the Polish United Workers' party (PZPR), and in 1949 the new United Peasant party absorbed the remnants of the old Peasant party. Significantly, the Soviet Marshal Konstantin Rokossovsky was appointed as Poland's commander-in-chief and minister of defense. When the presidency was abolished (1952) in favor of a State Council, Bierut, while retaining his secretaryship of the PZPR, became prime minister, to be succeeded by Józef Cyrankiewicz in 1954.

The year 1956 represented for Poland, as for Hungary, a turning point. Bierut died in March, and the following June workers in Poznań demonstrated against one-party rule and Soviet domination. Profiting from a national mood of protest, anti-Stalinist party members staged a bloodless coup, the "Polish October," and the resurgent Gomułka was elected secretary-general of the PZPR. For several months the government's reforms suggested a departure from Stalinism, involving as they did a liberalization of culture, improved church-state relations, decollectivization of agriculture, the dismissal of Rokossovsky and other Soviet military personnel, economic aid from the United States and growing contacts with the West. But the lesson of Hungary in 1956 and Gomułka's political conservatism combined to disappoint the advocates of change. The 1957 elections confirmed Cyrankiewicz as prime minister and Aleksander Zawadzki as chairman of the State Council (to be succeeded on his death in 1964 by Edward Ochab). A state of political apathy, bureaucratic immobilism, economic stagnation and cultural restiveness began to prevail; church-state rivalry and relations with the West became a substitute for intraparty or interparty debate. In a country where religion is so emphatically equated with national identity, the Roman Catholic church assumed a quasi-political role, and in 1966 the PZPR was obliged to find a counterattraction to the church's millenary celebrations. The Polish episcopate was accused of interfering in the nation's foreign affairs when, as a conciliatory gesture, it invited West German bishops to Poland; Western ecclesiastics including the pope were refused entry. The personal intransigence of both Gomułka and Cardinal Wyszyński symbolized the resulting impasse. Anti-Semitism was rife in 1968 and has reappeared during each subsequent period of crisis.

Workers' riots in December 1970 provoked a political crisis that led to the replacement of Gomułka by Edward Gierek, with Piotr Jaroszewicz succeeding Józef Cyrankiewicz as chairman of the Council of Ministers. During the 1970s, Poland's economic climate steadily worsened as a result of poor harvests, higher fuel costs and mounting foreign debt. As a result, Jaroszewicz was forced in 1980 to step down in favor of Edward Babiuch, who reconstituted the Council of Ministers and announced an austerity program that called for a reduction in imports, improved industrial efficiency and the gradual withdrawal of food subsidies. In July 1980 the government began its implementation of this program with a 60% rise in beef prices. Workers throughout the country responded by striking for wage adjustments and against higher food prices. By August these work stoppages had assumed political overtones, with unofficial workers' committees replacing official trade unions. The dissident groups joined forces under the name of the Committee for Social Self-Defense. On August 14, 17,000 workers at the Lenin Shipyard at Gdańsk struck, occupied the plants and issued a list of demands, including the right to organize independent trade unions, a rollback of the meat prices, higher wages, family allowances and pensions, and the erection of a monument honoring workers killed in the 1970 riots. A second list of demands, issued by other workers in Gdańsk, went further and called for an end to censorship, the recognition of the right to strike and the release of political prisoners. By August 21 the strike had spread to Szczecin and involved over 150,000 workers. Two days later the Politburo's representative, Mieczysław Jagielski, met with delegates of the Gdańsk interfactory committee headed by Lech Wałęsa, a former shipyard worker who had helped to organize the 1970 demonstrations. They reached a historic agreement recognizing the new self-governing trade unions as "authentic representatives of the working class." The government made a number of concessions, including a wage settlement, a five-day work week and reconsideration of the censorship laws.

Following the settlement, most of the Baltic-coast workers returned to work, but strikes continued to break out in other areas, particularly in the mining region of Silesia. As the situation worsened, Gierek and Babiuch resigned and were replaced by Stanisław Kania and Józef Pińkowski. On September 18, 250 representatives of the new independent labor groups established at Gdańsk the National Committee for Solidarity (*Solidarność*), with Lech Wałęsa as chairman, and on November 10 it was officially registered under the new rules. By December, 40 free trade unions were registered, and on January 1, 1981, the official Central Council of Trade Unions was dissolved. The success of the registration of independent unions fueled further labor unrest, and Pińkowski resigned on February 11, to be succeeded by Gen. Wojciech Jaruzelski, who initially enjoyed the support of the moderate elements of Solidarity. On May 12, Rural Solidarity—the Independent Self-Governing Trade Union for Private Farmers—with 3.5 million members, was registered.

At an extraordinary congress of the ruling PZPR, only four former members were reelected to the Politburo in the first multicandidate secret balloting for office in party history. The Solidarity unions held their first national congress at Gdańsk, at which Wałęsa was reelected as chairman and numerous radical resolutions were approved. As the relations between the state and the unions worsened, the government arrested most of the Solidarity leadership, including Wałęsa, while the Council of State declared martial law on December 13, 1981. A Military Council for National Salvation was established under Jaruzelski, who had by then been elected to the post of first secretary of PZPR as well. By 1982, most of the repressive measures were eased, although violent demonstrations occurred on the second anniversary of the 1980 Gdańsk accord. On October 8, 1982, the *Sejm* (diet, or parliament) approved legislation banning autonomous trade unions. The Solidarity underground leadership responded by calling for a nationwide protest strike, which, however, drew little public support. Wałęsa was released from prison on November 12, and was awarded the Nobel Prize for Peace in 1983. Martial law was lifted in the same year but many restrictions on political activities remained as the military powers were expanded. In 1984 the government held nationwide local elections in which voters were permitted to choose between two candidates. Although Solidarity boycotted the elections, the government claimed a 75% turnout. Later in the year, the Polish Parliament voted to grant amnesty to all political prisoners jailed since the imposition of martial law in December 1981.

Poland's foreign policy generally follows the Soviet line and since, for the first time in history, it has treaty arrangements with all its neighbors, it is firmly committed to the present German frontiers and in 1950 secured East German recognition of the Oder-Neisse Line. During the 1970s, Poland expanded ties with Western Europe, the United States and the Third World. As a result of the recent domestic crises, however, a decline in Poland's international status has occurred. Its credibility as an ally of the Soviet Union was undermined, and, at the same time, Western states have maintained constant criticism of the Polish government's policies during the 1980s.

Defense (1983): Military service is compulsory, for two years in the army and air force and three years in the navy. Strength is estimated at: army 230,000, navy 22,000, air force 88,000, paramilitary forces 85,000. 1980 defense expenditure was $4,300 million, representing 3.1% of GNP. Poland is a member of the Warsaw Pact and accommodates a number of Soviet troops.

ECONOMY

Background: Next to the Soviet Union, Poland is the largest and most populous of the Eastern-bloc states, with a strong agricultural base and mineral resources, yet it lags behind East Germany, Czechoslovakia and Hungary in per capita income, and its economy is disorganized and failing. Its aggregate GNP recorded a negative growth in 1979–80 and has fared even worse since then. Although it has extensive agricultural farmlands (two-thirds in private hands), the country is not self-sufficient in grain and imports a substantial volume of food products. The extensive mineral resources have helped to establish a number of heavy industries, including ships, railroad cars, generators, mining and construction equipment, machine tools and automotive equipment. Chemicals, textiles and clothing are produced for export as well as for the large domestic market.

Polish leadership has been more responsive to popular needs than other Eastern-bloc states, even reversing orthodox communist policies to suit current conditions. Yet Poland's economic performance during the late 1970s was the worst in three decades as a result of economic mismanagement, poor harvests, rising petroleum costs and, above all, heavy trade deficits. Polish hard-currency debts to the West totaled approximately $27 billion by 1983—some $16 billion borrowed on commercial terms. Debt-service payments absorbed an ever-higher percentage of the value of exports. Beginning in 1980, Poland experienced unprecedented labor unrest and political turmoil. Although most of the foreign debt was renegotiated during the next five years, Prime Minister Jaruzelski issued a warning in 1983 that Poland "stood on the brink of a great catastrophe."

Foreign trade: Trade policy is formulated by the Ministry of Foreign Trade, which sets targets, issues import and export licenses, and allocates foreign exchange. Actual trade negotiations are conducted by foreign trade organizations established for various types of products. More than half the trade is with COMECON countries, including two-thirds of exports and over half of imports. Trade between the United States and Poland greatly expanded in the 1970s through credits extended by the U.S. Import–Export Bank and the Commodity Credit Corporation. Because of the upheavals of the 1980s, Poland has been running heavy trade deficits with both East and West. Other Eastern European countries that depended on Polish industrial exports have also suffered as a result of these troubles. Although 90% of Poland's foreign indebtedness is with the West, the Soviet Union has also borne a substantial share. Most of the Polish deficit in bilateral trade with the Soviet Union is a result of petroleum imports, which cover 70% of national needs. The higher price of Soviet oil, combined with cutbacks in delivery, has forced Poland to buy oil in the international market, creating additional strains on an already overburdened economy.

In 1982, merchandise exports amounted to $13.249 billion and merchandise imports to $15.476 billion, leaving a trade deficit of $2.227 billion. The annual average growth rate during 1970–82 was 6.7% for exports and 6.0% for imports. The percentage share of merchandise exports was 17% for fuels, minerals and metals; 8% for other primary commodities; 7% for textiles and clothing; 47% for machinery and transport equipment; and 21% for other manufactures. The percentage share of merchandise imports was 18% for food, 20% for fuels, 10% for other primary commodities, 31% for machinery and transport equipment and 21% for other manufactures. Poland's principal export partners are the Soviet Union (31%), West Germany (8%), East Germany (7%) and Czechoslovakia (7%). The principal import partners are the Soviet Union (33%), West Germany (7%), East Germany (7%) and Czechoslovakia (6%).

Employment: In 1982, the total labor force was estimated at 17,043,000, of which 31.4% was employed in agriculture and 29.4% in industry. Approximately 27.6% were employed in the private sector, compared with about 30% in 1970. The number of employment vacancies has risen dramatically, from 40,000 in 1970 to 248,000 in 1982, while the registered number of unemployed has fallen from 79,000 in 1970 to 9,000 in 1982. The recently reformed workers' councils provide a forum for the majority of worker grievances.

Prices and wages: Recent government attempts to phase out massive food subsidies and introduce a more realistic price structure have resulted in large-scale price and wage increases. In 1983, inflation reached 23%, while industrial wages increased by 25%. Since 1981, the average monthly wage has increased by about 400%. Most recently, in 1984, food price increases averaging 10% went into effect.

Consumption: There has been a bottleneck in the supply of consumer goods during the last few years, with a high level of demand for imported products. Such key commodities as meat, butter, sugar and flour have been in short supply, leading to the introduction of rationing for all of them. The country's standard of living fell in 1983 for the fourth year in a row. The total retail trade turnover of commodities for 1983 was 3.64 trillion zlotys, of which 46.8% was for food and 53.2% for nonfood commodities.

SOCIAL WELFARE

Social insurance, which is supervised by the Ministry of Labor, Wages and Social Affairs and financed from state budget allocations, covers all working people. There are special systems for miners, railroad employees, police and independent farmers. Locally, the system is administered by the health and social welfare departments of the presidia of the people's councils, and the local branches of the Social Insurance Institute.

Health Services: Free health facilities are available to all workers (or pensioners) and their families, and to students and servicemen. Emphasis is placed on separate clinics for industrial enterprises and on a network of outpatient clinics, health cooperatives and mobile units in rural locations. A worker is entitled to sick pay amounting to 100% of average earnings over the previous 13 weeks, if he/she has been employed for at least eight years. 80% of average earnings is granted to workers employed for three to eight years, 75% if employed less than three years. This benefit is payable for up to 26 weeks and may be extended to 39 weeks if a cure is probable. This may be followed by a sickness pension for up to 12 months at 75% of earnings, if recovery is likely. A worker may receive 100% of earnings payable for up to 60 days to care for a sick child under the age of 14 and for up to 14 days to care for a sick adult family member. A maternity benefit of 100% of earnings is granted to a working mother for 16 weeks for the first birth, 18 weeks for subsequent births and 26 weeks for multiple births. Lump-sum grants are given for each birth and, in additon, for each birth of a child with Polish nationality. Insured workers, excluding pensioners, must pay 30% of the cost of medicines. Medical benefits for dependents of insured workers are the same. In 1980, the maternal mortality rate was 11.7 per 100,000 live births and the infant mortality rate was 21.3 per 1,000 live births. The average life expectancy in 1980 for the Polish male was 66.1 years and for the female 74.6 years.

Pensions and other benefits: The pensionable age for men employed at least 25 years is 60 and for women employed 20 years is 55. For men with 20 years of employment, the pensionable age is 65; the age is 60 for women with 15 years of employment. Those in mining or unhealthy work, teaching, aviation and maritime work may qualify at earlier ages. The old-age pension is 100% of average monthly earnings below 3,000 zlotys during the previous 12 months, or the best two of the previous 12 years, plus 55% of the remainder. Pensions are increased by 1% per year of work in excess of 20 years. There is a 15% increase in pension for aviation and maritime work. Temporary and permanent disability pensions are available for victims of occupational injury or disease. The temporary disability benefit is 100% of earnings, payable for up to 26 weeks. Workers permanently disabled receive 100% and 65% of earnings for total and partial disability, respectively. Family allowances are provided, ranging from 70 zlotys a month for the first child to 155 a month for the fourth and each other child. The rates are increased for families without farming land. The worker is entitled to a family allowance for his wife if she is not gainfully employed and rears at least one child under eight, or if she is 50 years of age or over, or incapacitated. Funeral allowances, primarily intended to cover funeral costs, are paid to the family in the event of a worker's death, and amount to two months' wages of the deceased. In the event of the death of a family member, the worker receives an allowance fixed at one month's earnings. Since officially unemployment is no longer a large-scale phenomenon there is no unemployment insurance. Any incidental needs of the unemployed are met from other funds.

Housing: Poland in World War II lost more housing stock per capita than any country in the world. This factor, coupled with an extremely dynamic postwar demographic growth and a doubling of the urban population during the 1950s caused an acute housing shortage that is only now being substantially alleviated. However, waiting time for an apartment in urban areas still averaged 15 to 20 years in the mid-1980s. In the 1980 Gdańsk agreement between the government and the workers' strike committee, there was a call for an improvement of the housing situation in order to reduce the waiting time for apartments. As a rule, the local people's councils allocate state housing to lower income groups, cooperative dwellings to middle and higher income groups. In the state sector, the principal investors are the municipal people's councils and various industrial establishments whose building projects are financed from their own budgets, in turn subsidized by grants-in-aid from the state budget. Cooperative housing is administered by the Central Housing Cooperatives Union, which is responsible for its own investment services and design institutes. Prospective tenants contribute 15% to 25% of construction costs, the remainder being financed by state credits over a 40-year period, whereas the state may grant additional aid by annulling up to one-third of the loan. To meet the cost of the contribution, a member of a housing cooperative can also obtain an additional personal loan of up to 10% from his or her place of employment. Construction of private housing, which is concentrated in rural and suburban areas, is supported by state credits averaging 50%, and never exceeding 75%, of construction costs, available for a period of up to 25 years. In Polish housing the emphasis is put on prefabrication and multiple units containing shopping precincts. Large-scale developments include the postwar renovation of Warsaw's Old Town, the reconstruction of the Muranów district (formerly Warsaw's Jewish ghetto) and the creation of new towns such as Nowa Huta and Nowe Tychy.

EDUCATION

In Poland's unified and secular system of education, primary, secondary and most higher institutions come under the Ministry of Science, Higher Education, and Technology, while medical schools are controlled by the Ministry of Health and Social Welfare. Fine arts colleges fall under the Ministry of Culture and Art, military colleges under the Ministry of National Defense, and colleges of physical education under the Central Committee for Physical Culture. Since 1961, several reforms have raised the compulsory school-leaving age to 14, strengthened the polytechnical element in primary and secondary schooling, expanded Western European language programs and extended the system of higher learning. Russian is taught at primary and secondary levels, while religion may be taken as an extramural option. There are two autonomous theological academies in Warsaw and a nonstate Catholic University at Lublin. Extracurricular activities are promoted and boarding facilities in hostels or private accommodations are provided for pupils in need of them. The illiteracy rate is about 2%.

Primary education: The free and optional kindergarten is run by the state, by institutions or communities. Eight-year primary education is free and obligatory for children aged seven to 14. By 1967, the basic eight-year primary schools (*szkoły podstawowe*) replaced the earlier seven-year system and added such subjects as workshop activities, aesthetic and civic training, music and physical drill to the traditional academic syllabus. The school curriculum is uniform throughout Poland. A small number of private schools exist and are run under state supervision. About 96% of those leaving primary school continue on in secondary schools, admission to which is by entrance examination. Of this number, some 77% proceed to vocational and technical schools; the remainder go on to general secondary schools.

Secondary education: The four-year general secondary schools (*licea ogólnokształcące*) complete the uniform twelve-year general education program on the combined primary and secondary levels. Matriculation is by means of examination in Polish, mathematics, history, one language and a science, and entitles the pupil to higher education.

Vocational education is organized on two levels. The lower vocational schools (*zasadicze szkoły zawodowe*) admit primary school leavers aged 15 to 17 and include three-year training schools for industry (*szkoły przysposobienia zawodowego*) and agriculture (*szkoły przysposobienia rolniczego*) in which basic vocational instruction is closely related to enterprises and cooperatives and may take the form of direct apprenticeship or workers' refresher courses. At a higher level are the one- to three-year technical schools (*technika zawodowe*) for graduates of general secondary schools; five-year technical schools (*technika zawodowe*) for graduates of the primary system who wish to combine practical with general education; five-year teacher training schools (*licea pedagogiczne*) and five-year schools of arts and applied arts (*licea i technika artystyczne*). Eligibility for further vocational training at teacher training schools for secondary school teaching (*technika przemysłowo-pedagogiczne*), postsecondary teacher training courses (*studia nauczycielskie*) and nursing schools (*szkoły pielęgniarskie*), is based on completion of two to five years of previous secondary education.

Special education; For the handicapped there are special schools in the primary, general secondary and lower and higher vocational categories. Board is provided for chronic cases and orphans, and treatment and tuition are free.

University and higher education: The institutions of higher education include 10 universities (Jagiellonian Univ. at Cracow, Warsaw, Poznań, Wrocław, Lublin, Łódź, Toruń, Catholic Univ. of Lublin, Gdańsk and Katowice) and 18 technical universities (*politechniki*), as well as specialized technical and professional institutions: 12 higher teacher training institutions, six higher schools of fine arts, seven academies and higher musical schools, three higher schools of drama and film, six academies and higher schools of physical training, and two higher maritime schools. Courses leading to the first (master's) degrees of *magistra* and *magistra inżyniera* last four to five years, while the degree of *lekarza* follows on six years for medicine and five and a half years for veterinary medicine. Art and music school diplomas are awarded after five or six years of study. Many of those enrolled in higher institutions are extramural students otherwise employed; those in certain sciences take degree courses of six rather than five years.

Educational Institutions (1982–83)

	Institutions	Staff	Students
Primary	14,341	244,800	4,465,300
General Secondary	1,171	22,800	380,800
Technical, art, vocational	9,973	84,400	1,555,800
Higher	91	56,600	396,600

Adult education: Full-time workers may take vocational day or evening courses as students enrolled in the "people's universities" and "rural universities." These institutions are set up as regular study groups for a minimum of 30 persons over the age of 17 who have completed primary school. Most courses last one or two years and include programs of general culture and practical training. In addition, various communities and educational organizations run highly popular correspondence courses, especially in foreign languages, at both secondary and higher levels.

MASS MEDIA

The Press (1983):

Dailies: Express Wieczorny (e), Warsaw, ind., 451,000; *Trybuna Robotnicza*, Katowice, PZPR, 685,000; *Trybuna Ludu*, Warsaw, PZPR, 1,000,000; *Dziennik Ludowy*, Warsaw, ind., 200,000; *Życie Warszawy*, Warsaw, ind., 369,600; *Słowo Powszechne*, Warsaw, Catholic, 85,780; *Dziennik Zachodni*, Katowice, ind., 198,200; *Echo Krakowa*, Cracow, ind., 81,800; *Dziennik Łódzki*, Łódź, ind., 98,400; *Głos Wielkopolski*, Poznań, ind., 144,500; *Sztandar Młodych*, Warsaw, youth, 210,000; *Ilustrowany Kurier Polski*, Bydgoszcz, Democratic party, 100,000; *Dziennik Bałtycki*, Gdańsk, econ./shipping, 96,200; *Głos Robotniczy*, Łódź, PZPR, 272,200; *Gazeta Robotnicza*, Wrocław, PZPR, 274,500; *Głos Szczeciński*, Szczecin, PZPR, 148,800.

Periodicals: Przyjaciółka (w), Warsaw, women's, 2,400,100; *Gromada-Rolnik Polski* (3 per week), Warsaw, 435,000; *Kobieta i Życie* (w), Warsaw, women's, 658,800; *Przekrój* (w), Cracow, illus., 514,500; *Panorama* (w), Katowice, illus., 496,900; *Nowa Wieś* (w), Warsaw, rural illus., 280,000; *Polityka* (w), Warsaw, polit., 371,600; *Twoje Dziecko* (m), Warsaw, mother's, 250,000; *Przegląd Sportowy* (four per week), Warsaw, sport, 200,000; *Sport* (five per week), Katowice, sport, 210,000; *Film* (w), Warsaw, film, 194,300; *Poznaj Świat* (m), Warsaw, geog. illus., 99,500; *Morze* (m), Warsaw, maritime, 107,300; *Spilki* (w), Warsaw, satirical, 95,300; *Żołnierz Polski* (w), Warsaw, military, 170,000; *Robotnik Rolny* (w), Warsaw, agric. union, 100,060; *Sportowiec* (w), Warsaw, sport, 160,000; *Głos Nauczycielski* (w), Warsaw, teacher's, 62,400; *Przyjaźń* (w), Warsaw, Soviet friendship, 97,100; *Życie Literackie* (w), Cracow, lit., 57,900; *Problemy* (m), Warsaw,

86

pop. science, 50,000; *Nowe Drogi* (m), Warsaw, polit., 60,000; *Stolica* (w), Warsaw, cult., 34,000; *Życie Gospodarcze* (w), Warsaw, econ., 68,300; *Teatr* (f), Warsaw, theater, 8,000; *Ekonomista* (six per year), Warsaw, econ., 10,000; *Sprawy Międzynarodowe* (m), Warsaw, internat. affairs, 5,100.

Broadcasting: Polish Radio and Television, a state monopoly controlled by the Committee for Radio and Television, maintains four daily radio programs. Foreign transmissions are made in 12 languages. There are two television programs, one transmitting for 13½ hours and one for seven and a half hours per day.

CONSTITUTIONAL SYSTEM

Constitution: The Soviet-type constitution of the Polish People's Republic dates from 1952. An amendment approved in 1976 officially described the republic for the first time as a socialist state.

Under a constitutional amendment passed in 1980, the Supreme Chamber of Control is directly responsible to the *Sejm*, rather than to the Council of State as it was until 1976, or to the Council of Ministers as it was from 1976. Martial law was lifted on July 22, 1983, and the Military Council of National Salvation was dissolved. Gen. Wojciech Jaruzelski, who had chaired the Council, remained the Communist party leader. Two days before martial law was revoked, the *Sejm* approved a constitutional change allowing the government to assume broad powers by declaring a state of emergency in response to national unrest. The government had previously been obliged to declare a state of war in order to obtain such powers, as it had done when it imposed martial law.

Legislature: The unicameral *Sejm*, convoked at least twice a year, is theoretically the supreme legislative organ, empowered to initiate and pass legislation, adopt the budget and national economic plan, declare a state of war, appoint and recall ministers, elect members of the State Council (*Rada Stanu*) and exercise control over the work of other organs of state authority and administration. The Parliament is elected for a four-year term by all citizens over 18 years. It is composed of 460 deputies. 99.5% of the electorate participated in the last elections (1980). Candidates are nominated by organizations strictly controlled by the PZPR. Nominally subordinate to the *Sejm* is a 17-member collegiate body, the State Council, whose extensive powers include the convocation of Parliament, the holding of general elections, the appointment and recall of diplomats, the ratification and abrogation of international agreements, the awarding of honors, the nomination of higher civil and military officers, the right to grant pardon, the definitive interpretation of laws and the issuance of statutory decrees such as martial law and mobilization. It also supervises the people's councils. There is no constitutional provision for the recall of its members. Also responsible to the *Sejm* is the Supreme Chamber of Control, which supervises the legality and functioning of legislation and administration at all levels and is required to make an annual report on the execution of the national economic plan. It is officially independent, with a chairman appointed and dismissed by Parliament.

Executive: The highest executive and administrative body is the Council of Ministers (*Rada Ministrów*) whose members are appointed and recalled by the *Sejm*. It is responsible to Parliament or, when the latter is not sitting, to the State Council and is composed of a chairman (i.e., prime minister), vice chairmen, 28 ministers, the chairman of the Planning Commission, the government press spokesman, and the president of the State Atomic Agency. It coordinates the work of ministries, frames and submits in the *Sejm* the annual budget and the draft of the national economic plan, ensures the execution of laws, establishes the annual conscription quota and directs the activities of the presidia of the people's councils.

Local government: Poland is divided administratively into 49 voivodships. In each of these units, government is exercised by the people's councils (*rady narodowe*) whose executive and administrative branches are the presidia. The latter are assisted by departments of the presidium, as, for example, departments of finance, health, agriculture, education.

Judiciary; Justice is administered through a Supreme Court (*Sąd Najwyższy*) and regional courts at the level of voivodship and district. The Supreme Court, which acts as both ordinary and extraordinary court of review, is elected for a five-year term by the State Council, while the regional courts, consisting of one judge and two lay assessors, are elected by the people's councils. District courts act as courts of first instance in most civil suits and less important criminal cases. Voivodship courts act as courts of appeal but also handle more serious cases. There are constitutional provisions for special courts, most of which (such as military tribunals) are outside the judicial system. The procuracy, based on the Soviet model, is separated from the judiciary, and the procurator-general, appointed by the State Council, heads a body of prosecutors theoretically independent of local government. Their functions are both to enforce observance of socialist legality and to prosecute in criminal cases. Capital punishment is maintained.

Party: There are in theory three main political parties, which collaborate in the Patriotic Movement for National Rebirth (formerly National Unity Front)—namely, the Polish United Workers' party (*Polska Zjednoczona Partia Robotnicza*, PZPR), which is the ruling party; the United Peasant party (*Zjednoesone Stronnictwo Ludowe*, ZSL); and the Democratic party (*Stronnictwo Demokratyczne*). The PZPR is predominant. Its structure, based on the Soviet model, includes periodic party congresses, a Central Committee and a Politburo. The PZPR had (1983) 2,340,900 members and the ZSL (1982) 463,100.

Leading government and party figures (1985): Gen. Wojciech Jaruzelski (chairman of the Council of Ministers, general secretary of the PZPR), Henryk Jabłonski (chairman of the State Council), Stefan Olszowski (foreign minister), Gen. Florian Siwicki (defense minister), Gen. Czesław Kiszczak (interior minister), Lech Dumaradzki (justice minister), Tadeusz Nestorowicz (foreign trade minister), Stanisław Nieckarz (finance minister), Kazimierz Zygulski (culture minister), Adam Łopatka (religious affairs minister). Vice chairmen of the Council of Ministers: Manfred Gorywoda, Zenon

Komender, Edward Kowalczyk, Roman Malinowski, Zbigniew Messner, Janusz Obodowski, Mieczysław Rakowski, Zbigniew Szalajda.

BIOGRAPHICAL SKETCHES

Cardinal Józef Glemp. Józef Glemp was born in 1929 in central Poland, a member of a farming family; during the war he worked as an agricultural laborer. He studied Polish language and literature in Warsaw and Toruń before entering the seminary in Gniezno, and was ordained in 1956. He pursued graduate studies at the Lateran and Gregorianum colleges in Rome in 1958–64; in 1967 he was transferred to the primate's office as Cardinal Wyszyński's secretary and chaplain. In 1979 he was made bishop of Warmia, where he was regarded as an able administrator. He was named successor to Wyszyński in July 1981 as archbishop of Gniezno and primate of Poland. His elevation came at a difficult time, in the midst of the Solidarity crisis. Initially, he generally supported Solidarity, though with moderation, but his task after the imposition of martial law was much more complex. He sought to steer a middle course between the extreme antagonism of the people and the demands of the authorities. He pressed for the release of internees and the restoration of civil rights, but was not willing to act as the leader of a political opposition to the communist regime. This middle course earned him criticism from both sides, but Glemp never lost sight of the church's pastoral role and religious duties. He was made cardinal in February 1983.

Wojciech Jaruzelski. Gen. Jaruzelski was born in 1923 to a landowning family. In 1939, having been deported to the Soviet Union, he worked as a manual laborer, then received military training and took part in the fighting both during the war and afterward in the antiguerrilla campaign in Poland. In 1956 he was promoted to general, the youngest in the Polish army at the time. In 1960 he was made head of the main political board of the armed forces; in 1962 he became deputy defense minister; in 1965 he was appointed army chief of staff; three years later he became defense minister, a post he held until 1983. He became a member of the Central Committee in 1964, candidate member of the Politburo in 1970 and full member a year later. He was appointed prime minister in the midst of the Solidarity crisis in February 1981 and took over as party first secretary from Stanisław Kania after the latter was voted out by the Central Committee in October of that year. Jaruzelski's accumulation of offices was unprecedented in the communist world. In December he masterminded the coup d'état that led to the suppression of Solidarity. Jaruzelski was, as his career indicates, always more of a political soldier than a serving general who occasionally played a political role; his links with the Soviet Union were generally close.

Czesław Kiszczak. Gen. Kiszczak, interior minister and deputy member of the Politburo, was regarded as a close supporter of Gen. Jaruzelski. Born in 1925 to a peasant family, he trained as an officer after the war and then worked in military counterintelligence. From 1972 to 1979 he was simultaneously chief of military intelligence and deputy head of the general staff; he took command of the Internal Military Service of the defense ministry in April 1979. In April 1981 he was placed in charge of the body that played a major role in preparing the military takeover later that year: the Coordinating Commission for Public Law and Order. Kiszczak became a full member of the Central Committee in 1981 and was appointed deputy interior minister. He supervised the campaign against Solidarity before the takeover, notably the harassment of its activities by the interior ministry. At the takeover, Kiszczak figured on the 20-man Military Council for National Salvation. As interior minister, he was responsible for the suppression of civil liberties in Poland after December 1981, and particularly for the role played by the security forces.

Stefan Olszowski. Olszowski, foreign minister from July 1982, had a highly checkered career. Born in 1931 in Toruń, he studied languages and literature at Łódź University. He was active in the Komsomol in the 1950s and then transferred to party work: as voivodship secretary in Poznań in 1960–63; as director of the Central Committee press office in 1963–68; as Central Committee secretary in charge of press affairs in 1968–71; and as Politburo member from December 1970 to February 1980. Promoted to foreign minister (1971–76), he returned to the Secretariat, but was stripped of this post and his Politburo membership by Gierek in February 1980 because of his critical stance. He returned to both offices in August 1980. During the Solidarity period he was widely regarded as one of the leading figures in the hard-line anti-Solidarity wing of the party leadership, and under Jaruzelski he maintained this stance.

Mieczysław Rakowski. Rakowski was born in 1926 to a peasant family. In 1945 he joined the army, then studied journalism in Cracow and history in Warsaw. He helped to launch and then was editor in chief from 1958 to 1982 of the weekly, *Polityka.* He became a candidate member of the Central Committee in 1964 and a full member in 1975. From February 1981 he was deputy prime minister with special responsibility for negotiations with Solidarity. Although he enjoyed a reputation as a moderate, his dealings with Solidarity were not regarded as a great success. After the imposition of martial law, he became one of the most prominent spokesmen for the middle road of "moderate" reforms under the guidance of Jaruzelski.

Florian Siwicki. Gen. Siwicki, a close associate of Gen. Jaruzelski, was made defense minister in 1983. Born in 1925 in eastern Poland (now the Soviet Union), he was deported after the invasion in 1939 to the Soviet Union and worked as a manual laborer. He passed subsequently through the communist Polish Officer's School in Ryazan, was commissioned and then returned to Poland in 1945, where he played an active role fighting anticommunist guerrilla units. He graduated from the Soviet Military Academy in Moscow in 1956. Eventually he became commander of the First Motorized Division in Warsaw (1964) and commander of the Silesian Military District, taking part, in this capacity, in the 1968 invasion of Czechoslovakia. In 1971 he was appointed first deputy head of the general staff of the Polish armed forces and was chief of staff in 1973. In 1968 he was elected a candidate member of the Central Committee, was a full member from 1975 and was elevated to the Politburo in 1981.

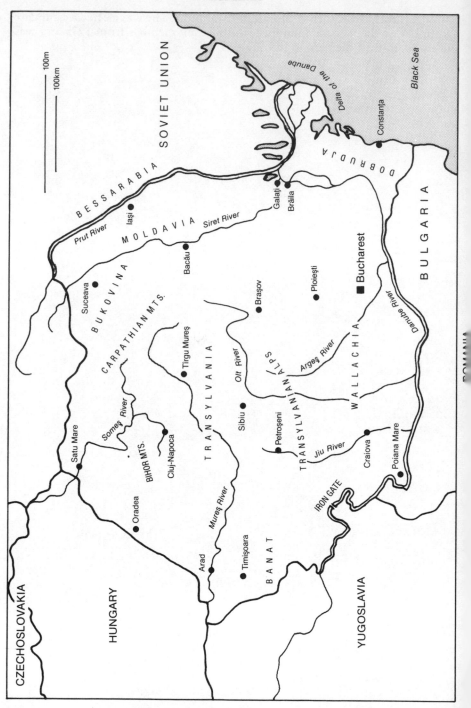

ROMANIA

Features: Romania is a symmetrically shaped country adjoining four other communist states—the Soviet Union, Bulgaria, Yugoslavia and Hungary. Its northeastern and southern political frontiers comprise in large measure the rivers Prut and Danube, respectively. It has 150 miles (250 km.) of coast on the Black Sea. The country may be subdivided into three almost equal parts: plains, mountains and hilly plateaus. The southern ranges of the arcuate Carpathian chain reach heights of over 7,000 ft/2,000 m. in several regions. The Transylvanian and Someş plateaus lie inside the semicircle of the Carpathians, while the Moldavian and Wallachian lowlands (or Romanian Plain) radiate to the east and south. The basins of the Tisza, extending westward into Hungary and Yugoslavia, and of the Danube, are low-lying and of recent lacustrine origin. The climate is continental with the transitional character peculiar to southeastern Europe, and is relatively uniform.

Despite the accelerated growth of industry in the last two decades, unparalleled in Eastern Europe, Romania is still primarily agricultural. With very fertile soils, especially in the Wallachian and Moldavian plains, it supports a wide range of crops and is agriculturally self-sufficient. With 26% of its area forested, it has a well-developed timber industry, and the reed resources of the Danube delta are exploited on an industrial scale. Romania is well endowed with mineral and fuel resources, including the second largest oilfields in Europe (in the Ploieşti and Bacău regions), methane gas in Transylvania, lignite and black coal, especially in the Jiu Valley and hydroelectric power, generated in several regions. The hydroelectric plant at the Iron Gate of the Danube, built in cooperation with Yugoslavia, is one of Europe's largest. A wealth of other minerals, including ferrous and nonferrous metals, manganese, bauxite and rock salt contribute to a variety of widely dispersed industrial complexes. Bucharest, Ploieşti, Braşov, Hunedoara, Cluj, the Banat, Galaţi and Constanţa are chief centers of the iron and steel metallurgical, chemical and petrochemical, textile, construction and light industries. Communications are easy in lowland areas and facilitated in the mountainous fringes of Transylvania by several low passes. The Danube is navigable. Constanţa and the Danubian city of Galaţi are chief ports. New resorts, such as Mamaia and Eforie, serve the needs of tourism on the Black Sea coast.

Area: 91,700 sq. miles/237,500 sq. km.

Mean max. and min. temperatures: Bucharest (44° N, 26° E; 270 ft/82 m.)

74°F/23°C (July) 27°F/−3°C (Jan.) Cluj (47° N, 24° E; 1,285 ft/392 m.) 68°F/ 20°C (July) 24°F/−4°C (Jan.) Constanţa (44° N, 29° E; 15 ft/5 m.) 71°F/22°C (July) 31°F/−1°C (Jan.).

Relative humidity: Bucharest 87%; Cluj 85%; Constanţa 83%.
Mean annual rainfall: Bucharest 23 in./595 mm.; Cluj 24 in./610 mm.; Constanţa 15 in./380 mm.

POPULATION

Total population (1983): 22,550,000.
Chief towns and populations (1981): BUCHAREST (2,165,997), Braşov (320,168), Cluj (289,808), Timişoara (288,237), Iaşi (279,753), Constanţa (279,753), Galaţi (267,962), Craiova (239,651), Ploieşti (219,890).

Ethnic composition: Romanians are 88.1% of the population, Hungarians 7.9%, Germans 1.6%. Other minorities include Turks, Greeks and Serbs.

Language: The official language is Romanian, although minority groups speak Hungarian, German and other languages.

Religion: 75% of the population is nominally Romanian Orthodox and 7% Roman Catholic. Religious minorities include Protestant, Serbian Orthodox and Muslim groups.

RECENT HISTORY

After the invasion of Romania by the Red Army in August 1944, King Michael led a coup d'état that removed the fascist Antonescu government and allied the country to the Soviet Union and the Western Allies. Elections in 1946 confirmed communists, under Petru Groza, in the key posts of a National Democratic Front government, even though in 1944 the party had only numbered 900 adherents; in 1947 Groza, with Soviet support, conducted a mass purge of political opponents. The king abdicated and the country was proclaimed a People's Republic. The 1947 Paris Peace Treaty assigned to Romania the frontiers of January 1, 1941 (i.e., ceding Bessarabia and northern Bukovina to the Soviet Union and southern Dobrudja to Bulgaria), with the exception of the frontier with Hungary, which was restored to the prewar configuration, Romania thus retaining all of Transylvania.

In 1948 the Romanian Communist party (RCP) and its subordinate Social Democrats merged to form the Romanian Workers' party with Gheorghe Gheorghiu-Dej as its secretary-general. Gheorghiu-Dej in 1952 succeeded Groza as prime minister, Groza becoming titular head of state. In the 1950s, the purges encompassed the veteran communist and foreign minister, Ana Pauker, and in general Romania suffered severe purges. Until the 1960s, Romania remained a model ally of Moscow and there were few reverberations of Hungary in 1956. In 1958, the Soviet army was quietly withdrawn from the country, while the role of agricultural and petroleum producer assigned to Romania as a member of COMECON was throughout the 1950s loyally performed.

The 1960 Party Congress in Bucharest, at which Khrushchev was to air the developing Sino-Soviet dispute, publicly marked the beginning of Romania's increasingly independent line. It could profit from bloc disunity and at the same time advocate conciliation. In 1964 the RCP proposed a tripartite meeting, with Romania as intermediary, to settle Sino-Soviet differences. In the 1960s it put national objectives first and rejected a "breadbasket" function within COMECON, embarked on a program of rapid industrialization and evolved a highly individual foreign policy, with the result that it became the most independent of all Soviet-bloc countries. After 1962 a policy of derussification was promoted; the Maxim Gorky Institute and Russian bookshops were closed, street names changed and the languages and culture of the West reinstated.

Gheorghiu-Dej died in 1965 and was succeeded as titular head of state by Chivu Stoica. Nicolae Ceauşescu was elected secretary-general of the RCP and a new constitution (superseding those of 1948 and 1952) declared Romania a Socialist Republic. Ceauşescu succeeded Stoica in December 1967, thus to head both the party and government apparatus. The current political leadership has inherited from the Stalin era a high degree of orthodoxy, and the paradox of Romania's volte-face in foreign, economic and cultural affairs is to be explained by the identification of the party with national independence, be it from the supranational planning of COMECON and the Warsaw Pact or from bloc ideological conformity.

For the past two decades, Ceauşescu has instilled a high degree of personalization of political power, combined with a tightening of ideological control internally and increasing independence in foreign policy. In addition to his other two posts, Ceauşescu was elected to the newly created position of president of the republic in 1974. He currently continues to hold all three positions. In addition, through regular reshuffles, Ceauşescu has gradually filled many government and party posts with members of his family as well as his personal followers. In 1977, his wife Elena was elected to the Permanent Bureau of the RCP, and in 1980 she became one of three first deputy chairpersons of the Council of Ministers. In 1984, Ceauşescu's youngest son, Nicu, became a candidate member of the Political Executive Committee. Cultural repression, denunciatory campaigns against religious groups and arbitrary emigration policies have been constant features of the Ceauşescu regime.

The fostering of a Latin consciousness, the irredentist issues of Bessarabia and northern Bukovina, and the creation of a unitary state despite the vexed question of the large Hungarian minority in Transylvania have served to consolidate the nation. Romania has succeeded in retaining a measure of independence, and Ceauşescu's nationalist postures draw a warm response from the majority of Romanians.

Romanian foreign policy is directed at a denuclearized Balkan region exclusive of great power influence, at a maximum of maneuvering within present economic, defense and ideological groupings, and at increasing economic cooperation with the noncommunist world. Romania has maintained relations with China, Egypt and Israel, sympathized with the Czechoslovak reformers in 1968, condemned the Moscow-backed Vietnamese invasion of Kampuchea and has repeatedly called upon Moscow to withdraw its forces from Afghanistan. It has cultivated friendly relations with Yugoslavia and with major Western countries, including the United States, West Germany and France. Until 1982 it was the only Eastern-bloc nation to belong to the World Bank and the IMF. Romania is also reported to have opposed Warsaw Pact nations in their efforts to increase defense spending.

Defense (1983): Military service is compulsory, for 16 months in the army and air force and two years in the navy. Strength is estimated at: army 150,000, navy 7,500, air force 32,000, paramilitary forces 37,000. 1980 defense expenditure was $1,350 million, representing 1.6% of GNP. Romania is a member of the Warsaw Pact, but does not participate in military exercises nor allow Pact troops on its soil. Soviet troops were withdrawn in 1958.

ECONOMY

Background: During the 1970s, Romania recorded the highest rate of industrial growth in Eastern Europe. This gain, however, was not reflected in the standard of living, which remained the lowest in Eastern Europe because growth was primarily in the industrial sector to the exclusion of agriculture and personal consumption. While Romania has asserted relative independence in foreign affairs, it retains a command economy heavily centralized on the Soviet model.

Until 1970 Romania was a predominantly agricultural country; according to COMECON development strategies, it was to supply agricultural commodities to its neighbors. This role was subsequently abandoned in favor of rapid industrialization. As a result, the agricultural sector has declined both in terms of output and contribution to the GMP. Adverse weather, an aging rural population, shortages of agricultural machinery and the deliberate transfer of agricultural labor to industry have compounded the problem. Private farms and plots account for about one-sixth of the acreage but one-third of the production. Yet Romania remains self-sufficient in foodstuffs and a net exporter of some, albeit at the cost of severe shortages for the domestic consumer.

About a third of the national income is devoted to industrial investment, particularly to the production of producer goods, such as machinery, metals, chemicals and construction materials. Consumer goods have received low priority in all the five-year plans. Petroleum production peaked in the 1970s, but increased consumption has caused the depletion of oil reserves faster than anticipated. As a result, the country has become a net importer of oil, most of it designed to supply the extensive petrochemical industry. The 1981–85 five-year plan, therefore, placed high priority on energy independence through greater use of coal, hydroelectric power and nuclear power.

Continuing deterioration in the balance of payments position forced Romanian planners to retool their economic strategy. Under the New Economic Mechanism that took effect in 1981, agriculture received greater input, a number of producer prices were supposedly brought into alignment with world prices, the complex exchange-rate system was simplified and profitability has been adopted as a yardstick in determining costs and prices. The government also revised the 1981–85 plan targets; industrial output growth was reduced to 7.6% from 9.1% and agricultural output was increased to 5%. Following these changes, Western banks rescheduled Romania's $10 billion debt, and the IMF extended compensatory financing facilities to cover shortfalls.

Foreign trade: Although the Soviet Union and the Eastern bloc countries account for nearly half of Romania's merchandise trade, it has developed important trade relations with the West, as well as with China and Japan. It was the second Eastern European country (after Poland) to be admitted to GATT and the first to be admitted to the World Bank and the IMF. In 1975, the United States accorded it most-favored-nation trading status and recognized it as a developing country eligible for preferential trade treatment. In 1980 it became the first COMECON country to enter a comprehensive industrial trade agreement with the EC. Trade exchanges with developing countries also have expanded greatly in recent years and now account for over one-third of foreign trade.

Although trade accounts were balanced until the late 1970s, subsequent years have witnessed a deterioration in these accounts. The nation's net hard-currency debt rose to over $10 billion by 1981, a large part of it in short-term obligations. Romania has also been forced to import oil from the Soviet Union, thus placing an additional burden on its trade structure.

In 1982, merchandise exports amounted to $11.714 billion and merchandise imports to $9.836 billion, leaving a trade deficit of $1.878 billion. The percentage share of merchandise exports was fuels, minerals and metals (29%); machinery, plant and vehicles (26%); raw and processed materials and foodstuffs (17%); and consumer goods (16%). The percentage share of merchandise imports was fuels, minerals and metals (43%); machinery, plant and vehicles (32%); and raw and processed materials and foodstuffs (13%). The principal exports partners are the Soviet Union (18%); West Germany (8%); East Germany (6%); Italy (5%) and China (5%). The principal import partners are the Soviet Union (16%); the United States (7%); Iraq (7%); West Germany (6%); Iran (5%) and China (5%).

Employment: The total labor force is estimated at 10,428,000, of which 29% is in agriculture and 36.6% in industry. The level of employment has risen steadily. Plans for the period 1986–90 envisage much of the country's economic growth coming from increased labor productivity. In 1983, however, labor productivity, targeted for an increase of 7.1%, rose by only 1.7%.

Prices and wages: During the years 1976–80, real wages rose by an average of 5.2% per year but subsequently fell by about 10% during 1981–83. The average monthly wage is currently a meager 2,600 lei. In 1983, a new wage system was introduced in the manufacturing industry that abolished the minimum wage and geared a worker's income to the factory's total output. Several price increases have been instituted during the 1980s. In response to soaring energy and production prices at home and abroad, the government in 1982 announced the first price increase in food products in 25 years—an average 35% increase in basic food products and a 65% rise in the price of meat.

Consumption: Following steady improvement during the 1960s and 1970s, living standards have stagnated in recent years and remain low in comparison to other Eastern European countries. The preliminary plan for the 1986–90 period promises only to maintain living standards. Basic commodities such as sugar, flour and cooking oil are rationed. Retail trade turnover was 265 billion lei in 1983, of which foodstuffs accounted for 52.8% and nonfoodstuffs for 47.2%.

SOCIAL WELFARE

Since 1967, social security has been the responsibility of the Ministry of Labor. A small portion is contributed by the employees themselves to the voluntary pension fund, but the system is mostly financed by the employers and the government. Local social insurance offices administer the system at the local level.

Health services: Free medical assistance is available to all citizens in hospitals, sanatoriums and polyclinics. Free medicine is granted to the entire population. A sick worker receives 50% to 85% of earnings, depending on number of years of employment, payable at half rate for the first three days of incapacity and at full rate from the fourth day until recovery or reward of invalidity pension. Working women receive a maternity benefit of 50% to 94% of earnings, depending on work history and number of children, payable for up to 52 days before and 60 days after childbirth. In 1981, there were 89.09 hospital beds per 10,000 population and 15.34 doctors per 10,000 population. The maternal mortality rate in 1981 was 139.9 per 100,000 live births. The infant mortality rate in 1980 was 29.3 per 1,000 live births. In 1980, the average life expectancy for the Romanian male was 68.2 years and for the female 72.7 years.

Pensions and other benefits: Old-age pensions are granted according to the category of work. Workers in the first category, which includes the hardest jobs (e.g., underground mining, ballet dancing) are entitled to retire at an age as low as 45, but the general retirement age is 62 for men and 57 for women. The lowest statutory pension is 650 lei per month. Pension schemes are basically noncontributory, but since 1967, in order to correct the imbalance between wages and pensions, a contribution of 2% of earnings has been payable, repayable at the appropriate pensionable age. In cooperative farming, where men are pensionable at 65 and women at 60, old-age pensions are financed from the individual cooperative's special pensions fund, which is set at 2% of annual income. Since 1978, noncollectivized farmers have been covered under a special system. Disability pensions, which are related to the degree of incapacity, are granted till old-age pensions are applicable. Other means of social assistance are available if a worker is ineligible for pension.

Family allowances are granted to families with an income of up to 1,600 lei per month. They may receive from 185 to 275 lei per month, depending on the number of children. There is a birth grant of 1,000 lei for the third and each succeeding birth. Awards are also granted to mothers with many children, ranging from 200 lei per month for five to six children to 500 lei per month for 10 or more children. A funeral allowance of 800 lei, distributed from trade union funds, is granted for the funeral expenses of a deceased industrial worker or functionary.

Housing: There are three sectors of housing—state, cooperative and private. While formerly all state dwellings were centrally allocated, individual enterprises are now empowered to finance housing for their own employees. Cooperative units, which are increasingly sought after and financed on the basis of cooperative members' contributions and savings bank credits, may also include privately owned dwellings. Private housing is purchasable through state grants at 1.5% interest and guaranteed by a mortgage. As a rule, credit for private construction is granted only to residents of the respective town, except where a citizen's new locality has fewer inhabitants than the usual town of residence. Private ownership is confined to one dwelling only (excepting holiday houses). In both the state and private sectors, special purchasing arrangements are available for technical and intellectual workers employed in rural areas. Most new urban housing (including private dwellings) takes the form of multiple units in housing developments.

EDUCATION

The Ministry of Education administers and supervises the school system as a whole, but local organization of education is entrusted to the regional and district people's councils, which each contain an education section. Art schools are controlled by the State Committee for Art and Culture. All institutions of higher education are directly administered by the Ministry of Education. All tuition is free; at the level of higher education, two-thirds of students receive state scholarships. Extracurricular activities, frequently sponsored by the Young Pioneer and Communist organizations, are fostered on a broad scale. The illiteracy rate is about 3.5%.

Primary education: Crèches (for one- to three-year-olds), controlled by the Ministry of Health, are set up in institutions, enterprises and communities. Following an optional preschool kindergarten (ages four to seven), primary schooling consists of the compulsory eight-year school (*şcoală de 8 ani*) for all children aged seven to 15. The curriculum has a unitary structure and includes humanistic, scientific and polytechnical subjects.

Secondary education is of five types, available to all who have completed the eight-year school. The general secondary school (*şcoală medie de cultură generală*), entrance to which is on the basis of an examination in Romanian and mathematics, provides further general education for pupils aged 15 to 18. The curriculum is standardized in the first year; subsequent specialization is in humanities or science, in both of which the polytechnical element is stressed. Every school maintains laboratory, workshop and sports facilities. 75% of the pupils proceed to specialized and technical schools or to universities. National minority pupils may also receive some lessons in their native language where Romanian-language schools are the rule. The pressing need for trained technical workers resulted in a new law, taking effect in 1966–67, which established specialized technical/vocational secondary schools (*şcoli profesionale de ucenici*). These schools offer both day and night classes, free of charge to pupils graduating from the eight-year school, also to older citizens in need of basic or remedial training. The course lasts four to five years and the curricula include both the main subject and a general education. Practical instruction is emphasized. The secondary art school (*şcoală medie de artă*) instructs in music, fine arts and choreography, but in structure and curriculum otherwise resembles the general school. The physical education secondary school (*şcoală medie de educaţie fizică*) follows the pattern of the general and specialized school but gives special physical training. There is also the teacher training secondary school (*şcoală pedagogică de învăţători* and *şcoală pedagogică de educatoare*) with six-year courses toward kindergarten and primary teaching. Matriculating pupils from all five systems may proceed to higher education. Boarding maintenance is given in special cases.

Special education: There are two types of school for handicapped children: general and vocational. Tuition, board and medical treatment are free. A research unit in the Cluj Institute of Pedagogy studies the problems of the handicapped.

University and higher education: An annual intake quota is imposed by the Ministry of Education in accordance with state planning. There are seven universities, five polytechnical institutes, four technical institutes (building, mining, oil and gas, under-engineers), five institutes of medicine and pharmacy, four agricultural institutes, an institute of architecture, two institutes of fine arts, two institutes of dramatic art and film, three music conservatories, eight institutes of higher education (both technical and pedagogical) and an institute of physical education. The usual higher education course is five years, but institutes for architecture and medicine (six years), drama (four) and teacher training (three) are exceptions.

Educational institutions (1981–82):

	Institutions	Staff	Students
Primary and General Secondary	15,200	205,043	4,305,862
Vocational Secondary	587	1,833	123,864
Higher	134	14,354	190,903

Adult education in postwar years has aimed at the elimination of illiteracy. Evening and correspondence courses are readily available at the secondary and postsecondary levels.

MASS MEDIA

The Press (1983):

Dailies: (Bucharest) *Scînteia*, Communist party. (RCP), 1,820,000; *Informaţia Bucureştului*, RCP and People's Council (PC), 215,000; *România Liberă*, PC, 414,000; *Scînteia Tineretului*, youth, 226,000; *Előre*, Hungarian, 90,000; *Neuer Weg*, German, 51,000.
(Provincial) *Făclia*, Cluj, RCP and PC, 42,000; *Igazság*, Cluj, RCP and PC, in Hungarian, 27,000; *Drum Nou*, Braşov, RCP and PC, 50,000; *Flacăra*

Iaşului, Iaşi, RCP and PC, 55,000; *Dobrogea Nouă*, Constanţa RCP and PC, 32,000; *Flamura Prahovei*, Ploieşti, RCP and PC, 65,000.

Periodicals: (Bucharest); *Femeia* (m), women's illus., 410,000; *Contemporanul* (w), polit./cult./social, 20,000; *Lumea* (w), internat. affairs, 130,000; *Flacăra* (w), lit./art illus., 300,000; *Luceafărul* (w), lit., 13,500; *Urzica* (f), satirical, 200,000; *Munkásélet* (w), trade union, in Hungarian, 25,000; *Pravda* (three per week), in Serbo-Croat; *Romanian Review* (q), lit., in English, etc., 5,000; *Munca*, trade union, 200,000.

Broadcasting: Romanian Radio and Television, which is a state monopoly controlled by the Radio and Television Committee, operates two daily radio programs and a third on Sunday evenings, with five regional variations that include programs in Hungarian, German and Serbo-Croat. Foreign broadcasts are made in 13 languages. Television transmissions are made daily on two channels. Broadcasting is financed by subscriptions.

CONSTITUTIONAL SYSTEM

Constitution: The 1965 constitution, largely based on the Soviet model, declared Romania to be a Socialist Republic, a sovereign, independent and unitary state of the working people of the towns and villages. Amendments were made to the constitution most recently in 1974, the most significant of which were the creation of the post of president of the republic and the decrease of the Grand National Assembly membership to 369.

Legislature: The unicameral Grand National Assembly/GNA (*Marea Adunare Naţională*) is theoretically the sole legislative organ, with the following main functions: adoption of the constitution; regulation of the electoral system; approval of the budget; organization of the Council of Ministers and ministries, and of courts, the procuracy and people's councils; the framing of foreign policy; the declaration of war; the appointment and recall of the supreme commander of the armed forces; the proclamation of a state of emergency; and the election and control of the State Council. The GNA is elected for five years by universal franchise (18 years and over). The 369 deputies (*deputaţi*) represent single-member districts. Since December 1965, one or more candidates may stand in each constituency. Ninety-nine percent of the electorate participated in the last elections (1980). Officially subordinated to the GNA is the State Council (*Consiliu de Stat*) or collective presidency currently consisting of a president, five vice presidents, a secretary, 16 members and six counsellors. This is a permanent body with executive functions that include the establishment of election dates, the appointment of military chiefs and diplomatic representatives, and the right of pardon and commutation of punishments. Party control of both the GNA and State Council is decisive, although nonparty members have occasionally been elected to head the State Council (formerly Presidium). In 1967, Nicolae Ceauşescu, the party leader, was appointed its president and has retained the position for two decades.

Executive: The president (head of state) is elected by the Grand National Assembly for a five-year term. He is the supreme commander of the armed

101

forces and chairman of the Defense Council. He presides over the State Council and meetings of the Council of Ministers when necessary, and may appoint or remove most officials when the legislature is not in session. The Council of Ministers (*Consiliu de Ministri*) is the supreme body of state administration, whose sweeping powers include the conduct of foreign affairs, the achievement of national economic plans, general management of the economy, defense and control of subsidiary government organs. The Council of Ministers consists of a chairman, vice chairman, ministers and the chairmen of the State Planning Committee, State Committee for Culture and the National Council for Scientific Research. Its chairman and vice chairmen form a Permanent Bureau. It coordinates ministerial activity and is in theory responsible to the GNA. The majority of its members are active in the Central Committee of the RCP.

Judiciary: Justice is administered by the Supreme Court, 90 regional courts (and the Capital Court in Bucharest) and people's courts. There are also special courts, such as military and railway workers' tribunals. The Supreme Court (*Tribunal Suprem*) directs the judicial activity of all courts, is elected by the GNA and is responsible to it, but has no power to review the constitutionality of statutes. It functions mainly as the highest court of appeal but can act as a court of first instance in special cases. People's Courts (*tribunale populare*), whose lay assessors are elected for five years, are the usual first instance tribunals, but regional courts handle both appeal and first instance cases. The procuracy, introduced in 1952 and based on the Soviet model, is independent of the judiciary and headed by a procurator-general who is elected by the GNA for the term of the legislature and is responsible to it. The subordinate procurators not only maintain the procuratorial function of supervising state administration but act as prosecutors in criminal cases. There is capital punishment.

Basic rights: The state guarantees equality; many social services; freedom of speech, assembly, demonstration (though these "cannot be used for aims hostile to the socialist system and to the interests of the working people"); freedom of religion and conscience; the right to personal property and inheritance; and the right of ethnic minorities to their own cultural self-expression and education in their own language.

Party: Romania is a one-party state and there is no parliamentary opposition. In 1965, following the March general elections in which 99.6% of the electorate participated, the Romanian Workers' party was renamed the Romanian Communist party. Electoral candidates are nominated by a mass organization, the Popular Democratic Front; the electoral law of December 1966 authorized nomination of more than one candidate in each constituency. The structure follows the Soviet example: periodic party congresses are held that elect a Central Committee, and this body, in turn, elects the Executive Political Committee. The RCP has a membership (as of 1982) of 3,262,125. The party leader is currently head of state.

Local government: Until early 1968 Romania was subdivided into 16 regions (*regiuni*), two cities with regional status (Bucharest and Constanţa), districts (*raioane*), towns and communes, but the system now operating is based on 39 counties (*judeţe*), 46 city municipalities and, at a lower level, towns and communes. Bucharest is further subdivided into sectors. Each unit has its people's council (*consiliu popular*) with an executive branch. The executive committees at the city municipality level are subordinate to their county equivalents, with the exception of Bucharest, which is centrally supervised. Members of people's councils are elected for five years except at commune level where the term is two and a half years.

Leading government and party figures: Nicolae Ceauşescu (president, general secretary of the RCP, president of the State Council), Constantin Dăscălescu (prime minister), Elena Ceauşescu (first deputy prime minister), Lt. Gen. Ion Dinca (first deputy prime minister), Gheorghe Oprea (first deputy prime minister), Stefan Andrei (foreign minister), Maj. Gen. Constantin Olteanu (defense minister), Gheorghe Homostean (interior minister), Stefan Birlea (State Planning Commission chairman), Petre Gigea (finance minister).

BIOGRAPHICAL SKETCHES

Elena Ceauşescu. The president's wife came to assume a growing role in the country's affairs during the 1970s and 1980s. She was born in 1919 and is said to have joined the party in 1937. She spent the postwar years working at the Central Institute of Chemical Research, becoming its head after 1965. Her political ambitions began to be realized when she joined the Central Committee in 1972 and the Executive Committee in 1973. From this point on she was a member of the inner circle of politics and was regarded as highly influential. Her formal status advanced when appointed to the Permanent Bureau of the Political Executive Committee in 1977; and she was created first deputy prime minister in 1980. Elena Ceauşescu was widely disliked in Romania, seen by many as wielding excessive influence over her husband.

Nicolae Ceauşescu. Ceauşescu, party leader from 1965 and head of state, was born to a peasant family in 1918 at Scorniceşti, near Piteşti. He joined the illegal communist youth movement in 1933 and the party in 1936. He was mostly in prison until 1944, when he was released. After the war he worked in the party's organizational department and in the political directorate of the armed forces. A candidate member of the Central Committee in 1948, he was appointed deputy minister of the armed forces in 1950, rising to full membership in the Central Committee in 1952. In October that year he was promoted to lieutenant general. A member of the Secretariat and a candidate member of the Politburo in 1954, he was made a full member in 1955—a very rapid ascent indeed. After 1960 he emerged as the heir to party leader Gheorghe Gheorghiu-Dej, whom he succeeded in 1965. In 1968 he became titular head of state as well, and president in 1974. His political career as leader falls into three phases. Between 1965 and 1968 he was consolidating his position and was no more than first among equals, flanked by a number of senior figures. His profile at this time was of a relatively youthful,

energetic leader, with some commitment to change; he continued his predecessor's policies of fostering Romanian nationalism and stressing his country's
independence from the Soviet Union. Between 1968 and 1971, Ceauşescu
introduced the nearest thing to liberalization that postwar Romania has
experienced. He purged the interior minister, Alexandru Draghici, and condemned the violations of legality of the 1950s. In 1971, however, he launched
the third phase of his career, insisting on high levels of discipline, mobilization
and accelerated industrial growth. During this phase there was a rapidly
increasing emphasis on Ceauşescu's personality, and numerous members
of his extended family were promoted to positions of power. His personality
cult, which on one occasion saw Ceauşescu termed Romania's "secular
God," broke all precedents. His strategy of extended industrial growth failed,
partly through internal difficulties of overregulation and partly because of
the two oil shocks of the 1970s, which shifted the terms of trade against
Romania. By the early 1980s the country was in serious economic difficulties;
the population saw itself enduring cutbacks in its living standards and the
prospect of many more years of privation. Ceauşescu, for his part, seemingly
cut off from Romanian realities, apparently felt that there was no need to
amend his political and economic strategy.

Constantin Dăscălescu. Dăscălescu, prime minister after 1982, was born in
1920. He made his career in the party organizations in Galaţi county
(1964–74), then moved to the center as head of a Central Committee department (1974), as Central Committee secretary (1976) and head of the party
organization department (1978). He was made member of the Permanent
Bureau of the Political Executive Committee in 1979. Evidently trusted by
Ceauşescu, Dăscălescu was essentially a political administrator. He was
regarded as a tough party activist and had no background in economics.

Mănea Manescu. Manescu, a member of the Ceauşescu clan by marriage,
returned to the Permanent Bureau of the Political Executive Committee in
1984. Born in 1916, he held a variety of posts, including that of prime minister
(1973–79). He was regarded as a Ceauşescu loyalist and as a reliable executor
of the president's policies.

Ilie Verdeţ. Verdeţ, related to the president by marriage, was a member
of the Permanent Bureau and of the Secretariat. Born in 1925, he was made
a candidate member of the Central Committee in 1955 and a full member
five years later. During the Ceauşescu years, he held a variety of high-ranking
posts, including that of prime minister (1979–82), but was from time to
time dropped, indicating that even membership in the Ceauşescu clan was
not an automatic guarantee of tenure of office.

SOVIET UNION

Features: The two most salient features of Soviet geography are size and latitudinal location. The Soviet Union stretches almost halfway around the world, covering 17% of the inhabited surface of the globe. Of this territory, one-third lies in Europe, two-thirds in Asia. Its total size is three times as large as the United States (including Alaska), and the European part is seven times the size of France. The distance from the Baltic Sea to the Pacific is 6,000 m./9,600 km., and from north to south 3,000 m./4,800 km. There are 11 time zones. The following states are contiguous with the Soviet Union: Norway, Finland, Poland, Czechoslovakia, Hungary, Romania, Bulgaria, Turkey, Iran, Afghanistan, China, Mongolia and North Korea.

The latitudes of much of the Soviet Union are comparable to those of Canada, Scotland and Scandinavia, Moscow being on a par with Edinburgh, and Leningrad with Oslo and southern Alaska. The Caucasus and Central Asia, however, are on the same latitudes as Italy or Utah.

Topographically outstanding is the generally low relief of the western half of the Soviet Union. Only at the southern periphery of this region and in the eastern sector are there extensive and high mountain ranges. In the western sector, the Great Russian Plain never reaches altitudes of more than a few hundred feet, the chief elevations being the Podolian Plateau, the Central Russian Uplands, Donets Ridge and Volga Heights. These have effected stream patterns of rivers that, like the Dnieper and Volga, are largely navigable. The Pripet marshes provide especially poor drainage in the west. The Ukrainian sector of the European Soviet Union is bounded in the south by the Black Sea, where the Crimean Peninsula contains elevations of over 5,000 ft/1,500 m. The northwestern sector (i.e. the RSFSR and Baltic republics) has a frontage on the Baltic, Barents and White seas. It was in the Great Russian Plain that the Russian state historically evolved; it is this core area of the Soviet Union that still contains three-quarters of the Soviet population and two-thirds of its national production.

As an extension of the fault system rising in the Crimea and continuing under the Sea of Azov, the Greater Caucasus, ranged between the Black and Caspian seas, attains heights of more than 18,000 ft/5,400 m. The Lesser Caucasus merges in the frontier zones of Turkey and Iran with the Armenian Plateau. At the geographical division of Europe and Asia, the plain is interrupted by the glaciated ridges of the Ural Mountains (av. height 2,000 ft/ 610 m.). These are sufficiently broken in places to allow unimpeded

SOVIET UNION: EUROPE

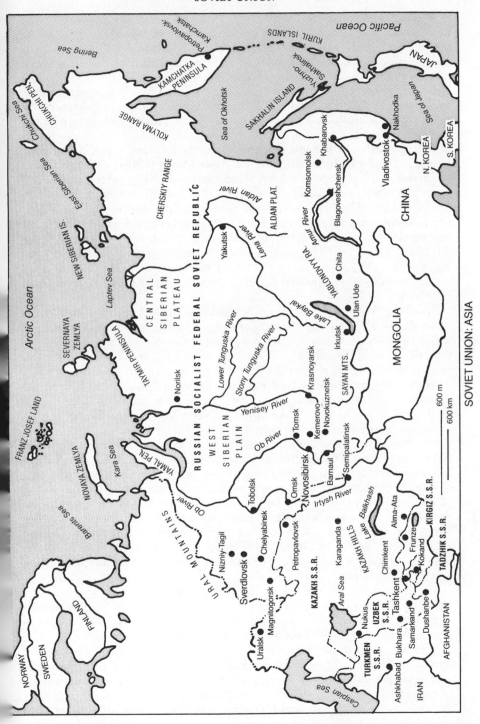

SOVIET UNION: ASIA

movement, settlement and industry. From the southeastern shore of the Caspian Sea, the Kopet Dag range forms an eastern frontier with Iran. At the political borders of Soviet Central Asia, Afghanistan, Pakistan, India and Chinese Sinkiang, the Pamirs, a northwestern spur of the Himalayas, contain the highest peak in the Soviet Union (Communism Peak 24,700 ft/7,500 m.) and together with the Tien-Shan to the north reach several heights well above 20,000 ft/6,000 m. The massive physical barrier represented by these ranges is broken occasionally by east-west valleys such as that of the Ili River and the Dzungarian Gate.

To the north of the high ranges of Central Asia lies the arid Turanian Basin, drained by rivers such as the Amu Darya (Oxus) and Syr Darya (Jaxartes), with outlets in three inland bodies of water: the Caspian and Aral Seas and Lake Balkhash. Extreme high summer temperatures are recorded here. The black-earth (*chernozem*) steppe of the Kazakh Virgin Lands constitutes a transitional stage between Central Asia and the forest and tundra regions of Siberia. Western Siberia, bounded on the west by the Urals and on the East by the Yenisey River, centers on the waterlogged basin of the Ob River, emptying northward into the Arctic Ocean. In its southeastern sector, western Siberia includes the Kuznetsk coal basin (Kuzbas).

From the Yenisey eastward to beyond the Lena (both of which rivers attain nearly 3,000 m./4,800 km.) lies eastern Siberia, covering one-third of the Soviet Union's territory, yet supporting only 4% of its population. In the middle of this region the immense desert-filled Central Siberian Plateau reaches an average height of 2,000 ft/610 m. while to the south is a series of much higher, more complex ranges, the Sayan, Yablonovyy and Stanovoy mountains. At its southern fringes lies the tectonic basin of Lake Baykal (5,700 ft/1,750 m. deep). From this lake rises the Angara River with its incomparable hydroelectric power.

Finally, between the Lena and the Pacific Ocean, is the Soviet Far East. Its several mountain ranges (notably the Verkhoyansk, Cherskiy and Anadyr mountains) extend offshore in a series of islands and peninsulas. The Kamchatka Peninsula has 100 active volcanoes (including Klyuchevskaya, 16,000 ft/4,800 m.). Only in the extreme southern part is there significant population, communications and economic development: in the valleys of the Amur and Ussuri rivers and the petroliferous, coal-producing island of Sakhalin. The Soviet Union's important Pacific seaport, Vladivostok, is largely icebound in winter (as are the main ports of the Baltic and Black seas; Murmansk remains ice-free).

The climate of the Soviet Union has all the characteristics of extreme continentality, ranging from Arctic conditions in the far north to Mediterranean-type in the Crimea, subtropical in the southern Caucasus, arid in Central Asia and monsoon-type in the Soviet Far East.

Although there is not, for climatic, soil and topographical reasons, a good correlation between size and cultivable land, the Soviet Union possesses a diverse agriculture and is a major world producer of wheat, maize, sugar beets and sunflower seeds. Grain is confined mainly to the European sector and to the new steppe lands of Kazakhstan and Western Siberia; sugar beets

Temperature, Relative humidity, Precipitation

Station	Height in ft	Position	Temperature (Mean max. and min.)		Relative humidity	Mean annual rainfall
Moscow	505	55°N,	July	66°F/19°C	84%	25 in./ 635 mm.
(European Russia)		37°E	Jan.	15°F/−9°C		
Riga (Baltic)	65	56°N,	July	64°F/18°C	86%	22 in./ 559 mm.
		24°E	Jan.	25°F/−4°C		
Pechenga	35	69°N,	July	54°F/12°C	83%	17 in./ 432 mm.
(Kola Peninsula)		31°E	Jan.	15°F/−9°C		
Odessa	215	46°N,	July	72°F/22°C	80%	14 in./ 356 mm.
(Black Sea)		30°E	Jan.	25°F/−4°C		
Sevastopol	75	44°N,	July	72°F/22°C	79%	12 in./ 305 mm.
(Crimea)		33°E	Jan.	35°F/ 2°C		
Batumi	10	41°N,	July	74°F/23°C	82%	96 in./2,438 mm.
(West Caucasus)		41°E	Jan.	42°F/ 6°C		
Lenkoran	60	38°N,	July	76°F/24°C	86%	49 in./1,245 mm.
(East Caucasus)		48°E	Jan.	37°F/ 3°C		
Astrakhan	45	46°N,	July	77°F/25°C	80%	6 in./ 152 mm.
(Lower Volga)		48°E	Jan.	19°F/−7°C		
Sverdlovsk	895	56°N,	July	62°F/17°C	82%	17 in./ 432 mm.
(Urals)		49°E	Jan.	0°F/−18°C		
Dudinka	140	69°N,	July	55°F/13°C	82%	8 in./ 203 mm.
(Central Siberia)		87°E	Jan.	−22°F/−30°C		
Verlhoyansk	330	67°N,	July	59°F/15°C	74%	4 in./ 102 mm.
(East Siberia)		133°E	Jan.	−58°F/−50°C		
Tashkent	1,570	41°N,	July	78°F/26°C	71%	15 in./ 381 mm.
(Central Asia)		69°E	Jan.	29°F/−2°C		
Vladivostok	25	43°N,	Aug.	69°F/21°C	80%	21 in./ 533 mm.
(Far East)		131°E	Jan.	7°F/−14°C		

to the Ukraine and the central part of European Russia. There is localized production of potatoes, vegetables, flax, hemp and tobacco (European sector), vines (Moldavia, Caucasus, Central Asia), cotton (Central Asia), tea and citrus (Caucasus) and rice (Central Asia and Far East). There is varied and extensive pastureland. Nonetheless, some nine-tenths of the country remains at present uncultivable on a commercial basis. Nearly one-half of the Soviet Union comprises forest, providing for the world's greatest timber industry. Hydroelectric potential is unequalled.

While inaccessibility has always been a major problem, the Soviet Union's overall fuel and mineral resources are the richest on earth. They include an estimated 58% of the world's coal deposits, 59% of its oil, 41% of its iron ore, 88% of its manganese, 54% of its potassium salts and 32% of its phosphates. The well-established industrial areas are the Central Industrial Region (centering on Moscow and Gorky), Leningrad, the Donbas-Dnieper complex, the Middle Volga cities, Baku and the Urals. Recent emphasis is placed on new centers east of the Urals, along the axis of the Trans-Siberian railway and its branches as far as Lake Baykal. These include Karaganda, east Uzbekistan, the Novosibirsk-Kuzbas complex and Baykal. The Amur and Ussuri valleys comprise the manufacturing hub of the Soviet Far East.

Area of Soviet Union: 8,600,000 sq. miles/22,402,200 sq. km.

Area of union republics: RSFSR 6,569,000 sq. miles/17,075,400 sq. km.; Kazakh SSR 1,102,300 sq. miles/2,717,300 sq. km.; Ukrainian SSR 231,100 sq. miles/603,700 sq. km.; Turkmen SSR 187,000 sq. miles/ 488,100 sq. km.; Uzbek SSR 153,000 sq. miles/447,400 sq. km.: Belorussian SSR 80,000 sq. miles/207,600 sq. km.; Kirghiz SSR 76,150 sq. miles/ 198,500 sq. km.; Tadzhik SSR 54,600 sq. miles/143,100 sq. km.; Azerbaidzhan SSR 33,400 sq. miles/86,600 sq. km.; Georgian SSR 27,700 sq. miles/ 69,700 sq. km.; Lithuanian SSR 25,000 sq. miles/65,200 sq. km.; Latvian SSR 24,600 sq. miles/63,700 sq. km.; Estonian SSR 17,300 sq. miles/ 45,100 sq. km.; Moldavian SSR 13,000 sq. miles/33,700 sq. km.; Armenian SSR 11,540 sq. miles/29,800 sq. km.

POPULATION

Total population of the Soviet Union (1983 est.): 272,500,000.

Population by union republic, with capital cities (1983 est.): Russian SFSR (RSFSR) (Moscow) 140,952,000; Ukrainian SSR (Kiev) 50,456,000; Uzbek SSR (Tashkent) 17,044,000; Kazakh SSR (Alma-Ata) 15,470,000; Belorussian SSR (Minsk) 9,806,000; Azerbaidzhan SSR (Baku) 6,400,000; Georgian SSR (Tbilisi/Tiflis) 5,137,000; Tadzhik SSR (Dushanbe) 4,236,000; Moldavian SSR (Kishinev) 4,053,000; Kirgiz SSR (Frunze) 3,803,000; Lithuanian SSR (Vilna/Vilnius) 3,504,000; Armenian SSR (Yerevan) 3,222,000; Turkmen SSR (Ashkhabad) 3,045,000; Latvian SSR (Riga) 2,568,000; Estonian SSR (Tallinn) 1,507,000.

Chief towns and populations (1983 est.): Greater Moscow 8,396,000; Greater Leningrad 4,779,000; Kiev 2,355,000; Tashkent 1,944,000; Kharkov 1,519,000; Minsk 1,405,000; Gorky 1,382,000; Novosibirsk 1,370,000; Sverdlovsk 1,269,000; Kuybyshev 1,243,000; Dnepropetrovsk 1,128,000; Tbilisi/Tiflis 1,125,000; Odessa 1,097,000; Yerevan 1,095,000; Omsk 1,080,000; Chelyabinsk 1,077,000; Baku 1,071,000; Donetsk 1,055,000; Perm 1,037,000; Ufa 1,034,000; Kazan 1,031,000; Alma-Ata 1,023,000; Rostov-on-Don 977,000; Volgograd 962,000; Saratov 887,000; Riga 867,000; Krasnoyarsk 845,000; Zaporozhe 835,000; Voronezh 831,000; Lvov 711,000; Krivoy Rog 674,000; Kishinev 580,000; Frunze 577,000; Dushanbe 530,000; Vilna/Vilnius 525,000; Tallinn 454,000; Ashkhabad 339,000.

Ethnic composition: The 1979 census identified over 100 distinctive nationality groups. Of these some 53 are recognized politically in administrative units ranked as union republic (SSR), autonomous republic (ASSR), autonomous region (AO) or national area (NO) in which a particular nationality is officially predominant although (as in the case of Kazakhstan) it may be numerically inferior. The 15 SSRs comprise the 15 largest nationalities. Of the total population of the Soviet Union, Russians constitute 52.4%,

Ukrainians 16.1%, Belorussians 3.6%. The remaining 28% are non-Slav nationalities. In the RSFSR, 82.6% of the population is Russian, but there are numerous other groupings, of which some 30 are organized in ASSR, AO or NO subunits. The largest minorities with special administrative status in the RSFSR are the Tatar (2.4%), Chuvash (1%), Daghestan (1%) and Bashkir (1%). Russians form large minorities in several non-Russian SSRs: Kazakhstan (40.8%), Latvia (32.8%), Estonia (27.9%), Kirgizia (25.9%), Ukraine (21.1%), Moldavia (14.2%), Turkmeniya (12.6%), Belorussia (11.9%), Uzbekistan (10.8%), Tadzhikstan (10.4%), Lithuania (8.9%) and Azerbaidzhan (7.9%). Ukrainians form minorities in Moldavia and Kirgizia. Other large minorities in SSRs include: Uzbeks in Tadzhikistan, Kirgizia and Turkmeniya; Armenians in Azerbaidzhan and Georgia; Azerbaidzhanis in Armenia and Tatars in Uzbekistan. The several minorities historically associated with territories outside the Soviet Union include Poles, Kurds, Germans and Jews (each constituting approximately 1% of the Soviet Union), while Finns (including Karelo-Finns), Bulgarians, Persians, Koreans and others each form less than 1% of the Soviet Union's population. Demographic trends indicate that the current rate of growth for the Muslim areas—mainly Central Asia and Kazakhstan—is significantly higher than that for the Slavic population.

Language: There are over 120 languages in the Soviet Union. Russian is the official language and lingua franca of the union. All SSRs and most of their constituent national subdivisions have, in addition to Russian, national languages with official status. Most of these languages are written in variations of Cyrillic, notable exceptions being the Baltic languages (Latin script); Georgian and Armenian use their own scripts. Language groups are 76% Slavic, 11% Altaic, 8% other Indo-European, 3% Uralian, and 2% Caucasian.

Religion: 70% of the population are said to be atheist, 18% Russian Orthodox, and 9% Muslim. Smaller percentages include Jewish, Georgian Orthodox, Roman Catholic, Baptist, Evangelical Christian and Buddhist groups.

RECENT HISTORY

The Soviet Union's two primary objectives at the end of World War II were to reconstruct the severely damaged home economy and to consolidate the territorial and ideological gains that had accrued to it. These goals have been largely realized, though often at the expense of individual liberties and of pacific relations with other states. The 1945 Potsdam Conference of the Soviet Union, United States and Britain practically sanctioned the wartime incorporation within Soviet borders of most of Poland east of the 1919 Curzon Line, part of Finnish Karelia and of Bessarabia, northern Bukovina, Carpatho-Ruthenia, Lithuania, Latvia, Estonia and the northern part of east Prussia. Peace with Japan likewise brought concessions in Manchuria, Port Arthur and northern Korea, the possession of the Kuril Islands and reincorporation of southern Sakhalin. Tannu Tuva was annexed in 1944. The Soviet military presence in most Eastern European countries subsequently formed the basis for the establishment of communist governments in eastern Germany, Poland, Hungary, Bulgaria and Romania. Liberated Yugoslavia was to maintain, till 1948, a close alignment with Moscow, while in 1948, a predominantly communist government wwas formed in Czechoslovakia. These, with Albania, were to be termed the satellite states of the Soviet Union. In 1949 they were conjoined in COMECON (CMEA), the Soviet answer to the U.S. Marshall Plan in Western Europe.

Europe was now divided by an "Iron Curtain," running from Szczecin to Trieste and, though the Soviet Union was a founder member of the United Nations, its former alliance with the Western Powers was converted into a cold war. Several major events were soon to reinforce the growing bipolarization of the world into Eastern and Western, communist and noncommunist, Soviet- and American-oriented power blocs. In 1946, UN pressures forced the withdrawal of Soviet troops from Iranian Azerbaidzhan. In 1948–49, the Soviet attempt to blockade West Berlin was defeated by an airlift undertaken by the Western allies. In Germany, cooperation between the Soviet Union and the West had come to a virtual standstill, and the formation of a German Federal Republic in western Germany was promptly countered (1949) by the establishment of a German Democratic Republic in the zone of Soviet occupation.

When NATO was instituted (1949) as a means of containing Soviet expansionism in Europe, the Soviet Union responded by establishing a network of bilateral defense treaties, which included the Soviet Union and all the communist states of Eastern Europe except Yugoslavia. In the same year, Mao Zedong obtained full control of mainland China, and an "eternal friendship" between the Soviet Union and People's Republic of China was proclaimed. The Western Powers were faced by the apparent monolithic unity of a much enlarged communist bloc; and from 1950 to 1953 war between the Sino/Soviet supported North Korean troops, which had crossed the 38th parallel, and the combined forces of South Korea and the United Nations posed the threat of a head-on collision between a Sino/Soviet alliance and the West. The 1951 defense pact between the United States and Japan, the admission to NATO of Greece and Turkey (1951) and of West Germany (1955), the creation of anticommunist defense systems on the Asian periphery of China and the Soviet Union (SEATO in 1954 and the Baghdad Pact/CENTO in 1955) and the detonation in 1953 of the Soviet Union's first thermonuclear device further served to intensify the Cold War. The Warsaw Treaty, the Soviet Union's military alliance system, was signed in 1955 in response to the rearmament of West Germany. Summit conferences at Geneva in 1955 and 1959 failed to solve the German problem, but in 1955, nonetheless, the Austrian peace treaty secured a Soviet signature.

This early postwar period was marked at home by the strengthening of the totalitarian system. Stalin's personal control of key positions in the party and government, of the secret police and army, of the judiciary and propaganda ensured the survival of his person and position, but after his death in 1953, the problem of succession was not immediately resolved. Georgi M. Malenkov succeeded as chairman of the Council of Ministers until 1955, to be replaced by Nikolai A. Bulganin. Real power, however, remained with the Communist party. In a secret speech to the 20th Congress of the CPSU in early 1956, the party first secretary, Nikita Khrushchev, made the first strong denunciation of some of Stalin's "crimes," and this led to a cultural thaw. The trend towards destalinization had already begun in 1953 when several of Stalin's associates were purged, some, like secret police chief Lavrenty Beria, to be executed—but now new personalities were to be matched by cautious modifications of the system itself. The cult of personality among political leaders was officially denounced and the use of terror was reduced. But few relaxations were tolerated in the Eastern European countries of the Soviet bloc, for the example of Tito was easily recalled. In 1956, partly in response to destalinization in the Soviet Union, riots in the Polish city of Poznań and subsequent events of the "Polish October" led to a temporary liberalization of the system within Poland. But a revolution in Hungary was, with the help of Soviet troops, ruthlessly suppressed. Soviet action was condemned by the United Nations and much of world opinion. In 1958, Bulganin, through his association with the discredited "antiparty group," was replaced as premier by Khrushchev who now held preeminent posts in both party and government. Collective leadership reasserted itself again in 1964 when the party's Central Committee removed Khrushchev. He was succeeded as first secretary of the CPSU by Leonid Brezhnev and as premier by Alexey Kosygin, and in 1965 Nikolai Podgorny was elected president in succession to Anastas Mikoyan. While the Khrushchev era was one of populism and reform, the ensuing 18-year period was one of conservatism, consensual decision making and political stability. Under Brezhnev's leadership, the Soviet political elite received job security for the first time in its history. In addition, the leadership created political and economic stability in the country as a whole by emphasizing agriculture and consumer-oriented programs, thus satisfying popular expectations for higher standards of living. The overall policy of the Brezhnev era, however, did not serve the Soviet Union's best interests. The country faces a prolonged period of economic stagnation and, at the same time, a very rapid turnover of a large proportion of the political leadership.

The passing away of the older political leadership with no provision for a smooth succession to the younger generation resulted in an ineffective leadership for the past several years. In 1977, an already ailing Brezhnev replaced Podgorny as president, becoming head of both party and government. In 1980, Kosygin retired because of failing health and was replaced by the elderly Nikolai Tikhonov. Upon the death of Brezhnev in 1982, Yuri Andropov, a former chairman of the State Security Committee (KGB), became party first secretary and was later elected president as well. Andropov quickly initiated a campaign to eliminate corruption and to increase labor productivity, but ill health resulted in his prolonged absence from public life until his death in February 1984. Konstantin Chernenko, a Brezhnev protégé and another aging figure, succeeded Andropov. Chernenko's tenure was decidedly uneventful, and he died in March 1985, after only 13 months in office. Mikhail Gorbachev, 54 years old, succeeded Chernenko as first secretary of the CPSU, the youngest leader to hold this post since the 1917 Bolshevik Revolution. Gorbachev moved quickly to assert his leadership, publicly proclaiming the need for significant economic reforms and promoting a number of his supporters to top party and government posts.

In general, the post-Stalin era has been notable for a decline in emphasis on heavy industry in the evolution of the economy; for the development of vast new regions, particularly in Siberia, Kazakhstan and Central Asia; for alternate thaws and freezes in the cultural and political climate; and for major contributions to science, especially in aerospace and military technology, nuclear power, medicine and transportation.

Soviet foreign policy since Stalin has been characterized by an increasing emphasis on the formula of peaceful coexistence with the West and with foreign capitalism, by growing trade and contacts with the entire noncommunist world, by a corresponding deterioration in relations with Peking (based on ideological, national and territorial differences), and by an unprecedented ideological and economic involvement in Third World countries, especially Cuba, India, Syria, Ethiopia, Nicaragua and, formerly, Indonesia, Ghana, Egypt and Guinea. A direct conflict of interests has, nonetheless, brought the Soviet Union and the West to the brink of war, as in the Middle Eastern crises of 1956, 1958 and 1967; in the Cuban missile crisis of 1962; and in Vietnam. In addition to conventional diplomacy, the Soviet Union uses the international network of Communist parties and front organizations in its pursuit of external policy, but its support of "national liberation" movements has been none too successful.

In 1961, another Berlin crisis led to the construction of the Wall, but since then the growth of nationalism and polycentrism in Eastern Europe, together with Soviet preoccupations elsewhere, have somewhat reduced Soviet direct domination of that region; but ideological ties of the party, regional integration within the Warsaw Pact and COMECON, and the retention of Soviet troops in four Eastern European states guarantee the preservation of a Soviet hegemony. The limits of reform and ideological deviation in the region were clarified by the Soviet invasion of Czechoslovakia in 1968. The liberal leadership of that country had far-reaching plans to adapt socialism to local needs, and it is clear that Moscow feared not only the strategic consequences of a "Czech road to socialism" but even more the infection of "heretical" policies that had already won the explicit sympathy of the Yugoslav, Romanian and Western Communist parties and of world opinion as a whole. The Solidarity movement in Poland also tested these limits. Pressure on the Polish government from Moscow was clearly a determining factor in that government's decision to impose martial law.

In another region, the Soviet Union was drawn into a massive military intervention outside the Soviet bloc. In the wake of a pro-Soviet coup in April 1978, the Soviet army swept into Afghanistan and virtually occupied the country in 1979. The move was widely condemned by both Muslim and Western governments, but formal action by the UN Security Council was blocked by a Soviet veto in 1980.

Relations with Western countries have fluctuated in recent years. A wide expansion of contacts was implemented during the détente period of the 1970s, culminating in the signing of strategic arms limitation agreements in 1972 and 1979. Recently, however, relations have hardened, each side accusing the other of treaty violations, human rights violations and disregard for international law, among other things. At the same time, Moscow has attempted to encourage the European peace movement in order to turn the tide of popular opinion against Western policies.

Defense (1983): Military service is compulsory, for two years in the army and air force and between two and three years in the navy and in the border force. Strength is estimated at: army 1,800,000, navy and naval air force 460,000, air force 365,000, paramilitary forces 450,000, strategic rocket forces 325,000, air troops 100,000, air defense forces 500,000, command and general support troops 1,500,000. Present total defense expenditure, including items related to defense but not in the declared defense budget was estimated at $130, billion, representing 10.7% of GNP (in market prices). In 1955, the Soviet Union signed the 20-year Warsaw Treaty of Friendship and Collaboration with Albania, Bulgaria, Czechoslovakia, East Germany, Hungary, Poland and Romania. This treaty was renewed in 1975. Soviet army divisions are stationed in East Germany, Poland, Hungary and Czechoslovakia. Albania formally abrogated its defense agreements with the Warsaw Pact countries in 1968.

ECONOMY

Background: The Soviet Union is the largest command economy in the world and it has never swerved from its goal of total centralization of all economic activities within its borders. Since 1928, the system has been subjected to stringent directives of successive economic plans, with the 11th five-year plan covering the period 1981–85. The planning process begins in the State Planning Commission (Gosplan), which drafts general guidelines that are published, evaluated, revised and ultimately approved by the Communist party congress. Somewhat more detailed plans are worked out within ministries representing various industries, based on output targets and resource availabilities, and Gosplan and Gossnab (the State Supply Committee) are responsible for making the necessary adjustments to the main plan. In addition to the five-year plans, Gosplan formulates schedules for both shorter and longer time periods. Sometimes goals are set that extend through several plan periods. The success of the plans depends on material balances that equate resources and uses. Gosplan supervises the myriad interrelationships of some 2,000 major commodities; Gossnab allocates some 15,000 inputs; and other ministries oversee the distribution of an additional 40,000. Planning departments also function within each union republic and smaller geographical division down to the level of production units with varying degrees of efficiency. Computer-generated input–output matrices have permitted a higher degree of sophistication in the planning process.

The tenth five-year plan (1976–80) was a failure, falling below both agricultural and industrial targets—the former achieving a growth rate of only 1.7%, and the latter of 4.4%. The 1981–85 plan included even more modest goals than its predecessor, which itself had lower targets than earlier ones. Industrial growth rate under the current plan is set at 4.7% to 5.1%, and agricultural expansion at 2.3% to 2.7%. In addition, priority is being given to the production of consumer goods, representing a shift from the traditional emphasis on heavy industry.

115

Even poor performance cannot conceal the fact that the Soviet Union is an economic giant with an extraordinary range of resources that few other countries can claim. The country ranks among the top 10 in 93 economic rankings, with particular strengths in agriculture, industry, energy, transportation and communications, and mining. It has been the world's largest oil producer for a number of years and its proved reserves account for 10% of the world total. It is a world leader in the production of iron ore, manganese, tungsten, chromite and gold. However, huge distances continue to create a number of logistical problems in both the extraction and transport of minerals.

Agriculture, dependent on weather and other natural conditions, is the bugbear of Soviet planners. Only one-tenth of the land can be cultivated, approximately one-sixth is suitable for pasturage and one-third is classified as forest and brushland. A sizable portion of the arable land is subject to periodic drought. As a result, the Soviet Union has been a net importer of food for a number of years, placing an additional burden on its foreign-exchange resources. Collectivization of agriculture, completed in the 1930s, offers few incentives for increased output. State farms cover 66% of agricultural land, collectives another 31%, and private farms the remaining 3%.

Marked regional inequalities still exist in the Soviet Union. The RSFSR is highly developed in comparison with northern and eastern Siberia. This inequality is being tackled by large-scale investments and above-average wages and salaries. Siberia is rich in coal, iron ore, natural gas, timber and diamonds, and has excellent potential for hydroelectric power.

Foreign trade: The Soviet Union's international commerce is conducted by special foreign-trade organizations in accordance with the country's long- and short-term plans. Because the ruble is not convertible (except for accounts within COMECON), trade with the noncommunist world is settled either in hard currencies or according to bilaterally balanced agreements.

The direction of trade has remained relatively stable over the years; nearly half is with COMECON, some 33% with developed countries and 17% with developing countries. Within COMECON, the Soviet Union has used trade as a strategy for achieving an integrated economy—more for its own good than for that of its partners. Trade with the West, however distasteful to ideologues in the Kremlin, has become a necessity in order to obtain both high technology on the one hand and grain on the other.

Although the Soviet Union has pursued a balanced bilateral trade as the ideal for many years, it has not achieved this goal in the recent past. Trade deficits soared in the early 1980s; these were somewhat offset by the sale of gold and by selling arms to Third World countries. Following OPEC trends, the Soviet Union increased its oil prices on deliveries to COMECON countries to 80% of the world rate. On the other hand, lower-priced natural gas is being supplied to Eastern Europe, and larger deliveries will become available to the West once the 2,700-mile pipeline from Urengoi, close to the Arctic Circle in western Siberia, is completed with the aid of a Western European consortium.

In 1982, Soviet merchandise exports amounted to $86.912 billion and merchandise imports to $77.752 billion, leaving a favorable trade balance of $9.160 billion. The average annual growth rate during 1970–82 was 5.6% for exports and 8.3% for imports. The principal exports are fuels, minerals and metals (48%); machinery, plant and vehicles (19%); chemicals and construction materials (18%); raw materials, foodstuffs and processed nonfood materials (12%). The principal imports are machinery plant and vehicles (38%); raw materials, foodstuffs and processed nonfood materials (27%); fuels, minerals and metals (15%); and industrial consumer goods (11%). The major export partners are East Germany (10%), Poland (9%), Bulgaria (8%), Czechoslovakia (7%), West Germany (6%) and Hungary (6%). The major import partners are East Germany (10%), Poland (8%), Czechoslovakia (8%), Bulgaria (8%), West Germany (7%) and Hungary (6%).

Employment: As of 1980, the Soviet labor force stood at 125,648,000, of which 20.1% was employed in agriculture and 29.4% in industry. The Soviet Union currently faces a serious labor shortage. During the 1970s, the estimated net increase in "able-bodied" persons was 24 million, but the increase during the 1980s will be less than 6 million. Regional distribution of the agricultural labor force is rather uneven, with areas of acute scarcity and areas of labor surplus. High priority is being given to measures to improve the mobility of the industrial labor force, with retraining to meet the needs of new technology; and the education system is biased toward the production of technicians and engineers. Management education is receiving more attention. In addition, attempts are being made to persuade older men and women, especially those nearing retirement age, not to stop working.

Prices and wages: Rural workers have benefited most from developments in recent years. Collective farmers now receive a guaranteed monthly wage related to state farm rates, in place of the old system of payment according to days worked, from the annual residual net income of the farm. In 1980, industrial wages averaged 185.4 rubles per month and agricultural wages averaged 149.2 rubles per month. For the country as a whole, the average monthly wage was 168.9 rubles per month. Real incomes of the population have risen an average of 3% since 1976. Nominal wages have risen at a slightly lower rate. Retail prices on ordinary food products have remained stable for the past two decades, but prices of luxury items have risen rapidly. In 1983, labor productivity rose by 3.5% over 1982 figures.

Consumption: Deliveries of consumer goods rose steadily through the mid-1960s and into the 1970s, but in recent years the rate of growth of the consumption sector has been slowing down significantly. In 1984, per capita consumption in the Soviet Union was approximately one-third of the US level, and about half that in France, West Germany and Great Britain. The rise in the stock of consumer durables has been at a slower rate than in many other Eastern European countries. Between 1970 and 1983, the stock of refrigerators per 1,000 rose from 89 to 270 (the lowest in the Eastern bloc), that of washing machines from 141 to 205 (the lowest in the Eastern bloc), that of television sets from 143 to 287 (the lowest in the Eastern bloc) and radio sets from 199 to 280 (the lowest in the Eastern bloc). In passenger cars per capita, the Soviet Union fares even worse; at 29 cars per 1,000, it ranks 73rd in the world (below such countries as Zimbabwe and Fiji) but above Poland in the Eastern bloc. Deposits in savings and other banks have grown by 401% since 1970 to 186.9 billion rubles, reflecting unsatisfied demand.

SOCIAL WELFARE

Social insurance (excluding medical services) is supervised by the USSR Central Council of Trade Unions, the central committees of trade unions and local trade union organizations. Trade union organs draft and approve estimates for social insurance determine specific expenditure and help formulate social insurance policy. The social insurance budget is a part of the Soviet Union state budget. Pensions, sick pay, maternity benefits and accommodations at vacation therapy centers are the main expenditure items of social insurance, which is financed from compulsory payments by plants, factories, enterprises and institutions. All citizens are constitutionally guaranteed welfare in old age, free medical attention and compensation for industrial disability. A five-day week was introduced in 1967. In 1980, the average working week was 40.6 hours for most industrial and administrative workers. In 1977, the average annual paid holiday of adult workers and employees was 21.6 days. In 1981, total expenditure on state social insurance was 37,417 million rubles, a more than 100% increase over expenditures in 1970.

Health services: Free health services are available to the whole population. All expenditure on public health comes out of the state budget and the funds of state bodies or cooperatives, trade unions and other mass organizations. In 1978, the state's health allocations amounted to 8 billion rubles. Industrial enterprises and *kolkhozy* (collective farms) provide buildings and equipment and bear the maintenance costs of their own health units.

Supervision over health services (including pharmaceutical industries) is exercised by the USSR Ministry of Health and its subordinate republican ministries of health. The *kray, oblast* (local or province) and city public health departments of local soviets, subdivided into medical, maternal/pediatric and hygiene departments and subordinated both to the local soviet and to the higher public health body, are headed by physicians. Operational units are based on the *oblast*, city and *rayon* and are further subdivided into health districts. The *rayon* hospital offers comprehensive and integrated health care for inpatients and outpatients, is responsible for health screening of the *rayon*'s population and is aided by a network of peripheral units ranging from the district unit proper, headed by a district doctor, to the smallest local health unit, the feldscher-midwife station. As a rule, district units possess small hospitals, maternity homes and health stations in rural areas. A 24-hour emergency medical service based on larger towns deals with an average 30 million calls a year, and mobile health units are available for emergencies in remote locations. While expansion of facilities has included rapid growth of urban medical institutions and services, there has been a tendency toward amalgamation or elimination of earlier establishments in rural areas, except in developing regions such as Siberia, where new wide-area hospitals with some 300 beds are the rule. The basic health philosophy in the Soviet Union is one of prophylaxis by health protection and public hygiene; formerly endemic diseases such as plague, cholera, smallpox and malaria have been eradicated.

Since 1968, all employees with a record of over eight years' service are entitled to full earnings during sickness leave; those with five to eight years of service receive 80% of earnings; those with three to five years receive 60%; and those with less than three years receive 50%. Benefits are payable from the first day of incapacity until recovery or pension, and are 50% lower for nonunion members. Disabled workers receive allowances of up to 90% of their pay, depending on length of service. In the event of occupational injury or disease, the worker is, on the recommendation of the trade union, entitled to disability pension equaling full pay. Incapacity persisting over four months is subject to board review and further benefits. According to age and length of service, the monthly minimum disability is 75 rubles, maximum 120 rubles. Fully paid maternity leave is granted for 112 days; postnatal leave with full pay is extended by 14 days after the birth of twins, or in case of complicated delivery. Gynecological and legal counseling is available to all mothers, and psychoprophylaxis is employed in a majority of childbirths. Mothers of large families and unmarried mothers receive monthly allowances.

In 1982, there were 127 hospital beds per 10,000 population and 39.5 physicians per 10,000 population. The official infant mortality rate has not been published since 1974; Western estimates, however, placed the rate in 1979 at a very high 39 or 40 per 10,000 population—more than three times as high as that of the United States. The average life expectancy in 1980, again according to Western estimates, was a low 61.9 years for males and 73.5 years for females.

Pensions and other benefits: Pensions are paid by the state from funds annually allocated in the Soviet Union's budget. Citizens eligible for various pensions simultaneously are granted one pension of their choice; pensions are not taxable. Pensioners in 1984 composed 13.5% of the population. Males engaged in industrial and administrative occupations and (since 1968) in collective farming are eligible for old-age pensions at 60 (with a record of 25 years service), females at 55 (with 20 years service). For certain categories of work (e.g. underground mining and Arctic services), men are pensionable at 50 or 55, women at 45 or 50. Pensions are computed on the basis of average monthly net earnings during the last 12 months of work, or, if the applicant requests, for the optimum five-year period out of the last 10 years preceding application. Old-age pensions average 60% to 70% of earnings. Pensioners in ordinary work categories are entitled to monthly benefits ranging from 30 rubles (where monthly earnings did not exceed 35 rubles) to 55 rubles (where earnings exceeded 100 rubles). The minimum statutory retirement pension is 50 rubles, maximum 120 rubles monthly. Favorable adjustment is made for workers in "hard" categories. Employees with insufficient service are ineligible for an old-age pension if they continue working; employees retiring before qualifying age are ineligible for pension till attaining that age. A pensioner with dependents is entitled to a maximum bonus of 15% of pension. Dependents bereaved of a working parent are eligible for pensions ranging from 26 rubles monthly (for one dependent) to 120 rubles monthly (for three or more dependents of an employee deceased as a result of occupational injury or disease). Since 1930, when the labor exchanges were abolished, there has officially been no unemployment in a planned economy which "guarantees the continuous expansion of production." There is thus no unemployment relief.

Housing and resettlement: Since 1917 the devastating internal upheavals and two world wars have caused a chronic housing deficit. In World War II, 1,710 towns and industrial settlements and 70,000 villages were destroyed by the enemy, and some 25 million persons were rendered homeless. Such cities as Stalingrad (Volgograd), Minsk, Voronezh, Sevastopol and Smolensk had to be reconstructed after 1945. During the period 1959–65, 84 million persons obtained new housing and by 1970 over 60 million more persons had moved into new or improved dwellings. Housing is still inadequate and overcrowded by Western standards. Cooperative units, increasingly popular, are purchased by the cooperative member on 10- to 15-year credit covering 60% of total cost, a 40% down-payment being required. For lower income brackets, state housing, financed by city, town and enterprise authorities, is still predominant; here rent is fixed at between 4% and 5% of monthly wages. As a rule, new Soviet housing comprises multiple, multistory units, largely prefabricated, incorporated in "microdistricts," i.e., self-contained neighborhood complexes. While much rural housing remains rudimentary, experimental schemes in the far north (e.g., at Aikhal and Norilsk) have, through use of glass and heating, suggested a pattern of the future.

Resettlement grants are awarded as a stimulus to settlement and economic exploitation of new areas. Workers volunteering for work in eastern and northern areas, following a public appeal, draw double the allowance fixed for workers contracting with ordinary recruitment organizations. Grants are the responsibility of the enterprise to which the worker is transferred. Workers who are officially transferred and young persons graduating from higher educational institutions or from certain secondary schools are entitled to immediate housing on arrival. As compensation for the harsher conditions and higher cost of living in Arctic and certain Siberian areas (where price levels may be 80% higher than in temperate zones), all workers and office employees of government, cooperative and public organizations and enterprises receive an increment on their monthly earnings (e.g., in several Arctic areas, 10% after a year's employment, with a 20% rise for each successive year) and up to 18 days of extra paid vacation. Travel costs of all officially sponsored work transfers are borne by the receiving enterprise.

EDUCATION

All but the oldest generations of Soviet citizens are products of an education that differs radically from Western systems. According to the 1979 census, approximately 63.8% of the population aged 10 years and over had been or were being educated above primary school level. Education is uniform and highly centralized, with ultimate control of primary and most secondary institutions vested in the 35 SSR and ASSR ministries of education, while some higher and all secondary specialized schools are placed under the USSR Ministry of Higher and Specialized Education. Vocational-technical schools come under the State Committee of the USSR Council of Ministers on Vocational-Technical Education. The RSFSR Ministry of Education in effect sets the pace and standards for the development of the entire structure and curricula of schools, whether Russian or non-Russian. Soviet and national patriotism, revolutionary pride, party loyalty and *grazhdanstrennost* (civic-mindedness) are the chief elements of communist morality inculcated at the earliest stages, and at every phase of administration the CPSU ensures ideological orthodoxy through its control of general educational policy and of local educational organizations, through its sponsorship of personnel and formulation of the curricula, and through parent-teacher consultations, Pioneer and Komsomol activities and media of information and guidance such as the teachers' journal, *Uchitelskaya gazeta*. A feature of today is the growing role of polytechnical and practical elements in the curriculum and the consequent expansion of vocational and specialized schools. Production training has become as integral a part of secondary education as traditional science and humanities. Other characteristics include coeducation at all levels (half the students in higher education are women), the emphasis on comprehensive primary and secondary education, the evolution of the boarding school, the increasing use of the Russian language in non-Russian republics and the development of schools for specially gifted children. In 1979 the illiteracy rate was 0.2%.

Language policy: The Russian language is the native tongue of half the Soviet Union's population and as a federal language has wide and growing application outside the RSFSR itself. Complete instruction is, in theory, available at all educational stages in Russian and the languages of the 14 non-Russian SSRs, although in rural areas there is often no choice. In major ASSRs, primary and some secondary education is provided in the native tongue; in minor ASSRs and NOs, schooling in the vernacular is seldom available above primary level. Other national minorities may or may not receive native language instruction at the lower grades. The non-Russian SSRs also support Russian-language schools that educate not only Russian residents but also, increasingly, non-Russians. These schools must, however, teach the SSR language. There are also some 700 primary-secondary schools in which many subjects are taught in English, German or French. Similar establishments are planned for Spanish, Chinese, Arabic, Hindi and Urdu. English, German and French are the most popular foreign languages at every level, and in higher institutions over 80 Soviet and foreign languages are taught.

Preschool education: The noncompulsory crèches (*yasli*) for infants aged three months to three years and kindergartens (*detsky sad*) for children aged three to seven, run by ministries of health, individual factories, farms, enterprises or other bodies, are fee-paying institutions organized on an annual or seasonal basis and in 1982 catering to approximately 15.3 million children.

Primary education: Universal compulsory primary education was introduced in the 1930s; in 1952, a basic seven-year compulsory system was instituted, and this was extended to eight years in 1958. The current eight-year school (*vosmiletnyaya shkola*), compulsory for all children aged seven to 15 (except those in special education), is divided into elementary and middle grades (*nachalnaya shkola* and *srednyaya shkola*) of four years each. In the middle grades, the curricula include a foreign language (usually English, German or French), production training, basic physics, chemistry and biology, and a high content of mathematics as well as Russian language, literature, history, geography and physical training. Labor training for girls includes elements of domestic science. In non-Russian schools, the Russian language is taught as a second tongue. Pupils successfully completing eight years receive a certificate (*svidetelstvo*). In 1973, a new educational law was passed which had as its aim the compulsory ten year schooling of all children from the age of seven. In addition to the eight years of schooling, children would receive two further years of teaching. Eventually, it was intended, schooling would be eleven years in all. The new policy was introduced gradually and was not operating fully by the mid-1980s.

Secondary education: The compulsory eight-year school course is followed by one of four main types of secondary schooling: (a) the three-year secondary general polytechnical school (*srednyaya obshcheobrazovatelnaya politekhnicheskaya shkola*), which forms a three-year extension of the continuous primary-secondary system (11-year school, *odinadtsatiletnyaya shkola*) and combines academic courses with vocational training (in factories, farms, enterprises) leading to a school-leaving certificate (*attestat*); (b) the four- to five-year secondary specialized school (*srednee spetsialnoe uchebnoe zavedenie*), which mixes a predominant proportion of vocational training (for some 400 professions) with general curricula, leading to a diploma (*diplom*); (c) the three-year vocational-technical school (*professionalno-tekhnicheskoe uchilishche*), which supplements institutionalized apprenticeship with a minimal academic course leading to a certificate (*udostoverenie*). Students here are paid at apprenticeship rates; (d) the three-year secondary general evening/shift school (*vechernyaya/smennaya srednyaya obshcheobrazovatelnaya shkola*) offering part-time or correspondence courses at the general polytechnical level to students unable, for reasons of employment, distance, etc., to enroll in day school. This also leads to the *attestat*. In theory, graduates from all four categories are entitled to apply to higher institutions, but those from secondary general polytechnical schools enjoy obvious advantages.

Special education is of three kinds, with 11-year courses where possible: (a) schools for the handicapped, run by either education, health or national insurance ministries, provide free treatment and general polytechnical tuition for the mentally or physically deficient; (b) children showing particular artistic promise may forgo the usual polytechnical and production training and combine general education with professional instruction at schools attached to music conservatories, ballet companies, etc. Since 1958, a few selective schools for the scientifically talented have also been established; (c) military schools, which give preference to children of war casualties and combine military training with a general curriculum.

Boarding-school education: The coeducational boarding school (*shkola internat*) system has been greatly expanded since 1956 to include several categories of deprived and dislocated children. Where applicable, parents are subject to a means test. A variant is the extended eight-year day school (*shkola prodlennogo dnya*) where pupils participate in supplementary daily extra-mural activities.

University and higher education: Every institute of higher education (*vysshee uchebnoe zavedenie, VUZ,* pl. *VUZy*) has the power to confer diplomas and postgraduate degrees and to conduct research. Higher education is co-ordinated on an all-union scale by the USSR Ministry of Higher and Specialized Secondary Education, which is also directly responsible for 29 major institutions. SSR and ASSR education ministries or committees have jurisdiction over the majority of their VUZy. Certain institutions come under specific ministries: transport VUZy are controlled by the USSR Ministry of Transport; communications VUZy by the USSR Ministry of Communications; agricultural, forestry, medical, art and trade VUZy are administered by their respective republican ministries, as are all teacher training colleges except in the Belorussian SSR where a composite Ministry of Higher Specialized Secondary and Vocational Education is responsible. Curricula are generally uniform throughout the Soviet Union. Admission to the VUZ is on the basis of successful completion of secondary schooling and of success in the competitive entrance examinations (taken in both general and specialized subjects), but may be facilitated by a reference from the Komsomol, etc. All tuition is free, and board for most students is covered by grants (*stipendii*) that are related to performance. Bonuses are awarded for excellence. Every student must attend classes in the theory and history of Marxism-Leninism, in the history of the CPSU and in scientific atheism, in addition to his or her speciality. Many specialized departments (e.g., medicine) operate independently of the universities and enjoy at least equal status. Courses last from four to six years and lead to the diploma (*diplom ob okonchanii VUZa*). Among the universities are: Alma-Ata, Ashkhabad, Baku, Cheboksary, Chernovtsy, Dnepropetrovsk, Donetsk, Dushanbe, Frunze, Gorky, Irkutsk, Kaliningrad, Kazan, Kharkov, Kiev, Kishinev, Leningrad, Lvov, Makhachkala, Minsk, Moscow (2)[1], Nalchik, Novosibirsk, Odessa, Ordzhonikidze, Perm, Petrozavodsk, Riga, Rostov-on-Don, Samarkand, Saransk, Saratov, Sverdlovsk, Tartu, Tashkent, Tbilisi, Tomsk, Ufa, Uzhgorod, Vilna, Vladivostok, Voronezh, Yakutsk, Yerevan.

Adult education: Part-time evening and correspondence courses leading to certificates or diplomas are increasingly popular at every level. These are sponsored and organized by factories, farms, enterprises, communities, etc., in formal collaboration with existing educational institutions. Theoretical training is closely linked to production work. The system of extramural VUZ education consists of correspondence and evening colleges. Students

[1]One of these being the Patrice Lumumba People's Friendship University, founded in 1960 for students from Asia, Africa and Latin America.

are entitled to annual supplementary paid leaves during workshop and examination sessions.

Educational institutions (1982–83)

	Institutions	Students
General	n.a.	44,300,000
Secondary specialized	n.a.	4,500,000
Vocational-technical	n.a.	4,000,000
VUZy (incl. extramural)	n.a.	5,300,000
Other professional courses	n.a.	45,100,000

MASS MEDIA

The Press (1983):[1]

Russian-language dailies: Izvestiya, Moscow (M), govt., 8,600,000; *Pionerskaya Pravda,* M, children's, 11,000,000; *Pravda,* M and major cities, CPSU, 10,700,000; *Komsomolskaya Pravda,* M, youth, 10,000,000; *Selskaya Zhizn,* M, CPSU agric., 9,000,000; *Sovyetskaya Rossiya,* M, CP and govt. of RSFSR, 3,200,000; *Sovyetsky Sport,* M, sport, 3,500,000; *Trud,* M, trade union, 13,500,000; *Krasnaya Zvezda,* M, military, 2,400,000; *Gudok,* M, communications, 641,000; *Moskovskaya Pravda,* M, CP and city soviet; *Moskovsky Komsomolyets,* M, youth; *Leninskoye Znamya,* M, CP; *Leningradskaya Pravda,* Leningrad, CP and city soviet; *Pravda Ukrainy,* Kiev, Ukrainian CP and govt.; *Rabochaya Gazeta,* Kiev, Ukrainian CP; *Sovyetskaya Belorussiya,* Minsk, Belorussian CP and govt.; *Sovyetskaya Estoniya,* Tallinn, Estonian CP and govt.; *Sovyetskaya Latviya,* Riga, Latvian CP and govt.; *Sovyetskaya Litva,* Vilna, Lithuanian CP and govt.; *Sovyetskaya Moldavia,* Kishinev, Moldavian CP and govt.; *Bakinsky Rabochy,* Baku, Azerbaidzhan CP; *Kommunist,* Yerevan, Armenian CP; *Zarya Vostoka,* Tbilisi, Georgian CP and govt.; *Kazakhstanskaya Pravda,* Alma-Ata, Kazakh CP and govt.; *Pravda Vostoka,* Tashkent, Uzbek CP and govt.; *Kommunist Tadzhikistana,* Dushanbe, Tadzhik CP; *Sovyetskaya Kirgiziya,* Frunze, Kirgiz CP and govt. (also in Kirgiz).

Non-Russian SSR language dailies: Radyanskaya Ukraina, Kiev, Ukrainian CP and govt.; *Zvyazda,* Minsk, Belorussian CP and govt.; *Rahva Haal,* Tallinn, Estonian CP and govt.; *Cina,* Riga, Latvian CP and govt.; *Tiesa,* Vilna, Lithuanian CP and govt.; 250,000; *Moldova Socialiste,* Kishinev, Moldavian CP and govt.; *Kommunisti,* Tbilisi, Georgian CP; *Sovietakan Aiastan,* Yerevan, Armenian CP and govt.; *Kommunist,* Baku, Azerbaidzhan CP; *Sotsialistik Kazakhstan,* Alma-Ata, Kazakh CP and govt.; *Sovyet Uzbekistony,* Tashkent, Uzbek CP and govt.; *Tochikistony Sovyety,* Dushanbe, Tadzhik CP and govt.; *Sovyet Turkmenistany,* Ashkabad, Turkmen CP and govt.

[1]Circulation figures generally unavailable.

Periodicals: (Moscow) *Zdorovye* (m), pop. science, 12,600,000; *Ogonyok* (w), illus., 2,100,000; *Krokodil* (3 per m.), satirical; *Za Rubezhom* (w), foreign news, 1,300,000; *Sovyetsky Soyuz* (m), Soviet Union illus., incl. 19 foreign languages; *Sovyetskaya Zhenshchina* (m), Soviet women's illus., incl. 11 foreign languages; *Literaturnaya Gazeta* (w), CPSU econ., 2,600,000; *Zhurnal Mod* (q), fashion; *Novy Mir* (m), progressive literary, 150,000; *Oktyabr* (m), conservative literary; *Kommunist* (18 per annum), CP theory; *Novoye Vremya* (w), foreign affairs, also in eight foreign languages; *Molodaya Gvardia* (m), youth; *Yunost* (m), literary youth; *Ekonomika Syelskogo Khozyaistva* (m), agricultural; *Kolkhozno-Sovkhoznoye Proizvodstvo* (m), agricultural; *Zemledeliye* (m), agricultural; *Iskusstvo* (m), art; *Inostrannaya Literatura* (m), for. lit.; *Planovoye Khozyaistvo* (m), economic; *Sovyetskaya Torgovlya* (m), trade; *Vneshnyaya Torgovlya* (m), for. trade, also in English, French and Spanish; *Muzykalnaya Zhizn* (f), music; *Teatralnaya Zhizn* (f), theater; *Sovyetsky Ekran* (f), film; *Moskva* (m), literary; *Nash Sovremmenik* (m), literary; *Russkaya Literatura* (q), literary; *Literaturnaya Rossiya* (w), conservative literary; *Sovyetskaya Meditsina* (m), medical; *Lesnoye Khozyaistvo* (m), forestry; *Rybovodstvo i Rybolovstvo* (m), fishing; *Sovyetskoe Kino* (m), film; *Futbol* (w), football; *Zhurnal Moskovskoy Patriarkhy* (m), Orthodox Patriarchate; *Bratsky Vestnik*, Baptist. (Other cities) *Neva* (m), Leningrad, literary, 235,000; *Zvezda* (m), Leningrad, literary; *Don* (m), Rostov-on-Don, literary; *Radyanska Zhinka* (m), Kiev, women's illus., in Ukrainian, 800,000; *Ukraina* (w), Kiev, illus., in Ukrainian, 180,000; *Raduga* (m), Kiev, literary, in Ukrainian, 15,000; *Literaturnaya Gruziya* (m), Tbilisi, literary, in Russian and Georgian; *Literaturnaya Armeniya* (m), literary, in Russian and Armenian; *Prostop*, Alma-Ata, literary, in Russian.

Broadcasting: Soviet broadcasting is supervised by the Committee on Broadcasting and Television under the USSR Council of Ministers and by similarly subordinate Committees in the SSRs. Radio Moscow, with eight main programs, provides the bulk of relay material for the entire country. There are also special broadcasts for separate regions, the Urals, Siberia, Central Asia and the Soviet Far East. There are also radio broadcasts in those regions that have their own radio stations operating local systems. Internal broadcasts are made in 68 languages. In 1977, program hours totalled 1,040 hours daily. Radio Moscow also makes overseas broadcasts in 64 foreign languages, covering Europe, Africa, the Middle East, the Far East and Australasia, and North and South America. The television system covers an area that includes four-fifths of the country's population. Broadcasts average 1,900 hours a day. There are six central TV channels, with a total operating time of 46 hours a day. In 1982, there were 450 television stations and 130 television centers. Eighty-one cities have two channels, and in 14 capitals of Union republics programs are presented in national and Russian languages. Moscow has six and Leningrad three channels. Color television is received in 120 cities.

CONSTITUTIONAL SYSTEM

Constitution: The present Soviet constitution of 1977 is the result of the work of the constitutional commission appointed by Khrushchev in 1962 and chaired by Brezhnev from 1964. The final version was adopted by the Supreme Soviet in 1977. Although the basic law does not depart significantly from the so-called Stalin constitution of 1936, the 1977 document is new in both form and details. A total of 69 articles, as against 27 in 1936, set forth the basics of communist ideology, while providing for a nominal democratic system with political and constitutional rights subjected to severe restrictions in actual practice. The remaining 105 articles describe the structure of the Soviet state and its various components.

The preamble identifies the Soviet Union as a "developed socialist society," having as its goal the building of a "classless communist society" through the efforts of the Communist party, which is described as the "vanguard of all the people" and "the leading and guiding force" of the nation. The intelligentsia is included for the first time with the workers and peasants as constituting the revolutionary base of the state. The foundations of the Soviet economic system are described as "the socialist ownership of the means of production in the form of state property, and collective farm and cooperative property." Personal property is limited to earned income, articles of everyday use, a house, savings, smallholding, and livestock and poultry; these may be inherited but not used as a means of deriving unearned income.

Territorial-administrative divisions: The Soviet Union is a federal state formed on the basis of a voluntary union of 15 Soviet Socialist Republics (SSRs). Each SSR is a nominally sovereign republic possessing the right to secede from the Soviet Union, to maintain its own army and to have direct relations with foreign states. The Presidium of the USSR Supreme Soviet includes the 15 presidents of the SSRs in the capacity of vice presidents; the USSR Council of Ministers includes the chairmen (prime ministers) of the SSR councils of ministers, and the USSR Supreme Court includes the chairmen of SSR supreme courts. Within the SSR the main subdivisions are the province (*oblast*), district (*rayon*) and rural localities. Cities are separately administered usually at the *rayon* level, but the larger ones fall directly within SSR jurisdiction and themselves include a number of municipal *rayony*. There are also units theoretically based on autonomy for ethnic minorities. Twenty autonomous republics (ASSRs) (of which 16 are inside the RSFSR) possess their own constitutions and state organs and send deputies to the Soviet of Nationalities of the USSR Supreme Soviet and one representative each to the Presidium of the SSR Supreme Soviet. The eight autonomous regions, or *avtonomnye oblasti* (AOs), are smaller subdivisions of the same type. Several large and remote areas within the RSFSR, classified as *kraya*, are administered like *oblasti*, but can themselves contain *oblasti* or AOs. Finally there are 10 national areas, or *natsionalnye okruga* (NOs), all within the RSFSR, small national entities sending one deputy each to the Soviet of Nationalities in Moscow.

Legislature: The legislative structure consists of a pyramid of soviets (councils) reaching from the level of rural localities to the highest organ of state power in Moscow, the Supreme Soviet of the USSR (*Verkhovny Sovet SSR*). The latter consists of two chambers having equal rights, the Soviet of the Union (*Sovet Soyuza*) and the Soviet of Nationalities (*Sovet Natsionalnostey*).

The Supreme Soviet adopts and repeals the laws of the Soviet Union, supervises observance of the Soviet constitution, approves Soviet external and internal policy by turning decrees into laws and regulates the functioning of state bodies. Formally speaking, it elects the USSR Presidium (i.e., collective residency), appoints the USSR Council of Ministers (i.e., government), elects the USSR Supreme Court and appoints the USSR procurator-general. Seven hundred and fifty deputies (*deputaty*) are elected to the Soviet of the Union and 750 to the Soviet of Nationalities. The Soviet of the Union is elected for a 4-year term by all citizens of 18 years and over. The Soviet of Nationalities is elected by the citizens of each national-administrative subdivision on the basis of 32 deputies from each SSR, 11 from each ASSR, five from each AO and one from each NO. Either chamber may initiate legislation; they sit simultaneously twice a year, and a bill becomes law when passed by a simple majority in both chambers. No vote to date has in fact been other than unanimous. Each chamber elects a number of standing commissions that meet between sessions of the Supreme Soviet, report to sessions and make recommendations to the Presidium. The Presidium of the Supreme Soviet of the USSR is elected at a joint sitting of the two chambers and is accountable to the Supreme Soviet. It consists of a president, 15 vice presidents (the presidents of each SSR), a secretary and 21 members. It convenes and dissolves the sessions of the Supreme Soviet, issues decrees, interprets operative laws and discharges other functions of state administration.

The highest legislative organs in the SSRs and ASSRs are their single-chamber supreme soviets.

Election of deputies is conducted on the basis of universal, equal and direct suffrage by secret ballot; the electorate is offered a single slate of candidates, all of whom are elected unless any of them obtain less than 50% of the vote, something that has happened only occasionally and at the local level.

Executive: According to the Soviet Union's constitutional separation of powers, the USSR Council of Ministers (*Sovet Ministrov SSSR*), i.e., the Soviet government, has no official legislative authority and is responsible to the USSR Supreme Soviet or, in the intervals between sessions of the latter, to its Presidium. In reality, much of the legislative as well as executive power is concentrated in the Council of Ministers, which operates in close association with the CPSU. It consists of a chairman (prime minister), first vice chairmen, vice chairmen, ministers, chairman of the State Planning Committee (Gosplan), chairman of the State Committee for Construction (Gosstroy) and chairmen of other state committees and agencies. The chief posts are held by prominent party members who form a presidium within the Council of Ministers. Ministries are of three kinds: all-union, which have no equivalent in the SSRs; union-republic, which have counterparts in the SSRs; republic, which exist only in constituent republics and are formally subordinate to the Council of Ministers of the respective SSR all-union ministries and state committees that administer affairs of all-union significance, e.g., communications.

127

Local government: The more than 47,000 soviets of working people's deputies constitute local organs of state power at the levels of *kray, oblast,* autonomous *oblast, okrug, rayon,* city and rural localities. The executive and administrative arm of the local soviet is the executive committee (*ispolkom*), elected by it and comprising a chairman, vice chairmen, secretary and members. Local soviets are elected for two-year terms.

Judiciary: The highest judicial organ is the USSR Supreme Court (*Verkhovny Sud SSSR*), which is elected by the USSR Supreme Soviet. Each republic has its own set of courts. Subsidiary regional courts hear appeals and more important original cases, but the latter function belongs mainly to the people's court (*narodny sud*) at the *rayon* level. There are also special courts, e.g., military tribunals and state arbitration bodies (*Gosarbitrazh*) that decide contract disputes between state enterprises. Courts are elected by respective soviets for a five-year period with the exception of the people's court, which consists of people's judge (*narodny sudya*) and two lay people's assessors (*narodnye zasedateli*), elected locally for five and two years, respectively. The people's court functions as the first instance court for the majority of civil and criminal cases. The USSR Supreme Court acts as the ultimate court of appeal. This highest judicial organ, however, lacks the right to judicial review of legislation (a procedure nonexistent in the Soviet Union) or the power to reverse the decisions of the CPSU or Council of Ministers. Judges, who are frequently CPSU members, are theoretically independent. In all courts, cases are heard in public with the exception of cases where this is deemed prejudicial to the preservation of state secrets. The accused is guaranteed the right to defense, although the defense lawyer is appointed only after the indictment has been drawn up. Court proceedings are conducted in the language of the SSR, ASSR or AO, and interpreting facilities are made available.

The 200,000 comrades' courts (*tovarishcheskiye sudy*) that are now operating purport to instill a sense of civic duty (*grazhdanstvennost*) in individual and collective alike by combating antisocial acts and violations of labor discipline.

The safeguarding of "socialist legality," supervision over the observance and application of laws by institutions, organizations and individuals, is vested in the procuracy (*prokuratura*) whose highest incumbent, roughly equivalent to the western ombudsman, is the procurator-general of the USSR (*generalny prokuror SSSR*). Elected for a five-year term by the USSR Supreme Soviet, and never a member of the USSR Council of Ministers, he directs a system of subordinate bodies at the various republican, regional and city levels. Procurators, who act both as watchdogs over the bureaucracy and as prosecutors in criminal cases, are independent of local authority and subordinate only to their procuratorial superiors; the procuracy, staffed as it is mainly by CPSU members, is in effect a strongly centralized and antifederal institution.

The chief agent of public order is the people's militia, but about 150,000 voluntary public order squads (*druzhiny*) currently function. Since 1950, capital punishment has been gradually restored for treason, espionage, sabotage, certain categories of murder, terrorism, brigandage, certain economic crimes and, in particular circumstances, attacks on militia and voluntary public order squads.

Party: The Communist Party of the Soviet Union (CPSU), whose supreme organ is the Party Congress (held in theory at least once in five years), purports to play the leading role in society and the state; unite the politically conscious sections of workers, peasants and intellectuals; lay the bases of communist society; raise the material and cultural level of the people; organize national defense and promote the solidarity of the international working class. The Soviet Union is a one-party state because its society is in theory morally and politically united. Its Central Committee (CC), elected by the Congress, meets at least twice a year and chooses a Politburo (currently numbering 11 members and six candidate members) to direct the functions of the CC between plenary sessions. The party's structure at regional and local levels approximates that of the state apparatus. It includes over 330,000 primary organizations. In 1983 the CPSU numbered over 17,400,000 members and the Young Communist League (*Komsomol*) (ages 14 to 28) 41,000,000.

Leading government and party figures: (1985): Mikhail S. Gorbachev (general secretary of the CPSU, chairman of the Presidium of the Supreme Soviet), Nikolai I. Ryzhkov (prime minister), Andrei A. Gromyko (chairman of the Presidium of the Supreme Soviet), Geidar A. Aliyev (first deputy prime minister), Vasily V. Kuznetsov (first deputy chairman of the Presidium of the Supreme Soviet), Ivan Arkhipov (first deputy prime minister), Marshal Sergei L. Sokolov (defense minister), Viktor M. Chebrikov (State Security Committee chairman), Nikolai Patolichev (foreign trade minister), Vasily Garbuzov (finance minister), Nikolai Baibakov (deputy prime minister, State Planning Commission chairman), Vitaly Fedorchuk (internal affairs minister), Edvard A. Shevardnadze (party first secretary of the Georgian SSR, foreign minister), Yegor K. Ligachev (Secretary in charge of ideology and personnel).

BIOGRAPHICAL SKETCHES

Mikhail Sergeevich Gorbachev. Gorbachev, who succeeded Chernenko as secretary-genereal of the Communist party of the Soviet Union (CPSU) in March 1985, was born in 1931 in the Stavropol region. Of Russian nationality and peasant background, he studied law at Moscow University, graduating in 1955. Earlier, he worked at a machine-tractor station and as a manual laborer (1946–50). He joined the party in 1952. His career thereafter was at first in Stavropol, as deputy head of a department (1955–56), then as first secretary of the Stavropol town Komsomol organization (1956–58). Continuing his career in the Komsomol, he was second and then first secretary in the Stavropol regional organization (1958–62). In 1962–63 he was party organizer of agricultural production in the Stavropol region, and after that was head of a CPSU department in the same region (Kraikom). In

1966–68 he was first secretary of the Stavropol town party organization (Gorkom), second secreteary of the regional organization (Kraikom), then first secretary (1970–78). In 1971 he became a full member of the Central Committee, and in 1978 Central Committee secretary for agriculture. A year later he was a candidate member of the Politburo, and in 1980 was made a full member. Gorbachev's career was unexceptional, except for the fact that he was able to avoid the political disgrace associated with many of his predecessors who had held the agricultural portfolio. His particular patron was Mikhail Suslov, who had had antecedents in Stavropol, and he was close to Yuri Andropov as well. Gorbachev's particular strength lay in his knowledge of agriculture; his experience of the West, having visited several Western countries before his succession; his evident flexibility, in that he recognized that some change in running the Soviet system was unavoidable; and, at the same time, his acceptability to much of the party machine. His image in the West was much enhanced by the good impression he made on his hosts; on the other hand, he had grown up entirely within the CPSU and could be regarded as a man of the system.

Andrei Andreevich Gromyko. Gromyko, long-serving foreign minister of the Soviet Union and member of the Politburo, was born in 1909, of Russian nationality. Having been deputy foreign minister from 1951, he was promoted to foreign minister in 1957 and was brought into the Politburo in 1973. Over the years he acquired extensive influence over the foreign policy establishment and was widely acknowledged as the senior Soviet specialist in East-West relations. Under Chernenko, Gromyko was in a position actually to formulate policy, not just implement it. In this role he proved to be relatively inflexible. In July 1985 he was made head of state.

Boris Nikolaevich Ponomarev. Ponomarev, head of the influential Central Committee international department from 1955 and as such, one of the powerful figures in the foreign policy establishment, was born in 1905, of Russian nationality. A candidate member of the Politburo from 1972 and a Central Committee secretary, Ponomarev wielded decisive influence over interparty relations for many years. After the death of Suslov in 1982, he was preeminent in ideological policy as well. In general, he was a strong supporter of the strictest orthodoxy and of the primacy of the Soviet Union in the world communist movement.

Nikolai Ivanovich Ryzhkov. Rzyhkov, born in 1929 of Russian nationality, was a technocrat of Gorbachev's generation. In September 1985, he succeeded the 80-year-old Tikhonov as prime minister: Gorbachev had successfully removed one of the last leading figures of the Brezhnev era. Ryzhkov was educated at the Ural Polytechnical Institute and served in various managerial posts in the Sverdlovsk area. From 1975 to 1982 he held various ministerial posts, including a spell in the Ministry of Heavy Engineering and in Gosplan. In 1982, thanks to his connections with Andropov, he was moved into the party Secretariat to head its economic department. In April 1985 he was promoted to full Politburo membership and was given the task of overhauling the economic administration. He was generally regarded as intelligent, fairly well educated, close to Gorbachev and in tune with his thinking.

Edvard Amvrosievich Shevardnadze. Shevardnadze, born in 1928 of Georgian nationality, was made foreign minister of the USSR in July 1985. Although of the Gorbachev generation, Shevardnadze differed in that he was not a Russian and in that he had a background in the Interior Ministry. Shevardnadze's capabilities were tested in the early 1970s, when he was put in charge of the Georgian party as first secretary to succeed the corrupt Mzhavanadze, with the task of cleaning up the republic. He proved relatively successful in this, and in 1978 he was made a candidate member of the CPSU Politburo, becoming a full member in July 1985. Although Shevardnadze had next to no international experience, he was regarded as having made a good start in his first few months in office.

Mikhail Sergeevich Solomontsev. Solomontsev, appointed head of the CPSU control commission in 1983 by Andropov, was born in 1913 near Lipetsk; he was of Russian nationality. His early career was in industry in Chelyabinsk. In 1959 he was first secretary of the Karaganda regional party organization; then, as second secretary to the Kazakhstan party (1962–64), he acted as Moscow's supervisor. In 1966 he was promoted to the Central Committee Secretariat and headed the department of heavy industry, until being transferred to the Russian (SFSR) premiership in 1975. He was made a full member of the Politburo in December 1983, under Andropov. His career had stagnated somewhat under Brezhev. He was regarded as closer to Andropov and, like Andropov, appeared committed to uprooting corruption.

Vitaly Ivanovich Vorotnikov. Vorotnikov, a full member of the Politburo, was born in 1926 in Voronezh, of Russian nationality. Trained in aeronautical engineering, he made his early party career in Kuibyshev and Voronezh. In 1975 he was first deputy prime minister of the Russian SFSR, but in 1979 was sent as ambassador to Cuba under Brezhnev. In 1982 he was brought back by Andropov as first secretary of the Krasnodar region, and in 1983 was promoted to the Politburo as candidate member and became prime minister of the SFSR.

YUGOSLAVIA

Features: Yugoslavia, a federation of six socialist republics (Serbia, Croatia, Bosnia-Hercegovina, Slovenia, Macedonia, Montenegro) including two autonomous provinces within Serbia (Vojvodina and Kosovo-Metohija), is situated on the Adriatic coast of the Balkan Peninsula and is contiguous with seven Western and Eastern European states (Italy, Austria, Hungary, Romania, Bulgaria, Greece, Albania). Its geology and relief are exceptionally varied. The inland Pannonian Basin, drained by the Danube, is separated from the Adriatic coastline of Dalmatia by the Dinaric mountain system. In Slovenia, the Karawanken and Julian alps contain the highest peaks in the country (Triglav 9,393 ft/2,863 m.) and south of the Ljubljana basin continue as the Karst-type Dinaric Alps (av. height 5,000 ft/1500 m.) to the Kosovo-Metohija (Kosmet) Basin. From the Iron Gates of the Danube, the northeast Serbian Mountains are ranged north-south and form a vertex with the Dinaric system in the Šar and Korab massifs of Kosovo and Macedonia (maximum elevations over 8,000 ft/2,400 m.). Glacial and Karst lakes are common, and in the southern frontier zones, lakes Ohrid, Prespa and Dojra are of tectonic origin. Much of the southern mountain system is faulted and subject to seismic disturbance. In Macedonia, a low watershed between the rivers Morava and Vardar (with outlets in the Danube and Aegean Sea respectively) permits of easy north-south connexions. The Dalmatian coast, always difficult for land access, is indented by several large bays, and only 60 of its 233 islands are inhabited. The coastal climate is Mediterranean, while conditions in the interior are of a continental type.

Of the total land area, over one-half is agricultural and one-third forest. Despite recent industrialization, the agrarian sector is still predominant. One-third of the arable land is located in the treeless fertile Pannonian Basin which, though liable to flooding and drought, produces half the nation's maize and wheat. Mixed farming is prevalent in the fertile regions of the Vojvodina, Serbia proper and Croatia. Fruit and vine production are widespread; citrus is confined to Dalmatia; and sheep grazing is predominant in mountain regions. Timber of many types is exploited.

Yugoslavia possesses one of the widest ranges of mineral and fuel resources in Europe and is a leading world producer of copper, lead, mercury and bauxite. Serbia, Bosnia-Hercegovina and Macedonia have major sources of copper, lead, zinc and gold; mercury is mined in Slovenia; bauxite in Dalmatia and Istria; and iron-ore in Bosnia, Serbia and Macedonia. Bituminous coal

YUGOSLAVIA

reserves, however, are poor, but there is lignite in Bosnia-Hercegovina. Petroleum and uranium are also worked.

Heavy industry is centered in Ljubljana, Zagreb and Belgrade and at new sites in the Sava Valley. Iron-steel combines operate at Zenica (Bosnia), Sisak (Croatia) and Skopje (Macedonia). Light industries are being promoted in the Vojvodina and the Drava Valley. Stress is placed on the industrialization of backward Bosnia-Hercegovina, Montenegro, Kosovo and Macedonia. Shipyards are located at the ports of Split (It. Spalato), Rijeka (Fiume) and Pula. Tourism, especially on the coast, is evolving fast. Hydroelectric potential is great and the project at the Iron Gate, built in cooperation with Romania, is outstanding.

Land relief impedes communication but road construction proceeds.

Area: 99,300 sq. miles/255,800 sq. km.

Mean max. and min. temperatures: Belgrade (45° N, 20° E; 450 ft/137 m.) 71°F/22°C (July) 32°F/0°C (Jan.). Zagreb (46° N, 16° E; 540 ft/165 m.) 70°F/ 21°C (July) 32°F/0°C (Jan.). Skopje (42° N, 22° E; 790 ft/241 m.) 73°F/23°C (July) 32°F/0°C (Jan.).

Relative humidity: Belgrade 80%; Zagreb 84%; Skopje 87%.

Mean annual rainfall: Belgrade 25 in./635 mm; Zagreb 35 in./890 mm.; Skopje 20 in./510 mm.

POPULATION

Total population (1981 est.): 22,427,000. Serbia: 9,313,000, Croatia: 4,601,000, Bosnia and Hercegovina: 4,124,000, Macedonia: 1,912,000, Slovenia: 1,892,000, Montenegro: 584,000.

Chief towns and populations (1981 est.): Federal capital and capital of Serbia: BELGRADE 1,470,000. Capitals of republics: Zagreb (Croatia) 768,000, Skopje (Macedonia) 506,000, Sarajevo (Bosnia-Hercegovina) 448,000, Ljubljana (Slovenia) 305,000, Titograd (Montenegro) 132,000. Capitals of autonomous provinces: Novi Sad (Vojvodina) 257,000, Priština (Kosovo) 210,000. Other major towns: Niš 643,000, Split 236,000, Rijeka 193,000, Maribor 186,000.

Ethnic composition (1981): 36.2% Serbs, 19.7% Croats, 7.8% Slovenes, 8.9% Bosnian Muslims (regarded as a separate ethnic group), 6% Macedonians, 7.7% Albanians, 2.5% Montenegrin Serbs, 2% Hungarians, 1% Turks. There are also smaller groups, including Slovaks, Romanians, Bulgarians, Czechs and Italians.

Language: Serbo-Croat, Macedonian and Slovene are official languages; Serbo-Croat is the lingua franca. In Serbia, Bosnia-Hercegovina and Montenegro, Serbo-Croat is written in Cyrillic script, while in Croatia it uses a Latin script. Slovene uses a Latin script; Macedonian is written in Cyrillic.

Religion: About 41% of the population is Serbian or Macedonian Orthodox (mainly in Serbia, Bosnia-Hercegovina, Montenegro and Macedonia), 31% is Roman Catholic (mainly in Croatia and Slovenia) and 12% Muslim (mainly in Bosnia and Kosovo). Protestants and Jews number less than 1% each.

RECENT HISTORY

The Yugoslav Partisans, under Josip Broz Tito, together with their Albanian colleagues, were the only communists in Eastern Europe to establish their postwar system without decisive Soviet intervention. In the 1945 elections, Tito won overwhelmingly, in part because the monarchists boycotted the ballot. The monarchy was subsequently abolished and the 1946 constitution declared a Federal People's Republic of Yugoslavia, consisting of six republics, which was soon recognized by the Great Powers. The government embarked on a ruthless purge of opposition factions, including the summary trial and execution of Serbian leader Mihajlović in 1946. In 1947, King Peter II and other members of the Karadjordjević dynasty were deprived of their nationality and their property confiscated. The Paris Peace Treaty with Italy provided for the cession to Yugoslavia of the greater part of Istria, although the fate of the Free Territory of Trieste was not settled till 1954, when the city of Trieste was finally awarded to Italy.

When in 1948 Tito refused to subordinate his party to Moscow, Yugoslavia was expelled from the Cominform and, alone among communist states, adopted a consistently independent program, despite periods of reconciliation with Stalin's successors (1955 and 1961) and a frequent coincidence of view with the Soviet bloc. This independence allowed Yugoslavia to turn West for support in the early 1950s and, as an advocate of nonalignment, to play a disproportionately large international role. The first reconciliation with Moscow (1955–57) followed Khrushchev's visit to Belgrade and foundered on China's unrelieved hostility to Yugoslav "revisionism" at a time when the Soviet leaders were making every effort to maintain good relations with Peking. The second reconciliation was highlighted by Tito's visit to the Soviet Union in 1962. The fortunes of more extreme liberals reflected changing Yugoslav-Soviet relations. Milovan Djilas, a former vice president who had been dismissed from the Central Committee of the League of Yugoslav Communists, was imprisoned in 1956 for protesting about government inaction during the Hungarian uprising and for the implicit criticisms of the bureaucracy in his book *The New Class*, later published in the West. Djilas was again arrested in 1962 as a proponent of a two-party political system and author of another publication that subsequently appeared in the West, *Conversations with Stalin.*

In 1963 Tito was reelected president for the fourth time, and a new constitution declared the state to be a Socialist Federal Republic. A reorganization in 1966 of the League of Yugoslav Communists (LYC) abolished the Politburo and replaced it with a Presidium and Executive Committee. Djilas was freed, and in 1967 the vice presidency was formally abandoned: the orthodox Aleksandar Ranković, a potential successor to Tito, was dismissed from his posts as vice president, cosecretary of the party and de facto head of the security police. In the same year, the young writer Mihajlo Mihajlov was imprisoned for disseminating hostile propaganda.

The rise of nationalist sentiment and its potential for political instability led Tito in 1971 to introduce a system of collective leadership and regular rotation of posts. In 1974, the country's fifth and most recent constitution was adopted. Tito was a strong advocate of decentralization and devolution of power from the federation to the republics and provinces, and this constitution reflects his desires.

President Tito died in 1980 three days short of his 88th birthday, and the leadership of the state and party thereupon passed to a collegiate body, the collective presidency. This system, planned with great care toward the end of the Tito years, has worked though not without friction; recently the Federal Assembly (parliament) has been critical of the government's inefficiency, saying ministry appointments should be filled on the basis of professional competence rather than on ethnic parity. In an apparent reaction, the president of the Federal Executive Council (prime minister), Milka Planinc, announced a major reshuffling of her government in mid-1984. A total of nine ministers were either dismissed or assigned to other posts in the government.

Internally, the principle of workers' self-management first introduced in 1950 has been reconfirmed by subsequent constitutions, and the Yugoslav road to socialism has led to a drastic liberalization of the economy, especially since 1965, and to significant administrative relaxations. There is now virtual freedom of movement, ready access to the ideas and commodities of East and West alike and a breadth and depth of political discussion unequalled in the communist world. The number of political prisoners, however, has increased significantly in recent years, due mainly to arrests on charges of nationalist sentiment, Yugoslavia's most serious long-term concern. In 1981, protests over living conditions by students in Priština led to demonstrations by Albanian nationalists throughout Kosovo province. The government declared a state of emergency, and the riots resulted in several deaths and many injuries. Many Albanian activists have since been imprisoned on charges of antistate activity. Similar charges have recently been leveled on groups of Muslim nationalists in Bosnia and Croatian nationalists in Zagreb.

Yugoslavia's place, along with India, Egypt and Indonesia, as a leading nonaligned nation, brought to Belgrade in 1961 the first major conference of nonaligned countries. Despite both the weakening of nonalignment as a world system and some closer cooperation with Soviet-bloc countries, Yugoslavia still maintains the most active and flexible foreign policy of all Eastern European states. Since 1971, Yugoslavia has largely succeeded in achieving one of its main foreign policy objectives: friendly relations with all states regardless of social systems, including the member countries of NATO and the Warsaw Pact. Despite Yugoslav criticisims of Soviet actions in Hungary (1956), Czechoslovakia (1968) and Afghanistan (from 1979), economic cooperation with the Soviet Union has increased in recent years. Good relations are also maintained with the United States, China and France, among others. Relations with Albania have become severely strained at times because of the often unstable situation in Kosovo.

Defense (1984): Military service is compulsory for men, for 15 months in the army and air force and 18 months in the navy. Voluntary military service for women was introduced in 1983. Strength is estimated at: army 191,000, navy 12,000, air force 36,000, paramilitary forces 15,000. 1984 defense expenditure was $1.6 billion. Yugoslavia maintains no military alliance.

ECONOMY

Background: The Yugoslav economy has several unique features distinguishing it from the other European socialist countries. Since the break with the Soviet Union in 1948, Yugoslavia has steered a middle course between a fully centralized planned economy and a free-market system. Small-scale private enterprises survive in many service industries and alongside the voluntary socialized units in the agriculture sector. Workers' councils exercise a strong influence on the pattern of management of enterprises.

The market mechanism plays a much greater role than in other Eastern European countries and planning is of a more indicative nature. There have been moves to establish a capital market. In 1967 a law was enacted enabling foreign companies to invest in Yugoslav firms, participation being limited to 49%, and this has been successful in attracting Western investment over a range of industry.

During the first half of the 1970s, the economic structure was further altered through the creation of "communities of interest," which were given some autonomy in setting production goals, and "basic organizations of associated labor," which functioned as production units at the shop level within factories. The latter participate in every level of decision making, including income distribution, social insurance, marketing, investment, and even foreign trade and international borrowing. Broad economic policies emerging from the federal government receive input from every economic level and often represent real consensus rather than simple high-level directives. Such policies are described as "social compacts," and are binding.

The country's economic growth during the 1960s and 1970s averaged 6.8% in gross material product (GMP), which, because it excludes personal, social and government services, is 13% to 15% below GNP. During this period, Yugoslavia moved from its status as a developing country to a middle-income, semi-industrialized country with a per capita GNP higher than that of Portugal and Romania—although, at $2,790, this rate is lower than that for most EC countries. Its per capita GNP growth rate of 5% during 1970–80 was higher than that of *all* the larger countries of Europe. This period also witnessed dramatic changes in the sectoral shares to GMP; agriculture dropped from 24% to 12%, services rose from 31% to 44%, while industry remained stable at 44%.

Economic policy has also been directed toward reducing disparities between the developed northern republics of Croatia, Slovenia and Serbia proper; the Serbian autonomous province of Vojvodina; the relatively poor southern republics of Bosnia–Hercegovina, Montenegro and Macedonia, and the province of Kosovo. In 1965 a permanent "federal fund for financing the accelerated development of the less-developed republics and the autonomous province of Kosovo" was established by law and additional aid was provided through the federal budget. Nearly 2.7% of the northern GMP was being sent into the south annually, along with an even greater proportion of international aid and technical assistance. Nevertheless, disparities persist, with Kosovo reporting a per capita income of only $627.

About 70% of the agricultural output is produced on 2.6 million privately owned farms. The Agrarian Reform Law of 1953 reversed the policy of collectivization and allowed individual farmers to hold up to 15 hectares of land. In 1982, private holdings accounted for 85% of cultivable land and 90% of the sectorial labor force. The giant state-owned *agrocombinats*, however, report much higher productivity and over 15 times the amount of capital investment per acre.

The fastest-growing components of manufacturing include capital goods and equipment, consumer goods and textiles. Between 1956 and 1975, industry recorded an average annual value-added growth rate of 9.4%, and between 1976 and 1980 of 7%. The country has extensive mineral deposits, as mentioned above, but is deficient in petroleum. Because official economic thinking favors import substitution rather than exports, trade deficits have been the rule. Yet, despite trade imbalances in every year since 1950, the overall current account has shown a surplus in most years because of the input from invisibles, such as foreign-exchange earnings from tourism, transit traffic from the several free-trade zones and, most importantly, worker remittances from abroad. The number of Yugoslavs working abroad peaked in 1973 at 1.1 million, but fell to about 800,000 by 1981 (of which 620,000 were in EC countries). Returning workers have added to the unemployment rate, which is much higher in the south.

A five-year trade agreement with the EC that expired in 1978 was renewed in 1980 soon after the death of Tito. This accord, scheduled to run through 1985, includes a $286 million low-interest loan from the European Investment Bank; it permits most Yugoslav industrial goods duty-free access and grants concessions to such agricultural exports as beef, wine and tobacco.

The five-year plan for 1981–85 is more modest than its predecessors and projects a substantially lowered investment growth rate of 1.5% per year in contrast to the 7% achieved during the 1970s. Exports, energy and agriculture receive considerable boosts, while imports of capital and consumer goods are reduced.

Foreign trade: Foreign trade accounts for 34% of the GMP and plays a crucial role in the economy. From 1949 to 1979 Yugoslav trade was equally divided between the East and West, but the balance tilted toward the East as Soviet oil and gas imports cost a larger share of the trade pie and were repaid with shoes, textiles, bauxite and alumina. However, more recent contracts for Mexican oil may shift the balance again to the West. More than 35% of Yugoslav imports come from the EC, while only 29% originated in the COMECON countries.

Guidelines for foreign trade and exchange are set by the federal Executive Council, while the federal Secretariat for Trade oversees commercial transactions, the issue of import and export licenses and bilateral trade balances. The federal Assembly is charged with the formulation of trade policies but each republic and province has its own councils to set export and import targets and determine borrowing and lending procedures. In 1981 the dinar was adjusted to a basket of convertible currencies, weighted in accordance with their importance in Yugoslav trade. Although export policy is relatively liberal, imports are subject to duties, licensing and quotas. Commercial imports are limited to registered organizations and major industrial enterprises, while quotas are enforced for certain raw materials, equipment, intermediate goods and consumer products. The import of food is the special province of the federal Office for Food Reserves, and special licenses are required for other items, such as tin, textiles and cotton.

Yugoslavia has special trade agreements with COMECON, the EC and the OECD, but is not a member of these organizations. On the other hand, it participates in GATT and belongs, unlike most other communist states, to the IMF and the World Bank. Yugoslavia is currently burdened with a debt of some $20 billion to Western creditors. In 1982, merchandise exports amounted to $10.265 billion and merchandise imports to $13.346 billion, leaving a trade deficit of $3.081 billion.

The percentage share of merchandise exports was 6% for fuels, minerals and metals; 15% for other primary commodities; 11% for textiles and clothing; 29% for machinery and transport equipment; and 39% for other manufactures. The percentage share of merchandise imports was 6% for food, 24% for fuels, 12% for other primary commodities, 28% for machinery and transport equipment and 30% for other manufactures. The principal export partners are the Soviet Union (28%), Italy (9%), West Germany (9%), Czechoslovakia (5%) and the United States (4%). The principal import partners are the Soviet Union (18%), West Germany (17%), Italy (7%), the United States (7%) and Iraq (6%).

Employment: In 1981, the total labor force was estimated at 9.4 million, of which 29% was in agriculture, 35% in industry and 34% in services. Unemployment has been a major problem for a number of years, reaching 900,000 in 1983. Nonagricultural employment has been very erratic, and is aggravated by seasonal unemployment in agriculture. Emigration has been on a large scale; some 800,000 Yugoslavs are now working abroad, mostly in Western Europe.

Prices and wages: Controls on wages were imposed in 1980 as part of a general austerity program, and real wages have declined in the first half of the 1980s. Controls on the prices of a large number of products were lifted in 1980, but when this resulted in general price increases, price freezes were imposed in 1981.

Recently, inflation rates have reached very high levels. In 1983, consumer prices rose by 39.2%. The government responded in late 1984 by lifting price controls on virtually all products and services. The prices of 37% of all goods are to be established through "self-managing agreements" between producers and consumers, while 55% of the prices are to be controlled by producers only.

Consumption: Rural living standards have been advancing, but there are still very great regional inequalities. Slovenia in the north is very prosperous but in the south, Serbia, Montenegro, Bosnia-Hercegovina and Macedonia remain comparatively backward despite significant investment in these areas by the richer republics. On average, per capita ownership of consumer durables, availability of social services and standards of living are low in comparison with other Eastern European countries.

SOCIAL WELFARE

Due to the system of social and financial self-management, the social security system in Yugoslavia differs markedly from systems operating elsewhere in Eastern Europe. Broadly supervised by the Union of Pension and Invalidity Associations on a national scale, social security is administered locally by the associations of social insurance of each commune. Each association is headed by assemblies elected directly by the insured persons. General social insurance covers all employees and self-employed, while partial insurance of private farmers was introduced in 1962. Social insurance funds accrue from the contributions of enterprises and institutions, i.e., contributions levied on the personal income of the insured. Maximum contributions (health, retirement, disability pensions and children's allowances) vary according to republic or autonomous region. Separate funds for health insurance and retirement and for disability pensions are formed from the contributions of enterprises. All funds are independent. Government spending on public health and social welfare amounted to 18.8% of the federal budget in 1981. All workers are entitled to paid annual leave of at least 14 working days (maximum 30 days). Women, and workers under 18 years of age, cannot be assigned to certain "hard" categories of work.

Health services: The health insurance system, compulsory for all workers and administrative employees, for the self-employed and for their families, provides insurance against sickness, injury, work injury and disease, and death. Since 1972, agricultural workers have also been fully insured. Public health institutions are independent, being managed by their own organs of self-government and financed on the basis of contracts concluded with local associations of social insurance. Free health services, preventive and curative, are available to all workers, including self-employed farmers, together with their families. Rates for sickness benefits are set by the local health insurance associations, with a minimum of 60% of the worker's net earnings. Working women are entitled to 105 days of paid leave during pregnancy. A maternity grant is also awarded, the amount being determined by the local health insurance association. Although health services in Yugoslavia have greatly improved in recent years, the infant mortality rate was a relatively high 32.8 per 1,000 population in 1981. The maternal mortality rate in 1980 was 17.8 per 100,000 population. There were 59.6 hospital beds per 10,000 population in 1980, and 14.85 doctors per 10,000 population in 1981. The average life expectancy in 1983 for the Yugoslavian male was 68 years and 73 years for the female.

Pensions and other benefits: All employees are entitled to old-age pensions, while the self-employed are insured on the basis of contracts concluded with the local association of social insurance. The minimum pension is 35% for men/40% for women of average earnings during the previous 10 years of work or the 10 highest-paid consecutive years. Increments are provided for each year of insurance beyond 15 years. The maximum pension is 85% of base earnings. The right to a pension is acquired upon reaching 60 years of age for men, 55 for women and a 20-year term of employment; or 65 years of age for men, 60 for women and a 15-year term of service; or 55 years of age for men, 50 for women after 35 years of employment. Pensions are paid at any age after 40 years of employment for men and after 35 years for women. There are lower requirements for arduous or unhealthy work. Workers temporarily disabled as a result of occupational injury or disease receive 100% of earnings, payable from first day of incapacity until recovery or award of permanent disability pension. Those permanently disabled receive up to 85% of base earnings, depending upon number of years of employment.

Family members of an insured person, including widows over 45, widowers over 60 and children registered at school, are entitled to a survivor pension. Widows younger than 45 qualify for a survivor pension if they look after children under 15. Survivor pensions amount to the following percentages of the basic pension rates: 70% for a widow, 80% for a family of two members, 90% for a family of three and 100% for a family of four or more. In case of an insured person's death, his family receives a cash payment (amounting to his last month's earnings) and a funeral allowance fixed according to local charges. Funeral allowances are also payable on the decease of any member of the insured's family.

There is no unemployment benefit as such, but in case of unemployment workers applying to the local labor exchange are entitled to compensation of 50% of average earnings in the last three months, payable for up to six months. Payment of these benefits is contingent upon the worker passing a needs test. All persons with an uninterrupted term of one year's employment, or 18 months with intervals, in the two years preceding unemployment are entitled to this compensation. Temporarily unemployed persons are entitled to health insurance and children's allowances.

Housing: As of 1982, Yugoslavia had over 6.4 million occupied dwellings, with an average of 2.5 rooms per dwelling. The decline in housing construction in recent years reflects a shortage of building materials, rising construction costs and difficulties in implementing self-managed housing. Wide disparities exist in housing investment betweeen the developed and less-developed regions.

EDUCATION

The basic principles of Yugoslav education (including curricula) for all six republics have been determined on a federal scale. The republican ministries of education have ultimate responsibility for supervision and maintenance, but schools are directly managed by their social communities through the school board, two-thirds of whose members are staff and one-third local citizens. Every school has its own statute outlining internal organization, jurisdiction and procedure. The entire system is fast expanding, and since 1961 the social communities, local enterprises and autonomous institutions have replaced the larger units as the main source of educational funds. Educational reforms instituted in the 1970s have attempted to standardize the subject matter in secondary schools and to integrate it more closely to the needs of the workplace. Instruction is in the language of the republic except in the case of national minority schools. The illiteracy rate is 15%.

Primary and secondary education: Primary instruction is the function of the eight-year elementary school (*osnovne škole*), free and compulsory for all children aged seven to 15. On completion of the primary course, pupils generally choose between one of the five types of secondary school, which

141

are not compulsory: (a) the gymnasium (*gimnazija* or grammar school) with a four-year course in general and optional academic subjects, and a quota of polytechnical training; (b) the technical/vocational school (*škole za srednji stručni kadar*) with two to four years of polytechnical and general instruction; (c) the vocational training school (*škole za kvalifikovane radnike*) whose predominantly practical three-year curriculum prepares the students for skilled work in such fields as agriculture, forestry, medicine, veterinary medicine, transport, business, library science and hydrometeorology; (d) four-year art school (*srednje umetničke škole*); and (e) five-year teacher training school (*srednje škole za nastavni kadar*). Some gymnasia in larger cities offer more extensive instruction in traditional humanities. Those who have attended the technical schools may enroll at one of the two-year postsecondary schools, created in response to the needs of industry and the social services. The majority of pupils graduating from secondary school proceed to higher education.

National minority education is provided at primary and secondary levels in the Albanian, Hungarian, Bulgarian, Turkish, Czech and Slovak, Romanian, Italian and Ruthenian languages—wherever there are large minority groups. Bilingual schools are established in some cases; one Yugoslav language is compulsory in all. The curricula of the national minority schools are similar to those in Yugoslav-language schools but include instruction in the national culture of the minority. In 1980–81, national minority institutions included, among others, 1,165 Albanian-language primary schools with 359,162 students, 165 Hungarian-speaking primary schools with 30,719 students and 63 Turkish-speaking primary schools with 6,801 students. There were a total of 274 secondary schools for various national minorities with a total student body of 409,923.

Special education: Special schools exist for handicapped pupils at all primary and secondary levels. Tuition, board and treatment are free.

University and higher education: Under the 1954 Universities Law, responsibility for university management was transferred from republican ministries to the universities and faculties themselves. Local autonomy was further reinforced in 1960. The faculties are independent of the universities but may unite in a university. Yugoslavia has 19 universities, nine of which have been set up in the last 15 years. The languages of instruction are Macedonian, Serbo-Croat and Slovene in the respective federal republics, as well as Albanian at the University of Priština and Hungarian at the University of Novi Sad. The two-year postsecondary schools make up the majority of higher educational institutions, and many specialize in technical areas such as pedagogy, social work, hotel management, dentistry, railway engineering and leather technology. Separate from the other institutions are the three autonomous faculties of theology (Orthodox in Belgrade, Catholic in Zagreb and Ljubljana). Most courses of higher education last four years, but certain humanities and forestry (three years) and medicine (five years) are exceptions. Since 1961, a system of three levels of study has operated in several institutions so that some, especially technical, students may enter jobs and postpone later stages of study. In the universities and faculties, attainment of the master's and specialist's degrees (equal first degrees) presupposes completion of third level study. Tuition is free; board for the great majority is covered by a "children's allowance" (available to students up to 25 years of age with at least one employed parent) or by scholarships based on academic merit and/or inadequate parental aid. Student credit funds in each republic may provide study loans, repayment being related to the student's academic performance.

Educational institutions (1980–81)

	Institutions	Staff	Students
Primary	12,660	131,728	2,808,575
Secondary	25,386	60,316	1,008,109
University and higher	356	20,250	411,175

Adult education: Facilities are available for adult education, at all levels, at evening schools and in part-time studies.

MASS MEDIA

The Press (1983):

Dailies: Politika, Belgrade, ind., 420,000; *Večernje Novosti* (e), Belgrade, 346,000; *Borba*, Belgrade/Zagreb, Socialist Alliance of Working People of Yugo. (SAWPY), 50,000; *Politika Ekspres* (e), Belgrade, ind., 248,000; *Vjesnik*, Zagreb, SAWPY, 87,000; *Večernji List* (e), Zagreb, 385,000; *Delo*, Ljubljana, SAWPY, 105,000; *Oslobodjenje*, Sarajevo, SAWPY, 80,000; *Sportske Novosti*, Zagreb, sport, 155,000; *Sport*, Belgrade, sport, 120,000; *Ljubljanski Dnevnik* (e), Ljubljana, 57,000; *Magyar Szó*, Novi Sad, SAWPY, in Hungarian, 31,000; *Slobodna Dalmacija*, Split, SAWPY, 65,000; *Nova Makedonija*, Skopje, SAWPY, 33,000; *Dnevnik*, Novi Sad, SAWPY, 30,000; *Sarajevske Novine* (e), Sarajevo, 19,000; *Privredni Pregled*, Belgrade, ind., 13,000; *Novi List*, Rijeka, SAWPY, 60,000; *Glas Slavonije*, Osijek, SAWPY, 14,000; *Rilindja*, Priština, SAWPY, in Albanian, 27,000; *La Voce del Popolo*, Rijeka, SAWPY, in Italian, 3,000.

Weeklies: Arena, Zagreb, illus., 224,000; *Ilustrovana Politiki*, Belgrade, illus., 270,000; *Politikin Zabavnik*, Belgrade, children's comic, 260,000; *Komunist*, Belgrade, communist, 520,000; *Nedeljne Informativne Novine* (NIN), Belgrade, info., 140,000; *Rad*, Belgrade, trade union, 70,000; *Mladost*, Belgrade, youth, 96,000; *Svijet*, Sarajevo, illus., 115,000; *Zadruga*, Belgrade, coop., 24,000; *Ekonomska Politika*, Belgrade, econ.; *Književne Novine* (f), Belgrade, lit., 7,500; *Narodna Armija*, Belgrade, milit.; *Medjunarodna Politika* (f), Belgrade, internat. affairs; *Socijalizm* (m), Belgrade, Communist theory; *Studentski List*, Zagreb, Yugoslavia Student's Union, 15,000; *Privredni Vjesnik*, Zagreb, Serbo-Croat.

Broadcasting: Yugoslav Radiotelevision (YRT) is a federal association of the state broadcasting institutions of the six republics and two autonomous provinces. While all-nation relays are used, each unit maintains its own programs. The units also broadcast regionally through a network of local stations, with special programs in Albanian, Hungarian, Italian, Romanian and Turkish. Radio Yugoslavia, the nation's foreign broadcast service, broadcasts in nine foreign languages. The all-nation TV network has stations in the republican capitals and broadcasts in the official republican languages. In 1983, there were 171 television sets per 1,000 population. Yugoslavia is a member of the European Radio Union (incl. Eurovision) and is in association with Intervision. Broadcasting is financed by revenue from subscriptions and advertising.

CONSTITUTIONAL SYSTEM

Constitution: The Constitution of the Socialist Federal Republic of Yugoslavia (SFRY), adopted February 21, 1974, is the country's fifth. The first constitutional act establishing Yugoslavia as a federated state was adopted in the form of decisions taken by the second session of the antifascist council of the National Liberation of Yugoslavia on November 29, 1943. The first constitution of 1946 introduced the system of people's democracy and state ownership of the means of production. The constitutional law adopted in 1953 inaugurated a system of self-management in the economy. The constitution of 1963 made self-management a constitutional right. A total of 43 amendments were made to that constitution, establishing relations between the federation and the constituent republics and provinces on the basis of full equality. These amendments were incorporated into the 1974 constitution, which contains 10 chapters dealing with basic principles.

Legislature: Under the 1974 constitution, the federal Assembly (*Savezna Skupština*) is a bicameral body consisting of a Federal Chamber and a Chamber of Republics and Provinces, both sitting for four-year terms. The Federal Chamber comprises 30 delegates from each of the six constituent republics and 20 from each of the two autonomous provinces. The Chamber of Republics and Provinces is composed of 12 delegates from each republican assembly and eight delegates from each provincial assembly. The presidents of the Assembly and of both chambers are elected on an annual basis, rotating among representatives of the republics and provinces.

The electoral process is relatively complex. At the first stage, delegates are elected by basic organizations of associated labor to some 12,000 local assemblies. These then elect delegates to some 510 communal assemblies, which, in turn, elect delegates to the assemblies of the republics and autonomous provinces. Finally, delegates to the Federal Chamber are elected by communal assemblies, while those to the Chamber of Republics and Provinces are elected by the assemblies of the territorial units.

Members of the Federal Assembly may not be reelected and are not career politicians. They are to retain their normal jobs during the four-year term of office. The Federal Assembly legislates; approves the budget and annual financial statement; ratifies treaties; and elects and removes members of the Collective Presidency, the Federal Executive Council, the Federal Court and the Constitutional Court. It exercises political supervision over other federal bodies, calls for a referendum, grants pardon, may declare war and generally determines internal and foreign policy.

Executive: Upon the death in 1980 of President Tito, the function of president of the Republic was terminated. The Collective Presidency is now the supreme executive and policy making authority. Its duties are to represent the federation at home and abroad, to protect the constitutional system and to harmonize the interests of the constituent republics and provinces. This body is composed of (1) a member from each republic and autonomous province elected for a term of five years by the Federal Assembly, and (2) the president of the presidium of the League of Communists of Yugoslavia. The positions of president and vice president of the presidency rotate annually. Members of the cabinet, known as the Federal Executive Council, are nominated by the Collective Presidency and are elected by the Assembly for four-year terms. Councillors may not be elected for more than two consecutive terms. The Federal Assembly's powers of appointment and recall of members of the Federal Executive Council, and of supervision over that body, underline the limitations placed on the chief organ of federal administration. There has been a general devolution of legislative and executive power from the federal to the republican level. Only the most important secretariats (foreign affairs, defense, finance, foreign trade) remain within federal jurisdiction, and their functions are explicitly coordinative.

Local government: Self-management (*samoupravljanje*) by the citizens in the commune (*komuna* or *opština*) is the political foundation of the sociopolitical systems in Yugoslavia. The supreme communal organ of communal government is the assembly, whose members are elected for a four-year term (half the members being elected every second year). Executive bodies are appointed from within the assembly. An assembly comprises a communal chamber (*komunalno veće*) and a chamber of working communities (*veće radnih zajednica*). Larger towns comprise more than one commune, and these may discharge their functions jointly. In all except the Slovene and Montenegrin republics another unit exists between commune and republic, namely the district (*srez*), whose precise competence varies according to republic but which discharges affairs of common concern to two or more communes. Members of district assemblies are elected by the communal assemblies from among their members. Within a given enterprise, workers' self-government finds expression in the workers' council (*radnički saveti*) whose members are directly elected for a two-year term and which determines the plan, program and development of the enterprise. It generally appoints a managing board (*upravni odbor*) for a term of one year.

Judiciary: Courts of general jurisdiction are the communal courts, county courts, supreme courts of the republics and the Federal Court of Yugoslavia (*Vrhovni Sud Jugoslavije*). The latter, consisting of a president and 24 judges, decides on appeals against decisions of the supreme courts of the republics and directs application of federal laws. Its judges are elected and removed by the Federeal Chamber of the Federal Assembly; supreme courts of the republics (*Vrhovni Sudovi Republika*) decide on appeals against decisions of county courts. Their judges are elected or removed by the republican assemblies. District courts (*sreski sudovi*) and communal courts (*opštinski sudovi*) comprise, except in certain single-judge cases determined by law, a judge (*sudija*) and two lay assessors (*porotnici*) elected and removed by the assembly of the corresponding sociopolitical community, except for some courts that may be directly elected by the citizens of that community. Court hearings are public, save where the safeguarding of secrets or the protection of public decency is involved. Proceedings are held in the national language of the republic, but provision may be made for interpreting. The Constitutional Court of Yugoslavia (*Ustavni Sud Jugoslavije*), consisting of a president and 13 judges elected for a term of eight years, decides on the conformity of law with the federal constitution and on the conformity of republican law with federal law; it also resolves conflicts between courts and federal organs on the territories of two or more republics. Economic cases and other forms of litigation concerning the economy are heard by district economic courts (*sreski privredni sudovi*), higher economic courts (*viši privredni sudovi*) and the Supreme Economic Court (*Vrhovni Privredni Sud*). Special courts include military tribunals and courts of arbitration. The judiciary is independent. The Public Prosecution (*Javno Tužilaštvo*) is an autonomous organ entrusted with criminal prosecution and also with ensurance of the uniform enforcement of law and protection of legality. This is headed by the federal public prosecutor (*Javni Tužilac Jugoslavije*) who is appointed and removed by the Federal Assembly. Capital punishment is maintained.

Party: There is only one political party, the League of Communists of Yugoslavia (LYC) with a current membership of 2,200,000 (1983), and there is thus no parliamentary opposition. The six republics are equally represented in the party Central Committee. The LCY Congress meets once every four years. It elects the Central Committee, which in turn elects the Presidium or Politburo. The Federation of Yugoslav Youth numbers at least 3,800,000 (1981). The Socialist Alliance of the Working People of Yugoslavia, which is a mass organization rather than a political party, contains over 14 million (1979) members.

Leading government and party figures (1985): Collective Presidency: Veselin Djuranović (president, April 1984–April 1985), Radovan Vlajković (vice president, May 1984–May 1985), Stane Dolanc, Sinan Hasani, Nikola Ljubičić, Branko Mikulić, Lazar Mojsov, Josip Vrhoveć, Ali Šukrija (president of Central Committee Presidium of LCY, ex officio member of the Collective Presidency), Milka Planinc (Federal Executive Council president), Raif Dizdarević (federal secretary for foreign affairs), Adm. Branko Mamula (federal secretary for defense), Vlado Klemenčić (federal secretary for finance), Milenko Bojanič (federal secretary for foreign trade), Dobroslav Čulafić (federal secretary for internal affairs).

BIOGRAPHICAL SKETCHES

Jure Bilić: Jure Bilić, a Croat, began to make his career after Tito's purge of the so-called nationalist leadership in 1971. By the mid-1980s he was in many respects the leading political figure in Croatia, particularly after the death of Vladimir Bakarić, the longtime republican political boss, in 1983. Bilić, born in 1922, joined the party and the partisans in 1941. After the war, he made his career in the Croatian party organization and government. In 1974 he was one of the six secretaries in the newly created Executive Committee of the League of Communists' Presidium, and was in charge of organizational and cadre questions. After holding a variety of federal and Croatian posts, in 1982 he became president of the Croatian Central Committee Presidium.

Veselin Djuranović: Djuranović, president of the eight-member state presidency (i.e., head of state) in 1984–85 and representative for Montenegro, was born in 1925. He joined the partisans in 1941 and made his career in the Montenegro party organization. During the 1950s he worked in radio and the press and was head of the Montenegro party organization's Central Committee commission on ideology (1958–62). In 1968 he was elected president of the Montenegro party organization. Between 1977 and 1982 he was federal prime minister. Djuranović, a member of the youngest partisan generation, is an experienced politician with a reputation for toughness.

Stane Dolanc: Dolanc, a Slovene and a member of the state presidency, was born in 1925. He joined the partisans in 1944 and served in the armed forces until 1960. In 1965 he became a member of the Slovene party's Central Committee, and in 1969 was elected a member of the federal party's Executive Bureau of the League of Communists' Presidium. In 1972, after Tito's reorganization, he became secretary of the Executive Bureau and one of the most influential party figures, often acting as Tito's spokesman. In 1982–84 he was federal interior minister. Dolanc, an influential and powerful political figure, was generally regarded as a centrist in Yugoslav politics—not a committed reformer, but not opposed to reform either.

Nikola Ljubičić: Gen. Ljubičić was one of the dominant figures on both the Yugoslav and the Serbian political stages. Born in 1916, he belonged to the older generation of former partisans, and in the 1970s was close to Tito as one of Yugoslavia's leading military politicians. Ljubičić had a lengthy career in the military, having started as a commander in the 1941 uprising in Titovo Užice, and was eventually defense minister from 1967 to 1982, an extraordinarily long tenure. Leaving the federal stage, he moved into Serbian politics, becoming president of the presidency of Serbia, a member of the Serbian Central Committee and of its Presidium.

Milka Planinc: Milka Planinc, a Croat, was federal prime minister from 1982, a particularly difficult time, when the economic crisis was beginning to spill over into politics. Born in 1924, she joined the partisans in 1941 and rose up the Croatian party and state ladder gradually; her career advanced noticeably after the 1971 purge. She sought to tackle the economic crisis with some determination, but the federal government's powers were found to be not effective enough for the purpose of imposing economic discipline.

COMPARATIVE STATISTICS

POPULATION, 1983

	Area (000 sq. km.)	Population (millions)	Density (per sq. km.)
Albania	28.8	2.84	99
Bulgaria	110.9	8.94	81
Czechoslovakia	127.9	15.41	121
East Germany	108.2	16.70	154
Hungary	93.0	10.69	115
Yugoslavia	255.8	22.85	89
Poland	312.7	36.57	117
Romania	237.5	22.55	95
Soviet Union	22,402.2	272.50	12
U.S.	9,372.6	233.70	25
U.K.	244.0	55.61	28

Source: *U.N. Demographic Yearbook*, 1983.

EMPLOYED CIVILIAN LABOR FORCE, BY MAIN SECTORS, 1982

	Agriculture (000)	(%)	Industry (000)	(%)	Other (000)	(%)	Total (000)
Albania[1,2]	128	21.9	221	37.8	235	40.3	584
Bulgaria[1]	929	22.8	1,406	34.5	1,741	42.7	4,076
Czechoslovakia	1,039	14.0	2,806	37.7	3,590	48.3	7,435
East Germany[1]	339	4.3	3,525	44.9	3,979	50.8	7,843
Hungary	1,144	22.9	1,605	32.1	2,248	45.0	4,997
Poland	5,357	31.4	5,015	29.4	6,671	39.2	17,043
Romania	3,025	29.0	3,813	36.6	3,590	34.4	10,428
Yugoslavia[1]	302	5.0	2,461	41.2	3,217	53.8	5,980
Soviet Union[3]	25,258	20.1	36.891	29.4	63,499	50.5	125,648
U.S.	3,571	3.6	22,742	22.9	73,213	73.5	99,526
U.K.	632	2.7	6,565	28.3	16,024	69.0	23,221

[1] Socialized sector.
[2] 1978.
[3] 1980.

Sources: *ILO Yearbook of Labor Statistics*, 1983; *Europa Yearbook*, 1984.

PER CAPITA NET MATERIAL PRODUCT AT CONSTANT PRICES, 1972–79
(1975 = 100)

	1972	1973	1974	1976	1977	1978	1979
Albania	n.a.	n.a.	n.a.	n.a.	n.a.	n.a.	n.a.
Bulgaria	80	86	93	107	114	121	126
Czechoslovakia	87	90	95	103	107	110	113
East Germany	85	91	97	106	111	113	115
Hungary	84	89	95	102	110	115	117
Yugoslavia[1]	87	91	98	103	110	117	124
Poland	79	86	94	106	110	113	109
Romania	75	83	92	110	119	127	133
Soviet Union	86	93	96	104	109	113	114
U.S.[2]	99	103	102	105	109	113	115
U.K.[2]	95	102	101	104	105	109	110

[1] Gross material product.
[2] Gross Domestic Product (GDP) at constant prices.
Source: *U.N. Statistical Yearbook*, 1981.

ORIGIN OF NET MATERIAL PRODUCT, 1983 (%)

	Agri-culture	Industry	Construc-tion	Transport and Commu-nications	Trade	Other
Albania	n.a.	n.a.	n.a.	n.a.	n.a.	n.a.
Bulgaria	17	56	10	8	7	3
Czechoslovakia	9	62	10	4	14	<1
East Germany	8	75	6	4	10	3
Hungary	13	38	11	8	11	20
Poland	18	50	11	5	14	2
Romania	n.a.	n.a.	n.a.	n.a.	n.a.	n.a.
Yugoslavia[1,2]	14	42	10	8	22	4
Soviet Union	20	46	10	6	18	<1
U.S.[3]	3	28	4	6	17	43
U.K.	2	31	5	6	12	45

[1] Gross material product.
[2] 1981.
[3] 1982.
(Note: Totals may not equal 100 because of rounding.)
Source: *U.N. Monthly Bulletin of Statistics*, Feb. 1985.

151

EXPENDITURE ON NET MATERIAL PRODUCT, 1983
(%)

	Government Consumption	Private Consumption	Increased Stocks	Gross Fixed Capital Formation	Net Exports
Albania	n.a.	n.a.	n.a.	n.a.	n.a.
Bulgaria[1]	4	72	12	16	−3
Czechoslovakia	8	69	5	14	4
East Germany	n.a.	n.a.	n.a.	n.a.	n.a.
Hungary	11	69	2	16	2
Poland	11	63	6	18	2
Romania	n.a.	n.a.	n.a.	n.a.	n.a.
Yugoslavia	n.a.	n.a.	n.a.	n.a.	n.a.
Soviet Union	(	72	)	(26)	2
U.S.	19	66	<1	17	−2
U.K.	22	60	<1	17	1

[1] 1972
Source: *U.N. Monthly Bulletin of Statistics*, Feb. 1985.

WARSAW PACT DEFENSE EXPENDITURE, 1980

	Defense Expenditure ($ million)	Defense Expenditure ($ per capita)	GNP ($ per capita)	Defense Expenditure as % of GNP
Bulgaria	1,180	133	4,219	3.2
Czechoslovakia	2,750	180	5,821	3.1
East Germany	6,020	360	7,226	5.0
Hungary	1,100	103	4,200	2.4
Poland	4,300	121	3,929	3.1
Romania	1,350	61	3,851	1.6
Soviet Union	130,000	490	4,564	10.7
Netherlands	5,277	373	11,399	3.3

Source: *World Military and Social Expenditures*, 1983.

EXCHANGE RATES OF COMECON CURRENCIES PER $
(as of Nov. 1984)

	Official Bank Rate	Free Market Rate (approx.)
Albania (new lek)	8.40	n.a.
Bulgaria (leva)	1.02	3
Czechoslovakia (koruna)	6.77	25
East Germany (mark)	3.05	11
Hungary (forint)	49.75	80
Poland (zloty)	125.39	600
Romania (lei)	5.04	n.a.
Soviet Union (ruble)	0.83	4
Yugoslavia (dinar)	222.20	300

EXTERNAL TRADE, 1983

	Imports $ million	Imports $ per capita	Exports $ million	Exports $ per capita	Balance[1] $ million
Albania	n.a.	n.a.	n.a.	n.a.	n.a.
Bulgaria	12,164	1,360	12,130	1,357	−34
Czechoslovakia	16,325	1,059	16,522	1,072	+197
East Germany	21,524	1,289	23,793	1,425	+2,268
Hungary	8,503	795	8,696	813	+193
Poland	9,995	273	10,951	299	+956
Romania[2]	9,836	436	11,714	519	+1,877
Yugoslavia	11,104	492	9,038	401	−2,067
Soviet Union	80,410	295	91,336	335	+10,927
U.S.	269,878	1,155	200,538	858	−69,341
U.K.	100,235	1,802	91,939	1,653	−8,296

[1] + Denotes export surplus, − Denotes imports surplus.
[2] 1982.
Source: *U.N. Monthly Bulletin of Statistics*, May 1985.

TRADE OF THE SOVIET UNION, 1970 and 1983
(% of Total)

Origin and Destination	Imports		Exports	
	1970	1983	1970	1983
Canada	1.1	2.1	0.1	<0.1
United States	1.0	2.6	0.5	0.5
Total North America	2.1	4.7	0.6	0.5
France	2.7	2.9	1.1	3.6
West Germany	3.2	5.6	2.0	6.0
Italy	2.7	2.4	1.7	4.4
United Kingdom	2.1	1.1	3.6	1.7
All EC	12.6	14.4	10.8	20.2
All EFTA	5.6	7.2	4.2	6.5
Rest of Western Europe	0.1	0.4	0.1	0.4
Total Western Europe	18.3	22.0	15.1	27.1
Bulgaria	9.2	8.5	7.3	8.1
Czechoslovakia	10.5	9.1	9.4	8.6
East Germany	14.7	11.1	15.1	10.0
Hungary	6.8	6.7	6.6	6.0
Poland	10.7	8.0	10.5	7.8
Romania	4.5	2.8	3.9	2.4
Yugoslavia	2.1	3.9	2.5	3.9
Total Eastern Europe	58.7	50.1	55.4	46.9
China	0.2	0.4	0.2	0.4
India	2.3	1.8	1.1	1.8
Indonesia	0.2	0.1	<0.1	<0.1
Japan	2.9	3.7	3.0	1.2
Rest of Asia and Oceania	3.6	2.9	5.5	4.3
Total Asia and Oceania	9.3	8.8	9.8	7.8
Africa	4.6	2.9	4.5	2.3
Central and South America	5.1	7.9	5.1	5.3
Middle East	1.1	2.2	3.3	2.3
Other	0.8	1.4	6.2	7.8
Total	100.0	100.0	100.0	100.0

Source: *U.N. Monthly Bulletin of Statistics*, July 1984.

TOTAL IMPORTS, 1976–83
(*$ million*)

	1976	1977	1978	1979	1980	1981	1982	1983
Albania	n.a.	n.a.	n.a.	n.a.	n.a.	n.a.	n.a.	n.a.
Bulgaria	5,626	6,393	7,651	8,514	9,650	10,801	11,527	12,164
Czechoslovakia	9,706	11,187	12,565	14,262	15,148	14,658	15,403	16,325
East Germany	13,196	14,334	14,572	16,214	19,082	20,181	20,196	21,524
Hungary	5,528	6,523	7,902	8,674	9,235	9,128	8,814	8,503
Poland	13,867	14,616	16,089	17,584	19,089	15,476	10,204	9,995
Romania	6,095	7,018	8,910	10,915	13,201	12,458	9,836	n.a.
Yugoslavia	7,367	9,633	9,983	13,240	18,279	15,817	13,346	11,104
Soviet Union	38,111	40,812	50,546	57,771	66,522	72,960	77,752	80,410
U.S.	129,896	157,560	186,044	222,228	256,984	273,352	254,884	269,878
U.K.	55,882	63,643	75,852	99,692	115,566	102,725	99,708	100,235

Sources: *U.N. Statistical Yearbook*, 1981; *U.N. Monthly Bulletin of Statistics*, May 1985.

TOTAL EXPORTS, 1976–83
($ million)

	1976	1977	1978	1979	1980	1981	1982	1983
Albania	n.a.	n.a.	n.a.	n.a.	n.a.	n.a.	n.a.	n.a.
Bulgaria	5,382	6,351	7,478	8,869	10,372	10,689	11,428	12,130
Czechoslovakia	9,035	10,302	11,747	13,197	14,891	14,876	15,638	16,522
East Germany	11,361	12,024	13,267	15,063	17,312	19,858	21,743	23,793
Hungary	4,932	5,832	6,345	7,938	8,677	8,712	8,767	8,696
Poland	11,017	12,265	14,114	16,249	16,997	13,249	11,174	10,951
Romania	6,138	6,979	8,077	9,724	11,401	12,610	11,714	n.a.
Yugoslavia	4,878	5,256	5,668	6,605	10,770	10,929	10,265	9,038
Soviet Union	37,169	45,159	52,219	64,761	76,449	79,003	86,912	91,336
U.S.	115,340	121,212	143,766	182,025	220,786	233,739	212,275	200,538
U.K.	46,257	57,585	67,912	86,422	110,156	102,215	97,075	91,939

Sources: *U.N. Monthly Bulletin of Statistics*, February 1985; *U.N. Statistical Yearbook, 1981.*

INDICES OF INDUSTRIAL PRODUCTION, 1977–84
(1980 = 100)

	1977	1978	1979	1980	1981	1982	1983	1984
Albania	n.a.	n.a.	n.a.	n.a.	n.a.	n.a.	n.a.	n.a.
Bulgaria	85	91	96	100	105	110	115	n.a.
Czechoslovakia	89	93	97	100	102	104	107	n.a.
East Germany	87	91	95	100	105	108	112	117
Hungary	94	99	102	100	103	105	106	108
Poland	96	99	101	100	86	85	90	95
Romania[1]	125	136	147	156	n.a.	n.a.	n.a.	n.a.
Yugoslavia	82	89	96	100	104	103	105	n.a.
Soviet Union	90	94	97	100	104	106	110	n.a.
U.S.	94	99	104	100	103	94	100	111
U.K.	100	103	107	100	96	99	102	103

[1] 1975 = 100.
Source: U.N. Monthly Bulletin of Statistics, May 1985.

INDUSTRIAL PRODUCTION (MAJOR PRODUCTS), 1983
(000 Metric tons)

	Pig Iron[1]	Crude Steel	Aluminum	Cement	Cotton Yarn	Plastics and Resins	Newsprint
Albania	n.a.	n.a.	n.a.	n.a.	n.a.	n.a.	n.a.
Bulgaria	1,632	2,820	n.a.	5,640	85	n.a.	n.a.
Czechoslovakia	9,624	15,024	36	10,500	140	1,004	67
East Germany	2,208	7,224	n.a.	11,784	134[2]	1,045	107
Hungary	2,052	3,612	74	4,248	56	337	n.a.
Poland	9,720	16,236	n.a.	16,164	178	526	83
Romania	8,184	12,588	n.a.	13,032	190[2]	n.a.	100
Yugoslavia	3,096	2,004	283	9,588	120	499	28
Soviet Union	110,496	152,496	n.a.	127,992	1,645[2]	4,392	1,526
U.S.	44,184	75,420	3,353	63,000	989[3]	12,418[4]	4,688
U.K.	9,636	15,972	252	13,392	97	1,966[3]	79

[1] Including ferrous alloys.
[2] 1981.
[3] 1982.
[4] 1980.

Source: *U.N. Monthly Bulletin of Statistics*, May 1985.

HOURS WORKED IN MANUFACTURING PER WEEK, 1977–83

	1977	1978	1979	1980	1981	1982	1983
Czechoslovakia	43.7	43.5	43.5	43.5	43.3	43.1	43.1
Hungary[1,4]	163.5	161.9	160.8	160.8	160.7	153.9	152.7
Poland[1,4]	165.0	163.0	163.0	160.0	n.a.	n.a.	n.a.
Soviet Union[4]	40.6	40.4	40.6	40.5	40.7	n.a.	n.a.
Yugoslavia[1,4]	185.0	185.0	n.a.	n.a.	n.a.	n.a.	n.a.
U.S.	40.3	40.4	40.2	39.7	39.8	38.9	40.1
U.K.[2]	43.6	43.5	43.2	41.9[3]	42.0	42.0	42.6

[1] Per month.
[2] Males only.
[3] Revised method of calculation.
[4] Socialized sector.
Source: *U.N. Monthly Bulletin of Statistics*, Feb. 1985; *U.N. Statistical Yearbook*, 1981.

ENERGY PRODUCTION, 1983

	Coal (000 metric tons)	Lignite (000 metric tons)	Crude petroleum (000 metric tons)	Natural gas (terajoules)	Electricity (million kWh)
Albania	n.a.	n.a.	n.a.	n.a.	n.a.
Bulgaria	240	32,124	n.a.	n.a.	42,876
Czechoslovakia	26,916	102,408	96	20,100	75,972
East Germany	n.a.	277,968	n.a.	n.a.	104,928
Hungary	2,832	22,392	2,004	246,000	25,704
Poland	191,064	42,528	252	192,780	125,880
Romania	7,788	36,732	12,000	1,680,000	68,004
Yugoslavia	372	58,188	4,128	65,592	65,772
Soviet Union	486,768	154,764	618,000	18,627,960	1,395,996
U.S.	660,504	51,516	427,512	15,879,972	2,367,636
U.K.	119,220	n.a.	110,832	1,576,956	276,204

Source: *U.N. Monthly Bulletin of Statistics*, May 1985.

LAND UTILIZATION, 1982

	Agricultural Area (000 hectares)	(% of total area)	Arable Land* (% of agricultural	Permanent Meadows and Pastures area)
Albania	1,254	43.6	56.5	43.5
Bulgaria	6,182	55.7	67.1	32.9
Czechoslovakia	6,840	53.5	75.6	24.4
East Germany	6,259	57.7	79.9	20.1
Hungary	6,582	70.7	80.5	19.5
Poland	18,891	60.4	78.5	21.5
Romania	14,967	63.0	70.3	29.7
Yugoslavia	14,218	55.6	55.1	44.9
Soviet Union	605,466	27.0	38.4	61.6
U.S.	428,163	45.7	44.5	55.4
U.K.	18,281	74.7	38.2	61.8

* Including land under permanent cultivation.
Source: *FAO Production Yearbook*, 1983.

AGRICULTURAL PRODUCTION, 1983
(000 metric tons)

	Wheat	Potatoes	Sugar beet	Cow's milk	Meat	Hen's eggs
Albania	583	136	320	347*	75	12*
Bulgaria	3,600	428	749	2,080	717	146
Czechoslovakia	5,820	3,105*	6,037*	6,496	1,382	261
East Germany	3,470	7,500*	6,400*	8,208	1,746	336
Hungary	4,800*	1,506*	4,800*	2,800*	1,664	215*
Poland	5,165	34,473	16,358	16,496	2,281*	423
Romania	5,000	6,100	4,819	3,137	1,612	348
Yugoslavia	5,519	2,580	5,700	4,550*	1,433	239*
Soviet Union	82,000*	83,000	82,000	96,000	16,196*	4,116*
U.S.	66,010	14,774	19,152	63,488	25,351	4,004
U.K.	10,880	5,849	7,600	17,252	3,143	736

* FAO estimate.
Source: *FAO Yearbook*, 1983.

RAILWAYS, 1982

	Length of Line (Km)	Passenger/km (millions)	Net Tons/km (millions)
Albania	n.a.	n.a.	160[1]
Bulgaria	4,273	7,092	18,276
Czechoslovakia	13,142	15,085	71,585
East Germany	14,231	24,785	54,016
Hungary	7,823	13,980	23,396
Poland	24,348	49,266	112,731
Romania	11,125	25,578[2]	71,110
Yugoslavia	9,393	10,200	26,166
Soviet Union	143,300[3]	347,900	3,464,500[4]
U.S.[5]	270,370	18,371	1,485,693
U.K.	17,568	27,360	15,876

[1] 1970.
[2] Includes passengers carried free of charge.
[3] Excludes industrial railways—approximately 99,300 km.
[4] Excludes industrial railways—approximately 77,400 net tons/km.
[5] 1981.
Source: *U.N. Annual Bulletin of Transport Statistics for Europe*, 1982.

MERCHANT SHIPPING, 1981
(000 gross registered tons)

	Total	Oil Tankers	Ore and Bulk Carriers
Albania	56	n.a.	n.a.
Bulgaria	1,194	338	438
Czechoslovakia	185	n.a.	103
East Germany	1,570	175	285
Hungary	83	n.a.	n.a.
Poland	3,579	547	1,262
Romania	2,032	340	776
Yugoslavia	2,541	267	913
Soviet Union	23,493	4,758	2,012
U.S.	18,908	8,125	1,931
U.K.	25,419	12,154	6,257

Source: *U.N. Statistical Yearbook*, 1981.

INLAND WATERWAYS TRANSPORT, 1982

	Total Length of Inland Waterways (km.)	Ton/km. (million)
Albania[1]	43	n.a.
Bulgaria[2]	471	n.a.
Czechoslovakia	483[3]	3,683
East Germany	2,319	2,290
Hungary	1,622	1,731
Poland[4]	3,894	1,868
Romania	1,659[5]	2,548
Yugoslavia	2,001	7,362
Soviet Union	138,900	262,400
U.S.[4]	41,403	1,494,464
U.K.	1,147	71

[1] 1979.
[2] 1973.
[3] 1969.
[4] 1981.
[5] 1975.
Sources: *U.N. Annual Bulletin of Transport Statistics for Europe*, 1982; *World Factbook*, 1984.

CONSUMER PRICE INDEX, 1974–80
(1970 = 100)

	1974	1975	1976	1977	1978	1979	1980
Albania	n.a.	n.a.	n.a.	n.a.	n.a.	n.a.	n.a.
Bulgaria	101	101	101	102	103	108	124
Czechoslovakia	100	101	102	103	105	109	112
East Germany	97	97	97	96	96	n.a.	n.a.
Hungary	110	115	120	125	131	142	155
Poland	110	113	118	124	134	144	157
Romania	102	103	103	104	106	108	110
Yugoslavia	195	243	271	312	356	429	559
Soviet Union	100	100	100	100	101	102	103
U.S.	127	139	147	156	168	187	212
U.K.	148	184	215	249	270	306	361

Source: *U.N. Statistical Yearbook*, 1981.

INTERNAL CONSUMPTION OF BASIC PRODUCTS, 1980

	Primary Energy[1] (kg per capita)	Steel[2] (kg per capita)	Newsprint (kg per thousand inhabitants)
Albania	1,131	70	n.a.
Bulgaria	5,341	312	5,203
Czechoslovakia	6,393	729	5,157
East Germany	7,271	583	8,367
Hungary	3,745	330	5,864
Yugoslavia	2,149	254	1,342
Poland	5,000	527	3,570
Romania	4,477	544	4,360
Soviet Union	5,551	n.a.	4,012
U.S.	10,628	508	49,480
U.K.	4,791	247	24,583

[1] Reduced to coal equivalent.
[2] Apparent consumption expressed in terms of crude steel.
Source: *U.N. Statistical Yearbook*, 1981.

HEALTH SERVICES (LATEST YEAR AVAILABLE)

	Doctors	Dentists	Pharmacists	Number of inhabitants per doctor
Albania (1977)	2,641	637	532	966
Bulgaria (1980)	21,796	4,839	3,648	406
Czechoslovakia (1980)	42,210	7,746	6,846	362
East Germany (1978)	32,397	8,864	3,481	517
Hungary (1980)	26,768	3,303	4,328	400
Poland (1979)	61,460	16,527	15,274	573
Romania (1979)	31,285	6,790	6,205	704
Yugoslavia (1978)	29,980	5,964	5,131	732
Soviet Union (1980)	995,600[1]		239,900	2,667[1]
U.S. (1978)	424,000	117,000	136,000	524
U.K.[2] (1978)	75,000	n.a.	13,018	654

[1] Includes dentists.
[2] England and Wales.
Source: *U.N. Statistical Yearbook*, 1981.

HOUSING, 1982 (or latest year available)

	Number of Occupied Dwellings (000)	Average number of Rooms per Dwelling	Average number of Persons per Room
Albania	n.a.	n.a.	n.a.
Bulgaria	2,969.7	2.4	1.0[1]
Czechoslovakia	5,370.0	3.8	n.a.
East Germany	6,057.0[2]	2.8	n.a.
Hungary	3,724.9	3.4	1.5[3]
Poland	10,131.8	3.9	1.2[4]
Romania	n.a.	n.a.	n.a.
Yugoslavia	6,404.7	2.5	n.a.
Soviet Union	n.a.	2.3[3]	n.a.
U.S.	91,561[5]	n.a.	n.a.
U.K.	21,842	4.4	n.a.

[1] 1975.
[2] 1970.
[3] 1980.
[4] 1978.
[5] 1981.

Source: *U.N. Annual Bulletin of Housing and Building Statistics for Europe*, 1983; *U.N. Statistical Yearbook*, 1981.

FACILITIES IN DWELLINGS, 1982

| | Percentage of Dwellings with | | |
	Electricity	Inside Running Water	Bathroom
Albania	n.a.	n.a.	n.a.
Bulgaria	99.8[1]	98.0	91.0
Czechoslovakia	n.a.	99.3	98.0
East Germany	n.a.	100.0	100.0
Hungary	98.1[2]	99.0	98.8
Poland	n.a.	96.6	93.6
Romania	n.a.	n.a.	n.a.
Yugoslavia	n.a.	92.7	87.6
Soviet Union[3]	n.a.	91.0	88.0
U.S.[4]	n.a.	99.3	n.a.
U.K.	n.a.	100.0	100.0

[1] 1975.
[2] 1980.
[3] 1981.
[4] 1977.

Sources: *U.N. Annual Bulletin of Housing and Building Statistics for Europe*, 1983; *U.N. Statistical Yearbook*, 1981.

MOTOR VEHICLES IN USE (latest year available)
(000 units)

	Year	Passenger Cars	Commercial Vehicles
Albania	n.a.	n.a.	n.a.
Bulgaria	n.a.	n.a.	n.a.
Czechoslovakia	1980	2,274.9	340.1
East Germany	1978	2,392.3	600.7[1]
Hungary	1980	1,013.4	162.8
Poland	1978	1,835.4	605.6[2]
Romania	1970	n.a.	45.1[3]
Yugoslavia	1978	1,857.1	256.9[4]
Soviet Union	n.a.	n.a.	n.a.
U.S.	1980	118,458.7	33,410.6
U.K.[5]	1978	14,309.0	1,798.0

[1] Including farm tractors.
[2] Excluding buses and tractors, but including special trucks.
[3] Buses and trucks.
[4] Excluding tractors and semitrailer combinations.
[5] Excluding Northern Ireland.
Source: *U.N. Statistical Yearbook*, 1981.

RADIOS, TELEVISIONS AND TELEPHONES IN USE, 1980

	Radio Receivers		TV Receivers		Telephones	
	(000)	(per 000 popu- lation)	(000)	(per 000 popu- lation)	(000)	(per 000 popu- lation)
Albania[1]	202	74	10	3.7	n.a.	n.a.
Bulgaria[2]	2,149	242	1,652	186	1,255	141
Czechoslovakia[2]	4,693	307	4,292	280	3,150	206
East Germany[2]	6,409	383	5,731	342	3,156	189
Hungary	2,700[1]	252	2,766[2]	258	1,261	118
Poland[2]	8,666	244	7,954	224	3,387	95
Romania[2]	3,205	144	3,714	167	1,196[3]	56[3]
Yugoslavia[2]	4,851	217	4,442	199	2,139	95
Soviet Union[1]	130,000	490	81,000	305	23,707[4]	89
U.S.[1]	477,800	2,099	142,000	624	180,424	788
U.K.[1]	53,000	947	22,600	404	26,651	477

[1] Estimated number of receivers in use.
[2] Number of licenses issued or sets declared.
[3] 1975.
[4] Excludes telephone systems of the military forces.
Sources: *UNESCO Statistical Yearbook*, 1984; *U.N. Statistical Yearbook*, 1981.

NATIONAL COMPOSITION OF THE SOVIET POPULATION
(according to the census, as of January 17, 1979)

	Population by nationality, thousand people		Population by nationality, thousand people
Total population	262,085	Kabardinians	322
Russians	137,397	Kara-Kalpaks	303
Ukrainians	42,347	Uighurs	211
Uzbeks	12,456	Gypsies	209
Belorussians	9,463	Ingushi	186
Kazakhs	6,556	Gagauzes	173
Tatars	6,317	Hungarians	171
Azerbaidzhanis	5,477	Tuvinians	166
Armenians	4,151	Northern nationalities, of whom:	158.5
Georgians	3,571		
Moldavians	2,968	Nentsi	29.9
Tadzhiks	2,898	Evenks	27.3
Lithuanians	2,851	Khanty	20.9
Turkmens	2,028	Chukchi	14.0
Germans	1,936	Evens	12.5
Kirghiz	1,906	Nanaians	10.5
Jews	1,811	Koryaks	7.9
Chuvashi	1,751	Mansi	7.6
Daghestan nationalities, of whom:	1,657	Dolghans	5.1
		Nivkhi	4.4
Avars	483	Selkups	3.6
Lesghins	383	Ulchi	2.6
Dargins	287	Saami	1.9
Kumyks	228	Udegheins	1.6
Laks	100	Eskimoes	1.5
Tabasarans	75	Itelmens	1.4
Nogaians	60	Orochi	1.2
Rutuls	15	Kets	1.1
Tsakhurs	14	Nganasans	0.9
Aguls	12	Yukaghirs	0.8
Letts	1,439	Tophalars	0.8
Bashkirs	1,371	Aleuts	0.5
Mordvinians	1,192	Nehidalsy	0.5
Poles	1,151	Komi-Permyaks	151
Estonians	1,020	Kalmyks	147
Chechens	756	Karelians	138
Udmurts	714	Karachias	131
Mari	622	Romanians	129
Ossels	542	Kurds	116
Koreans	389	Adyghei	109
Bulgarians	361	Turks	93
Buryats	353	Abkhazians	91
Greeks	344	Finns	77
Yakuts	328	Khakas	71
Komi	327	Balkars	66

	Population by nationality, thousand people		Population by nationality, thousand people
Altais	60	Assyrians	25
Dungans	52	Tats	22
Circassians	46	Shorians	16
Persians	31	Other nationalities	136
Abazians	29		

NATIONAL MINORITIES IN EASTERN EUROPE
(estimated figures)

Albania		Gypsies	229,986
Greeks	35,000	Ukrainians	54,429
Vlachs	35,000	South Slavs	34,034
		Russians	20,253
Czechoslovakia		Jews	25,686
Hungarians	550,000[1]	Turks	23,303
Germans	40,000	Tatars	23,107
Poles	60,000	Slovaks	22,037
Ruthenes	100,000	Czechs	7,756
		Bulgarians	10,467
East Germany		Greeks	6,607
Sorbs	30,000	Poles	4,756
		Armenians	2,436
Hungary			
Germans	200,000	*Yugoslavia* (1981 census figures)	
Slovaks	120,000	Albanians	1,753,605
South Slavs	100,000	Hungarians	426,865
Romanians	20,000	Gypsies	148,604
		Turks	101,328
Poland		Slovaks	80,300
Ukrainians	200,000	Romanians	54,721
Belorussians	200,000	Bulgarians	36,642
Germans	200,000[2]	Vlachs	32,071
Slovaks	25,000	Ruthenes	23,320
Lithuanians	25,000	Czechs	19,609
		Italians	15,116
Romania (1977 census figures)		Ukrainians	12,809
Hungarians	1,705,810[3]		
Germans	348,444[4]		

[1] Hungarian sources claim, with some justification, that the total number of ethnic Hungarians in Czechoslovakia is as high as 700,000.
[2] The exact number of Germans in Poland is impossible to determine, because quite substantial numbers of people can opt for either German or Polish ethnicity when this is to their advantage. This explains the high number of applications to emigrate to West Germany, around 150,000 in the 1970s, as well as the significant numbers who have indicated their desire to do so.
[3] This is the official figure. Hungarian sources argue that this underestimates the size of the minority, because it does not enumerate Hungarians who live outside Transylvania and who number at least 300,000. If this is accepted – and Romanians do not accept it – then the number of Hungarians in Romania may be estimated at around 2 million.
[4] Emigration and assimilation have reduced this number to c.20,000 or less.

PART ONE

HISTORICAL

RUSSIA AND THE SOVIET UNION TO 1985

JOHN KEEP

INTRODUCTION

Two major themes run through the history of modern Russia and provide an element of continuity between the imperial and postrevolutionary epochs. One constant preoccupation of the Russian people, and more particularly of their rulers, has been the effort to overcome swiftly the country's historic legacy of backwardness vis-à-vis most Western nations. Forced industrialization at a rapid tempo has involved a radical reshaping of the traditional social order and of people's attitudes to their environment. Their next most important concern has been the endeavor to adapt the political system to 20th-century conditions in such a way as to maintain an abnormally high degree of central control over the thoughts and actions of individual citizens. In Russia, the state authority has always loomed larger in people's lives than has been the case in countries with a democratic tradition. The czarist autocracy pursued aims of a quite conventional character, judged by the standards of the day. It sought to preserve the empire's external and internal security and to increase the national wealth insofar as this was compatible with political and social stability. The Soviet regime, on the other hand, has pursued much more far-reaching goals. Ever since the Bolshevik revolution of October 1917, it has striven to effect a complete transformation of Russian (and international) society: to achieve socialism, and ultimately full communism, as defined by Marx and Lenin. The raison d'être of the ruling Soviet Communist party is to fulfill this ideological mission.

These two themes—socioeconomic change and a tradition of political authoritarianism—are closely connected, as we shall see by examining each of them in turn.

SOCIOECONOMIC CHANGE IN RUSSIA

Russia's relative underdevelopment was the product of long-range geographic and historical considerations. Its vast size hindered communications and the exploitation of its rich mineral resources. Agricultural progress was impeded by the harsh climate and the poor quality of the soil in most areas of the country. Despite modern scientific and technological advances, these

173

factors remain important even today. So long as the bulk of the population lived close to the subsistence margin, it was difficult for autonomous social forces to emerge, strong enough to challenge the power of the state, which from the 15th century onward had been the architect of national unity. The Russian nobles preferred to follow careers in the state service, as officers or officials, rather than to make their mark as independent farmers or businessmen. Of the peasantry, the bulk of the population, a large element was economically passive or inert. Serfdom, abolished as recently as 1861, left deep traces upon the popular psychology. Russia conspicuously lacked an enterprising middle class able to take the initiative in modernizing its economy, so that this role fell mainly to the state. After defeat in the Crimean War (1854–55) brought home the urgent necessity for economic progress, the government assisted private entrepreneurs to build railways and establish new mines and factories. An important part in this development was played by foreign capital, notably in the Ukrainian metallurgical industry and in petroleum extraction in Transcaucasia. To attract investors (predominantly French or British), the government stabilized the currency and built up a sizable gold reserve. From 1885 to 1900, Russian industrial output forged ahead, and in the last years of the 19th century its growth rate was second to none.

A business recession, war with Japan (1904–05) and consequent internal disturbances temporarily interrupted this progress, but it was resumed in the years before the outbreak of World War I. In 1913, Russia was the world's fifth largest industrial producer. In relation to its rapidly growing population, however, manufacturing output was very low. The per capita growth rate in the period 1885–1913 has been put at 1.25 percent per annum. Savings bank deposits rose twelvefold between 1890 and 1913—eloquent testimony to increased well-being. Imperial Russia had yet to attain the take-off point for self-sustaining growth, but it did have an industrial base in terms of equipment, manpower and technological know-how upon which later Soviet planners could build.

There were two large blots on this happy picture. In the first place, labor obtained so little immediate benefit from Russia's industrial progress that social tensions in the cities were acute. The industrial wage earners, some 3 million strong in 1913, earned more than most peasants, but wages lagged far behind newly aroused expectations. Working hours were long, factory conditions poor. Elementary protective legislation for women and juveniles was introduced in the 1880s, but the law had many loopholes and adult men often worked a 14-hour day. After 1905, some industrialists adopted more enlightened attitudes, but all too many behaved shortsightedly. Where ethnic and class discrimination were combined, as in factories employing highly paid foreign foremen, an explosive situation often resulted. World War I brought additional hardships for most groups of wage earners.

The second major defect was the imbalance between industry and agriculture. To travel from the cities in to the Russian countryside was to go back centuries in time. The muzhiks had their virtues, notably an ability to withstand every kind of adversity with uncomplaining good humor, but their general cultural level was abysmally low. They obtained precious little uplift or enlightenment from the clergy or landowning gentry. The peasants lived in a world of their own, remote from authority, barely touched by modern influences radiating from the cities. Juridically they were free, but until the early 20th century the village commune (*mir*) retained extensive administrative powers. It could allocate the heavy tax burden among the individual householders, penalizing the thrifty to subsidize the idle or unfortunate. In Great Russia, the commune held legal title to the land, which it redistributed periodically among its members according to their needs. This egalitarian system, highly regarded by some romantic intellectuals, was a serious disincentive to productive investment. Crop yields were extremely low, except on large estates; it was the latter that provided most of the surplus needed to feed the cities and for export. In areas of extreme overcrowding, many peasants were dependent upon landowners who leased land at extortionate rates—as in Ireland or India.

These conditions explain why there was serious agrarian unrest in 1905. Thereafter, the prime minister, P. A. Stolypin, embarked upon a major reform designed to create a strong class of individualistic peasant proprietors who could reinforce the declining landed gentry as a bulwark of conservatism. Householders were encouraged to leave the commune and to gather their scattered strips into consolidated farms on the Western model. The reform evoked a positive response in the more advanced regions of the country, but in Great Russia the results were modest. It was probably launched too late for it to have realized the government's high hopes. Greater success attended other measures taken to promote migration to new lands in Russian Asia, crop diversification, primary schooling in rural areas and farm mechanization. It was the regime's misfortune that this progress was disrupted by the outbreak of World War I in 1914. This led to widespread social disaffection and eventually to a turbulent revolution. In 1917, when authority in the countryside collapsed, the peasants renewed their ancient cry for a general distribution of the land and embarked upon a new wave of violence from which not only the gentry but also their better-off fellows suffered. This spontaneous and anarchic agrarian revolution, sanctioned by the Bolsheviks, eliminated the more productive farms and turned Russia into a country of some 25 million smallholders, more addicted than ever to their communal traditions and eager to enjoy their new wealth free from outside interference. Such a situation posed intractable problems for any government, especially one committed to Marxist proletarian socialism.

SOCIALIST ECONOMIC PLANNING

The Soviet regime inherited a grim legacy in the economic field. War and revolution had upset the whole pattern of international trade. From 1914 until the civil war ended in 1920, Russia was all but isolated from its normal markets and sources of supply. Industrial production was dislocated by territorial losses, lack of raw materials and fuel, and labor unrest. In 1918–19, the richest areas were outside Moscow's control altogether. In 1917 the transport system had broken down, serving as a potent stimulus to revolution in the famished cities. To escape starvation, many workers fled to the villages.

The financial system, too, collapsed as successive governments covered their expenditures by issuing vast quantities of paper money. By 1920, the ruble had become practically worthless and trade had to be conducted in the form of barter. To add to the chaos, the new regime adopted doctrinaire socialist economic policies. All sources of wealth were nationalized, and an attempt was made to replace the capitalist profit motive by coercion coupled with moral exhortation. Some enthusiasts hailed the dying out of trade and money as a sign that full communism was around the corner. Lenin was more realistic and inveighed against bureaucratic inefficiency, but his instructions on matters of economic policy were often ambiguous. Not until March 1921, when his regime was gravely imperiled by popular uprisings, did he persuade his colleagues to adopt a somewhat more rational approach.

The New Economic Policy (NEP) was construed ideologically as a compromise between socialism and capitalism, a transitional phase of unspecified duration. In practice it meant concessions to the peasant farmers and small private traders. The former were no longer subject to arbitrary and violent requisitions of allegedly surplus produce, but had their dues fixed—at first in kind, later in cash—in relation to their property or earnings. Although crude, this arrangement did at least afford them some incentive to produce for the market. Ultimate ownership of the land remained vested in the state, but peasants were permitted to farm their land more or less as they wished, and even to employ hired labor on a limited scale. Meanwhile the top-heavy industrial bureaucracy was simplified. In less essential branches, managers, often members of the old intelligentsia, were given wider decision making powers, although within the factory they had to take account of the local trade union branch and party activists, and overall policy was still determined by the planners in Moscow. The controlling heights of the economy—heavy industry and foreign trade—remained under close state control, but stress was now laid upon improving output and efficiency. As a result of these moderate policies, agricultural, and later industrial, output within a few years reached and surpassed their prewar level.

The next stage in economic strategy was the subject of intense debate within the party. The right-wing leaders, notably Bukharin, advocated a cautious policy: to conciliate the peasants by providing them with sufficient industrial consumer goods in exchange for their surplus produce. The left-wingers, notably Trotsky, took an alarmist view of the peasants' individualistic propensities, and urged that a policy of severe fiscal pressure be applied against the wealthier elements in order to obtain funds to promote rapid industrialization, with the accent on producers' goods. In the event, neither formula was adopted, since under Stalin politics determined economics, not vice versa. Stalin first took an intermediate line, which won him support in the party; then, having suppressed his main opponents on the left and right, he embarked upon an ultraleftist course more extreme than anything hitherto conceived.

First five-year plan
Stalin's first five-year plan (1929–33) set out, by mobilizing ideological enthusiasm and applying force on a massive scale, to effect a drastic transformation

of the economy. A large volume of capital, contributed by the population through heavy indirect taxation, restrictions on consumption and cheap labor, was invested in the development of heavy industry. Production was boosted at a rapid tempo, regardless of the cost to working-class living standards. Fulfillment of targets assigned by the central plan became the prime legal obligation of all Soviet citizens. The peasants were cajoled or coerced into voluntarily abandoning their independent properties and joining large mechanized collective or state farms, where their activities were subject to close administrative control. The collective farms had to meet heavy delivery quotas and other obligations before they could share out the residue of their income among their members. By 1936, 90 percent of Soviet peasants had been brought within the new system of socialized agriculture. The reform was carried through so violently, and with so little regard either for peasant interests or for economic rationality, that it was exceedingly unpopular. But those who protested (or were deemed likely to protest) were arrested and either shot as alleged kulaks or deported to forced-labor camps. Many of those who remained, threatened with loss of their property and mass starvation, slaughtered their horses and cattle. This was a contributory cause of the catastrophic man-made famine of 1932–33. Stalin himself later privately estimated the total loss of life at 10 million, but in public he claimed that his policies had succeeded. In a limited sense they had; the procurement agencies obtained surpluses with which to supply the urban population, but at an incalculable human and material cost.

Wasteful and inefficient use of resources became one of the hallmarks of the Stalinist planned economy, in industry as in agriculture. The main incentive for all state employees, whether workers or managers, was fear of punishment for real or alleged shortcomings. At the same time, to provide a material stimulus, income differentials were widened, with privileges for "shock workers" who exceeded their production norms or otherwise excelled. Educational opportunities were greatly improved. By the late 1930s, a new managerial elite had come into being, a technologically minded Soviet intelligentsia, which henceforward served as the principal bulwark of the regime. This stabilization of Soviet society, and the high priority given to industries of significance to national defense, enabled the Soviet Union to meet the great test of war in 1941. The system of centralized planning was well suited to perform such tasks as evacuating entire factories to the rear and boosting production in new industrial areas (for example, the Kuzbas in western Siberia). The transport system, which had been extended and modernized, withstood wartime strains much better in 1941–45 than it had done in 1914–20. The population, accustomed to total mobilization in peacetime, by and large accepted stoically the new burdens imposed upon them in order to defeat the Nazi invader. In the occupied areas, however, the artificial collective farm system swiftly collapsed.

Postwar economic reconstruction
When Stalin set about the formidable tasks of postwar economic reconstruction, he adhered to the earlier system of priorities. Agriculture was once again starved of investment funds, while political controls over the farmers

Table 1
OUTPUT OF SELECTED GOODS IN THE SOVIET UNION 1928–82

	1928	1940	1960	1970	1980	1982
Crude oil (million tons)	11.6	31.1	148	353	603	610
Gas (billion cubic meters)	—	3.2	45	198	435	501
Coal (million tons)	36	166	510	624	716	718
Electric power (billion kilowatt hours)	5	48	292	741	1,294	1,367
Steel (million tons)	0.3	18	65	116	148	147
Pig iron (million tons)	3.3	15	47	86	107	107
Mineral fertilizer (000 tons)	0.03	800	3,300	13,100	24,800	26,700
Locomotives (000 horsepower)	?	927	1,699	1,808	7,231	7,327
Tractors (000)	1.3	31.6	239	459	555	555
Fabrics (million square meters)	207	3,320	6,368	8,852	10,746	11,080
Leather footwear (million pairs)	58	212	419	679	743	734
Watches (million)	0.9	2.8	26	40	67	69
TV sets (000)	—	0.3	1,726	6,682	7,528	8,345
Refrigerators (000)	—	3.5	529	4,140	5,925	5,800
Cameras	?	355	?	2,045	4,255	4,058
Canned food (million tins)	—	1,118	4,900	10,678	15,270	16,605
Meat (000 tons)	678	1,501	4,606	7,144	9,140	9,269
Sugar (000 tons)	1,283	2,165	6,363	10,221	10,127	12,070
Cereals (gross yield, million tons)	?	96	121	187	[182]	?
Vegetables (million tons)	?	13.7	?	21.2	27.3	30.0
Cattle (stock as of Jan 1, million head)	?	55	76	95	115	117
		(1941)	(1961)		(1981)	(1983)

were reinforced. The prices paid for deliveries of produce were so low that many peasants earned little or nothing. The government feared that any concessions would encourage bourgeois individualist tendencies. Instead, it embarked upon grandiose schemes for the transformation of nature, which could not bring any short-term return. In foreign trade, autarkic tendencies prevailed, while in industry the traditional emphasis on producers' goods was enhanced by the need to develop nuclear energy for military purposes.

Thus, when Stalin died in March 1953, the Soviet economy suffered from striking disproportions. The Soviet Union had become the world's second largest military and industrial power. It disposed of ample resources of fuel (oil, coal, natural gas) and had developed a national electric grid. Production of steel, which in 1913 had been a mere 4.2 million tons, had by 1956 reached 48.6 million tons. New branches of industry, such as aircraft construction, as well as new regions had been opened up. The gross national product rose annually by an estimated 6.9 percent over the period 1928–55 (5.8 percent, if population changes are taken into account). Yet in 1953, per capita agricultural production was less than it had been in 1928, and the consumer was badly served. The output of footwear, for example, sufficed to give each citizen only one pair of shoes or boots a year. Clothing was expensive and shoddy in design. There were few private telephones, refrigerators, or television sets and still fewer private cars. Much more serious from the standpoint of average citizens were the deficiencies in their diet. Grain products played an inordinately large role, meat was an expensive luxury and even fruit and vegetables were scarce. The distribution system was so inefficient that the urban householder might have to spend several hours accumulating the ingredients for a simple evening meal. Some 40 years after the revolution, and 20 years after socialism had been officially promulgated, life for ordinary working people was still monotonous and grim (see Table 1).

Khrushchev's new course
In such circumstances, Stalin's successors could hardly fail to embark upon reforms. Nikita S. Khrushchev, who soon rose to prominence as first secretary of the Communist party of the Soviet Union (CPSU) regarded himself as something of an agricultural expert. He boosted the prices paid to collective farmers for produce delivered to state procurement agencies and reduced their obligatory quotas, thus raising agricultural incomes. But he resisted enlargement of the peasants' private plots that supplied, via the free-price collective-farm markets, much of the foodstuffs (especially perishables) consumed by the urban population. Instead, he encouraged mergers in order to form larger units that were expected to be more efficient, and improved the quality of their management. Some were converted into giant state farms. These became the norm in the so-called Virgin Lands and marginal lands—pasture, mainly in western Siberia and Kazakhstan—which were brought under the plough in a massive drive to increase the area sown to cereals. The results of this campaign, as of the one to force planting of maize as a fodder crop, were uncertain. In good years grain output soared, but when drought struck key regions it had to be imported from the West. Many agronomists warned of the perils of soil erosion and held that capital could

179

have been invested more wisely. Another reform that had mixed results was the compulsory sale to the farms, at prices they could ill afford, of agricultural machinery previously operated by the machine-tractor stations (MTSs), which had served Stalin as agencies of control. There was still too much administrative interference in day-to-day decisions, too little incentive to stop wasteful practices and introduce innovations. Khrushchev's proud boast that by 1960 the Soviet Union would overtake the United States in per capita output of meat and dairy products was soon an embarrassing liability; nor could Soviet agriculture realistically expect to create, by 1980, the material abundance deemed necessary to support a fully communist (as distinct from socialist) society, forecast in the 1961 CPSU program.

These failures played a part in Khrushchev's ouster (October 1964) on charges of "hare-brained scheming." So too did his ill-received plan (1962) to split local party agencies into separate industrial and agricultural sections. This measure seems to have been a desperate response to obstruction by officials in the central ministries, who did not relish his somewhat demagogic insistence that they should relinquish their comfortable offices for the work-bench or the plough. Their passive resistance slowed up, and eventually reversed, a 1957 scheme to decentralize industrial management. Yet these were years of high (if declining) economic growth rates. Production of certain consumer durables (e.g., TV sets, refrigerators) leaped. Industrial wage earners secured higher pay and better pensions. Many hoped that further reforms would lead to closer relations with the capitalist West, which a favored few were now permitted to visit as tourists. Commercial and cultural exchanges with foreign countries, although carefully controlled, were expanded. The modest liberalization in the cultural field (see below) and the feats of Soviet cosmonauts engendered a public mood of cautious optimism.

Brezhnev and "mature socialism"
These hopes slowly dissipated under the stern rule of Khrushchev's successors. Leonid I. Brezhnev (1964–82) was a stolid conservative who catered to the interests of the bureaucratic elite. First priority in allocation of scarce economic resources went to heavy industry, especially those sectors catering to the needs of the military. Humiliated by the 1962 Cuban crisis, the Soviet Union built up its armed forces to unprecedented levels, thus straining the country's economy and keeping consumers deprived of nonessential goods. The system of five-year plans continued, with decisions on output, prices and countless other matters being centrally determined, although in a more methodical and less hectic manner than hitherto. The output and range of products increased (see Table 1). Particularly important was the development of the fuel base (notably the natural gas fields in western Siberia). In the late 1960s, the number of plan indicators ("targets") that managers had to meet were reduced and rewards were geared more closely to sales. However, this reform, for which prime minister A. I. Kosygin bore special responsibility, was not allowed to go as far as some Soviet economists, E. G. Liberman, for example, had suggested; nor was the picture much changed by subsequent efforts to group interconnected enterprises into socialist firms (corporations)

or to set up so-called territorial production associations. Soviet leaders looked askance on the Hungarian new economic model, let alone the market socialism of Yugoslavia. Yet during the 1970s, the Soviet Union did become more closely involved in the world market—not least because it depended on industrialized Western countries for imports of advanced technology, especially in the electronics field. Some foreign companies were allowed to set up entire factories in the Soviet Union (e.g., Fiat at Togliatti on the Volga, 1967–72), but care was taken to prevent such ventures leading to "capitalist ideological contamination."

By the late 1970s, the built-in rigidities of the planning system were contributing to a serious decline in growth rates. Another factor was that large reserves of underutilized labor were no longer available. Shortages of foodstuffs developed in the towns. Although the Brezhnev regime invested massive sums in agriculture, notably increasing supplies of mineral fertilizer and introducing more powerful machinery, this effort often brought disappointingly low returns. The farms suffered from a steady flow of able-bodied young people to the towns, where social and cultural amenities were better and career advancement easier than in the countryside. Proportionately far fewer peasant children entered higher educational establishments than did those of workers, not to mention those of functionaries. Residence permits for Moscow and other large cities were hard to come by; nevertheless, from 1975 peasants bore the same internal passports as others. This ended their legal attachment to their farms—a concealed form of social discrimination— and encouraged mobility. From 1965, collective farmers were incorporated into the state pensions scheme and as of 1966 received a guaranteed wage. The total income at the rural population's disposal increased markedly, narrowing the gulf between town and country.

Differences between manual and nonmanual workers were generally less marked than in free-enterprise economies, but privileged functionaries enjoyed many hidden perquisites, e.g., shops with restricted access and special holiday arrangements; some party members even got extra cash in their pay packets. All this fostered corruption and the growth of a semilegal second economy to furnish goods and services not provided under the plan. Elimination of such abuses was a major aim of Yury Andropov, an ex-police chief who succeeded Brezhnev in November 1982. However, he was physically incapacitated before his tough measures could produce any startling results. Nor could mere administrative action of this kind—partially continued after his death in February 1984 by Konstantin U. Chernenko—cure the underlying economic malaise. This was rooted in the irrelevance to a modern sophisticated, diversified economy of the doctrine to which the ruling party was so intransigently committed. Socialist ideology had helped to mobilize the masses for certain limited tasks, but once these had been accomplished routine set in. Industrial maturity undermined the credibility of cherished Soviet beliefs—and institutions.

THE RUSSIAN AUTHORITARIAN TRADITION

During the 19th century, Russia's autocratic monarchs had stoutly resisted any change that would infringe on their sacred prerogatives. In practice, their power rested on loyal service by a phalanx of officials and a large standing army that could be used for internal security duties in an emergency. Another bulwark of the imperial regime was the Orthodox church, which had inherited from Byzantium a spiritual tradition that emphasized obedience to the temporal power. Although the church lost its hold over many educated Russians as secular influences penetrated from the West, religion remained a potent force in the lives of the common people, especially the peasants, and this would endure into the atheist Soviet epoch.

The great reforms of the 1860s made two major breaches in the traditional absolutist order. Semi-autonomous elected councils were set up for local government, and courts of law were made genuinely independent of the executive. These moves toward what is now called pluralism were resented by many conservatives, and often insufficiently appreciated by radical intellectuals. The latter, swayed by romantic myths posing as scientific social theory, argued that only violent revolution, not gradual reform, could ensure happiness for the Russian people, whom they idealized. The government's heavy-handed efforts to suppress dissent by press censorship and administrative interference in universities and schools merely served to make radical ideas more plausible and attractive to the growing number of educated professional people. By 1900 it was plain that the autocracy would have to yield to their demands.

The first explosion came in 1905, after the unsuccessful war with Japan. Nicholas II (1894–1917) reluctantly consented to introduce a constitution (although the word was officially avoided). The crown preserved far-reaching powers, but laws ordinarily had to pass through a two-chamber legislature, in which the lower house (the imperial duma) was elected on a restricted and indirect franchise. This quasi-parliamentary system did not work smoothly, owing to the accumulated mistrust on both sides. Political tensions mounted during World War I, when the administration assumed emergency powers, bypassing the legislature, but proved incompetent. Once again military defeat discredited the monarchy, which in March 1917 collapsed, leaving a political vacuum.

REVOLUTION AND CIVIL WAR

Initial rejoicing soon gave way to bitterness as orderly government failed and various segments of the population pressed for immediate satisfaction of their pent-up demands for change. The provisional government, comprising inexperienced politicians with liberal and democratic socialist sympathies, delayed taking important decisions and forfeited much public support by trying, at the western Allies' behest, to keep Russia in the unpopular and fruitless war. Upon this groundswell of opposition, Lenin's Bolshevik party rode to power without much difficulty in October 1917.

The takeover cost little bloodshed, at least in Petrograd (now Leningrad, then the capital), but in January 1918 forcible dissolution of the democratically elected Constituent Assembly starkly revealed Lenin's intention to establish a single-party dictatorship, using terrorist methods wherever necessary. He saw the coup simply as a prelude to a general revolutionary upsurge by war-weary proletarians all over Europe, where conditions seemed riper for Marxist-style socialism. The victorious workers in the industrialized West, he hoped, would come to the rescue of the Russian Bolsheviks—a group of extremists with only an unstable popular following, slighter in the countryside (where the bulk of the population lived) than in the towns or in the army. But these expectations were not borne out by events. Europe by and large turned its back on communism, whereas the Bolsheviks succeeded, against tremendous odds, in suppressing internal dissent and then extending their power over most of the former Russian empire. Victory in this bitter civil war (1918–20) was due in large part to the Red Army, under Leon Trotsky, and also to the security police (*cheka*). The conservative White forces, aided intermittently by the Allies and the various national-minority movements, were liquidated, but efforts to extend Soviet power abroad by force of arms were rebuffed. By 1921, the Bolsheviks (communists) unexpectedly found themselves ruling a nominally socialist country encircled by capitalist foes. Revising their ideological assumptions, they now set out to construct a socialist society by direction from above, in a single country until such time as a new international crisis broke, which they could hope to exploit.

THE SOVIET PARTY-STATE

This meant that they had to improvise political institutions to govern the new Soviet state. Such a state seemed to many revolutionaries a contradiction in terms. Naively, they had looked forward to the elimination of all public coercive authority, to a communist order run on ultrademocratic lines. The soviets (councils elected informally by workers, soldiers and peasants) were seen as symbols of this new kind of polity. At first these bodies did indeed represent mass opinion and exercised considerable influence; but the Bolsheviks, as devotees of organization and discipline, could not tolerate this freedom, especially in a time of civil war. There was a rapid drift toward administrative centralization. The soviets were subordinated to their central executive and to the government, which existed independently. Although the 1918 (Russian SFSR) and 1923 constitutions formally vested supreme power in elected soviet congresses, these deliberative assemblies were soon reduced to rubber-stamp status and the federal structure had no real meaning. An increasingly important part came to be played by the Communist party, the only political grouping allowed to exist. It was organized on strict, hierarchical lines. Decisions were taken in the Politburo, an inner organ of the Central Committee, and put into effect by a rapidly growing apparatus of full-time officials. The party was supposed to supervise, not supplant, the state administration, but in practice this distinction ceased to matter; many functionaries served simultaneously in both apparatuses. In this way, the dictatorship of the proletariat became the dictatorship of a small group—indeed, of a single individual: Lenin, succeeded on his death in 1924 by Stalin (secretary-general of the party from 1922). The more idealistic communists were shocked by this development, which seemed to recreate in a new form the evils of autocracy; the more realistic, Lenin and Stalin included, understood that only in this way could the system be made to function.

THE STALINIST ERA

The party did not publicly acknowledge its usurpation of power from the people, but disguised the fact by propaganda fictions—for example, that the Soviet state was more democratic than any other since the masses allegedly helped to implement public policy. The divorce between the reality of Soviet political life and its official image widened appreciably after 1929, when Stalin, having disposed of Trotsky and other deviationists, consolidated his personal dictatorship in a totalitarian form. Totalitarian rule was designed to insulate Soviet society from hostile outside influences, to eliminate all autonomous institutions and to subordinate the individual wholly to the all-encompassing demands of the state power. The 1936 constitution, promulgated after Stalin had announced the achievement of socialism in the Soviet Union, embodied many progressive principles, including guarantees of civil and political rights for every citizen; but the leadership freely ignored these provisions whenever expedient, since it considered itself above the law and responsible solely to history for its actions.

This discipline was crudely manipulated to make the record conform to current political requirements. Trotsky, for instance, became an unperson. In 1937, Stalin published an official textbook of party history that became a new, unchallengeable orthodoxy, to which all thought and learning had to be adjusted. Intellectual life atrophied. The repetition of meaningless ideological concepts and slogans served to condition people to accept the status quo and to react, like Pavlov's dogs, in the correct manner to each new signal from above. Writers and artists had to suppress their individual consciences and to identify themselves wholly with the party's current line.

Stalin was remarkably successful in constructing a facade of total public conformity, but in doing so sacrificed the communist movement's revolutionary dynamism. His efforts to reshape human nature were much too ambitious. By denying all individual autonomy, he forced people to be false to their true selves. Often they adopted a dual system of values: one for their public, another for their private conduct. Although the regime boasted of its universal public support, it could not really trust the people and relied heavily on its mighty coercive machinery. Stalin skillfully exploited rivalries within the bureaucratic hierarchy to maximize his power. The most important body was the security police (now called the NKVD), which managed a vast network of secret agents and informers whose duty was to seek out and eliminate not only actual but also potential opponents of the regime. This "prophylactic terror" produced a climate of fear and suspicion. Denunciation by one's closest associates for some allegedly counterrevolutionary act normally brought summary arrest, trial by an extra-judicial tribunal and a heavy sentence: death or exile to a forced-labor camp. These notorious establishments, run by the police, held some 10 million prisoners at their peak; countless millions died in them. About 1 million Communist party members were also imprisoned during the Great Purge of 1936–39, of whom about half perished. It is still unclear to what extent the purges were deliberately staged by Stalin to ensure his paramountcy, and to what extent there was genuine opposition within the party apparatus to his disastrous policies.

The terror eased slightly during the most critical years of World War II, but was subsequently resumed. Stalin was particularly afraid of ex-prisoners of war and others who returned to the Soviet Union after seeing something of better conditions abroad. An iron curtain was lowered to limit contact between Soviet citizens and foreigners. A campaign against bourgeois cosmopolitanism (from 1948) claimed many Jews among its victims. Stalin seemed to be preparing a new bloody purge of his party when he died.

THE POST-STALIN EPOCH

As soon as the tyrant's controlling hand was removed, pressure groups began to form within the establishment. A struggle for succession developed, in which the security police soon lost power. In 1955, Khrushchev, who identi-fied himself primarily with the Communist party apparatus, curbed the eco-nomic managers whose chief patron was G. M. Malenkov. Two years later he humiliated Marshal Zhukov, the army leader who had previously helped defeat an effort to unseat him attempted by conservatives in the Presidium.[1] The Leninist principle of party primacy was thus established. Khrushchev may have decided that terrorist excesses were counterproductive. In any case, he found it politically expedient to dissociate himself in part from Stalin and his crimes. Millions were released from the camps and silently rehabili-tated; but the revelations produced a shock wave that temporarily imperiled the whole Soviet edifice in Eastern Europe (as of 1956). In the Soviet Union, the regime granted certain concessions in an effort to maintain its credibility. Attempts were made to encourage more active public participation in soviets, youth organizations and trade unions, although without weakening the over-all control system. New fundamental principles of criminal law (promulgated in 1958) gave accused citizens somewhat better protection against judicial abuse. Writers and artists were afforded a little more leeway. The most pro-gressive elements in the new intelligentsia resumed their prerevolutionary role as the conscience of the nation and pressed for more freedom to discuss sensitive issues.

Their greatest success came with the publication in 1962 of Aleksandr I. Solzhenitsyn's novella *One Day in the Life of Ivan Denisovich*, which broke the taboo on mentioning the prison camps. But the censors soon stopped the leak, and none of Solzhenitsyn's major novels (let alone his documentary work, *The Gulag Archipelago*) was allowed to appear in the Soviet Union. By the mid-1960s there had emerged a democratic movement, small in numbers but rich in ideas, which comprised men and women of various national groups and religious or philosophical views. It reached its climax in 1968, when a public demonstration—the first for 40 years—was held in Moscow's Red Square to protest against Soviet intervention in Cze-choslovakia. Manuscripts circulated widely in samizdat, and a clandestine journal, *The Chronicle of Current Events*, registered repressive actions taken

[1] The Politburo bore the name of Presidium from 1952 to 1966.

by the KGB (as the security police was now called) and the courts. The authorities often ignored the new legal norms and sternly punished even those defenders of basic human and civil rights who took their stand on the provisions of the Final Act of the Helsinki Accords (1975), which the Soviet government was formally pledged to respect. A few prominent dissidents were permitted to go abroad, as were, after strong international pressure, tens of thousands of Soviet Jews; but would-be emigrants had to endure much official harrassment and the flow later diminished to a trickle.

In such matters, as in other areas of domestic policy, Brezhnev took a more consistent and harsher line than Khrushchev. There was no revival of massive terror, but neither was there any advance toward genuine discourse on matters of public concern. The political void was patched over by pompous anniversary celebrations, for example, the centennial of Lenin's birth (1970). The 60th anniversary of the Bolshevik coup in 1977 was marked by promulgation of a new Soviet constitution, which spelled out more clearly some of the citizens' rights and duties but introduced no basic changes; it was little more than a propagandist device to demonstrate the regime's purported commitment to socialist humanism. Meanwhile, Brezhnev strengthened his power base by bringing army, police and foreign affairs representatives into the Politburo, in 1973; two years later, he became a marshal of the Soviet Union, and in 1977 president.[2] This accumulation of offices was accompanied by a personality cult, but on a less grandiose scale than that fostered by his predecessors. Many functionaries appreciated the greater job security and other benefits they enjoyed under his policy of care for cadres.

Yet the apparent stability of Soviet public life concealed pressing and intractable problems. First, there was the aging of the leadership, which was scarcely consonant with revolutionary élan. At the Twentieth Congress of the CPSU in 1956, five percent of Central Committee members had been 40 or under, and nine percent were 61 or over; at the Twenty-sixth Congress, in 1981, the figures were 0.3 percent and 54 percent, the average age being 62. When Brezhnev died at 76, the surviving oligarchs played safe by choosing Andropov (69); his replacement, Chernenko, was two years older than Andropov. The old guard seemed to be clinging to power as though fearful even of their experienced middle-aged junior associates.

Second, the disaffection current among Ukrainians and other national minorities sometimes affected people in official positions; and the high birthrate in the Central Asian and other traditionally Muslim republics implicitly threatened continued control by the formally internationalist but actually Russocentric CPSU. Third, the party's ideology was becoming ossified and relativized in the thinking of ordinary citizens. It could not easily be updated and brought closer to reality without shaking the legitimacy of party rule; yet endless repetition of stereotyped exhortations and promises, couched in a wooden jargon, left many young people, in particular, bored, apathetic or indifferent. The lack of any prospect of self-generated radical change, the difficulties of daily life and the regime's failure to satisfy people's spiritual

[2]More precisely, chairman of the Presidium of the Supreme Soviet.

needs, helped to account for the high incidence of alcoholism, divorce and suicide. Some foreign observers feared for the mental health of a population that for so long had been kept artificially isolated from "harmful" external influences and subjected to intense psychological pressure—while at the same time psychiatric institutions could be used as jails for perfectly sane dissenters. The ruling elite had acquired a vested interest in the status quo and the technical means to perpetuate it. Like the czarist autocracy, it was unwilling to surrender its prerogatives voluntarily; yet a totalitarian state, even an effete one, could not readily be overthrown by revolution while its nuclear capability protected it against military defeat and allowed it to expand its power abroad. The stalemate boded no good for anyone.

FURTHER READING

Barry, Donald D. *Contemporary Soviet Politics: An Introduction*, 2nd ed. Englewood Cliffs, New Jersey: Prentice-Hall, 1982.

Bergson, Abram. *The Real National Income of Soviet Russia since 1928*. Cambridge, Massachusetts: Harvard University Press; Oxford: Oxford University Press, 1961.

Binyon, Michael. *Life in Russia*. London, 1983.

Brown, Archie et al., eds. *The Cambridge Encyclopedia of Russia and the Soviet Union*. Cambridge, 1982.

Campbell, Robert W. *Soviet Economic Power: Its Organization, Growth and Challenge*, 2nd ed. London: Macmillan, 1967.

Chamberlin, W. H. *The Russian Revolution, 1917–1921*, 2 vols. New York: Grosset and Dunlap, 1965.

Charques, R. *The Twilight of Imperial Russia*. London and New York: Oxford University Press, 1967.

Conquest, Robert. *The Great Terror*. London: Macmillan, 1968.

Fainsod, Merle. *How Russia Is Ruled*, 2nd ed. Cambridge, Massachusetts: Harvard University Press; London: Oxford University Press, 1963.

Gregory, Paul R. and Stuart, R. C. *Soviet Economic Structure and Performance*, 2nd ed. New York: Harper and Row, 1981.

Jasny, Naum. *The Socialized Agriculture of the USSR*. Stanford, California: Stanford University Press, 1949; London: Oxford University Press, 1950.

Medish, Vladimir. *The Soviet Union*, 2nd ed. Englewood Cliffs, New Jersey: Prentice-Hall, 1983.

Nove, Alec. *The Soviet Economic System*. London: Allen and Unwin; New York: Frederick A. Praeger, 1977.

———. *Stalinism and After*. London: Allen and Unwin, 1975.

Schapiro, Leonard B. *The Communist Party of the Soviet Union*. London: Methuen; New York: Vintage Books, 2nd ed., 1970.

Seton-Watson, Hugh. *The Russian Empire, 1801–1917*. London and New York: Oxford University Press, 1967.

Shub, David. *Lenin: A Biography*. London: Penguin Books, 1966.

Ulam, Adam B. *A History of Soviet Russia*. New York: Praeger, 1976.

———. *Stalin: the Man and his Era*. New York: Viking, 1973; London: Allen Lane, 1974.

Zinoviev, Alexander. *The Reality of Communism*, trans. C. Janson. London: Gollancz, 1984.

EASTERN EUROPE, 1944–85

GEOFFREY STERN

SOVIET INFLUENCE ON POSTWAR EVENTS IN EASTERN EUROPE

WHEN the Soviet Union became virtual arbiter of Eastern European affairs in the late 1940s, its behavior helped to give wider currency to a conviction many had held since the Bolshevik revolution—that the Soviet leaders aimed at world conquest and had a blueprint for the purpose. The idea that the creation of a bloc of Eastern European client states furthered Stalin's master plan was later called in question, especially by "revisionist" historians for whom the bloc was largely an improvised response to an apparently threatening international environment. If the origins of the iron curtain are still in dispute, there is no doubt of Stalin's crucial role in redrawing the map of Eastern Europe in the wake of the Red Army's advance at the end of World War II.

In July 1944, for example, Moscow, having broken with the Polish government-in-exile in London after the Katyn revelations of the year before, established its own Polish administration, the Lublin Committee, in Soviet-controlled territory. With the virtual destruction of Poland's noncommunist resistance following the Warsaw rising from August to October 1944 against the retreating German forces, Poland was assured of a pro-Soviet communist regime, despite the country's Catholic, nationalist and anticommunist traditions. By September 1944, Soviet-trained political agents were conveying instructions and financial assistance to communists in Romania and Bulgaria—pro-Axis powers that had just capitulated to the Red Army. By the end of the European war in May 1945, Soviet pressures and inducements served to raise Communist party fortunes in Hungary, Czechoslovakia and those parts of Austria and Germany under Soviet occupation. Only in Yugoslavia and Albania did communists succeed largely independently of Soviet power. In the meantime, Stalin used the understandings with his wartime allies as justification for territorial changes and political intervention. At Teheran, in November–December 1943, the Big Three had agreed to divide Europe into Anglo-American and Soviet zones of operation; at Moscow, in October 1944, Stalin and Churchill had talked informally about "spheres of influence;" and at Yalta, in February 1945, Roosevelt and Churchill had acknowledged the security interests of the Soviet Union, reached an ambiguous compromise with Stalin regarding the geographical and political con-

188

figurations of postwar Poland, and agreed to joint four-power rule over Germany.

By the time of the Potsdam conference, in July–August 1945, at which the United States and Britain accepted, if only as provisional, changes in Poland's eastern and western frontiers and conceded some at least of Moscow's territorial claims, the Soviet Union had enlarged its European domain almost to the dimensions of the Russian empire of 1914. Eastern Poland, the Baltic states, part of Finland, Bessarabia and northern Bukovina were in Soviet hands. The former Czechoslovak territory of Sub-Carpathian Ruthenia, annexed by the Hungarians in 1939, went to the Soviet Union, likewise part of northeastern Prussia. Stalin, meanwhile, in a move never formally accepted as final by the Western powers, turned over to the Poles the area east of the Oder-Neisse line as compensation for Poland's loss of eastern territory to the Soviet Union.

Whether part of a long-term strategy or not, Stalin's subsequent treatment of his Eastern European neighbors stemmed in large measure from his conception of the Soviet Union's security needs—a conception that was rooted as much in Marxist dialectic as in Russia's historical experience. After all, the Nazi invasion, which had just cost the Soviet Union some 20 million lives and the destruction of much of its industry, agriculture and transportation, had been only the latest in a series of foreign interventions launched by way of Eastern Europe. And since Stalin believed that yet another conflict with a union of capitalist powers was inevitable, he thought it vital for the governments of Eastern Europe to be kept out of the hands of what remained of the prewar generation of anti-Soviet and anticommunist leaders. At the same time, Eastern Europe was to contribute to the Soviet economic and military advance by serving as both an economic reservoir and a strategic base for the deployment of Soviet troops. These objectives would obviously be difficult to achieve unless the countries in question were led by Soviet nominees. The Communist party became Stalin's major instrument for effecting the requisite control.

To begin with, Stalin behaved with extreme caution in the area. When, for example, certain Bulgarian communists sought to establish a one-party state immediately after the liberation, Stalin dispatched Foreign Minister Molotov to dissuade them. Ironically, it was Tito's overhasty establishment of a one-party state along Stalinist lines in 1945, and his success in persuading Albania's Enver Hoxha to follow suit in 1946, that precipitated Moscow's subsequent break with Yugoslavia. The insurgence in Greece received scant assistance from Moscow after the communist revolt of December 1944.

Stalin's main reason for attempting to temper his more overzealous comrades in Eastern Europe was doubtless to avoid provoking the Western powers into a holy alliance with anticommunist forces in the region. Perhaps he also needed time to reassert his authority over the more nationally orientated communist leaders—especially those, like Tito and Hoxha, who had come to power largely without the aid of Soviet bayonets. In addition, he had to bear in mind the sheer administrative difficulty of turning over to communist control an area of such political, economic and social diversity—hence the employment, in those Eastern European countries amenable to

Soviet influence, of what the Hungarian communist leader Mátyás Rákosi termed "salami tactics," the technique of progressing slice by slice, as it were, to communist victory.

THE ESTABLISHMENT OF COMMUNIST PARTY RULE

At first, the Communist parties generally combined with Social Democratic, Liberal and other political elements on a relatively uncontroversial program for reconstruction. At the same time they spoke of "separate roads to socialism" and made strenuous efforts to win support by identifying themselves with popular aspirations. In Poland, for example, the party championed the cause of recreating the devastated capital, when other groups, more pessimistic, needed to be convinced of its feasibility. In Poland, Czechoslovakia, Yugoslavia and to a lesser extent in Hungary, the party's campaign for the expulsion of ethnic German citizens and the expropriation of their property had considerable popular appeal. Over such disputed areas as the Oder-Neisse territories, Transylvania and Macedonia, the communists of each country took an appropriately patriotic line.

At a later stage, however, the communist bid for popularity took second place to the drive to increase control over political and economic life. During this period the communists infiltrated the key ministries of security and defense, and established an extensive secret-police network. They further enhanced their power by penetrating political, economic and cultural organizations and sponsoring frequent purges against "fascists"—a term used to include most of the Communist party's influential opponents. Divisions within and among rival political groups were successfully exploited; soon the communists were able virtually to determine the leadership of the parties with which they nominally shared power. By the time of the Czechoslovak coup of February 1948, active opposition to communist rule had been more or less suppressed throughout the region.

The transition to monolithic Communist party rule did not occur at a uniform pace, and there were significant variations from one country to another. Yugoslavia and Albania, both somewhat beyond Moscow's reach geographically and hence relatively resistant to Soviet pressure, were, as we have seen, the first countries to experience communist control. Such control was reached in Poland more slowly, but at no time was there any semblance of a genuine coalition between parties. Even though, in return for recognition, the Western powers managed to secure the inclusion into the Soviet-sponsored government of a few members of the London-based Polish government-in-exile, these were heavily outnumbered and in no position to resist communist demands. The most distinguished of them, Stanisław Mikołajczyk, was forced in 1947 to flee the country after the destruction of his Peasant party. Within a year, Communist and Socialist parties had been merged into a Polish United Workers (i.e., Communist) party; other political organizations survived in name only.

The Soviet Zone of Germany, likewise, produced no "coalition of equals." After the communists failed to attract more than 20 percent of the votes cast in local elections in the autumn of 1945, the Soviet Union decided on the fusion of the Communist and Social Democratic parties in the zone, and in April 1946 set up the Socialist Unity party (SED) under Walter Ulbricht's leadership. Almost immediately, the other parties tolerated under the Soviet occupation were rendered politically impotent, and soon most of the former Social Democrats in the SED hierarchy were deprived of effective power.

In the ex-enemy states of Romania and Bulgaria, the "genuine coalition" was of short duration. In March 1945, King Michael of Romania yielded to a Soviet ultimatum and appointed Petru Groza, leader of the leftward-looking Ploughman's Front, as premier of a new National Democratic Front government in place of the former coalition. All the vital posts in the new administration were held by communists, even though in 1944 the party's membership had barely exceeded a thousand. By November 1946, the front, after much intrigue and intimidation, was able to obtain four-fifths of the parliamentary seats at a general election. Within a year, Michael abdicated, Communist and Socialist parties were merged and all effective opposition was eliminated.

If there was some logic in the communist decision to curtail parliamentary activities in countries with a strong anticommunist tradition, there was much less justification for treating Bulgaria in like fashion. After all, the Bulgarian Communist party had enjoyed considerable popularity in the days before 1923, when it was forced underground, and its Soviet connections were no obstacle in a country traditionally pro-Russian. On the other hand, Bulgaria's prewar political organizations had remained largely intact at the end of the war, and the communists felt that if they were to achieve control their rivals had to be rendered politically impotent. In January 1945, they forced the resignation of a leading official in the Agrarian Union, the most influential group in the Fatherland Front coalition, and increasingly established their own domination of the front. By October 1946, the government had been placed in the hands of the veteran communist, Georgi Dimitrov, after a communist-sponsored general election, and whatever active opposition remained crumbled after the execution in September 1947 of Nikola Petkov, leader of the Agrarian Union. Within two years, all noncommunist parties were disbanded.

In Hungary, another ex-enemy state, whose experiences under Béla Kun's Soviet-style regime in 1919 had rendered the country strongly anticommunist, the parliamentary system was allowed to survive unfettered for somewhat longer. In November 1945, a general election in which the communists polled only 17 percent of the votes brought the Smallholders (i.e., Peasant) party to power, but its authority was soon threatened when the communists formed a leftist bloc with the Social Democratic and National Peasant parties. In February 1947, Moscow ordered the arrest of the secretary general of the Smallholders party, and in May the communists forced the prime minister, Ferenc Nagy, to resign. The ruling party disintegrated and the leftist bloc, having disenfranchised some 500,000 voters and intimidated others, was able to obtain a small lead over its opponents in the general election of August 1947. Within a year, the Socialist and Communist parties were fused into a single political organization, and the last independent political party was dissolved in 1949.

It was in Czechoslovakia that the "genuine coalition" lasted longest. Here the Communist party, which had not been associated with the betrayal of the country at Munich in September 1938, became the largest parliamentary party, having obtained 38 percent of the votes in the free elections of May 1946. With its leader, Klement Gottwald, as prime minister and a number of communists in the cabinet, it looked as if communist ambitions were being achieved by parliamentary means. But when the party suffered reverses in local elections, it began police operations against its rivals, and several noncommunists resigned from Gottwald's cabinet in protest. The communists retaliated with strikes, demonstrations and the occupation of premises belonging to the noncommunist parties; and on February 25, 1948, Gottwald staged his coup, creating a new administration that omitted all those opposed to communist rule. Soon the takeover was complete. On March 10, Jan Masaryk, the noncommunist foreign minister, died after a fall (possibly induced) from his office window, and in September President Beneš died, having resigned three months earlier.

STALINIST CONTROL OVER "SATELLITE" STATES

While organized opposition to communism was crumbling, Stalin's hold over the Communist parties of Eastern Europe was being tightened. In part, this was Stalin's response to the gradual consolidation of the Western powers into a bloc dedicated to the containment of communism. For with each successive Western measure for greater economic and military security—the Truman doctrine of aid to Greece and Turkey, Marshall Plan aid, the Brussels Treaty between Britain, France and the Benelux countries, the airlift to block-aded West Berlin and the creation of NATO—Soviet control was further extended. In part, however, it was also an answer to the growing tendency of the communists in Eastern Europe to pursue their own line, as when Poland and Czechoslovakia showed interest in Marshall Plan aid, and Yugoslavia and Bulgaria moved to establish a Balkan confederation of their own design. In order to crush such independent tendencies, Stalin took measures to strengthen the Soviet Union's political, economic and military links with Eastern Europe.

The creation in September 1947 of the Cominform—an information Bureau linking the Soviet Communist party with the Communist parties of Eastern Europe, France and Italy—was symptomatic of the new trend. Perhaps more crucial in the creation of the bloc of client states were the bilateral treaties of friendship and mutual assistance between the Soviet Union and its neighbors that legalized the stationing of Soviet troops in the area and facilitated the work of the Soviet security services. At the same time an actual iron curtain of barbed wire, watchtowers and ploughed minefields was erected between Communist countries to keep them isolated both from each other and from the West. Meanwhile, the reorientation of trade following the Coordinating Committee for Export to Communist Countries (COCOM) embargo on strategic goods to Communist-dominated countries gave the Soviet Union a further lever of control over its trade-dependent allies.

Admittedly, Eastern Europe, even after the tightening of Soviet control, was never quite as monolithic as is often assumed. There were differences of emphasis as well as minor variations in political and economic institutions, reflecting to some extent divergences in national tradition. For example, in Poland, now ethnically more homogeneous than for centuries, the terror tactics employed elsewhere against both the church and the private peasant were somewhat muted as was the personality cult of Bierut, the Communist leader. However, in basic aspects of internal and external policy, similarities far outweighed differences. From 1948, a reign of terror was unleashed throughout the bloc (as in the Soviet Union itself) during which thousands of communists and noncommunists were arrested, imprisoned, or executed. The Hungarian minister of the interior, Rajk; a Bulgarian deputy prime minister, Kostov; the Czechoslovak foreign minister, Clementis; and the general secretary of the Czechoslovak Communist party, Slánský, were among those charged with "national deviationism" and executed after carefully staged show trials. Those arrested during this period included Władysław Gomułka, János Kádár, Gustáv Husák and Josef Smrkovský, who were to be prominent in post-Stalin Eastern European politics. That more than 20 Bulgarian ministers were purged is sufficient indication of the extent of the upheaval.

Not surprisingly, between 1948 and 1953 little was heard of "independent roads to socialism." Each country under Soviet control was dubbed a people's democracy—a halfway house to socialism. Each became a mere replica of the Soviet Union in political, economic and cultural life, and each modeled its constitution on the Soviet Constitution of 1936, ignoring, as did the Soviet leadership, its more liberal aspects. Most were headed by a dictator who developed his own personality cult alongside that of Stalin—for example, Hoxha of Albania, Chervenkov of Bulgaria, Gottwald of Czechoslovakia, Rákosi of Hungary, Ulbricht of East Germany (the former Soviet Zone of Germany before the collapse of the four-power administration) and Gheorghiu-Dej of Romania. All secondary schools were obliged to teach Russian, and strict censorship was imposed on all forms of literature and art. Religious activities were placed under state control and several prominent clergymen were imprisoned. Moreover, following Moscow's lead, the Eastern European countries took to persecuting Jews under the pretext of fighting Zionism—even though the Soviet Union was one of the first countries to recognize the state of Israel.

The economies of Eastern Europe were reorganized to accord with Soviet requirements. Farming began to be collectivized, and industry and trade were nationalized and regulated by Soviet-style central planning techniques. Consumer production languished, while the planners emphasized heavy industry, especially steel production. Labor discipline was tightened, and trade unions became mere transmission belts for the party line.

Given Stalin's preference for bilateral rather than multilateral ties, little use was made of the Council for Mutual Economic Assistance (COMECON), created in January 1949 ostensibly for facilitating economic cooperation between bloc members. Nonetheless, by the time of Stalin's death in March 1953 their economic relationships had been completely reorientated, with little more than a quarter of their total trade done outside the bloc. In the meantime, they had become increasingly dependent on the Soviet Union's vast market, its technology, credits and raw materials. But their dependence enabled Moscow to weight the terms of trade heavily in its favor—e.g., buying Polish coal at a fraction of the world price and overcharging Hungary for iron ore. The Soviet Union also took the lion's share of the profits of the joint stock companies established to manage former enemy property in East Germany, Romania and Hungary, even though the Eastern Europeans had contributed most of the capital. Finally, the heavy reparations Moscow exacted from East Germany, Hungary and Romania meant the stripping of assets and large-scale transfers of resources.

Yugoslavia

Stalin's chain of satellite states had, however, one weak link—Yugoslavia. Having won national power largely through his own efforts as a wartime partisan leader, Tito did not feel as beholden to Moscow as did many fellow Communists. Moreover, his original admiration for Stalin began to wane when the Soviet leader appeared to make a deal with Churchill regarding Yugoslavia's future and refused to back either the country's irredentist claims against Austria and Italy or its one-party socialist system, introduced without consultation with Moscow in 1945. Soviet-Yugoslav economic relations and the fate of the abortive Balkan Confederation were further irritants; but when Stalin recruited Yugoslavs to subvert the Tito regime, the simmering dispute proceeded to open rupture and in June 1948 Yugoslavia was expelled from the Cominform. A Communist embargo on trade with Yugoslavia and other pressures organized from Moscow occasioned a reorientation of Belgrade's policies and alignments. Geographical distance, Tito's political and military repute, and Western financial assistance enabled Yugoslavia to develop the first independent and viable Marxist-Leninist alternative to the Soviet model. In place of Stalin's centralized bureaucracy, Yugoslavia began to devolve much economic and some political power to the constituent regions and gradually replaced the command economy, forced industrialization and collectivization with a decentralized, socialist market economy. As against Stalin's monolithic conception of communism, Tito argued for the independence of each communist country and party.

Continued pressure from his former communist allies led Tito at first into a pro-Western stance, and in 1954 Yugoslavia joined Greece and Turkey (both NATO members) to form the Balkan Pact. In subsequent years, as relations with Moscow somewhat improved, Tito's Yugoslavia sought a more equidistant stance between the power blocs—a position that was to be reflected in Belgrade's sponsorship of the nonaligned movement of developing countries. Thus, even though it was not until 1956 that "polycentrism" entered the political vocabulary, Tito was already indicating the possibility of independent centers of communist decision making and ideology by the time Stalin died.

THE REVOLUTION OF RISING EXPECTATIONS

After Stalin's death in March 1953, his successors in the Kremlin tried to establish a new relationship with the bloc. As at home, so throughout Eastern Europe the power of the Soviet security police was curbed and many of its agents recalled. Economic exploitation was reduced, and Moscow now seemed willing to concede a measure of diversity in the region as it took stock of its changing interests in the world at large. For example, in Hungary during Imre Nagy's first premiership (July 1953 to March 1955), it encouraged a New Course of economic and political development far more radical than that in the Soviet Union. For Nagy shifted the emphasis from heavy industry to agriculture and the production of consumer goods, ended forcible collectivization and allowed peasants to set up small commercial undertakings. He also permitted some freedom of expression and movement, while legal procedures slowly began to replace police despotism.

But Stalin's demise had also generated the kind of unrest characteristic of revolutions of rising expectations. In June 1953, there were workers' demonstrations in Plzeň and other Czech and Slovak towns, and a revolt in East Berlin that could only be quelled with the aid of Soviet troops. But neither this exercise of Soviet power nor the creation in May 1955 of a formal Eastern European alliance—the Warsaw Treaty Organization—silenced the dissidents. And after Khrushchev's efforts to embrace Tito, his endorsement of "different roads to socialism" during his visit to Belgrade in May 1955 and his denunciation of Stalin at the Soviet Communist party's 20th Congress in February 1956, unrest mounted. After all, those communists punished only a few years earlier for their "Titoism" had not yet been rehabilitated, and Stalin's nominees were still in power.

In Albania, Bulgaria, East Germany and Romania, the party rode out the crisis by keeping a tight rein on dissidents and finding scapegoats to demote for their "errors" during the period of the "cult of personality." In Czechoslovakia, on the other hand, intellectual discontent was allowed to surface, but events in neighboring Poland and Hungary led the party to impose new restrictions in the summer of 1956.

THE POLISH OCTOBER

In Poland, the regime was already both divided and under heavy criticism as a result of the revelations of a security police chief, Colonel Światło, who defected to the United States in 1953. But the disaffection became much more visible after Khrushchev's denunciation of Stalin, the death in Moscow in March 1956 of the Polish leader, Bierut, and the vain attempt by Khrushchev to influence the Polish succession. The new party chief, Ochab, bowing to popular pressure, disregarded the residual Stalinists in the leadership and propelled the party in the direction of reform. Significantly, the trial of workers whose strike in Poznań in June 1956 had turned into an insurrection was open to Western journalists and was conducted with scrupulous fairness. Each of the accused had an able defense lawyer, and most were given light sentences or acquitted. Nonetheless, party credibility was low and it appeared that only the reinstatement of the former secretary general, Władysław Gomułka, imprisoned for four years for his nationalist views, could restore communist self-respect and earn the confidence of the country. On the other hand, his return to power was strongly opposed by Moscow, and in October 1956, Khrushchev arrived in Warsaw with Molotov, Mikoyan, Kaganovich and several Soviet generals to try to reestablish Moscow's authority and to curb the liberalization process. But the Poles, enjoying Chinese and Yugoslav support, refused to retreat, and issued counterthreats following reports of Soviet troop movements in and around the country. In the end, Warsaw's firmness combined with its pledge to maintain communist control and allegiance to the Warsaw Pact led to Moscow's acceptance of Gomułka's leadership and his plans for continued reform. It was a turning point in Eastern European history. Henceforth, Moscow could no longer expect total subservience from its communist clients.

THE HUNGARIAN UPRISING

Yet within two weeks of Gomułka's victory, Khrushchev was to demonstrate the limits of Eastern European autonomy. The test was to come in Hungary, which had been seething with discontent since March 1955, when party leader Rákosi ousted Nagy from the premiership and attempted to put his reforms into reverse. By June 1956, the Hungarians, both outside and within the party, had become so antagonistic to Rákosi that he was being openly attacked in the party press and could no longer maintain control. To try to defuse the crisis the Soviet leaders agreed to Rákosi's removal, but in substituting Gerő, one of Rákosi's close associates, they merely intensified national frustration. In the months that followed, the pattern of communist rule began to disintegrate, amid demonstrations of solidarity with the Poles and demands for the return of Nagy and a free and independent Hungary. But when Gerő called on Soviet troops to aid Hungary's security police (AVH) in putting down what appeared to be a popular uprising, there was a critical spiral of violence that Nagy, restored to the premiership on October 24th, was powerless to stop. Nor could he resist, even had he wanted to, the popular demands for the removal of Soviet forces, Hungary's withdrawal from the Warsaw Pact and the reintroduction of the multiparty system Hungary had known in the immediate postwar years. But coming so soon after the Kremlin's capitulation in Warsaw, these developments constituted for Moscow a grave ideological and political threat to the bloc, at a time of apparent Western military superiority. Hence ensued the suppression by Soviet tanks of the Nagy administration, its bloody aftermath and the reinstatement of party rule under János Kádár, a reform-minded communist who had deserted Nagy.

Although Moscow's military intervention in Hungary was not to be its last in Eastern Europe, it did not presage a return to Stalinist hegemony. For the Soviet role in international society had been considerably enlarged since Stalin's day, and the Soviet leaders knew that without a drastic overhaul of its relations with Eastern Europe the Soviet Union would be handicapped in its bid to convince the peoples of the developing countries of the superiority of the socialist system. In any case, with the nuclear stalemate and the development of East–West economic ties, Eastern Europe no longer had quite the same critical importance for Soviet policy makers as in the Stalinist era. There were, moreover, the daunting political and economic costs of the use of force in Eastern Europe which made it an increasingly unattractive option for Moscow. In addition, the politics of the widening Sino-Soviet rift and the emergence of a younger generation of more nationally minded communists in Eastern Europe facilitated political and economic differentiation. On the other hand, Moscow could not be indifferent to developments in an area so closely bound up with its perceptions of security, welfare and prestige—and hence its periodic and forceful reminders since 1956 of its determination to exercise at least the power of veto.

POLYCENTRISM, 1956–68

Despite the suppression of the Hungarian revolution, the trend toward greater autonomy in Eastern Europe survived. In Poland, Gomułka decollectivized agriculture and permitted some decentralization of industry and a limited return to private enterprise in the trades and professions. Religious and other traditional values were allowed freer expression, as the church won back some of the rights of instruction and dissemination lost in the Stalinist era, and the arts were freed from the constraints of socialist realism. In foreign affairs, too, Poland showed some autonomy as it dissociated itself from the rest of the bloc in the U.N. vote on Hungary and secured U.S. economic assistance. But soon, the Polish October was in retreat, and as Gomułka sought to mend his fences with Moscow, others began to step out of line.

By the early 1960s, those most anxious to chart their own course were the dogmatists opposed to Khrushchev's renewed campaign for de-Stalinization. In 1961, Albania chose to link its fortunes with Peking and break with Moscow rather than submit to Khrushchev's revisionism. An attempted coup against Albania's leader, Enver Hoxha, following an alleged plot to incorporate Albania into Yugoslavia, and severe economic pressure coordinated through COMECON had brought matters to a head, while Tirana's resistance was facilitated by its geographical distance from the Soviet Union. Behind the decision lay Hoxha's determination to maintain tight control of his small, mountainous and impoverished country with its history of foreign occupation and tribal strife.

Though no other country went to such extremes, Khrushchev's summons to hasten de-Stalinization brought resistance from East Germany and Romania. Ulbricht completed forced collectivization of agriculture in 1960, thereby unleashing a chain of events that eventuated in a further tightening of political and economic controls and an added boost to the already massive exodus of able-bodied East Germans worried about Khrushchev's intentions toward West Berlin. It took the erection of the Berlin Wall in August 1961 to stem the flow of refugees.

In Romania, Gheorge Gheorgiu-Dej withstood Soviet demands with an unexpected display of national self-assertion. If the withdrawal of Soviet troops in 1958 provided the opportunity, Moscow's attempt to persuade Bucharest to abandon plans for rapid industrialization to become an agricultural reserve for COMECON provided the pretext. Romania refused the role of minor partner in a Soviet-sponsored scheme for integrating the economies of Eastern Europe, and the project had to be shelved. But the successful use of the veto over Soviet policy had set a precedent on which Gheorgiu-Dej was anxious to capitalize. It suggested a way of courting domestic popularity without the need to relax political or economic control—and its apparent benefits encouraged Nicolae Ceauşescu, who inherited the party leadership in 1965, to make a still more ambitious bid for national autonomy. What had begun as a polemic with Moscow and East Berlin over COMECON widened into a rift over the running of the Warsaw Pact, and soon Romania was at odds with both Moscow and Budapest over territorial questions—in particular, Bessarabia and Transylvania. Romania was further estranged from its allies by its decision to maintain friendly ties with Peking and Tirana, to recognize Bonn and upgrade its embassy in Tel Aviv after the Six-Day War of 1967. Such policies accorded with Romania's determination to diversify its economic and political contacts so as to give added protection to its now much vaunted sovereignty.

Though Romania's southern neighbor, Bulgaria, proved a more reliable Soviet ally it, too, had periods of disaffection. In the late 1950s, Sofia had a brief flirtation with China's "great leap forward" policy, and while Khrushchev succeeded in bolstering the fortunes of the pliable Todor Zhivkov, who in 1962 emerged as both party leader and prime minister, Bulgarian communist politics were to be permeated with factionalism, culminating in an attempted coup in April 1965. In the meantime, Bulgaria alternated between de-Stalinization and re-Stalinization, while in foreign policy it was slow to effect a policy of peaceful coexistence either with the West or with neighboring Yugoslavia.

Ironically, the country that most eagerly seized on Khrushchev's renewed call for de-Stalinization was Hungary, which had suffered four years of intense repression after the revolution. At the end of 1960, however, the terror was suddenly lifted and soon it was Hungary rather than Poland, now retreating further into communist orthodoxy, which led the reformists within the bloc. Most of those arrested in connection with the 1956 events were released, many Soviet advisers to the Hungarian government were returned to Moscow and increasingly merit rather than political reliability became the key to promotion. Such measures were a prerequisite of the introduction in 1967 of a New Economic Mechanism to decentralize economic decision making. And though the Kádár regime remained a firm supporter of Moscow in foreign policy, it allowed greater opportunities than its allies for foreign travel and at the same time began to intensify its economic contacts with the West.

THE PRAGUE SPRING

The one country that failed to gauge accurately the limits of Moscow's tolerance of polycentrism was, paradoxically, the one with the most pro-Soviet and procommunist tradition—Czechoslovakia. Here, de-Stalinization had been slow, but in 1963 a major economic crisis combined with a sudden upsurge of national feeling among Slovak communist intellectuals led President Novotný to undertake a policy of reform. But it was not enough to satisfy popular aspirations for change, especially when the economy continued to stagnate—its problems compounded by an aid and trade policy determined largely in Moscow. By the end of 1967, after brutal displays of police power against demonstrating students and workers, discontent reached its climax. Visiting Prague in December, the Soviet leader, Leonid Brezhnev, who had succeeded Khrushchev in October 1964, realized the dangers and gave the signal for Novotný's removal. In the absence of any clear successor, Alexander Dubček, the party leader of Slovakia, emerged to lead the country.

Within days there began what was to become known as the Prague Spring—a ground swell of seemingly unstoppable reform. The lifting of censorship and of restrictions on freedom of assembly, together with the appearance of noncommunist pressure groups brought a flurry of discussion and debate, much of it critical of the communist system. The party itself was in process of transformation as many of the old guard Stalinists were either retired or else threatened with defeat in the projected secret ballots. In the economy, steps toward the decentralization of decision making along Hungarian lines were already far advanced, as were the plans for large-scale Western credits. Constitutionally, the Slovaks were promised a better deal in a proposed Federal Union of Czechs and Slovaks.

In the face of such upheaval, Dubček's repeated assurances that the one-party system and Czechoslovakia's loyal adherence to the Warsaw Pact would be maintained, carried little conviction with its more hard-line allies, who in any case had reason to fear that the Prague Spring might prove contagious. In Poland, slogans in support of Czechoslovakia had been in evidence in the serious rioting in the major universities in March. In the Soviet Union, the trials of liberal writers were provoking criticism from intellectuals, while in East Germany there was the fear that Prague's new trade policies would give West Germany a dangerously strong foothold in Eastern Europe. Hence there was the Soviet-led invasion of August 20–21, the bloodless but thoroughgoing purge that followed it and the Brezhnev Doctrine of the "limited sovereignty" of socialist states by which it was justified. At last the Soviet Union had clarified its position on polycentrism. Separate roads to socialism were permitted, but Moscow reserved the right to intervene in countries where there were threats to the Communist party's monopoly of political power, to its democratic centralist structure, or to its alliance commitments.

POLYCENTRISM AFTER 1968

The invasion of Czechoslovakia, involving East German, Polish, Bulgarian, Hungarian as well as Soviet forces, brought existing rifts in European communism to a head. Immediately afterward, its major communist critics, fearing that the Brezhnev Doctrine might be used against them, made significant shifts in foreign policy. Albania formally left the Warsaw Pact and began improving state-to-state relations with Yugoslavia and cultivating ties with Greece, Italy and a number of other Western countries. Romania held a series of joint consultations with Yugoslavia, possibly with a view to a secret alliance. In addition, having welcomed President Nixon to Bucharest in August 1969, President Ceauşescu may have acted as an intermediary to facilitate the first formal contacts between Washington and Peking in 1971. Yugoslavia intensified its contacts with the nonaligned and began to patch up its long-standing quarrel with China, which was in the process of launching a diplomatic offensive to outflank Moscow.

As the communist opponents of the Brezhnev Doctrine strengthened ties with each other, they also sought to tighten ideological and political controls at home. In Yugoslavia, however, the process was delayed. Indeed, the trend toward greater democratization, decentralization and regional autonomy, which had gathered pace after the disgrace in 1966 of the secret-police chief and vice president, Aleksander Ranković, persisted for some considerable time. But in 1971, President Tito felt obliged to stem the process of liberalization that he now saw as threatening Yugoslavia's residual socialist structure and national integrity. Mounting regional and ethnic rivalries, seccessionist threats, runaway inflation and the need to provide for orderly succession caused some recentralization of political and economic life, the replacement of the elected governments of Croatia and Serbia and a purge of unreliable officials. Among Moscow's closest allies, too, there was a general tightening of controls in the immediate aftermath of the intervention. However, save for Czechoslovakia, the renewal of constraints was relatively short-lived. In Poland, the widespread resentment at the country's role in the forcible normalization of Czechoslovakia only further increased the growing gulf between a government that had failed to live up to expectations and its people, and fueled the sentiments that in December 1970 erupted in the bloody riots in Gdańsk and Szczecin that eventually toppled Gomułka. His successor, Edward Gierek, appeared more conciliatory, and Moscow approved his more easygoing approach. Moscow also warmed to the Hungarian economic reform, which was serving to raise living standards. Soon, it was giving cautious welcome to a Bulgarian economic experiment that, among other things, allowed more private enterprise in the countryside.

The Kremlin's newfound tolerance may have stemmed in part from the conviction that after the events of 1968, both communists and noncommunists now understood and would respect the Soviet stake in Eastern Europe. But there were two additional and related considerations: the need to encourage dynamism in the flagging economies of the bloc lest another economic crisis should spark off a further political conflagration; and the economic as well as political value of maintaining East–West détente, which had been developing apace since 1970, when Bonn initiated a series of agreements seemingly recognizing the territorial status quo in Eastern Europe.

However, Moscow soon became increasingly ambivalent about the impact of détente on Eastern Europe. On the one hand, East–West trade was flourishing, and generous Western credits and technology transfers were helping to bolster communist economic prospects. On the other hand, this burgeoning of East–West commerce was undermining Moscow's attempts at strengthening socialist integration, reaffirmed in COMECON's comprehensive program of 1971. And when Moscow's ambitions seemed further threatened—as the Helsinki accords, which had concluded the 1975 Conference on Security and Cooperation in Europe, became a rallying cry for the promotion of human rights rather than acceptance of political boundaries in Eastern Europe—Moscow again called for tighter discipline and cohesion. A sudden deterioration in the international political climate and an upsurge of dissident activity in the Warsaw Pact's vital northern tier ensured that Moscow's call did not go unheeded.

Politically, relations between Moscow and Washington had been under strain since the fall of President Nixon, Brezhnev's partner in détente. But with the superpowers increasingly at odds, East–West relations in general suffered, while the slackening of interbloc commerce toward the end of the decade—in part the product of adverse trends in the world economy in the wake of successive oil-price rises—only made things worse. Against such a background, the Kremlin's renewed emphasis on inter-COMECON joint ventures now seemed attractive, even to Romania. And as human rights activists in Czechoslovakia, East Germany and elsewhere began taking the provisions of the Helsinki Final Act a little too literally, their governments moved to close ranks politically as well. Developments in Poland in 1980–81 gave urgency to the move toward greater bloc coordination.

THE RISE AND FALL OF SOLIDARITY

The emergence of Solidarity, Poland's independent trade union, after a series of strikes in the Baltic ports prompted by an unheralded set of government-induced price rises, reflected a serious crisis of confidence in the communist system. Economically, the country was a shambles, with wages and production costs soaring above official price levels, and productivity in decline; peasants hoarding their surpluses; officials squandering much of the country's $27 billion credits on personal luxuries and uneconomic projects; and adverse terms of trade intensifying the already severe economic imbalances. Politically, lacking any legal opposition party, Poland's workers needed a safety valve for their growing frustrations, and they found it in Solidarity, whose de facto existence Gierek recognized in the Gdańsk agreements of August 1980. Soon, Solidarity had an estimated 10 million members—one-third of the population—and became the vehicle for a nationwide and largely spontaneous struggle for a significant share of power. But ready resort by Poland's workers and peasants to striking merely compounded the legacy of years of inept administration, contributing to a further economic decline and a possible threat to public order.

Moscow, Prague and East Berlin made no secret of their fears, and called on party leader Stanisław Kania, who had replaced Gierek in September 1980, to reestablish firm control. Instead, however, the party, itself in ferment, introduced reforms at its Ninth Congress, in July 1981, designed to give the rank and file more say. Moscow's temptation to apply the Brezhnev Doctrine must have been strong, but the difficulties in applying it to a country like Poland were formidable. In any case, there was a potential strong man in reserve. Defense Minister Gen. Wojciech Jaruzelski had become prime minister in February 1981 and party leader the following October. On December 13, alleging that the country stood in mortal danger, he became Eastern Europe's first communist leader to promulgate martial law.

Moscow's key demand was swiftly met. Solidarity was banned, as was KOR, an organization of intellectuals that had been assisting dissident workers since the riots of July 1976; and though Solidarity still exists underground, its ability to marshal resistance has been steadily undermined by resolute government action, which continues despite the lifting of martial law in July 1983. Military-style government has had a paradoxical effect on the economy. It has contributed to a tightening of labor discipline and a lowering of expectations, and has facilitated the cutting of subsidies as a prerequisite of thoroughgoing economic reform. But it has also increased worker resentment, and has engendered Western sanctions for which the infusion of Soviet and allied credits cannot wholly compensate. Thus, although there are signs of economic improvement, many of the problems Gen. Jaruzelski sought to solve persist and have a knock-on effect throughout COMECON, at a time of declining growth rates and mounting debts.

With the countries of Eastern Europe having to cope with economic stringency and yet another crisis of political legitimacy, these are testing times. Most face dynamic forces impelling them in the direction of reform. But there are constraints—the product, in part, of their political, economic and military interdependence, in part of the Brezhnev Doctrine, which survives its creator and his successors and gains in importance in times of East–West tension. Thus, no matter how far Eastern Europe evolves from satellite status and prepares to jettison discarded ideological baggage, it remains in the shadow of a superpower to which it owes its political system and on which, in the final analysis, its fate must largely depend.

FURTHER READING

Bornstein, M. et al., eds. *East–West Relations and the Future of Eastern Europe: Politics and Economics.* London: George Allen and Unwin, 1981.

Brzezinski, Z. K. *The Soviet Bloc: Unity and Conflict.* Cambridge, Massachusetts: Harvard University Press; London: Oxford University Press, 1960.

Clawson, R. W. and Kaplan, L. S., eds. *The Warsaw Pact: Political Purpose and Military Means.* Wilmington, Delaware: Scholarly Resources, 1982.

Dawisha K. and Hanson, P., eds. *Soviet-East European Dilemmas: Coercion, Competition and Consent.* London: Heinemann, 1981.

Djilas, M. *Conversations with Stalin.* New York: Harcourt Brace; London: Rupert Hart-Davis, 1962.

Fejtö, F. *A History of the Peoples Democracies: Eastern Europe since Stalin.* Harmondsworth: Penguin, 1974.

Fischer-Galati, G. S., ed. *Eastern Europe in the 1980's.* London: Croom Helm, 1981.

Gati, C., ed. *The International Politics of Eastern Europe.* New York: Praeger, 1976.

Jones, C. D. *Soviet Influence in Eastern Europe: Political Autonomy and the Warsaw Pact.* New York: Praeger, 1981.

Kuhlman, J., ed. *The Foreign Policies of Eastern Europe: Domestic and International Determinants.* Leiden: Sijthoff, 1978.

McCauley, M., ed. *Communist Power in Europe, 1944–49.* London: Macmillan, 1977.

Micunovic, V. *Moscow Diary.* London: Chatto and Windus, 1980.

Mlnar, Z. *Nightfrost in Prague.* New York: Karz, 1980.

Narkiewicz, O. *Marxism and the Reality of Power 1919–1980.* London: Croom Helm, 1981.

Neuberger, E. and Tyson, L., eds. *The Impact of International Economic Disturbances on the Soviet Union and Eastern Europe.* New York and Oxford: Pergamon, 1980.

Polonsky, A. *The Little Dictators: The History of Eastern Europe since 1918.* London: Routledge and Kegan Paul, 1975.

Rakowska-Harmstone, T. *Communism in Eastern Europe.* 2nd ed. Bloomington: Indiana University Press; Manchester: Manchester University Press, 1984.

Remington, R. A. *The Warsaw Pact: Case Studies in Communist Conflict Resolution.* Cambridge, Massachusetts: MIT Press, 1971.

Valenta, J. *Soviet Intervention in Czechoslovakia 1968: Anatomy of a Decision.* Baltimore and London: Johns Hopkins University Press, 1979.

PART TWO

POLITICAL

GENERAL

IDEOLOGY AND POLITICS

MARCUS WHEELER

INTRODUCTION

THE role of ideology in politics and society often appears mysterious to natives of the Anglo-Saxon countries. This is because the concept (which stems from Germany) is associated with a system-building style in philosophy that has largely been discarded in these countries in the last 50 years and with a totalitarian practice in politics that is felt to be still more alien. Yet anyone who has any interest in the Soviet Union or other communist states is likely to seek answers to such questions as "What is the practical impact of the communist creed?" and "Do the citizens of these states really believe in communism?" And this is what the study of communist ideology is about. Unfortunately, the simple essence of the matter is befogged by the special jargon employed by communist ideologists themselves, and any attempt to assess the function of ideology in the Soviet Union or other communist states today presupposes some understanding of the basis of their official creed—Marxism–Leninism.

THE PHILOSOPHY OF MARXISM

The core of the philosophical teaching of Karl Marx is what is known as dialectical materialism (or, in relation to the philosophy of history in particular, historical materialism). Marx opposed, on the one hand, the idealism of the German school led by Hegel, which was in the ascendant in his own formative years and, on the other hand, what he called "mechanical materialism"—in effect, the mainstream of French and British 18th-century philosophy. He sought to refute the former in much the same way as Dr. Johnson thought that he himself had refuted the idealism of Bishop Berkeley—by suggesting simply that it contradicted common sense. As his friend and collaborator, Friedrich Engels, put it, Marx's achievement was to recognize "the palpable but previously overlooked fact that men must first of all eat, drink, have shelter and clothing, therefore must work, before they can fight for domination, pursue politics, religion, philosophy, etc." In short, *cogito quia sum* as opposed to *cogito ergo sum*—or, as Marx himself expressed it, "it is not the consciousness of men that determines their existence, but, on the contrary, their social existence determines their consciousness." From this observation springs the notion, which is central to Marx's thought and links his philosophy with his analysis of the politics and economics of his time, that the essence of social reality is productive activity. This idea also influenced Marx's opposition to the classical form of materialism, which portrayed reality as something both static and independent of human perception. And, although for Marx the basic reality was matter and not spirit, his criticism of this body of doctrine owed most of all to the Hegelian idea of "dialectics"—hence the phrase "dialectical materialism."

Dialectics is defined by Engels as "the science of the general laws of the motion and development of Nature, human society, and thought." But this is an unilluminating account of a conception that amounts, crudely, to the following propositions: First, change or process is a universal feature of the world; second, the world-process comprises not random change but an advance from the less perfect to the more perfect; third, this progress is not direct but proceeds through tensions between conflicting forces and the resolution of these tensions. For Hegel, the development of the ultimate reality—Spirit, or the Absolute Idea—was manifested in the history of human society in the successive rise and fall of nations (from ancient China, through Greece and Rome, to his own Prussia). For Marx, however, the crucial "unit" was the social class and the crucial conflict the struggle between classes that, at certain points in history, explodes as a result of an intolerable disharmony between means and methods of production and the property relations prevailing at that stage of society. But whereas from the conception of history as development through conflict and synthesis, Hegel drew the conservative conclusion that the society of his own day and nation was the highest manifestation of the universal Spirit, Marx and his adherents saw in it on the contrary the justification for revolution. One more cataclysm at least, was scheduled, namely the decisive conflict between the two currently opposed classes—bourgeoisie and proletariat—which would result in the achievement of the final goal, the classless society. Why should this society be a *communist* society? Because, according to Marx, the new system of production ushered in by the Industrial Revolution was already a "socialized" one, in which the product was the fruit of the pooled labor of the many and not, as in the old handicraft economy, of the special skill of one person—hence, individual ownership of this product, or appropriation of the market value thereof, was no longer in order. Moreover, the classless society resulting from the triumph of the proletariat would also neatly demonstrate another aspect of dialectics, the "negation of the negation." As the system of private property had "negated" the primitive communism that (according to the largely speculative anthropology of the mid-19th century) prevailed in early human society, so, in its turn, it would be "negated" by communism of a higher type.

Mention should be made, finally, of one aspect of Marxian thought that springs directly from its Hegelian antecedents, but which has resulted in the seemingly cynical indifference of some of Marx's followers to the choice of means in achieving their goal. This is his relativism with regard to values, which he expressed in the proposition that beliefs about good and evil (and, by implication, social, political, and aesthetic values and concepts) are in no sense absolute but are inevitably a reflection of class interests. Marx did indeed criticize the French socialist thinkers of the early 19th century as "Utopians," because their condemnation of existing society sprang from abstract notions of justice and injustice rather than from "scientific" study of the "laws" of social development; and, conversely, his advocacy of the interests of the proletariat was ostensibly based on an unsentimental conviction that history was on the side of that class. Marx's own life, however, to some extent belies his reasoning, in that he was clearly motivated by a humane detestation of the evils of the raw industrialized society of his time and by an idealistic longing for a better future for humanity.

MARXISM AND LENINISM IN RUSSIA

In the movement of radical thought and of action against the czarist system that developed in Russia during the 19th century, Marxism was a foreign and unexpected growth. Until the last quarter of the century, the economy of the vast Russian empire remained overwhelmingly agrarian. Industry was concentrated in two or three centers and, excluding certain special branches (such as the Tula armaments works and the Urals metal-working industry), the workers were recent immigrants from the country who remained solidly peasant in outlook. Moreover, among the radical intelligentsia who headed the movement for reform and later—disillusioned with the emancipation of the serfs and other reforms conceded from above in the 1860s—for more extreme action, a majority retained an uncritical faith in the peasant commune as the ready-made instrument for securing "Russian socialism." It is a measure of the insignificant impact made by the "specter of communism" that the first volume of Marx's *Capital* was able to be published in Russia in 1872 without hindrance from the czar's censors. The greater number even of the "Westernist" intellectuals continued to believe that Russia could, with the aid of the commune, reach communism bypassing the capitalist stage (and, ironically, Marx himself gave qualified assent to this view). Debate about this question, however, was soon overtaken by events; the Russian Marxists, whose movement gained momentum rapidly after 1880 with the failure of attempts to "revolutionize" the peasantry or to hasten change by individual acts of terror, rightly judged that capitalism had already arrived. As one of the early leaders, Georgy Plekhanov, put it, "Is Russia to go through the school of capitalism?" We may answer: "Why should she not complete the schooling on which she has already entered?"

What of Lenin's contribution to the communist ideology? The official present-day designation of the latter as "Marxism–Leninism" may be misleading, for Lenin (1870–1924, real name: Vladimir Ilyich Ulyanov) made no appreciable addition to the philosophy of dialectical materialism. His great contribution lay in the field of political theory, in formulating the strategy of revolution and of the transition through revolution from capitalism to communism—a branch of the ideology now known as "scientific communism." The seminal elements of Lenin's thought are often obscured by the turgid style and polemical character of his voluminous writings, a large part of which took the form of ad hominem diatribes; but his most important theoretical statements are to be found in two works—*What Is to be Done?*

(1902) and *The State and Revolution* (1917). In the former, he asserted (in opposition to the so-called economists) that the revolutionary movement must be guided by a revolutionary political theory and not reduce itself to an opportunist workers' struggle merely for improved economic conditions; and he expounded his view of the revolutionary organization as a tightly knit clandestine party network, whose ranks must be limited to dedicated professionally trained revolutionaries. In the latter, he expounded and expanded the views of Marx and Engels on the need for violence in bringing about the replacement of the bourgeois state by the proletarian state; on the functioning of the "dictatorship of the proletariat," which was to ensure the suppression of the bourgeoisie on the morrow of the revolution; on the nature of socialist democracy; on the phases of the transition to full communism; and on the eventual "withering away" of the state. These are the doctrines that may properly be called "Leninism."

IDEOLOGY AND POLITICS TODAY

Since the death of Marx, Engels and Lenin, and since the Russian Revolution, the principles constituting communist ideology have undergone certain modifications—on the one hand, as a result of the pressure of external circumstances that its originators could not or did not foresee; on the other hand, as a result of what is euphemistically known as the "creative development of Marxism–Leninism." Lenin himself in 1921 sanctioned, albeit as a temporary expedient, a departure from ideology in initiating the New Economic Policy, which provided for a limited reintroduction of private economic enterprise. Stalin is considered in his later years to have jettisoned Marxist –Leninist principles in the administration of the country in favor of "subjective" doctrines prompted by a paranoid determination to maintain by whatever means his own personal power against enemies, real or imagined. The posthumous condemnation of Stalin in 1956 was followed by a much-publicized reintroduction of "Leninist norms" in the direction of the country's affairs; and Khrushchev in large measure rehabilitated ideological indoctrination as a substitute for terror. Yet he, too, after his fall from power in 1964, was charged with wanton tampering with hallowed Leninist principles. His successors, Leonid Brezhnev, Yuri Andropov and Konstantin Chernenko, died in office and have not (to date at least) been accused of excesses or aberrations. Brezhnev was politically and temperamentally a more cautious and less colorful man than Khrushchev, and he took care to respect "the norms of party life." Vain enough, however, to seek a niche in the Marxist –Leninist pantheon, he was responsible for the promulgation, in 1977, of a new Soviet constitution, the preamble to which contained the claim— seemingly intended to register an advance on that of 1936—that the Soviet Union was now "a developed socialist society." Nor was this all; in his report to the 26th Congress of the CPSU in 1981 (the last of his lifetime), Brezhnev spoke of the necessity "of restructuring—yes, that was not a slip of the tongue, I said restructuring—many sectors and areas of ideological work"; and the Congress approved a resolution instructing the Central Committee to draft a new party program to replace the one adopted in 1961—a document imbued with Khrushchev's lofty but perfectionist eschatology (see below).

How far does ideology at present impinge on the formulation of internal or foreign policy? How far does it affect the lives of ordinary people? Before an attempt is made to answer such questions, it should be noted that, in the Soviet Union, the term "ideology" has both a wider and a narrower meaning. In the former, more familiar sense, it connotes a whole body of philosophical, political, economic, ethical and aesthetic doctrine. In the narrower usage, it relates to the application of such doctrine to day-to-day life. Thus, the party program adopted in 1961 specifies as the principal element of ideological activities "the inculcation in all the working people of a spirit of high principle and of dedication to communism and of a communist attitude to work and the economy of the society, the complete overcoming of relics of bourgeois views and mores, the all-around, harmonious development of the personality, and the creation of a genuine wealth of spiritual culture." Shorn of detail, this amounts to what is usually described as the "formation of the new person."

"Creative development of Marxism–Leninism" may be illustrated, at a fairly rarefied level, by the doctrine of phases in the building of communism and of the corresponding role of the "dictatorship of the proletariat." Marx, as far as can be discerned, saw the transition period between the overthrow of capitalism and the achievement of communism as a single phase. Lenin, however, developed the idea of two phases—the first, lower phase being the building of *socialism*, marked by the termination of private ownership, the conclusion of the struggle between "antagonistic" classes and the stabilization of society on the basis of the formula "From each according to his ability, to each according to his work" (as opposed to the formula for *communism* of ". . . to each according to his needs"). This milestone was deemed to have been reached in the Soviet Union in 1936. Nevertheless, authoritative documents continued until after the death of Stalin (in 1953) to lay down that the dictatorship of the proletariat shall remain in operation until the achievement of full communism. Khrushchev, however, inspired a new formula: the need for the dictatorship of the proletariat terminates with the achievement of *socialism* and thereafter gives way to "the state of the whole people." This change of formulation, which was subsequently an important issue between the Soviet Union and China but, notwithstanding its source, is firmly predicated in article 1 of the new constitution, belongs to an area of ideology that shades off, in one direction, into mythology; in another direction, it moves into the language of public relations.

In the sciences and the arts

In other spheres, those of the sciences and the arts, the impact of ideology not only on policy but on ordinary human lives has been direct and palpable. In the case of the natural sciences, dramatic conflicts developed between freedom of research and constraints imposed by ideologists who assessed scientific work by reference to the nature of the society in which it was carried out. Leaving aside the bizarre episode of Lysenko and the condemnation of "bourgeois" genetics, the rejection, while the cold war lasted, of relativity theory and cybernetics as suspect "pseudo-science" threatened at one point to jeopardize the Soviet defense and space research programs. In this field, at least, the national interest, rationally appraised, appears to have won a resounding victory over ideological absurdity, but with the important proviso—indicated by the treatment of Andrei Sakharov—that the application of scientific, Westernist rationalism to the criticism of political institutions and practices is no more acceptable in Russia today than it was in the time of Peter the Great.

The freedom of writers and artists to experiment is less obviously related to national security and prestige, and their position is more complicated. In the Soviet Union, the Marxian tenet that the work of writers and artists necessarily reflects the interests and values of the class or society to which they belong was reinforced by the 19th-century tradition of "civic" writing as a vehicle of political protest. It is open to question whether the Soviet rulers, or even the supervisors of cultural matters, attach a precise meaning to the mandatory formula of socialist realism (defined in the statutes of the Union of Soviet Writers as the "truthful, historically concrete representation of reality in its revolutionary development"—a definition sometimes parodied as "writing about life today as it will be tomorrow"); but they would certainly endorse the following admonition addressed by Khrushchev in 1963 to a meeting of party leaders with Soviet writers and artists:

> It is the highest duty of the Soviet writer, artist and composer, of every creative worker, to be in the ranks of the builders of communism, to put his talent at the service of the great cause of our party, to fight for the triumph of the ideas of Marxism–Leninism. We must remember that a sharp struggle is going on in the world between two irreconcilable ideologies—the socialist and the capitalist.
>
> It is the task of the artist actively to contribute by his works to the assertion of communist ideas, to deal crushing blows to the enemies of socialism and communism and to fight against the imperialists and colonialists.

Since the early 1930s, strict control of the arts by the Communist party has been maintained, with only brief intervals of relaxation in 1953–54, 1956–57 and 1962, and the situation has worsened since the fall of Khrushchev. Despite his somewhat primitive and military-sounding conception of the duty of creative artists, Khrushchev personally intervened in 1962 to secure publication of Aleksandr Solzhenitsyn's powerful anti-Stalinist story, *One Day in the Life of Ivan Denisovich*. The subsequent fate of Solzhenitsyn has in some respects been as melodramatically unique as the further unfolding, through his *Gulag Archipelago* and public statements and letters to politicians, of his idiosyncratic view of the past, present and future of Russia. Nevertheless, the willing or unwilling procession Westward of a number of prominent Soviet writers (Aksyonov, Brodsky, Nekrasov, Sinyavsky, Voynovich and others), musicians, ballet dancers and other figures from the arts world must—whether these people are regarded as martyrs or traitors—betoken a malaise in Soviet society.

Soviet leaders have frequently spoken, as did Brezhnev at the 26th Communist Party of the Soviet Union (CPSU) Congress, of "the visible sharpening of the ideological struggle" between capitalism and socialism. It is likely that they sincerely believe that their country is the target of a cultural offensive from the West of unprecedented strength. This, since their professed ideology leads them to see connections and totalities in phenomena often regarded in the West as quite discrete, is linked in their statements to acts either of espionage in the ordinary sense or—as attributed to tourists, exchange students and the like—of financial, spiritual or political "sabotage." In addition, they evidently believe that a removal of limitations upon freedom in the artistic sphere would be followed by dissemination of critical attitudes in the sphere of politics proper. As Khrushchev once put it, "Let us see what would in fact happen in Soviet art if the adherents of peaceful coexistence of various ideological trends in literature and the arts gained the upper hand. As a first step, a blow would be dealt to our revolutionary gains in the sphere of socialist art. By the logic of struggle, things would hardly end there. . . ."

In the eyes of communist ideologists, freedom in the arts is very closely related to freedom of the press. The penalties imposed on Sinyavsky and Daniel for unauthorized publication of their work abroad sprang from the same logic as the restrictions imposed on the distribution of foreign newspapers and magazines, other than the organs of foreign Communist parties. From the Soviet point of view, one of the gravest "errors" of the Dubček regime in Czechoslovakia was the lifting of press censorship. This type of reasoning is probably not invalidated by the case of Yugoslavia, where over a number of years the availability of capitalist newspapers and the large measure of freedom accorded writers and artists (at least in matters of form) does not appear in any way to have undermined the regime. The strength of Yugoslav communism rests in very large measure on nationalist sentiment, and although in the last few years Soviet–Yugoslav relations have been generally cordial at state level, Yugoslavia is not a member of the Warsaw Pact or COMECON, and is excluded in Soviet statements from the list of members of the "socialist commonwealth."

In internal affairs
What of internal affairs generally? Does the introduction of advanced technology and the recognition of consumer choice as an inevitable aspiration betoken the end of ideology, or imply that the leaders of the country or the people as a whole have become disillusioned with Marxism–Leninism? If so, are the continuing stress on indoctrination and the anathema on "ideological coexistence" merely a last stand? To answer these questions it may be helpful to draw a distinction between Marxism–Leninism as an ideology and communism as a political goal. Khrushchev was primarily a man of action, a somewhat crude expounder of doctrine, but a firm and sincere believer in the reality of the communist goal. He thus felt able, at the 22nd Congress in 1961, to offer a timetable for the achievement of the "material and technological basis of communism" and to proclaim that "the present generation of Soviet people will live under communism." No such promise has been repeated by his successors, but it would be wrong to conclude from this that they do not share his faith, although some Western commentators share the plausible view that, since the mid-1960s, the gap has widened between "official ideology" and "operating ideology." Moreover, the style

of the Soviet leaders since Khrushchev has been very different from his; they are more cautious, less given to flights of fancy or rhetoric, more concerned with the problems of today than with the distant horizon, more orthodox in their practices, less disposed to replace traditional governmental or legal organs by premature forms of "communist self-government." This mistake was made, in their view, not only by Khrushchev, but by the Chinese with their "Great Leap Forward" and "people's communes," and by the Yugoslavs with their workers' self-management. The Chinese, in the eyes of Soviet ideologists, also sinned against a fundamental tenet of Marxism–Leninism when they gave the peasantry equal status with the workers as a revolutionary force and when, during the Cultural Revolution period, they allowed power to pass from the Communist party to the army and the youth. In the same way, the ruling party in Poland is held by the Soviets to have come, during 1980–81, perilously near to conceding authority to a rival mass organization—Solidarity—which, though manifestly a free association headed by industrial workers, had therefore to be labeled counter-revolutionary.

Legitimacy
The kernel of the Soviet leadership's position is what may be called the dogma of party legitimacy, that is, that the party has an unquestioned right to a monopoly of power in the country. This dogma stands at the apex of the ideology, it is not itself part of it, but is a brute fact to be shored up by the ideology—for example, by the doctrine of "intraparty democracy," according to which continued opposition to a party decision, once formally adopted, constitutes "factionalism" or, in effect, treason. It is instructive, in this context, to compare article 2 of the Soviet constitution—"All power in the USSR belongs to the people"—with article 6, which describes the Communist party as "the leading and guiding force in Soviet society, the nucleus of its political system and of its state and voluntary organizations." The unstated corollary of this is, of course, that no other party is permitted. (Other parties are permitted in some Eastern European countries, but on condition that they adhere to a "national front" and pledge loyalty to the socialist state.) In this way, opposition can be construed not only as a breach of ideological principle but as a potential threat to the interests of the country. Hypothetically, the development of an opposition communist faction would not jeopardize the Marxist–Leninist faith, but it would certainly threaten the dogma of party legitimacy. This is why the rival revolutionary parties in existence at the time of the Russian Revolution—the Mensheviks and the Socialist Revolutionaries—had to be suppressed. This is also why the split in the world communist movement in the 1960s, together with the formation in some countries of rival, schismatic Communist parties, was, in the short term, seen as a greater threat than disillusionment with communism as such. The importance accorded legitimacy explains also the rabid hostility of the CPSU to all forms of ideological "revisionism," whether outright innovation—as in the Yugoslav variant—or criticism, from Euro-communists and others in both Eastern and Western Europe, of shortcomings in the implementing of socialist democracy in the Soviet Union itself.

215

Corresponding to the internal dogma of party legitimacy is a dogma—similarly unstated in formal documents—that the position of the CPSU, as the party of Lenin, is at any given moment the measure of orthodoxy in the communist world. Here one may contrast the abstract doctrine of "proletarian internationalism" with what came to be called in the West the "Brezhnev doctrine," which effectively claimed for the Soviet Union the right to determine what circumstances require action to "safeguard revolutionary gains." These gains may be held to be threatened from within, as in the case of Czechoslovakia in 1968, or from without, as in the case of Vietnam when, as Brezhnev put it, that country in 1979 "became the target of a barbaric aggression by Peking." By contrast, Romania's independent stand on some international issues (for example, its participation in the 1984 Olympics at Los Angeles), although associated with the garish "cult" of the dictator Ceauşescu and his family, does not pose a major threat because it is based on nationalism, not on ideological heterodoxy.

The interplay of ideological principles with the interests of the Soviet state, as interpreted by its rulers, and the modification of the former by reference to the latter, are strikingly displayed not only in relations between the Soviet Union and other communist states but in Soviet foreign policy generally. In the post-1945 period, the development of the hydrogen bomb and the emergence of the Soviet Union as one of the two superpowers, with the resulting global power stalemate, have resulted in the formulation that a world war between the socialist and capitalist systems is not "fatally inevitable" (the related doctrine of "peaceful coexistence" was not wholly new, being piously traced by Soviet apologists to Lenin). These factors have also conduced to the modification of Lenin's doctrine that the revolutionary process must necessarily involve violence. There has been, in addition, an oscillation in foreign policy between the "ideological" aim of promoting revolution throughout the world and the "political" aim of extending Soviet national influence through the cultivation of good relations with established noncommunist regimes. This Jekyll-and-Hyde approach was always a factor in relations with the major Western powers but, since the death of Stalin, it has transformed policy toward the developing countries of the Third World. At various times, the Soviet Union has appeared to be prepared to pursue good relations with the governments of Middle Eastern, Asian, African and Latin American countries at the expense of local communists. Conversely, most notably in Afghanistan since 1979, it has crudely exaggerated the significance of indigenous "progressive forces" and the threat to these of "the export of counterrevolution," using both as an ideological screen for the pursuit of an historical Russian foreign-policy goal. In its attitude to the Islamic fundamentalism of the Iranian Revolution, it has oscillated uncertainly between applauding and deploring actions based on an ideology that appears, bewilderingly, now progressive, now reactionary.

CONCLUSION

It would be foolish to believe that communist ideology is a totally spent force in the Soviet Union. However, its impact is probably being diminished and its character modified by such factors as: the stabilization of "merito-cratic" incentives; the increased attraction—unmatched by availability—of material luxuries; the chauvinism engendered by superpower status—always latent in Russia, and now reinforced by "neo-Slavophilism"; the inability of an aging leadership and an arid jargon to kindle the enthusiasm of the younger generation—and, conversely, the appeal of new or revivified foreign interpretations of the communist ideal; and the worldwide spread of national-ism, which has not only contributed to the proliferation of "national" forms of communism but must, it would seem, sooner or later be a threat to the unity of the multinational Soviet state.

FURTHER READING

Berlin, I. *Russian Thinkers*. London: Hogarth Press; New York: Viking, 1978.

Brzezinski, Z. K. *Ideology and Power in Soviet Politics*. London: Greenwood, 1976.

Conquest, R., ed. *The Politics of Ideas in the USSR*. London: Greenwood, 1976.

Keep, J. L. H. *The Rise of Social Democracy in Russia*. London and New York: Oxford University Press, 1963.

———. *On Stalin and Stalinism*. London: Oxford University Press, 1979.

Medvedev, R. *Khrushchev*. Oxford: Blackwell, 1982.

Meyer, A. G. "The Functions of Ideology in the Soviet Political System." *Soviet Studies*, Vol. XVII, No. 3, January 1966.

Reddaway, P. "The Development of Dissent and Opposition," in A. Brown and M. Kaser, eds., *The Soviet Union since the Fall of Khrushchev*. London: Macmillan, 1978.

Schapiro, L. *The Communist Party of the Soviet Union*. London: Methuen, 1970; New York: Random House, 1971.

Walker, R. *Ideology in the USSR: The Jabberwocky of Soviet Studies*. University of Essex Russian and Soviet Studies Centre Discussion Paper No. 3, July 1984.

Wesson, R. G. "Soviet Ideology: The Necessity of Marxism," *Soviet Studies*, Vol. XXI, No. 1, July 1969.

Zaslavsky, V. "Socioeconomic Inequality and Changes in Soviet Ideology," *Theory and Society*, Vol. 9, No. 2, March 1980.

THE SOVIET UNION AND THE WARSAW PACT: MILITARY AND SECURITY AFFAIRS

JOHN ERICKSON

Of the several phases and periods in Soviet military development since the early 1950s, it can now be argued with some plausibility that the mid-1970s to the mid-1980s decade, stamped indelibly as the Ustinov–Ogarkov era, has been one of unprecedented change, both radical and innovative, though not free from the effects of serious internal and external turbulence. Revision of threat assessments, elaboration of doctrine, modification in force structures, change in deployment patterns, expansion of the competence of the general staff of the Soviet armed forces, enhanced mobility in senior command appointments, advances in both offensive and defensive weapons systems, and, not least, preoccupation with improved command and control systems (C_3) designed to combine centralized strategic control with decentralized battle management—these are the elements of restructuring and rethinking that have marked the Soviet effort over the past decade and that might even be projected as far forward as the year 2000.

None of this was without its portents. Consistency over the past two decades has certainly attended the Soviet buildup and steady modernization of strategic nuclear forces, leading to the present total of 1,398 silo launchers (818 of which have been rebuilt since 1972) housing 520 SS-11s, 60 SS-13s, 150 SS-17s, 308 SS-18s and 360 SS-19s. The SS-13 is currently being replaced by the SS-25 ICBM, which has been under development for the past six years and housed in a mobile silo with a sliding roof, designed also to carry six to nine warheads over some 6,000 miles. Meanwhile, the Soviet Union maintains the world's largest ballistic missile submarine force, 64 vessels fitted with 936 nuclear missiles—not to mention the world's single largest ballistic missile submarine, the 25,000-ton TYPHOON class with one ship operational, one currently on trials and three to four under construction; potentially, the complete class will consist of eight vessels. Over the past two decades (1964–84), the Soviet Union has built no fewer than 15 new classes of submarines (180 ships in all), with maximum speed for craft increasing from 28 to 42 knots (force average increasing from 16 to 24 knots) and diving capability over the same period extending from 1,000 feet to about 3,000. Submarine-related weapons include four new cruise missile types and seven new ballistic missile models.

Nor has strategic defense gone unrecognized. The only operational antiballistic missile (ABM) system in the world, that deployed around Moscow, has been steadily upgraded since 1980 within those limits permitted by the 1972 ABM Treaty. The original 64 surface-based launchers are being replaced by 100 silo-based long-range exoatmospheric interceptors supported by new battle management radars. Two new missiles, the SA-10 and the SA-12, might well be dual mode, that is, related both to air defense and antiballistic missile defenses—denounced by some as a specific breach of the 1972 ABM Treaty. Conventional air defense includes some 1,200 interceptors and 10,000 surface-to-air missiles (SAMs), with a further 2,000 interceptors held in Soviet border areas and high-energy lasers lurking in the background for use with SAMs in point defense, a system that could become operational in the late 1980s.

Soviet ingenuity, energy and industry have also been applied over the past decade to the modernization and expansion of theater nuclear forces. These range from 378 longer-range intermediate-range mobile SS-20 missiles with triple warheads—designed to replace the elderly, cumbersome and vulnerable SS-4s and SS-5s (some 243 SS-20s being at present targeted against NATO, plus 11 new bases under construction)—to the newer family of tactical nuclear missiles: the SS-21 to replace the aging FROG-7; the SS-22 to replace the SCALEBOARD missile; and the SS-23 to take over from the SCUD as a brigade/army-level weapon. The SS-21 can also be loaded with a 1,500-pound conventional warhead that can be delivered up to 100 nautical miles within an accurate range of 50 meters. It is suited to strikes against airfields, command posts and gun or launcher positions.

Norms and numbers certainly dominated the years 1964–74, years of the "Soviet military buildup," bringing an end, in the early 1970s, to Soviet strategic inferiority and the attainment of rough parity with the United States, even a margin of advantage that was duly confirmed in the SALT-I agreements. Expansion and diversification of both strategic nuclear and general purpose forces remained the order of the day, inducing and increasing a degree of flexibility for which the Soviet command had long pressed, as well as widening the range of military options available. The rudimentary nuclear theorems advanced by Marshal Sokolovsky in *Voennaya strategiya* would no longer suffice in a world of increasing strategic complexity, a point made publicly in 1976, with some asperity and not a little abrasiveness, by Gen. (later Marshal) V. I. Kulikov, chief of the general staff. Improved Soviet capabilities and revised threat assessments prompted Kulikov to stress the danger inherent in the comprehensive arc of threat facing the Soviet Union (not merely an East–West collision), the need to develop new tactical forms embracing all branches and implementing the combined arms principle, and the crucial importance of sustaining favorable ratios of military force.

Kulikov's tenure on the general staff (1971–77) marked a start, albeit an imperfect one, of the process of greater coordination of the Soviet military effort and integration of Soviet military forces, particularly the fit between strategic and theater forces. In addition to flexibility, however, other ideas, related to the possibility of more protracted war, began to creep in, notably the need for survivability and sustainability (subsumed under the term *zhivu-chest*) in the system at large. The shape of a strategy of *tous azimuths* was emerging, requiring planning and preparation for coordinated operations on a global scale and responses to security threats not hitherto perceived; but other hands—principally those of Defense Minister Ustinov and Marshal Ogarkov, who succeeded Kulikov in 1977 as chief of the general staff—took up the task, intensifying rethinking and restructuring in a process that is not yet complete.

The thrust of Ogarkov's program involved the integration and reorganization of what had hitherto been separate, even scattered, assets, and the development of a unified command structure. In Ogarkov's own words, this required radical alteration of the "organizational structure of the armed forces and control organs," sweeping aside the traditional "harmonious development" designed to maximize the "combat might of the army and the navy." In effect, Orgarkov's planned development envisaged structuring the Soviet armed forces along the lines of their missions as opposed to their land, sea, and air responsibilities. Careful to protect himself with extensive Marxist–Leninist formulations, as if to insist on his orthodoxy, Ogarkov laid out the guidelines and the priorities of this new program designed to assure Soviet security. He emphasized the accelerating pace of technology that would enlarge the scale of military operations—no longer the front, but the strategic operation in the theater of military operations. He underlined the role of strategic weapons, together with their operational control, as determinants of the final outcome of any military confrontation. He stressed the growing complexity of command and control systems (*upravlenie*), which demand in turn a new approach to the organization and emplacement of strategic command systems. Above all, Ogarkov held, the element of surprise in modern warfare is strategically important in its own right, necessitating not only greater effectiveness in air defense but also mechanisms to guarantee extremely rapid transition from peacetime status to a war footing, involving, in turn, effective coordination between local party organs and the Soviet military.

Dialectical materialism apart, it is this logic that has informed the development of a force posture which uniquely combines regional (theater) military capabilities (groups of forces, military districts, naval and air elements) with intercontinental offensive-strike power. The result, in brief, has been the development of twin triads, one at the theater level and the other at the intercontinental level. An inevitable and deliberate overlap between theater and intercontinental operations provides added flexibility and versatility. A great deal of debate has centered on the role and the optimum structure of these theater force packages, continuing a theme developed in the mid-1950s. At that time there was concern with the concept of a combined-arms force operating in a theater battlefield, which has emerged with its own triad—namely, air power, air defense capability and field forces possessing greater firepower and maneuverability. This concept has ramifications extending beyond the confines of the Soviet military establishment itself, impinging, for example, upon command and control capability within the Warsaw Pact at large, and encouraging the development of joint operational staffs at all levels (one significant factor being the presence of Soviet and Polish officers at the Friedrich Engels Staff Academy in East Germany).

Integration and reorganization of the Soviet air defense command went almost hand in hand with the restructuring of Soviet air assets. Air defense forces have been reorganized to provide all-around air and aerospace protection with the establishment of the *Voiska PVO*, or air defense troops. The result of merging the assets of the National Air Defense Command (*PVO Strany*) with the air defense components of the ground forces, *Voiska PVO* is a huge new entity charged with tasks as diverse as controlling air space, meeting the challenge of the cruise missile and countering helicopters on the battlefield. It has also taken over the interceptor aircraft, previously part of tactical (frontal) aviation, as well as ground-based air defense elements in the Soviet army. Restructuring has also reached into the regional command arrangements. The disbanding of the Baku Air Defense District has left Moscow as the only regional air defense command; the 10 remaining districts were absorbed into the headquarters of military districts, with *Voiska PVO*, as elements of a military district receiving public mention in January 1980.

The merger of strategic and tactical air defense assets in the key border areas of the Soviet Union is part of a major restructuring that has visibly changed the face of the Soviet air force (VVS). Later in 1979, there was public mention of a new command position in the military district/groups of forces, a position designated as deputy district/group commander of air forces (as opposed to the earlier designation, aviation commander). Numbered air armies (such as the 16th group of Soviet forces/Germany) have disappeared, replaced by a new structure, air forces of the district/group, comprising *all* air assets within specific district/group geographic areas (save for strategic-strike aviation and air transport, VTA). Air assets in the four fleets have been similarly reorganized into air force commands.

Operational-strategic air armies (*udarnaya aviatsiya*, or air armies of the Soviet Union) have retained their numbering and, though located within military districts, are directly subordinated to the high command, with Col. Gen. (Aviation) Reshetnikov acting as commander in chief (C-in-C). Of the five operational-strategic air armies, three (the 24th at Legnica in Poland, the 46th based at Smolensk and the 4th at Vinnitsa) are deployed forward for operations in the European theater; both the 24th and 4th air armies deploy the SU-24 FENCER in considerable strength (five regiments to each army), thus increasing both night and adverse-weather capability (the aircraft are on a par with the USAF-F-111). The 30th air army is deployed for operations in the Far Eastern theater.

The third leg of this theater triad, supplementing and complementing air power and air defense, has involved steady improvement in the firepower (particularly the artillery resources) and maneuverability of the field forces. In the three main theaters—Western, Southern and Far Eastern—the Soviet command maintains 30 divisions (groups of forces) deployed forward in east-central Europe: 60+ divisions in the western districts of the Soviet Union, 30 divisions in the Southern theater and 52 divisions in the Far East (including the two divisions in the Mongolian operational group). Non-Soviet Warsaw Pact divisions present a formidable tally on paper: 53 tank and motor-rifle divisions all told, plus three specialized divisions (one Czechoslovak artillery division, one Polish airborne division and one amphibious division), but quantity and quality, not to mention overall reliability, vary considerably; Romania drags its military feet, such as they are, while it may well be that the much vaunted East German divisions (two tank and four motor-rifle) have been excluded from the Soviet first echelon. The major Soviet deployment/mobilization exercise, which ran from June 28 to July 5, 1984, involved only Soviet elements, testing theater coordination in time and space and drawing in the groups of forces plus the Baltic, Carpathian and Belorussian military districts—the 11th Guards Army, 38th Army and 28th Army, respectively, bringing in staffs at all levels from the general staff down to division and regiment.

The artillery/missile elements of the ground forces (Soviet army) have received special attention, since Soviet doctrine insists that artillery can and must play a role similar to that of air power in providing concentrated firepower and clearing the way for tank and motor-rifle units. In particular, in any conventional mode or phase, artillery and air power would have to compensate by weight of fire for the effects wrought by nuclear weapons. In sum, the decline in the role of conventional artillery has been dramatically reversed, a process reflected in the upgrading of the status of artillery/missile commander at district/group level. Elsewhere, the tendency continues to be development in both tank and motor-rifle divisions, designed to transform them into genuine combined-arms formations, an example of which is the addition of an artillery battalion to tank regiments, with an increase in artillery assets (towed and self-propelled) in both divisions. This preoccupation with all-arms/combined-arms is also implicit in the revised rank structure introduced in April 1984 for ground forces officers, abolishing individual designation and organic rank structure for tank, engineer, signal and technical troops, thereby reducing 14 categories within the officer corps to five—a move designed, no doubt, to align "teeth" arms and technical branches more closely.

Though the Soviet field forces, with air and artillery/missile support, train for rapid conventional attack, pursuing operations in depth involving sequential destruction of enemy groups and the fire destruction of the enemy, this does not preclude constant readiness to use nuclear weapons. Rather than there being a nuclear/conventional dichotomy in Soviet usage, the trend continues to be a form of nuclear/conventional integration. Indeed, the widely advertised operational maneuver groups (OMGs) might be better interpreted as a form of substitute for battlefield nuclear weapons, in that they are a means of effecting the quasi-simultaneous destruction of the enemy at middle depth, literally filling the space between the operations conducted by the mobile (tank) arm and the heavier combined-arms formations, though the principle is the same—to move far and fast in order to destroy particular objectives. On the other hand, air support for the OMGs, not to mention logistics and command/control, presupposes the need for a radically decentralized mode that sits uneasily with present Soviet practice. This once more highlights Soviet difficulties at the level of regiment and battalion, not least the scope of initiative and subunit performance.

It is not only the organization of force but also its employment that has attracted Ogarkov's reforming zeal. The main operation of contemporary war must now be considered strategic operations in the theaters of military operations (TVDs)—in short, a transition from front operations in World War II-style to one of TVD operations. Theaters of war (TVs) are duly divided into their own TVDs and, logically, the Soviet navy now operates its maritime theaters of operations (MTVDs) in conjunction with the all-arms TVDs, where geographically appropriate. As before mentioned, the Eurasian landmass comprises three main TVs—Western, Southern, Far Eastern—each of which is duly divided into its TVD/MTVDs; the main Western theater of war, for example, splits into three TVDs, the Northwestern, Western (Central) and Southwestern, with naval adjuncts operating in the Atlantic and Arctic theaters.

Recent Soviet promotion patterns indicate that there is a sustained effort to man the senior tier of strategic commands, even at the expense of lowering the seniority of commanders in key military districts. One item worthy of attention is the recent replacement of Gen. Gerasimov, latterly general officer in command (GOC) of Kiev Military District, by Lt. Gen. V. V. Osipov. Gen. Gerasimov has hardly disappeared from the scene and may well emerge as the commander/Southern theater. In no dissimilar fashion, Gen. I. M. Tretyak, erstwhile GOC Far Eastern Military District, exchanged that post for one more senior, that of C-in-C Far Eastern theater. Meanwhile, at the general staff, Gen. Varennikov could well be charged with the coordination of the several TVDs, making him a military overseer of some importance. All this merely underlines the fact that every significant sector and segment of the Soviet military system—general staff, the several arms and services, as well as the Warsaw Pact—is affected in varying degrees by the Ogarkov initiatives.

The theater triad (air power, air defense, field force firepower), or the TVD combined-arms force package and mission-related organization, is only one part of the evolutionary change in Soviet military structures. In paradoxical fashion, much depended on what Marshal Ogarkov did *not* say rather than his explicit references. Beginning with the 1980s, Ogarkov made diminishing mention of the strategic missile forces, as such, and long-range aviation, though clearly these had not vanished from the order of battle of Soviet strategic-intercontinental forces. Between 1981–82, Ogarkov referred to Soviet strategic nuclear forces in terms of a dyad, namely, ICBMs and submarine-launched ballistic missiles (SLBMs), but latterly he enlarged upon this to include elements of the Soviet air force, in short, a Soviet triad and an integrated strategic-strike force. The net result was to eliminate mention of the strategic missile forces as the premier Soviet arm, indeed even as a separate arm, bringing about a marked change in the style of ranking within the Soviet military, which now reads: strategic nuclear forces, ground forces (Soviet army), Soviet air force, air defense troops and the Soviet navy.

There are grounds for thinking that E. V. Boichuk, appointed a marshal of artillery in November 1980, was responsible for working out plans to restructure the Soviet strategic nuclear forces. He was obviously connected with other members of the Ogarkov think tank, a hand-picked brain trust of experienced senior officers that included Col.-Gen. V. N. Karpov, charged with investigating strategic organization under war conditions. We can assume, therefore, that a new directorate was established within the general staff, not unconnected with Marshal Boichuk and dealing with the integration and coordination of Soviet strategic nuclear forces, together with the establishment of a nuclear command.

In general, the Soviet command has cause for a certain satisfaction with the composition of Soviet strategic nuclear forces, with improved accuracies providing the means to attack the entire hard/soft target array in the United States with any mix of Soviet systems, as well as the facility to match minimum yields against target vulnerability. The Soviet command can also look to the prospect of favorable exchange ratios, plus survivable reserve forces (not to mention reload and refire capabilities). It is the latter, together with assumed full MIRV-ing, that complicates the issue of assessing Soviet warhead holdings. With minimum force loadings, that stockpile could amount to some 18,000 warheads; but assuming full ICBM MIRV-ing, MIRV-ing of SLBMs, reload/refire capability and dual systems nuclear armed, plus nuclear-armed long-range cruise missiles, then that figure could leap to about 40,000, far outstripping U.S. stockpiles.

A centralized organization for Soviet strategic nuclear forces has apparently been achieved, with Marshal Akhromeyev installed earlier as the first nuclear C-in-C; however, with Akhromeyev's elevation to the post of chief of the general staff, his duties may be handed to another senior officer. Operational control over ICBMs, the SSBN/SLBM force and strategic aviation—the air armies of the Soviet Union—now comes under centralized command, with the respective arms commanders (Tolubko, Gorshkov and Kutakhov) acting only as managers (for training and peacetime organization) for these elements. On the whole, it appears that the Soviet air force has readily accepted the new centralized command, turning over its strike air armies (soon to be augmented by the BLACKJACK intercontinental bomber and supplemented with long-range air-launched cruise missiles) to the new strategic entity— with the added bonus of having advanced its position in the pecking order of the Soviet services. Not so the Soviet navy, however, with Gorshkov and his adherents (principally Stalbo) clinging to the notion of an independent naval mission and the distinctiveness of the naval role, only to be challenged by other senior naval officers bent on reexamining the nature of Soviet naval requirements.

At the end of 1981 and the beginning of 1982, it was clear that a fundamental review of Soviet naval doctrine had begun, or was publicly disclosed, with Adm. Chernavin, the newly appointed chief of the main naval staff (and likely successor to Gorshkov), in the van. In demanding a radical revision of the principles of naval art, Adm. Chernavin argued, in essence, that the naval role in defense of the Soviet homeland should be seen from the vantage point of the entire Soviet defense community, adducing at the same time the combined-arms principle and invoking the necessity for integration, much in the Ogarkov style. A number of issues had already come to the fore, some of them of long-standing nature, such as the role of naval forces in more protracted war—survivability in an extended campaign as opposed to a first-salvo shootout—as well as the form and future of the antisubmarine warfare (ASW) fleet, the expansion of naval aviation and the fit of naval capability with theater operations (partly solved by the alignment of the MTVDs with TVDs).

Newer Soviet surface combat units have demonstrably increased range, greater endurance, improved firepower and more survivability. They will serve at least to extend the geographical limits of the MTVDs and the KIROV class CGN. The latter are nuclear-powered and capable of independent operations, with optional nuclear or conventional warhead-targeting of Western carrier task groups; they operate in a combined-arms role with BEAR-D targeting aircraft, shore-based air striking, and the full coordination of air, surface and subsurface strike. The new destroyers, SOVREMENNYI ships, have an antiship capability and the UDALOY have an ASW role; both are more specialized ships, with twice the volume of the KASHIN ships and greater sustainability. The UDALOY class seems destined for large-scale production, since it incorporates the best of existing Soviet naval systems (the gas turbine of the KASHINs, the SS-N-14 ASW system, the 100-mm gun mounts from the KRIVAK-2 and the KRIVAK VDS). Fleet replenishment and amphibious warfare ships have also made their appearance; large new types such as the BEREZINA replenishment ships (36,000 tons), the two IVAN ROGOV 13,000-ton amphibious warfare ships and 11 of the ROPUCHKA landing ships (3,600 tons), plus hydrofoils and hovercraft for close-in operations, possibly related to egress operations in the Baltic and Black seas.

The Soviet naval command appears to have changed its requirement from a navy suited to a first-salvo exchange, in a short war scenario, to one committed to the protection of its SSBNs, keeping them safe for an indefinite period and protecting the SSBN holding stations in the Barents and Norwegian seas and the seas of Japan and Okhotsk. New large multi-purpose ships would be better suited to this purpose, able to keep at sea for extended periods without returning to ports that may have been obliterated. At the same time, Soviet experiments with space-based and airborne submarine tracking devices represent a very considerable technical achievement (using synthetic aperture radars–SARs—on the SALYUT manned space station to track DELTA SSBNs off the Pacific coast by nonacoustical means). There is also a discernible trend whereby Soviet SSBNs may be used to take on U.S. SSBNs, thus augmenting the growing capabilities of nuclear attack submarines (SSNs)—hence the development of a new class of attack submarines based on the high-speed deep-diving ALFA-class of boats, the MIKE-class (9,700 tons) and the SIERRA-class (8,000 tons)—high technology submarines with pressure hulls manufactured from titanium. In addition, the Soviet navy has commissioned three of the KILO-class and five of the TANGO-class diesel submarines to supplement the attack force, making a total of eight SSN/SSGN/SS classes in all. Soviet missile submarines linked with ocean surveillance satellites for detection and information are used for attack on distant mobile targets, in addition to wake-homing weapons and a form of towed accoustic arrays, amply displayed on a recently disabled Soviet submarine. Space-based ASW assets undoubtedly play a prominent and increasing role in Soviet programs, hence added Soviet incentive in deterring the United States from proceeding with an American antisatellite interceptor weapon, ASAT.

In short, the Soviet navy like every other Soviet service is being given greater staying power, as well as being integrated into a new strategic war management system, one that is capable of responding to a wide range of threats and contingencies, whether short, sharp, intensive local wars or more protracted war on a global scale. The move toward the integration of strategic-strike forces and the emplacement of theater commands with their own triad has been accompanied by an extensive mobilization base that can, in theory at least, effect a rapid buildup or call on select assets over time. Clearly, the objective is to reduce the impact of the surprise factor, a factor recently heavily emphasized by Marshal Ogarkov, to ensure large-scale, extremely accurate actions on the part of the defender and, if at all possible, to prevent any conflict becoming nuclear, presumably by a form of conventional preemption. Within this design, Marshal Ogarkov over the past decade has rammed through a long-term plan for strategic defense, which has combined centralized strategic control with greater flexibility of command of regional-theater force packages on the several vital strategic axes covering each arc of threat. This imprint, deep as it is, will persist for years, as will Ogarkov's publicly declared misgivings (reported in *Krasnaya Zvezda*, May 9, 1984) on the direction of Soviet defense policies, in particular, the obsessive massing of ICBMs—missile mania all at the expense of investing in advanced technology related to conventional weapons, which promises to be the wave of the future. Nuclear weapons simply piled on top of each other fail to enhance deterrence, since neither side can amass enough to carry through a successful disarming strike—hence the need for new ideas on deterrence and force employment, not least, the exploitation of advanced technology. Here is an idea whose time is not yet come, to judge by the reaction of the entrenched Soviet military bureaucracy; but Marshal Ogarkov will assuredly be vindicated.

THE WARSAW PACT AND THE FUTURE

Not entirely by coincidence, the year 1985 is stamped with singular significance for both Soviet and non-Soviet Warsaw Pact affairs. With the current Soviet five-year planning cycle ending in 1985, there is no reason to be surprised at the brouhaha raised by Marshal Ogarkov's policy proposals, which must inevitably mean a switch in resource allocation, to the probable disadvantage of the missile men. Meanwhile, Article 11 of the Warsaw Treaty, signed on May 14, 1955, measured out the legal lifespan of the Eastern alliance system. The treaty was to remain in force for 20 years and without notice of denunciation to the government of the Polish People's Republic on the part of contracting parties; then to extend a further 10 years—30 years in all. On the whole, the Pact's record of attainment is mediocre. By the end of the first decade of the Pact's existence, the initial consensus of what constituted the threat had visibly eroded; the eruptions in Hungary, the irruption into Czechoslovakia and the flaring crisis in Poland all contributed to undermine any sense of cohesion. Latterly, nationalist revivals have brought fresh problems, whether Romanian obduracy or East German stirrings. Failing absolute unity, of which there is no sign, the best that might be said for the Pact is that it can be used to minimize or regulate discontents. Yet, for all the political turbulence and economic constraints, the Pact still appears to hold a central place in Soviet military thinking, perhaps most pertinently as an intermediate coalition organ of strategic command/control at large. If this is the case (and it was a case set out by Kulikov, now a Marshal and Warsaw Pact C-in-C), then it is possible to make greater sense of certain developments within the Pact and what its worth is to the Soviet military command. Under these circumstances, the renewal of the Pact seems to be a foregone conclusion.

Although integration seemed to be promised with the creation of the joint command of joint forces, this has hardly been the case. Even if the designation "joint" is translated as "unified," this does not mean integrated forces, since on both Soviet and non-Soviet testimony, even assigned or earmarked forces remain under their own national deputy commanders and remain responsive to national control. Command responsibilities ran more or less on conventional lines with each national ministry in charge of its own affairs, save for the air defense system, which came under overt Soviet control (a place being found quite automatically for the head of the Soviet *PVO Strany* within the joint/unified staff). Control exercised through the Warsaw Pact mechanism operates at three levels: (a) the senior representative of the C-in-C of the Pact's joint armed forces (for example, Col.-Gen. V. K. Meretskov, newly appointed representative in East Germany), responsible for those first-line non-Soviet troops assigned to the Pact, though also able to request additional military assistance; (b) the office of the Soviet military attaché working closely with national central committees and political administrations of the national formation; and (c) the KGB/GRU officers in contact with both civilian and military agencies (a component the Czechs in 1968 perhaps too precipitately sent packing).

Operational control, however, is another matter. Clearly, the establishment of separate, autonomous TVD commands affects Warsaw Pact organization and, not least, the position of the Pact C-in-C, Marshal Kulikov. The joint command does provide an overall strategic structure in terms of protocol (organization along the lines of socialist internationalism), legitimizes Soviet control over non-Soviet forces in time of war and is itself a pattern of any joint (Soviet/non-Soviet) staff, again applicable to wartime conditions. But if actual operational control rests with the TVD commander(s), then Kulikov's role is sensibly diminished, his command being little more than a supersized military district, committed to training, logistics support and a mobilization function. On the other hand, Kulikov's joint command is a form of centralization, with the staffs—jointly manned at all levels—providing both flexibility and a form of continuity. Multinational staff training, using not only the Frunze and general staff academies but also the East German academy, provides both personal and institutional associations.

We must assume, therefore, that Soviet control is activated through the TVD(s), which in turn lead back to the Soviet general staff, while Kulikov's joint command is a form of control organ, with the particular function of multinational staffing responsive to Soviet prompting and direction. Warsaw Pact exercises are designed to implement this program, with a deliberate attempt to intermingle the non-Soviet rank and file with their Soviet opposite numbers. This still falls far short of actual integration, but it seems to pass muster; as the restructuring of the air defense systems proceeds, however, more immediate Soviet intrusion into and inspection of national military units can be anticipated, perhaps reaching as far down as subunits.

Qualitative and quantitative aspects of the non-Soviet military establishments continue to vary, with the permanent differentiation between the northern tier and its southern counterpart, the latter embodying the relative military backwardness of Hungarian, Bulgarian and Romanian forces. In the southern tier, only Bulgarian forces have anything approaching a defined mission, but even that is subordinate to the Soviet mission of controlling the Bosphorus and northern Aegean; too often it seems to be a matter of holding out the military begging bowl. In the northern tier, the largest military establishment, that of Poland, is tangled in a protracted internal political crisis, with modernization held back by economic difficulties. The East German *Volksmarine* bids fair to overtake the Polish navy and become the most important non-Soviet naval force as obsolescence creeps over Polish naval units, though the East German military machine is not without its own difficulties. Thus, rather than looking at nominal order of battle and a simple tally of divisions, it may be more profitable to anticipate further specialization within the economic possibilities and political inclinations of northern-tier states. The SHIELD-82 exercises, held in northeast Bulgaria, could well illustrate this principle, with an East German general, Horst Skerra, acting as deputy to Gen. Dzhurov of the Bulgarian army, deploying Soviet, Bulgarian and East German units in the first assault wave and Hungarian and Czech units in the second, following up paratroopers of the 6th Polish Airborne Division. Soviet (and other) troops were moved by sea (heavy equipment shipped on RORO ships) from Odessa to Varna, the Romanians having declined to permit air transport across their territory.

The Warsaw Pact is unlikely to fade from the scene; renewal may offer the occasion for some display of contrived consensus over threats, an affirmation of peaceful purposes and policies linked at the same time with the celebration of the 40th anniversary of the defeat of Nazi Germany and Japan. But this will not of itself eliminate nationalist resurgence or dissipate the economic burdens of joint defense. Paradoxically, modernization, particularly in the field of C_3, may serve only to exacerbate the frustrations of non-Soviet military professionals, their sense of subservience previously sharpened by Soviet hauteur.

MEN, MONEY AND MACHINES

The strains of this massive effort, given the relative constrictions of the Warsaw Pact economies, are beginning to show. Eastern European economists and others complain of the social and political cost of heavy defense burdens, while the Soviet side is unhappy at Eastern European contributions, a mere three to six percent of gross national product compared with 14 percent for the Soviet Union. Soviet military spending is the subject of endless controversy, encouraged by the absence of truly hard data. For those bent on demonstrating "an unprecedented Soviet military buildup," Soviet defense outlays grow apace, never slackening, with the Defense Intelligence Agency disputing the CIA estimate that Soviet spending had not increased much above two percent—the CIA case for a slowdown being based on technological problems, industrial bottlenecks and shifts in policy, with the real surge in expenditure having occurred in the previous decade (1966–76).

Soviet military production efforts, however, speak for themselves. Over the past 15 years, the Soviet military industry has produced six new series of advanced fighter aircraft, two new bombers (with a third under test), 10 new types of transport aircraft, two new series of helicopters every five years, 10 new ballistic missile systems (with 13 modifications to ICBMs and five to SLBMs), six new SAM missile systems, 14 new submarine classes since 1970 (including the UNIFORM-class nuclear-powered experimental vessel), 10 major classes of surface warships, and one new tank every five years. In addition, since 1980 the Soviet Union has become the world's leading arms exporter. Quantity is impressive enough, but it is increasingly enmeshed with quality and with more complex weapons systems, increasing procurement costs by as much as 10 percent and promising to make further inroads into Soviet expenditures, particularly if the Soviet military is bent on responding to the Western technological challenge—the issue raised in specter-like fashion by Marshal Ogarkov. The days of advantage conferred by "rugged simple equipment," plus a bonus in manpower, are on the wane, with advanced aircraft, space programs and electronics coming to the fore in this race, further diverting funds from procurement to research and development. The realignment of Soviet research efforts is also closely connected with the need to speed the pace of technological innovation, using new associations linking scientific organizations with production facilities, designed to reduce lead times and promote modernization.

Marshal Ogarkov raised some very awkward questions at a very inconvenient time. While his "unpartylike tendencies" scarcely make sense, except to fob off further questions, Ogarkov, in arguing that a nuclear stalemate now exists, that more for more missiles makes little sense, was arguing for resources, money and technology, to match the U.S. program for deep-strike conventional weapons—resources that both the party and the government knew could not be provided under the present scheme of things. He might not be forgiven, but he will certainly not be forgotten soon.

FURTHER READING

Berman, Robert P., and Baker, John C. *Soviet Strategic Forces: Requirements and Responses*. Washington, D.C.: Brookings Institution, 1982.

Clawson, Robert W., and Kaplan, Lawrence, S., eds. *The Warsaw Pact: Political Purposes and Military Means*. Wilmington, Delaware: SR Inc., 1982.

Drachkovich, Milorad M. *East Central Europe: Yesterday—Today—Tomorrow*. Stanford, California: Hoover Institution/Stanford University Press, 1982.

Erickson, J., and Feuchtwanger, E. J., eds. *Soviet Military Power and Performance*. London: Macmillan, 1979.

Kulikov, Marshal V. G. *Kollektivnaya zashchita sotsializma*. Moscow: Voenizdat, 1982.

Lewis, William J. *The Warsaw Pact: Arms, Doctrine and Strategy*. New York: McGraw-Hill, 1982.

NATO. *The CMEA Five-Year Plans (1981–1985) in a New Perspective*. NATO Economic Colloquium 1982. Brussels: (Especially, M. Checinski, "CMEA Defense Spending," pp. 237–55.)

Oldberg, Ingmar, ed. *Unity and Conflict in the Warsaw Pact*. Stockholm: Swedish National Defense Research Institute, 1984.

Organizatsiya Varshavshovo Dogovora. Dokumenty i Materialy 1955–1980. Moscow: Politizdat, 1980.

Ogarkov, Marshal N. V. *Vsegda v gotovnosti k zashchite Otechestva*. Moscow: Voenizdat, 1982.

———. "Zashchita sotsializma: opyt istorii i sovremennost." *Krasnaya Zvezda*, May 9, 1984, pp. 2–3.

Rakowska-Harmstone, Teresa, et al. *Warsaw Pact: The Question of Cohesion*. Phase II, Vol. 1. ORAE Extra-Mural Paper No. 29, February 1984.

Ross Johnson, A., et al. *East European Military Establishments: The Warsaw Pact Northern Tier*. New York: Crane Russak, 1982.

Scott, Harriet Fast, and Scott, William F. *The Soviet Control Structure: Capabilities for Wartime Survival*. New York: Crane Russak, 1983.

Tiedtke, Stephan. *Die Warschauer Vertragsorganisation*. Munich/Vienna: Oldenbourg Verlag, 1978.

U.S. Congress. *Allocation of Resources in the Soviet Union and China—1983*. Hearings... Joint Economic Committee, U.S. Congress (Pt. 9). Washington, D.C., 1984.

Vladimirov, S., and Teplov, L. *Varshavskii Dogovor i NATO: dva Kursa, dve politiki*. Moscow: "Mezh. Otnosheniya," 1979.

Vorontsov, G. F. *Voennye koalitsii i koalitsionnye voiny*. Moscow: Voenizdat, 1976.

Whence the Threat to Peace. 3rd ed. Moscow: Military Publishing House, 1984.

THE SOVIET UNION

RUSSIAN NATIONALISM

NEIL HYAMS

ORTHODOXY, AUTOCRACY AND NATIONALITY

THE history of Russian nationalism presented here concentrates particularly on the uses that centralized regimes, over the past 150 years, have made of a broadly defined Russian national consciousness and Russification policies. Quasi-official and unofficial expressions of Russian nationalism will also be addressed; in the very different circumstances of the czarist regime and its successor, discernible tensions arose between official and unofficial Russian nationalist views.

The largely peasant masses of 19th-century Russia were inspired by patriotism—particularly during the "patriotic war" against Napoleon—rather than by nationalism as such. Centuries of foreign invasion and struggles for supremacy in the borderlands had left a profound sense of insecurity, a suspicion of foreigners and a disdain for foreign political institutions that were exploited by the czars and particularly by their communist successors.

During the reign of Nicholas I (1825–55), *narodnost*—the principle of Russian nationality—became part of official ideology. The slogan of "Orthodoxy, autocracy and nationality" was proclaimed in the first circular issued (in 1833) by the new minister of education, Count Uvarov. It remained in force, theoretically at least, until the fall of the monarchy. The czar and his officials emphasized the special character of the Russians and, not least, their language. Such policies were intended to buttress a divinely ordained monarchy at a time of political change in Europe. Reacting to the events of 1848, Nicholas I himself wrote a well-known manifesto maintaining that every Russian would respond to "the ancient battle cry: for faith, czar and fatherland!" According to a better-known manifesto also published in 1848, however, workers had no fatherland. Yet this last element of Nicholas I's triad has, ironically, stood the test of history rather better than the ringing declaration of Marx and Engels.

A deliberate process of Russification was initiated in the borderlands— parts of Poland, Belorussia and Lithuania. After the suppression of the Polish rebellion of 1830–31, the administration, economy and educational system were Russified. In 1847, a secret Ukrainian society was suppressed. The outstanding Ukrainian national poet, Taras Shevchenko, was exiled to Siberia for 10 years; his fellow conspirators were treated more leniently. In general, however, advancement was open to loyal and suitably Russified subjects. Jews, restricted since the late 18th century to the Pale of Settlement in the western and southwestern provinces, were subjected to assimilatory and discriminatory measures. In 1827, they became liable to compulsory military service (six years of training followed by 25 in the ranks).

The official, essentially static, concept of nationality began to diverge from the more dynamic views derived from German romantic nationalism that gained ground among intellectuals, writers, journalists (two of the most influential being Russified Poles), officers and students. The undertones of revolutionary change and messianic, Pan-Slavic ideas became most apparent in discussions of foreign policy. These sentiments grew in strength during the reign of Alexander II (1855–81), which was also marked by imperial expansion, particularly into Central Asia. Gen. Skobelev, a hero of the Central Asian and Bulgarian campaigns, remains a hero to Russian nationalists to this day.

The policy of Russification was stepped up when Alexander III (reigned 1881–94) succeeded his assassinated father, Alexander II. Even such peoples as the Finns and Armenians who had shown loyalty to the throne were persecuted. The position of the Jews, in particular, deteriorated sharply; not surprisingly, many joined radical or nationalist movements. In the ethnically tense borderlands they were subjected to pogroms by gangs of "Black Hundreds" who enjoyed a degree of official support. More discriminatory legislation against them was enforced. Armenians also suffered through official connivance at pogroms. The revolutionary year of 1905 also saw the establishment of several reactionary, protofascist groups with support from landowners and the clergy.

The Bolsheviks, after their seizure of power in 1917, further developed such czarist institutions as censorship and the secret police, and, in due course, exploited their total control of publications and systems of education and indoctrination. However, they were faced with a problem of their own making—how to deal with the national consciousness of the ethnic Russians—by far the largest nationality in their multinational state—under the conditions of an "internationalist," class-based ideology.

LENIN AND THE EARLY SOVIET PERIOD

Before the revolution, Lenin was alive to the exploitable discontent felt by non-Russians, and declared "war to the death" against Russian chauvinism. He rejected the enforced use of Russian, supporting education in vernacular languages. He looked forward to a time when all national mistrust would disappear and nations would merge on the basis of an international proletarian culture. After the fall of Nicholas II, however, nationalist governments and parties arose throughout the former Russian empire. The Bolsheviks initially made certain tactical gestures toward averting the traditional nationalism of the White Russian enemies of these groups, for example by issuing a declaration on the rights of all the peoples of Russia and an appeal to Muslims; banning Russian settlement in certain areas; and returning historic relics to certain peoples. Under the pressure of events, Lenin was forced to abandon his objections to (enforced) federation, and in 1922 the Soviet Union was formed of nominally independent republics. Lenin insisted, however, on a single, centralized, ruling party—a factor of crucial political significance.

A certain ambiguity was inherent in the official reaction to the Polish invasion of the Ukraine. An appeal of April 29, 1920 (signed by Lenin, among others) "To All Workers, Peasants and Honest Citizens of Russia" was essentially couched in class terms—but "honest citizens" (i.e. patriots) were also directly addressed. The former czarist general, Brusilov, appealed in *Pravda* to fellow officers to help in the defense of the homeland. Subsequently, however, the official stress on the class nature of the conflict predominated.

The Polish campaign, the enforced return to private enterprise (the New Economic Policy) and the suppression of the 1921 Kronstadt revolt caused certain émigrés, notably N. Ustryalov and V. Shulgin, to suggest (in the words of the former) that "the revolution is evolving" and (of the latter) that while the Bolsheviks thought they were fighting for the glory of the International: "In reality, they are only spilling their blood to restore Russian power protected by God . . . ." Ustryalov called himself a "National Bolshevik," thus synthesizing two theoretically incompatible concepts. This was not to be the last time émigrés believed that the balance had tilted against the proclaimed internationalist ideology.

It is impossible to understand the revival of Russian nationalist trends in the USSR in the 1960s without recognizing the iconoclasm of the immediate postrevolutionary years—in particular, the attacks on Orthodoxy (including the martyrdom of many priests), the sexual license and weakening of family bonds, and the denigration of great figures from Russian history. Nor should it be forgotten that many of Lenin's fellow revolutionaries were not Russian, while Lenin himself was of ethnically mixed origin.

STALIN AND SOVIET PATRIOTISM

In the power struggle after Lenin's death in 1924, Stalin made use of the (borrowed) slogan "socialism in one country." A strong socialist base had to be built in the USSR before thoughts of world revolution (as propounded by his rival, Trotsky) could be entertained. The time was not yet ripe, however, for significant concessions to the Russians. In his report to the 12th Party Congress (1923), Stalin had stated that Russian chauvinism was "the principle force impeding the merging of the republics into a single union." Local nationalisms, also attacked, were viewed as a lesser danger.

By the late 1920s, Stalin had fought off the challenge from the right wing of the party and was able to enforce an intensified drive for industrialization and the collectivization of the peasantry. The social upheavals involved, particularly traumatic as regards the peasant culture that had long exercised a grip on the Russian imagination, were to have a delayed impact on expressions of nationalism. At the 17th Party Congress (the "Congress of the Victors") in 1934, Stalin maintained that it was pointless to argue which deviation (Russian or local nationalism) constituted the greater danger. "The deviation against which we have ceased to fight" was the more dangerous.

He went on to discuss the rise of Ukrainian nationalism without admitting, however, that it had probably been fanned by the horrors of collectivization and famine.

Hitler came to power in 1933; at the same time, in the Far East, Japanese militarism was embarking on an expansionist course. Stalin evidently judged it expedient to mobilize the Soviet population against external threats by inculcating a "Soviet patriotism," heavily based on Russian national symbolism (as well as hysteria about foreign spies). A major reassessment of the czarist past took place in history and the arts. Historical monuments and battlefields were restored. In the Red Army, most of the old czarist ranks were reinstituted and soldiers swore an oath to defend the "fatherland"—a term once more in vogue. However, the most symbolic of all these gestures, the introduction of a Soviet national anthem to replace the *Internationale*, did not occur until 1944. In the social sphere, new legislation outlawed abortion on demand and divorce was made progressively more difficult. In 1937, a government decree advanced the theory that although the annexation of non-Russian territories under the czars had been an evil, it was a lesser evil than absorption by other imperialist states would have been. In 1938, the Russian language became a compulsory subject in non-Russian schools. From about this time, it was stated that "a single Soviet people" existed (a proposition elaborated in subsequent decades). However, there were limits to Stalin's refurbishing of Russian attributes. The Russian SFSR, by far the largest of the constituent republics, was not permitted to have its own party organization—a situation that has remained in force, although some institutional tinkering took place under Khrushchev. (In a well-known unofficial document of 1971, an anonymous "group of Russian patriots" drew particular attention to this discrimination.)

The "perfidious aggression" of Stalin's Nazi ally in June 1941 led to more symbolic gestures, such as the institution (in 1942) of decorations in the names of great czarist commanders. The very name chosen for the hostilities—"The Great Patriotic War"—was a deliberate echo of the campaign against Napoleon. Most tellingly, concessions were made to the Orthodox church whose hierarchy had supported the war effort from the outset. In his book *Conversations with Stalin*, Milovan Djilas reported the head of the Soviet mission to Yugoslavia, Gen. Korneev, as saying that many responsible people considered turning toward Orthodoxy as a more permanent ideological motive force. "We would have saved Russia even through Orthodoxy if that were unavoidable!" To the young Yugoslav, Korneev's hypothesis "seemed absurd. Yet I was not at all amazed—so widespread had Russian patriotism, not to say nationalism, become.... Stalin understood intuitively that his... social system could not withstand the blows of the German Army unless they leaned for support on the older aspirations and beliefs of the Russian people."

In 1943, Stalin and Molotov received three Russian Orthodox metropolitans in the Kremlin and permission was granted for a long overdue Church Council to be convened in order for a Patriarch—the first since 1925—to be elected. Antireligious publications had been banned since 1941; the Moscow Patriarchate was now permitted to publish a journal.

After the victory, Stalin delivered a famous toast at a reception for military commanders, in which he paid tribute to the preeminent role of the Russian people. With the onset of the cold war, a new campaign against foreign influences was launched, in which a renewed emphasis on communist ideology was grafted onto boasts about the achievements of Russian inventors, men of letters, etc. Jewish writers were shot and "rootless cosmopolitans" denounced; even more drastic anti-Semitic measures were only halted by Stalin's death in 1953. Non-Russian historians were attacked once again for local nationalism, and attempts were even made to suppress national epics. The acquisition by the czars of non-Russian areas was henceforward regarded not just as a "lesser evil" but a positive good. The Orthodox church was not, however, deprived of its wartime gains, possibly because Stalin understood the uses to which a subservient hierarchy could be put to further Soviet foreign policy.

In his unsuccessful bid for power, Stalin's last secret-police chief, his fellow Georgian L. Beria, seems to have made a bid for non-Russian support by stressing the evils wrought by Russian chauvinism. One of the more believable charges brought against Beria and his associates was that they had sought to stir up national feelings in the republics to the detriment of the friendship between their peoples and the Russians.

KHRUSHCHEV BREAKS THE MOLD

Khrushchev's (partial) revelations, in 1956 and subsequently, of Stalin's crimes led to a well-attested loss of faith among Soviet youth in particular, and a search for alternatives. This was particularly ironic because Khrushchev, for all his idiosyncrasies, was a relatively conventional communist. His onslaught on the Orthodox church, in which some 10,000 churches are thought to have been closed down, provided evidence on this point. Leninist nationality policy was given a new lease on life: the rapprochement and flourishing of peoples would, it was averred, result in their ultimate fusion. Mixed marriages were regarded as highly desirable. The 1961 Party Program asserted that the borders between the republics were increasingly losing "their past significance." Such postulates probably aroused the apprehension of Russian and other nationalists. At the same time, however, linguistic Russification was encouraged—a policy that has been strengthened repeatedly in subsequent years with the aim, in particular, of enabling the entire population to make fluent use of Russian at work and in the services.

BREZHNEV AND RESURGENT RUSSIAN NATIONALISM

Khrushchev, ousted in 1964, bequeathed an ideological and spiritual vacuum. Some young people and intellectuals (the best known of them abroad) pressed for greater political freedoms and opposed any return to Stalinist ways. Others urged the resurrection of an untainted "Leninism"; yet others, a return to genuine national traditions. Unofficial groups sprang up and expressed their views in samizdat writings. The works of philosophers like Berdyaev and Bulgakov enjoyed a vogue, while Russian classical writers—especially Dostoevsky—inspired the nationally conscious. Dostoevsky has, understandably, always proved a difficult nut to crack for the ideologists; writings about him continue to arouse controversy and censure.

Nationalist concerns were also articulated by a group of writers anguished by the fate of the depopulated Russian countryside and the social upheavals of rapid urbanization. Known as the *derevenshchiki* ("ruralists," "village prose" writers), they came into prominence in the 1960s although their origins can be traced back further. Included in this school are such leading writers as V. Belov, V. Shukshin, V. Astafiev, F. Abramov, V. Soloukhin and V. Rasputin. A story by Aleksandr Solzhenitsyn published in 1963, "Matryona's Homestead," exemplifies their respect for a (Christian-based) peasant ethic and regret at its passing. Rasputin has written: "The fact that the centuries-old village way of life has been fully destroyed and its moral climate destroyed with it (from time immemorial villages were the custodians of the people's moral values) could not, of course, fail to be reflected in literature, which always reflects such changes very sensitively." (*Literaturnaya Gazeta*, March 26, 1980)

Rasputin was obliquely referring to the brutal policy of collectivization. When trying to explain how the *derevenshchiki* have implicitly been able to criticize such a fundamental party policy, the writer A. Sinyavsky has suggested (*Index on Censorship* No. 4, 1980) that the ultimate peasant origin of the political leadership meant that "secretly they also mourn the passing of the old way of life and the ravages wrought by collectivization.... You might even say that they experience a certain sense of guilt toward the peasantry—toward the intelligentsia not at all, but toward the peasantry, yes." These views are speculative, but the significant fact remains that the *derevenshchiki* have not only managed to publish their works and achieve great popularity with them (a cult has evolved, for example, around the late V. Shukshin), but some of them have even won official prizes. At the same time, party ideologues often denounce their championing of "patriarchal ways" and their implied criticisms of "progressive social transformations" in industry and agriculture.

After Soloukhin published a book lyrically evocative of his ancestral region (*Vladimir Back Roads*, 1957) he received 6,000 letters from readers. His subsequent *Letters from a Russian Museum* (1966) and *Black Boards* (1969) dealt with the emotional issues of the destruction of the Russian cultural— particularly religious—heritage. In 1982, Soloukhin, a party member for three decades, incurred heavy party criticism for a suggestion he had published the previous year in the officially tolerated nationalist magazine *Nash Sovremennik* (Our Contemporary), to the effect that a "higher rational principle" obtained in the universe.

Literature has not been the only art form in which a nostalgia for prerevolutionary traditions has been accompanied by apparent criticisms of later developments. No discussion of recent overt expressions of Russian nationalism can proceed for long without reference to the painter I. Glazunov. Born in Leningrad, Glazunov has achieved great success, measured by such Soviet criteria as the ability to travel abroad extensively and have dealings with foreigners at home, to live in style in central Moscow, etc. He is no stranger to controversy and distrust (reportedly by lower-level party officials as well). In 1976 he won a libel action in a West German court against the suggestion that he was an agent of the KGB. One-man exhibitions of his works in Moscow (1978) and Leningrad (1979) were extraordinarily popular; they were said to have attracted some 1,500,000 visitors. The visitors' books (published abroad) contained effusive thanks, for example, "for telling the truth about Russia," and such exclamations as "For Holy Russia!" A touring exhibition in 1984 evidently evoked similar responses. Glazunov has achieved the rare distinction of being eulogized both in nationalist samizdat and in the official press. In 1980 he was made a People's Artist of the USSR. Although he is by far the best-known artist to strike an emotional Russian chord in his works, he is not alone (see, for example, the article about the late K. Vasiliev in *Komsomolskaya Pravda*, March 13, 1980).

In 1964, the *Rodina* ("Motherland") Club was established with official permission. Its membership evidently consisted of *rusity* ("Russites"), fervent Russian nationalists. (Various colloquial terms have been used of such people since; in the 1980s, "the Russian party" became the most current.) A Jewish emigrant, G. Svirsky, described in *Le Monde* (April 8–9, 1973) the conspiratorial atmosphere surrounding the club and his unwelcome presence at one of its meetings. Glazunov was a prime mover in the creation in 1965 of a mass public organization: the All-Russian Society for the Preservation of Historical and Cultural Monuments (Russian initials: VOOPIK). It was not the first such society in the USSR; in 1959–64, similar bodies had been set up in the three Transcaucasian republics. By January 1983, VOOPIK had more than 15 million members in 98,000 primary organizations. The much older All-Russian Society for the Conservation of Nature—another area of concern to Russian nationalists, among others—had more than 35 million members by the same date, including junior affiliates.

Apart from the conservation of the cultural heritage and the environment, several other burning social and demographic issues began to be discussed openly in the press, particularly rural depopulation in the Russian SFSR, rising divorce and alcoholism rates, and the declining birthrate of Russians (and other Slavs) in contrast to the dynamic birthrates of certain Muslim peoples of the USSR. The censuses of 1959, 1970 and 1979 provided unwelcome data. Dissident nationalists spelled out their anxieties emotionally: "Our so-called nationalism . . . is a manifestation of the instinct of self-preservation on the part of a vanishing nation. . . . I believe that even the question of human rights in the USSR is less important at this juncture in history than the problem of the dying Russian nation." (V. Osipov in a letter to an émigré journal published in 1972)

After 1967, official "anti-Zionist" propaganda began increasingly to draw on traditional anti-Semitic themes, even, on occasion, recycling czarist fabrications and raising the specter of a "Jewish-Masonic" conspiracy. Those with their own anti-Semitic axes to grind, such as the writer I. Shevtsov and the extreme conspiracy theorist V. Emelyanov (reportedly committed to an asylum in 1980 after murdering his wife), sought to exploit the situation.

In the late 1960s, the main officially tolerated nationalist outlet was the magazine *Molodaya Gvardiya* (Young Guard), issued, significantly, by the Komsomol. It published two essays by V. Chalmaev that attempted to define the historical Russian ethos and which led to particularly vigorous polemics. In 1970, the Politburo was (unofficially) reported to have criticized the magazine. Its editor was replaced. More significant, however, was the manner in which Chalmaev had managed to rally support (in the mass-circulation slick magazine *Ogonek*, published by *Pravda*) against the liberal journal *Novy Mir* (New World), which had, somewhat ironically in the circumstances, attacked him from an orthodox Marxist standpoint. It was rumored that two of the departments (these departments supervise virtually every aspect of Soviet life) of the Central Committee of the Communist party of the Soviet Union (CPSU)—the Department of Culture and that of Agitation and Propaganda—differed over the desirability of supporting Russian nationalist trends. The Department of Agitation and Propaganda had certainly been involved in censure of Chalmaev (*Zhurnalist* No. 5, 1969). Its acting head, A. Yakovlev, published a major article in the weekly *Literaturnaya Gazeta* on November 15, 1972, aimed at many targets but particularly at Russian nationalists in the arts, including the antiindustrial "ruralists." Not long afterward, Yakovlev was demoted to the post of ambassador to Canada, where he remained until Andropov brought him back to Moscow in 1983 to head an important institute. More than any other, this episode appeared to reveal that the issue of a response to Russian nationalism was causing dissension in the highest councils of the party.

Dissident nationalist groups, however, discussed issues without restraint in their samizdat. Program proposals began to be drawn up. An early such group, the Leningrad-based All-Russian Social Christian Union for the Liberation of the People (Russian initials: VSKhSON) had 28 members and 30 candidate members when the KGB decided to strike in 1967. Its program presented a specifically Russian blueprint for the future, emphasizing the role of the Orthodox church and the family. The best-known samizdat nationalist magazine, *Veche* (Rumor), began circulating in 1971. Nine issues came out under the editorship of V. Osipov who, in a distant echo of Dostoevsky's political evolution, had become a nationalist in the prison camps. The KGB appears to have engineered an eventual rift among *Veche*'s editors. Osipov managed to circulate two issues of another samizdat magazine, *Zemlya* (Land) before being arrested. In 1975 he received a sentence of eight years in a labor camp. There is speculation that he had been protected by an allegedly pronationalist member of the Soviet leadership, D. Polyansky, who was himself dropped from the Politburo in 1976 and appointed ambassador to Japan—an intriguing apparent parallel with the antinationalist Yakovlev mentioned above.

Osipov is one of the relatively few dissident Russian nationalists per se to have been tried, in comparison to religious and human rights activists and non-Russian, such as Ukrainian and Baltic, nationalists. However, when the authorities do decide to impose punishment it can be draconian; in 1983, L. Borodin, a former member of VSKhSON who had issued a quickly suppressed nationalist magazine himself in the mid-1970s, was sentenced to 10 years in a labor camp to be followed by five in internal exile.

Veche provided a useful insight into a wide range of nationalist aspirations, apprehensions and views on subjects both current and historical. Although it was the mouthpiece of a relatively moderate group, occasional anti-Semitic notes could be discerned; however, the journal also featured relatively constructive exchanges on the Jewish question. Certain other examples of nationalist samizdat, usually pseudonymously or anonymously written, have been outspokenly racist or anti-Semitic. The first issue of *Veche* emphasized especially that nationalism was inconceivable outside Christianity. Such a point of view is evidently not shared by more extreme nationalists, who now include small-scale fascist groups reliably reported to have demonstrated in public in several Russian towns in the 1980s (in particular on Hitler's birthday).

The most celebrated of all contemporary Russian nationalists is the writer Solzhenitsyn. Briefly lionized under Khrushchev, who made use of him in his de-Stalinization campaign, Solzhenitsyn was increasingly forced into a dissident role under Brezhnev before being expelled from his native land in 1974. In his *Letter to the Soviet Leaders* (written in 1973), Solzhenitsyn urged the renunciation of Marxism, with its international commitments, in favor of a genuinely national policy and a concentration on building up Russia's own resources (particularly in northeastern Siberia). Solzhenitsyn's focus on the need to cure Russia's own social and economic ills, with its concomitant isolationism in foreign policy, is shared by other moderate dissident nationalists. Also in 1973 he contributed to a collection of essays entitled *From under the Rubble*. His letter and essay can be seen as part of the nationalist response to the writings of members of the dissident "democratic movement." The positions held by the two sides echo the 19th-century controversy between Slavophiles and Westernizers.

Solzhenitsyn's appeals to patriotism and Orthodoxy, his tendency to idealize prerevolutionary (and particularly pre-Petrine) Russia and his firm rejection of the introduction of a Western-type democracy into a society unprepared for it, provoked direct criticisms from the country's best-known dissident, Academician A. Sakharov, who insisted that the need was for more democracy. There can be little doubt, however, that of the two Solzhenitsyn is closer to the concerns and traditions of most Russians than the liberalizing "Westernizer" Sakharov. Soviet conditioning has, of course, maintained negative attitudes toward the West. Fear of radical changes that might lead to violent anarchy is, however, very probably a potent factor in the psyche of many Russians, even those not particularly enamored of the regime. Among the "third wave" of emigrants from the 1970s onward, the relatively respectful exchanges between Sakharov and Solzhenitsyn have been replayed in more acrimonious form—with one side (mainly, but not exclusively, Jews) expressing fears that the outright adoption of a Russian nationalist ideology by a Soviet leadership unconstrained by internationalist considerations would lead to bloody disaster both within and outside the USSR, while the other side insists that the only cure for Soviet ills lies in the rejection of the alien import of Marxism and in a genuinely national and religious renaissance. The alarm of the first faction, fueled by historical precedents and by what they see as mounting evidence of overt Russian nationalism in the official media, is understandable. However, there is limited evidence to suggest that the nationalists themselves do not feel they are receiving positive support from the regime. Even if a Soviet leadership wished to permit Russian nationalism its full expression (and despite rumors about the sentiments of individual Politburo members in recent years, there is no evidence to suggest that this has been the case), Russian and Soviet history provides potent warnings of the danger of anti-Russian reactions in a multinational state; an example is the wartime collaboration of many non-Russians with the Nazi invaders. It is for this reason, no doubt, that non-Russian nationalities, particularly the more volatile ones, are themselves permitted certain symbolic outlets for their nationalism.

The ideas of what a leading expert on contemporary Russian nationalism, J. B. Dunlop, has called the *vozrozhdentsy* (from the Russian for "renaissance") are also open to qualification. In Dunlop's view virtually all dissident nationalists are aligned with this tendency, as well as many of those who try to publicize their views in the media. There can be no doubt of the connection between a renewed interest in Orthodoxy and the aspirations of certain nationalists. However, the future prospering of this moderate tendency would appear to depend heavily on the removal of the shackles inhibiting the church and the shedding of the compromises forced on it by the state, as well as on a significant reversal of the process of secularization. There is no indication that the Soviet authorities wish to be accommodating in these respects.

The other main current tendency singled out by Dunlop is "National Bolshevism," the attempts by Semanov, Chalmaev and others to promote a fusion of Russian patriotism with aspects of the official ideology but, crucially, without Christianity. In his 1983 book *The Faces of Contemporary Russian Nationalism*, he draws useful parallels between certain elements in fascism and National Bolshevism.

Brezhnev, to judge by rumor and a disparaging reference to "round dances, peasant huts and headdresses" that occurred in the third volume of his autobiography (published in 1978), appeared to be personally irritated by aspects of the renewed interest in Russia's roots. Under his leadership, however, not only were several of the main nationalist grievances openly aired, but some efforts to placate the nationalist constituency were also undertaken. In 1974, a massive plan to develop the so-called non-blackearth zone of the Russian SFSR (the republic where most Russians still live) was announced. This zone encompasses the ancestral Russian heartland, the dereliction and depopulation of which had been described both in public print and in samizdat. At the 26th Party Congress in 1981, Brezhnev appealed to other republics for assistance ("and in as short a time as possible") in tackling the area's complex problems. Also in 1981, the proposals of certain demographers were accepted and some welfare benefits became payable on a regionally differentiated basis that happened to favor (initially) areas of the Russian SFSR. From 1976, various laws on conserving cultural monuments and the natural environment were also enacted, if not always observed. The Brezhnev administration procrastinated over schemes to divert Siberian waters to the south, including Central Asian regions whose political spokesmen were loud in their demands that the main scheme must proceed. Russian intellectuals seemed to be apprehensive about the loss of cultural and historical monuments involved in such schemes, while scientists debated the environmental aspects.

With the experience of the last war and the possibility of hostilities against China or the West in mind, the leadership particularly encouraged "military-patriotic" indoctrination, into which the cult of czarist military commanders was incorporated. In February 1982, for example, a statue of Generalissimo Suvorov was unveiled in a busy Moscow square in the presence of two Politburo members. However, popular interest in the ancien régime—demonstrated, for example, by the sensation caused by a documentary account of the last days of Nicholas II's family, serialized in the magazine *Zvezda* (Star) in 1972–73, and by V. Pikul's pulp novel *On the Edge* in 1979—left the authorities uneasy. In 1977, according to a reliable samizdat source, the house in Sverdlovsk (formerly Ekaterinburg) where the royal family had been incarcerated prior to execution, was demolished at night, after being surrounded by soldiers and police. More than 300 people gathered nevertheless. It had apparently become a place of pilgrimage. Monarchist sentiments are clearly discernible among certain dissident nationalists and others as well. Novels published in 1969 and 1981 by the otherwise politically opposed writers V. Kochetov and Y. Yevtushenko contained lampoons of monarchistically inclined intellectuals.

AFTER BREZHNEV

Brezhnev's immediate successor as general secretary of the party, the former KGB Chairman Yuri Andropov, evidently did not favor "the Russian party." After M. Suslov's death in January 1982, Andropov took over as party secretary in charge of ideological matters. At about this time, some dissident Russian nationalists were arrested and others interrogated. The well-known "National Bolshevik" S. Semanov was sacked from the editorship of a mass-circulation legal journal and eventually given a much humbler publishing post. Brezhnev died in November 1982, and in a major speech the following month Andropov stressed the significance of Lenin's view about an ultimate fusion of all nationalities—an unpopular concept shunned by Brezhnev. One of the few senior party officials to use the same Leninist language was K. Chernenko, the new secretary in charge of ideology (*World Marxist Review* No. 12, 1982). It was also Chernenko who, at the June 1983 Central Committee plenum on ideology, attacked the incorrect treatment of collectivization—an oblique criticism of the ruralist writers.

Andropov's short tenure of office ended in February 1984. As party chairmen, both Chernenko and Mikhail Gorbachev have generally abandoned the policy of relative laissez-faire concerning nationalist trends. It remains to be seen, however, whether Gorbachev's relative youth and energy can counter traditional sentiments of long standing.

CONCLUSION

Not only is a broad range of nationalist aspirations and sentiments flourishing among by far the largest and most politically significant of the Soviet Union's peoples, but for about half a century the leadership has exploited aspects of such nationalism with greater or lesser enthusiasm. Although there is no reason to doubt that Lenin's statement at the Eighth Party Congress in 1919—"Scratch some communists and you will find Great Russian chauvinists"—still applies at various levels of the system, the practical purpose of such exploitation is the mobilization of a population no longer responsive to the revolutionary, internationalist rhetoric of earlier years (the grass roots disapproval of aid to Soviet clients abroad is notorious, for example). Not the least of the ironies that abound is that in a country and under a system commonly identified with "Russia" and "the Russians," many Russians themselves would agree with the words of the ruralist V. Rasputin (in an interview published abroad in 1982): "It seems to me that in our country Russians live no better, but perhaps even worse, than other peoples." Such sentiments have even found their way into the official press; see, for example, the article by the demographers B. Urlanis and G. Litvinova in *Sovetskoe Gosudarstvo i Pravo* (Soviet State and Law) No. 3, 1982. At the same time, Russians sense that their political tutelage is resented by other Soviet peoples who are not necessarily grateful for what the former perceive to be their self-sacrifice in war and peace. Dissatisfaction among the peoples of the world's first workers' state—Russians and non-Russians alike—is all too apt to acquire a nationalist hue.

FURTHER READING

Allworth, E., ed. *The Dilemma of Dominance.* New York: Pergamon, 1980.

Barghoorn, F. C. *Soviet Russian Nationalism.* New York: Oxford University Press, 1956.

Dunlop, J. B. *The Faces of Contemporary Russian Nationalism.* Princeton: Princeton University Press, 1983.

———. *The New Russian Revolutionaries.* Woodside, New York: Nordland, 1976.

Holdworth, M. "Lenin and the Nationalities Question," in L. Schapiro et al., eds. *Lenin: The Man, The Theorist, The Leader—A Reappraisal.* London: Pall Mall 1967.

Hosking, G. A. *Beyond Soviet Realism: Soviet Fiction Since Ivan Denisovich.* London: Granada/Paul Elek, 1980.

Riasonovsky, N. V. *Nicholas I and Official Nationality in Russia, 1825–1855.* Berkeley and Los Angeles: University of California Press; Cambridge: Cambridge University Press, 1959.

Seton-Watson, H. *The Russian Empire 1801–1917.* New York and London: Oxford University Press, 1967.

Yanov, A. *Détente After Brezhnev: The Domestic Roots of Soviet Foreign Policy.* Berkeley: University of California Press, 1977.

———. *The Russian New Right: Right-Wing Ideologies in the Contemporary USSR.* Berkeley: University of California Press, 1978.

(The two last-named works are controversial but contain useful material.)

THE STRUCTURES OF GOVERNMENT AND POLITICS

PETER FRANK

FROM 1917 to the end of World War II, the Soviet Union was the world's only socialist state (pace Mongolia and Tannu Tuva). That alone was sufficient reason for foreign communists to regard it as a model to be emulated, if and when their own countries followed the socialist path. Between 1944 and 1948, such hopes were fulfilled in several Eastern European states. In some cases (Albania, Yugoslavia and, later, Czechoslovakia), this came about largely because of the efforts of the indigenous Communist parties; elsewhere (Poland, East Germany, Hungary, Romania and Bulgaria) it was the result of intervention or imposition by the Red Army.

The Soviet Union emerged from the war as a world power; Stalin's prestige and dictatorial power were at their height. By precept or force, the "people's democracies," while retaining certain national or cultural characteristics, in however attenuated a form, adopted the structural and organizational patterns of the Soviet Communist party and state.

The Communist party of the Soviet Union (CPSU) had its genesis as an illegal, clandestine, revolutionary political party. It placed great emphasis upon security and secrecy, to which ends cells of party members were formed not in the area of residence (as in open democracies, where governmental power is transferred by electoral means), but in places of work. This strategy enhanced the cells' security, but also enabled them to exert their maximum disruptive influence at the point of production. When linked with the doctrine of "democratic centralism," this "production principle" made for a centralized, military type of organization that was highly responsive to party leadership. These traits had obvious utility after the revolution, given the CPSU's mobilizing and modernizing objectives. Today, they are the salient features of all Leninist parties.

The CPSU has a membership approaching 19 million people of diverse national, ethnic, occupational and educational backgrounds. Every communist belongs to a "primary party organization" (as the cell is now called), which exists wherever three or more party members work together. Above that primary tier are party committees corresponding to the territorial divisions of the Soviet Union: towns, rural districts, regions, constituent republics. At the apex of this pyramid stand the central party organs, the All-Union Central Committee, the Politburo and Secretariat. At the heart of every

244

party organization, from bottom to top, is an executive official (the first secretary) who is assisted by a permanent staff (the *apparat*).

Whereas the CPSU is a unified, strictly centralized organization, the Soviet state is, ostensibly, a federal or quasi-federal system made up of legislatures (soviets) that elect executive committees. So at the top, parallel to the CPSU's All-Union Central Committee, there is the USSR Supreme Soviet. The Central Committee appoints the Politburo; the Supreme Soviet appoints the Council of Ministers. The general secretary of the CPSU is appointed by the Central Committee to head the Politburo; the Council of Ministers has its chairman, the prime minister. Unique to the system of soviets is the presidium of the USSR Supreme Soviet with its chairman, the president.

There are thus two organizationally separate structures. One structure, the party, is superior to the other, the state. Article 6 of the Soviet Constitution describes the CPSU as the leading and directing core of the entire Soviet political system. This parallel but unequal relationship is expressed in Soviet theory and practice in the strict separation of the two main elements of government. Decision making and policy formulation (the superior element) are monopolized by the party; policy implementation (administration) is the function of the soviets and other public organizations, such as the trade unions and Komsomol, the youth organization. In Russian, the leadership role is known as *rukovodstvo*; administration is *upravlenie*. Citizens are exhorted to involve themselves in *upravlenie*; the party alone (in practice the party *apparat*) exercises *rukovodstvo* over society.

Formally, the supreme party institution is the congress, which meets every five years. Congress names a Central Committee (CC), consisting of several hundred members whose task is to manage the party's affairs between meetings of the congress. Because the CC usually convenes only twice a year, it appoints a political bureau (meeting at least weekly), which is serviced by the Secretariat headed by the general secretary. It is this Politburo, with its overlapping Secretariat membership, that, in the superior decision making sense, is the de facto government of the country.

Table 1 depicts, in functional terms, the composition of the CPSU Politburo and Secretariat as of September 1984 (although the pattern is remarkably consistent). The core consists of Politburo members who are simultaneously CC secretaries, while certain candidate members (those with only a consultative vote) also have dual membership in these two interlocking bodies. Then there are secretaries who attend Politburo sessions, but who have no formal voice at all. Together with the chairman of the Party Control Committee (an institution responsible for intraparty discipline) and the first secretary of the Moscow city party organization, this constitutes the Moscow-based party element in the Politburo. There are also the regional party representatives, first secretaries of certain republic party organizations. Taken together, the party *apparat* element forms a majority.

The "nonparty" or governmental element in the Politburo (all long-standing party members, of course) is made up of the prime minister (chairman of the USSR Council of Ministers) and one of his first deputy chairmen, the prime minister of the Russian Soviet Federated Socialist Republic (Russian SFSR), the largest constituent republic, and two ministers with the portfolios

245

Table 1
FUNCTIONAL COMPOSITION OF THE POLITBURO CC CPSU
(*as of September 1984*)

Full Members
   general secretary CC CPSU and chairman (president) of the presidium of the USSR
   Supreme Soviet
   2 secretaries of the CC CPSU
   first secretary of the capital city party organization
   2 first secretaries of republic party organizations
   chairman of the Committee of Party Control
   chairman (prime minister) of the USSR Council of Ministers
   first deputy chairman of the USSR Council of Ministers
   first deputy chairman of the USSR Council of Ministers and minister for foreign
   affairs
   USSR minister of defense
   chairman (prime minister) of the Russian SFSR Council of Ministers

Candidate Members
   2 secretaries of the CC CPSU
   1 first secretary of a republic party organization
   first deputy chairman (vice president) of the presidium of the USSR Supreme Soviet
   USSR minister of culture
   chairman of the USSR State Committee for State Security (KGB)

(There are also five CC secretaries who attend Politburo meetings but have no vote,
either full or consultative.)

of foreign affairs and defense. Culture and internal security are represented
among the candidate members, as is the state in the person of the first deputy
chairman of the presidium of the USSR Supreme Soviet. Linkage of party
and state has been exemplified by the fact that general secretaries Brezhnev,
Andropov and Chernenko have each in turn assumed the presidency.
   Once policy has been set, the party's chief role is to supervise (*kontrol'*)
its implementation. Supervision should not extend to outright control (in
the direct, English sense of the word); that would be usurpation (*podmena*)
of the functions of the soviets and other public organizations. In practice
the distinction is very fine, and party committees all too often interfere in
the implementation of policy decisions and the management of enterprises
or elected soviets. In one rural district alone, for example, the party committee sent out 500 documents in a six-month period; another party committee
required 122 persons from the same collective farm (*kolkhoz*) to report to
district headquarters at harvest time, the *kolkhoz* chairman making the
journey 12 times and his deputy 14 times. Such examples, especially in the
agricultural sector, are not uncommon.
   Attempting to ensure compliance with its wishes, the party has evolved
various mechanisms of control over society. The party membership itself,
scattered in varying density throughout all occupational and social groups,
is seen as the active ingredient among the masses, rather as yeast activates
flour in bread making.

As well as exercising *kontrol'* over the management of the workplace, the party element within such elective bodies as the soviets and trade-union committees acts as a caucus to ensure that the party line on all matters is adopted and carried out. The common denominator in these practices is the strict enforcement of democratic centralism, the organizational principle underpinning the fundamental tenet of Soviet-type systems, "the leading role of the party."

All these mechanisms of control are clearly prescribed in CPSU statutes and are frequently discussed in the party press. Mentioned far less often, yet critically important—some consider it the crucial feature of communist systems—is *nomenklatura*.

Suppose that every party committee, from the Politburo in Moscow down to the most remote district or town committee, maintains two lists. One consists of the names of members (usually referred to as cadres), with details of their personal histories, professional qualifications, career background, social and political activeness, and so on; the other list is of posts, the *nomenklatura*. All these posts, both party and nonparty, are situated at the interstices of power and authority in the territorial area falling within the purview of a given party committee. In a city with a population of around a million, the local party committee's *nomenklatura* might consist of 800 posts. Many other posts in that city would belong to the *nomenklatura* of the next-highest party committee at regional level, and a few, no doubt, would be included on the Politburo list at the center. The Politburo itself would decide who should be the editors of the main central newspapers and other media managers, the chief military commanders, the head of the All-Union trade union movement, the head of the Komsomol, and so on. The art consists in placing the cadre most suitable—according to the party's criteria—in the appropriate *nomenklatura* slot. An untypically frank account of how the system of *nomenklatura* works appeared in an authoritative party source:

> Party committees play the decisive role in the selection and placement of leading cadres in all the most important sectors of party, state, economic and social activity, and in scientific organizations, educational institutions, cultural establishments, in health, public education, law-enforcement organs, and other spheres of activity. How, concretely, is this role expressed? There exists an extensive *nomenklatura* of posts, the filling of which is carried out according to the decisions of, or with the consent of, the appropriate party committee. Every nominee for a *nomenklatura* post must be considered on a personal basis by the party organs.[1]

The same source cites as an example the *nomenklatura* of the Kursk regional party committee, the *obkom*, which contains 1,840 posts. Twenty-six percent of these are party offices comprising the *obkom apparat*—the secretaries, the heads of department and deputy heads of department of subordinate town and district party committees, and the secretaries of major primary party organizations. In the nonparty sector, but entirely at the party's disposal, the distribution is as follows:

> A significant part of the *nomenklatura* (22 percent) consists of soviet cadres: leading officials of the regional soviet executive committee and regional boards, chairmen

[1]E. Z. Razumov, *Problemy kadrovoi politiki KPSS*, Moscow, 1983, p. 58, author's translation.

247

and deputy chairmen of town and rural district soviet executive committees. About four percent of *nomenklatura* posts are occupied by trade union and Komsomol cadres; 12 percent are cadres in industry, construction, transport and communications. The most numerous group of *nomenklatura* offices (36 percent) are in agriculture [Kursk is an agricultural region], including ... directors of state farms and *kolkhoz* chairmen.[2]

A Soviet-type political system, then, is one in which the Communist party plays the leading, directing role. The party guards and interprets the ideology, sets the long-term policy agenda and formulates shorter-term goals. It exercises a monopoly of political power and preserves that monopoly partly through formal, institutional structures, and partly through informal mechanisms, notably *nomenklatura*. Less to the fore, yet still available to the leadership should the need arise, are organs of coercion such as the KGB (which likes to describe itself as "the sword and shield of the party"). In neighboring Eastern European socialist states, there is another powerful coercive constraint upon internal political behavior. This is the Soviet Army, which, as a last resort, may be deployed in order to maintain the existing system (as it was in East Germany in 1953, Hungary in 1956 and Czechoslovakia in 1968).

The salient features of the Soviet system are fundamental, too, to the other socialist states. There are, however, some local variations. Half of the eight countries of Eastern Europe have multiparty political systems (Bulgaria, Czechoslovakia, East Germany and Poland); the rest, like the Soviet Union, are single-party systems (Albania, Hungary, Romania and Yugoslavia). In Bulgaria, for example, as well as the Communist party with its membership of 826,000 (in a population approaching 9 million), there is also the Bulgarian Agrarian People's Union with 120,000 members. In Czechoslovakia, in addition to the Communist party of Slovakia, which is a component part of the Communist party of Czechoslovakia, there are four other, ostensibly distinct, political parties. This formal "pluralism" is reflected in the composition of the parliaments of these countries, where members sit under the various party labels. In practice, however, the non-Communist parties long ago "recognized the Communist party's leading role" in society and state. Indeed, in seven countries (Yugoslavia is the exception) there exists a National Front, behind which are united all the political parties led by the communists, together with various cultural and sporting organizations. Even in countries where there is a single party (such as Albania) there is still a front (in Albania its chairman was, until his death on April 11, 1985, Enver Hoxha, the party's first secretary). Where the front is headed by a nonparty chairman, control is in the hands of the Communist party, since this is a key *nomenklatura* appointment. In the legislatures, all deputies vote as a bloc according to the leading party's instructions; abstentions or dissenting votes occur only very rarely (as when the decision was taken to impose martial law in Poland). Nevertheless, the regime can never be quite sure that different traditions or interests will not reassert themselves through the non-Communist parties, and there have been critical moments, as in Czechoslovakia in 1968, when

[2]*Ibid.*, p. 60.

248

these "rump" parties have shown signs of reasserting a truly separate and independent existence.

There is one respect in which Eastern European practice appears to have affected political behavior in the Soviet Union. When Stalin was alive, most Eastern European leaders modeled their behavior on him. Not only was their personal style of rule the same (they used terror and repression, and fostered personality cults), but they also emulated Soviet practice by tending to occupy the equivalent, titular institutional posts.

There are three leadership offices in the Soviet Union; the general (or first) secretaryship of the Communist party, now recognized to be of first importance; the chairmanship of the Council of Ministers, the prime minister; and the chairmanship of the presidium of the Supreme Soviet, usually referred to as the presidency. Since Soviet constitutional theory is hazy as to which office in particular is the supreme leadership position, in practice the three may be held separately or in combination. Stalin, having risen to preeminence by exploiting the power potential of the party general secretaryship, chose ultimately to hold that office and the premiership simultaneously. As part of the de-Stalinization process, the new Soviet leadership separated these offices and required the client socialist states to do likewise.

Although Khrushchev was the prime de-Stalinizer, it was he who in 1958 once again added the government post to the party office, much to the subsequent discomfiture of his Politburo colleagues who, in 1964, ousted him from the leadership and stated that never again would the party and government posts be linked in the same person. However, such are the exigencies of supreme Soviet leadership, especially in the realm of foreign policy, that it became evident by the mid-1970s that the party general secretaryship by itself was not enough.

In Eastern Europe, meanwhile, in the somewhat more relaxed climate of "separate roads to communism," patterns different from the Soviet one evolved. In Yugoslavia, Tito (once anathematized by Moscow) was head of party, government *and* state; in Czechoslovakia, the office of president retained an aura of great prestige from the precommunist era, and was held by the party general secretary; while in Romania, Ceauşescu in 1974 assumed the newly created post of president of the republic. Elsewhere in the communist world, such charismatic leaders as Ho Chi Minh and Mao Zedong headed both party and state. In the era of détente, Brezhnev perceived the utility of linking party and state posts, as well as the personal honor and prestige that would accrue to him, and so in 1977 he assumed both offices. Since then, Andropov and Chernenko have followed suit, and Gorbachev may eventually to do so too. As indicated below, the party-state linkage is now dominant:

Leader holds party post only: Hungary, Soviet Union

Party post and government post linked in same person: Poland

Party post and state posts linked in same person: Albania, Bulgaria, Czechoslovakia, East Germany, Romania

(Note: Yugoslavia, since Tito, has adopted a complicated, institutionalized collective leadership with rotating heads of party and state.)

Since Stalin died, the Eastern European socialist states have either been given or (as in the cases of Yugoslavia, Albania and, to a somewhat lesser degree, Romania) have taken for themselves varying amounts of autonomy with respect to domestic affairs. In Hungary, innovatory economic mechanisms have produced impressive results compared with neighboring economies; in Poland, independent economic initiatives have brought the country to the brink of disaster. Romania has stayed ultraorthodox and at the same time pursued a risky foreign policy line. Yet, again with the exception of Albania and Yugoslavia, there has never been any doubt that the Soviet Union would physically intervene should any of the fundamental structural or organizational principles of a Soviet-type political system appear to be in danger. The formulation of the Brezhnev doctrine of limited sovereignty in the wake of intervention in Czechoslovakia in 1968, and Soviet pressures on Poland more recently, have made it crystal clear that the leading role of the party, democratic centralism and the primacy of *nomenklatura* remain the inviolable core of the communist political system.

FURTHER READING

Brown, Archie and Kaser, Michael, eds. *The Soviet Union since the Fall of Khrushchev*. London: Macmillan, 1975.

Byrnes, Robert F., ed. *After Brezhnev—Sources of Soviet Conduct in the 1980s*. Bloomington: Indiana University Press, 1983.

Schapiro, Leonard B. *The Communist Party of the Soviet Union*. London: Methuen; New York: Vintage Books, 1964.

Voslensky, Michael. *Nomenklatura—The Soviet Ruling Class: An Insider's Report*. New York: Doubleday, 1984.

THE SOCIAL AND POLITICAL SIGNIFICANCE OF DISSENT IN THE SOVIET UNION

PETER REDDAWAY

It was in the late 1960s that many of the dissident groups in the Soviet Union started organizing themselves and publicizing their concerns—social, political, economic, humanitarian, cultural, religious, legal, emigrational, and so on. I use the term "dissent" to designate those movements that have expressed either opposition to particular government policies or the desire to emigrate. The broad questions I want to pose are the following: What have been the main successes and failures of these groups? What concessions has the regime made to them? Which groups have proved stronger, which weaker, and why? How important has the West been in supporting or failing to support them? What effect have such external developments as the Czechoslovak events of 1968 or the 1979 Soviet invasion of Afghanistan had on them? Why did the regime treat the dissident groups with relative tolerance until 1979–80? Why did it then switch by stages to a policy of virtually halting emigration and trying to suppress all open dissent? Can this policy be maintained without provoking an unacceptable growth of underground activity, terrorism or other acts of violence? Finally, have the groups had a noticeable overall impact on the regime's perceptions and self-confidence?

RESPONSES TO DISSENT

The crucial initial success of the groups consisted in overcoming the social atomization that had been induced by Stalinism and in breaking down some of the political taboos associated with it. The classical freedoms of association and of expression were boldly asserted in order to report the truth and to press demands on the regime publicly. The openness with which this was done, the lack of secrecy or conspiracy, made infiltration of the groups difficult and, therefore, rare. Apart from a brief moment of euphoria during the Prague Spring of 1968, the groups have maintained a sober approach, scarcely ever raising their supporters' hopes above the expectation that the road ahead would be long and arduous—as indeed it has been. Many

251

individuals, including Andrei Sakharov, have been motivated by a moral imperative that requires them to act, even when the chances of any substantial success seem minimal or nonexistent.

The movements have communicated their views, reports and demands effectively—given the circumstances—to three main audiences outside their own memberships: a certain proportion of their fellow citizens (thereby gaining sympathizers and recruits); appropriate Soviet authorities; and individuals and organizations abroad. The main channels have been samizdat (typescripts passed from hand to hand), foreign journalists in the USSR, foreign radio broadcasts to the Soviet Union in Russian and other languages and direct representations, either to Soviet bodies via delegations and the mails or to foreign bodies via, for example, supporters who have emigrated.

In general, the Soviet authorities have responded to such representations by ignoring or rejecting them. Perhaps only in three cases have clear-cut concessions been made on broad issues. The most notable so far has been the decision of 1971 to allow emigration on a significant scale for the first time since the 1920s, though this momentous concession was to be retracted a decade later. Second, in 1973 the Jewish emigration movement, backed by crucial support from the U.S. Congress, achieved the de facto abolition of the heavy education tax on emigrants that had been introduced a year earlier. A third clear-cut concession was made in 1967 when the Crimean Tatars were exonerated from the charge of having committed mass treason during World War II. However, this group's main demand—that they be allowed to return from Central Asian exile to their Crimean homeland—has been consistently rejected.

Appeals by Soviet dissidents to foreign audiences have, by contrast, quite often evoked a positive response. Most helpful of all have been nongovernmental bodies with professional, political or religious concerns directly related to those of the Soviet group or individual. Obvious examples are scientific organizations that want to protect persecuted scientists like Sakharov.

International bodies to which the USSR belongs have been, not surprisingly, generally unresponsive to appeals. This has been especially true of U.N. organizations. Non-U.N. bodies have, in some cases, however, been forums for protracted struggles between the Soviet organizations that belong to them and other members who support the demands of the Soviet dissident groups in the relevant fields. In the World Psychiatric Association (WPA), a struggle of this sort was waged for over a decade on the issue of Soviet use of psychiatric facilities to suppress dissent. In 1983, the Soviet psychiatric society finally resigned from the WPA rather than be expelled by that body. By contrast, officials of the Soviet churches that belong to the World Council of Churches have successfully prevented the Council from responding in any effective way to numerous appeals from persecuted groups of Soviet Christians.

Some unlucky dissident movements have found little or no support abroad, mainly because bodies that might have helped them have either remained passive or are virtually nonexistent. It is only recently that one or two Muslim governments have shown interest in the Crimean Tatars because of the common bond of Islam. Dissenting Russian nationalists have been viewed with some caution in the West because of their seeming lack of commitment to pluralist democracy, although they have received more support since the expulsion in 1974 of their leading figure, Aleksandr Solzhenitsyn. And nationalist movements in the Ukrainian, Baltic and Trans-caucasian republics have suffered above all from Western hesitation about supporting forces that could conceivably lead to the breakup of the Soviet Union.

All this said, however, the outside world has been of great importance to every Soviet dissident group for two reasons. First and foremost, Western radio stations are likely to broadcast back to the USSR any serious document that a group can smuggle out. Second, the outside world is a source of international declarations and covenants on citizens' rights that have been signed by the Soviet government (like the 1975 Final Act of the Helsinki Conference on Security and Cooperation in Europe) and have, therefore, repeatedly been used by groups to underpin their demands.

REGIME POLICIES TOWARD DISSENT

In view of this and of the other successes of the dissident groups, an important and intriguing question arises that has puzzled many observers for a decade and a half: Why did the Politburo allow these groups to develop, interact, multiply, generate worldwide publicity and find foreign support? Above all, why did it not nip in the bud in 1968 the only two integrating elements— the human rights movement and the more political democratic movement (whose informal memberships widely overlapped)—that were just coming into existence? Had it done so, first, the other groups, diverse and scattered, would have remained ignorant of each other. Second, since the Moscow-based "integrators," or "democrats" for short, were the only dissidents with constantly available foreign contacts, very few samizdat documents and very few interviews with foreign journalists would ever have reached the West.

The operation would not have been difficult technically and could have been achieved at very little real political cost. Only about 100 arrests of key individuals would have been needed (on top of the small number actually made) to stop the democrats' activity. If the situation had been handled firmly, the domestic and hence the foreign protests would have been few and muted and the country's social and economic cohesion would scarcely have been badly upset. As for the timing, late 1968 would have been an ideal moment to strike. At that time the KGB had already had nearly a year in which to investigate the 700 or so individuals who had signed the democrats' early documents and to identify the organizers. The organizers had only just begun to develop their information networks outside Moscow. And finally, the invasion of Czechoslovakia, just carried out smoothly, pro-vided a perfect occasion on which to ram it home that liberal ideas would not be tolerated in the USSR any more than they would be in Czechoslovakia.

Only informed speculation can be offered on why the above scenario was not actually carried out. In 1968 the post-Khrushchevian leadership had still to achieve stability; throughout that year it was overwhelmingly preoccupied with Czechoslovakia. Although its outlook was not very anti-Stalinist, it did not want to appear Stalinist. The leadership's view of the newly emergent democrats in August 1968 may well have been that they were a worrisome phenomenon, but that the KGB could probably soon complete the task of reducing them to near silence. At any rate there was no good reason to resort to a wave of arrests of well-established individuals; indeed, there were many persuasive reasons not to. After all, the arrest in 1967 of a mere half-dozen young unknowns from the fringes of the "suspect 100" had provoked 700 members of the intelligentsia to protest in late 1967 and early 1968—a troublesome escalation from the few dozen who had signed protests over the trial of Andrei Sinyavsky and Yuli Daniel in 1966.

Such an evaluation of the Soviet leaders' views in 1968—if reasonably accurate—suggests, in retrospect, that they underestimated the potential threat to their interests. The late 1960s and early 1970s were the crucial years in which taboos were broken and wholly new patterns of thought and action were worked out by the dissidents. It was then that the far-flung dissenting groups were first linked together by the networks devised by the democrats, that they perceived the interests they had in common, saw the importance of publicizing their cause and learned to play their part in the elaborate mechanisms required for doing so.

Certainly the KGB leadership (and hence the Politburo) seems to have underestimated the strength and significance of the whole dissent phenomenon, even as late as 1973. In early 1972 it launched an orchestrated, but not massive, wave of arrests. It was clearly designed to break the democrats and their Ukrainian allies, and also to convey the message that the incipient détente with the West did not portend any relaxation of political or ideological controls. The trials of two key democrats, Viktor Krasin and Peter Yakir, were indeed blows to the group. But at this difficult moment, Sakharov and Solzhenitsyn stepped into the front line and when a furious press campaign was mounted against them as a clear prelude to their arrest, the Kremlin was taken aback by the unprecedentedly loud chorus of Western protests that this provoked. In the face of this, the Politburo retreated from what it had apparently expected to be a fairly simple destruction of the democrats. As a result, the democrats' activities continued and in 1974–76 they and associated groups regained the ground lost in 1972–73 and forged ahead in new directions.

A further reason for the authorities' retreat in 1973 was that they had already been thrown more and more onto the defensive over the issue of emigration. In early 1971, the rapidly growing militancy of the Jewish movement, plus its foreign support, had forced Moscow to half-open the gates. The alternatives to doing so had become unacceptable. To imprison a few hundred activists would have infuriated American and world Jewry and threatened the détente package already being actively planned with the West. But no sooner were the gates ajar than a much larger number of Jews, Germans, Armenians and others wanted to press through them than the KGB had apparently anticipated. Before long, however, the Jackson-Vanik amendment was launched in the U.S. Congress to try to have the gates opened wide, with the explicit threat that if they were not, the USSR would be denied one of the economic fruits of détente—most-favored-nation status—

and perhaps other benefits too. In 1973, the Politburo was responding to this threat by sharply increasing the rate of emigration and arresting only a very few Jews.

The low rates of arrest for dissidents in all categories in the years 1974–78 should probably be attributed in the main to the Soviet leadership's desire to stabilize détente by bringing to a successful conclusion the Conference on Security and Cooperation in Europe, which it had long sought. During the many stages leading to the Helsinki Final Act in August 1975, it became clear that the West would insist on strong humanitarian provisions.

When, however, the human rights movement and associated groups of democratic nationalists in four of the USSR's republics decided to monitor Soviet noncompliance with the Final Act's humanitarian clauses, and when the Belgrade Review Conference began to loom, the Politburo was forced to reconsider its policy on dissent. It had doubtless been uneasy about the policy for some time, as its initial assessment had proved faulty and the attempt of 1972–73 to suppress key groups had had to be abandoned in midcourse. Now a highly embarrassing stream of reports was issuing from Helsinki monitoring groups in different parts of the country, documenting systematic abuses of human rights, tying the abuses to specific provisions of the Final Act and thus exposing the Soviet government as a major violator of an international agreement of which it had itself been the keenest promoter.

The policy decided upon is (most unusually) known to the West, if only in a secondhand and summary form. It was spelled out at a closed high-level party meeting and later leaked. An official speaker said: "The editors of newspapers and journals receive numerous demands from Soviet people that, at last, firmness be shown and the dissidents silenced. It has been decided to imprison the 50 most active dissidents and deal severely with their associates. It is time to show strength and not pay attention to the West."

Coincidentally, however, just after this policy began to be applied in December 1976, President Carter launched his human rights campaign, striking a chord in a number of countries. The first arrests (of Yuri Orlov and others) therefore provoked an unprecedented outcry of world condemnation. With only 20 of the "most active dissidents" arrested, the Soviet leaders once again beat a retreat. As a result, almost all the Helsinki and other groups survived.

The next crisis came in 1979–80, initially because of the predictable "pre-Olympics" purge of dissent. The aim was to initimidate, imprison or force abroad as many as possible of the dissidents or malcontents who might spoil the image of a universally popular regime that was to be presented to foreigners during the 1980 Moscow Olympic Games. In December 1979, however, a few months after the campaign began, a critical extra factor entered into the reckoning and accelerated its development. The Politburo decided to occupy Afghanistan. Amid the storm of world condemnation and embargoes that ensued, the political and economic price to be paid for conducting the purge more thoroughly than ever went down sharply and could be paid. At last the main constraints of 1968–69, 1972–73 and 1977 no longer applied.

What, concretely, has the new approach entailed? First and most decisively, from autumn 1979 onward the rate of arrest for dissidents and would-be emigrants was more than doubled. Since then, it has been running at a steady rate of around 200 known arrests per year—a number probably far below the actual total. Second, the key individuals in each group or movement have been systematically jailed or otherwise removed from the scene, whatever their social status. Dr. Sakharov, who is still living in internal exile in Gorky, is the most important and obvious example. Even the Marxist historian, Roy Medvedev, dedicated to the idea of a loyal, nonprovocative opposition, was ordered in January 1983, at a formal interview in the offices of the USSR procurator general, to keep quiet or face prosecution. Third, the average length of the sentences has risen sharply, 10 years now being common; and dissenters who do not promise to keep silent on release are often subjected to a new trial. Fourth, physical abuse has been used more than in the past, both in places of captivity and outside, and a number of dissidents have died in circumstances suggesting they were killed at official instigation. Fifth, the number of Jews allowed to emigrate has come down from a high of 51,000 in 1979 to 1,315 in 1983; the number of Germans from almost 10,000 in 1976 to 1,447 in 1983; and of Armenians from 6,000 in 1980 to fewer than 400 in 1982. Sixth, since 1980 the jamming of foreign radio broadcasts in Russian and other Soviet languages, which was lifted in 1973, has been reimposed. Seventh, the number of phone circuits with the West has been reduced by about two-thirds. And eighth, a prolonged Soviet press campaign has boasted of the final crushing of dissent, offering predictable ideological justifications for the new tough line. Especially ominous for the national minorities has been the revival of references—by Andropov among others—to the desirability of the "merger" (*sliyaniye*) of the Soviet peoples, a well-understood code reference to Russification. In short, a logical series of police measures has been taken, in a consistent way, just as the Politburo would presumably have ordered instinctively in any year since 1967, had it not been inhibited by a mixture of domestic and foreign policy considerations.

DURABILITY OF DISSENT

Perhaps the emigration movements have the best prospect of effecting eventual change in Politburo policy. The American, Israeli, West German and other governments will not forget the aspirations of prospective Soviet émigrés, since countless family ties link them to relatives in those countries. In their prolonged frustration, these movements seem bound to spawn extremist underground groups of a sort even more feared by authoritarian than by democratic governments. And the Soviet regime may well prove unable to resist indefinitely the temptation to barter emigrants away at a good price in future diplomatic deals.

Groups concerned with religious freedom seem to be dividing into two categories—those among the Russian Orthodox and those among other denominations. The latter—notably Baptists, Roman Catholics, Adventists and Pentecostals—have felt the full blast of the KGB's drive of the last four years, contributing about half of all new prisoners. In 1983, only one formal dissident group was still operating above ground—Lithuania's Catholic Committee for the Defense of the Rights of Believers. However, these denominations have a strong social base in the working classes and a long tradition of resistance to persecution. Already they have formed underground groups, which continue to provide their own communities with literature and also to smuggle abroad information about arrests, house searches, police breakups of prayer meetings and so on. With the assurance of moral and practical support from a growing number of Christians abroad, these groups appear indestructible.

By contrast with these denominations, very few Russian Orthodox have been imprisoned, probably because the regime has long been edging its way, slowly and hesitantly, toward a smoother, less tense relationship with the Orthodox church as a whole. The reasons for this would seem to be the desire of some elements in the regime to harness Russian nationalism more decisively to Marxism–Leninism, and also to try to use the church's influence to combat the erosion of moral values in society. In any case, those few Orthodox selected for imprisonment have been individuals who are regarded either, like Father Gleb Yakunin, as members of the human rights movement, or like the young people's Christian Seminar, as dangerous meddlers, merging Orthodoxy with anticommunist Russian nationalism in the manner of Solzhenitsyn. Yakunin's highly effective Christian Committee to Defend Believers' Rights, which had promoted cooperation among denominations, was forced underground in 1980 and has since operated in more spasmodic ways.

To turn to the question of nationalism among the minorities, the strength of nationalism has, predictably, depended in some cases on whether or not it is interwoven with a strong national religion. Thus, Catholic Lithuania stands out clearly as the republic where this interweaving obtains in a high, almost "Polish" degree, and where national dissent is therefore endemic and ineradicable. The same church-nation relationship exists in western Ukraine, but official policy has made the situation there radically different. The Uniate Catholic church, the region's traditionally dominant church, has been outlawed since the mid-1940s precisely because of its intimate association with Ukrainian nationalism. Since nationalism in the USSR's second largest republic is potentially a serious threat to Soviet rule, Ukrainian nationalists of all hues have been suppressed with special vigor, and demands for the legalization of the Uniate church have been rejected. Nonetheless, these demands appear to be growing stronger.

Also foreseeable has been the equally severe suppression of nationalism in eastern Ukraine. The Ukrainian Helsinki group, which was based in Kiev, was crushed with special severity, many of its members receiving prison camp terms of 10 to 15 years. As a result, nationalist dissent in the Ukraine had, by 1983, been driven almost entirely underground.

In Georgia, the nationalist movement has tended to be strong but amorphous. It has intertwined more with the local clans than with the church. Although the Georgian Helsinki group was quickly suppressed, Georgian nationalism seems to be growing stronger. Certainly the very low level of political arrests suggests official fears of provoking the nationalist movement in counterproductive ways.

In Estonia, the level of dissent rose dramatically in the years 1979–81, stimulated in part by developments in Lithuania and Poland and by an incipient sense of Baltic unity. By 1983, however, the sentencing of a few dozen key figures had brought the situation more or less under control. In Latvia, by contrast, dissent has been much weaker, and nationalist feeling has not yet developed into even a loosely organized movement.

As for the Muslims of Central Asia and the Caucasus, the rise of Islamic fundamentalism in Iran and Muslim resistance to the Soviet occupation of Afghanistan have clearly provoked official nervousness and led to the jailing of a small number of militant Muslims in the Soviet Union. However, dissent still remains at an apparently unthreatening, nonpublic level.

If we turn now to general political and social dissent, two broad points should be made. First, whenever party members have gone public with dissent of any substance, the party has been quick to expel them, unless they promptly recant. Second, whenever a group has formed around more than a few discrete issues, i.e., around a political program of some sort, it has been broken up as soon as the authorities learned of it. In other words, when the border between dissent (which may perhaps be tolerated) and opposition (which is not) has been crossed, the regime reacts immediately.

Since 1979–80, however, any formal group, even if it dissents on a single narrow issue that is not political in any normal sense, has been liable to suppression. And almost all of them have been suppressed. Beyond this, individuals who have circulated critical views on a political issue have in most cases been arrested too. Thus, the democratic movement—always a very loose "community" of individuals and formal and informal groups—has been virtually destroyed. Surviving remnants have fallen silent, emigrated or been driven underground.

Groups with social, economic and cultural concerns have fared as badly as those with more political aims. Artists, feminists, free trade unions, the group for the rights of disabled people, the Lithuanian movement to combat alcoholism, editorial boards issuing sociopolitical and cultural samizdat journals—had all been reduced to total or near silence by 1983. The free trade union known as SMOT was naturally enthusiastic about the rise of Solidarity in Poland. However, this enthusiasm could not, in Soviet conditions, be translated into a mass membership. Its leaders, most of whom were arrested, claimed a few hundred members in a dozen or so cities.

The human rights movement, by contrast, has demonstrably withstood the KGB's assaults to date, at least regarding its informational role. Although bodies like the Moscow Helsinki group and the Working Commission to Investigate the Use of Psychiatry for Political Purposes have succumbed, the movement's informal networks have mostly continued to function. These have, as before, gathered information on arrests, trials and political prisoners in places of captivity and funneled it to Moscow and abroad.

CONCLUSION

As the failure of free trade unionism indicates, the Politburo is not—as yet, anyway—especially alarmed by the dissenting groups and movements, because they have made little or no headway among the mass of ordinary people in the Russian heartland. For this reason, there has been no serious domestic danger in conducting the post-1979 purge of dissent. But why have ordinary Russian people been so inert? First, the general demoralization and loss of autonomous values so vividly described by Andrei Amalrik and Aleksandr Zinoviev evidently still obtain. Second, police controls remain overwhelmingly strong. And third, the regime's constant propaganda, relating all dissent to the malign influence of foreigners or to mental illness doubtless has a certain effect, if only for a time.

Nonetheless, the tenacity of dissent, the KGB's relative difficulty in infiltrating groups and coopting members, the failure of ideology as an instrument of control, the need to resort to straight coercion on a broad front, the realization that the dissidents have convinced important sections of Western opinion of their case and the fear that Western governments will continue to capitalize on this over the indefinite future—all this seems to arouse real if largely unacknowledged concern in the leadership.

To date, the Politburo has had no stomach for meeting any of the dissidents' main grievances. However, some of its policies do seem to be addressed, at least in part, to the need to keep the Russian masses immune from contagion. The campaign—since the rise of Solidarity in Poland—to try to make Soviet trade unions more responsive to workers' complaints is the most obvious example. Apart from this, the abolition of federalism, which would, it is presumably hoped, both inspire the Russians and make it easier to contain the minorities, has definitely been tempting the Politburo for some years.

The biggest short-term risks of the current policy on dissent would seem to be the development of underground groups that the KGB cannot easily monitor and a sharp rise in acts of violence, which so far have been fairly rare. Yet, given Russian traditions of the 19th century, the contagious violence of the modern world and the extreme rigidity of the Soviet system, these closely related trends could become threatening quite quickly and might in due course force a reversal of policy. This consideration may be one reason why the post-1979 purge has been steady and systematic, rather than sudden and dramatic.

But whether or not official policy becomes less intolerant in the foreseeable future, the currents of dissent will not just fade away as ideology prescribes and the leadership often seems to expect.

FURTHER READING

A fairly complete summary record of most of the dissident movements has appeared since 1968 in the samizdat journal originating in Moscow, *A Chronicle of Current Events*, published in English by Amnesty International Publications, London. Since 1978, a semiweekly record of dissident developments, *USSR News Brief: Human Rights*, has been edited by Conrad Lubarsky (48 rue du Lac, 1050 Brussels, Belgium).

Bloch, Sidney, and Reddaway, Peter. *Russia's Political Hospitals*. London: Gollancz, 1977.

———. *Soviet Psychiatric Abuse: The Shadow over World Psychiatry*. London: Gollancz, 1984.

de Boer, S. P., et al., eds. *Biographical Dictionary of Dissidents in the Soviet Union 1956–75*. The Hague, Boston, London: Martinus Nijhoff, 1982.

Chalidze, Valery. *To Defend These Rights*. London: Collins-Harvill, 1974.

Reddaway, Peter. *Uncensored Russia: The Human Rights Movement in the Soviet Union*. London: Cape, 1972.

Religion in Communist Lands. Quarterly.

Rigby, T. H., et al., eds. *Authority, Power and Policy in the USSR*. London: Macmillan, 1980.

THE UKRAINE

VICTOR SWOBODA

THE Ukrainian Soviet Socialist Republic has a territory of 603,700 sq. km. (233,090 sq. mi.) and a population of over 50 million. This figure comprises nearly one-fifth (18.6 percent) of the total population of all 15 republics of the Soviet Union, and is second only to that of the Russian SFSR.

In theory, according to the constitution, the Ukraine, like all other republics, is a sovereign national state, belongs to the Union voluntarily and enjoys equality of rights, including that of secession, which right may be neither repealed nor restricted by the Union government. The Ukraine has the right, in theory, to establish its own international relations, which it has exercised only by its representation at the U.N. since 1958. (Belorussia is the only other Soviet republic also represented.)

The republic's sovereign power is theoretically vested in its Supreme Soviet, which appoints the Council of Ministers. Its sovereignty is, however, limited by the fact that all spheres of activity within the jurisdiction of the Union government are outside the republic's control; a varying number of joint Union-Republican ministries are in fact under the Union's control. The number of the latter had increased by the early 1980s to 31, and they included, among others, foreign and internal affairs; trade; finance; the coal, steel,building materials and food industries; light industries; communications; power; agriculture; health; culture; and education. The republic is solely responsible only for a dwindling circle of activities, such as the ministries of roads and road transport, housing, communal services and social insurance.

These considerable limitations of sovereignty are compounded by the fact that the Communist party of the Ukraine (CPU) is accurately described in Soviet documents as "the leading power of the society and State of the Ukraine." As the CPU forms part of the Communist party of the Soviet Union (CPSU), has no program or policy of its own and is entirely controlled by the CPSU leadership, the supreme de facto power over the Ukraine rests with the CPSU leadership in Moscow.

ECONOMIC ROLE

The Ukraine has considerable natural resources. The Donbas coalfields, the most important coal producing basin in the Soviet Union, are, on a world scale, second only to the Appalachian coalfields in the United States. They were considerably expanded in the early 1950s, and another coalfield was discovered in the Lvov-Volynia region soon after World War II. Oil, earlier drilled only in the western Ukraine, has been struck in several eastern regions and in the Crimea. Large natural gas sources have been discovered in the east, adding to the old sub-Carpathian deposits. The Ukraine produced over 30 percent of all Soviet gas until 1972; about one-fifth of this was supplied to Russia and several other republics, and also abroad. Since then, the Ukraine's share of output has been thrown into the shade by the rapid development of deposits east of the Urals; and now the Ukrainian sources are approaching exhaustion. Iron ore, mined mostly in Krivoy Rog, much less in Kerch and since 1970 in Kremenchug, accounts for more than half of the total Soviet output. The Nikopol manganese basin near Krivoy Rog is the world's largest manganese producer (over 27 percent of the world total in 1973). The Ukraine has been a major world producer of titanium since about 1958. There have been several reports of a major uranium mining operation in the north of the Krivoy Rog, where the largest uranium-plutonium plant in the country has apparently been constructed.

The Ukraine has well-developed industries (the chemical industry has expanded particularly fast in the 1950s and '60s) and a diversified agriculture. Gross output in the key industries approaches and, in certain cases, exceeds that of advanced European countries. The Ukraine produces more pig iron than any other European country, and more coal and steel than Britain or France. Per capita, the Ukraine's production of iron, steel and iron ore leads the world.

The part played by Ukrainian industry within the Soviet Union is considerable; it accounts for some 50 percent of the pig iron and coke output, over 40 percent of steel and nearly half of metallurgical equipment. The Ukraine leads in computer technology and cybernetics (it is significant that in 1973 a two-volume *Encyclopedia of Cybernetics*, the first of its kind in the Soviet Union, was published in Ukrainian in Kiev). The Ukraine also exports much agricultural produce. On balance, in various ways it contributes more to the Soviet exchequer than it receives from it.[1]

PRESOVIET HISTORY

The Ukrainians, the southern branch of the Eastern Slavs, are descended from the inhabitants of the southwestern regions of the ninth to 13th century Kiev state; these regions, comprising the Dnieper valley and the principalities of Kiev, Galicia and Volynia, passed in the 14th century to the Grand Duchy

[1]No complete balance sheets of the financial relationships between the Ukrainian SSR and the Soviet Union budget have been published; among the chief unknown quantities are the Ukraine's share of the Union administration and defense costs, of income from transport undertakings and of "hidden" payments in the form of the supply of goods to other republics at less than cost price. Nevertheless, comparison of incomplete balance sheets suggests that some republics (such as the Central Asian republics) receive more from the Union exchequer than they contribute, and others vice versa.

of Lithuania and the Kingdom of Poland, while the northeastern principalities, together with their future center, Moscow, were subjugated in the 13th to 15th centuries by the Golden Horde.

From the 15th century, growing numbers of peasants and serfs, as well as burghers and nobles, chiefly Ukrainians, chose the free life of hunting and fishing in the no-man's-land of the south Ukrainian steppes. They had to fend off the Crimean Tatars' encroachments, and soon organized themselves into an independent military-political force. The Polish government attempted to put the Cossacks (as they came to be called) under its control, but in the 17th century they led a successful Ukrainian rebellion against the Polish overlordship, which because of the militancy of the Jesuits was oppressive both socially and economically. The Cossacks were led by Hetman Bohdan Khmelnytsky, who set up the Cossack State and concluded a treaty with its coreligionist, Muscovy, in 1964. For the next 50 years, the Cossack State was only loosely tied to Muscovy, and the elective Hetmans were virtually independent sovereigns. This independence was, however, gradually eroded by the Muscovite czars, and so in 1708–09 Hetman Ivan Mazeppa tried to break away by siding with Charles XII of Sweden against Peter the Great; Peter's victory at Poltava was the beginning of the end of Ukrainian autonomy.

The culture of the Ukraine followed on from that of medieval Kiev, but it was also subject to strong Western influences through Poland. In the 17th century, the Ukraine contributed greatly to the education and culture of Muscovy, while its own population had a very high level of literacy. Educational standards were also maintained in the following century; in the 1740s there was one school with Ukrainian as the language of instruction for every 746 persons. The loss of autonomy was followed throughout the 19th century by increasing restrictions on printing and instruction, which resulted in a drastic drop in literacy to 13 percent by 1897. Some of these restrictions were imposed in reaction to the Ukrainian revival led by the poet Taras Shevchenko (1814–61). Many restrictions were swept away by the 1905 revolution, but new repressions soon followed.

The Ukrainian Central Rada (Council), established on March 17, 1917, proclaimed on November 20 the independent Ukrainian People's Republic. The Central Rada did not recognize the authority over the Ukraine of the Bolshevik regime recently established in Russia. On December 25, a Bolshevik Soviet government was formed in opposition to the Rada and proclaimed the Ukrainian People's Republic to be federative part of, and actively supported by, the Russian Republic. This government was, however, unable to assert itself against a succession of national Ukrainian governments in a conflict that also involved occupation by the Central Powers, landings of allied expeditionary forces, the campaigns of Denikin's White Russian armies, and, in 1920, a Polish invasion. On November 17, 1918, a new provisional government of the Ukraine was formed in Moscow by the Central Committee of the Russian Communist party (Bolsheviks)—RCP(B)—and a Red Army offensive was mounted. On January 6, 1919, the Ukrainian Socialist Soviet Republic was proclaimed and on March 10 its first constitution was adopted, in which the Republic's independence was implied. On

June 1, 1919, by Lenin's directive, a military alliance was formed among all the Soviet republics (Russia, the Ukraine, Belorussia, Latvia and Lithuania). The eventual frontier between the Soviet Ukraine and Poland left a six million-strong Ukrainian minority in Poland.

THE SOVIET UKRAINE: THE DRIVE AGAINST UKRAINIAN NATIONALISM

The Red Army had finally gained the Ukraine for the Bolsheviks by March 1920. Under pressure from Lenin, the Comintern dissolved the Ukrainian Communist party (UCP, or Borotbists)—a national Communist party founded in 1919, which stood for a completely independent communist Ukraine and whose strength rivaled that of the Communist party (Bolsheviks) of the Ukraine (CP(B)U). A large section of the UCP then joined the latter party and contributed to its pursuance of policies directed toward the safeguarding of the interests of the Ukrainian Republic and its people, and the policy of "Ukrainization." The new Ukrainian government concluded a military and economic union treaty with the Russian SFSR, in which the parties acknowledged their mutual independence and sovereignty. The Ukrainian SSR was a sovereign state, recognized by several European countries including Britain, and having diplomatic representatives in six.

The Soviet Union was formed, according to Lenin's plan, as "a union of equals" on December 30, 1922, and the union treaty, at the Ukrainian SSR's insistence, included the right to secede for each member republic (Article 72 of the present Soviet Constitution and Article 69 of the Ukrainian SSR Constitution, of 1977 and 1978 respectively). Yet there were no provisions for redress against any violation of a republic's sovereignty, and CP(B)U delegates were unsuccessful in their demands for such at the 1923 RCP(B) Congress.

The industrialization of the Soviet Union brought with it a speedy collectivization of agriculture. In 1929, the Ukraine was selected "to provide an example in the shortest time," and those who resisted were exiled, imprisoned, or killed (in all 650,000, men, women and children) while another 350,000 fled from the villages. The speed of the collectivization without the necessary machinery and the exorbitant demands for grain from Moscow culminated in the catastrophic famine of 1932–33. A Soviet Union law authorizing the OGPU to shoot on sight anyone who attempted "to steal socialist property" was applied throughout the Ukraine, sometimes against starving children. It has been estimated that not less than 10 percent of the population, some 5 to 7 million, perished in the famine.

Collectivization of agriculture was accompanied by increased attacks on "Ukrainian bourgeois nationalism," accompanied by mass arrests, mostly secret trials and sentences to long terms in concentration camps. Most were accused of belonging to organizations (actually fictitious) working toward the restoration of a bourgeois-democratic independent Ukraine. Although lip service was paid to Lenin's declaration that "a distinction must necessarily be made between the nationalism of an oppressor nation and that of an oppressed nation," and although it was constantly reaffirmed at Moscow party congresses (attended by delegates from all the Soviet republics) until

1930 that Great Russian chauvinism was the chief menace to communism, in fact there were no prosecutions for Russian chauvinism, while thousands were deported on charges of Ukrainian bourgeois nationalism. In November 1933, the party line was reversed, Ukrainization was replaced by a drive to Soviet patriotism and Ukrainian nationalism was declared to be the main threat to communism.

The OGPU terror of 1929–33 was not directed against noncommunists alone; any manifestations of "national communism" were also punished. When the CP(B)U leaders repeatedly appealed to Moscow to alleviate the 1932–33 famine by reducing grain delivery quotas from the Ukraine, the Central Committee of the CPSU(B) refused, accused the CP(B)U leadership of nationalism, blamed it for the nonfulfillment of the quotas and a new wave of OGPU terror was unleashed. Between June 1, 1932 and October 1, 1933, 75 percent of officials of local soviets and 80 percent of the local party committee secretaries were dismissed, and by late 1934 half of the CP(B)U's 520,000 rank and file were purged. Most were shot or exiled. There were also mass arrests among intellectuals. The OGPU fabricated charges of "nationalism"[2] against the victims, while the real purpose of the terror was to exterminate even the potentially nationally minded leadership.

The secret police terror, after some slackening, intensified after October 1936 when Yezhov became its chief, reaching unprecedented proportions. By late 1938, nearly a million people in the Ukrainian SSR had been imprisoned, sent to concentration camps or shot. They were mostly Ukrainian intellectuals of the new Soviet school, officials, technicians and many CP(B)U members. The highest CP(B)U bodies were wiped out; of the 115 Central Committee members elected in 1934, only 36 remained in May 1937, when the 13th Congress elected a new Central Committee of 102 members; of these, only three remained in March 1938, while of the entire Politburo only one member survived in exile. The break in the continuity of leadership was absolute.

With Khrushchev, who arrived early in 1938 from Moscow with new men to fill the void, came a more militant policy of Russification, while the CP(B)U became merely a local branch of the CPSU(B).

The Ukraine had barely begun to recover from one bloodbath before it was plunged into another with the devastation and losses suffered in World War II. Two million Jews were exterminated; deaths at the front and in German prisoner-of-war and forced-labor camps, mass German reprisals against the civilian population, and executions of resistance members and partisans accounted for at least another 3 million dead. These nearly matched the 1930–38 "peacetime" human losses. Ukrainian nationalist guerrillas were destroyed both by the Germans and, right into the early 1950s, by the Soviet security forces.

After the war, Russification continued unabated. The Russian population of the Ukrainian SSR increased from 8.1 percent in 1926 to 21.1 percent

---

[2] Though regularly punishable by death or concentration camp since about 1930, this "offense" has never been defined in Soviet law.

in 1979; moreover, 10.9 percent of Ukrainians (who comprised 73.6 percent of the total population) gave Russian as their native language in the 1979 census, while non-Russian minorities are mostly Russian-speaking. Four-fifths of all Russians, and most other Russian speakers, live in cities and towns, where practically all administration, industry, trade and further education have been Russified. New campaigns against alleged Ukrainian nationalism were launched in 1946–47 and in 1951–53.

After Stalin's death, the Central Committee of the CPU in June 1953 criticized Russification for the first time since the 1920s and removed the first secretary, L. Melnikov, for having pursued it. A. Kirichenko was appointed in his place—the first Ukrainian to occupy this post since the founding of the CP(B)U/CPU in 1918. Protests against the Russification of education and culture penetrated—although only for a few months—into the Kiev press.

RUSSIFICATION OF UKRAINIAN CULTURE

In the specifically national field of culture, the Ukraine's position in the Soviet Union is decidedly inferior to that of several other republics. The disastrous effect upon literacy of the 19th-century restrictions on printing and teaching in Ukrainian has been mentioned; much was done after the creation of the Ukrainian SSR to establish education in Ukrainian at all levels, but since the mid-1930s Russification of all education has been under way. The process is least advanced in general education schools, where the percentage of pupils in Ukrainian schools was 73 percent in 1958, the same as the percentage of population who stated Ukrainian to be their native language in the 1959 census; but by 1965, only 66 percent of all pupils went to Ukrainian schools. The downward trend has since continued, but precise figures are no longer published; by 1973, the ratio had authoritatively been said to have dropped to "around 60 percent." This noticeable drop may be only partly accounted for by the continued trend in the Ukrainian population at large to adopt Russian as their native language, for this process could hardly have proceeded so fast; it is, rather, caused by administrative and economic pressures.

Schools in cities and towns are being Russified the most; Ukrainian schools, which served solid Ukrainian settlements in other parts of the Soviet Union until the mid-1930s, were liquidated under Stalin and have not yet been restarted. By contrast, Russians have more than ample numbers of Russian schools in every non-Russian republic. (Armenians are the only nationality partially to share this privilege outside Armenia.) All professional, secondary, technical and higher education, about 50 percent Ukrainian in the early 1930s, has now been almost completely Russified. This, in varying degrees, also applies to most other republics. A quota system, and very likely unofficial preferential measures, have the effect that in the noncompulsory sector of education the percentage of Russians is above, and the percentage of Ukrainians and several other "titular" (republican) nationalities, is below their respective percentages of the total Soviet population. Thus in 1980–81, there were 217 Russian students in higher education per 10,000

Russian population, but only 164 Ukrainian students per 10,000 Ukrainians (the USSR average being 196). Also above average were the Georgians (247), Kazakhs (227), Lithuanians (224), Armenians (209), Estonians (199) and Kirghiz (198), while the Moldavians (126) were the lowest. In secondary technical education, on the other hand, the Lithuanians (207), Kazakhs (199) and Russians (187) were above the average (173), with the Belorussians reaching it, and being followed by the Ukrainians (161) and down to the Tadzhiks (89).

An objective indication of the position of a national culture may be found in its book-publishing figures. In 1982, while 6.8 copies of books were produced per person in the Soviet Union, the language ratios per capita varied considerably among the republics. Thus, per Estonian in Estonia there were 12.2 books in the language; the Latvians with 8.7 were also above average; the Lithuanians were only just below average, with 5.7 books per capita; the others ranged from 4.3 (Georgians) to Moldavians (2.3) and Ukrainians (2.2), and to the Belorussians (0.8) at the bottom of the scale. If it is assumed that book consumption in all republics (except Latvia and Estonia) is around the average, the lower figures quoted may be assumed to be made up by a correspondingly larger import of Russian books, and may be seen as a measure of the Russification of any given republic. Thus, by this criterion, Russification is most advanced in Belorussia and to a lesser extent in the Ukraine. Nor is the low number of Ukrainian books due to low readership demand: there are constant complaints about editions being insufficient and books being sold out immediately upon publication. Editions are, in fact, kept artificially low by a central authority in Moscow allocating a disproportionately low total of paper to the Ukrainian SSR. Such discrimination has developed immensely since 1930; in 1982 only one-third the number of Ukrainian book titles and 95 percent of copies were published, compared with those produced in 1930, while the Ukrainian population of the Republic had meantime increased (mainly owing to the annexation of the western Ukraine) by some 30 percent. During the same time, the total Soviet book production in all languages grew to 152 percent of book titles and 218 percent of copies. Russian-language figures, if analyzed separately, would show an even steeper increase, thus reflecting, in conjunction with the drop in Ukrainian-language publishing, the progress of Russification between 1930 and 1982.

Ukrainian-language publishing compares unfavorably also with that of smaller and economically much less developed neighboring communist states. Thus in 1981, Hungary produced 9.6 copies of books in Hungarian per capita; Bulgaria, 6.8 books in Bulgarian; Romania, 3.9; and Poland, 3.7.

THE POST-STALINIST PERIOD

Khrushchev's de-Stalinization, begun at the 20th CPSU Congress in 1956, was rather half-hearted in the sphere of nationality policies. Although there was a definite relaxation of pressures, there was no posthumous rehabilitation of the victims of anti-Ukrainian terror and the proscription of national communism in 1929–38; nor was the genocidal character of collectivization in the Ukraine (or in the Cossack lands of the northern Caucasus and in Kazakhstan) ever admitted. Moreover, the party showed no intention of resuming the Ukrainization policy that had been cut short by the terror campaign of the early 1930s. On the contrary, Stalin's Russification policy has never been abandoned.

In this atmosphere, several clandestine opposition groups, some numbering a dozen or two dozen members, originated in the late 1950s and 1960s. Believing that the Ukraine's membership in the Soviet Union was against Ukrainian interests, they mostly advocated peaceful secession in accordance with the constitution. They were all savagely suppressed by the KGB; some individuals were sentenced to death and shot, most others sent to prison camps for up to 15 years. The best documented organization among them was the 1959–61 Lukyanenko-Kandyba group of seven men (three of them jurists; four, CPSU members) who planned the formation of a Ukrainian Workers' and Peasants' Union (UWPU). Their draft program severely criticized, from the Marxist-Leninist standpoint, the party and government policies during the famine and the terror of the 1930s, the shortcomings of the post-Stalin period, economic bureaucracy, oppression of the peasants and the policy of Russification. It concluded that in order to develop normal statehood, the Ukraine must secede by implementing Article 17 of the Soviet constitution then in force (corresponding to Article 72 of the present constitution mentioned above). To this end, the UWPU was peacefully and constitutionally to conduct secessionist propaganda and ask the Ukrainian SSR Supreme Soviet for a referendum. If the majority favored secession, an independent Ukraine would still be a Soviet-type socialist state, staying within the socialist commonwealth and evolving toward communism; it would be a Ukraine "in which all citizens could effectively enjoy their political freedoms and determine the direction of the Ukraine's economic and political development," and the UWPU's immediate aim was to be "the gaining of democratic freedoms." The draft's final words were: "The triumph of Soviet law will also be our triumph." In the event, however, Soviet law did not triumph; the court had to bow to the dictates of the KGB and, accepting the latter's fabricated charges, sentenced Lev Lukyanenko to death (on appeal, the sentence was commuted to 15 years by the Supreme Court of the Ukrainian SSR) and the others to long prison terms. In common with all other political trials of the later Stalin and Khrushchev periods, this one was held in camera, in clear violation of the Soviet law on criminal procedure.

UKRAINIAN SAMIZDAT

In the field of Ukrainian literature, a younger generation, free from the reflexes ingrained in their elders from the Stalinist past, arose in the early 1960s. They experimented with form as well as content, and one of them, Vasili Symonenko, wrote deeply felt Ukrainian patriotic and civic poetry. Some of his poems, unacceptable for publication, circulated in early samizdat on paper and on tape (he read them in public), and so did his politically outspoken diary after his untimely death in December 1963. Another important samizdat document, an anonymous pamphlet claiming that the arson in May 1964 at the State Public Library of the Ukrainian Academy of Sciences in Kiev was a deliberate act of Russian chauvinism, aimed at the spirit of the Ukraine. Some 600,000 books and archives relating to Ukrainian history and culture, including the archives of the 1918–20 non-Bolshevik governments, were said to have perished. This pamphlet also gave the first outline ever of the Lukyanenko case.

A year after Symonenko's death, his samizdat poems and diary were published in the West. In August–September 1965, the KGB struck. In Kiev and various Ukrainian cities, they arrested some two dozen intellectuals, who were charged with writing, reading, copying and passing on various samizdat publications; among them was the well-known literary critic and research worker at the Academy of Sciences, Ivan Svitlychny, who was accused of "smuggling Symonenko's poetry and diary abroad." In Moscow, at the same time, Sinyavsky and Daniel were arrested for smuggling their works abroad. Svitlychny was released after eight months without trial—it was decided to treat the late Symonenko as a faithful communist, because of his published works. In January–February 1966 the first two Ukrainian trials, followed by the trial of Sinyavsky and Daniel in Moscow, made Soviet legal history; they were the first attempt at open political trials—a legal form forbidden by Soviet law—for nearly three decades. This visibly perpetrated injustice stimulated the rise of a human rights movement, with an ever-growing samizdat. Among the most important early works in the Ukraine were Ivan Dzyuba's *Internationalism or Russification?*, originally a December 1965 memorandum to Petro Shelest and Vladimir Shcherbitsky (the latter at the time was prime minister of the Ukraine), a carefully documented indictment of present-day Russian chauvinism as working contrary to Leninist nationalities policy; Chornovil's examination of the 1966 trials (*The Chornovil Papers*); and the documents collected in *Ferment in the Ukraine*. The next important development was the appearance of the samizdat journal, *The Ukrainian Herald*, of which four issues appeared in 1970 documenting Russian chauvinism and the developing protest movement against it.

The role of Petro Shelest, until May 1972 first secretary of the Central Committee of the CPU, seems to have been a moderating one. He pledged the party's support for the development of the Ukrainian language and culture and, more concretely, required that new textbooks in science and technology be published in Ukrainian. He apparently also ordered the changeover to Ukrainian as a medium of instruction in higher education. The latter two moves were blocked, either by the local Russian lobby or by Moscow,[3] and he was unable in 1968 to save from condemnation *The Cathedral*, a novel by his friend Oles Honchar, chairman of the Writers' Union of the Ukraine and a member of the CPU's Central Committee. Party ideologues condemned the novel chiefly for its glorification of the Ukrainian Zaporozhian Cossacks, who flourished from the 16th to the 18th centuries, and

[3] Though the Ukrainian-language *Encyclopedia of Cybernetics*, referred to above, was prepared for publication when he was in power.

whose organization, Sich, was described in Marxian terms as a "democratic republic." Shelest was apparently able to stave off the arrests or expulsions from the Writers' Union of some dissident writers, though in 1966 he could not produce the open trials, with their maximum press coverage and their greater chance of justice which he had promised in November 1965.

As a part of a new general drive against dissent throughout the Soviet Union, the heaviest single KGB assault on any dissenting group in the post-Stalin period was launched in the Ukraine on January 12, 1972. Scores of patriotic Ukrainians, many of them far from "dissidents," were sentenced to prison terms of up to 15 years for "anti-Soviet agitation and propaganda"; among them was Ivan Svitlychny. Several writers had their works condemned, and were refused all future publication. The publication of Symonenko's works was stopped after he was accused of "an exaggerated and distorted display of national feelings." The culmination came in May 1972, when Shelest was removed from his post by Moscow (not by his own Central Committee) and replaced by Vladimir Shcherbitsky. It was the task of the latter, after eliminating all real or potential Ukrainian dissidents, along with many of Shelest's like-minded subordinates in the party, to work toward the desired "drawing together" of Russians and Ukrainians (as a part of the drawing together of all nations of the Soviet Union) through the process of Russification. The following April, the party journal, *Kommunist Ukrainy*, attacked Shelest's book *O Ukraine, Our Soviet Land* (1970) for its idealization of the Zaporozhian Sich as "some sort of absolute democracy," its failure to show Russian culture's beneficial effect upon Ukrainian culture, and its advocacy of Ukrainian economic self-sufficiency. These were clearly some of the reasons for Shelest's removal.

Since the adoption of the Helsinki Final Act in 1975, reemerging dissent in the Ukraine has centered on the Ukrainian Public Group to Promote the Implementation of the Helsinki Accords. (Similar groups have been active in Moscow and some other republics.) Its leader was the well-known writer Mykola Rudenko, a party member and wartime political commissar in the armed forces, who had occupied high positions in Ukrainian publishing and the Writers' Union. Rudenko and more than 20 other members of the group were imprisoned for long terms during its four-year existence, but they managed to produce a sizable body of documentation on human- and national-rights violations in the Ukraine.

The late 1970s and early 1980s have been marked by a degree of ambiguity. Some writers, banned since 1973, whose very names could not be mentioned in print, gradually resurfaced from the mid-1970s onward, though obviously they were allowed to write only within the limits of orthodoxy. Some of them, such as R. Ivanychuk, received high literary honors; even Symonenko was rehabilitated and republished in 1981. The treatment of dissidents, on the other hand, has been growing ever more harsh; many of them, on completion of their terms in labor camps, are given further long terms of imprisonment, a revival of the infamous practice under Stalin. It remains to be seen how successful the carrot-and-stick policy will be.

FURTHER READING

Armstrong, J. A. *Ukrainian Nationalism*. New York and London: Columbia University Press, 1963.

Borys, Jurij. *The Sovietisation of Ukraine, 1917–1923: The Communist Doctrine and Practice of National Self-Determination*. Edmonton, Alberta: Canadian Institute of Ukrainian Studies, 1980.

Browne, Michael, ed. *Ferment in the Ukraine: Documents by V. Chornovil, I. Kandyba, L. Lukyanenko, V. Moroz and Others*. London: Macmillan; New York: Praeger, 1971; Woodhaven, New York: Crisis Press, 1973.

Dzyuba, Ivan. *Internationalism or Russification?*, 2nd ed. London: Weidenfeld and Nicolson, 1970; 3rd ed. New York: Monad Press, distributed by Pathfinder Press, 1974.

Farmer, Kenneth C. *Ukrainian Nationalism in the Post-Stalin Era: Myth, Symbols and Ideology in Soviet Nationalities Policy*. The Hague, Boston, London: Martinus Nijhoff, 1980.

Hodnett, G., and Potichnyj, P. *The Ukraine and the Czechoslovak Crisis*. Canberra: Australian National University Press, 1970.

Krawchenko, Bohdan, ed. *Ukraine after Shelest*. Edmonton: University of Alberta Press, 1983.

Kubijovyč, Volodymyr, ed. *Ukraine: A Concise Encyclopaedia*. 2 vols. Toronto: University of Toronto Press, 1963, 1971.

Liber, George, and Mostovych, Anna. *Nonconformity and Dissent in the Ukrainian SSR, 1955–1975: An Annotated Bibliography*. Cambridge, Massachusetts: Harvard University Press, 1978.

Mace, James E. *Communism and the Dilemmas of National Liberation: National Communism in Soviet Ukraine, 1918–1933*. Cambridge, Massachusetts: Harvard University Press, 1983.

Nahaylo, Bohdan, and Peters, C. J. *The Ukrainians and Georgians*. London: Minority Rights Group, 1981.

Sahaydak, Maksym. *The Ukrainian Herald, Issue 7–8: Ethnocide of Ukrainians in the USSR*. Baltimore, Paris, Toronto: Smoloskyp, 1976.

Swoboda, V. "Cat and Mouse in the Ukraine," *Index on Censorship*, Vol. II, no. 1, Spring 1973.

The Ukrainian Herald Issue 6: Dissent in Ukraine. Baltimore, Paris, Toronto: Smoloskyp, 1977.

Verba, Lesya, and Yasen, Bohdan, eds. *The Human Rights Movement in Ukraine: Documents of the Ukrainian Helsinki Group, 1976–1980*. Baltimore, Washington, Toronto: Smoloskyp, 1980.

THE BALTIC REPUBLICS

DAVID KIRBY

TO 1918

THE pagan tribes inhabiting the present-day territory of Estonia and Latvia were subjugated by crusading Teutonic Knights in the 13th century, and military-ecclesiastical rule was established that lasted until the middle of the 16th century. In ensuing wars, Estonia and Livonia came under the rule of the Swedish crown. In spite of the efforts of successive Swedish kings to alleviate the servile conditions of the peasantry, the German-speaking gentry continued to enjoy far-reaching autonomy in peasant affairs and the dominance of this group was not substantially weakened with the incorporation of Estonia and Livonia into the empire of Peter the Great after 1710–11. Not until the latter half of the 19th century was the economic and political grip of the German upper class weakened by the measures of the imperial Russian government and by socioeconomic changes brought about by industrialization.

Medieval Lithuania managed to withstand the onslaughts of the crusaders and of its eastern neighbors, and eventually entered into union with Poland in the 14th century. Lutheranism took firm root in Estonia and Livonia, but the Lithuanians remained faithful to Catholicism. The national revival was also slower to develop in the economically backward Lithuanian lands (for centuries subjected to polonization) than in the more advanced northern provinces, though by the beginning of the 20th century, considerable advances had been made in all three nations. In Latvia, the most industrially advanced region, with a major port at Riga (558,000 inhabitants in 1910), a strong labor movement developed and played an important part in the revolutions of 1905 and 1917. The Bolsheviks won 72 percent of the vote in the elections to the All-Russian Constituent Assembly held in the unoccupied areas of Latvia, and exercised de facto power between November 1917 and February 1918. The Bolsheviks were also strong in Estonia, but the occupation of the whole Baltic area by German troops in February–March 1918 extinguished any hopes of establishing either a Soviet regime or a national independent state.

THE PERIOD OF INDEPENDENCE, 1918–40

All three modern states experienced a difficult birth. The Germans, who had occupied Lithuania in 1915 and taken Riga in August 1917, were not

272

disposed to favor truly independent national states, and the victorious Allies viewed the prospects of independence for the three countries with little enthusiasm. Soviet Russia signed treaties with all three states in 1920, formally recognizing their independence and territorial integrity.

Economic and financial problems dogged the early years of independence, although by the late 1930s, sufficient stabilization had been achieved to allow for a degree of progress in agricultural production and certain manufacturing industries, with expanding exports of dairy and meat products to Western European markets. The large estates of the German-speaking gentry were broken up and lands distributed to the peasantry; radical land reforms were also carried out in Lithuania. Estonia and Latvia were unable to sustain the industrial growth that had occurred during the last years of the Russian empire, and the number of people employed in industry declined, especially in the textile and metal industries. In 1930, 17.4 percent of the Estonian work force was employed in industry, compared with 13.5 percent in Latvia and a mere six percent in Lithuania.

The ultrademocratic parliamentary systems created in the first flush of independence soon ran into difficulties, with scores of small parties making the task of forming stable governments ever more onerous. By 1926, an authoritarian presidential regime had emerged in Lithuania, and similar strongman governments were established in Latvia and Estonia in the early 1930s. The great wave of support for Bolshevism manifested in the revolutionary year of 1917 was not sustained. Communist parties attracted little popular support in the 1920s, and party membership in all three countries dwindled to a few hundred during the years of underground activity in the 1930s. There were several protofascist groups, but their activities were generally kept under control by the authoritarian regimes, which preferred to create their own rather vacuous ideologies and personal political systems rather than embrace radical doctrines imported from abroad. Genuine attempts were made in the 1920s to provide a degree of autonomy for the national minorities in Latvia and Estonia, and the whole period was generally free of serious conflict between the ethnic groups.

THE WAR YEARS

The authoritarian regimes began to show signs of disintegration as the clouds of great-power conflict loomed over the Baltic before World War II. The loss of Memel (Klaipėda) to Germany in March 1939 provoked a serious government crisis in Lithuania. The demands made by the Soviet Union upon all three Baltic republics in the wake of the Nazi-Soviet pact caused further despondency and confusion. Unable to offer any resistance or to coordinate their efforts, the three countries agreed to sign mutual assistance treaties with the Soviet Union in the autumn of 1939, with provision for Soviet troops to be stationed in each country. For the time being, however, the Soviet Union refrained from interfering in the internal affairs of the Baltic states; but in June 1940, as Germany was preoccupied in the West, the Soviet Union accused the Baltic governments of failing to comply with the terms of the agreements and insisted on the formation of new governments and the admission of unspecified numbers of troops. Zhdanov, Vyshinsky and Dekanozov were sent to supervise the process of setting up acceptable governments and arranging the elections of assemblies in all three states. In August 1940, these assemblies voted for admission of the republics into the Soviet Union.

The process of sovietization had hardly got under way before German troops swiftly overran the Baltic area. Four years of German occupation did nothing to raise the hopes of the indigenous peoples for a restoration of national independence. Soviet rule was restored in 1944–45, and Soviet-trained functionaries began to replace the disparate collection of native-born figures originally chosen to head the new regime. There was now widespread resistance, with thousands "going to the woods." Thousands more were deported in the drive for agricultural collectivization.

POPULATION AND DEMOGRAPHIC CHANGE

It has been estimated that the loss of population between 1939 and 1945 as a result of deportations, emigration, evacuation and flight, and executions, amounted to 25 percent for Estonia, 30 percent for Latvia and 15 percent for Lithuania. Certain ethnic minorities virtually disappeared, either as a consequence of evacuation (the German minority in 1939–40) or extermination. In the postwar years, there was a high influx of immigrants from other Soviet republics into Estonia and Latvia; the Estonian share of the population of the Estonian SSR fell from 94 percent in 1945 to 72 percent in 1953, while the Latvians in the Latvian SSR declined from 83 to 60 percent over the same period. The Lithuanians, with a much higher birth rate and a predominantly rural economy less attractive to immigrants, managed to maintain the native proportion of the population at around 75–80 percent. (See Table 1.)

Table 1
POPULATION AND ETHNIC COMPOSITION OF THE BALTIC REPUBLICS, 1939–80

Year	Total Population (in millions)			Percentage Belonging to Republic Nationality		
	Estonia	Latvia	Lithuania	Estonia	Latvia	Lithuania
1939*	1.05	1.93	3.1	92	77	76(?)
1945	0.85	1.4	2.4	94(?)	83(?)	80(?)
1950	1.09	1.94	2.57	76(?)	63(?)	75(?)
1960	1.2	2.11	2.75	74.1	61.7	79.4
1970	1.35	2.36	3.12	68.2	56.8	80.1
1980	1.47	2.52	3.42	64.5	53.3	80.1

* Adjusted to postwar borders.

A second major wave of immigration began at the end of the 1960s, and the major cities were a favorite area for settlement. Latvians are no longer in a majority in Riga, and the Estonians in Tallinn may well have suffered the same fate. The degree of urbanization in Estonia is the highest in the Soviet Union; Lithuania, once an overwhelmingly rural country, now has over 60 percent of its inhabitants living in towns and cities. The population of Riga and Vilnius has more than doubled since 1940, that of Tallinn has almost trebled. (See Table 2.)

THE ECONOMY

In comparison with the rest of the Soviet Union, the Baltic republics enjoy an enviably higher standard of living. Per capita national income and retail sales rates in Estonia and Latvia are about 40 to 50 percent above the Soviet average. Consumption of meat, fish, eggs and milk was also considerably higher in these two republics during the relatively prosperous 1960s and early 1970s. On the other hand, the proportion of personal income spent on food is still much higher than in the West, and consumer goods—which are often manufactured in the Baltic republics—are often shoddy and in short supply.

Table 2
URBAN POPULATION IN THE BALTIC, 1940–80

Year	Percentage of population living in urban areas			
	Estonia	Latvia	Lithuania	Soviet Union
1940	33.6	35.2	24.0	32.5
1950	47.1	45.3	28.3	38.9
1960	57.1	53.7	39.3	48.8
1970	65.0	62.5	50.2	56.3
1980	70.1	69.0	62.0	62.8

The economic councils (*sovnarkhoz*) of 1958–64 probably marked the high point of autonomy within the Baltic republics. Since their abolition, the central ministries' control has been greatly extended. In Latvia, for example, only three percent of industrial production was under union control in 1960; 10 years later, this had risen to 34 percent, with union-republic ministries controlling a further 56 percent. An attempt by the local Communist party leaders to secure greater economic autonomy for Latvia came to grief in 1959, though the more cautious Estonian leaders managed to avoid a confrontation on similar issues three years earlier.

Within the framework of ever-increasing integration, certain activities have been encouraged, though talk of specialization within the three republics has come to nothing. The Estonian Cybernetics Institute has pioneered new methods of computerized economic management, and the Kirov fishing collective in the same republic has become something of a showpiece for Soviet and foreign visitors. With respect to manufacturing industries, the Baltic republics produce a large proportion of the Soviet Union's output of motorcycles, and stereo, radio and television equipment. Oil shale production in eastern Estonia has continued to expand in spite of the changing pattern of Soviet energy supplies and needs, and in defiance of environmental and ecological considerations. The oil discovered in the 1960s near Klaipėda has not been considered worth exploiting, however. Plans to build a large refinery for Siberian crude oil near the Nemunas River delta in Lithuania aroused opposition on environmental grounds, and the refinery was eventually sited near the Latvian border.

The level of agricultural efficiency in the Baltic republics is higher than that of most other Soviet republics, and some wealth has been generated by auxiliary industries such as canning, sawmilling and the manufacture of derivatives such as starch and maltose. Private plots of land continue to contribute a large portion of collective farm income—44 percent in Latvia in 1970, 43 percent in Lithuania in 1975—and a significant share of marketed produce such as potatoes, fruit and vegetables.

The rapid expansion of industry and the pace of urbanization in the Baltic has created labor shortages that cannot be met from the small reserves of indigenous rural labor. The influx of Russians and other non-Baltic peoples into the area has thus added another dimension to the urban problems of overcrowding—that of national friction.

RUSSIFICATION AND NATIONALISM

The governments set up in the three Baltic republics in 1940 were of the popular front type, composed largely of left-wing intellectuals and politicians. Soviet-trained communists played a relatively minor role. This pattern was to change after 1945. A number of Estonian ministers and officials were purged as "bourgeois nationalists" in 1950. By 1952, almost half the members of the Communist party in Estonia were nonnative, and the senior party offices were occupied largely by Russians or Russian-educated "Yestonians" (a pun on their poor command of the Estonian language). The party secretaries Johannes Käbin (served 1950–78) and Karl Vaino (since 1978) were both educated in the Soviet Union, as were their Latvian counterparts, Arvīds Pelše (1959–66) and Augusts Voss (since 1966). The long-serving (1936–74) party secretary in Lithuania, Antanas Snieckus, was Lithuanian-born, and Lithuanians also constitute a higher proportion of Communist party membership than is the case in either of the two northern republics. (See Table 3.)

The numerical insignificance of the Baltic peoples, the low birth rate of the Latvians and Estonians and the influx of non-Baltic peoples—not to mention the sanctions and measures against national autonomy taken by the central government—would seem to bode ill for the future. However, the Baltic peoples seem possessed of a remarkable degree of resilience, and are not without certain advantages. The existence of well-organized émigré communities, which Moscow has deemed it wise to acknowledge, has been an important source of cultural contacts. The Estonians and Latvians in particular, with their traditional contacts with Western culture and their inheritance of Lutheran ideas of education and self-improvement, have maintained a high level of literary output. Many non-Soviet works are first translated into one or more of the Baltic languages, and there are many authors

Table 3
COMMUNIST PARTY MEMBERSHIP AND ETHNICITY, 1930–80

Estonia	Year	% Estonian	Total membership
	1934	—	387
	1938	—	110
	June 21, 1941	65	3,750
	1946	48.1	7,140
	1956	44.6	22,500
	1965	51.9	54,800
	1980	—	95,400

Latvia	Year	% Latvian	Total membership
	1939	—	400
	June 21, 1941	—	3,130
	1949	53	31,200
	1959	35	61,400
	1965	39(?)	95,700
	1980	—	158,000

Lithuania	Year	% Lithuanian	Total membership
	1937	—	1,499
	1941	53.3	3,138
	1945	31.8	3,500
	1953	38	36,200
	1959	55.7	49,100
	1970	67.1	116,600
	1980	—	165,800

unknown to Russian readers through translation whose works are available in the Estonian, Latvian or Lithuanian languages. The international successes of athletes, artists and scientists have also helped maintain national self-esteem.

It might also be argued that the indigenous populations have a sense of belonging that is denied the immigrant, and an ethnic cultural milieu that is still thriving, in spite of the increase in the amount of Russian-language programs on television and radio. The younger generation shows little desire to be assimilated. There is a low rate of intermarriage between natives and immigrants in the republics; a survey of the children of such marriages in Tallinn between 1960 and 1968 showed that most opt for an Estonian identity when they reach the age of 16. Teenage rebelliousness manifests itself mainly in the flouting of convention and official lines—hippies and punks are a not uncommon sight in the Baltic cities, and the flaunting of plastic bags from Western supermarkets and the wearing of emblazoned T-shirts are virtually universal—but there have also been serious anti-Russian demonstrations and riots. The self-immolation of a student in Kaunas in 1972 provoked serious rioting, as did the cancellation of a pop concert in Tallinn in 1980.

In Lithuania, the Roman Catholic church is a major rallying point for the national cause, and religion has proved to be an inspiration for much samizdat literature. Mass petitions calling for freedom of conscience were organized in 1971, 1973, and again in 1979. The *Chronicle of the Lithuanian Catholic Church* first appeared in 1972, and has managed to keep going in spite of harassment. In the northern republics, it is the Baptists who have provided the main impetus for religious dissent.

Evidence of political dissidence continues to trickle through to the West. In October 1980, 40 Estonian intellectuals, in an open letter to *Pravda* —which was not published—complained of food shortages and itemized the anxieties felt by the indigenous population about the influx of immigrants and the propaganda in favor of Russian. In recent years, the number of dissidents arrested and tried has increased, evidence of mounting dissatisfaction and of official determination to crack down on such discontent.

Writers and artists have helped sustain a sense of separate national identity, sometimes in remarkably outspoken language, as in this poem by Māris Čaklais (Karogs, 1970):

> Alas, many have come to remake us,
> to give us their faith, their gods,
> to take our harbors—ice-free!
> to occupy our shores—amber shores!

The future survival of the peoples of the Baltic lands may not appear very bright in demographic perspective; but small nations have experienced a renaissance in Western Europe since 1945, and there are very evident signs of vitality in the Soviet Baltic republics. Contacts with the diaspora are important, though these are bound to change as the generation of wartime emigrants dies off. It is not inconceivable that the flow of immigration will slacken and even dry up, and that a section of the nonnative population will become assimilated, at least in the regions where they constitute a small minority. This is unlikely to occur in the big cities, however, and the oil shale district of Estonia is already virtually a Russian-speaking area. Dissidence is unlikely to take the form of national opposition to the regime, as in Poland, with its strong historic traditions and much larger indigenous population. As the poem by Čaklais suggests, invasion and occupation have been the lot of the Baltic peoples from time immemorial, and the period of independence was short-lived. On the other hand, the rulers of Russia and of the Soviet Union have been prepared to tolerate a degree of autonomy and freedom in the Baltic and have from time to time recognized the benefits of superior skills. It was Peter the Great who sent Estonian peasants through Russia to demonstrate the technique of harvesting with scythes; and Baltic experts in the sciences are still able to impart information to their Russian counterparts. Much will depend on the composition and attitudes of the leadership in Moscow, and on the military situation, for it must be remembered that the area of *Pribaltiki* is an important advance base for Soviet naval forces. The balance between Soviet domestic aims and policies and the aspirations of the indigenous peoples of the Soviet Union is a delicate one; and if the Baltic peoples are only a small fraction of that welter of nationalities, their cultural and social standards are such that they offer an interesting "Western" dimension for the outside observer.

FURTHER READING

Allworth, Edward, ed. *Nationality Group Survival in Multi-Ethnic States: Shifting Support Patterns in the Soviet Baltic Region.* New York: Praeger, 1977.

Misiunas, Romuald J., and Taagepera, Rein. *The Baltic States: Years of Dependence 1940–1980.* London: Hurst, 1983.

Parming, Tönu, and Järvesoo, Elmar, eds. *A Case Study of a Soviet Republic: The Estonian SSR.* Boulder, Colorado: Westview, 1978.

Rauch, Georg von. *The Baltic States: The Years of Independence, 1917–1940.* London: Hurst, 1974.

Remeikis, Thomas. *Opposition to Soviet Rule in Lithuania, 1945–1980.* Chicago: University of Chicago Press, 1980.

Sprudzs, Adolf, and Rusis, Armins, eds. *Res Baltica.* Leiden: Sijthoff, 1968.

———. *Lithuania under the Soviets: Portrait of a Nation, 1940–1965.* New York: Praeger, 1965.

Vardys, V. Stanley. *The Catholic Church: Dissent and Nationality in Lithuania.* Boulder, Colorado: Westview, 1978.

Ziedonis, Arvids, et al., eds. *Problems of Mininations: Baltic Perspectives.* San Jose, California: Association for the Advancement of Baltic Studies, 1973.

SOVIET FOREIGN POLICY

MALCOLM MACKINTOSH

SOVIET foreign policy can be analyzed under three general headings: its guiding principles, the main areas of its activity and the conclusions that can be drawn from this activity.

GUIDING PRINCIPLES

In a survey such as this, it is inevitable that certain unprovable assumptions must be made about the leadership of a foreign power. It is probably true, however, to say that the following principles guide the Soviet leaders:

a. The Soviet Union must survive as a state and as a world superpower, with some degree of parity with the United States.

b. There must be no military-strategic confrontation with the United States involving active hostilities.

c. There should be no foreign commitments, beyond the reasonable capability of the Soviet armed forces to fulfill them.

d. Communist ideology must to some degree be injected into foreign policy, especially within the world communist movement, where China continues to represent an ideological threat.

e. Wherever consistent with the first two principles, Soviet political influence and prestige must increase throughout the world. In any clash between survival and ideology or prestige, survival will always win.

f. An active role in the United Nations should be retained, with the proviso that decisions running counter to Soviet national or ideological aims will be unacceptable.

AREAS OF ACTIVITY

Relations with the United States

Historically, there has always been a Russian urge to come to bilateral terms with the world's strongest power—the czars with Napoleon and with Bismarck's Germany, and Stalin with Hitler. The relationship with the United States, including the strategic dialogue carried on during the 1970s, as well as the Soviet and American involvement in détente, helped the two superpowers avoid a military clash through miscalculation. It ensured acceptance of the Soviet Union's claim to superpower status, and raised possibilities for bilateral deals and joint action to control unwanted crises. It also acted as a spur to the Soviet Union to formulate policies confirming its parity with the United States. In the field of armaments, this meant both a continued arms race and some moves toward controlling strategic-weapons competition through the SALT process.

The Soviet Union, therefore, believed during the 1970s that one of its main postwar goals had been achieved through a bilateral political, strategic, commercial and crisis-management relationship with the United States. This relationship allowed it to divert energies and resources to policies in Europe, the Far East and the Third World. In the Soviet view, however, events since 1981 appear to have seriously undermined this achievement in Soviet–U.S. relations. President Reagan's buildup of American military power and the virtual cessation of the SALT process, the redress of the NATO–Warsaw Pact military balance in Europe, the growth and suppression of Solidarity in Poland, lack of progress in Soviet–Chinese relations and setbacks for Soviet policies in the Middle East and Africa, the continued war in Afghanistan, the Korean airline disaster and, at home, the death of three Soviet leaders in quick succession—these events have thrown the Soviet Union back on the defensive. In foreign policy, the instinctive reaction of its elderly leadership as a result of the breakup of the Soviet–U.S. relationship of the 1970s has been to hold the fort, to secure gains already achieved and to adopt attitudes of defiance toward the outside world. This has been the essential element in Soviet foreign policy through the first quarter of 1985.

Europe
The Soviet Union's primary requirements in this critical area are to retain military predominance in Eastern Europe, to create a buffer zone politically and militarily and to create opportunities for the USSR to exploit its long-standing goal of increasingly influencing what goes on in Western Europe. The Warsaw Pact is one of its main instruments in carrying out those tasks and in countering divisive trends in Eastern European countries. Employing the Warsaw Pact in this latter role was a main feature of Soviet foreign policy in the Czechoslovak crisis of 1968. It was available and ready to act in the Polish Solidarity crisis of 1980–81, although, in the event, this course was not followed. The Polish crisis was brought under control by the Poles themselves (with Soviet approval) imposing martial law in December 1981. The situation in Poland remains complex and potentially tense for both the Poles and the Soviet Union, and is bound to affect Soviet foreign policy in Europe for some time to come. The USSR certainly showed that it will not tolerate divergence from loyalty within the bloc, and such countries as Romania, Hungary and East Germany will have to recognize this fact today, as they have had to in the past.

During the 1970s, however, the Soviet Union seemed to believe that events in Western Europe were moving their way. If they played their cards well, they believed, the initiative in Europe might fall to them and they might be able to influence Western European politics and security. There were five main reasons for this: U.S. involvement in Vietnam; the new West German approach to Eastern Europe, and its decreasing rigidity toward East Germany (a trend unpopular in Moscow—hence the Soviet attempts to discredit it and to distract attention from Bonn's Ostpolitik); the Greek–Turkish tensions; and last, the somewhat remote possibilities of revitalizing certain Western European Communist parties, perhaps by forming leftist popular fronts. This last idea seemed especially to appeal to Brezhnev, and the 1968 conference of Communist parties in Budapest was a sign of this interest.

In fact, none of these situations produced results sought by the Soviet Union in Europe. With the end of the Vietnam war, Western European–U.S. tensions lessened, and the Helsinki process on security and cooperation in Europe demonstrated that the Western Europeans and the Americans were able to coordinate their policy making and bring the treaty to a satisfactory conclusion. The relationship between East and West Germany was influenced largely by the German Federal Republic's desire to build a special German relationship, one that might encourage the German Democratic Republic to exercise a greater degree of freedom in its policies toward the Soviet Union. Greece and Turkey remained at loggerheads over Cyprus, but this situation offered no major opportunities for the Soviet Union to exploit. The Western European Communist parties fell increasingly under the influence of the Eurocommunist movement, especially in Italy and Spain, against which the Soviet ideologists were forced to divert more and more of their efforts trying to discipline the nonruling Communist parties in Western countries.

The main European issue for the Soviet Union, as it turned out, was a military one. Since the mid-1960s, encouraged by NATO's abandoning the medium- or intermediate-range land-based nuclear missiles of the Thor type, the Soviet Union had come to believe that NATO accepted Soviet superiority in the European theater with respect to those missiles—the SS-4 and SS-5—that had been deployed in western Russia since the late 1950s. When the Soviet Union began in 1976–77 to modernize these missiles by deploying the SS-20—a mobile missile with three warheads—Soviet leaders apparently assumed that the new missile would be automatically accepted by NATO, which would continue to accord the Soviet Union superiority in this area.

To NATO, however, the SS-20 was a weapon far too powerful and dangerous to be accepted without response. While seeking negotiations with the Soviet Union on the issue, NATO asked the United States to dispatch a matching capability to Europe. The Cruise and Pershing-II land-based missiles would go to the NATO countries wanting to deploy them—Britain, West Germany and Italy. This was enshrined in the dual-track decision of December 1979. The Soviet Union declined to negotiate on the issue except on its own terms, seeming to hope that the antinuclear movements in the Western countries concerned would force their governments to abandon deployment. As the deployment date approached the Soviets, whose policy planning had been dominated by the worsening Soviet–U.S. relationship, awoke to the fact that the antinuclear movements and Soviet propaganda had failed to force cancellation of deployment. They therefore turned, in mid-1983, to diplomacy, offering a number of proposals on weapons levels in Europe, on condition that the new NATO missiles not be deployed. But it was too late. Deployment began in late 1983, and unless the Soviet government can negotiate an agreement with NATO to limit the number of these kinds of missiles acceptable to both sides, it is possible that full deployment of Cruise and Pershing-II weapons will be completed on schedule in 1986.

In general, the Soviet Union's European hopes of the 1970s have not been realized as of early 1985. In this area, as well, there has been a tendency to hold on to existing gains and to fortify the Soviet bloc politically, ideologically and militarily in the European theater.

The Middle East

The Soviet Union has continued to accord great importance to the Middle East in planning its foreign policy, although it has suffered a number of setbacks in the region, especially in Egypt. After the death of President Nasser in 1970, President Sadat decided to lessen Egypt's dependence on the Soviet Union. He subsequently tried, in 1973, to regain by military action Egyptian territory occupied by Israel after the 1967 Yom Kippur war. This war was followed by a diplomatic process, dominated by the United States, that left the Soviet Union without its main power base in the Middle East. The Soviets then had to witness the Camp David agreement between Egypt and Israel. The Soviet Union, it is true, retained footholds in Syria and Iraq and, initially at least, benefited from the overthrow of the shah in Iran. But the USSR has been unable to exercise control over the long, divisive civil strife in Lebanon, has failed to save Syrian forces from defeat at Israeli hands there in 1982, and has been unable to influence the war between Iraq and Iran or to dominate events within the Palestine Liberation Organization. Moreover, the increasing spread of Islamic fundamentalism, some of which originated in Iran, is deeply troubling to the Soviet Union, which fears its effects on its own Muslim population in Central Asia.

The Soviet Union in the mid-1980s continues to enjoy a position of influence in Syria, partly through its military aid; it has military links with Iraq, to which it is still supplying weapons; and further afield, it has a fairly strong position in South Yemen, where the port of Aden is heavily used by the Soviet navy. The Soviet Union has, however, made little progress in restoring its former position of influence in Egypt, and has had difficulty formulating a consistent policy on the Iran–Iraq war. Diplomatically, the Soviet Union seeks support for a new regional conference on the Middle East, perhaps under joint Soviet–U.S. direction; some Middle Eastern countries have indicated support for at least the idea of such a conference.

Little progress, however, is likely to be achieved here unless the United States wishes, or is able, to change Israeli attitudes to the region's problems; this appears unlikely in the near future. The Soviet rulers will probably continue to rely on arms sales and military assistance to their friends, and to maintain and upgrade their ocean-going naval capabilities in the Indian Ocean and the Mediterranean Sea as demonstrations of Soviet superpower status and military power.

China

Even after the death of Mao Zedong in 1976 and the end of the Cultural Revolution, Soviet leaders seem determined to confront China on all important

283

issues—political, military and, to some extent, ideological. These include the main territorial issues, the problems of the "unequal treaties," and the role of China in the East Asian "Quadrilateral" relationship (China, Japan, the Soviet Union and the United States) and also in the Third World, where Soviet interests and prestige have to be protected by constant vigilance on all fronts.

Although China has adopted a more moderate approach to the Soviet Union under Deng Xiaoping and now negotiates with Moscow on trade and some border issues, it has continued to insist on three major demands, on which no compromise with the Soviets seems possible. The first is the withdrawal of Soviet troops from the Sino–Soviet border area and from Mongolia; the second is the removal of Soviet forces from Afghanistan; and the third is an end to Vietnamese operations in Kampuchea. The Soviet Union cannot consider any of these demands, especially in the present period of international tension, given its attitude of defiance toward the outside world. Moreover, the Soviet Union's relations with Japan seem particularly uneasy, based on its feeling that Japan is moving closer both toward its traditional partner of the postwar era, the United States, and to China.

The Third World

The Soviet Union appears to have divided the Third World—in which it claims the full rights of a superpower to pursue active policies for national and ideological reasons—into two broad categories: peripheral areas, close to the Soviet borders; and more distant regions. In the peripheral areas, Soviet leaders believe that for political, geographical and strategic reasons they must ensure some form of control or influence. When a pro-Soviet communist regime in neighboring Afghanistan appeared to be disintegrating in late 1978, the Soviet army invaded to restore loyal communist control. The Soviets clearly expected that the army, which had not suffered defeat since 1942, would quickly overcome all Afghan resistance.

Events moved differently, however, and Soviet foreign policy has suffered in the last five years. The failure of the Soviet army and air force to suppress Afghan opposition has had a grave effect on the Soviet Union's reputation abroad, especially in the Third World. It is seen to be following what Third World countries regard as a traditionally imperialist policy, using military power against a small, nonaligned state. Even more worrying for Soviet leaders is that this continuing conflict in Afghanistan, like the shooting down of the Korean airliner in September 1983, has shown that Soviet armed forces are unable to carry out vitally important military tasks. No doubt some Soviet forces are gaining professional experience in the Afghan campaign, but active and hostile international repercussions are still apparent.

The Soviets are also active in more distant areas of the Third World—in Africa, Southeast Asia and Central America. They support both procommunist revolutionary movements, as in El Salvador, and established pro-Marxist governments, as in Nicaragua, Angola, Ethiopia and Vietnam. In Africa and Central America, the burden is borne mainly by Cuba, whose leaders have been ready to send expeditionary forces to Angola and Ethiopia and to help guerrilla movements in the Caribbean area. In Southeast Asia, Vietnam is militarily active in Laos and Kampuchea, and provides a military irritant to China along China's southern border. All these actions, along with Soviet economic- and military-aid programs, assist Soviet policy in these areas of the Third World. They do not, however, have a high priority in the formulation of Soviet foreign policy, and are basically opportunistic both strategically and tactically. Yet they do provide a further justification for the Soviet ideological claim to be on the side of world history in international affairs, and for maintaining very impressive global naval and air power.

CONCLUSIONS

It seems likely that Soviet foreign and military policy will continue to follow strategies similar to those described above, most of which involve an element of threat to the West or Western interests. Whatever the Soviets can achieve in the Third World, especially by developing military, naval and air power, as well as by subversion and propaganda, they will pursue with vigor, based on opportunism. Yet such actions will always take second place to the preservation of the Soviet political system at home and in Eastern Europe, and to the advancement of Soviet interests in the areas that really matter. These vital areas will remain the strategic balance with the United States; the improvement of the Soviet position in Europe; the present and longer-term confrontation with China; the expansion of Soviet power in border areas; and the attaining of some influence in the more distant areas of the Third World.

There may be probes and experiments, some of them locally highly risky. As long as the West retains its ultimate deterrent, however, the Soviets will not regard nuclear war as a feasible way of achieving the foreign policy goals that, according to the composition and convictions of the Politburo, they may set themselves now and in the years ahead.

FURTHER READING

Brown, J. F. *The New Eastern Europe*. New York: Frederick A. Praeger; London: Pall Mall, 1966.

Brzezinski, Zbigniew K. *The Soviet Bloc*. Cambridge, Massachusetts: Harvard University Press; London: Oxford University Press, 1960.

Dallin, David J. *Soviet Foreign Policy after Stalin*. Philadelphia: J. B. Lippincott, 1961; London: Methuen, 1962.

Gelman, Harry. *The Brezhnev Politburo and the Decline of Détente*. Ithaca, New York: Cornell University Press, 1984.

Horelick, Arnold L., and Rush, Myron. *Strategic Power and Soviet Foreign Policy*. Chicago: University of Chicago Press, 1966.

IISS *Strategic Survey*. (Annual).

Luttwak, Edward N. *The Grand Strategy of the Soviet Union*. London: Weidenfeld and Nicolson, 1983.

Mackintosh, J. M. *Strategy and Tactics of Soviet Foreign Policy*. London: Oxford University Press, 1962; New York, 1963.

Ulam, Adam B. *Expansion and Coexistence: The History of Soviet Foreign Policy, 1917–1967*. London: Secker and Warburg; New York: Frederick A. Praeger, 1968.

EASTERN EUROPE

NATIONALISM IN EASTERN EUROPE

J. F. BROWN

HISTORY OF PRESENT-DAY EASTERN EUROPE

HISTORY has been unkind to Eastern Europe on a number of accounts, not least in its indiscriminate dumping of a large number of nations into its relatively small area. The area of Eastern Europe is about two-thirds the size of Western Europe, yet, whereas the one is almost exclusively covered by five large nations—British, French, German, Spanish and Italian—the other has more than 15 nations jostling within its boundaries. Nor are these nations compact units; all have sizable minorities of other nations in their midst and members of their own nation enveloped by others. The events that have produced this situation are complex and bitter and still influence the attitudes and actions of the Eastern European nations today.

The history of the Eastern European nations has largely been one of struggle for existence, against outsiders or against each other—or against both simultaneously. For the most part these nations themselves are not indigenous to Eastern Europe but settled there, through outside pressure, between the sixth and the 10th centuries. The peaceful Slavs, later to become divided into many nations, came from the interior of Russia and had by the year 1000 settled the area between the Elbe and Oder in the west and the approaches to the Byzantine empire in the south. The Hungarians, coming from the steppes of southern Russia, had finally been forced to settle in the central plain of Eastern Europe. Of the nations that inhabited Eastern Europe at the time of the Roman empire, the only three that survive today are the Wallachians of Romania, the Albanians and the Greeks.

Between the beginning of the 11th century and the end of the 18th, these Eastern European nations were subjected to constant pressures from literally all points of the compass. From the west came pressure, both warlike and peaceful, from the Germans and from the Italians, particularly the Venetians in southeastern Europe; from the south from the Turks; from the east, first from the Tatars, then from the Russians; even from the north, the Swedes in the 17th century made damaging incursions into Poland. Not all nations suffered the same degree of pressure or for the same period of time, but it was *the* constant factor in the existence of all of them and in the end

288

all succumbed to it. Those states that the various nations of southeastern Europe had created were the first to disappear. The Serbian and Bulgarian fell at the end of the 14th century, the Albanian shortly afterwards in the middle of the 15th century; Constantinople was finally overrun in 1453—all fell to the Ottoman Turks. Early in the 16th century, Moldavia and Wallachia (later to become Romania) and most of Hungary fell also to the Turks. In central and northeastern Europe different conquerors took the spoils. Early in the 17th century, Czech independence was finally snuffed out for 300 years by the Germans; at the end of the following century it was Poland's turn, divided by Prussia, Austria and Russia in the course of three partitions.

However, it was during this period of what in retrospect is now seen as gradual, inexorable liquidation that some of these nations—those that were to reappear again as states in the 20th century—had built up states and empires impressive in size and often in civilization. This had mostly been done, not at the expense of those outside nations bearing down on them, but of the other nations in the same area and under the same threat. Thus, in southeastern Europe, first the Bulgarians and then the Serbs created empires between the 10th and 14th centuries that covered, in part, the same territory. Further north, the Hungarian kings extended their domain to include territories inhabited not only by Magyars but by Romanians and Slavs. (Much later, after the establishment of the Austro-Hungarian monarchy in 1867, Hungary was to reestablish its hold over these regions; from a subjugated nation it became an imperialist power.) Poland, at the height of its power in the 16th century, held sway over a vast conglomeration of non-Polish peoples.

These periods of greatness, medieval or modern, remained clearly in the minds of the successive generations of Eastern European peoples submerged in the long night of foreign occupation. Their country to them was their country at the very peak of its power, and when their long night ended in the course of the 19th century and at the beginning of the 20th, this was the country they claimed as both their heritage and their birthright.

PRESSURES ON THE NEWLY INDEPENDENT STATES

Thus, independence when it came usually meant not fulfillment, but at best only partial satisfaction; only too often it meant bitter frustration and resentment. Bulgaria, for example, at the very dawn of its independence from Turkey, considered itself cheated by the Congress of Berlin in 1878 because a large part of the territory it had gained a few months earlier was taken away by the great states in the interests of the "balance of power." In efforts to recover part or all of this territory from Serbia, Romania and Greece, Bulgaria took the losing side in the second Balkan War, and the two World Wars. Poland, restored to independence after World War I, hankered after its frontiers of before the first partition of 1772, and Polish territorial dissatisfaction led to embittered relations with Germany, Soviet Russia and Czechoslovakia. This was despite the fact that the new Poland still contained several million non-Polish inhabitants. The case of Hungary was different, in that it had been the one local imperialist power in the period before World War

I. The treatment it received subsequently was extremely severe. As a result of the Treaty of Trianon, not only were large "historic" territories lost but at least one-third of the Hungarian nation found itself outside the borders of the motherland, enveloped by peoples once its subjects, now its masters. Hungary became an embittered rump state, its foreign policy dictated by the desire to recover its lost territories and peoples.

Nor was this dissatisfaction, caused by nationalist and imperialist frustrations, confined to the interstate level. The peace treaties after World War I created one binational and one multinational state in Eastern Europe: Czechoslovakia and Yugoslavia, respectively. Czechoslovakia was the most advanced state in Eastern Europe between the wars, but relations between Czechs and Slovaks deteriorated steadily largely because of Slovak frustration at Czech domination. In Yugoslavia, the situation was much more explosive. Here the Croats and Slovenes, relatively advanced culturally and economically, formerly part of the Habsburg empire, were put into a state dominated by the Serbs, far less advanced and, to them, still showing unmistakable signs of over four centuries' membership in the Ottoman empire.

All these historical factors made a veritable witches' brew in Eastern Europe between the wars. Add to it the bubbling ingredient of ethnic minorities in every country, left in the wake of empires, invasions and emigrations, and one had a situation lacking almost every prerequisite for both internal and international stability. The Wilsonian concept of self-determination was certainly the wisest and the most equitable for Eastern Europe. But it posed almost as many problems as it solved, and developments in the rest of Europe, leading inevitably on to World War II, soon made a peaceful solution of these problems impossible.

One important reason why the new problems could not be solved was that the old dangers remained. What the 20th century has shown is that the external pressures on Eastern Europe continued unabated. Up to and including World War II, Italy, then Germany, then the new Russia reassumed their predatory interest. After World War II, the Soviet Union assumed domination over the whole region. This it did partly by the reincorporation of those territories that had previously been part of czarist Russia (and some that had not)—the independent Baltic republics of Estonia, Latvia and Lithuania, large slices of eastern Poland, Sub-Carpathian Ruthenia, northern Bukovina and Bessarabia—but mainly by installing or engineering communist governments in Poland, Hungary, Romania and Bulgaria. In Yugoslavia and Albania, communist governments were installed largely without Soviet support. Finally, Czechoslovakia fell into the Soviet sphere through a brilliant coup in 1948, actively or tacitly supported by a large minority of the population.

SOVIET DOMINATION OF EASTERN EUROPE

The Soviet domination in Eastern Europe contained a historically new element, in that most states affected did not lose their identity. They were not physically incorporated into the Soviet Union as previously Poland had been swallowed up by Russia, Prussia and Austria, or Bulgaria and Serbia

by the Ottoman empire. The essential framework for nationalist expression
—the state—was, therefore, preserved. But according to communist theory,
the factors that had caused the bitter nationalist and chauvinist enmities
of the interwar years had now been swept away. The old ruling class had
gone and with it the old feudal and capitalist system. The new concept of
proletarian internationalism now embraced the area. Previous antagonisms
would be replaced by cooperation between governments of the same type,
led by new leaders operating a new system that, by definition, precluded
both inward exploitation and outward imperialism.

So much for the theory. The practice was quite different. For one thing,
the Soviet Union exploited the Eastern European states economically to
an extent that made the previous imperialisms look almost charitable. Countries like Hungary, Romania and East Germany, which had fought against
the Soviet Union in the war, had to pay grievously damaging war reparations,
and states like Romania and Bulgaria were also plundered of their mineral
wealth by means of joint stock companies, owned "equally" by the Soviet
Union and the states concerned. Finally, all the Eastern European states
were subjected to a trading relationship involving cheap exports to the Soviet
Union and relatively expensive imports in return. For another, even with
communist governments installed, national distinctions soon appeared, and
Stalin was hardly partial to any peculiarities except his own. There was
also evidence that, proletarian internationalism or not, some communist
states still heartily disliked others for reasons mainly based on the old rivalries. Finally—and most dangerous of all—some communist leaders were
not prepared to accept the principle of exclusive Soviet control over their
affairs. There were clear examples of this in Poland and Bulgaria, where
Władysław Gomułka and Traicho Kostov, albeit convinced communists,
were bent on policies conceived, first and foremost, according to the requirements of their own countries.

It was Yugoslavia, however, that disproved the idealistic claims of proletarian internationalism. Tito and the other Yugoslav leaders—again, convinced
communists and at first blindly loyal to the Soviet Union—soon clashed
with Stalin on how things were to be run in Yugoslavia. For these men,
veterans of an epic struggle for communism in Yugoslavia, it was inconceivable that they could not be trusted with the effective government of their
own country. Thus began the bitter dispute between Belgrade and Moscow
that led to the break in June 1948. It was, therefore, the Soviet imperialism
practiced by Stalin that brought out the latent nationalism in Yugoslav communism and showed that nationalism was by no means incompatible with
a creed that was supposed to make it irrelevant. Stalin's answer to the Yugoslav disaster—the only kind he knew—was not to relax the grip but to tighten
it, to try to stamp out the signs of a reviving Eastern European nationalism.

His organizational response to the danger was the Cominform (Communist Information Bureau), founded in September 1947. This was a harmless
enough title for a body designed to check the centrifugal forces already at
work in Eastern Europe, forces deriving their sustenance from national and
historical peculiarities. It recalled, as it was designed to, the Comintern
of the interwar years, an organization that Stalin soon perverted for Soviet

rather than purely communist aims. Later, after the break with Yugoslavia, Stalin began the *Gleichschaltung* (elimination of the opposition) in earnest. Communist leaders, whose experience had been gathered mainly or exclusively in their own countries and were therefore suspected of "nationalist deviations," were replaced by "Muscovites," leaders who had spent long years of exile and education in Moscow. Kostov in Bulgaria and László Rajk in Hungary were executed after nightmare trials; Gomułka and Lucrețiu Pătrășcanu in Romania were publicly disgraced (the latter was eventually executed in 1954). Large-scale purges were carried out in all parties. Down to almost the last detail of public life, the Soviet model was the only one to be followed. The Stalinist era in Eastern Europe had begun in earnest.

It was only to last till Stalin died in March 1953. But during this short period, Eastern European nationalism was effectively submerged under a thick layer of ice that gave the area east of the Elbe a blank appearance of uniformity and cohesion. It looked durable but was not; it could last only as long as Stalin. His was a system that could not be bequeathed because without him it was unworkable.

Stalin's successors, mainly Khrushchev as he elbowed his way to supreme power, fumbled toward a new policy that had two layers. First, the Eastern European satellites were to be granted more autonomy in running their own affairs, and Moscow's economic exploitation of them, at least in its crudest forms, was to stop. Second, the governments of the satellites themselves were urged to make themselves more acceptable to the people they were governing. Both layers of this policy tended to encourage the reemergence of Eastern European nationalism. The more autonomy the satellites received, the more diverse they again became and, if their leaders were to hope for any kind of consensus with the population, then they had, in some degree, to embrace—or pay lip service to—the national sentiments of these peoples. Khrushchev's rapprochement with Tito in 1955, very much on Tito's own terms, gave considerable impetus to this national revival. It was a de facto Soviet recognition of the existence of national communism and could not fail to have a considerable effect throughout Eastern Europe as a whole. Nor could the significance of the abolition of Stalin's Cominform in April 1956 go unnoticed.

The effects were not long in coming. In October 1956, a revolutionary situation in Poland resulted in the return to power of Władysław Gomułka, who had been purged in 1949 for resisting Soviet attempts at the complete domination of Poland. In Hungary, an actual revolution, also in October 1956, succeeded for a few days in toppling the Stalinist regime and had to be crushed by the Soviet army. In the immediate sense, these outbursts were prompted by local dissatisfaction at local oppression. But, basically, they were nationalist outbursts against the system of empire Stalin created and were possible because that system was being deliberately dismantled.

After Poland and Hungary, Khrushchev showed both courage and statesmanship by refusing to stop this dismantling process despite the near-disasters it had caused. But he was very much aware that the centrifugal forces were gathering pace. Reformer though he was, he was not prepared to preside over the dissolution of Soviet hegemony. He therefore cast about for a new and more viable means of cohesion, and by 1958 it was obvious what he had in mind.

COMECON had been founded in 1949 as the communist bloc's (very ineffectual) answer to the Marshall Plan. It had been virtually ignored by Stalin and had never really assumed real importance after his death. Khrushchev now saw it, however, as an instrument for economic integration leading eventually to political integration. What he had in mind was indicated in a remarkable passage during a speech made in East Germany in March 1959. After referring to the future communist society and its benefits, Khrushchev went on:

> In these conditions the old concept of borders as such will disappear. . . . In all likelihood only ethnic borders will survive for a time and even these will probably exist only as a convention. Naturally these frontiers, if they can be called frontiers at all, will have no border guards, customs officials or incidents. . . . Speaking of the future, it seems to me that the further development of the socialist countries will, in all probability, proceed along the lines of consolidation of the single-world socialist economic system.[1]

Obviously, Khrushchev here was ruminating on rather than actually outlining a scheme for serious work to be done. But there was in Khrushchev a streak of the old revolutionary idealism not shared by most of his contemporaries or successors. Strangely, for a man politically groomed in the Ukraine, he seems seriously to have underestimated the durability of nationalism both in the Soviet Union itself and in Eastern Europe. The pursuit of economic integration through COMECON and the use of the newly established Warsaw Treaty Organization (founded in 1955) for political as well as military integration was the basic theme of his Eastern European policy. The coercive power of the Soviet Union, so the reasoning went, would be needed less and less as the mechanics of internationalism became more efficient and its promise more apparent.

But by the time Khrushchev was making that speech in East Germany in 1959, his differences with China had already passed the point of no return. Although these differences were for several years to be couched in ideological terms, two of their powerful generating impulses were Chinese historical resentment and mutual nationalistic antagonisms. And within the COMECON and the Warsaw Pact, the two instruments designed to promote internationalism, nationalist differences were beginning to ferment and some were even starting to appear. Romania's resentment, for example, at the notion—evidently propounded by East Germany and Czechoslovakia and accepted in Moscow—that it should abandon the scope of its industrialization drive and concentrate on agriculture, had already been voiced. It was to develop into a quite serious nationalist challenge to the Soviet Union's hegemony in Eastern Europe and to weaken even further its power in the Balkans. Albania, too, fearful of a renewed Soviet rapprochement with Yugoslavia and carefully monitoring the growing Sino-Soviet schism, was in the process of changing its patron and openly defying Moscow.

[1]*Pravda*, March 27, 1959; quoted by Zbigniew K. Brzezinski, *The Soviet Bloc: Unity and Conflict*, Cambridge, Mass., Harvard University Press, 1960.

By late 1964, therefore, when Khrushchev was removed from power, nationalism in Eastern Europe, rather than being mitigated or sublimated, had already resulted in Yugoslavia and then Albania breaking away from Soviet tutelage, and in Romania having gained a unique status of semi-independence. But this was not all. In Czechoslovakia, forces of reform, in which nationalism played an important part, were gathering strength. At first this nationalism was not directed so much against the Soviet Union; it revolved around the Slovaks' self-assertiveness in their relations with Czechs. But the demands quietly being made in Prague for a revision of Czechoslovakia's military role in the Warsaw Pact, for example, were very much addressed directly to Moscow.

The drama of the Prague Spring of 1968 and its abrupt termination were followed by a massive effort by the Brezhnev leadership in Moscow to reimpose Soviet leadership in Eastern Europe in a way that would make the Czechoslovak trauma and the subsequent need for invasion impossible and unnecessary in the future. Against a background of a massive drive for ideological reinvigoration and conformity, Brezhnev expanded the scope of COMECON and reshaped certain aspects of Warsaw Pact policy and organization in an effort to give the Soviet alliance more motivation and viability. And in the first half of the 1970s, he appeared to be enjoying some success in these efforts.

In retrospect, however, this success was short lived indeed. In fact, the very illusion of success was fostered by the extraordinary economic prosperity of the early 1970s. It was this fortuitously based "consumerism" that mainly gave Soviet policy in Eastern Europe its deceptive appearance of effectiveness. This became evident after 1975, when the prosperity steadily waned and, in varying degrees, all the Eastern European economies were affected by sharply rising Soviet raw-material prices, the Western recession and, in almost every case, the problem of repayments on massive loans contracted with either Western governments or banks. From August 1980, when the free trade union Solidarity was founded in Poland, until its suppression in December 1981, the Soviet-imposed system in Eastern Europe faced its most serious and fundamental challenge. For what Solidarity amounted to was an open rejection—by practically the whole of Polish society—of the communist system and, by implication, of Soviet hegemony. Nationalism, with its predominantly anti-Russian connotation, was obviously not overtly part of Solidarity's platform, but the whole movement was imbued with it, and animosity for the Soviet Union was never far from the surface.

Since the suppression of Solidarity, Eastern Europe has been quiet. The swift efficiency shown by Poland's forces of coercion and the awareness that, behind them, stood the might of the Red Army itself may well have had a numbing effect on those actual and potential forces of dissent that the situation, both in the Soviet Union and Eastern Europe itself, would otherwise seem likely to encourage. A weak and aging Soviet leadership; potential succession problems in Eastern Europe itself; serious economic problems and the prospect of declining living standards; lack of self-confidence among the ruling elites—these were some of the more obvious defects of the system in the 1980s. But the most basic defect remains that communism has not only failed to solve the national question, it may in some respects actually have exacerbated it.

Eastern European nationalism has, as already mentioned, two dimensions: one directed by most of the nations and states in the region against the Soviet Union; the other directed by them against each other. This second dimension has often seemed the more important and evident, and it could well continue to be so in the foreseeable future. Both dimensions will be touched upon in the following country-by-country survey.

Albania: Historically, Albania's nationalism has been totally defensive in character, prompted by fear of encroachment, even extinction, at the hands of more powerful neighbors: Yugoslavia, Greece and, earlier, Italy. More recently, however, this defensiveness has been less pronounced, although the paranoia with which Albania's leaders seem permanently to be gripped is still occasionally evident. Obviously, the danger from Italy can now be discounted if the situation is viewed in Tirana with even a modicum of realism. That from Greece, arising from long-standing Greek claims to "Northern Epirus" (or "Southern Albania" as the Albanians insist), has also receded. It is Yugoslavia that remains the great historic enemy. But, whereas the issue used to be Yugoslav designs, real or simply feared, on Albania's sovereignty, the issue now is more the burgeoning assertiveness of the Albanian community of Kosovo, the autonomous region in Yugoslavia. Albanian nationalism vis-à-vis Yugoslavia has, therefore, now gone from defensive to offensive. Albanians now outnumber Serbs four to one in Kosovo, which in the Middle Ages was the heartland of the great Serbian kingdom. Their numbers have been steadily increasing for over 200 years, but until the last 20 years they were repressed, often brutally, by the ruling Serb minority. Now the Serbs (and Montenegrins) are leaving Kosovo in droves—many through intimidation and fear—and the Albanians are demanding separate republic status for Kosovo within the Yugoslav federation. Few at present would want reunion with Albania itself, and Tirana has formally renounced any claim to the territory. But this could change, and it looks likely that Kosovo will remain one of Eastern Europe's flash points of nationalism.

Yugoslavia: Kosovo has for several years—certainly since the serious Albanian rioting there in 1981—been Yugoslavia's most volatile ethnic trouble spot. But many would argue that, in terms of gravity and potential seriousness, it is still Serb-Croat rivalry that presents the greatest national problem. An uneasy calm has prevailed since the Croatian crisis of 1971, but there is nothing to suggest that relations between Yugoslavia's two largest nations have substantially improved. Perhaps the most serious element of concern is over future Serb behavior. The Serbs were, of course, the "nation of state" in royal Yugoslavia. And for some 20 years, in federal socialist Yugoslavia, despite the constitution and many official protestations to the contrary, and despite the fact that Tito himself was not a Serb, it was the Serbs who still exercised the dominant role—not least because of their control of the federal secret police and their predominance in the military officer corps. Recently, however, this dominance has declined and the Serb role in the Yugoslav state substantially weakened. The humiliation in Kosovo at the hands of the Albanians is only the most recent indignity, but for many Serbs the least bearable of all. Many observers fear a Serbian backlash, taking the form of rioting against Albanian communities in cities like Belgrade, and the possible rise of Serbian separatism. On the political level they fear an increasing lack of cooperation in the affairs of the federation, on the international level an increasing susceptibility to Soviet intrigues.

Bulgaria: Most of Bulgaria's history since the modern state emerged in 1878 has been bedeviled by the urge to regain the so-called San Stefano frontiers. These included not just present-day Bulgaria but also large parts of what are now Yugoslavia and Greece. They were given to the new Bulgaria by the treaty of San Stefano between Russia and the defeated Ottoman Empire in March 1878, then were taken away a few months later at the Congress of Berlin at the insistence of the Western powers, which saw the new "San Stefano Bulgaria" as indirectly strengthening Russia. The focal point of Bulgaria's continuously frustrated ambitions has become more and more centered on Yugoslav Macedonia.

For their part, the Yugoslavs incorporated Macedonia as a constituent republic of the federal state they established after the communist victory in 1945, and they officially regard the Macedonians as a separate, distinct nation with its own language, history and culture. This the Bulgarians, with some historical justice on their side, refuse to accept, maintaining that the Macedonians are part of—or a branch of—the Bulgarian nation and that the "new" Macedonian language is an artificial contrivance. While formally renouncing any *territorial* designs on Yugoslav Macedonia, the Bulgarian regime, with the undoubted support of most Bulgarians, refuses to accept the separateness or distinctiveness of the Macedonians. Polemics between Sofia and Belgrade (or, more often, Skopje, the capital of the republic of Macedonia) flare up periodically over the issue. They occur especially on the occasion of Bulgarian historical anniversaries, because so much of the history of Bulgaria is intertwined with that of present-day Macedonia, the heartland of the medieval Bulgarian kingdom. The Yugoslavs reply by pointing to the alleged disappearance of the "Macedonian minority" in Bulgaria itself. This minority, they point out, was recognized as existing in the late 1940s and in the 1950s, but has since been steadily integrated into the Bulgarian majority. There is a strong suspicion that Moscow has in the past prompted Sofia to stir up the Macedonian issue to embarrass Belgrade when relations between the Soviet Union and Yugoslavia have been strained. This may be so, but the specific Bulgarian component in the controversy and the strength of Bulgarian feeling on the issue should not be ignored. It remains a constant in Bulgarian national life. What has probably changed is that, having fought three wars between 1913 and 1944 to regain Macedonia, without success but with huge loss of life, wealth and reputation, Bulgaria is now not likely to engage in any maneuvers to attempt its recovery.

Romania: The Romanians' ability to carve out a considerable degree of autonomy in bilateral relations with the Soviet Union and multilateral relations within the Soviet alliance has won many admirers for their skill and nerve. These are qualities they acquired over centuries of struggle to gain statehood and to preserve it against often more powerful enemies. Russia has invaded Romania 13 times, and for centuries Transylvania was part of, or associated with, the Kingdom of Hungary—later within the Habsburg Empire. Transylvania was integrated into Romania after World War I, partially lost in 1940 and then totally regained after World War II. In fact, the only territory lost by Romania after World War II was Bessarabia and Northern Bukovina to the Soviet Union.[2] This was a concession for which ethnically there was little justification, and it only served to fuel the historic Romanian resentment against Russia.

It is a resentment, though, that has largely remained impotent simply because of Russian power. Romanian nationalism, therefore, has always been focused on Transylvania—gaining it, then keeping it and now integrating it. It is this third phase, integration, that is occurring now and is causing increasing friction between Bucharest and Budapest.

The history of the Hungarians in Transylvania is irrelevant here; what is relevant are the measures taken to integrate them into the Romanian state proper, and the national antagonisms thus aroused. In retrospect, the Romanian moves to resist certain aspects of Moscow's policy in the late 1950s can be seen as part of the same manifestation of nationalism as the steady dismantling of the Hungarian Autonomous Region and the disbanding of the separate Hungarian university in Cluj that took place at about the same time. These moves were understandably resented by most Hungarians living in Romania, but the Kádár regime in Budapest, still recovering from the effects of the revolution in 1956, was hardly in a position to try to check the Romanian move. In the last 15 years, however, as the Kádár regime has grown in self-confidence and as popular feeling in Hungary has been exacerbated by what is considered to be increased discrimination against their compatriots in Transylvania, relations between the two countries at both state and societal level have deteriorated considerably.

Czechoslovakia: Just about the only achievement of the Prague Spring to have survived is the legislation making Czechoslovakia a federal state, by which Slovakia achieved home rule and full equality of status with the Czech lands. There is little doubt that this achievement satisfied the ambitions of most Slovaks and that this nationalist goal, rather than political liberalization, had been the main objective of many of them during the brief reform period. Anti-Czech feeling in Slovakia has subsided since 1968, particularly among the younger generation. However, whether this welcome development has so far served to strengthen the federation, and Slovak feeling for the integrity of Czechoslovakia as such, remains doubtful. What most Slovaks now feel about Czechs and the Czech lands is their essential irrelevance. In the first republic, and for some 20 years after 1948, Czechs dominated many aspects of Slovak life. Now, with federation and the growth of an all–around Slovak national intelligentsia, Slovaks have moved into positions of responsibility once occupied by Czechs in Slovakia. Not only that: with a Slovak (Gustáv Husák) as Czechoslovak president and party leader and many Slovaks in

[2] In 1940 Romania was forced to surrender to Bulgaria South Dobrudja, where the majority of the population was clearly Bulgarian.

senior federal posts in Prague, the traffic has to some extent been reversed. Perhaps the bitterest national feeling in Czechoslovakia at present is that harbored by frustrated Czechs, impatient at what they now regard as a Slovak equality that sometimes looks to them like dominance.

In Slovakia itself, two forces have been struggling to capture and represent Slovak nationalism: the Communist party and the Catholic church. This has led to a severe and sometimes bloody persecution of the church. But despite, and perhaps because of, this persecution, the church is regarded by growing numbers—and by many young people—as the very embodiment of the Slovak spirit. The party, with all the massive material means at its disposal, must resort to persecution as it realizes it is unable to meet the church's challenge.

A darker side to this growing Slovak nationalism, however, is increasing discrimination against the Hungarian minority, numbering over 600,000. The discrimination is not massive; it certainly does not amount to persecution. But in terms of careers, education, culture, social and economic life, Hungarians—the master ethnic group in Slovakia for 800 years—are increasingly suffering disadvantages, similar in many respects to those they suffer in Transylvania.

Hungary: Massively dismembered by the Treaty of Trianon, the draconian provisions of which were never permanently reversed, Hungary in this century has found itself the victim of the nationalism of others. Parts of the former territory and some 3 million ethnic Magyars are now divided among Romania, Czechoslovakia, Yugoslavia and the Soviet Union. In between the wars, therefore, irredentism was not simply widespread but practically de rigueur. Since 1945, four factors have tended to reduce the volume and shrillness of the former irredentism: (1) official discouragement by the ruling Communist party; (2) the huge losses suffered in pursuing the policy; (3) the loss of national reputation and honor in pursuing it; (4) the postwar realization of its futility. There may be the lingering hope in Budapest, of course, that Moscow might seek to punish Romania for its continuing recalcitrance by threatening border revisions. But no one can realistically expect the Soviet Union to begin a process that may have no end.

But abandoning irredentism has definitely not signified a lack of concern in Hungary, among both rulers and ruled, for their compatriots abroad. In fact, that concern is growing as the condition of Hungarians in Romania and Czechoslovakia worsens. It could become a major point of tension in Central and Eastern Europe in the next decade.

Poland: Perhaps because the Poles as a nation have encountered greater threats to their existence than almost any other, nationalism in Poland is the strongest evident characteristic. Since 1945, its political expression has been directed against the Soviet Union. Russia, with Germany, has always been the greatest threat to Poland's very existence; now, with the Soviet Union controlling Eastern Europe and with Germany militarily emasculated and territorially divided, it is the former that, directly and indirectly, drastically curtails Polish national and individual freedom. Since 1945 Poland has, for the first time in its history, also become an ethnically unified state without substantial national minorities. Nationalism, therefore, so often directed (or misdirected) within Poland's state borders, can now be directed almost solely against the historical enemy to the east.

Internally, since World War II, what was described above as occurring in Slovakia—the struggle between the communist regime and the Catholic church to embody and represent the national spirit—has been happening also in Poland, but on a much more important scale. And more clearly than in Slovakia, the church in Poland has triumphed. In fact, the church in Poland has not only continued in its role as defender of the nation but has expanded it.

During the brief rise of Solidarity in 1980 and 1981, it seemed as if a second powerful nationalist force was emerging that, though cooperating with, and blessed by, the church, could have developed into a position of rivalry with it. But the possibility was never tested. After the crushing of Solidarity, the church, though often falteringly led by Caradinal Glemp, successor to the great Cardinal Wyszyński, resumed its role as both the symbol and focus of Polish nationalism. The church's strength and influence have also been incalculably bolstered by the fortuitous circumstance of a Polish pope in Rome, and there is little reason to believe that its role will appreciably diminish in the future. Two factors will serve to strengthen and perpetuate it even further: Soviet hegemony and a local communist control that is manifestly dependent on that hegemony. As for state persecution of the church, this has counted for little since the early 1950s. Harassment and legal disabilities continue but, unlike in Slovakia, the church in Poland is simply too powerful to be the target of real persecution.

The German Democratic Republic: It might seem unusual, even grotesque, to include East Germany in any survey of nationalism in Eastern Europe. This, after all, is perhaps the most artificial state ever created in European history.

But East Germany deserves, indeed, a special consideration in this context, not, obviously, as a case of organic nationalism but of the opposite—an attempt at induced nationalism from above. After the building of the Berlin Wall in 1961 and the blocking of the last open escape hatch, the Ulbricht regime began a systematic attempt to induce a distinctive sense of "East Germanism," which, it was hoped, would develop into a more genuine sense of nationalism. The regime depended on two instruments to achieve this: (1) increasing prosperity, or "consumerism;" (2) the nurturing of specific social strata with a vested interest in East German survival and no interest in reunification. Obviously, as in any orthodox communist state, the workers' stratum received great attention, although this was often more ritualistic than substantial. More intriguing, however, was the deliberate cultivation of the technical-managerial classes. These people got considerable social and economic privileges but also, more importantly, a considerable say in the running of the economy at all levels. It was this class that Ulbricht envisaged as the technical-managerial elite, developing a special sense of identity with East Germany.

This policy was continued after Honecker's accession in 1971. In the meantime, East Germany was achieving international recognition as a sovereign state, de facto by West Germany, de jure by everybody else. It was also (a factor not to be ignored) winning worldwide recognition as a sporting nation. The success of its athletes, indeed, has been one of the few factors uniting the East German state and society.

In the second half of the 1970s, however, the Honecker regime was persuaded that genuine historical roots were necessary if a real sense of nationalism was to be induced. There followed the bewildering rediscovery and rehabilitation of such previously excoriated symbols as Frederick the Great, Martin Luther, Bismarck and even Prussia, so long dismissed as the cradle of Nazism and militarism.

From what can be gathered, the impact of the campaign on the East German population was hardly what the regime had hoped. Bemusement and derision were the main initial reactions and, if the campaign was taken at all seriously, it only tended to show East Germans the common history they had with their West German neighbors. But the campaign is likely to continue. The Honecker regime seems to be striving for the "Austrianization" of East Germany—not, one hastens to emphasize, in the sense of neutralization, but in the sense of detachment from the German historical mainstream. Austria finally achieved this, not in 1918 but after 1955. Success is doubtful in East Germany's case, but its efforts to achieve it could be an important factor in the Central European scene of years to come.

Several conclusions could be drawn from this sketchy survey of the condition of nationalism in the Eastern European countries. The most obvious, and probably the most important, is that while the resilience of nationalism continues to present the Soviet Union with serious problems in Eastern Europe, it also presents it with considerable opportunities for the classic strategy of divide and rule.

FURTHER READING

Blazynski, George. *Flashpoint Poland.* New York and Oxford: Pergamon, 1979.

Brock, Peter. *The Slovak National Awakening.* Toronto: University of Toronto Press, 1976.

Brown J. F. *Bulgaria under Communist Rule.* New York: Praeger, 1970.

Brzezinski, Zbigniew K. *The Soviet Bloc—Unity and Conflict.* Cambridge, Massachusetts: Harvard University Press; London: Oxford University Press, 1960.

Jelavich, Barbara. *History of the Balkans—Twentieth Century.* Cambridge: Cambridge University Press, 1983.

Jowitt, Kenneth. *Revolutionary Breakthroughs and National Development: The Case of Romania, 1944–1965.* Berkeley and Los Angeles: University of California Press, 1971.

Kolarz, Walter. *Myths and Realities in Eastern Europe.* London: Lindsay Drummond, 1946.

Seton-Watson, Hugh. *Eastern Europe between the Wars.* London: Cambridge University Press, 1945.

———. *Nations and States.* London: Methuen, 1977.

de Weydenthal, Jan, et al. *The Polish Drama 1980–1982.* Lexington, Massachusetts: Lexington Books/D. C. Heath, 1983.

NATIONAL MINORITIES IN EASTERN EUROPE

GEORGE SCHÖPFLIN

INTRODUCTION

EASTERN Europe is renowned for its problem of national minorities. The ethnic complexion of the area has become very mixed over the centuries and hence the newly established nation-states that emerged from the Paris Peace Settlement (1918–20) were bound to include some national groups alien to the ruling nation. The difficulty of drawing just frontiers, ones drawn in such a way that the number of individuals separated from the main body of their conationals should be the lowest possible, is recognized; nevertheless, in a number of cases the professed principle of self-determination was blatantly disregarded by the peacemakers in favor of some other principle, such as the need to guarantee the security or communications of the new states. The post-World War I frontiers were left largely unaltered after 1945. The only significant change was that the powerful German minorities of Poland, Czechoslovakia and Yugoslavia were expelled, the majority to West Germany, while a few found their way to East Germany and Austria.

A distinction must be made between a minority proper and a coequal nationality. Thus in a state which is multinational in character, that is, made up of two or more constituent national groups (*Staatsvölker*), each of these constituent national groups enjoys full rights, precisely because it is one of the constituent national groups. The rights of a minority, on the other hand, tend to be more circumscribed. The question of relations between constitutionally equal national groups forming the state—as in Czechoslovakia and Yugoslavia—will not be treated in this chapter, which is concerned only with minorities.

Minorities may be classified in a number of ways. For instance, they may be distinguished as minorities that are cut off from the main body of their conationals by an arbitrarily drawn state frontier; as minorities that live separated by a great distance from their conationals; and as minorities that are in effect a nationality of their own, having no conationals anywhere (only the Lusatian Sorbs of the Bautzen area of East Germany fall into this category in Eastern Europe; in Western Europe, the Bretons provide another example). However, for this chapter another classification has been thought more useful, namely, a classification in terms of political power. Hence minorities are divided into those that are large enough to occasion political

302

concern to the majority nationality and those that are not. A list of the latter, excluded from discussion in this chapter by reason of their lack of political importance, is given in an appendix to Part One of this volume. The former, which will be looked at in some detail, are the Hungarians in Czechoslovakia, the Turks in Bulgaria, the Albanians and Hungarians in Yugoslavia, and the Hungarians in Romania.

Official communist policies toward minorities stem from Lenin's belief that class was more important in practical terms than nationality. Lenin was fully prepared to support national demands where this suited his purposes, but for purely tactical reasons. Thus in framing his policies vis-à-vis czarist Russia, he accepted the demands of the non-Russian nationalities for autonomy or even independence. Once the Soviet state was established, minorities retained a fair measure of formal local rights, notably press and education in the local languages, but the basic philosophy of these institutions was that of communism. Essentially, Lenin saw the local languages as little more than the most intelligible and hence the most effective vehicle for communist propaganda. Subsequently, all communist governments have professed the principle of local linguistic rights in the treatment of minorities—a principle often summed up in the slogan "national in form, socialist in content." In fact, theory and practice have diverged in a number of cases, and where in a communist country the population suffered totalitarian rule, the weight of this bore especially heavily on the minority that found itself under a double pressure. With the growth of the national element in the policies of the communist states of Eastern Europe in the late 1950s and early 1960s, the pressure on the minorities tended to increase. On the other hand, where liberalization had made a major breakthrough (as in Yugoslavia after July 1966), then the treatment of the minorities tended to improve parallel with other fields.

CZECHOSLOVAKIA: THE HUNGARIAN MINORITY

According to the 1981 census, Hungarians in Czechoslovakia number 582,000 (some 11.2 percent of the population of Slovakia), an increase of only 41,000 in 20 years. They live in compact groups in southern Slovakia, in areas bordering on Hungary. The majority are employed in industry, although the proportion employed in agriculture is still well above the overall Czechoslovak average even while there are disproportionately fewer of them in nonmanual jobs.

Relations between Slovaks and Hungarians have been traditionally poor and this became, if anything, worse after 1945 following a brief interlude, from 1938–45, of Hungarian rule over the Hungarian-inhabited southern marches of Slovakia. The postwar Czechoslovak government applied the principle of collective guilt against the minority. This policy was not reversed until the communists took power in 1948. From then until 1960, the Hungarians enjoyed moderately good treatment, given the otherwise oppressive policies of the Czechoslovak government in the Stalinist and neo-Stalinist periods. In other words, Hungarians were seldom subjected to extra discrimination on the grounds of their nationality alone, though there were individual

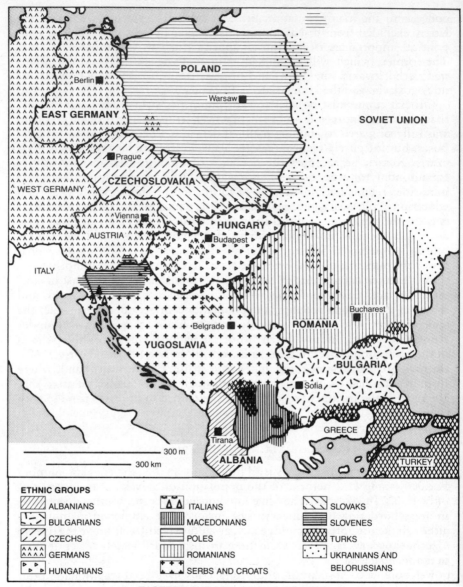

ETHNIC GROUPS

▨ ALBANIANS	◭ ◭ ITALIANS	◫ SLOVAKS
〰 BULGARIANS	▥ MACEDONIANS	▤ SLOVENES
▧ CZECHS	▤ POLES	▩ TURKS
⋀⋀⋀ GERMANS	▦ ROMANIANS	⋰ UKRAINIANS AND BELORUSSIANS
▷ ▷ HUNGARIANS	+ + SERBS AND CROATS	

EASTERN EUROPE: ETHNIC GROUPS

instances of discrimination. Around 1960 there came a certain change in attitude toward the Hungarian minority. Possibly as a late reaction to the Hungarian revolution of 1956, which the Hungarians in Slovakia followed with sympathy, the Prague government, with the support of Bratislava, decided on a new policy toward the minority. The essence of this policy was to encourage as far as possible the assimilation of the Hungarians. As a first step, three changes were undertaken. Administrative boundaries were changed, with the result that Hungarians were left in a majority in only two districts after the reorganization (*okres* Dunajská Streda and *okres* Komárno). However, whatever its impact on the Hungarian minority, the reorganization of local government districts did make local administration more efficient. Second, changes were initiated in education. Great emphasis was placed on the inculcation of a "state patriotism," of absolute and over-riding loyalty to the Czechoslovak nation-state in all fields. And third, a campaign was undertaken to induce the Hungarians to learn Slovak.

The Dubček reforms of 1968 did not leave the Hungarian minority untouched. On March 12, 1968, the Central Committee of Csemadok, the Hungarian Workers' Cultural Organization, adopted a policy declaration that called for separate political organizations for the minority; for the reorganization of local government districts in order to end the situation where Hungarians were in a minority in areas where they would have formed the majority had Slovak-inhabited districts not been attached to Hungarian ones in 1960; for equality of opportunity in participating in all aspects of public life; for improved educational facilities; and for full autonomy in culture.

On October 27, 1968, the Czechoslovak National Assembly adopted a new Minorities Statute, which by means of legislation of constitutional authority guaranteed the position of the minorities and incorporated most of the demands of Csemadok. The willingness on the part of the Czechoslovak authorities to do this was without a doubt encouraged by the stand of the minority during the invasion of the country by Warsaw Pact forces. The Hungarian-inhabited area was garrisoned largely by troops from Hungary, and contrary to expectations, the minority remained absolutely loyal to the Dubček leadership, something that was recognized even by the most nationalistic Slovaks. The Minorities Statute came into force on January 1, 1969. However, this statute was never fully applied. As the 1970s drew on, it became increasingly clear that the Slovak authorities were proposing to dismantle Hungarian-language educational and cultural institutions, in the expectation that this would speed up the integration and assimilation of the minority. From the late 1970s, Slovak policies began to encounter resistance from the members of the minority, particularly over the threatened closure or merger of minority schools. An unofficial body, the Committee for the Legal Rights of the Hungarians of Slovakia, emerged around 1980 and circulated a number of documents detailing the grievances of the minority. An ethnic Hungarian geologist, Miklós Duray, was twice arrested by the authorities as the instigator of this unrest. In 1984 a protest movement over the new education law, which would give the Slovak authorities the power to curtail Hungarian-language schooling, attracted the support of many thousands. The Budapest government, which keeps a watchful eye on the fate of the minority, is thought to have intervened from time to time on its behalf.

BULGARIA: THE TURKISH MINORITY

The exact size of the Turkish minority is not known because the Bulgarian authorities have sought to keep it a secret in order to preserve the appearance of Bulgaria's ethnic homogeneity. However, estimates of the size of the minority run between 800,000 and 1.1 million. To the Turks, who are all Muslims, should be added the Pomaks, whose mother tongue is Bulgarian but who tend to identify themselves with their coreligionists. In other words, around 10 to 13 percent of the population is Muslim. The Turks are concentrated in the northeast and the south and locally they form majorities. They are mainly employed in agriculture, though there has been some movement by Turks into industry.

The Turks in Bulgaria are in part the descendants of Turkish colonists and in part assimilated Bulgarians who have adopted Islam. There is no doubt that the Turkish minority has not reconciled itself at all to communism —especially, being devout Muslims, to its antireligious policies—and that the great majority of the Turks would wish to emigrate to Turkey. In 1950–51, the Bulgarian government announced that it would permit the emigration of 250,000 Turks and some 150,000 did leave, often under circumstances that were hardly different from expulsion. During the 1950s, the Bulgarian authorities put considerable pressure on the minority to conform to national policies and, up to a point, to assimilate. Some of the assimilatory policy was relaxed in the 1960s, but it revived with renewed strength in the 1970s as part of the promotion of Bulgarian nationalism by the authorities. It was from this time that unconfirmed, though widespread, stories of discrimination began to circulate. These seemed to concentrate on the removal of the visible signs of the existence of non-Bulgarians, like forced name changes (from Muslim to Christian names) and the transformation of Islamic into Christian cemeteries. Turkish-language education and publishing was limited, and the authorities placed great emphasis on antireligious propaganda directed against Islam. Sometimes, official measures met with resistance, and reports of violence were occasionally heard. Emigration to Turkey was down to a trickle and although the Turkish government regularly raised the question of the minority with Sofia, it was reluctant to accept immigrants at a time of economic and political difficulty.

YUGOSLAVIA: THE ALBANIAN MINORITY

The Albanian minority living in Yugoslavia presents a particularly difficult problem for the Yugoslav authorities. The minority has been steadily increasing in size, and with their demographic growth the Albanians have begun to demand a commensurate share of power in the context of the Yugoslav political system. This the Yugoslav authorities have been unwilling and unable to grant, and the result has been deadlock. There were 1,730,878 Albanians in Yugoslavia in the 1981 census; there were more Albanians than there were Macedonians (1.34 million) and Montenegrins (0.58 million), and there were almost as many Albanians as there were Slovenes (1.75 million). The great majority of these Albanians (1,226,000) lived in the autonomous Kosovo province, and almost all the remainder (504,000) were to be found in Macedonia. In the Kosovo, the Albanians constituted the overwhelming majority of the population—77.4 percent as against 13.2 percent Serbs. The dynamics of the statistical picture were even more striking. The Albanians had not only been increasing in absolute terms, but also relatively, at the expense of the Serbs, who in 1971 still made up 18.4 percent of the population (23.6 percent in 1971; 23.5 percent in 1961). The Albanian percentages were 67.2 percent in 1961, 73.7 percent in 1971 and 77.4 percent in 1981. This major demographic turnaround was caused by a very high Albanian birthrate (32 per 1,000, the highest in Europe) and accelerating Serbian outmigration, which resulted in a fall in the absolute figure for Serbs between 1971 and 1981 (down from 228,000 to 209,000).

The story of the Kosovo and of Yugoslavia's Albanians is long and convoluted. Historically, the area was one of the centers of medieval Serbdom and the Serbs have continued their strong attachment to the territory on these grounds, even while the province gradually acquired an Albanian majority by the 20th century. The cultural gap between the Muslim Albanians and the Orthodox Christian Serbs is enormous. In post-1918 Yugoslavia, the Serbs ran the Kosovo in effect as a colony, which intensified resentments. In 1944 there was an Albanian uprising against the Yugoslav state—then dominated by Tito's partisans—which was finally put down with considerable force. Thereafter, until the fall of the Yugoslav security chief Aleksandar Ranković in 1966, the Kosovo was administered as a kind of security police fief in the Serbian interest. With the post-1966 liberalization, however, the rights of the Albanians began to receive recognition. Two years later, major rioting erupted principally over demands that an Albanian-language university be established at Priština, the capital of the Kosovo. In the event, this was granted, and during the 1970s the Kosovo acquired more and more the political characteristics of an autonomous republic within the Yugoslav federation, although it actually lacked this status in legal terms.

Tito's strategy toward the Kosovo in the 1970s was to try to create a state of affairs giving Yugoslavia's Albanians some stake in Yugoslavia, but without going so far as to intensify Serbian resentment over concessions to the Kosovo, which remained technically a part of Serbia. As far as Albania was concerned, a state with which Yugoslav relations were poor during most of this period, Tito applied the "bridge" principle: that the Kosovo Albanians should serve as a bridge between the two states, by which Yugoslav influence would be brought to bear on Albania. This strategy failed on all counts. The Kosovo Albanians were not satisfied; Serbian resentments did intensify; and the "traffic across the bridge" tended to be from Albania into Yugoslavia, rather than the other way round.

In essence, the Yugoslav authorities, by creating all the appurtenances of a separate Albanian cultural and economic unit in the Kosovo, but without the appropriate political autonomy to go with them, had struck a very poor bargain. Expectations were aroused and then left unsatisfied. Albanian cultural autonomy, which was very far-reaching indeed, included the use of the standard language devised in Tirana, the import of books, the exchange of delegations and, generally, the building of closer ties with Albania. Huge sums of money were poured into the Kosovo, but to little avail. The area remained chronically backward (though more developed than Albania); its standard of living was around one-sixth of that in prosperous Slovenia, and, in consequence, unemployment in the Kosovo grew alarmingly. By the early 1980s, the unemployment rate was over 25 percent, and three-quarters of the unemployed were people under 25. Worst of all, the large numbers of graduates poured out by the hyperinflated University of Priština (about 50,000 students) had no jobs to go to. An unemployed intelligentsia had been created and this predictably proved fertile ground for unrest.

The time bomb exploded in March 1981, just 10 months after Tito's death. Ironically, Tito's last public speech (December 1979) had been a warning against the resurgence of Albanian nationalism. The 1981 riots began at the university and spread. The slogan was "Kosovo Republic," a demand the federation could not possibly grant for fear of exacerbating Serbian resentments. Even more alarmingly, there were calls for the unification of the Kosovo with Albania, though how serious this was to be taken was another matter. Large numbers of people took to the streets and, after the central authorities intervened, many were purged and imprisoned. The party and state leaderships were sacked and the province was placed under military and security control. In 1982 there was another round of demonstrations and new reprisals.

Matters remained uneasy and unsettled in the Kosovo. The Albanians were sullen, their aspirations frustrated and their economic expectations unsatisfied. The Serbs were equally dissatisfied. Not only was the Kosovo, the mystical symbol of Serbdom, slipping from Serbian political control, but the outmigration of Serbs from the Kosovo increased. There was plenty of evidence that this outmigration was often the result of active intimidation by Albanians; sometimes it was the passive recognition by Serbian families that there was no future for them in an overwhelmingly Albanian province. In effect, the situation in the mid-1980s was intractable.

YUGOSLAVIA: THE HUNGARIAN MINORITY

At the 1981 census, there were 426,867 Hungarians in Yugoslavia, an absolute decline from 477,374 in 1971 and 504,368 in 1961. The great majority of Yugoslavia's Hungarians live in the Vojvodina (385,356, or 90.2 percent of them), while the rest are mostly in Croatia and Belgrade. In the multinational autonomous Vojvodina province, Hungarians make up 18.9 percent of the population and constitute the second-largest ethnic group there after the Serbs. There are thought to be several thousand Hungarians from Yugoslavia employed as guestworkers in the West. On the whole, Yugoslav policy toward the Hungarians has been fairly successful, unlike the policy toward the Albanians of the Kosovo. It has been based on a similar idea, namely that the Hungarians of Yugoslavia and the South Slavs of Hungary should constitute bridges between the countries. The explanation of why it has worked better with the Hungarians than with the Albanians lies partly in the low political importance of the Hungarians in the Vojvodina; partly in the willingness of the Hungarian state (unlike Albania) to support the bridge principle on more or less equal terms; and partly because the economic situation in the Vojvodina was, until the early 1980s at least, markedly better than in Hungary itself. The absence of any major Hungarian cultural tradition in the Vojvodina and the weakness of the Hungarian intelligentsia in the province, coupled with their relative readiness to accept whatever the Yugoslav authorities have offered in terms of concessions, are also contributory factors. Nevertheless, occasional disquiet has been expressed, both in Hungary itself and in Yugoslavia, about the situation of the minority. The seemingly inexorable decline in their numbers has been a major concern. There is no question of the readiness of a section of the minority to assimilate, partly as the offspring of mixed marriages who opt for the "other" nationality (that is, Serbian rather than Hungarian), and partly through the decision of a sizable number of Hungarians to declare themselves "Yugoslav." Second, there have been occasional complaints of discrimination voiced in the Hungarian-language press in the Vojvodina. Although these have been quickly denied by the Vojvodina authorities, there can be little doubt of their reality, especially in the realm where discrimination is as much a matter of feeling as of objective reality. All the same, by general consensus, the Hungarians of Yugoslavia have enjoyed fairly favorable treatment by comparison with the other ethnic Hungarian minorities in the successor states.

ROMANIA: THE HUNGARIAN MINORITY

The Hungarians of Transylvania form the numerically largest minority in Eastern Europe: 1,705,810 in 1977 (a small increase over the 1,619,592 recorded in 1966), according to the official census figures. Unofficial estimates put their number at over 2 million, not least because the census figures do not appear to record many Hungarians outside Transylvania, whereas it is known that several hundred thousand Hungarians live in the Regat (Wallachia and Moldavia), notably in the capital, Bucharest. The greatest concentration of Hungarians in Romania is to be found in the so-called Szekler counties, lying roughly between Tîrgu Mureş and Braşov; the area bordering Hungary itself also has a Hungarian majority; and there are considerable pockets in the Banat. Until 1945, the Hungarians were in a majority in most towns in Transylvania, and although they still constitute a substantial proportion of the urban population, they are in a majority probably only in Oradea as a result of the great influx of Romanians from the countryside. (It is difficult to be precise on this since the detailed figures of the 1977 census have still to be released.)

The political fortunes of the Hungarians have gone through enormous fluctuations in the last 50 years. The rulers of Transylvania until 1918, they were incorporated into Romania unwillingly and felt that they owed it little loyalty. About two-thirds of the Hungarian population of Transylvania again came under Hungarian rule in 1940 as a result of the Second Vienna Arbitration, only to be returned to Romania in 1945 with the restoration of the 1918 frontiers. During the early years of communist rule, the Hungarians enjoyed extensive political and cultural privileges, including a separate Hungarian-language university at Cluj and a Hungarian Autonomous Region comprising the Szekler counties. However, with the reemergence of nationalism as a force in Romanian politics in the late 1950s, the privileges of the Hungarians were gradually suppressed. The Hungarian university was merged with the Romanian one (1959), thereby effectively ending its role as an institution of Hungarian culture. Hungarian-language schools were merged with Romanian-language schools, with the result that education

became gradually Romanianized, in spirit at least, The Hungarian Autonomous Region was first reorganized (1960) in such a way that its Hungarian
population fell and its Romanian population rose. At the end of 1967 it
was abolished altogether in the territorial reorganization. From about 1959
to 1966, the Hungarian minority was subjected to extensive discrimination,
a judgment borne out by the report of the International Commission of
Jurists (December 1963).

However, in about 1966 or 1967 there came a change in policy. It is
difficult to pinpoint it exactly, but it is certain that by the summer of 1968
the Romanian leadership was in favor of accommodation with the Hungarians. Nicolae Ceauşescu, the Romanian party leader, was for a long time
regarded as an archnationalist and as a committed anti-Hungarian. Yet as
early as 1966 he toured Transylvania and lost no chance of stressing the
historical links between Hungarians and Romanians. Certainly, among the
Hungarians these speeches were regarded as window dressing. Nevertheless,
the situation did improve, or at least, the atmosphere of terror and intimidation that prevailed in the early 1960s was being dispelled.

It seems not implausible that the Romanian leadership was aware of disaffection among the minority and recognized that by promoting Romanian
nationalism against the Soviet Union, which in turn spilled over into hostility
against the Hungarians, they had totally alienated the Hungarian minority.
The handling of the territorial reorganization at the end of 1967, which
extinguished the Mureş-Hungarian Autonomous Province (actually it had
only existed in name after the first reorganization), was another indication
of a greater sensitivity toward the minority. The new system of local administration created 39 counties out of the former 16 regions and in two of
these, Covasna and Harghita, the Hungarians are still a large majority. They
also constitute sizable minorities in Bihor, Satu Mare and Tîrgu Mureş
counties.

The 1967–71 period coincided with the only time when the Romanian
authorities pursued anything resembling relative liberalization, and during
this time the position of the Hungarians was not unfavorable. However,
after Ceauşescu launched his recentralization drive, the policy toward the
Hungarians tightened. In effect, they came to be regarded as constituting
an obstacle to Romania's economic and political development, the essential
ordering principle of which was Romanian nationalism. In this context, Hungarian culture was regarded as an obstacle to be eliminated and the Hungarian
intelligentsia, which grew more and more reluctant to accept that all development in Romania had to be pursued according to an exclusively Romanian
model, became a main target for those looking to an ethnically homogeneous
Romania. Thus, since 1971 there has been considerable evidence of assimilatory pressure.

This has taken two main forms. There have been "passive" measures—the
result of economic modernization—like the building of a new industrial base
in Transylvania, which has inevitably drawn statistically significant numbers
of Romanians into Transylvania from the Regat. Equally, many of the jobs
in the managerial-technical field have gone to Romanians, while Hungarians
with the appropriate qualifications have received such jobs only outside

Transylvania. The development of the urban centers, notably of Cluj, Oradea and Braşov, in the 1970s and 1980s has seen some discrimination in favor of Romanians in the field of housing.

"Active" discrimination has included the partial dismantling or underfunding of Hungarian cultural institutions, such as education and the mass media, and generally the possibility of pursuing a Hungarian cultural life. According to estimates, something like two-fifths to one-half of school children of Hungarian nationality receive their education in Romanian, and even in Hungarian-language schools up to one-third of the curriculum may be taught in Romanian. As the economic situation in Romania deteriorated sharply after 1980—the result of the regime's overambitious industrialization policies—the Hungarians saw a worsening of their position. A new wave of Romanian nationalism swept through a section of the Romanian intelligentsia and the primary characteristics of this nationalism were anti-Hungarianism and anti-Semitism.

Around this time, sections of the minority began to feel that trying to improve matters within the system was hopeless, and that only by drawing the attention of the West to what was happening could things be remedied. The first such moves in this connection were the letters of protest sent by Károly Király, onetime party secretary of Covasna county, in which he outlined the discriminatory practices against the minority. These were followed by the publication (in samizdat) of the journal *Ellenpontok* (Counterpoints), which reached nine numbers before it was silenced by the secret police in 1982. But protest documents have continued to reach the West, mainly through Hungary, where the unofficial democratic opposition has placed great emphasis on human rights for the minorities in the successor states.

The international context of the Transylvanian question has become broader, with the partial inclusion of Western opinion. Still, the main players in the game in addition to Romania, have been the Soviet Union and Hungary. Since the early 1960s the Soviet Union has used the vague threat of a Hungarian interest in Transylvania as an instrument of pressure on the Romanian government's aspirations for an independent foreign policy. Although never going as far as giving the Hungarians overt and direct support, hints and veiled allusions have served to maintain a sense of unease and uncertainty in Bucharest over Soviet intentions. For the Hungarian authorities, the problem has been different. As the 1970s wore on, Hungarian opinion grew increasingly concerned over what it regarded as the intolerable discrimination practiced against a sizable body of their conationals. By the early 1980s, the sense of popular indignation was too strong for the Hungarian government to ignore entirely. Hungary began to play a more active and more visible role in appearing to protect the rights of the minority, although it is questionable whether very much was actually achieved in real terms. In 1977 the Hungarians were successful in getting the Romanians to accept the "bridge principle" (see above), but the Romanians have studiously ignored any possible consequences that might flow from this. Since this time, however, Hungary has had a formal political basis from which to raise questions over the treatment of the minority.

In the West, too, the image of Romania, which was positive during the 1970s, changed as the repressive nature of the Ceauşescu regime became better known. Above all, the strategy of rapid industrialization was seen to have failed. The growing emphasis on human rights created a new context in which ethnic minority rights were discussed more openly than before. In the United States, pressure was put on the Senate to deny Romania its most-favored-nation status because of its antiminority policies. In France, traditionally a country well disposed to Romania, attitudes began to change as several espionage scandals involving Romania became public. Likewise, in West Germany, there was concern over the fate of the German minority in Romania, and some of this rubbed off on the Hungarians. None of this changing attitude in the West had any concrete effect on Romanian policies, but it served notice on Ceauşescu that the real nature of the Romanian situation was known and that the sympathy that he had labored long to create was dissipating. From the standpoint of the Hungarian minority, the 1970s and 1980s seemed to be a time of general deterioration in the economic well-being of their country and a shrinking of their cultural rights at the same time.

FURTHER READING

Biberaj, Elez, and Pavlowitch, Stevan K. *The Albanian Problem in Yugoslovia: Two Views.* Conflict Studies No. 137–138, 1982.

King, Robert R. *Minorities under Communism: Nationalities as a Source of Tension among Balkan Communist States.* Cambridge, Massachusetts: Harvard University Press, 1973.

Klein, George, and Reban, Milan J., eds. *The Poltics of Ethnicity in Eastern Europe.* New York: Columbia University Press, 1981.

Schöpflin, George. *The Hungarians of Rumania.* London: Minority Rights Group, 1978.

Sugar, Peter F., ed. *Ethnic Diversity and Conflict in Eastern Europe.* Santa Barbara, California: A.B.C.–Clio, 1980.

POLAND — THE "BLOODLESS REVOLUTION" AND ITS AFTERMATH

ABRAHAM BRUMBERG

WHEN the Polish government announced a steep increase in the price of meat on July 2, 1980, 17,000 workers at the Ursus tractor plant near Warsaw—the seat of labor disturbances four years earlier—laid down their tools. Within a matter of days, thousands of other workers throughout the country followed suit, and by mid-August 150 factories and more than 100,000 workers, including streetcar operators and garbage collectors, were on strike. It was once again Gdańsk—where mutinous shipyard workers had helped to topple the government of Władysław Gomułka in December 1970—that became the focal point of the new wave of unrest.[1] In tandem with representatives of 20 other local striking units, the Lenin Shipyard workers set up an "Interfactory Strike Committee" (MKS) that was to coordinate strike activity and, as it turned out, to negotiate with management and with central party and government authorities. Soon, numerous other MKSs sprang up along the Baltic coast and elsewhere. Faced with a challenge so massive and well organized, the government finally agreed to discuss the workers' grievances and demands. Two weeks later Solidarity was born, an organization that in record time was able to claim a membership of nearly 10 million Polish citizens.

Solidarity described itself as an "independent and self-governing trade union." Throughout its turbulent 16-month existence as a legally functioning body (September 1980–December 1981), its most active disciples and principal spokespeople came from the ranks of Poland's new industrial proletariat—mostly skilled, well-educated workers, whose expectations had been conditioned by Edward Gierek's short-lived and disastrous "boom strategy" of the early 1970s.[2] Yet it was clear from the outset that Solidarity was bound to transcend the narrow confines of a conventional trade union. The 16 points drawn up by the Gdańsk MKS on August 17 included demands for freedom of speech and information, for an end to censorship and for the

[1] For a survey of previous Polish upheavals, see Jakub Karpinski, *Count-Down*, New York, 1982.
[2] See chapters by Włodzimierz Brus and Alex Pravda in A. Brumberg, ed., *Poland: Genesis of a Revolution*, New York, 1983.

313

freeing of political prisoners. The famous "21 Points" of the Gdańsk accord, as well as the agreements signed by government representatives and workers in Szczecin (an important port) and Jastrzębie (in the heart of the Silesian coal mining district) were, indeed, notable more for their political than for their economic content. In addition to such matters as pensions, improved work conditions, salaries, health care, and the like, the accords included provisions for opening the public media to "expressions of different points of view," for untrammeled public discussion of a "program of economic reform" and for the introduction of "the principle of cadre selection on the basis of qualifications, not on the basis of membership in the party." The last point, which also called for the abolition of "special privileges" for the police, security services and "party apparatus," struck at the very heart of the system of party control over nearly all areas of public life, the *nomenklatura*.[3]

PRECEDENTS AND LESSONS

The potentially revolutionary demands embedded in the Gdańsk and other accords, and the remarkable organizational élan evinced by the striking workers in the summer of 1980, can only be understood against the background of 35 years of communist rule. With the possible exception of the brief period following Gomułka's return to power in October 1956, communism never succeeded in establishing its legitimacy in the eyes of a profoundly nationalistic, anti-Russian, religious and generally conservative population. This was glaringly illustrated in the periodic upheavals that rocked the country—in 1956, 1968, 1970 and 1976. Each of these was short-lived, and in each case the achievements gained by the protests were eventually annulled by a party leadership determined to maintain its monopoly of power and to thwart any movement, however gradual, toward pluralism. At the same time, however, each episode became a political school for the self-tutelage of restive social groups. For one thing, intellectuals and workers alike became aware that no change could occur without a common effort. For another, the alarming political and economic crisis of the late 1970s bred the conviction that nothing short of a drastic overhaul of the entire system could rescue Poland from its creeping malaise. It was the Workers' Self-Defense Committee (KOR), formed in 1976 in response to the industrial strife of June of that year, that first elaborated a new oppositional strategy as well as, in time, a set of sweeping goals. Soon other groups came to the fore, all of them articulating similarly holistic visions of the future.[4]

Thus the workers who entered the fray in the summer of 1980 brought with them an experience born of past failures and aspirations nurtured and heightened by the writings of numerous Polish intellectuals, some of whom had actively participated in prior political battles. In January 1971, for instance, the Szczecin shipyard workers had raised the demand for free trade unions, but because they were inexperienced and lacked the support of the

[3] See chapter by A. Smolar in Brumberg, *op. cit.*
[4] For relevant documents, see Peter Raina, *Political Opposition in Poland, 1954–1977*, London, 1978, and *Independent Social Movements in Poland*, London, 1981.

intellectual community, they found themselves easily outmaneuvered by Gierek's perfunctory excuses and largely meaningless economic promises. In 1980, however, they clearly benefited from the lessons of the past, as well as from the daily advice proffered both by KOR and by distinguished intellectuals from Catholic lay circles. (KOR, in fact, immediately set up a clearing house and information center for the nascent Solidarity.) An additional impetus to the workers' confidence and resolve was provided by the election of Cardinal Wojtyła as pope, and by his visit to Poland in June 1979. The church hierarchy initially showed little enthusiasm for the striking workers, and the primate, Cardinal Wyszyński, preached a sermon on August 26, 1980, advising workers to modify their demands and go back to work. Nevertheless, the presence of priests celebrating daily mass and offering communion to the strikers, the impact of John Paul II's encyclical *Laborem Exercens* (which explicitly defended the right of workers to form trade unions) and some of Wyszyński's sermons from 1976 and 1977 all helped create a climate in which workers felt they had the support of the major moral authority in Poland.[5]

After September 1980, as more and more people joined Solidarity, the union became the outlet for demands not merely economic or even broadly political; in the eyes of the majority of Poles, it became the only institution capable of rectifying the wrongs of communist misrule. Industrial disputes, discriminatory practices against religious believers, cases concerning corruption, police brutality and academic freedom—all these, and other issues, became part of the daily agenda of Solidarity's increasingly harassed leadership. Inevitably, too, Solidarity became a catalyst for the revitalization of certain political ideologies dormant since the war, and for the proliferation of groups boldly calling themselves "political parties."[6] None of them

[5] Contrary to conventional wisdom, the Roman Catholic church has never been eager to throw its support behind the various upheavals that have rocked Poland over the past 30 years. Only the militancy of its flock has compelled it to challenge the government directly and explicitly. In 1956, Wyszyński made common cause with Gomułka in exchange for considerable concessions, including the teaching of catechism on school premises. In 1968, his condemnation of the brutal beatings of students was tepid, especially striking for its failure to mention the anti-Semitic campaign waged at that time. The church remained silent during the workers' demonstrations of June 1976, and only later protested against their treatment by the police and the courts. During the Solidarity period, some of the prelates close to Wyszyński showed a marked hostility toward KOR. Cardinal Glemp, who became primate after Wyszyński's death in 1982, openly displayed his lack of enthusiasm for Solidarity, which he felt was not sufficiently Catholic, and which had become, in his words, "a sack into which everything had been thrown, all the opposition Marxists, all the Trotskyites. ..." This last epithet, as is well known in Poland, is a code word for "Jews." See Maya Latynski, "The Church: Between State and Society," *Poland Watch*, No. 5, 1984, and Tadeusz Kaminski, "Poland's Catholic Church: A Parting of Ways?," *loc. cit.*, No. 6, 1984.

[6] The most notable were the Confederation for an Independent Poland (KPN), a militantly nationalistic, explicitly anti-Soviet party founded in 1979, which grew rapidly during the Solidarity period; and the Polish Labor Party, formed in the summer of 1981, which defended the cause of workers' self-government.

was affiliated with Solidarity; neither would they have risen to any prominence without the union. To all intents and purposes, therefore, Solidarity became at once a trade union and a corporate ombudsman, a carrier of national traditions, a social movement and even in some respects a religious movement.[7] This very multiplicity of roles was bound to engender difficult problems.

FROM "SOCIAL CONTROL" TO POLITICAL POWER

Solidarity's most ticklish dilemma—present, if only implicitly, from the very beginning—was how to reconcile its goal of remaking Poland into a functioning democracy with its reluctance to participate in the country's decision making process. To resolve the dilemma, Solidarity at first defined itself as, in effect, a pressure group representing the interests of its constituents, who were the Polish nation writ large. It would represent these interests, negotiating with the authorities on any issues affecting the welfare of the union's constituents, and insisting that the authorities seek its approval for any piece of legislation connected with the provisions of the Gdańsk accord. Although exercising the function of "social control," it would leave the apparatus of power entirely in the hands of the authorities, abjuring any overtly political role.

Solidarity's position could be viewed on the one hand as a semantic sleight of hand, on the other as a potentially reasonable way of avoiding a challenge to the party's leading role.[8] The union did not want to become involved in the business of running the country, and surely not of ruling it. The union at first even rejected the idea of setting up workers' councils in factories, on the grounds that any attempt to give workers a voice in managing the enterprises would eventually be coopted by the party or eradicated—as were the workers' councils that emerged in 1955–56. Solidarity's strategy was to force the party into undertaking the necessary reforms, but not, under any circumstances, to collaborate with it.

This position was unprecedented; it was also, as became increasingly obvious, unworkable. Putting pressure on the party was a tactic aimed at achieving dialogue and compromise; it produced instead conflicts and confrontations, the more so given the party's distinct lack of enthusiasm for honoring its commitments to the Gdańsk accord. Faced with deepening unrest, and with the growing impatience of Solidarity's own radicals (or "fundamentalists," as they were dubbed), who criticized the union leadership and its intellectual advisers for timidity and "lack of true Polish spirit," Solidarity was gradually compelled to revise its approach. By the spring of 1981 it came out strongly not only for self-management in factories, but for a number

[7] For many workers who joined Solidarity, Catholicism (whose symbols and rituals were in fact incorporated into Solidarity's modus operandi) was synonymous with their basic social, political and economic aspirations.

[8] In October 1980, Solidarity's legal registration was held up for two weeks because the union's statutes had failed to incorporate a statement recognizing the "leading role of the party." See T. Garton Ash, *The Polish Revolution: Solidarity*, London: 1983, pp. 79–85.

of basic reforms of the political system. Nonetheless, it still backed away from producing a credible explanation of how such goals could be achieved without changing the existing system of authority. In June, the celebrated journalist and novelist Stefan Kisielewski chided Solidarity, in the pages of its own *Solidarity Weekly*, for excessive caution. Any reform of Poland's system, he wrote, is inevitably "a political reform: you can't get out of politics, no matter how much you publicly declare yourself against it." Four months later, on the eve of its first and only national congress, Solidarity published a 50,000-word program effectively acknowledging the truth of Kisielewski's words and stating:

> The birth of the mass social movement that is Solidarity has brought about a fundamental change in the situation of the country . . . It has altered the conditions in which power is exercised. . . . The authorities should have taken into consideration the will of society and should have acted under its control, in keeping with the principles laid down in the social accords of Gdańsk, Szczecin and Jastrzębie.

But more than a year had passed, the document continued, without any progress in this direction. As a result, "the country has been brought to ruin," and the public is "weary and impatient":

> Faced with a national tragedy, Solidarity can no longer confine itself to expectations and to exerting pressure on the authorities. . . . We are the society's sole guarantor. Therefore, our union has recognized as its basic duty the initiation of all immediate and long-term actions aimed at saving the country from collapse, and society from poverty, despair and self-destruction. There is no other way of attaining this goal than through democracy and a concerted public effort to rebuild the state and economy.

What followed was no longer a relatively modest list of political demands, but rather an elaborate blueprint for the radical restructuring of Poland's political and social system. It was a call for a decentralized economy "linking market laws to socialist planning" and resting firmly on "supply and demand mechanisms"; for self-management in almost all enterprises, except those connected with the armament industry; for the creation of "independent and self-governing institutions in all areas of public life"; for "democratic elections to people's councils" (that is, local administrative bodies) and to the parliament; for reforms of the penal system and of the judiciary; and for freedom of the press and of expression in general. To achieve these far-reaching goals—finally spelled out in unmistakable terms—Solidarity was no longer asking for "social control," but for a share of political power.

THE ADVERSARIES

Not surprisingly, the party reacted with fury. Indeed, for the ruling elite Solidarity's challenge may well have recalled the slogan of the Polish gentry in the 17th century: *Rex regnat sed non gubernat* (The king reigns but does not govern). There can be "no agreement with those who . . . reach out for power," said the party daily, *Trybuna Ludu*, on October 23, 1981. Shortly thereafter, the Soviet commander-in-chief of the Warsaw Pact, Marshal Kulikov, paid a visit to General Jaruzelski, recently elected as party first secretary in addition to his government posts of premier and minister of defense. To be sure, such visits had become commonplace. But secret Polish and Soviet documents, if ever revealed, may well show that the final decision for the military crackdown was taken at that time.

If so, the decision to implement martial law was the culmination of a year in which the party was most conspicuous for its disarray. For many rank-and-file members, more than a million of whom joined the union, Solidarity spoke with an authentic workers' voice. By the spring of 1981 many disaffected party members formed a "horizontal linkage" movement, demanding that party organizations be free to consult with one another and to work out common programs and objectives without direction from above—a clear challenge to the Leninist principle of democratic centralism. As for middle-level apparatchiks, who had the most to lose from Solidarity's assault on their power and privileges, some of them consistently pressured the party leadership toward a more implacable stance, while others organized various distinctly hard-line—and sometimes anti-Semitic—discussion clubs and "forums." The ruling elite was itself split, if not over the goal of curbing Solidarity's might, then over the tactics by which that goal could best be accomplished. While it is clear that at no time did the ruling echelons seriously consider honoring promises made to Solidarity, neither did they have any idea how to disarm their opponent and reassert their own power and authority. The result was a series of confrontations and a crippling political stalemate. It was not until the extraordinary party congress of July 1981, which effectively neutralized the horizontal movement and left the entrenched party bureaucracy in power, that the party could congratulate itself on putting an end to the internal rot and turn resolutely against its adversary.

The Soviet leaders were no more agile than the Poles. What they wanted was obvious: a strong party and an emasculated union. How to achieve the two was more problematic, given their deep aversion to direct military intervention. The alternative was to intimidate the population (not altogether successfully) by such means as the Warsaw Pact maneuvers held intermittently throughout 1980–81, and to pressure the party leadership via threatening letters and sporadic articles in the Soviet press, which praised the hard-line party forums and attacked the faint-hearted. It was in part Soviet pressure that resulted in the hard-liners' victory at the congress, and in the subsequent election of Jaruzelski as first secretary. Indeed, although hard-liners occasionally challenged Jaruzelski's strategy in 1983 and 1984, it would be mistaken to regard them as having enjoyed Moscow's support; both during martial law and since, Moscow actually regarded Jaruzelski as representing most accurately its own view of how to deal with Poland.

The months preceding the imposition of martial law saw a further deterioration of the Polish economy, growing restiveness within the ranks of Solidarity and a hastening of confrontation with which Solidarity was ill equipped to deal. Negotiations between the union and the government repeatedly broke down, partly because of the regime's denial of promised access to the mass media, partly because of its decree nullifying all proposals on economic reforms for an indefinite period of time and partly because of its insistence that Solidarity join the sham Front of National Unity as a precondition for negotiations on all other matters. Efforts by the church—manifestly alarmed by the growing extremism on both sides—to mediate between Lech Wałęsa and Jaruzelski were equally unsuccessful. Demands escalated, and with that escalation came a hardening of positions within union and regime alike. In retrospect, the signs of approaching confrontation were patent; certainly Jaruzelski had already made his plans, as attested by the October extension of military service by two months. This move ensured that there would be no new influx of young, pro-Solidarity draftees. He also, in November, dispatched into the countryside many military units, ostensibly to resolve various administrative problems. In the union, however, while a few individuals recognized the likelihood of imminent action, the mood was at once too militant and too euphoric to permit serious consideration of such an eventuality. When martial law was declared on December 13, therefore, Solidarity was caught off guard; nearly its entire leadership was swept up in Jaruzelski's brilliantly executed dragnet.

MARTIAL LAW AND BEYOND

Martial law lasted 18 months. It was suspended in December 1982 and abolished six months later. The military action that began it, including the arrest of thousands of Solidarity activists, was accompanied by a series of measures designed to vitiate most of the achievements of the previous 16 months. The union was suspended. Newspapers were suppressed, and only gradually allowed to reappear. Free student organizations were dissolved, as were all vestiges of public autonomy, such as the actors', journalists', artists' and writers' unions. Academic freedom was curbed for faculty, administrators and students.

High on Jaruzelski's list of priorities was the resuscitation of the economy. Yet despite the party's pronouncements guaranteeing the scheduled implementation of economic reforms, its policies were contradictory and ambiguous. Laws requiring the abandonment of command planning and the establishment of market relations were enacted. But the de facto power of branch ministries was hardly diminished, the self-sufficiency and self-financing of individual enterprises (which would, in theory, close down unprofitable ones) were undercut by government intervention and workers' self-management remained a distant goal. When economic indicators continued to show decline, the regime increasingly resorted to administrative interference in the form of extensive "operational programs," which endowed ministerial commissars, or "plenipotentiaries," with comprehensive powers over their enterprises. Thus the market approach gave way to the continual growth of bureaucratic controls that circumscribed market forces.

By the time martial law was formally lifted, on July 21, 1983, many of the "temporary" powers assumed by the state had been codified into permanent law. Substantial amendments to the censorship law increased government controls over all forms of publishing. The right of workers to quit or change jobs was severely limited, and enterprise directors were empowered to impose compulsory overtime, up to a total of 46 hours per week. An amendment to the penal code stipulated a prison sentence of up to three years for anyone belonging to an organization that had been disbanded or had not been officially approved, as well as for anyone who "organizes or directs a protest action contrary to the existing legal regulations."

Under such conditions, Solidarity's options were few. At first, with most of its leaders under arrest and the country in a state of shock, the union seemed paralyzed. By January 1982, however, those Solidarity leaders who had managed to elude Jaruzelski issued appeals to the population not to engage in acts of wanton violence, but to resist martial law by organizing themselves into an underground movement. Soon the first clandestine newspapers began to appear, initially in Warsaw and Gdańsk, then in other cities; in time, their number grew to more than 500. Underground Solidarity chapters arose in factories throughout the country; some engaged in publication activities, issuing lists of "collaborators" and "traitors," and collected funds for the families of arrested workers; others mounted occasional work stoppages and demonstrations. On April 22, 1982, several fugitive Solidarity leaders set up a Provisional Coordinating Committee (TKN), which continued to function, although with a changed membership. Oddly enough, Solidarity's strategy was still to compel the government to enter into negotiations leading to a "national understanding"—this despite the palpable failure of such a strategy prior to martial law, and despite every indication that the regime had no intention of recognizing Solidarity, in any form, as a negotiating partner.[9]

Indeed, Jaruzelski's policy could be described in two words: never again. Never again would any movement threatening the regime's monopoly of power be permitted, let alone negotiated with. This stark formula, implemented during the period of martial law and beyond with single-minded determination—so different from the vacillations and ad hoc measures characteristic of the regime's past responses—explains Jaruzelski's policies. It explains the suspension of Solidarity and the gradual lifting of the most onerous provisions of martial law; it explains the creation of new trade unions deprived of the right to strike and to organize regionally (the source of Solidarity's greatest strength); and it explains the creation of new professional bodies shorn of "antisocialist elements" and pledged to uphold the "leading role" of the party. And it also explains the media's concerted campaign to portray Solidarity as an initially legitimate trade union movement that fell into the hands of antisocialist forces determined to seize power and annul the great achievements of Polish socialism.

Given such a policy, Solidarity's hope to mobilize the population in protest and to force the regime into eventual negotiation was futile. More and more voices advised Solidarity to concentrate on building a well-functioning underground organization—an "underground society"—to keep the spirit of resistance alive and prepare for the next eruption. The success of Solidarity's underground organization is debatable; that it still speaks for the values and aspirations of most Poles is not.

[9]See chapters by Jan de Weydenthal and Bruce Porter in de Weydenthal, et al., *The Polish Drama: 1980–82*, Lexington, Mass., 1983.

CONCLUSION

The history of Poland since its three partitions at the end of the 18th century is largely that of rebellions against occupying powers, each inspired by millennial hopes, each crushed by overwhelming force, each resulting in profound spiritual depressions that invariably spawned yet another round of hope, revolt and reprisal. Will Poland's "bloodless revolution" of 1980–81 follow the same historical trend? Some observers maintain that the Polish revolution, having lasted 16 months and having deprived the regime of any claim to legitimacy whatever, will—unlike earlier upheavals, or those in Hungary and Czechoslovakia—leave an enduring imprint on the Polish consciousness. According to this reading, Jaruzelski may have succeeded in crushing Solidarity, but he is destined to rule without consent in the face of pervasive and sullen hostility. Unable to placate Poles with a heavy dose of prosperity, and unwilling to institute the kind of reforms that would secure at least passive popular cooperation, he will continue to preside over a permanent crisis that will sooner or later ignite yet another rebellion.

This possibility cannot be excluded. Yet looked at from 1984, any "rebirth of freedom" in Poland seems a rather tenuous idea. The cruel disappointments of martial law and its aftermath have left Poles with a legacy of hatred for the regime, but also with a sense of enormous despair, fatigue and impotence. Hopes both within and outside Poland that the rise of Solidarity marked a gradual secularization of Polish political culture have also been dashed. Although the episcopate's desperate attempts to reach a modus vivendi with the government, frequently at the expense of Solidarity, have evoked outrage from both Solidarity activists and from some of the more militant lower clergy, the church has succeeded in consolidating its influence over millions of Poles and in fostering a spirit of messianic and exclusivist religiosity far removed from the teachings of Vatican Council II. For many Poles, the only hope of their "Catholic nation" now lies in the unbridled cult of the Virgin Mary, Queen of Poland, and in miracles. Exhaustion and desolation on one side, prayers and miracles on the other—this is not, perhaps, the stuff of which revolutions are made.

321

HUNGARY

GEORGE SCHÖPFLIN

HUNGARY during the 1980s enjoyed an extraordinary reputation in the West as for all practical purposes the one Eastern European country that had been successful in making the communist system work. According to these arguments, which were put forward by Western journalists and diplomats, the Hungarians had introduced a series of reforms demonstrating that a Soviet-type system need not be bound by the iron hoops placed on it by Moscow, and that there was room for maneuver from which both rulers and ruled could benefit. The Hungarians themselves did not argue in quite this way, but tended to say that they were not doing anything extraordinary in the communist world; that the Hungarian system was nothing more than the adaptation of the Soviet Union's programs to Hungarian conditions and involved no significant deviation; and that there was no question of there being any Hungarian model. It was also true, however, that Hungarian officialdom did nothing to discourage the positive image of Hungary being spread in the West. It was good for business and enhanced the country's creditworthiness. The reality of the situation lay elsewhere.

The key event determining Hungary's history in the postwar era was the failed revolution of 1956. The revolution was put down, but the event itself—the disintegration of the party in a matter of days—was a severe warning to the country's communist rulers that their power would have to be exercised within the limits that the population was prepared to tolerate. For the ruled, the revolution was also a signal that popular expectations and hopes must be curbed, otherwise the Soviet Union would intervene with force. The inexorable suppression of popular aspirations between 1956 and 1961, in which at least 2,000 people were executed and perhaps 10 times that number imprisoned, marked a new terror. But this twofold shift of attitudes, affecting both rulers and ruled, formed the basis of the compromise that emerged during the 1960s.

THE OPENING TO THE POPULATION, 1962–72

The essence of this compromise was the offer by the party leader, János Kádár, that the rules of the political and economic game were going to be subtly modified. The Communist party would still remain the sole and exclusive ruler of the country, and would retain its monopoly of all major and minor political initiatives, but the definition of what constituted politics would be interpreted in a more relaxed fashion. Above all, not all areas of economics would come under the rigid, central control characteristic of the 1950s.

On this basis, the rule of terror was discontinued and the Ministry of the Interior was instructed to make a distinction between political crime and political error. People were no longer expected to attend compulsory political meetings, but could opt out of politics entirely if they wanted to. Nonmembers of the party were told that the party was interested in their skills and that as long as they did an honest day's work, this would be recognized, so that advancement was no longer made solely dependent on political loyalty. All these moves contributed greatly to the relaxation of tensions between rulers and ruled during the 1960s. A major debate among the political elite was held on how the economy should be run, and the result of this was the New Economic Mechanism (NEM), introduced in 1968.

The NEM rested on three, possibly four, pillars. First, it created a new set of principles for planning. Whereas under classical Soviet planning, the center is responsible for instructing enterprises how much to produce (plan targets) and for the allocation of supplies, the NEM did away with compulsory plan targets and functioned instead by indicators. The criterion was supposedly profitability, so that a new and in many respects freer price structure was introduced, and enterprise managers were encouraged to make decisions independently of the center and to free themselves from the tutelage of the branch ministries. Enterprises were to pay much more attention to quality than before, to make their output equal to the demands of the world market. Second, the NEM involved a shift away from emphasis on heavy industry toward light industry and infrastructure—this latter being the Cinderella of Soviet-type planning because it appears in the books as "nonproductive." And third, the NEM envisaged a new role for agriculture, in which collectives would be very largely freed of restraints on their activities, would be able to make their own investment decisions and would be able to create a new and profitable relationship with the private agricultural sector, the household plot.

As a fourth, very putative pillar, the party offered the prospect of a new political mechanism to follow from the economic one. Very little of this was implemented, above all because the suppression of the Czechoslovak reform program of 1968–69 discouraged experimentation in this area. A few ideas, however, did remain. The party recognized that communist societies, like all other modern societies, would be beset by conflicts of interest and that there was nothing undesirable in this—on the contrary. The problem was how to create institutions through which these conflicts could be articulated, while at the same time retaining the political monopoly of the party. Various experiments were attempted. Trade unions were encouraged to play a more active role in defending the interests of the workers against enterprise managers. They were given the right to veto certain management decisions. The press was encouraged to play an "ombudsman" role, to report on local or even middle-level abuses of power, though never going so far as to criticize the fundamentals of the system. Parliament was similarly urged to become

323

more active in debating the laws and policies put before it by the government. In parliamentary and local elections, there were experiments with multiple candidacies, so that electors could at least choose among personalities, if not among policies. The government was given a little greater autonomy from direct party control. And the judiciary was given greater latitude in administering justice that was no longer purely "political," but was determined by legal criteria. The problem with all of these experiments was that they fairly quickly ran up against the party's determination to hang onto its monopoly, and they left nobody satisfied.

PARTIAL RECENTRALIZATION, 1972–79

The difficulty with this partial reform was not just that it aroused expectations that it could not satisfy, but that Hungary, having been run for many years on a very short leash, suddenly found that the removal of restraints brought to the surface all sorts of conflicts and unresolved issues that until then had been hidden by the restraints. But for those who were not committed to the reforms in the first place, the emergence of conflicts of this kind was proof positive that the reforms had caused them and that reform was undesirable. This was not merely born of a generally hostile disposition to change, something that clearly characterized a section of the party and state bureaucracy, who were fearful for their own privileged positions, but also wider sections of society whose economic status was threatened by change. Thus, those employed in outdated industries found that the switch to profitability placed them in a worse position financially. They resented, too, the access that other workers, employed in more modern industries, had to higher incomes. And special irritation was caused urban workers by the sharp rise in agricultural incomes, which had actually fallen way behind those in industry, but which, many workers felt, should stay that way. Added to these factors was the international climate in Eastern Europe in the early 1970s, conservative and unfavorable to serious experimentation.

Utilizing these various levers, the sections of the party that disliked the new, relaxed atmosphere and the greater expression of individual autonomy forced the reformers to retreat. Theirs was not a complete victory, however. The reforms were not abandoned entirely; above all, the language of reform was retained and the party was anxious to reassure the population that no serious change had taken place. Nor was the switch complete as far as personnel was concerned. One or two noted reformers left political life in 1974 and 1975, but quite a few remained in the upper levels of the elite, with the result that there was no wholesale clearing out of those committed to reform (unlike what happened in Czechoslovakia at much the same time).

The mid-1970s saw other events that reinforced the position of the anti-reformers—the world oil crisis and the massive deterioration of the terms of trade against Hungary at this time. They were able to argue that the reforms had done nothing to cushion Hungary against these shocks, that it was unacceptable that what happened in the capitalist world should prejudice the position of the Hungarian working class and that the standard of living should not be allowed to decline in consequence. For around half a decade, prices were supported by central subventions, enterprises once more came under the tutelage of the branch ministries, the economy stagnated and, to pay for all this, Hungary took on substantial credits in the West, then awash with oil-money liquidity.

In many respects these were the wasted years, for which Hungary was to pay a high price in the 1980s—the price of many lean years indeed. But it was not until the statistics for 1978 demonstrated incontrovertibly, even to the hardliners, that the country's economy was in a major crisis that renewed consideration of reform came on the agenda. The problem was that conditions for reform were far less favorable in 1978 than they had been a decade earlier and, what was even more discouraging, they were actually worsening.

THE SECOND REFORM WAVE

It was in this rather poorer international and domestic climate that the authorities once again gave the green light to a discussion of reform. The debate after 1979, and particularly in 1982–83, was wide-ranging and raised major, fundamental issues. The thrust of the reformists' argument was that excessive central control over the economy paralyzed innovation and initiative, acted as a hindrance to the most rational use of resources and ensured that Hungarian industry would remain in a perpetual state of inefficiency. How to dismantle this central control without setting off serious waves of either domestic opposition or Soviet concern proved to be a more complex proposition. Essentially, the radical reformers, who were calling for a "reform of the reform," were ignored and their arguments for the introduction of genuine market conditions were left unanswered. Above all, the debate raised the question of political power and how far arguments in favor of greater economic efficiency could be used as a counterweight to the power of the party. The answer that emerged was that although the core of centralized power was inviolate, modifications were possible, albeit only if introduced very cautiously.

The main changes brought in between 1979 and 1985 were the removal of the enterprises from the very close supervision of the branch ministries, in an attempt to promote greater enterprise independence. A certain range of subsidies was removed or reduced in size. Very large enterprises or trusts were broken up in order to encourage greater flexibility. Thus the Csepel iron and steel works was divided into 15 different units in 1983. Some attempts were also made to improve the mobility of capital, a notoriously difficult problem in Soviet-type systems. By 1985, there were the beginnings of a bond market in Hungary.

More significantly, the experiment of letting the state (or socialist) sector develop a symbiotic relationship in agriculture (for this was what the collective-private plot relationship had become) was to be extended to industry. Workers employed in a factory were permitted to make a bid for the enterprise equipment and use it in their own time, and were allowed to keep the profit. This experiment had the objective of promoting productivity and of releasing the energies of the labor force. Another potentially important move was the creation of enterprise supervisory councils on which the workers would have directly elected representatives.

HUNGARIAN PATTERNS IN THE 1980s

None of this really added up to a pattern of rule radically different from what obtained in other countries in the Soviet sphere. Where the Hungarians differed was in the recognition by the elite that monopoly power could not be exercised in an unbridled fashion and that certain restraints were essential—otherwise the possibility of mass unrest spilling over into upheaval could not be excluded. There was also the recognition that the party needed the talents and energies of the population as a whole to promote the prosperity on which stability was based. In this intelligent operation of the system, the Hungarian leadership was distinctive in Eastern Europe.

In its approach to various social groups, the relationship between rulers and ruled functioned differently, according to which group was in question. Toward the intelligentsia, the party's offer (which was accepted with alacrity) was that intellectuals would be allowed to use their specialist knowledge as long as they did not challenge the sole right of the party to rule. In exchange, they would be left alone and not have to profess Marxism–Leninism publicly, they would be guaranteed material benefits and they would be given access to the outer fringes of power. The great bulk of the intelligentsia, particularly those whose specializations did not bring them into serious conflict with the party—engineers, planners, economists and physicians, for example—found this system highly to their liking. Only a small minority responded (and this happened only in the late 1970s) by challenging the party's political monopoly and going into opposition. The Hungarian opposition was small, restricted to the intelligentsia and concerned primarily with questions of alternative strategies of rule, rather than with day-to-day, bread-and-butter issues. The members of the opposition issued very considerable amounts of unofficially circulated material (samizdat) and organized a number of alternative activities. The authorities harassed them but allowed them to survive.

The relationship between the party and the working class was somewhat differently arranged. Here, the party offered an arrangement whereby the workers would be guaranteed a cradle-to-grave welfare system (not as efficient as in the West but better than that which had existed before in Hungary), a steady increase in the standard of living, price stability, full employment, the right not to work excessively and the right not to be compelled to participate in politics. Less obviously, the party also accepted that certain members of the working class would be better off than others, regardless of the value of their work, so that some, such as miners and heavy-metal workers, would earn more than those in, say, textiles.

In the late 1970s, however, this arrangement began to shift toward differentiation rather than a notional equality. Price stability was abandoned, the Hungarian population became used to one or more price rises a year and to virtually no improvements in their real wages for several years from 1980 onward. Inflation between the mid-1970s and the mid-1980s was around

100 percent. The absence of any upheaval, unlike the situation in Poland, was explained by three factors: the legacy of 1956 and the suppression of high aspirations; the growing income differentials within the working class; and the availability of foodstuffs and consumer goods at a price. These, taken together, diverted potential political activism into economic enterprise through the secondary economy, which in turn served to intensify differentials and create new inequalities. The growth in the importance of the secondary, or unregistered economy, in which—it was estimated—two-thirds of the population participated, meant that official figures on income differentials had become meaningless. Nevertheless, estimates suggested that, discounting the elite, about 5 percent of the people could be regarded as very rich (those who run the fashionable boutiques in Budapest, for example) and 30 percent lived at or below the poverty line.

As far as the peasantry was concerned, the relationship devised by the party could be regarded as something of a success. Essentially, the party recognized that prosperous agriculture was necessary as a firm foundation for the health of the economy as a whole, that relying on the specialist knowledge of the peasantry was the best way of achieving this and that the most useful policy the party could pursue was to leave the agricultural sector alone, even while permitting a higher level of investment than had been the case in the 1950s. The system that evolved, which turned out to be highly effective, relied on peasant initiative both in the collective and on the private plot. Agricultural output rose as did peasant incomes, resulting in a transformation of the countryside, and food supplies to the towns were not in danger. At the same time, the peasantry was recruited as a source of support to the system.

The party had changed too. Whereas in the 1950s it had been the sole institution controlling all activity, by the 1980s it had ceased to be the disciplined Leninist organization run by a single center. In effect, its role had been subtly transformed from having been the exclusive initiator and executor of all policies to something more resembling an arbiter among different social interests. This did not mean that the party had ceased to be the dominant political force, but it did exercise its political power in a more diffuse way. Thus the central party apparatus had lost or abandoned its hegemonic power over the regions, and central directives could only be enforced after bargaining. Control over personnel at the county level had largely passed to the counties. At the county level, party secretaries tended to share power, at any rate informally, with other local people of rank, such as the senior officials of the local administration, the judiciary, the economic bureaucracy and the police. In this sense, the territorial and functional bureaucracies had to some extent merged. What took place at the center was the crucial debate over the allocation of resources and the direction of future strategy. The whole system was held together by the personal authority of the party leader, Kádár, himself.

SOURCES OF WEAKNESS

The system appeared stable enough after a fashion, but it did contain a number of sources of weakness. On its own, none of these potential weaknesses would have been sufficient to destabilize the system, but if crises sparked off by two or more occurred simultaneously, then Hungary would face very serious problems indeed. It was all the worse from the party's point of view that all four sources of weakness were very largely outside its control.

The first of these potential weaknesses was the fact that so much of the stability depended on the survival of Kádár as party leader. Despite having been regarded as the man who betrayed the revolution in 1956, he had by the 1980s built up an enormous personal prestige and commensurate authority. What he said went; it was accepted that whatever he decided was the best strategy to follow. The trouble with this pattern of rule is that it cannot be transmitted to a successor, and Kádár, born in 1912, would obviously not remain on the political stage forever. There was no indication that any provision was being made for the succession, and in any case, succession mechanisms are difficult to establish in a Soviet-type system. So at the point when Kádár left the political scene, there would be a significant gap in the system and the various contending forces would seek to fill it, certainly recruiting allies. Something like a power struggle could then emerge, with unpredictable consequences.

The second source of weakness was the national question. Hungary was highly homogeneous nationally. German, Slovak, South Slav, Romanian and Gypsy minorities accounted for no more than 7 or 8 percent of the population (and Gypsies were not recognized as a national minority, only as a social problem). On the other hand, around 3 million ethnic Hungarians lived in the contiguous states; Romania had about 2 million, Czechoslovakia about 0.6 million, Yugoslavia about 0.45 million and the Soviet Union about 150,000. Throughout the 1970s, the authorities permitted and even encouraged the gradual expression of a Hungarian national consciousness as a way of strengthening identification between rulers and ruled. Even if the communists were never accepted as ruling fully in the interests of the Hungarian nation, because of the ultimate dependence of the party on the Soviet Union, on an everyday level this was less true. Inevitably, this emerging consciousness of nationhood placed the question of the ethnic minority Hungarians on the political agenda. The problem for the Hungarian authorities was that while they needed the support from Hungarian society and had to appear as the effective protagonists of all Hungarians, abroad as well as at home, there was very little that they could do to allay Hungarian anxieties that their conationals were being subjected to discrimination (see the chapter on National Minorities, p. 302). There was considerable evidence in the 1980s that on the issue of the Hungarians of Transylvania, opinion in Hungary was running very high. Unless checked by continuous government attention, it could spill over and shake the party itself. Within the party, there were enough people who would support a much tougher policy toward Romania than Hungary was actually pursuing. The party had to tread a delicate line.

The third source of weakness was the economy. Hungarian public opinion appeared ready to tolerate considerable privation, and although the strategy of differentiation seemed to be working, it was not without its strains. In the event of another international downturn and a worsening of the terms of trade (Hungary was one of the most trade-dependent countries of the world, earning around half its gross national product from foreign trade), the authorities could face serious difficulties and would have few remaining resources with which to meet them.

The fourth source of weakness was that Hungary was, after all, ultimately dependent on Soviet goodwill. In the event of a new Soviet leadership coming to power with a stricter view of what constituted ideological orthodoxy, much of the freewheeling in the economy might be declared unacceptable. A tightening-up could then ensue, leaving the leadership with repression as its principal resource for meeting disaffection.

All in all, the Hungarian road looked highly attractive from many points of view, especially to other Eastern European countries that had been far less successful in maintaining a leadership intelligent enough to run the system with some semblance of efficiency. Yet it was still far from being the successful, reformed system that its many admirers in the West claimed it to be.

FURTHER READING

Kovrig, Bennet. *Communism in Hungary from Kun to Kádár*. Stanford, California: Hoover Institution, 1979.

Toma, Peter A., and Volgyes, Ivan. *Politics in Hungary*. San Francisco: W. H. Freeman, 1975.

Hare, Paul, Radice, Hugo, and Swain, Nigel, eds. *Hungary: A Decade of Economic Reform*. London: Allen and Unwin, 1981.

Schöpflin, George. *Hungary between Prosperity and Crisis*. London: Institute for the Study of Conflict, 1981.

THE LEGACY OF
THE PRAGUE SPRING

VLADIMIR V. KUSIN

WHEN the tide of World War II began to turn in his favor, Stalin probably did not expect that Czechoslovakia would fall fully under his boot. Virtually nothing was said about this country at the Teheran and Yalta conferences. The weakness of the Czech democratic Parties and of President Edvard Beneš, no less than the able tactics of the local communist leadership, led nevertheless to a takeover in February 1948. Communism has repeatedly proved itself to be incongruous with the disposition of a country that had embraced democracy as a mode of government as much as a way of life before the war. The communist rulers have repeatedly had to act with special dogmatic cruelty in order to suppress the internal "enemy."

A significant part of the population believed in 1945–48 that it ought to be possible to experiment with nonorthodox communism in a country like Czechoslovakia. After tens of thousands had fallen victim to communist rule and the country's formidable economic potential had been mismanaged to a state of dire inadequacy in the 1950s, communist intellectuals, burdened with guilty consciences, joined forces with other aggrieved and disaffected groups in the 1960s to set in motion the reformist process. A package of proposals for change evolved, culminating in the 1968 program for action. It centered neither around a self-management blueprint, as in Yugoslavia, nor around national emancipation, as in the Hungarian revolution of 1956, but rather around the twin concepts of democratization and liberalization. It was to be both a political and an economic reform, with an injection of cultural freedom, called by some observers unprecedented and an attempt to square the circle. The party's leading role was to be preserved, albeit in a modified way, but society as a whole was to have much more input into politics as well as into the formulation of rules that governed the life of the individual.

GESTATION OF THE REFORMIST CONCEPT

The intellectual became the prime moving force of reform in Czechoslovakia. A few young lecturers in philosophy and history, as well as some writers at their congress in 1956, set the tone in response to the first round of de-Stalinization. They proposed more debate and less enforcement inside

330

the party, a more benign relationship between party and nonparty people, a look at past injustices with a view to rectifying them and wider freedom in scholarship, which should cease to be a servant of power politics.

The party leadership withstood early post-Stalin criticism well, not the least because Klement Gottwald, the pillar of Czechoslovak Stalinism, had died in 1953 and it could be proclaimed that dogmatism had already been overcome. The country was also doing reasonably well, and there was much less economic pressure for change than elsewhere in the Soviet bloc. A modest reform of parts of the economic mechanism was, nevertheless, initiated in 1958, and by the beginning of the 1960s two further factors entered the scene: the second round of Khrushchev's de-Stalinization campaign and the disaffection of the Slovaks. Reformism thus gathered momentum.

The power-political and national position of Slovakia within an essentially unitary Czechoslovak communist state has never been satisfactorily resolved. In the new "socialist" constitution of 1960, the powers of such Slovak political bodies as were allowed to exist came to be further curtailed. Party first secretary Antonín Novotný had a vision of communist centralism that offered little room for Slovak power-sharing, and he was deeply suspicious of Slovak national traditions. He also intensely disliked Gustáv Husák, the man who embodied for many Slovaks a continuity with communist nationalism as it had manifested itself during the war. Husák had spent nine years (1951–60) in jail for the crime of "bourgeois nationalism"; while he was not given any high office after release and rehabilitation, he gradually became a rallying point for his discontented countrymen. When Alexander Dubček became Slovak party chief in 1963 and a number of the old centralists were ousted from politics under Khrushchev's pressure, the way was open for collaboration between Slovak nationalists and Czech liberal reformers.

The absence of economic adversity had helped the leadership sail through the heavy weather of 1956, but by the early 1960s the imbalance between Czechoslovakia's economic capital of the past and the roughshod methods of communist management was affecting performance and output. The break with China, Czechoslovakia's customer of substance, was an important factor contributing to the decline. The regime, always ready to bulldoze intellectuals into submission, became acutely afraid for its own future when faced with negative economic growth in 1962 and 1963. It reluctantly permitted the design of an economic reform plan, and in the process the tenets of a command economic system were shown to be intimately linked with politics.

The period 1956–68 can best be seen as one of gradual coalescence of the various strands of change-orientated attitudes. Intellectuals and social scientists, people of culture and the arts, Slovaks, students and economists, while motivated by an assortment of differently perceived goals, found themselves advocating change in essentially the same direction. They all meant to reshape the precepts of one-party rule to allow room for the articulation of individual interests, and to attain efficiency through more liberal human interplay.

REFORMIST GOVERNMENT ATTEMPTED

Two more prerequisites for the successful launching of an experiment in reformist government were needed, and both were forthcoming. The concept of reformist change had to take root in the party leadership, and the public at large had to respond favorably to it. Commitment to reform reached the higher echelons of the party through the good offices of the party intellectuals, or "insiders," and their growing influence on a number of politicians. It became clear at the 13th party congress in 1966, then at several central committee meetings in 1967, that discontent with the Novotný group was not confined to certain writers or historians who happened to be party members, but had already permeated the party apparats. Power struggle along with reform ambition became a factor of change. There had never been any doubt about popular acceptance or reform, even if some misgivings about the effect of the market forces could be sensed among the workers. While many "outsiders" considered the nascent reformist concept as little more than the subject of a family quarrel in the communist camp, there had emerged a more or less general preference for reform communism over the neo-Stalinist, or Novotný, variety. After some hesitation as to what the people's role might be when two factions of the party were in combat, popular input became one of the essential features of the Prague Spring. The public forced the pace of reform, often presenting the communist reformers with requests for solutions that the party-based change-seekers had not been prepared to advance.

The program of the Prague Spring was novel in that it entailed reformist action in all areas of the party's power, and in that the party had to accept pressure from nonleadership sources as a legitimate contributory factor in policy formulation. The Dubček leadership wanted the party's leading role preserved by means of restoring public confidence in a consistent program of democratization. Debate within the party and in the media was to be reasonably free, and censorship was lifted. Politicians were no longer to meddle in cultural and literary affairs. Religion would cease to be a target of official atheism and many restrictions on religious life would be lifted. People would be allowed to associate in clubs and societies of their choice, but the formation of new political parties would not be permitted. Trade union and youth organizations were decentralized; however, while the young were given almost unlimited freedom to create associations of their own or abstain altogether from any such membership, the party preferred at least a formally united labor union structure.

A thoroughgoing economic reform was initiated and vigorously pursued, based on market relations between highly independent enterprises and even considering consumer needs. Later in 1968 the element of self-management was put on the agenda in the form of "enterprise councils" as a factor of the work force's influence on, and in some respects dominance over, management. Limited private enterprise was envisaged for sections of retail trading, for small producers and for craftspeople, but no hints of a return to private farming were detected amid an almost fully collectivized agriculture.

The party and government action programs of April 1968, together with the other decrees of the Prague Spring, went a long way toward comprising an all-embracing blueprint for liberal reform that would require some time before a final version could be implemented. It was a dynamic and open-ended program, which grew in scope and depth as it developed. By the summer of 1968, its contours were much clearer than could have been foretold barely six months earlier, but its future was still far from obvious.

SOVIET INTERVENTION

The expansionist potential of the reform process, together with its perceived impact on the other countries in the bloc (especially Poland, which experienced a smaller upheaval of its own at the same time), made Moscow start intervening early. The Soviet leadership and its allies in East Germany and Poland went through the whole gamut of responses, from public criticism to barely concealed pressures and threats. Four top-level conferences, in Dresden, Warsaw, Čierna nad Tisou and Bratislava, were devoted to censure of the Czechoslovak reformist course. The Romanians and the Yugoslavs showed sympathy for Prague, and the Hungarians were less than eager to rattle their sabers, yet it was soon evident that Moscow was determined to set limits on the Czechoslovak reform, limits that could not be obeyed without abandoning the essentials of the reform. Soviet objections ostensibly focused on the strategic tilt in the European power balance that would result from a reformed and liberalized Czechoslovakia. The fact that the Dubček leadership trod with special caution in the field of foreign policy, repeatedly professing loyalty to Soviet-bloc commitments, made no dent in Moscow's intransigence. Military maneuvers of Soviet troops were held on Czechoslovak territory from late June to early August, and large armed concentrations were massed on the border. The moment of attack was chosen to prevent the beginning of a special party congress in early September. Moscow leaders feared that the rout of a the dogmatic wing that would probably occur would force them to face a totally reformist party, thus repeating their painful experience with Yugoslavia in 1948–50, and, allowing for differences, with China in 1959–61. Soviet troops, together with contingents from East Germany, Poland, Hungary and Bulgaria, invaded Czechoslovakia on August 20, 1968, in the name of the theory of "limited sovereignty," later known as the Brezhnev doctrine. According to this tenet, which is apparently still in force, whenever Moscow perceives that developments in a fraternal country are dangerous to the collective interests of communism, it has the right to intervene militarily.

COUNTERREFORMATION

Moscow's first plan to govern Czechoslovakia through an alternative "revolutionary" power center failed, becuse of unexpected defiance by the public in general and by the reformist section of the party in particular. A more difficult and gradualist course was therefore adopted. With a quarter of a million Soviet troops in the country, Moscow forced the Dubček leadership to begin dismantling its own reforms. At the same time, the Soviets gradually started to chip away at the composition of this leadership, aiming to replace it once popular support for it had been eroded. In April 1969, Alexander Dubček was forced to make way as party first secretary for Gustáv Husák, the man who had been dumped by Gottwald and spurned by Novotný, but who was now able to reach the top on the sinking Dubček's shoulders.

Quite a few people held to the belief that a reasonably moderate form of government could be preserved once the invasion's dust had settled. They based their expectations on faith in Husák's commitments to reformism during his short alliance with the change-orientated faction, and on the hope that the economic reform and the Czech-Slovak federal arrangement would be retained as a legacy of the Prague Spring. From this, they hoped, a slow climb back to overall relaxation could be started again.

Czechoslovakia was federalized by act of parliament in October 1968, to take effect on January 1, 1969; but almost immediately steps were taken to disrupt the formal symmetry of the arrangement by barring the existence of an autonomous Czech Communist party and, the following year, by curtailing the powers of the Slovaks in both party and government. The shell of a federation has since then been preserved as a training camp for Slovak administrators, but for most practical purposes Czechoslovakia remains a unitarily ruled communist state, where national devolution serves a purely bureaucratic end, devoid of any power-political substance. The number of Slovaks in federal positions has increased considerably.

Contrary to some expectations, Moscow evidently decided—and its agents within the Czechoslovak party were only too willing to oblige—to break the back of reformism. "Normalization," as the excision of reformism from communist rule came to be known, evolved rapidly and with a vengeance. The party and all the political apparats were purged to an extent only comparable to the Chinese cultural revolution. About a million people, including nearly half a million party members (a third of the January 1968 total), were affected. All liberalizing processes were reversed, no matter what damage was caused to the nation's ability to see to its cultural, scholarly and scientific needs. Economic reform was buried and command practices reintroduced. Dogmatic ideology triumphed once again, as did the coercion typical of early communist rule. Well over 100,000 people emigrated, considerably more than after 1948. With Hungary's experience after 1956, Czechoslovakia's normalization was the second case of the successful restitution of totalitarianism on a national scale.

Relying on coercion, yet allowing some room for the pursuit of private pastimes, the Husák leadership concentrated on economic improvement. Consumerism flourished during the first half of the 1970s, but the successive oil price explosions, coupled with the assertion of the old failings of the command system of economic management, put an end to hopes that the country would stay "normal" forever. "Really existing socialism," an official slogan, has turned out to be an organism in which the party-police can rule without having to fear reformism from within, but an organism which cannot be governed properly. During the early 1980s, Czechoslovakia warded off economic disaster only with difficulty. Forced into reduced circumstances by normalization, it has been unable to modernize its economy or to exhort an apathetic population to heroic labor feats.

NEW DISSENT

The first reemerging dissident groups of the early 1970s realized that a program similar to that of the Prague Spring could no longer claim active popular support; most people feared another invasion. The normalizing leadership easily suppressed their reformist ex-comrades in a series of political trials in 1972, yet the intellectuals kept the flame of discontent burning. A lively and growing network of samizdat literature—books, essays, personal depositions, petitions—became a major part of the dissident scene and has remained so to this day. In January 1977, the manifesto of Charter 77 began an orientation toward human rights that was directly caused by the government's repressive practices, by passage of the Helsinki Final Act and by Czechoslovak ratification of the U.N. covenants on human, political, economic, social and cultural rights. In 1978, the Committee for the Defense of Unjustly Prosecuted Persons was formed. The group remained unbroken by a series of incarcerations, by trials in 1979 and by the enforced emigration of several of its leaders. The committee had issued more than 400 statements on political persecution by the end of 1984. The Charter 77 organization itself, originally formed by some 1,200 people, circulated several hundred documents, ranging from petitions and appeals to informed commentary on the social ills rampant under the Czechoslovak form of communism. Charter 77 also gave impetus to a specific form of peace movement, the basic tenets of which have come to be accepted by several leaders of similar campaigns in the West. Peace and human rights are indivisible, Charter 77 stated, and a government that does not want to be at peace with its own citizens, against whom it feels compelled to wage constant ideological war, cannot be trusted to seek genuine peace internationally.

A revival of religious activity since the late 1970s, especially among the young, can be traced to the activism of the Polish pope, John Paul II, as well as to the existential impasse created by a regime that calls itself socialist but is generally felt to be a mere exercise in preserving a power-political status quo. Even with a much weaker hierarchy than in Poland, religion in general and the Roman Catholic church in particular have perceptibly enhanced their influence on the ruling elite and on the population at large, especially in Slovakia.

Fearing and opposing reformism of even the mildest variety, the regime has found it difficult to see its precepts through by means of mobilization campaigns. The public, including the lower and middle ranks of management, has become adept at diluting, circumventing or plainly ignoring most decrees and exhortations. Dissent by noncooperation is widely practiced.

The Czechoslovak regime of normalized socialism has in reality not solved any of the problems addressed to communist rule even before the Prague Spring, except those of keeping itself in power and of eliminating revisionism within its own ranks. In this sense it is stable. It has also socialized, as all regimes do, a constituency of office holders at all levels of the apparats who would lose status and material well-being under any other arrangement. The police-centered machinery of vigilance against all political deviance is also quite reliable. The Soviet preference for the current state of affairs in

Czechoslovakia is central to this stability, and there is no reason to doubt Moscow's unwavering backing, under either Chernenko or Gorbachev.

The problem with this kind of stability is that it equals virtual stagnation, because of its inherent inability to increase the country's wealth or to meet people's growing expectations. Because of both economic challenges and continuing intellectual and spiritual disaffection, the coercive stability of the Czechoslovak regime will be increasingly difficult to uphold in the future.

FURTHER READING

Golan, Galia. *The Czechoslovak Reform Movement: Communism in Crisis 1962–1968.* Cambridge: Cambridge University Press, 1971.

———. *Reform Rule in Czechoslovakia: The Dubček Era 1968–1969.* Cambridge: Cambridge University Press, 1973.

Kusin, Vladimir V. *From Dubček to Charter 77: A Study of "Normalization" in Czechoslovakia 1968–1978.* New York: St. Martin's Press, 1978.

———. *The Intellectual Origins of the Prague Spring.* Cambridge: Cambridge University Press, 1971.

Mlynář, Zdeněk. *Nightfrost in Prague: The End of Humane Socialism.* New York: Karz, 1980.

Skilling, H. Gordon. *Charter 77 and Human Rights in Czechoslovakia.* London: Allen and Unwin, 1981.

———. *Czechoslovakia's Interrupted Revolution.* Princeton: Princeton University Press, 1976.

Tigrid, Pavel. *Why Dubček Fell.* London: Macdonald, 1971.

Valenta, Jiri. *Soviet Intervention in Czechoslovakia 1968: Anatomy of a Decision.* Baltimore: The Johns Hopkins University Press, 1979.

THE GERMAN DEMOCRATIC REPUBLIC: INTERNAL AND INTERNATIONAL

MARTIN McCAULEY

THE German Democratic Republic (GDR, or East Germany) is one of the 12 most industrialized nations in the world today. From an economic point of view it has been a success story. Born amid defeat and despair in 1945, the country has now achieved internal stability and a modest prosperity. The GDR came into being on October 7, 1949—between 1945 and 1949 the territory was known as the Soviet Zone of Occupation—in direct response to the founding of the German Federal Republic (West Germany) a few weeks earlier. The GDR is now the most developed and prosperous country in the communist world. It can be viewed as one side of a triangle. West Germany is another side, but the most important influence on East Germany's evolution has been exercised by the remaining side, the Soviet Union. East Germany has always had to maneuver between these two stronger powers and over time has developed considerable skill in defending its own interests.

As a member of COMECON and the Warsaw Pact—the most important member of both after the Soviet Union—it is firmly ensconced in the Soviet bloc. Article 6 of the 1974 constitution maintains that "the German Democratic Republic is forever and irrevocably allied to the Soviet Union." Under the Soviet East German treaty of friendship, cooperation, and mutual aid, signed in October 1975, East German troops would likely be fighting alongside their Soviet comrades in the event of a Sino-Soviet conflict.

The ruling Communist party, the Socialist Unity party (SED), is modeled on the Communist party of the Soviet Union; as a Marxist–Leninist party, it observes democratic centralism. The key political body is the SED Politburo, which in October 1984 contained 21 full members and four candidate members. Erich Honecker heads the party with the title of secretary general. He succeeded Walter Ulbricht as party leader in 1971. Until then he had specialized in youth and security affairs, but he soon revealed himself to be an astute politician by outmaneuvering Willi Stoph, prime minister and a senior member of the Politburo, to become national leader in 1973. Stoph then lost his position as prime minister but regained it in 1976 and has retained it ever since. Honecker has been able over time to strengthen his position, and in May 1984 was able to promote Werner Jarowinsky and Günther Kleiber to full Politburo membership. The most startling promotion, however, was that of Professor Herbert Häber to full membership without his going through the normal candidate stage. These promotions emphasize Honecker's two main concerns: the economy and intra-German relations. Jarowinsky's expertise is in foreign trade; Kleiber is a specialist in advanced technology; Häber is the leading expert on East–West German relations.

East Germany is a resource-poor country and must import much of its raw materials and energy. The main indigenous source of energy is lignite, or brown coal, and of this it is the world's largest producer: 278 million tons in 1983. Opencut mining is the norm, and 2,000 to 3,000 hectares of new land must be cleared annually. Lignite, however, is becoming more expensive to mine. In 1960, only 2.85 cubic meters had to be mined to secure a ton of lignite, but the figure is now 4.4 cubic meters and is expected to reach 10 cubic meters by the end of the 1980s. The Soviet Union has reduced its deliveries of oil, but supplies of natural gas are plentiful. The need to conserve energy is ever present and considerable success has been recorded.

Since the East German economy is based on created value, economic efficiency is of paramount importance. Central-planning controls are tight and industry is concentrated in over a hundred *Kombinate*, which direct the activities of all enterprises in the various industrial sectors. *Kombinate* can engage in foreign trade on their own account. During the 1981–85 five-year plan, the performance of the East German economy was one of the best in the communist world; during the first half of 1984 it was above the planned targets. As examples, national income rose by 5.1 percent, or 0.7 percent above plan; retail-trade turnover, at 4.4 percent, was double that planned; and foreign trade revealed the same result. The overall picture, however, is less rosy than these successes would suggest.

The terms of trade turned against East Germany after 1973. Since then, the price of imports has been increasing faster than that of exports, obliging the country to export more to import the same amount of goods. The jump in the price of hydrocarbons over the last decade has caused East German trade with the Soviet Union to run into the red. At the end of 1983, the national deficit had reached 3.03 billion transferable rubles (about U.S.$4 billion). In the communist world, the hard-currency indebtedness per capita of East Germany is second only to Poland. In 1981, for instance, 61 percent of hard-currency earnings had to be spent on servicing the hard-currency debt.

THE SED AND THE POPULATION

The SED is only one of five political parties. The others are the Christian Democrats (CDU), the Liberal Democrats (LDPD), the National Democrats (NDPD), and the Peasant party (DBD). The communists, however, have a monopoly of political power; the other parties all acknowledge the SED's leading role and proclaim the building of communism to be their goal. The

SED resulted from the fusion of the Communist party (KPD) and the Social Democrats (SPD) in April 1946, and ever since the party has contained many who are more social-democratic than communist in outlook. It was called the "Russian" party by the population, most of whom had little sympathy for Soviet-style socialism. Those who opposed the direction the SED was taking could always move to the West, and between 1949 and 1961 about 2.7 million did. About 60 percent of these, moreover, were of working age and about one-quarter were under 25. The vitality of the West German economy, which commonly recruited labor in the East, exacerbated the situation. The decision to complete the collectivization of agriculture in 1960 brought matters to a head. Khrushchev, then the Soviet leader, finally agreed to the building of the Berlin Wall, which began on August 13, 1961. Ulbricht, the SED leader, conceded in July 1961 that the party had failed to present the "basic facts of the policy of worker and peasant power to the masses in such a way as to convince them of their correctness." Ulbricht thereby conceded that his party's legitimacy in the eyes of the population was still quite low.

Things improved for the SED thereafter, and the New Economic System (1963–70) was a period of great optimism. Those who gained most were the technical intelligentsia and the skilled industrial workers, as the SED placed great hopes on the scientific-technical revolution. By 1970, however, the economic goals were proving unattainable—this was one of the reasons why Honecker replaced Ulbricht in 1971. Honecker eschewed experimentation and adopted a very orthodox political and economic approach. Whereas Ulbricht had proved intractable during the Berlin agreement negotiations, Honecker was amenable to Soviet wishes. His first five years in office were Honecker's golden years; thereafter, the terms of trade began to bite, so that by the early 1980s living standards were stagnating.

LEGITIMATION OF SED RULE

The SED has always faced an uphill task in the struggle to legitimate its rule. Initially, the party based its legitimacy on the fact that it was the vanguard of the working class, but it was the working class that spearheaded the uprising of June 17, 1953. This taught the SED the lesson that it could not demand too many sacrifices from the workers. It has heeded that lesson ever since. During the 1960s and 1970s, the party could claim success for its policies, and the advent of modest prosperity increased its standing. Economic expansion allowed the party to place greater stress on social policy, and under Honecker the unity of economic and social policy has been underlined: tangible improvements in social policy can only come if the economy grows. The main plank in social policy under Honecker is housing. Between 1971 and 1980s, almost a million new dwellings were built and over 400,000 renovated. Between 1976 and 1990, it is hoped that 2.8 million to 3 million dwellings will be constructed or renovated. By 1980, over 6 million citizens, or about 40 percent of the population, had improved accommodation. Workers' cooperatives building their own homes, and private builders accounted for 56 percent of new dwellings in 1980.

By 1977, 87 percent of women between the ages of 16 and 60 were at work, many of them part-time. This was due to the state's desire to see every able-bodied person at work, but also to the need for both spouses to earn if the East German version of the good life is a family's goal. A price, however, had to be paid for this. The birthrate declined to an all-time low of 10.6 live births per 1,000 of the population in 1974; the East German population was in serious decline. A pronatal campaign was launched to halt the trend, and it has had some success. The number of mothers able to go out to work has been enlarged because of the increase in crèche and kindergarten places made available. In 1980, 92 percent of children aged from three to six years were attending kindergartens, and 60 percent of those up to three years attended crèches.

Admissions to universities and technical colleges reached an all-time record of 158,000 in 1971, but declined sharply to 129,000 in 1979. Women, however, have improved their position. Where in 1971, 37 percent of the total student population was female, in 1979 it had risen to 48.1 percent. Women have been even more successful in obtaining university places, and now make up over half the student body.

Pensions under Honecker have also increased sharply, but those of pensionable age are encouraged to remain at work. All basic foods and services are subsidized; this now amounts to over a hundred marks per person annually.

Social expenditure per capita doubled between 1971 and 1982, about twice the growth of national income. Housing, again, was accorded the greatest priority; the outlay in 1982 was about 3.5 times that of 1971. On the other hand, expenditure on health only rose by about a quarter over the same period, and it remains the Cinderella of the social policy.

The fact that expenditure on social policy has increased at about double the rate of national income growth under Honecker means that other sectors have suffered, notably industrial investment. The proportion of the East German national income invested annually is now the lowest in the communist bloc. If fewer resources were channeled into social policy, however, the party fears social tension would increase. Economic and social policy are thus of paramount importance in the battle for legitimacy.

The SED seeks legitimation on two other planes, the national and the state. The first East German constitution of 1949 claimed to speak for all Germans, emphasizing that there was only one German nationality. Several appeals were made by the SED and the Soviets to establish an all-German state. In 1955, both East Germany and West Germany had their sovereignty restored, which caused the SED to change tactics. It no longer claimed that the solution to the German problem was an all-German state, but favored a German confederation in which both states would enjoy equal rights. The concept of the socialist nation surfaced in 1962, and East German citizenship was proclaimed in 1967. The 1968 constitution defined East Germany as a "socialist state of the German nation," implying that there was one German nation divided into socialist and capitalist parts. Willy Brandt's *Ostpolitik*, the Berlin agreement and the basic treaty between East Berlin and Bonn fundamentally altered the situation. Between 1949 and 1972, the Federal

Republic had refused to recognize East Germany diplomatically, providing the SED with many opportunities to put forward solutions to the German problem. After 1972, however, the SED became defensive and sought, through the policy of *Abgrenzung* (demarcation), to keep the two German states apart. The party now argued that class defined a state and nation, and that there were two German states and two German nations, one socialist and the other capitalist. Throughout the 1970s, East Germany began to reassess German history in order to create a "progressive" pedigree. The evaluation of Martin Luther, for example, underwent a complete change—once condemned, he is now seen in a positive light. It was claimed that since the SED was securely in power, it could take a more relaxed view of the German past. There is also a strong sense among East German citizens of being heirs to a common German past. Since the Soviet and Eastern European (mainly Slavic) way of life has little appeal for the average East German, building on German tradition could be an astute policy. East German citizens are slowly recovering their self-confidence and taking pride in the achievements of the German past. By stressing that past, however, the SED is making it more difficult to instill in East Germans the notion that they are distinctly different from their West German neighbors. East German thinking about the nation is clearly still evolving.

As far as the state is concerned, the SED is on stronger ground. The average citizen is much more willing to identify with East Germany as a state than with the SED. A primary party SED goal has thus always been the establishment of a strong East Germany. The gradual rehabilitation of the Prussian state during the 1970s is part of this process, which allows the party to stress the citizen's duty to serve the state.

The SED has regularly employed these and other devices to legitimate its rule. The East German state is now firmly established, but the East German nation is still a nebulous concept. The economic performance and the educational, health and social security systems of East Germany are among the best in the communist world. Indeed, the SED could claim, for example, that the educational system is the best available anywhere. Hence the party's standing in the eyes of the population has risen, and will remain high as long as citizens believe there is no alternative to SED rule.

FOREIGN POLICY

The function of East German foreign policy is the security and strengthening of the state. To this end, the most important foreign capitals are Moscow and Bonn. The Soviet Union is of greater significance, since without its support East Germany would not have come into being nor would it have achieved diplomatic recognition by the West in the 1970s. East Germany may be called an accidental state, for the Soviet Union in 1945 did not expect two German states to come into existence. Moscow reluctantly concluded only in 1955 that the two German states had come to stay. During the first postwar decade, therefore, the East German elite was in constant fear that a deal would be concluded between the Soviet Union and the West undermining their position. The Soviets have never been able to decide

341

whether their interests are better served with one Germany or two. If Soviet –East German relations are one side of the triangle, then Soviet–American relations are the umbrella under which all contacts take place. From Moscow's point of view, its interests take obvious precedence: East German development should take the path favored by the Soviets, and East German –West German relations should be subservient to Soviet–West German relations. East Germany's main diplomatic concern before 1972 was to secure diplomatic recognition by Bonn and the West. Afterward, East Berlin could look out into the wider world and begin defending its own national interests. The Soviet attitude to East Germany was personified by Pyotr Abrasimov, Soviet ambassador in East Berlin between 1962 and 1971, and again between 1975 and 1983. He saw his role as that of a proconsul and regarded the SED as being always in the debt of the Soviet Union because of the blood that was shed to liberate Germany from fascism. His style was abrasive and imperious, and he crossed swords with Honecker on many occasions. It says much for Honecker's skill and standing that during Andropov's rule he was able to engineer the recall of Abrasimov, who was replaced by Vyacheslav Kochemasov, an old acquaintance of Honecker's from his days as leader of the Free German Youth. East Germany has been moderately successful in the battle to assert its own interests, yet every time the Soviets have opposed an East German initiative, they have won. Two examples of this stand out. In 1971, during negotiations over the Berlin agreement, Ulbricht insisted on better terms, was overruled, and eventually lost his post. In 1984, Honecker wished to make his already postponed visit to West Germany, but had to postpone it once again under pressure from Moscow. East Germany seeks to influence Moscow by presenting itself as the Soviet Union's most reliable ally in Eastern Europe and the most important military ally in the Warsaw Pact. It provides military, security and cadre training in those Third World states that are allied to the Soviet Union. Doubts about the reliability of the Polish and Czechoslovak armed forces have enhanced the role of the East German armed forces. Economically, the Soviet Union took 38 percent of East German exports in 1984 and would like more. Because of East Germany's need to earn hard currency to import high technology, however, it is not in the nation's interest to become too dependent on the Soviet Union and COMECON.

East German–West German relations have improved considerably since the late 1970s, when East Berlin abandoned its policy of *Abgrenzung* and sought a closer relationship with Bonn. Since 1979, East Berlin has sought to protect these bilateral German relations from the storms of the superpower relationship, and in this effort has so far had considerable success. A DM1 billion credit in 1983 was followed by a DM950 million credit in 1984, money used mainly to service East Germany's hard-currency debts. West German chancellor Helmut Schmidt visited East Germany in December 1981, but Honecker's return visit was postponed in both 1983 and 1984. Honecker remains committed to improving relations with Bonn, but will have to proceed more slowly. Recognition of East German citizenship and of East Germany as a foreign country are two long-term goals vis-à-vis Bonn. Reunification is not considered a realistic prospect in this century.

INSTRUMENTS OF COERCION

The East German armed forces (NVA) were formed in 1956. More than half of the approximately 160,000 members are conscripts who serve for 18 months. All males are required to do national service except theology students and other special party and state categories.

The instruments of coercion have increased their influence in East Germany over the last decade, but this is not due to the weakness of the SED. The NVA does not stand particularly high among the population, and many young men are unwilling conscripts. Conscientious objectors (not officially recognized) have increased from an estimated 250 in 1975 to 1,000 in 1984. They may opt to work in construction brigades but must wear uniforms; the alternative to construction work is usually prison, but only a tiny minority choose this path. The NVA is the best-equipped army in the Warsaw Pact, after that of the Soviets. Over the last decade, defense expenditure has increased more rapidly than national income, and over the same period East Germany has spent more on defense as a proportion of national income than any other Eastern European state. Considerable attention has been paid to the navy in the last few years, and its equipment has been updated. The NVA is probably more efficient than the Soviet Army, thereby gaining East German influence in Moscow. The minister of national defense is Gen. Heinz Hoffmann, a full member of the SED Politburo.

The ministry of state security (STASI) controls a staff of about 18,000 and a guards regiment. It is headed by Gen. Erich Mielke, also a full member of the Politburo. Expenditure on the security forces has also increased substantially. The STASI and the KGB are assumed to work closely together; this may be an area of policy where Honecker is not completely in control.

OPPOSITION AND DISSENT

There is no organized opposition in East Germany because of the STASI's effectiveness. Individual protesters are quickly silenced by imprisonment, then pushed over the West German border. Many literary figures have also been obliged to leave. An unofficial peace movement, centered in the Protestant churches, has developed to oppose the creeping militarization of East German society. Church–state relations have improved since 1978, but believers are discriminated against by the state in education and jobs. A current objective of the movement is to secure the introduction of civil duty to replace military service for conscientious objectors.

The great majority of East German citizens are conformists or realists, and seek expression in an active private life. To pave the way for a new loan in 1984, the authorities agreed to allow about 30,000 citizens to move to West Germany. Many more than that number, however, then began to think about leaving, and it is clear that the SED badly miscalculated the numbers wishing to go. It is thus very difficult to assess the SED's legitimacy, since on the surface almost everyone conforms. The potential for unrest is probably still there, especially if living standards are perceived to decline and if more people are allowed to emigrate legally. Yet the SED has appeared to handle the difficult 1980s with considerable skill.

FURTHER READING

von Beyme, Klaus, and Zimmermann, Hartmut, eds. *Policy Making in the German Democratic Republic.* Aldershot, Hampshire: Gower, 1984.

Childs, David. *The GDR: Moscow's German Ally.* London: Allen and Unwin, 1983.

McCauley, Martin. *The German Democratic Republic since 1945.* London: Macmillan, 1983.

———. *Marxism–Leninism in the GDR The Socialist Unity Party (SED).* London: Macmillan, 1979.

Schulz, Eberhard, ed. *GDR Foreign Policy.* New York and London: M. E. Sharpe, 1982.

THE NATURE OF GOVERNMENT AND POLITICS IN YUGOSLAVIA

K. F. CVIIĆ

WHEN, after four bitter years of civil war and enemy occupation, Marshal Tito came to power in Yugoslavia in 1945, he did so as a dedicated communist wholly committed to the cause of international communism. The conflict with Moscow, which broke out into the open in 1948, was not—as the Soviet side tried to make out—about the "undemocratic" conditions inside the Communist party of Yugoslavia (an odd complaint from a party dominated by Stalin). Nor was it, as Moscow also alleged, about the ambitious Yugoslav comrades being inconsistent; rushing headlong into industrialization while dragging their feet over the collectivization of agriculture.

When a specially convened meeting of the Cominform, the organization Stalin set up in 1947 as a successor to the Comintern (disbanded in 1943), expelled Yugoslavia from its membership in June 1948, it did so not in order to cure an ideological deviation but to defeat a power challenge. Unlike other communist leaders in Eastern Europe, who were brought to power by the Red Army and were totally dependent on Soviet support, Tito had come to power at the head of a large and loyal partisan movement and an army with hundreds of thousands of supporters drawn from all of Yugoslavia's nationalities: Croats, Serbs, Slovenes, Montenegrins, Macedonians, as well as the national minorities. Stalin feared and mistrusted his most successful pupil, and when Tito showed signs of wanting to extend his influence in the Balkans and possibly to a still wider area, the axe fell; or it fell as far as membership in the Soviet bloc was concerned. Internally, Tito's position was secure and he was able to accept Stalin's challenge.

The manner of that acceptance showed that Tito and his colleagues were hoping for a reconciliation in the relatively near future. Yugoslavia's foreign policy remained pro-Soviet and anti-Western for over a year after the break. At home, Yugoslav communists tried to prove their orthodoxy by introducing a number of ultraleft measures, including a new collectivization campaign in the countryside. As part of that campaign, the number of collective farms (*seljačke radne zadruge*) jumped from 1,217 in 1948 to 6,238 in 1949 and 6,913 in 1950. But Moscow was not impressed. As the propaganda war waged from Moscow and the satellite capitals became more intense, accompanied by attempts to subvert key personnel in the Yugoslav army and the security service and to stir up trouble among the national minorities, the Yugoslav leaders were forced to rethink their whole domestic and foreign strategy. In order to repair the damage done to their economy both by the Soviet economic blockade and their own mistakes, they were obliged to turn to the West for help. They quietly withdrew from the Greek civil war, in which they had been aiding the communist side, and began to produce and disseminate their own propaganda criticizing Soviet foreign and domestic policies.

To appease the badly disaffected peasantry, which still formed the bulk of Yugoslavia's population, the authorities began to slow down the collectivization drive in 1951. By the end of 1952, there were only 4,225 collective farms, compared with 6,913 in 1950, the peak year for collectivization. By 1953 their number had dwindled to 1,165. Most of these, too, were later either disbanded or transformed into agricultural enterprises. However, the ideological sting arising out of the party's fear of the peasantry as a "reserve force" for a future "restoration of capitalism" in the countryside remained. It was reflected in the decision made in 1953 to fix at 10 hectares (25 acres) the maximum amount of land that could be owned by a private peasant family. The private peasant continued to be heavily taxed and discriminated against in other ways. Having decollectivized, the Yugoslav regime embarked on a series of fundamental reforms. The important thing about them was that they were practical measures, imposed on the regime by the new political and economic circumstances—notably the Soviet economic blockade—and designed to help the regime retain its monopoly of power at home and independence of both East and West abroad.

THE FIRST REFORMS

One of the earliest, and to this day best known, innovations of the Yugoslav regime was the creation of workers' councils (*radnički savjeti*) as the basis of what later became the system of socialist self-management (*sistem socijalističkog samoupravljanja*). It was at the end of 1949 that the federal government and the trade union leadership jointly instructed 215 state-owned enterprises to set up the first organs of workers' self-management. By the middle of 1950 there were 520 workers' councils in existence. On June 27, 1950, the Federal Assembly in Belgrade passed the basic law on the management of state economic enterprises and higher economic associations by work collectives, which formed the basis of the new workers' self-management system. The self-management system had several purposes. One was ideological: to provide a Yugoslav alternative to the "bureaucratic socialism" in the Soviet Union, which the Yugoslavs had rejected. The second was political; by announcing measures designed to give greater management rights to the workers, encourage local participation and reduce the role of central authority, the regime hoped to broaden its base of support and increase its popularity. The third purpose was economic: by mobilizing local initiative in factories to increase output and improve efficiency.

By the end of 1953, the framework of a decentralized, self-managed system had been created. Central planning had been replaced by general, indicative plans. Enterprises were obliged to work for the market. The government continued to intervene through price controls, wage controls and investment allocations, but the factory manager was given increased scope for independent initiative. In theory, it was the workers' councils that made major business decisions and exercised control over the selection of factory managers. In practice, however, managers were appointed by the local authority (which meant the local Communist party committee), mainly on political grounds. These managers continued to run their enterprises as they had done before. But they were at least obliged to submit their plans to workers' councils and to answer questions.

The new system brought about rapid improvements in the quality of goods and services. Productivity rose. As regards new investment, factory managers actually had little or no capital under their direct control, but they could press for funds through local party officials and win approval for new projects from the government and the banks. Thanks to Yugoslavia's growing links with the West, the country could draw on Western technology and Western grants and credits to finance new investments and imports of raw materials and components. Between 1953 and 1963, industrial production grew at the (very high) annual rate of 13.7 percent. Labor productivity increased at the annual rate of 3.9 percent during the same period. Real net personal wages per worker rose by 6.2 percent each year in the 1953–60 period.

But there were problems, too. Yugoslavia continued to run a persistent trade deficit that amounted to three percent of the country's gross domestic product (GDP) in the 1953–60 period. Most of this was covered by Western (mainly U.S.) aid. By 1959, the United States had given Yugoslavia more than $1 billion in aid, mainly in the form of foodstuffs, fuels and raw materials. Foreign indebtedness continued to rise, however. Another problem was the enormous drain of funds from enterprises into public investment. The share of gross investment in the country's GDP was more than 35 percent in each year from 1953 to 1960 (except in 1958, when it was 33 percent). That meant that the scope available to self-managed enterprises for disposing of their own product remained small. In 1959, in all factories, 53 percent of gross value added was paid in taxes, social security contributions and interest on loans; 19 percent was gross saving; and only 28 percent was received in net cash incomes by the work force.

This situation provoked many questions and considerable dissatisfaction, first, because it reduced the scope for workers to improve their living standards, second, because it gave the authorities the final say in the use of more than half of the surplus generated within the enterprises. Instances of wasteful investment abounded, notably in Serbia and Montenegro. Even Tito started referring to the need to stop building "political factories." Efficient factories from Yugoslavia's more advanced areas (notably Slovenia and Croatia) felt particularly aggrieved by this drain of resources, which they thought they could have used more profitably. These grievances fueled national discontent; many Croats and Slovenes (in and out of the party) began to voice the view that their republics of the Yugoslav federation were being disadvantaged, even "robbed," by a central government manipulated by the Serbs. (Belgrade, Yugoslavia's capital, is situated in Serbia, and also serves as Serbia's capital.)

By the early 1960s, the pressure for changes in the system coming from a number of quarters had become very strong. The government was concerned about the balance of payments; workers and managers in profit-making enterprises objected to surrendering a large part of their enterprises' income to the government; more developed republics were aggrieved at what they regarded as the wasteful use of resources transferred from them to less developed areas by the central government in Belgrade.

The first tentative stab at reform in 1961 failed, mainly because of the opposition of hard-line forces in the party. But the push for reform continued, and in the end it came in the shape of a dozen laws, regulations and orders passed by the Federal Assembly on July 24, 1965. The reform had both political and economic ends. Its main economic goal was to increase the role of the market, reduce the state's role in investment and liberalize foreign trade with a view to increasing competition within the Yugoslav economy. The declared political aims of the reform were: an increase in the decision making role of ordinary citizens as "self-managing producers," and a major reduction in the party's role in the economy.

The immediate economic impact of the 1965 reform was severe. The sharp devaluation of the Yugoslav dinar, coupled with steep increases in prices of raw materials and farm products, resulted in high inflation. The switch in funds from government to enterprises—the result of a drastic reduction in taxes and contributions payable by enterprises—led to a fall in government-financed investment that was not immediately offset by a rise in enterprise investment. A recession followed. There was a sharp fall in the growth rate of the GDP. As money-losing enterprises began to close down, unemployment increased. Large numbers of Yugoslavs began to leave for temporary work in West Germany, Austria, France, Sweden, Switzerland and other Western countries. The government let them. By 1970 an estimated 1 million Yugoslavs were working in the West and, by sending hard currency home to their families, making an important contribution to Yugoslavia's balance of payments. (These Yugoslav guestworkers are estimated to have sent home about 20 billion marks in the 1968–82 period.) Meanwhile, private peasants were given the right to buy farm machinery, including tractors, and the opportunity to obtain bank credits for the purpose. Thanks to a 60 percent increase in the prices paid to the farmers for their products, the lot of that hitherto severely disadvantaged group improved. But the 10-hectare land maximum for private peasants remains in force even today.

SELF-MANAGEMENT IN POLITICS

The first Yugoslav parliament, elected in November 1945, was a typical communist rubber-stamp parliament modeled on the USSR Supreme Soviet. Its main role and that of Yugoslavia's six republican parliaments was to ratify decisions already reached by the Politburo of the party.

The picture began to change when, in the early 1950s, the conventional political parliamentary assemblies, elected by all voters in a constituency, were supplemented by a new type of assembly. These were elective at all levels, from that of the local district to that of the republic and then the federation, by all those working in industrial enterprises, in public services and institutions, and in the collectivized sector of agriculture (private peasants were excluded). This new type of assembly, called the producers' council (*vijeće proizvodjača*), represented an attempt to extend the workers' management principle into politics. Those who were elected to the producers' councils felt themselves to be spokespeople for the new pressure groups that the decentralized economy tended to produce. Another step toward decentralization was the establishment in 1955 of the new unit of local government—the commune (*komuna*)—which took over many of the administrative and economic functions formerly vested in the central or republican apparatus.

A new constitution was adopted in 1963 that reflected the policy of extending self-management to all spheres of public life while also continuing to pay attention to the principle of federalism, important in a multinational state such as Yugoslavia. The Federal Assembly in Belgrade was given five chambers (instead of two as under the 1946 and 1953 constitutions). These were: the Economic Chamber, the Health and Welfare Chamber and the Culture and Education Chamber, each with 120 deputies elected indirectly by delegates of communal assemblies and corresponding enterprises and institutions; the Sociopolitical Chamber with 120 deputies elected directly by voters in all the communes; and the Chamber of Nationalities with 140 deputies—20 for each of the six federal republics and 10 for each of the two autonomous provinces of Kosovo and Vojvodina. The Chamber of Nationalities was designed to act as the guardian of the interests of the republics and the provinces vis-à-vis the federal government and its organs. Any decision taken by a chamber in the Federal Assembly had to have the approval of the Chamber of Nationalities whose deputies were elected by the republics and the provinces and acted as their delegates. This pattern (without, of course, the Chamber of Nationalities) was reproduced at the level of the republics and the provinces. The communal assemblies continued to have two chambers only.

THE STRUGGLE WITHIN THE PARTY

At its Sixth Congress in Zagreb in November 1952, the Communist party of Yugoslavia (*Komunistička partija Jugoslavije*) changed its name to the League of Communists of Yugoslavia (*Savez komunista Jugoslavije*). The congress adopted new and more liberal party statutes, thus tempering the severity of the old Leninist principle of "democratic centralism." But when Milovan Djilas, one of Tito's closest collaborators in the Politburo and an enthusiastic reformer, suggested at the end of 1953 that the party's monopoly of power should be abolished and that a "loyal opposition" should be allowed in Yugoslavia, he was condemned at a special session of the Central Committee, expelled from the Central Committee and given a "final warning" by the party. At the end of 1954, following his criticisms in a U.S. newspaper of the purge of "Djilasists" going on in the party, he was tried and sentenced to six months, but his sentence was suspended. In December 1956, in an an article in a U.S. magazine, Djilas criticized Tito's support of the Soviet intervention in Hungary the month before. He was again put on trial, sentenced to three years in prison and was sent to Srijemska Mitrovica where, before World War II, he had served a similar sentence under the then royalist regime for his activities as a communist. The publication in English in August 1957 of his *New Class*, a Marxist critique of contemporary communism, led to the extension of his three-year sentence to a nine-year one.

But even after Djilas's fall from grace and eventual imprisonment, pressure for liberalization continued both within the party and outside. The continuing conflict between the "liberal" and "conservative" wings of the party came to a head over the question of the 1965 economic reform. Unable to secure its postponement, the party hard-liners tried to sabotage its implementation. Their fear was that economic and political decentralization would weaken the party's control over the country and undermine the Yugoslav state itself. They were extremely influential and confident.

The most prominent of these party conservatives was Aleksandar Ranković, founder of Yugoslavia's security police (first called OZNA, then UDBA), for years the party's powerful cadre secretary and since 1963 also the vice-president of Yugoslavia (slated to become Tito's successor). But the liberal wing secured Tito's support—a vital step in the struggle. At a dramatic session of the Central Committee in Brioni, Tito's island residence in the northern Adriatic, in July 1966, Ranković and his closest collaborator, Svetislav ("Ćeća") Stefanović, then head of Yugoslav security, were charged with a variety of offenses, including that of putting even top party leaders under surveillance. (Hidden microphones had been discovered in Tito's own bedroom by a team from KOS, Yugoslavia's counterintelligence service, working under the direction of Ranković's enemies.) Both were deprived of their posts, but were not put on trial. Their defeat led to a wholesale purge of the security service and later to its reform. A drastic decentralization of the service left the central security organs with responsibility only for such matters as counterintelligence. Public security was placed in the hands of the republics.

THE LIBERAL ERA, 1966–71

The fall of Ranković was reflected in the country's political life in a variety of ways. Some of the most notable changes occurred in the country's parliamentary institutions. Until 1963, the same people continued to be elected into parliamentary bodies and there were only as many candidates as there were seats to be filled. But at the elections held in April 1967, seats for republican and federal assemblies were contested by two, three, or even four candidates. Out of 60 newly elected members of the Sociopolitical Chamber in Belgrade (the other 60 had been elected in 1965), no fewer than 59 were new. The principle of rotation introduced in 1963 forbade deputies to run again for seats in the same assembly. The same principle applied to holders of high posts in the federal government and the governments of the individual republics. Party leaders, who wanted to alternate between parliament and government, found it difficult to be nominated or elected in 1967. A number of prominent party candidates were defeated by lesser known people. The nomination procedure, which had been relaxed still further since the 1967 election, made it relatively easy for groups of citizens to put forward names of their own candidates, sometimes even against the wishes of the local party leadership. In a small town in Serbia, a former partisan general was elected in 1967 as the candidate of the local old partisans' association, despite official party opposition. It took many months of pressure, including a direct intervention by the Central Committee in Belgrade, to have him unseated at the end of 1967. In another Serbian town, friends of one candidate mined a number of bridges in the constituency in order to prevent a rival candidate from addressing the voters. Some hard-liners, sacked in 1966 and earlier, made a comeback. The election generated so many conflicts that cases were still being heard by the courts a year later.

Once they were elected to parliament, deputies took part in vigorous and prolonged debates and frequently petitioned the government on a variety of issues. All assemblies, federal, republican, provincial and communal, met frequently and their deliberations were fully reported in the press and on radio and television. A debate on an important financial bill led to the resignation of the Slovene republican government in December 1966. This resignation, subsequently withdrawn after a compromise was reached, created a precedent. A year later the national press reported, in what was clearly a calculated leak, that the federal government had used the threat of resignation to force the passage of another controversial financial bill. The bill was passed, but at least one dissatisfied government, that of Slovenia, had queried the final decision in the context of the rapidly developing debate on the rights of the individual republics in the federation.

The liberals' victory brought with it, however, more problems than it solved. In the aftermath of the July 1966 confrontation, it became a matter of the utmost urgency for the regime to begin seriously to tackle the problem of nationalism. Touched upon at the Eighth Congress of the party in 1964 and even earlier, the problem came into the open in the great "investment debate" between the developed and undeveloped republics. The Croats and the Slovenes had for years resented Belgrade's policy of heavy investment in the less developed republics of Montenegro, Macedonia, Bosnia and Hercegovina, and Serbia itself at the expense of their own development and modernization. And when, under the economic reform of 1965, drastic action to close down uneconomic industrial enterprises became imperative, the axe was bound to fall first on the "political" factories of Montenegro, Serbia and Macedonia. The conservatives' defeat, which also meant the victory of the school that had advocated the concentration of investment in areas where it would bring maximum returns, i.e., in the developed republics, led to further complications. Leaders from the less developed republics lobbied in Belgrade to protect their interests. This in turn led to the republican authorities in Croatia and Slovenia to demand fuller sovereign rights for themselves vis-à-vis the federation.

While this controversy gathered strength, the party itself became a battleground for bitter nationalist struggles. Basically, Yugoslavia faced the same problems that eventually destroyed the first Yugoslav state before the war—

that of relations between the Serbs and the other nations. The economic debate had brought to light the resistance of Yugoslavia's non-Serbs to what they saw as the return of the old Serbian hegemony in a new guise. When Ranković fell, it was disclosed that Serbian security officials had been pursuing an oppressive chauvinistic policy against the Albanian minority in Kosovo. It was also disclosed that similar offenses had been committed against the Croats and the Muslims in Bosnia, an area historically claimed by both the Serbs and the Croats.

The regime tried to rectify the situation, particularly among the Albanians in Kosovo, which borders on Albania proper. More encouragement was given to various forms of cultural expression among the Albanians, who are the majority in the province. The Albanian flag was permitted to fly and the Albanian language was given fully equal status. The constitutional amendment passed in December 1968 gave the Kosovo authorities the right to plan their own economic and social development with full control of their financial resources, within the framework of a separate provisional constitution for Kosovo.

The implementation of these far-reaching concessions to the Albanians in Yugoslavia had undoubtedly been speeded up in order to contain the rising wave of Albanian nationalist propaganda in Kosovo and elsewhere in Yugoslavia. Riots in Priština and other major Kosovo cities in November 1968 and then again in Tetovo in western Macedonia, where there is a strong Albanian element, were evidence of the strength of Albanian nationalism in Yugoslavia and of the urgent need for constructive measures to prevent it from getting out of control.

These concessions to Yugoslavia's ethnic Albanians provoked a bitter reaction among the Serbs, Yugoslavia's largest nationality. Kosovo had been the center of Serbia's medieval kingdom and its church. It had an Albanian majority, and the local Kosovo Albanians were given political control—even though it was still shared with the local Serbs, now a minority of the population. For opposing the new policy and arguing that it would lead to the Serbs being pushed out of Kosovo altogether, Dobrica Ćosić, a prominent Serbian novelist and a wartime partisan commissar, was expelled from the Serbian Central Committee in May 1968.

Macedonia represented another bitter pill for many Serbs. Before World War II, the royalist regime had, unsuccessfully, tried to Serbianize the province by, among other things, settling Serbian war veterans there (the same policy was followed in Kosovo). This deeply unpopular policy was certainly one of the reasons why there was relatively little resistance to Bulgarian rule in the 1941–44 period. Tito made Macedonia a republic of the Yugoslav federation in 1945. The development of the Macedonian language and identity was deliberately fostered by the authorities, not least in order to preempt a future revival of the old Bulgarian claim on the province. In 1967, the Macedonians even got their own Macedonian Orthodox church. This move angered the Serbian Orthodox church, under the jurisdiction of which the Macedonians had been since the 1920s. Only government pressure prevented the Serbian partriarchs from issuing an anathema against the Macedonian clergy. (The Serbian Orthodox church still refuses to recognize the Macedonian church and has persuaded other Orthodox churches not to recognize it.)

Bosnia and Hercegovina, another region to which Serbia had previously laid a claim, became a federal republic in 1945 in the teeth of considerable opposition from some Serbian party leaders who wanted it to be a province of the Serbian republic—like Kosovo and Vojvodina. The fall of Ranković in 1966 opened the way for the rapid advance, both cultural and political, of the Bosnian Muslims, the descendants of an original local Roman Catholic population (and of the Bogomils, a sect persecuted by the Catholic church and the secular authorities alike). Many of them had embraced Islam during the period of Turkish rule that lasted from 1463 to 1878 when Austria wrested Bosnia from Turkey. Mistrusted and discriminated against by the prewar regime and for two decades after 1945, the Bosnian Muslims came into their own after Ranković's fall in 1966. They were accorded the status of an ethnic group on a par with the Serbs, the Croats and other Yugoslav nations. There was much building of mosques and religious schools, partly financed by Yugoslavia's Muslim friends in the nonaligned movement. By the end of the 1960s, Bosnia had a Muslim plurality (there were 39.6 percent Muslims in the census of 1971, 37.2 percent Serbs and 20.6 percent Croats). Resenting what they saw as a rising Muslim ascendancy, a number of Serbs, particularly among the intelligentsia, left for Serbia.

In Croatia, too, Ranković's fall produced a startling change of mood. The purge of the secret police brought to light the fact that in Croatia no fewer than 1.5 million people—more than one-third of the population—had secret police dossiers. This included the most prominent party members. Miko Tripalo, a popular young party leader in Croatia, had played an important part (in alliance with similar figures from other republics, notably Krste Crvenkovski in Macedonia) in the toppling of Ranković. He and a group of colleagues in the Croatian Central Committee waged an open campaign for further decentralization and democratization of the party. They demanded constitutional changes that would give the individual republics more power at the expense of the federal center in Belgrade; a modification of the rules of "democratic centralism" within the party to allow for minority voices to be heard; a purge of old party cadres opposed to the reforms; and an increased say for ordinary citizens in direct competitive elections. In the economic field, Tripalo and his supporters demanded a further reduction in federal taxes and fiscal powers to allow individual enterprises to retain more of their earnings. They attacked former federal banks in Belgrade, which had taken over the funds previously administered by the federal government, and powerful foreign trade enterprises (also with their headquarters in Belgrade and also founded, staffed and financed by Serbian-dominated federal institutions in the pre-1965 period) as instruments of state "centralism." This campaign enjoyed (at least initially) a good deal of support in non-Serbian parts of Yugoslavia. But it was in Croatia that the campaign enjoyed the greatest popularity. Despite the trappings of the federal system (and the fact that Tito himself was at least partly a Croat—his father was Croat and his mother Slovene), many Croats had felt themselves to be citizens of the second rank in post-1945 Yugoslavia. This feeling was strengthened and inflamed by the powerful role played in Croatia by the republic's Serbian minority, a role far greater than its numbers warranted. (Many of these Croatian Serbs still nursed bitter anti-Croat feelings as a result of their persecution under the notorious 1941–45 regime of Ante Pavelić.)

In March 1967, *Telegram*, the leading Croatian literary weekly, published a document signed on behalf of 19 Croatian cultural institutions by 140 prominent scholars, writers and other intellectuals. More than half of them were party members and included Miroslav Krleža, Croatia's greatest living writer, a member of the Croatian Central Committee and Tito's personal friend. The document, called "The Declaration Concerning the Name and the Position of the Croatian Literary Language," demanded constitutional recognition of full equality for four languages: Croatian, Macedonian, Serbian and Slovene, and the publication of all federal laws and other federal acts in these four languages (instead of, as until then, three: Macedonian, Serbo-Croatian and Slovene). The declaration also demanded the use of standard Croatian in schools and mass media in the Croatian republic. The declaration caused a public uproar. Some of its signatories were expelled from the party. Tito himself condemned it. In October 1967, as part of an official campaign to curb Croatian nationalism, Gen. Većeslav Holjevac, one of the most famous of partisan war heroes and a former mayor of Zagreb, was expelled from the Croatian Central Committee for alleged "nationalist deviation."

At the end of 1969, the Croatian party's leadership was attacked in a series of articles in *Borba* (the former party daily that had become the organ of the party's mass organization, the Socialist Alliance) for not fighting Croatian nationalism energetically enough. The leadership closed ranks and, at a special session of the Central Committee in January 1970, condemned the articles' author, Miloš Žanko, a prominent party figure and vice president of the Federal Assembly in Belgrade, as a "unitarist." The meeting condemned Croatian nationalism, but indicated that "unitarism" (another name for Belgrade centralism) was the chief enemy for the party in Croatia.

The main protagonists of this line were Miko Tripalo, elected in 1969 as one of the two Croatian members of the party's new top body, the executive bureau (*izvršni biro*) in Belgrade; and Mrs. Savka Dabčević-Kučar, an economist, who became the party president in Croatia in 1969. (Before that she had been the prime minister of Croatia, the first woman to hold that job anywhere in Europe). The line enjoyed the support of Vladimir Bakarić, the other Croatian member in the executive bureau. Bakarić was Croatia's most important party figure in the post-1945 period and a leading reformer, notably in the economic field. The reformist line helped to increase the party's prestige among the population and brought in many new members. For the first time, Croatia's communist leadership felt itself to be at one with the population. At the same time, the membership of Matica Hrvatska, Croatia's oldest cultural institution, which had been accused by Žanko of acting as an alternative political party, also increased its support. A weekly, *Hrvatski Tjednik*, launched by Matica Hrvatska in March 1971, achieved instant popularity and a large circulation far outstripping that of the "official" weeklies. In April 1971, Matica Hrvatska renounced the so-called Novi Sad Agreement of 1954, which had proclaimed Serbo-Croatian (or Croato-Serb) to be one language with two scripts (Latin and Cyrillic) and two "variants" (*ijekavski* and *ekavski*), on the ground that the agreement had been signed by the Croats under strong political pressure by the party. The Novi Sad agreement had already been repudiated earlier in the year by writers in Bosnia and Montenegro.

The mood of optimism and self-confidence in Croatia seemed to be justified. In April 1970, the Yugoslav party presidium passed a resolution officially recognizing the principle of the sovereignty of the individual republics of the Yugoslav federation. The Yugoslav state was defined as "an institutionalized agreement and cooperation among the republics." The federal authorities in Belgrade were to be restricted to looking after foreign affairs, defense and mechanisms needed for the operation of the single market for the whole of Yugoslavia. Both the federal authorities and the Yugoslav army were enjoined to pay due heed to the so-called "ethnic key" (fair representation for all nations and minorities). In September 1970, Tito announced that a collective state presidency consisting of an equal number of representatives from the republics and provinces would be set up with a view to succeeding him (he was then 78). On June 30, 1971, the Federal Assembly in Belgrade adopted a series of constitutional amendments, the net effect of which was to transform Yugoslavia into a very loose federation. The federal government in Belgrade retained the responsibility for defense, foreign affairs and broad economic policy. But no major investment projects could be started without the agreement of the republics, which retained the right of veto over decisions contrary to their interests. Various mechanisms were set up for the harmonization of different interests. There were also procedures for resolving disputes. Yugoslavia's new collective presidency, with Tito at its head, was elected on July 1971. Apart from Tito, it had three representatives from each of the republics (Bosnia had insisted on three so that the three main groups—Muslims, Serbs and Croats could each be represented) and two for each of the two autonomous provinces, Vojvodina and Kosovo.

THE HIGH POINT OF LIBERALISM

This movement toward a semi-confederated Yugoslavia was welcomed by Croats and most other non-Serbs in Yugoslavia. Among the Serbs, the prospect of greater independence for the republics was viewed with fear and mistrust. Many speakers at a three-day debate about the 1971 constitutional amendments at Belgrade University's law faculty described the amendments as "the beginning of the end of Yugoslavia." Others professed to be worried about their fellow-Serbs in Bosnia and Croatia. There were also misgivings in Yugoslavia's (predominantly Serbian) officer corps. An opinion poll in the spring of 1971 revealed that the majority of officers thought "chauvinism" and "separatism" greater threats than those from an external enemy. Yugoslav army chiefs had been angered and upset by demands voiced in Croatia and Slovenia for changes in the practice since 1945 of having the Serbian "variant" as the only language of command in all units.

Tito kept his own counsel. Outwardly he gave his backing to the new constitutional changes and to the general reformist thrust of party policy.

He even visited Croatia in September 1971 and publicly praised its leaders as "being on the right path." He said that he had seen no sign of "nationalist deviation" in Croatia. But less than three months later, he struck. Interestingly, this was shortly after his meeting with Dušan Dragosavac, a Serbian hard-line leader from Croatia, and a number of generals. At a special session with the Croatian leadership at the end of November, Tito attacked Tripalo and his colleagues for pandering to nationalists and separatists and displaying "rotten liberalism" in the face of a creeping counterrevolution.

TURNING AWAY FROM LIBERALISM

Tito's meeting with the Croatian leadership at the end of November 1971 marked the beginning of a new, illiberal phase that was to last till his death in 1980. In the wake of their meeting with Tito, Tripalo, Mrs. Dabčević-Kučar and some 400 Croatian party officials resigned. Several dozen intellectuals associated with Matica Hrvatska were arrested and sentenced to terms of imprisonment, including people like Gen. Franjo Tudjman, a wartime commander and later party historian, accused of "counterrevolution." Thousands of party members were expelled in Croatia, often also losing their jobs. In 1972, all 40,000 copies of a new Croatian orthography handbook were burned as a "nationalist act of sabotage."

The purge did not stop in Croatia. Tito wanted a clean sweep of all the "rotten liberals" in other republics, even those who did not necessarily agree with the Croats. His intentions became quite clear when, after the sacking of the Croat leaders, he repeatedly accused the sixth party congress in 1952—which had marked the start of the era of political and economic liberalization—of being the source of many of the present evils, the time when the rot set in. In due course, a number of senior figures associated with the liberal era were purged: Krste Crvenkovski, vice president of Yugoslavia, from Macedonia, accused of being too close a friend of Tripalo; Stane Kavčič, Slovenia's prime minister, condemned as a proponent of "people's capitalism"—the idea that enterprises should, under controlled conditions, sell shares to private individuals (Kavčič was also accused of forming close links with the neighboring Western states); and, last but not least, Marko Nikezić, the respected party president in Serbia and former foreign minister. He was removed at Tito's direct insistence in October 1972, again for "liberalism," together with the party secretary in Serbia, Latinka Perović, and a number of senior party figures. Koča Popović, prewar surrealist poet, famous wartime top commander, postwar foreign minister and holder of many other posts, resigned from the collective state presidency of Yugoslavia. But, unlike Croatia, there were no arrests and trials in Serbia.

Tito embarked on a new course with the assistance of Edvard Kardelj, his longtime chief ideologist and effective number two, and Stane Dolanc (another Slovene), the new executive secretary whose career had mainly been in army counterintelligence. Tito's new course was outlined in a letter he sent jointly with Dolanc to all party organizations throughout the country in September 1972, a month before the purge of the Serbian leadership. The letter denounced "etatism," "unitarism," "technocracy," "nationalism," "pseudoliberalism" and "leftism," and made a strong appeal for a "class" approach to all political and economic questions. The party was called upon to ensure that in future "only true communists held positions of responsibility in public life." The letter reflected Tito's (and many other party members') disillusionment with the results of the 1965 reforms in the economic field and with the post-1966 liberalization. In the 1965–68 period there had been rapid inflation, a serious recession and a rapid rise in unemployment. Liberalization had produced liberalism, nationalism and other threats to the party's dominant position.

THE PRESENT CONSTITUTION

Tito's and Kardelj's answer was the new 1974 constitution and the subsequent legislation, notably the Associated Labor Law (*Zakon o Udruženom Radu*) of 1976. The new constitution had three main aims. The first was to break down the larger enterprises into smaller units in order that—so it was said—the workers could exercise more direct control over management and the most important policy decisions. These "basic organizations of associated labor" (*osnovne organizacije udruženog rada*) were to be the controllers of a large part of the political system, the banks and the social services. By implication, local party bodies would find these easier to control. The second aim of the constitution was to eliminate direct elections and thus the possibility of a return to Western-style democracy via contested elections. Under the new system, every stage of the electoral process was to be under strict party supervision, with the possibility of reversing unacceptable decisions at an early stage. The third aim was to solve the old problem of combining (or rather, reconciling) a market economy with central political control via a system of "voluntary social planning."

The 1974 constitution abolished direct elections of members of legislative bodies and replaced them with a system of indirect elections by delegates. Delegates to communes elect delegates to republican and federal assemblies. The electorate consists of workers, citizens and members of political organizations (the party, the Socialist Alliance, trade unions, and so on). Workers elect their delegations in their "basic organizations of associated labor"; citizens elect delegations in local communities; members of political organizations, however, do not elect delegations: their delegates for appropriate assemblies are appointed by their governing bodies. Nomination lists are prepared by the trade unions and the Socialist Alliance after a formal opportunity has been provided for the electors to put forward nominations. Armed forces also elect delegations. Delegations from basic organizations elect delegates to the Chamber of Associated Labor; delegations from local communities elect delegates to the Chamber of Local Communities. Political and social organizations appoint delegates to a third chamber—the Sociopolitical Chamber.

Assemblies of the republics and provinces are elected from below as follows: the Chamber of Associated Labor by members of the corresponding commune chambers from a list drawn up by the Socialist Alliance; the Chamber of Communes by delegates of lower communal or city assemblies;

the Sociopolitical Chamber by the delegates of the corresponding commune chambers.

The Federal Assembly has two chambers. Each is composed of equal quotas from each republic and smaller quotas from the provinces. The 220-strong Federal Chamber consists of 30 delegates from each republic and 20 from each province. They are selected from basic delegations nominated by the Socialist Alliance and voted on by the assemblies of communes in each republic (or province). The 88-strong Chamber of Republics and Provinces consists of 12 delegates from each republic and eight from each province. They are elected by joint sessions of the three chambers in each republic or province from among their own members. Members of this chamber continue to sit also in their republic and provincial assemblies.

The Federal Executive Council (federal government) is elected by the Federal Assembly for four years on the nomination of the Socialist Alliance. Its president, the prime minister, can serve only one term of four years; the ministers for only two terms. The federal ministry is appointed on the basis of a combined republican (provincial) and ethnic quota. The presidency of Yugoslavia consists of one member from each republic and province plus the current president of the League of Communists (party) sitting ex officio.

The collective presidency's members are elected by their assemblies for five years and they elect their own president and vice president each year. The presidency has formal duties but also important real powers such as ordering mobilization, declaring war, passing decrees with the force of law in an emergency and taking, if necessary, extraconstitutional measures. The presidency can summon a meeting of the federal government, place an item on its agenda and hold up the enforcement of a government decision while it is referred to one of the legislative bodies. The republics and provinces have their own presidencies and governments.

The federal government looks after foreign affairs, defense, criminal law, foreign economic relations, the preservation of the self-management system, general economic plans and policies, and state security. Republic and provincial government have considerable powers, particularly in the economic sphere, as have the communes. The Chamber of Republics and Provinces of the Federal Assembly has the exclusive power to decide all major economic questions. All proposals on those questions are voted on in the Chamber by the delegations of the republics and provinces acting on instructions from their own assemblies. Normally, no proposal is carried unless it is by a unanimous vote, but the Chamber may pass "temporary measures" by a two-thirds majority. Such measures are proposed by the presidency of Yugoslavia and are valid for one year.

Central planning in the sense in which it is understood in the Soviet Union and most other Eastern European countries was long ago abolished in Yugoslavia. In both the "social" and private sectors, the market is regarded as the main instrument of coordination of Yugoslav enterprises. But it is supplemented by "self-management agreements" between various units of the social sector, and by "social compacts" that involve at least one government authority and are designed to set norms of behavior (but without the force of law). Government interventions occur frequently and affect the allocation of finance, foreign currency, imports (and, generally, goods in short supply), prices, rents and the rate of interest. Then there is a "social plan," supposed to provide a framework within which the market, the agreements, the social compacts and government policy operate.

The workers have little or no influence on the management of a Yugoslav enterprise. The system gives them a chance to raise issues that directly concern them: pay, working conditions, promotion, holidays, accommodation and so on. Two groups vie with each other for power: the party and the managers. In the 1950s the party, having opted for self-management and a market economy, was obliged to surrender some of its powers to the managers. This transfer of power accelerated after the 1965 reform. But when the party looked as if it was losing too much power, it struck back in 1971–72. The purpose of the 1971–72 crackdown, and eventually the 1974 constitution, was to reestablish the predominance of the party over the managers by breaking up enterprises into smaller, more easily controllable units. It did so in two ways: by its control over the informal party group in the enterprise— the *aktiv*, and by its control over the banks on which Yugoslav enterprises are totally dependent for credit because of their lack of independent finance. (The trade unions have no independent or influential role but act as the party's instrument.)

The advantages of self-management are that it provides a political justification for a market economy (without it, there would be more calls for a return to more full-blooded socialism) and gives the workers a chance to raise issues about which they feel strongly. They can even sack a manager they dislike. On the negative side, self-management is time-consuming and leads to lower discipline and enormous increases in paperwork and bureaucracy.

In the political field, the adoption since 1974 of the system of delegations in all elections has reduced even the limited degree of electoral choice that had existed in the late 1960s and has strengthened party control over delegates in the assemblies. The 1974 constitution helped to strengthen the party's influence in two other ways: first, by the creation of separate "sociopolitical" chambers in communal and republican assemblies composed of delegates chosen by the party and party-controlled organizations; and second, by decreeing that delegates to assemblies no longer give up their normal occupations. In general, despite the fact that a million or more delegates are elected every four years, power remains concentrated in the hands of a relatively small number of people, as Yugoslav social scientists themselves admit. All of the power-holders are members of the about 2 million-strong party.

The two checks on the ruling party—or rather, its leadership—are: the federalization of the party itself, which means that republican and provincial parties quite often express different points of view, especially on matters of local importance; and the fact that Yugoslav enterprises are not centrally planned but "self-managed," however limited their real independence may be.

In response to growing public demand, particularly among the intelligentsia, for a greater degree of genuine pluralism in politics and culture, Edvard Kardelj formulated a theory of "pluralism of self-managing interests" in 1977.

He admitted that legitimate clashes of interest could occur even under socialism and that they had to find an expression and be represented. But he explicitly rejected the idea of a multiparty system for Yugoslavia just as he rejected calls for a return to stricter socialist discipline, the policy of the "firm hand."

The most public challenge from the intelligentsia since the fall of Ranković in 1966 occurred when a group of ex-party members (mainly Montenegrin and Serbian) was arrested in Montenegro and Serbia in the late summer of 1974. It was revealed in September that the alleged leader of the group, Komnen Jovović, had got in touch with pro-Soviet (Cominformist) Yugoslav exiles during a trip to the Soviet Union in 1973. His group held a secret party "congress" in Montenegro in April 1974, at which a new party program was adopted. At several subsequent trials, a number of these alleged Cominformists were sentenced to varying terms of imprisonment. Mileta Perović, a former Yugoslav army colonel, who had defected to the Soviet Union after 1948, but later came to live in the West, was subsequently kidnapped by Yugoslav agents, brought to Yugoslavia and sentenced to 20 years imprisonment. He was alleged to have been chosen as the new party's leader. A similar fate befell Vlado Dapčević, also a pro-Cominform defector who was kidnapped while on a visit to Romania from Belgium. These trials probably nipped in the bud a potential pro-Soviet challenge. The Soviet Union distanced itself from these Cominformists. Despite occasional political and ideological skirmishes, Moscow did not attempt internal subversion during Tito's lifetime.

THE POST-TITO ERA

President Tito died on May 4, 1980, just a few days before his 88th birthday and after 35 years of power. The transition to the post-Tito era was impressively smooth. The collective leadership he had set up during his lifetime took over from him without any upheavals. Yugoslavia did not disintegrate or return to the Soviet bloc. Tito's successors declared their loyalty to all the main tenets of Titoism: self-management, economic decentralization and, in foreign policy, nonalignment between East and West. Yet within less than a year, the country was in the grip of a serious crisis affecting the leadership, the economy and the nationalities.

The leadership problem arose less out of the admittedly cumbersome system of regular rotation within the collective leadership than the purges in the 1970s, the last decade of Tito's life—notably in Croatia and Serbia. These had deprived Yugoslavia of modern-minded leaders with an assured following in their republics. Mediocre people put in their place by Tito after the 1971–72 purges lacked any wide base of support. The system of rotation of all senior offices was politically unpopular and was widely seen as a political game of musical chairs. Among his successors, differences over ideological matters have deepened since Tito's death.

This post-Tito leadership, disunited and lacking Tito's authority, is facing an economy that is out of control. The great borrowing spree of the 1970s has landed Yugoslavia with a huge debt of around $20 billion. Borrowing made sense for factories and other institutions at a time of high inflation and negative interest rates, but from the country's point of view it proved to be a disaster. Yugoslavia's borrowing amounted to 1.7 percent of the gross material product in the 1971–75 period and 3.5 percent in the 1976–80 period (in 1979 it reached the six percent level). Meanwhile, the trade deficit, which was 7.6 percent of the gross domestic product in the 1971–75 period, rose to 8.3 percent in the 1976–80 period. (In 1979 it climbed to 10.2 percent.)

The country faced bankruptcy, which was staved off with the aid of the International Monetary Fund (IMF) and sympathetic Western governments anxious to prevent Yugoslavia's collapse and possible slide into political unrest that could endanger its stability and ultimately its independence from the Soviet Union. The austerity measures imposed by the need to control and, finally, reduce and eliminate the debt, led to a drastic drop in living standards in the first half of the 1980s. Yugoslavia had to live with high unemployment (14 percent—and particularly high among the young) and rampant inflation (around 60 percent in 1984 and rising, despite occasional price freezes). Some of the problems were recognized as having been caused by external circumstances, notably the world recession. But the part played in the economic crisis by the deficiencies of the Yugoslav system itself has increasingly become the focus of debate, both within the political establishment and outside it. How to change the system—and how far to go in so doing—has been the major topic of debate ever since the high-powered Kraigher Commission's economic reform proposals in 1981–82 failed to get off the ground—despite their formal acceptance at the 1982 party congress.

The nationality problems, the chief headache of Yugoslavia's prewar royalist regime, have emerged as the most difficult challenge facing Tito's successors. Less than a year after Tito's death—in March and April 1981—there occurred something akin to a widespread insurrection in Kosovo. Small-scale student demonstrations in Priština, the province's capital, turned into a major confrontation between the province's Albanian majority and massive security forces brought in from all parts of Yugoslavia. The clash was over the popular demand for the upgrading of the province—still a part of Serbia—to the status of a full republic of the Yugoslav federation, on a par with Slovenia, Croatia and Serbia itself. This demand provoked a powerful counterreaction in Serbia and among Serbs elsewhere. Kosovo's remaining Serbian population (13.2 percent in 1981, compared with 18.3 percent in 1971) continues to emigrate from the province at a steady rate—for ordinary reasons of economic betterment, according to the Albanian interpretation; under threats and intimidation, according to the Serbian one. This Serbian exodus from Kosovo has particularly inflamed Serbian opinion. Measures to reassure Serbs, such as the appointment for the first time since Ranković's days of a Serb as party chief in Kosovo, have failed in their effect. But the effect on Albanian opinion in Kosovo has been to alienate it even further from Yugoslavia. The same is true of attempts to bring back Serbs who have emigrated from Kosovo; and of continuing trials for alleged "irredentism" of (mostly young) Kosovo Albanians (more than 1,000 were sentenced in the 1981–84 period). If anything, the demand for Kosovo to become a republic has become even more vociferous. It is argued on the ground of natural justice: Yugoslavia's ethnic Albanians (7.7 percent of the total population of the federation in the 1981 census) have no republic, while the smaller populations of Montenegrins (2.6 percent) and Macedonians (six percent) and the near-equal Slovenes (7.8 percent) have had one from the start. The proposition that Kosovo Albanians would, if given a republic, secede from Yugoslavia is met with the riposte that a Kosovo republic would have no cause to secede. The Serbian backlash provoked by the Kosovo crisis has expressed itself in two ways: demands for a reintegration into Serbia of the two provinces, Kosovo and Vojvodina (now de facto republics), and for a tightening of Yugoslavia's federal center at the expense of the powers of the republics. The first demand has provoked strong opposition, not just from Kosovo Albanians but also from the (predominantly Serbian) leadership in ethnically mixed Vojvodina. There has also been a strong reaction in favor of the broad constitutional status quo in other parts of Yugoslavia where there is also evidence of nationalist ferment—in Croatia, Bosnia, even Slovenia. The emerging confrontation between (largely Serbian) "neo-centralists" and the (predominantly non-Serbian) defenders of the status quo is probably the most serious development of the post-Tito era—probably far more dangerous than the purely political and ideological divisions in the party. The renewed national tensions are exacerbated by the country's present economic predicament. The peoples of Yugoslavia no longer have, as they had under Tito, the feeling of standing on an up escalator, with ever more development and prosperity within reach. Instead, there is a feeling of a movement back to the postwar conditions of scarcity. Inevitably, in this climate of austerity the apportionment of burdens becomes a subject of national rivalries.

Fortunately for Tito's successors, the self-management system has continued to act as a safety valve and a shock absorber at the same time. Strikes that do occur usually do not last long. Explosion is usually averted. Here fragmentation within the system has certainly come to the aid of the rulers. A Polish-style confrontation between the regime and the alienated population is less easy to envisage. How long the Yugoslav population's tolerance will last is a question the leaders themselves keep asking. The answer is that nobody can tell and that trouble could still come from unforeseen directions.

Another help to the post-Tito leadership is, undoubtedly, the absence of a credible opposition alternative. In a nationally divided state, the emergence of such an alternative is extremely difficult—though of course national divisions also affect the leadership. Yugoslavia has many dissidents but no coherent opposition. The critics attack the regime from different standpoints and are, not infrequently, more at loggerheads with each other than with the regime itself. Within the party itself a "liberal" group, of sorts, exists but its problem is that a really radical liberalization policy could endanger the party's monopoly of power. That is why such a policy is not easy to advocate from within the party. But the hard-liners too have a problem. Memories of the Ranković era are still fresh, particularly in Bosnia, Croatia and Kosovo. In Slovenia, too, probably the most liberal part of Yugoslavia, any attempt to bring back the policy of the "firm hand" (through an army coup) would be fiercely resisted. The deadlock between the liberals and the hard-liners gives the Yugoslav system another chance to renew itself. Whether or not it takes up that chance will probably depend on the outcome of the battle for economic and financial stabilization and the willingness of Yugoslavia's Western creditors to underpin the Titoist experiment they first backed in the 1950s. That experiment may survive and still provide new surprises. But the famous Yugoslav model, once so eagerly studied by would-be reformers in other communist countries, is now seen as something of a warning, even a failure. Characteristically, the Hungarians, the Chinese and other communist reformers look elsewhere for their inspiration. To that extent, Titoism has not survived Tito.

FURTHER READING

Auty, Phyllis. *Tito: A Biography*. Rev. ed. Harmondsworth: Penguin, 1974.

Bićanić, Rudolf. *Economic Policy in Socialist Yugoslavia*. Cambridge: Cambridge University Press, 1973.

Clissold, Stephen. *Yugoslavia and the Soviet Union: A Documentary Survey*. London: Oxford University Press for the Royal Institute of International Affairs, 1975.

Dedijer, Vladimir. *Tito Speaks*. London: Weidenfeld & Nicolson, 1953.

Djilas Milovan. *Conversations with Stalin*. London: Rupert Hart-Davis, 1962.

———. *Tito: The Story from Inside*. London; Weidenfeld & Nicolson, 1981.

———. *The Unperfect Society: Beyond the New Class*. London: Methuen, 1969.

Gruenwald, Oskar. *The Yugoslav Search for Man: Marxist Humanism in Contemporary Yugoslavia*. South Hadley, Massachusetts: J. F. Bergin, 1983.

Kardelj, Edvard. *Reminiscences: The Struggle for Recognition and Independence: The New Yugoslavia, 1944–57*. London: Blond & Briggs, 1982.

Lydall, Harold. *Yugoslav Socialism: Theory and Practice*. Oxford: Clarendon Press, 1984.

Maclean, Fitzroy. *Disputed Barricade*. London: Cape, 1957.

Pavlowitch, Stevan K. *Yugoslavia*. London: Ernest Benn, 1971.

———, and Biberaj, Elez. *The Albanian Problem in Yugoslavia: Two Views*. Conflict Study No. 137/138. London: Institute for the Study of Conflict, 1982.

Rusinow, Dennison. *The Yugoslav Experiment, 1948–74*. London: C. Hurst for the Royal Institute of International Affairs, 1977.

Singleton, Fred, and Carter, Bernard. *The Economy of Yugoslavia*. London and Canberra: Croom Helm, 1982.

Sirc, Ljubo. *The Yugoslav Economy under Self-Management*. London: Macmillan, 1979.

Tudjman, Franjo. *Nationalism in Contemporary Europe*. Boulder, Colorado: East European Monographs, 1981.

Wilson, Duncan. *Tito's Yugoslavia*. Cambridge: Cambridge University Press, 1979.

ROMANIAN FOREIGN POLICY
UNDER DEJ AND CEAUŞESCU

MICHAEL SHAFIR

HISTORIANS and political scientists alike are supposed to remember that the owl of Minerva spreads its wings only with the falling of dusk. Yet all too often, twilight is mistaken for a state of perfect knowledge, and instead of reading the present with an eye on the past, we readily give in to the temptation of interpreting the latter in terms of the former. Such self-beguilement, usually carrying the elegant label of "continuity," is better designated as "the telescoping of history." In monopolistic regimes, where historiography and the study of politics play a major role in the process of directed socialization, the telescoping of history results in constant reinterpretations of the past. In pluralist societies, social scientists do not have to succumb to the pressures of the powers that be. These scholars do not telescope history because they have to reinterpret. They merely misinterpret.

This proposition is perfectly illustrated by some contemporary analyses of Romanian foreign policy, which attributed to the former leader of the Romanian Communist party (RCP), Gheorghe Gheorghiu-Dej, "nationalist," "home communist" and similarly designated postures from as early as the beginning of the 1950s. Building on the incontestable division that existed in the party leadership between those communists who had spent the war years in the Soviet Union, returning to Romania on the tail of the Red Army, and the faction that had remained in the country during the war, the partisans of this approach attributed to the Dejist group anti-Soviet attitudes from its cradle. However, the equation of "home communism" and "anti-Sovietism" is by no means warranted. Not only does it rest on telescoped historical evidence, but it is also guilty of disregarding the fact that continuity and change are in most cases intertwined processes.

Dej was a convinced Stalinist and a faithful and obedient pupil of the Kremlin till well into the late 1950s. The turning point in Romanian foreign policy (as well as in derivative strategies pursued on the home front) originated in what Khrushchev saw as the appropriate division of labor within the Council for Mutual Economic Assistance (CMEA). The scheme would have turned Romania into a main supplier of agricultural products to the industrially advanced members of the community.[1] Dej was thus faced with the dilemma of having to opt for either the Soviet Union or the Soviet model. Paradoxically enough, it was to a large extent his total endorsement of the Leninist-Stalinist values of industrialization that generated Bucharest's autonomous foreign policies. The process was gradual and by no means unilinear,[2] for change is seldom the outcome of a one-time decision.

By the end of the 1950s, there were already signs of an unmistakable reorientation in foreign trade, with the total Soviet share reduced from 51.5 percent in 1958 to 47.3 percent in 1959 and 40.1 percent in the following year.[3] This shift was the outcome of Moscow's unwillingness to support the further expansion of Romania's modernization programs. In the face of Khrushchev's attitude, the RCP leadership turned to its own society in search for domestic support, to the world at large in quest for political assistance and to the West in particular for credits.

In so far as the regime's internal policies are concerned, their backbone consisted (and still consists) of a strategy of "simulated change," which encourages alleged grassroot participation in the political process, combining it with genuine encouragement of nationalism as a way of deflecting dissent, while at the same time avoiding the slightest infringement on the leading role of the RCP. In the arena of international politics, Romania's strategies are best defined in an analogous fashion, i.e., as displaying a "simulated presence" in the camp led by the Soviet Union. Constrained by the Soviet "bear," the Romanian "fox" simulates lodgment in Moscow's organizational (Warsaw Treaty, CMEA) forest. Yet at the same time, it cultivates such ties as would render the permanency of the allegiance minimal. Ronald H. Linden's metaphor (*Bears and Foxes: The International Relations of the East European States*, 1979) thus provides an interpretative background helping to explain the strategy of "simulated permanency."

These strategies can also be viewed as a case of partial alignment. For a policy of partial alignment to succeed, it is necessary for the less powerful state to avoid creating a situation where the leading member of the system would be faced with no other alternative but to terminate the partiality of the relationship. This is why declarations of intention to maintain membership in the alliance must be aired and emphasized by Romania even as it pursues policies conducive to loosening the bonds that tie it to the organizational structure dominated by the head of the alliance. The Romanians are known to advocate warmly (and genuinely) the dissolution of both the Warsaw Treaty Organization (WTO) and NATO. Since the beginning of their deviance they have taken measures such as ending WTO maneuvers on Romanian soil and restricting participation of their troops in military maneuvers elsewhere to symbolic dimensions; advocating reorganizational measures aimed at ending the domination of the WTO command structure

---

[1] K. Jowitt. *Revolutionary Breakthroughs and National Development: The Case of Romania, 1944–1965*. Berkeley and Los Angeles: University of California Press, 1971, pp. 174–228.
[2] *Ibid.*, pp. 198–232.
[3] M. Shafir. "The Socialist Republic of Romania," in B. Szajkowski, ed., *Marxist Governments: A World Survey*. London: Macmillan, 1981, pp. 603–05.

by the Soviet military; condemning the Pact's intervention in Czechoslovakia and adopting in its wake a new defense law and an "all-horizons" defense doctrine of "people's war"; refusing to increase defense expenditure despite Soviet insistence, etc. However, Bucharest has always been careful to pay due respect to its allegiance to the socialist camp. For example, in May 1967, Dej's successor at the helm of the RCP, Nicolae Ceauşescu, stressed that "whether the Warsaw Pact will exist or not, should imperialism unleash war, Romania, a socialist state, would fight alongside other socialist states."[4]

At first sight, the simulated change/simulated permanency might appear to contradict any linkage between internal and external policies. In reality, the opposite is the case. It is precisely because of the RCP's orthodox attachment to the principle of party domination of society that Moscow has condoned (albeit grudgingly) Romania's foreign policy postures. In other words, the RCP could achieve a certain degree of autonomy in the international arena because no doubts arose in the Kremlin about the Romanian leadership's determination to preempt and to contain autonomy internally. Simulated permanency thus signifies autonomous, *but not independent* postures.[5]

The basic aims of Romanian foreign policy were established in the famous 1964 statement of the party—quoted in the Romanian party daily, *Scînteia*, April 23, 1964—according to which every Marxist-Leninist party has "a sovereign right ... to elaborate, choose or change the forms and methods of socialist construction." This precludes the existence of a "parent" and a "son" party, or "superior" parties, or "subordinate" parties. The foremost objective of this policy has been, and remains, the counteraction of any possible attempt by Moscow to force Bucharest back into the fold. Motivated by this purpose, the Romanians entertain innumerable contacts and attempt to construct semialliances—with the international communist movement, the Third World and the Western world. China and Yugoslavia are Romania's foremost communist partners, while its most immediate opponents among the communist countries are the USSR and Hungary.

The Sino-Soviet split, which first came into the open at a congress of the Romanian party in 1960, was the essential precondition for Bucharest's successful challenge of Moscow. Unlike other Soviet allies in Eastern Europe, the Romanians initially adopted a position of strict neutrality, and in so far as appearances are concerned, this attitude is still maintained to date. When in June 1963, the Communist party of the Soviet Union (CPSU) and the Chinese Communist party (CCP) exchanged acrimonious letters, the *Scînteia* printed both epistles, thus hinting at negation of the Soviet right to "excommunicate" any member from the international movement. In 1964, a Romanian delegation visited Peking, ostensibly in a mediation effort. Such endeavors notwithstanding, Bucharest began to realize that a policy of autonomy would be best served by continued Soviet-Chinese differences, provided

[4] N. Ceauşescu. *România pe drumul desăvîrşirii construcţiei socialiste.* Bucharest: Editura politică, Vol. 2, p. 326.

[5] A. Braun. *Romania Foreign Policy Since 1965: The Political and Military Limits of Autonomy.* New York: Praeger, 1978, p. ix.

both countries remained acknowledged members of the socialist alliance.[6] Consequently, the RCP opposes any Soviet attempt to convene an international gathering of Communist parties with the purpose of ostracizing the Chinese or other "deviants." The Ussuri river incidents of 1969 gave Bucharest the opportunity to illustrate not only its strict neutrality in the conflict, but, to Moscow's obvious dismay, to insist on the strictly European and defensive character of the WTO. On the other hand, such neutral postures have not hindered the Romanians from employing, on several occasions, typical anti-Soviet Chinese jargon, such as denouncing hegemony.[7]

That Moscow views these developments with little sympathy is not surprising, even less so as Chinese support for the Romanian position is sometimes volunteered in formulas that are deliberately provocative. Shortly before the Romanians revived the issue of Bessarabia in 1964, for example, Mao spoke in one breath of Russian expansionism in the Far East and in Eastern Europe, mentioning Bessarabia (incorporated into the Soviet Union in 1940) as an illustration of the latter. More sensitive to the limitations of their autonomous postures, and uneasy about the timing chosen by the "Great Helmsman" to air these Romanian grievances, Bucharest chose to ignore the remarks, and they were never mentioned by the media. However, at times Romania itself underestimated the Soviet reaction to cultivation of its ties with the Chinese. Ceauşescu's 1971 visit to Peking, for example, coming as it did in the wake of evidence concerning the active role played by the Romanians in the Sino-American rapprochement, triggered a strong reaction in the Kremlin, the more so as this display of autonomy had been preceded by refusal to allow passage of Soviet troops through Romanian territory on their way to Bulgaria. In a thinly veiled hint of intimidation, WTO maneuvers were conducted close to Romania's borders, in the southern part of the Soviet Union. The implicit threat was clear enough to persuade Ceauşescu to make an unscheduled stop in Moscow on his return journey in an obvious effort to soothe the Soviet leadership.[8]

This incident was symptomatic of the nature of the Chinese-Romanian relationship. "Distant waters," as Zhou Enlai put it, as quoted in the Yugoslav publication *Vjesnik* in August that year, "cannot quench local fires." The lesson was certainly not lost on the Romanians, who already in 1968 had witnessed China's limited value for their own defense in the (unlikely) event of Soviet intervention against Romania.

Yet awareness of the limitations of a semialliance must not necessarily lead to its discontinuation. Both sides may find that, while restricted in scope, collaboration may still render mutual benefits. Bucharest, for example, is reported[9] to have extended its "good services" in an attempt to mediate between China and Vietnam, and Romania is China's most important trading partner in CMEA. For their part, the Romanians purchased in China not

[6] R. R. King. "Romania and the Sino-Soviet Conflict," *Studies in Comparative Communism*, No. 4, 1972, p. 376.
[7] Cf. M. Shafir. *Romania: Politics, Economics and Society. Political Stagnation and Simulated Change*. London: Frances Pinter, 1985, Chap. 10.
[8] Braun, *op. cit.*, pp. 133–34.
[9] *The Far Eastern Economic Review*, March 17, 1983.

only urgently needed petroleum and other raw materials (see below), but also naval military equipment.[10] The two sides exchange visits at the highest level of state and party leadership, and there are frequent exchanges of military delegations, the value of which rests in emphasizing their determination to pursue their respective separate, but occasionally intersecting, roads.

The development of the close Yugoslav-Romanian relationship has been determined by similar considerations. Belgrade's long experience of success-ful confrontation with Moscow, as well as Yugoslav prestige in the Third World, made Tito Romania's natural ally once the rift with Moscow had reached the point of no return. Initially, Dej's all too recent conformist past proved somewhat of an impediment. Following Ceauşescu's advent to power in March 1965, however, the relationship intensified considerably. In April 1966, Tito came to Romania in what subsequently proved to be the first in a series of regular annual encounters. Tito's heirs show no signs of disavowing these by now traditional consultations on coordination of policies and development of economic and technical cooperation.

The most impressive sign of economic cooperation between the two states are two projects on the Danube, designed to provide a source of electric power and to improve rail and water communication. More importantly, perhaps, on the military side the Romanians have clearly modeled their doc-trine of "all-people's war" on the Yugoslav blueprint, which is not surprising in view of the fact that Belgrade is likely to be Bucharest's only partner in an attempt to resist eventual Soviet intervention. Furthermore, the two countries have collaborated in the construction of a twin-jet fighter equipped with Rolls-Royce engines, the first non-Soviet aircraft to be introduced in a Warsaw Pact country.[11] This does not signify, on the other hand, that Belgrade and Bucharest view every issue from an identical perspective. In 1967, the Yugoslavs chose to follow the Soviet example and break off relations with Israel, whereas the Romanians refused to do so. In the more recent past, the post-Tito leadership appears to resent Ceauşescu's all too obvious efforts to cast himself as Tito's successor in the nonaligned movements, efforts that were ill-timed and undiplomatically exhibited at the Yugoslav leader's funeral.[12]

Out of similar considerations, the RCP pursued within the international communist movement a policy of support of the Eurocommunist parties. On the other hand, such support was carefully qualified to indicate that although generating from the principles of noninterference in other parties' affairs, it did not signify to any extent that the RCP intended to adopt Italian or Spanish stances vis-à-vis Romanian society.[13] This partially explains why, despite official support of Eurocommunism, or rather *because* of it,

[10] R. H. Linden. "Romania's Foreign Policy in the 1980s," in D. N. Nelson, ed., *Romania in the 1980s*. Boulder, Colorado: Westview Press, 1981, p. 252.
[11] A. Alexeiev. "Romania and the Warsaw Pact: The Defence Policy of a Reluctant Ally," *Strategic Studies*, No. 1, 1981, p. 10.
[12] A. Braun. "Romania's Travails," *Problems of Communism*, No. 3, 1982, p. 55.
[13] R. L. Tőkés. "Eastern Europe in the 1970s: Détente, Dissent and Eurocommu-nism," in R. L. Tőkés, ed., *Eurocommunism and Détente*. New York: New York University Press, 1978, p. 489.

the doctrine enjoys little support among Romanian dissidents, in contrast to countries where it is castigated, such as Czechoslovakia or East Germany.[14]

Since 1968, the leitmotiv of Romania's relations with the Soviet Union has been the explicit rejection of the "Brezhnev Doctrine," which was accompanied by implicit measures designed to render credibility to the Romanian determination to resist an eventual Soviet intervention. In the 1970s and the 1980s, Bucharest used every possible internal or foreign channel of communication in order to convey its unambiguous message concerning determination to entrench its autonomous postures. The new treaty of friendship and mutual aid, signed by the Soviet Union and Romania in July 1970, clearly reflects these positions. Unlike similar documents signed by Moscow with other members of the WTO, the treaty makes no mention of the obligation of the socialist community to come to the rescue of socialist achievements.[15] On foreign policy issues, there is mere mention of the two sides' agreement to consult. These consultations, however, only seldom proved fruitful from Moscow's vantage point. A visit paid by Foreign Minister Andrei Gromyko to Bucharest in January–February 1984, with the purpose of bringing the Romanians closer to bloc positions on issues such as the counterdeployment of SS-20 missiles in Europe, ended in apparent failure.

Criticism of the Soviet attitude vis-à-vis their allies can often be encountered in the Romanian press and, what is at least as important, in reports destined for foreign consumption. Shortly after the release of a declaration of the Political Consultative Council of the WTO concerning, among other things, the "new type of relations between socialist countries," the official daily *România liberă* published an article (on January 10, 1983) dealing with this subject. The author complained that although the right of nations to build socialism the way they choose was paid lip service by some (unmentioned) Communist parties, in reality some countries assumed "the right to claim that one's own socialism [is superior] to that built in other countries." The insinuation came not long after the new Soviet party leader, Yuri Andropov, had stated (in *Pravda*, on April 23, 1982) that "the basic principles of the socialist system ... its class nature and its essence are the same for all countries and for all peoples." The official news agency Agerpres disseminated the Romanian article extensively, thereby making sure that it came to Western knowledge.

Ceauşescu and Andropov were not on very close terms, the more so as the Romanian leader feared Andropov's alleged pro-Hungarian sympathies. Andropov's succession by Chernenko did not bring a significant improvement in relations with the Soviet Union. Disregarding the temporal nature of the succession itself, the former first secretary of the Moldavian SSR did not view with benevolent eyes the continued, if somewhat diluted, Romanian hints at the historical injustice of the Bessarabian questions. These allusions were first openly aired in 1964, when Bucharest enlisted the aid of Karl

[14] R. Wesson. "Eurocommunism and Eastern Europe," in M. M. Drachkovitch, ed., *East Central Europe: Yesterday–Today–Tomorrow*. Stanford, California: The Hoover Institution, 1982, p. 72.

[15] Braun. *Romanian Foreign Policy since 1965*, p. 92.

Marx and his anti-Russian manuscripts, published as *Notes on the Romanians*. Although in 1976, in an attempt to appease the Soviets, Ceauşescu paid an official visit to Soviet Moldavia, Romanian books and articles continue to deal with the topic in a manner likely to cause alarm in Kishinev and Moscow. Moreover, Chernenko's position on the issue of party equality was hardly different from that of his predecessors. History, according to Chernenko in a comment reported by Tass (January 4, 1983), "has demonstrated that there is not, nor can there be, any path of socialism in circumvention of the general laws discovered by Marxism-Leninism and confirmed by the experience of the USSR and other countries of existing socialism." Gorbachev is unlikely to diverge much from this classic statement of principle.

By promoting the class criterion as the unique determinant of interparty relations, the Soviets advance the view that real socialism is essentially similar everywhere and that conflicts among members of the socialist community are by definition nonantagonistic. The Romanians reject both the axiom and the implication. According to an article published in the RCP's ideological journal, *Era socialistă*, at the end of 1982, "the national state is far from being merely 'another name' for 'class'. ... It expresses a distinct reality, entrenched not only in class criteria." In other words, relations among the members of the socialist community being by no means the sole function of class criteria, the latter cannot be invoked in justifying interference in the internal affairs of a member of the community. "Contradictions in international life will develop ... in connection with differences, opposition and even antagonism specific to the problem of affirmation of values or of essential determinants of the nation and its state." Such antagonisms, the article went on, could be the outcome of a state's defense of "a true and multilateral independence and sovereignty," as well as of that entity's "economic and political development objectives and manifestation of its capability to adopt a certain [line in] internal and external politics." Socialist states, it transpired from these esoteric pronouncements, are national not only in form, but also in content—a tenet propagated by Bucharest as early as the 1960s. This is why "proletarian internationalism" is a term never employed by the Romanians, who would rather use "international solidarity"—a designation with implications extending to the Third World and occasionally cutting across East-West divisions.

In a similar, if not identical, manner, an article in the Bucharest weekly *Contemporanul* on March 5, 1982 insisted on the primacy of the national state criterion, adding that in the contemporary world the main contradictions were not those dividing capitalist from socialist states, but rather those between rich and poor countries. These contradictions stemmed from "the difference between the potential and the [actual] level of economic, technical and scientific development," rather than from differences in their social order. Consequently, similar contradictions could "arise in relations between socialist states"—a veiled allusion to Soviet refusal to foot the bill for Romania's economic development on terms of brotherly aid. These pronouncements undoubtedly aim at diminishing the effects of expected Soviet wrath by enlarging the circle of Romania's semialliances. In this particular case, one was witnessing an attempt to emphasize the common bonds that allegedly link Bucharest with the nations of the Third World (see below).

For their part, the Soviets often chose to respond to Romania's display of simulated permanency by using proxies, and it is not accidental that the most vociferous critics of Bucharest's attitude vis-à-vis proletarian internationalism have been the Hungarians, whose denunciations of narrow nationalism were by no means unconnected with the problem of Romanian mistreatment of the large Hungarian minority in Transylvania. After a speech delivered by Ceauşescu in May 1966, in which he castigated Soviet policies in the Comintern and raised the Bessarabian question,[16] Zoltán Komócsin, the chief ideologist of the Hungarian Socialist Workers' party (HSWP) and a member of its Politbureau, published in *Problems of Peace and Socialism* (No. 6, 1966) a strongly worded article in which the Romanian arguments in favor of party autonomy were rejected one by one. The incident was followed by a declaration by János Kádár himself, in the course of an interview with a UPI correspondent, in which he referred to the Trianon Treaty as an "imperialist diktat" that had "dismembered the territory of Hungary," and by a reference to the same treaty at the Ninth Congress of the HSWP in November 1966, in which the Hungarian leader employed similar terminology.

With Romania refusing to join in the chorus of WTO critics of the Prague Spring and later criticizing the invasion of Czechoslovakia, Hungarian-Romanian polemics were substantially intensified. Although Kádár could by no means be counted among the partisans of military intervention in Czechoslovakia, he openly criticized the Romanian position in a speech delivered before the National Assembly in April 1968. In an article published in *Pravda* two days later, Transylvanian-born István Szirmai, the head of the ideological section of the Hungarian Central Committee, warned against the danger of neglect of internationalist duties, prompted by the pursuit of selfish national interests. Neither Kádár nor Szirmai mentioned in any way the Hungarian minority in Romania, but on October 19 *Népszabadság* had the statement that "No people would sever its ties with its torn-away parts, which speak the same language and have an identical history and culture. ... We have an inalienable duty to preserve and cultivate these relations."

In March 1969, WTO maneuvers were conducted in Hungary,[17]shortly after the leadership of the RCP had undertaken the first measures designated to cope with invasion by Romania's allies. According to a law passed by the Grand National Assembly shortly before the intervention in Czechoslovakia, the Romanian parliament is the only body entitled to authorize the entry of foreign troops into the country. With the adoption of the Bill on the Organization of the National Defense in 1972,[18] Romania's defensive strategies became obviously geared *against* its partners in the WTO, the USSR in particular.[19]

[16] Ceauşescu, *op. cit.*, Vol. 1, pp. 352–61.
[17] See Braun, *Romanian Foreign Policy since 1965*, p. 130.
[18] *Ibid.*, pp. 150ff.
[19] I. Völgyés. *The Political Reliability of the Warsaw Pact Armies: The Southern Tier*. Durham, North Carolina: Duke University Press Policy Studies, 1982, pp. 16–17.

In June 1977, Ceauşescu and Kádár met on their common border and agreed to set up consulates in Cluj-Napoca and Debrecen, respectively. The Romanian side, however, was less than keen on implementing the agreement, suspecting attempts to establish links with the Hungarian minority and possibly to monitor its persecution. The two consulates were opened only in August 1980 and December 1981, respectively.

In the meantime, the doyen of Hungarian letters, the writer Gyula Illyés, published a two-part article in *Magyar Nemzet* calling attention to the plight of ethnic Hungarians living abroad. In a somewhat veiled manner, he accused the Romanians (whose name, however, was not specifically mentioned) of pursuing discrimination against the minorities. In a stiff reply (in *Luceafărul*, May 6, 1978), Mihnea Gheorghiu, the president of the Romanian Academy of Social and Political Sciences, accused Illyés of anti-Romanian obsessions and of having become a tool in the hands of the émigré fascist Hungarian circles.

Although the leadership of the HSWP, in contrast to that of the RCP, has been known to try to defuse the Transylvanian issue (except at times when Romanian-Soviet tensions can be exploited), the intensification of persecutions against the Hugarian minority during recent years[20] has produced mutual accusations verging on an open feud. In 1982, Ion Lăncrănjan, a Romanian writer of the Nationalist, neotraditionalist school, published a collection of essays entitled *Cuvînt despre Transilvania* (Discourse on Transylvania). Despite official claims concerning a shortage of paper, the volume was circulated in an edition of 50,000 copies. It was full of invective directed not only against what the author took for official Hungarian revisionist pronouncements (he "quoted" a distorted version of Kádár's declarations on the Trianon Treaty), but also at fellow writers of Hungarian origin. More importantly, however, a book written by the Romanian president's brother, party historian Ilie Ceauşescu, entitled *Transylvania: Ancient Romanian Land* and published in 1983, employs language that is almost as offensive toward the Hungarian minority as Lăncrănjan's. On two occasions in October 1982 and in March 1983, *Népszabadság* published satires and a cartoon of Ceauşescu, ridiculing his personality cult. When two Hungarian cultural high officials paid a visit to Bucharest in late 1982, *Scînteia*, which is usually very careful in retouching the photographs it prints, showed their faces in a grimace.

Negation of the right of one state to interfere in the affairs of another, alongside efforts aimed at evincing the common bonds that allegedly unite Bucharest and the Third World, determined Romania to adopt postures on Afghanistan different from those of the bloc. Subsequently, however, Romanian diplomacy demonstrated its awareness of the limitations of autonomy, proving that if and when the need arises, Bucharest knows it must make concessions on issues the priority of which is high in Moscow. Whether such malleability would have been displayed had the intervention occurred in Romania's immediate neighborhood, as in 1968, is, however, doubtful. Although Bucharest's delegation at the United Nations did not vote for

[20] See, e.g., Shafir, *Romania*, Chap. 9.

the nonaligned resolution demanding immediate withdrawal of foreign troops from Afghanistan in January 1980, neither did it join the rest of the camp in casting its vote against the invasion. Rather than provoke the displeasure of one side or the other, the delegation declared itself absent from the ballot. Romania's ambassador to the United Nations, Teodor Marinescu, declared that his country could not support the majority's resolution because this was likely to damage détente, but neither was it willing to condone interference in the internal affairs of a nonaligned state and the infringement of international law. Several months later, nevertheless, Soviet pressure must have persuaded the Romanian leadership to change its mind. On April 27, *Scînteia* published a message of congratulations addressed by Ceauşescu to Babrak Karmal on the occasion of the Afghan "revolution," and in May the Romanian president agreed to sign a declaration issued by a WTO summit, endorsing Moscow's position.

Such "deviance from the deviance" notwithstanding, Romanian courtship of the Third World remains intensive. With the Soviet Union unwilling to supply crude oil on the same favorable terms from which other CMEA partners benefit, and having developed a refining capacity well beyond its producing capabilities, Romania became an importer of oil from Third World countries starting in 1976. As a consequence, Bucharest began to devote increasing attention to developing trade with lesser developed countries (LDCs). These countries' share in Romanian foreign trade increased from a mere 8.2 percent in 1970 to 25.2 percent in 1980 and nearly 29 percent in 1981. The LDCs initially appeared as ideal trade partners, for their demand for quality products was less serious than the West's, and long-term agreements could provide a solution for Romanian needs of raw material imports.[21] In addition, it was hoped to use these countries as a means of avoiding Western technology export bans[22] and penetrating the Western European and North American markets via the back door.

The shrewdest step in the direction of intensifying contacts with the Third World was the official proclamation of the country as a socialist developing (rather than developed) state, at the National Party Conference in 1972. As Colin W. Lawson argues, no one believes Romania is as developed as most industrial market (or, for that matter, some planned) economies, but on the other hand there is little evidence that the country is an LDC in the normally accepted sense of the word. Official statistics supplied to the United Nations were subjected to manipulation in order to overemphasize the country's underdevelopment.[23] Contradictory as such initiatives may be in view of pronouncements concerning economic achievement under RCP leadership, they were motivated by endeavors to diversify trade and, above all, to enjoy the benefits extended to LDCs by the advanced countries and by U.N. agencies. Pursuing these aims, Romania joined the General Agreement on Tariffs and Trade (GATT) in 1971 and became the first CMEA country to gain International Monetary Fund (IMF) membership in 1972.

[21] R. R. King, "Romania and the Third World," *Orbis*, No. 4, 1978, p. 878.
[22] C. W. Lawson, "National Independence and Reciprocal Advantages: The Political Economy of Romanian-South Relations," *Soviet Studies*, No. 3, 1983, p. 364.
[23] *Ibid.*, pp. 369–70.

In 1976, Romania was admitted to the Group of 77. As a result of these steps, from 1974 onward Romania benefited from the developed countries' system of general preferences, the most important aspect of which was the agreement signed with the Common Market.

Courtship of the Third World also determined Bucharest to adopt postures favoring the establishment of a New International Economic Order (NIEO), much in contrast to the positions displayed by other CMEA members. The latter subscribe to the Soviet thesis, which declines any moral obligation to aid the LDCs and shifts the blame for the state of their economies onto Western shoulders alone. In a speech delivered at the Eleventh RCP Congress in November 1974, Ceauşescu dealt at length with the NIEO, intertwining it with the long-established Romanian principles of sovereignty, independence, equality and noninterference in internal affairs. This position may be suspected of attempting to serve purposes other than sheer support of the South. For example, Romania's refusal to distinguish between socialist and capitalist developed states in their duty to aid the LDCs appears to be strikingly consonant with the demand that CMEA industrialized countries extend intensive aid and advantageous terms to the community's less developed members, and that integration within COMECON is not feasible before all countries reach a similar level of development. The suggestion made by former Deputy Prime Minister Corneliu Burtică, at the U.N. Special Session on the NIEO, advocating "moratorium or postponement of payment without interest,"[24] is liable to suspicion of pursuing more than disinterested objectives, for by that time Romania's heavy borrowing in the West and failure to match investments with exports to developed markets had produced a huge deficit. By 1983, the country's foreign debt was estimated to be some U.S. $9.5 billion.

The decision to develop ties with the LDCs paid off until about 1975, when Bucharest was still registering a significant surplus in the balance of trade with the developing economies. According to official data, in the years 1971–75 commercial exchanges with the LDCs produced a favorable balance of 483 million rubles. For the period 1976–80, however, they rendered a deficit of 713 million rubles. It is true that the deficit was illustrative of the country's generally negative balance of foreign trade, which for the second half of the decade stood at 2,362 million rubles. However, it is not less obvious that the LDCs had ceased to be the profitable partner of the past. This was due to the 1978 explosion of prices on the international petroleum market which, unlike the 1973–74 rise in oil prices, was *not* accompanied by a parallel increase in the costs of oil products—in which Romanian exports specialized to a large extent. These developments were further intensified by the Iranian revolution and by the war in the Gulf. The economic rationale of Romania's courtship of the Third World, in short, proved quite mistaken. Instead of finding itself an exporter to the markets of the South, Bucharest ended up importing huge quantities of expensive petroleum. Moreover, the opportunities opened by recognition as a developing country were largely missed by economic mismanagement. What Romania has been left with is

[24] *Ibid.*, p. 368.

diplomatic pomp (apparently highly valued by the president in his attempts to establish himself as a statesman of international renown) and the questionably valuable diplomatic support of some Third World countries, which failed to satisfy expectations. In their quest to add to the web of semialliances, in April 1975 the Romanians requested the Yugoslavs to support their application for observer status at the nonaligned summit conference scheduled for Colombo in 1976. At their conference of August 1975, however, the nonaligned summit granted Romania only permanent guest status, and neither efforts at Colombo nor at New Delhi in 1983 met with further success.

At times, Bucharest's endeavors to defuse situations of potential friction, likely to generate renewed Soviet pressure for integration and coordination, have brought about Romanian attempts to play a mediation role in the international arena. Apart from the yet unconfirmed endeavor to serve as mediator between Vietnam and Kampuchea, the most famous instances of involvement in world affairs were the role played in the U.S.-Chinese rapprochement and in the preliminary stages of the Israeli-Egyptian talks.

In both instances, economic interests were not absent, for both the United States and Israel had come to occupy significant, though proportionately different, places among Romania's trading partners and in its quest for hard currency. In the former case, total trade had jumped from some 70.6 million lei in 1965 to 6,222.5 million lei in 1980, and although constantly in deficit until 1979, the balance of trade between the two countries showed signs of closing the gap. In the latter case, trade turnover has been constantly favorable to Bucharest since 1967, a price Israel paid not unwillingly in exchange for the Romanian position vis-à-vis the Arab-Israeli conflict.

Yet not only commercial considerations determined the Romanian stand. Recruiting support in the West was (and remains) a high priority, one that, it should be added, had also prompted Ceauşescu's other 1967 autonomous gesture—the establishment of diplomatic relations with West Germany. A second consideration, present at least in the case of U.S.-Chinese feelers, clearly stemmed from the benefits Bucharest envisaged deriving from a prospective collaboration between the Soviet Union's most formidable adversaries. Yet such tactics could also prove counterproductive, for an insecure Kremlin is not necessarily conducive to security for Bucharest.

The Romanian dilemma in foreign policy initiatives consequently rests in having to decide whether to promote measures conducive to the weakening of (a) Soviet motivation to exercise pressures for stricter discipline in the camp (hence the active advocacy of détente), or (b) Soviet capabilities to acquire superiority over adversaries. Like the Chinese-U.S. rapprochement, the pax Americana that the Camp David agreements seemed to initiate belongs to the second category, since it signified a substantial diminution in the strength of Moscow's position in the Mediterranean.

On precisely the same grounds, viewed from the opposite side of the superpowers' confrontation table, U.S.-Romanian relations received a boost with President Nixon's visit to Bucharest in 1969, shortly after Romania had castigated the WTO intervention in Czechoslovakia. In August 1975, after having granted most-favored-nation (MFN) status to Romania (in March), President Ford visited the Romanian capital; and in September 1983,

Vice President Bush came to Bucharest. On his part, Ceauşescu visited the United States in December 1967, in January 1973 and in April 1978.

During the first half of 1983, relations between the two nations were shadowed by the American decision to react against the infringements of human rights by the Romanian regime, which reached a peak with the announcement that an education tax was about to be imposed on emigrants. The administration threatened to withdraw MFN status. However, the problem was settled on Bucharest's promise not to enforce the legislation. Although one is likely to continue to witness yearly inquiries in the U.S. Congress concerning various forms of discrimination in Romania, no American president is likely to pursue a course feared to lead to the estrangement of the maverick. Moreover, American public opinion is likely to be more impressed with such displays of autonomy as Romania's participation in the Los Angeles Olympic Games than by what are largely perceived as the lamentations of oversensitive liberals or of recent immigrants concerning the fate of the occasional Romanian dissident.

The same applies to Western Europe, where Ceauşescu has cultivated with particular consistency the image of independence. In October 1984, for example, he paid a visit to Bonn shortly after Honecker and Zhivkov had canceled their planned visits to West Germany in the wake of Soviet pressure. Western Europe fulfills an important role in the Romanian strategems for entrenched autonomy. In 1980, West Germany was Romania's most important trade partner in the Western world, and, what is at least as important, Romanian exports to that country exceeded imports in 1970–71, 1977 and in 1980–81. Trade with France, while in deficit in every year except 1980, was in 1981 second only to that with West Germany among Romania's European Community partners. In addition, both countries participate in several joint production schemes, one of the most important of which involves the manufacture of French cars under license. Alongside the British, the French and the Germans have also been involved in the Romanian effort to produce military equipment, which was triggered by Moscow's reluctance to deliver modern armaments to an unreliable ally.[25]

No scrutiny of Romania's foreign policy can be concluded without reference to the personality factor. Like all other aspects of life in this Balkan corner of the world, foreign policy making has been completely dominated by one man—Nicolae Ceauşescu. More than any other aspect of life, however, the process came to reflect a gradual but constant replacement of rationality by empty grandiosity, and of substance by gesture. For example, Romania's role in the Middle East settlement served rational purposes, and even the most severe critics of the regime would credit Ceauşescu with a splendid performance. On the other hand, his subsequent insistence that his country (i.e., its president) be represented alongside the superpowers, at a prospective international conference dealing with the Middle East, verges on the ridiculous and serves little purpose other than that of satisfying the Romanian leader's thirst for personal glorification. More dangerous, as Aurel Braun observes, have been some of Romania's challenges to the Soviet Union

[25] See Shafir, *Romania*, Chap. 10.

in recent years. These appeared to be gratuitous and to indicate that Ceau-şescu might be succumbing to his own personality cult. According to but one of the more ridiculous versions of the canonization theory, he is the direct spiritual descendant of the Moldavian prince, Stephen the Great, and, like him, the champion of Western civilization. Likewise, his courting of various Third World leaders seemed almost farcical at times, and undertaken more for the glorification of his ego than for the sake of tangible benefits for Romania.[26]

It is true that prominence in international affairs may contribute to internal legitimation, the more so as Ceauşescu's hyperactivism in world affairs should be viewed as part and parcel of what Linden fittingly labels as "'the psychic payoffs' paid to the population in the currency of Romanian nationalism." The deplorable state of the Romanian economy, on the other hand, is reported to generate some doubts as to the wisdom of the autonomous course. The Hungarians or the Bulgarians, it is whispered in Romania, may have no foreign policy of their own, but their stomach is not empty either. It therefore looks as if Linden's doubts concerning the regime's ability to "purchase legitimacy with a nationalized foreign policy" are beginning to materialize.[27] The dusk nowadays falls early on Bucharest's poorly lit streets, because of the crisis in energy consumption. But whether the darkness is gloomy enough to cause the owl to spread its wings, no sage social scientist would dare prophesy. Minerva's pet, after all, may also be scared by the watchful eye of the security police, like everyone else in Romania.

FURTHER READING

Farlow, R. "Romania and the Policy of Partial Alignment," in J. A. Kuhlman, ed. *The Foreign Policies of Eastern Europe: Domestic and International Determinants*. Leiden: Sijthoff, 1978.

Forrest, R. "Romanian-American Relations, 1947–1975," in S. Fischer-Galati, et al., eds. *Romania Between East and West: Essays in Memory of Constantin C. Giurescu*. Boulder, Colorado: East European Monographs, 1982.

Schöpflin, G. *The Hungarians of Rumania*. Minority Rights Group Report No. 37. London: Minority Rights Group, 1978.

[26] Braun, "Romania's Travails," p. 55.
[27] Linden, *op. cit.*, pp. 238–39.

OPPOSITION AND DISSENT IN EASTERN EUROPE

WALTER D. CONNOR

The path followed in the post-Stalin era by Eastern European dissidents is a complex one, both in ideological development and in organizational tactics and strategy. It reflects both internal developments within the dissident groups and developments in the immediate political system and society, as well as changes in the tenor of Soviet-Eastern European relations. While the "modern" history of opposition and dissent is typically traced from events in 1968, a better starting point is in the "prehistory," which takes us back to 1956.

Just as Hungary's revolution was seen as a national paroxysm, where *all* had been lost (because, from the point of view of many observers, too much had been sought), the "Polish October" of 1956—the restoration of Gomułka to power and the evident legitimation of a distinct "Polish road to socialism"—was seen as a triumph of "revisionism." A ruling party, in the hands of a person viewed as a Pole first and a communist second, was seen to be engaged in a process of reconstruction on a "national" base. That this was tolerated by the Soviet leadership—that the "Polish road" remained in the category of *variations* on the Soviet model, rather than a challenge to its validity, as was Tito's alternative in Yugoslavia—augured well for the future. But by 1958, that future looked very different. The post-October "stabilization" had withdrawn many concessions to citizens as consumers, to intellectuals' freedom, to workers' management participation. Only the restoration of private farming remained.

Revisionism was to have one more "go," in the Czech reform movement of 1968. Here, in manner and ideology much less ambiguous than 12 years earlier in Poland (for Gomułka could, rightly, have been seen to have responded to pressures ranging from the Poznań workers' revolt to the mobilization of antiregime intellectuals over a year before October 1956), a reformist leadership "core" took control of the Czechoslovak party in early 1968, and proceeded with rapid strides to reduce censorship and travel restrictions to virtually nil and plan for a broader institutionalization of political and economic reform, while assuring all of their intent to remain loyally within the Warsaw Treaty Organization and the Council of Mutual Economic Aid. "Socialism with a human face" was to be accomplished by a party exercising its "leading role." In this the Soviets perceived a contradiction, for socialism

378

with such a face left no leading role for a party; the contradiction was resolved by the August 1968 invasion.

This, surely, was the death knell of the notion that reform handed down, albeit sincerely, from above by a party, was feasible or durable. The tendency to return to bad old habits by the Eastern European regimes was one problem; the Soviets' clearly signaled lack of tolerance for such transformations was even more compelling evidence that revisionism was a dead letter.

FROM REVISIONISM TO CIVIL RIGHTS

It is in the response—ideological and organizational—to 1968 that the history of Eastern European opposition and dissent in the recent period emerges. In his essay on "Hope and Hopelessness," the Polish philosopher Leszek Kołakowski confronted the stark alternative of no systemic change or complete overthrow of socialist regimes, rejected these limitations and argued for the mobilization of pressure by independent social forces on regimes whose weak points were frequently overlooked.[1] Kołakowski sought a way out of the hopelessness of conceiving of the regimes as unchangeable, and the equal hopelessness of awaiting their (improbable) total overthrow. Instead, he saw moderate, but promising, vulnerabilities in the post-Stalinist balance of regimes that sought unity, yet whose servitors also craved individual security (denied in Stalin's time), thus placing a limit on the unity that could be imposed. Hence, as had not been true earlier, the regimes were subject to pressures from society.

Such an approach rationalized the participation of broad spectra of opinion in the process of applying pressure. Thus, it is not surprising that in Poland, in Czechoslovakia and in Hungary, the trend in dissident thought in the 1970s (both before and after the Polish events of 1976, which put dissidents on a new course, and the foundation of Charter 77 in Czechoslovakia a year later) was toward a broad front. Dissidents whose frame of reference was (or had been) Marxist, social democratic, religious or nationalist/traditionalist moved toward alliance and away from the internal divisions that had limited their potential effectiveness. The new focus—added by the Eastern European regimes' signing of the Helsinki Final Act in 1975—was on civil rights, on freedom for all expressions of opinion, without ideological prejudice. Charter 77 linked Czechs of many diverse predispositions, including ex-party reformers who had earlier, in the post-1968 period, held themselves aloof from other, non-Marxist critics of the regime.[2] In Poland, the church hierarchy moved from a tendency to regard the opposition of "secular left" dissidents to the regime as merely "a fight among communists," while the secular left dissident Adam Michnik acknowledged the sterility

[1] Leszek Kołakowski, "Hope and Hopelessness," *Survey*, 3 (80), Summer 1971, pp. 37–52.
[2] See Vladimir V. Kusin, "Challenge to Normalcy: Political Opposition in Czechoslovakia, 1968–77," in Rudolf L. Tőkés, ed., *Opposition in Eastern Europe*. Baltimore and London: Johns Hopkins University Press, 1979, pp. 26–59.

of a previous view that saw the church, as well as the party apparatus, as an enemy, and had thus placed the secular opposition in the position of rejecting any collaboration with an "ally on the right."[3]

There were—and are—exceptions to this pattern. In Bulgaria and Romania, active dissent has never really emerged in a coherent manner. Fairly steady repression, the economic and political backwardness of the Balkan populations and their greater degree of habituation to despotism account to some degree for Bulgaria's continuing quiescence and for the episodic nature of Romanian outbreaks; the Jiu valley miners' militancy of 1977 was handled with ad hoc concessions and later elimination of the strike leaders, and intellectual dissent has been the enterprise of a few individuals, not of groups.

In the German Democratic Republic, a Marxism of a comparatively narrow sort remained the basis of critiques of regime and society by writers such as Harrich, Havemann and Bahro. "Sectarian" in its rejection of "bourgeois" democracy, alarming in its ambivalence toward (or positive endorsement of) the one-party system, utopian and, presumably, unappealing to a broad audience in its designs for more rational, "authentic" communism, East German dissent seemed cut off at the intellectual level from the broader society and from currents elsewhere. In the 1980s, however, the churches —Protestant and Catholic—have provided a focus and some organizational "cover" for those concerned about the East's contribution to a worsening of East-West tension, have formed the base for an authentic peace movement, and in a less ideological way have responded to mass and youth concerns —this, much to the consternation of a Honecker regime wary of any reassertion of an independent role, even over limited issues, by the religious communities and obviously sensitive to complicating factors in its own conduct of the Federal Republic of Germany-GDR relationship, so central in East-West relations.

Yugoslavia is a system—and a set of nations—unique unto itself, where the bounds of discussion and action have been fairly broad. Where criticism ends and opposition begins is hard to specify, but across the bounds the language of the debate is Marxist. The Marxism, however, is of its own Yugoslav variety—loose, creative, imprecise—whether employed by the intellectuals around the journal *Praxis* who tested the sytem's limits in the 1970s, or the regime that answered that they had exceeded them. In the post-Tito era, facing the severe economic problems of a "weak" and regionally diverse country trading with the developed West, and the political problems of a multinationalism always volatile, Yugoslavia is perhaps best seen as an arena in which contending groups struggle to direct the future. By 1984, judicial crackdowns on critics had increased, but it seems early to render any verdict on the long-term paths the regime and the dissidents may take, and whether these paths will diverge to the degree that an "opposition" takes shape and becomes the object of sustained and consistent repression—and if so, what the major issues will be.

[3]Adam Michnik, "The New Evolutionism," *Survey*, 3/4 (100/101), Summer/Autumn 1976, p. 173.

ISOLATION AND ORGANIZATION

In the more uncertain situations of Czechoslovakia, Poland and Hungary, the organizational experiences of the opposition diverged broadly. The Czech Charter 77 and other groups such as the Committee for the Defense of the Unjustly Prosecuted (VONS) were the objects of sharp regime crackdowns, a species of probable overkill considering that post-1968 dissident appeals have had no really broad resonance in the society as a whole. Among the charter signatories—now some thousands—intellectuals, urbanites and Czechs are overrepresented, Slovaks, rural people and workers (at least, those who are workers by origin and not ex-intellectuals forced downward in the vengeful policies of the earlier 1970s) are underrepresented. In all, while Czech dissent has reaffirmed and thus kept alive the democratic tolerant traditions of Czech political culture, the current combination of Soviet and internal repression seem to have convinced the public that they cannot affect the shape of politics by offering support to the words and ideals of smallish bands of opposition activists. Dissident appeals, thus far, have fallen on sterile ground, and the organization of Czech dissent reflects the relative absence of linkage between the masses and the opposition.

Very different has been the situation in Poland, where an effective linkage between the concerns of dissident intellectuals and the broader urban working class was forged before 1980 and remains a part of the context that limits what the Jaruzelski (or any successor) regime can do, either under or outside of martial law. The thought of people like Kołakowski, broadening the potential base of pressure against the system, played some role in preparing the way, but so did experience. In 1970, dissident intellectuals silently "sat out" the worker riots over price increases that toppled Gomułka, partially, at least, because in the crackdown on Warsaw University students and faculty and the anti-Semitic campaigns of 1968 they had perceived the workers as an inert, uncaring and unsupportive mass. But the sterility of a view that made impossible the linking of the intellectuals' relatively permanent commitment to opposition—limited in its effects by their small numbers—to the large working class's volatility over economic and social welfare issues, expressed only episodically (1956, 1970), must have become clear to some intellectuals; with the workers' riots of 1976—again touched off by price increases—the pattern altered.

The group of intellectuals who founded the Committee for Self-Defense of Workers (KOR) in mid-1976 signaled not only their support for workers arrested or fired as a result of the disturbances, but their acceptance of the fact that the workers' material concerns were as critical a national issue as the intellectuals' more abstract political preoccupations. The immediate roll-back of the price rises was one indication of the Gierek regime's weakness, the flourishing of dissident organizations over the next few years another. The Movement for Defense of Human and Civil Rights (ROPCiO) emerged as an independent organization, more traditional and Catholic than the predominantly ex-Marxist KOR (which about a year after its founding, and after the release of the recently jailed workers, broadened its mandate to include other issues of political concern and changed its name to Committee on Social Self-Defense (KSS/"KOR")). These, and other organizations, took the route of "alternative" publishing as well as open organization. KSS/"KOR"'s *Information Bulletins*, its workers' newspaper *Robotnik*, ROPCiO's *Opinia* (which publicized the regime's violation of citizens' rights and published the names and addresses of its advisers in major Polish cities to which aggrieved citizens were invited for recourse) and other periodicals (including literary journals) went beyond samizdat limits and formed a context of freer opinion and information in the Poland of the late 1970s than many could have expected even at the height of earlier optimism. The "flying university"—offering an alternate educational program in the history and problems of Poland and the Soviet bloc—emerged, scheduling regular lectures by academics and opposition activists in private apartments; these were periodically disrupted by public raids and the temporary detention of lecturers.

The four years from mid-1976 to mid-1980 provided a "prelude," important in itself, to the emergence of Solidarity in August of the latter year. The emergence of active and organized dissident groups, the visit of the newly-elected "Polish pope," with the experience of coordinating large events it gave to lay Catholics and clerics alike, the regime's direction of its harshest measures against early, regional attempts to form free trade unions (then as short-lived as similar efforts in Romania and the USSR), all accompanied what hindsight reveals to have been a "maturation" of the working class in its organizational capabilities.

The maturation was manifest in the events of 1980: the strikes in the Gdańsk shipyards, which, in contract to earlier responses to price rises, took the form of nonconfrontational sit-ins; the foundation of an interfactory strike committee to negotiate with the regime's representatives; and finally, the foundation of Solidarity itself. Solidarity grew to the status of an organization representing not only workers, but (and especially with the foundation of Rural Solidarity) one representing Polish society as a whole, drawing support while remaining distinct from the church. Its fate goes as do succeeding events in Poland, beyond the scope of this brief essay. In any case, opposition became a national movement, crossing class boundaries, and for a time assumed in an organized framework what the dissident Adam Michnik saw as the politics of the "new evolutionism": an increasing struggle for reforms, in favor of evolution which will extend civil liberties and guarantee a respect for human rights.[4] Martial law and the aftermath, the submergence of Solidarity as an open organization, were indeed brutal setbacks. Yet it is a measure of the strength of the public's pressure in Poland that the Jaruzelski government has been unable to achieve many of its desiderata, and in summer 1984 even found it politic to release, without securing their emigration, eleven KOR and Solidarity leaders who were among its most committed opponents.

The political, economic and social context of Hungary place opposition intellectuals in a different position from that of their Czech or Polish counterparts. The relatively moderate politics of Kádár have, since the 1960s, avoided

[4] See Adam Michnik, "The Church and the Left: A Dialogue," in František Silnitsky, et al., eds., *Communism and Eastern Europe*. New York: Karz Publishers, 1979, pp. 51–95.

broad repression; coopted many intellectuals by providing a place (and rewards) for their expertise, access to the West and other benefits; and dealt with dissident intellectuals by expatriation, exile or sackings rather than harsher means. Economically, the New Economic Mechanism (NEM) provided a spur to the economy and, despite the pullback on its innovations lasting from 1972 to later in the decade, generated substantial improvements in living standards and economic opportunity for large categories of the population. A realism in economic policy and in its presentation to the public allowed for the price rises that proved so provocative in the Polish context. Hungary's workers, in large numbers, lacked the basis for disgruntlement that affected their Polish counterparts. Socially, the benefits of the NEM were broadly, but unevenly, distributed—pensioners, and workers in industrial sectors that gave them little chance to earn supplementary income in the "second economy," benefited less than others. But by and large, the Hungarian context yielded little in the way of the problem potential that could "nationalize" responses to appeals by dissident intellectuals—with the single, sensitive exception of concerns over the fate of the Hungarian minorities in Romania and Czechoslovakia, and the public's feeling that the Kádár regime was doing less about it than it might.

In this situation, opposition and dissent in Hungary have remained predominantly an intellectual, and indeed Budapest, enterprise. Ideologically broader-based with time, yet still heavily drawn from the Marxist or ex-Marxist secular left and reflecting the influence of the "Lukács school," the dissidents have aimed more at consciousness-raising among the broader professional and intelligentsia strata than at direct appeals to workers or peasants.[5]

Characteristically, action has taken the form of writing, and Hungarian samizdat, rich in complex analyses of social and political reality as well as in explorations of the relevance of Marxist critical thought to those realities, takes the dialogue between the "marginalized" opposition intellectuals and the establishment intellectuals beyond the already rather broad (for Eastern Europe) limits of an official journal like Valóság. Samizdat collections such as Marxism in the Fourth Decade (wherein some 21 young intellectuals explored their own views on Marxism, which tended toward broader, more critical perspectives on earlier idealistic commitment) and Profile (unpublished manuscripts that did not "fit the profile" of official journals, and were largely non-Marxist in perspective) were anything but broadsides aimed at a mass audience outside the intelligentsia. Targeting a relatively narrow audience has made for depth, however; as an analytic, intellectual product, Hungarian samizdat has achieved a level of sophistication on the whole greater than that elsewhere in Eastern Europe. Konrád and Szelényi's Intellectuals on the Road to Class Power (published in the West),[6] a complex and erudite treatment of the role and future of intellectuals in the socialist system of "rational redistribution," confronted the intelligentsia with an image of itself as a "class' whose interests were different from those of the

[5] See George Schöpflin, "Opposition and Para-Opposition: Critical Currents in Hungary, 1968–78," in Tőkés, ed., op. cit., pp. 142–86.
[6] New York: Harcourt Brace Jovanovich, 1979.

workers—rather than as the workers' natural ally—and conceded that intellectuals might liberate themselves from their own class concerns to take the workers' part. The difficulty of intellectual-worker linkage was also reflected in the work *Towards an East European Marxism*,[7] wherein two younger dissidents, György Bence and János Kis, writing pseudonymously as "Marc Rakovski," contrasted the development of a group consciousness among the intelligentsia—which works in complex ways both for and against the "marginalized" nonconformist segment—with the difficulties of reaching a working class that, whatever degree of group consciousness it may have achieved, is not capable of organizing itself to communicate, to receive messages from the "outside" and thus to establish contact with the dissident intelligentsia.

Though their analyses on the whole provide a modest assessment of the prospects of Polish-type organizational activism, Hungarian dissidents have not been writers only. An organization for voluntary aid to the poor (SZETA) emerged to focus attention on and render some assistance to pensioners and the other poor who are not among the numerous beneficiaries of the NEM. Lászlo Rajk's samizdat "boutique," which kept regular hours in a Budapest apartment, selling (from a catalogue!) works by Hungarian and other Eastern European dissidents, operated for some time before being closed down by the authorities. Religious dissent has not achieved a high profile or linkage with the dissident secular left; some of it has come from smaller Protestant denominations, is not Budapest-centered and has been handled more harshly by the regime than the activities of intellectual dissidents. Hungary's main religious denominations, Catholic and Calvinist, have not been foci of dissent in themselves or active sources of support for other groups engaged in dissent, in the fashion of the Polish church, although opposition to conscription did emerge as an issue to trouble the Catholic hierarchy, as well as the state in the 1980s.

PRESENT AND FUTURE

Thus the picture of opposition in Eastern Europe is a mixed one, combining many elements. National variations are marked, with Poland, Czechoslovakia, Hungary and the GDR each presenting its own pattern of relations between regime and dissidents; and Bulgaria and Romania lacking evidence of any sustained movement or challenge to the regimes. In the first four countries, culturally part of the West, a certain ideological maturation or broadening of the ideological base of the opposition movement, is marked. The mutually tolerant strands of Polish dissent, the mixing of elements originating from different political standpoints under the umbrella of Charter 77 in Czechoslovakia and similar trends in the very different circumstances of the GDR and Hungary, all point toward a realization that the fundamental civil rights issues—the freedom of each to speak and be heard, the necessity of mutual and joint respect, the indivisibility of the freedoms of regime

[7] New York: St. Martin's Press, 1978.

critics, from whatever angle of attack—have been recognized as central, and indispensable. This, probably, provides a potential base for broader, nondoctrinaire public support of the dissident agenda.

Organizational maturation is another matter. No movement, obviously, has gone as far as did Solidarity in establishing itself as a force or in linking together the hitherto disparate concerns of workers and intellectuals. If Solidarity is fated to be "only" a chapter in Polish history, it seems clear that no Polish regime has the strength or resolve to close the book entirely. Neither in Czechoslovakia nor in Hungary have opposition intellectuals managed to "link" with broader masses in the Polish manner (the Hungarians have not, under the conditions of Kádárism, seen this as a reasonable goal in any case), but the survival of Charter 77, its succession of spokespeople, and the ability of so many Hungarian critics to avoid cooptation and inclusion in Kádár's flexible authoritarian system cannot be counted as unimportant.

The future prospect depends on many variables, both external and internal, with respect to those strata and categories of the population that have provided the personnel of opposition in the recent past. Economic issues, sharpened by the circumstances in which regimes in the late 1980s will either opt for or reject economic reforms, may prove inflammatory, as may national-integrity questions, wherein intellectuals and the mass may ask whether compromises their regimes make with the USSR do not fall outside of what has seemed bearable in the past. Perhaps the links between secular dissent and that based, partly at least, on religious values and convictions will grow stronger, fed by increasing autonomous action by churches and churchmen once thought effectively coopted or domesticated (as in the GDR and Czechoslovakia). This would signal the importance of the enlivening of once-independent "old" institutions, without detracting from the relevance of new organizational forms. One can be sure that, before the 1980s are over, a post-Brezhnev generation set of leaders will rule in the Kremlin, and that many of the Eastern European leaders of today will also be gone. Given the intractability of the social and economic problems that will be part of the inheritance of Eastern Europe's new leaders, this set of successions cannot fail to raise new questions about the role and prospects of the opposition.

FURTHER READING

Connor, Walter D. "Dissent in Eastern Europe: A New Coalition?" *Problems of Communism*, XXIX, (Jan.–Feb., 1980), 1–17.
Silnitsky, František, et al., eds. *Communism and Eastern Europe*. New York: Karz, 1979.
Tőkés, Rudolf L., ed. *Opposition in Eastern Europe*. Baltimore and London: Johns Hopkins University Press, 1979.

PART THREE

ECONOMIC

ECONOMIC PLANNING IN COMMUNIST SOCIETIES

FRANCIS SETON and DAVID DYKER

ORIGINS

"FROM each according to his capacity, to each according to his need." This was the Marxist vision of the communist society that was to replace capitalism in the fullness of time. It demanded a moral transformation of human beings, but even more a technological transformation of machines to create an era of material plenty. Without this, the "nonutopian" visionaries could not admit the practical possibility of communism, as they saw irresistible pressures for expanding production perpetuating differential incentives, economic inequalities and rewards according to social class. Only when capitalism had exhausted all its potentialities for technological progress could society legitimately take the first steps toward communism. Conditions were ripe for this in highly developed economies—in Britain, France or Germany—but not in the backward East which would have to await rescuing operations from the victorious proletariats of the West.

Yet it was in the czarist empire of the East that the doctrine fell on the most fertile ground. The Russian intelligentsia had long cherished the dream of a socialist millennium in which the age-old traditions of human equality enshrined in the Russian village commune would coalesce with their own individualist aspirations and searching spirit—a marriage of Russia's soul with Russia's mind—to create a promised land of free and equal people. The Populist movement had called for such an alliance with messianic fervor and had urged its consummation in Russia *before* all other countries, *precisely* because Russia was backward and therefore uncorrupted by the virus of bourgeois capitalism that had already sapped the moral fiber of the West to the point of incapacity for socialism. Russia alone might still be able to escape the fatal infection if action were taken in time, and might yet save the world by her example. The utter failure of the Populist movement in the 1870s and 1880s created widespread disillusion and despair, but also immense receptivity for the more "muscular" form of socialism that the Marxist doctrine seemed to offer.

First, however, the doctrine had to be adapted to Russian soil and to the needs of the Russian intelligentsia, which would never reconcile itself to the role of a passive victim of backwardness condemned to wait for liberation at foreign hands. It was left to Lenin to perform this adaptation, and he performed it brilliantly. His theory of imperialism unveils a late and degenerative phase of capitalism dominated by financial power, monopoly and international cartels which had developed weaknesses and contradictions that Marx could not have foreseen. In the place of a single powerful yoke, removable only by a massive proletariat at the peak of its strength, the new capitalism had forged a worldwide chain of exploitation that could best be broken at its *weakest* link. This weakest link was Russia, where capitalism had entered only in its latest moribund phase and yet was having to struggle against the strong survivals of a feudal absolutist order. It was therefore the historic mission of the Russian proletariat and intelligentsia to set the spark to world revolution, in spite of their relative weakness and immaturity. What was lacking in the material preconditions for the survival of the revolution in Russia would soon be made good by the newly roused proletariats of more advanced countries who, once the revolution was won, would quickly come to its aid.

Lenin provided the strategy and tactics of revolution in Russia as well as its ideological justification. But even more crucial to an understanding of the origins of Soviet planning is his concept of the role of Soviet power in Russia as a holding operation while revolution spread throughout the world, a stewardship undertaken on behalf of an international proletariat that was still to rouse itself. There could be no question of realizing communism in Lenin's Russia any more than a military base could aspire to turn itself into a new Jerusalem. The task was survival, resistance and consolidation.

In such conditions, planning itself concentrated on the commanding heights of the economy, those areas which the regime must control to prevent a recrudescence of capitalism (foreign trade, banking, grain procurement and certain key industries). The rest of industry was put under a regime that came to be known as state capitalism, i.e., the retention of former owners in management functions, subject to surveillance from above and below, but without the requirement to work to a plan. In retail trade and on the land there was at first no substantial departure from private capitalism. Lenin justified this New Economic Policy as a tactical maneuver essential to the survival of the regime. Meanwhile, the ground could be prepared for the eventual annexation to the state of *all* sectors by the creation of a network of central organs of planning and administration (State Planning Commission, established August 23, 1923; Supreme Economic Council, established August 8, 1918, etc.); and a long-term plan (GOELRO, 1920–21) to establish the technological preconditions for socialism within 15 years ("communism = Soviet power + electrification").

SOCIALISM IN ONE COUNTRY

When it became clear that world revolution was nowhere within sight, a longer-term accommodation had to be found. Moreover, popular faith in Lenin's New Economic Policy and the mixed economy in general was soon to be rudely shaken. In 1923–24 the "scissor crisis" erupted as a violent price movement against the agricultural producer that threatened the country with a full-scale peasant withdrawal from the market (into subsistence farming) and imminent starvation for the towns. The crucial link between agriculture and industry that the New Economic Policy had been invoked to save was now endangered by the very market forces that policy had unleashed.

It was only now that planners found themselves face to face with the fundamental problem of planning: deciding the direction in which the economy *as a whole* was to move. A right-wing faction under the influence of Bukharin supported a policy of high and differential incentives to private farmers until such time as enough agricultural surplus had been created to sustain a voluntary movement of resources into industry.[1] The opposing faction, inspired largely by Trotsky, Preobrazhensky and Pyatakov, argued for the immediate and forcible transfer of those resources and took their stand on the need for industry to embark on the "primitive accumulation" of capital through the deliberate exploitation of peasant agriculture—much as an imperial country exploited its colonies, or an emergent social order in the Marxist scheme of things was said to draw its initial fund of strength by parasitic action on the predecessor it was about to supplant. The intellectual weapons of the contestants were historical analogy and dialectical materialism rather than the analytical tools of the professional economist, but the controversy found its reflection on a more technical level inside the State Planning Commission and other bodies where the economic and planning implications of alternative policies occupied the forefront of attention.

THE PLANNING CONTROVERSY

The older school of economists, led by such impressive figures as Kondratyev, Groman and Bazarov, advocated—and practiced—what came to be known as "geneticist" planning. Essentially, they took their starting point from a forecast of the harvest (as the least controllable variable in the economy) with the consequent surpluses available for urban consumption, and built around these estimates a balanced system of performance indicators (output, employment, investment, etc.) for the guidance of the urban and the rural economy alike. The indicators were presented as feasible ideals to be aimed at rather than binding targets, and their mutual consistency was tested by means of structural coefficients derived from the experience of normally functioning unplanned economies, including that of prerevolutionary Russia. The opposing "teleological" school, in which Strumilin was steadily gaining in prominence, rejected such procedures as a retreat from the "conscious choices" made possible by socialism toward voluntary submission to the "elemental forces" at work in lower-type economies. This school advocated a method of planning that was to take its starting point from the final aims, rather than the initial possibilities, which characterized the period to be covered. It was the planners' task to single out the leading

[1] The industrialization controversy was in full swing during the years 1925–27.

links in the economy whose development was desired by the party on political or social grounds, and to draw up the concrete investment projects to serve them. From these were derived the targets for output or other performance which the rest of the economy would have to meet to support the postulated investment program. Overall consistency was tested by a system of supply-and-requirements balances drawn up separately for each key commodity or commodity-group with the aid of technological input norms. If the original program turned out to be unrealizable with existing resources, this was remedied by further shifts from consumption to investment, a tightening of input norms or, as a last resort, a lowering of the initial targets; but at each stage of the adjustment process the leading links were assured of absolute priority.

As the 1920s wore on, the annual economic plans or "control figures" (which were issued from 1925–26 onward) became more and more oriented toward the teleological school, and by the end of the decade the advocates of geneticism had completely lost out or disappeared in political purges.

COLLECTIVIZATION AND AFTER

Meanwhile the party leadership had veered abruptly to the left, and the country was radically transformed by the forced collectivization drive of 1929–32. Henceforth, the food surplus exacted from the peasants passed under the political control of the government, the risks of the harvest devolved entirely on the rural population and the terms of trade between country and town could be dictated at will without endangering the supply situation, present or future. Accordingly, the crucial questions concerning the pace of industrialization, the rate of investment and consumption, etc., ceased to be debated in *economic* terms (i.e., as choices between competing ends, given scarce means) and largely assumed the character of *technological* or *military* problems in which the ends were preconceived and unassailable, and only the means to their fulfillment remained open to choice.

This was the basic premise on which economic planning proceeded throughout the Stalinist period. The aims were unalterably given by the Stalinist understanding of the Soviet Union's historical setting. The economy was treated as a single gigantic factory in which agriculture provided manpower as a kind of raw material for industry. Industry concentrated overwhelmingly on the production of capital equipment for its own use. Food and amenities were produced in quantities sufficient to keep the wheels turning, but consumer satisfaction as an end in itself had no place in the scheme of things. It is to this concept of an economy geared to the secular transformation of one basic resource into another (surplus peasant labor into industrial capital) rather than to the traditional optimum allocation of *given* resources, that the nature and purport of economic planning under Stalin must be linked.

THE MECHANICS OF INDUSTRIAL PLANNING

The great Five-Year Plans[2] marked out the stage of the transformation process to be covered in each quinquennium. They were political documents setting out the major projects, production capacities and output targets to be achieved. Their starting point was a set of party directives, usually published six to 18 months before the plan, in which the aims were given in rough outline. It was then the task of the Planning Commission (Gosplan) to translate this into concrete targets for the major branches of industry. Theoretically, the commission was supposed to reach its decisions after a form of dialogue with subordinate organs, dealing simultaneously with those in charge of the separate branches of industry (people's commissariats, later ministries) and with those responsible for separate geographic divisions (republican or regional planning commissions). These organs would receive an outline plan in the nature of a bid from Gosplan and were required to answer with a counterplan that was to be at once a confirmation of feasibility (with corrections) and a pledge for the future. The counterplans themselves were seen as the result of a lower-level dialogue proceeding meanwhile between the branch authorities and their own executive organs, so that the ultimate source of the counterbids and pledges reaching the Planning Commission would be the enterprises' own assessment of what they were able and willing to do. The Planning Commission was then required to coordinate, integrate and summarize these responses into the final plan document for submission to the political authorities as the concretization of the original directives.

Once the Five-Year Plan was ratified, the State Planning Commission was required to retail its provisions once again as specific orders to subordinate organs that would then do likewise to the lower rungs of the hierarchy, until all industrial enterprises at the grassroots of production had been provided with detailed targets.

A similar procedure (with minor variations) generated the annual plans that were in theory emanations of the Five-Year Plans but soon took on a life of their own—and, indeed, could trace their historical ancestry to the yearly control figures which antedated the quinquennial plans by four to five years. It was the annual plans that eventually acquired the greater operational significance. Factory directors and ministers could expect rewards or sanctions according to the degree to which they fulfilled them, while their commitment to the Five-Year Plans was at best moral and general.

The procedure, interaction and time pattern of the plans has remained substantially unaltered to the present day. There were occasional departures of longer-term planning into three- or seven-year plans, and occasional extensions of an annual plan to cover a period of two years. Occasionally also the chain of command along which the planning dialogue and the eventual

[2] The great Five-Year Plans: First FYP 1928–29—32–33 (declared fulfilled by end of 1932); Second FYP 1933–37; Third FYP 1938–40 (interrupted by war); Fourth FYP 1946–50; Fifth FYP 1951–55; Sixth FYP 1956–60 (superseded by Seven-Year Plan); Seven-Year Plan 1958–65; Eighth FYP 1966–70. Five-Year Plans continue to form the basis of Soviet economic planning up to the present day.

retailing of targets was conducted changed from the "branch principle" (economy/major sector of industry/subsector-enterprise) to the "territorial principle" (economy/regional council/locality) and the two principles, when allowed to operate simlutaneously, received different emphasis from time to time. More recently, there have been experiments with rollover Five-Year Plans subject to annual revision as the new opportunities opened up by each year's achievement became clear. Nevertheless, the principle of political guidelines receiving progressively finer detail in a prescribed sequence of bid and counterbid and culminating in a set of mandatory targets for all producing enterprises has not so far been departed from.

What has changed—and is still in the process of change—is the nature of the targets set and the kinds of incentives offered for their fulfillment.

TARGETS AND INCENTIVES

Up to the mid-1950s, the overriding task facing each enterprise was fulfillment of the gross output target expressed in physical units (tons, gallons, kW/h, etc.) or in terms of constant prices. There were bonuses for fulfillment and often a steeply rising scale of management rewards for varying degrees of overfulfillment. Not surprisingly, the managers strove to excel in this at the expense of all other aspects of economic performance—quality, profits, productivity and costs—and the authorities were forced to devise more and more subsidiary targets (input limits, cost reduction, etc.) to minimize the damage done by "output-fetishism." As the number and complexity of targets multiplied, it became increasingly difficult to secure a proper coordination between them, and soon typical managers saw themselves faced with a welter of contradictory targets and supplementary orders which it was impossible to fulfill. The only way out was a judicious choice between them according to the managers' assessment of the political pull behind each target and the ease or difficulty of simulating the required result. The upshot of this situation appears to have been the continued enthronement of the output target as by and large the most worthwhile task to be pursued.

Clearly, this cost the economy dearly as the structure of production shifted to needlessly output-biased assortments (heavy items where the target was in tons, long items where it was in yards, high-cost items where it was in value, etc.). Above all, output was pursued regardless of its usefulness to the purchaser in the next link of the production chain, as the high output targets themselves created perennial shortages and a seller's market. There was no need to please the customers who would in any case take whatever they got, and the pipelines of production became choked with ill-adapted or unusable hardware. The emphasis on sheer output also resulted in serious backlogs in technology, as managers were reluctant to make room for innovations and new products that required retooling and irksome interruptions to the smooth flow of output. Some of the most spectacular technological revolutions of Western economies were missed or long delayed in the Soviet Union, for example: the shift from metals to plastics, from natural to artificial fibers, from steam traction to diesel locomotives, and from coal to oil and gas in general. Not all of this can be laid at the door of output-fetishism, but the comparative absence of cost consciousness and regard for allocative efficiency must bear the major share of responsibility. The fact that industry nonetheless developed at an unprecedented pace must be ascribed to its "transformative" character, its lavish absorption of rural labor and cheap raw materials, and its tight hold on the consumer who was forced to sacrifice everything to investment.

The picture changed abruptly, however, when the potentialities of surplus labor were nearing exhaustion and further advances became dependent on the productivity of those already working in industry. From that time onward, low standards of living became a hindrance rather than a help. The need to keep a nucleus of skilled workers on the land enforced higher food prices, and the need to raise the skills of those in towns demanded higher consumer standards all around. Meanwhile, the upward trend in energy material extraction costs brought into stark relief the dangers of crude output maximization. Resources were no longer free to be fed into an undiscriminating sausage machine, but had to be husbanded and judiciously allocated where they could do the most good.

It was against this background that the Soviet authorities started to tinker with the planning system in the late 1950s and early 1960s, finally introducing in 1965 a general industrial planning reform, which substituted sales and profits for gross output as key success indicators, and introducing capital charges for the first time. Since then, the issue of planning reform has never been altogether off the Kremlin's agenda, and we are, indeed, currently in the middle of yet another industrial planning experiment. Let us try to pinpoint the main elements in this evolution of the planning structure.

PLANNING AND DECENTRALIZATION— THE COURSE OF DEVELOPMENT SINCE 1965

There can be no doubt that the 1965 planning reform did give a fillip to Soviet economic performance. The downward trend in capital productivity was checked as enterprises were compelled by the new capital charges to unload surplus equipment. Partly as a result of that, partly for reasons quite unconnected with the planning system like the run of good harvests in the late 1960s, growth rates of national income rose in the period 1965–70 by comparison with those in the immediately preceding period. The new success indicators, coupled with the introduction of new technologies, a number of them from the West, helped to produce some improvement in the quality of goods. But the reform failed to eradicate any of the fundamental weaknesses of the Soviet planning system. It did little to modify the general level of centralization of the system, and the planners in Moscow continued to determine the great majority of prices and contractual links. With customer enterprises unable to switch suppliers in the face of unsatisfactory deliveries, the sales success indicator was in practice only a marginal improvement on gross output. The temptation to profiteer, in a situation where market pressures were not permitted to force excessively high profit margins down, proved too strong for Soviet industrial managers to resist. The continued insistence on regular quarterly and annual plan fulfillment inevitably meant that enterprise-level resistance to technical change survived vigorously into the new system. Attempts to give the enterprise more of a stake in reequipment by permitting it to accumulate substantial funds for decentralized investment were hampered by the clumsiness and inflexibility of an overcentralized supply system that could not cope with orders for supplies and equipment coming from *below*. In practice, the ploy of granting enterprises a degree of financial autonomy, without backing that up by any decentralization of the supply system, produced an unintended flowering of the second economy, as enterprise directors strove to obtain supplies in any way possible. This in turn seriously destabilized centralized investment plans in the early 1970s. The Communist party apparatus, with suspicions already aroused by developments in Czechoslovakia in the late 1960s, took that as an indication that the attempt to marry market elements with their centrally planned system had been fundamentally misconceived. The quadrupling of oil and gold prices at the end of 1973 seems to have given Brezhnev the idea that purchase of foreign technology, financed by raw material exports, could provide an adequate substitute for economic reform.

In the event, that hope was to be disappointed, as sharply rising costs of extraction in the Western Siberian oil and gas fields began to squeeze profit margins on energy exports; and the planning system showed itself to be as slow in assimilating and diffusing imported technology as any other technology. By 1979, the growth rate of national income had fallen to below three percent for the first time since the beginning of Stalin's industrialization drive. It came as no surprise, then, when that year saw the publication of a new decree on the planning system. This minireform bore all the marks of intellectual uncertainty and political compromise. With the "marketizers" among the economists under a cloud, and a new confidence in the capacity of computers to revolutionize the technicalities of planning, the new decree was essentially centralist in tendency, thus confirming the trend of the 1970s. The idea that profit might serve as a unique, key planning indicator was explicitly rejected, and there was, indeed, a return to the pre-1965 notion that different technical dimensions of the production process could be planned directly. In particular, there was a renewed emphasis on direct physical planning of output and cost reduction. At the same time, the minireform attempted to introduce more sophisticated value-added indicators under the rubric of "normed net output" (NNO), while minor elements showed that the idea of transforming the administered supply system into a system of wholesale trade was not completely dead. But in any case the decree had little policy impact in a period when the political establishment, already looking forward to a succession struggle, was intent on sitting tight.

The succession of Andropov to the general secretaryship in 1982 brought a breath of fresh air to Soviet economic policy making. At the simplest level, the new leader sponsored a campaign to improve work discipline and encourage job conflation as a way of cutting down on the overmanning inherited from the labor-surplus days. But he was evidently quite clear that you cannot expect better discipline from workers when a defective supply system continually breaks the rhythm of production and leaves people with nothing to do. Thus for Andropov, improved *planning discipline* was an indispensable condition of improved *labor discipline*. Sure enough, a decree was published in July 1983 setting up an industrial planning experiment, to run in selected ministries as of January 1, 1984.

In practice, the industrial planning experiment has turned out to be less than revolutionary. After Andropov's departure, and Chernenko's interim tenure as general secretary, it is likely that the experiment will receive renewed political impetus under Gorbachev. In any case, the details of the new system hold out little prospect of a radical revamping of Soviet planning. The success-indicator system seems to have become, if anything, even more complex, and while there is a new emphasis on the fulfillment of contracts there is little more in the way of flexibility in the establishment of interenterprise contractual links. Renewed emphasis on autonomous enterprise investment funds has run into exactly the same problem as it did last time around, namely the difficulty in obtaining appropriate investment supplies to spend the money on. The experimental system aims to embody the principle of "stable norms" within Soviet planning, i.e., to replace the bureaucratic arbitrariness of the traditional system with a set of parameters, constant over the five-year period, which would predetermine the relationship between incentives and performance on given indicators. But this clause of the new decree must be treated with some caution, for the principle of stable norms has been proclaimed in every Soviet reform since 1965. Plan targets and bonus coefficients have in the past been unstable, principally because overcentralization in planning has created insurmountable informational problems for Gosplan and made it impossible to achieve full consistency between the different parts of the plan. The application of computers has only marginally modified the severity of these problems. Thus planners have been compelled to feel their way toward aggregate plan fulfillment by trying to spot areas where there may be hidden reserves and adjusting accordingly. Even if the industrial planning experiment were generalized throughout Soviet industry, it would do little to ease that burden of overcentralization, so that it is difficult to see how the planners can in practice eschew the time-honored principle of "planning from the achieved level." By declaring that enterprises failing to fulfill all contracts will be deprived of all bonuses, the experimental system does in fact place a premium on capacity concealment at the grassroots level. This will merely make the central planners' job that much more difficult.

The industrial planning experiment should not be dismissed altogether. At the shop floor level it does appear to be making a substantial impact, and some enterprises involved in the experiment report striking reductions in work forces. But the Soviet authorities may be reluctant to generalize something that must present the threat of the emergence of large-scale pockets of unemployment, while enterprise managers may well prefer to hang on to surplus labor "just in case," as long as the supply system remains unreformed and unreliable. The industrial planning experiment was extended on January 1, 1985, and there is talk of a new "Program for the Complex Perfecting of the Management Mechanism." The cause of planning reform in the Soviet Union, then, has clearly still not run its course.

THE GROWTH AND STRUCTURE OF SOVIET INDUSTRY

The long persistence of output-fetishism and rigid centralization favored rapid growth in terms of physical weight and volume. In the quarter century from the inception of the Five-Year Plans (1928) to the mid-1950s, Soviet industry was undoubtedly one of the fastest growing in the world. Opinions differ on the proper measure of this growth performance and the Soviets' own claims up to 1955 are rightly discounted by Western observers (not without some implied support from Soviet commentators). Nevertheless, the annual growth rate of industry was probably comparable to—and may have exceeded—those rates achieved by the most spectacular "industrializers," such as Japan (from the turn of the century to the early 1930s) and South Africa (from about 1910 onward). With the approach to economic maturity, industrial growth rates slowed down and by the early 1960s Soviet industry had dropped well behind that of West Germany, Japan and Italy in the league table.

Table 1 displays the record of different periods and compares Soviet manufacturing growth with that of the main developed nations of the West. The fall in official Soviet growth rates up to 1966 is conspicuous, and would be more so if the first quinquennium of the 1960s were analyzed year by year. Equally conspicuous, however, is the recovery in 1967 in the wake of the preceding bumper harvest and as implementation of Kosygin's planning reform proceeded. As the industrial planning reform ran out out of steam in the early 1970s, so industrial growth rates started to trim again. They recovered in 1974 and 1975—the bumper windfall gain years for the Soviet Union in relation to world raw material prices—but then fell continuously in the late 1970s and early 1980s. Whether Andropov's energetic approach contributed to the upturn in 1983, and whether that upturn can be sustained under Gorbachev, remains to be seen.

The last column of Table 1 has been added as a sensitive barometer of the hardness of economic policy. Throughout the early period, the doctrine that fast industrial expansion demanded the "predominant growth" of producer industries held undisputed sway. Its justification, though often speciously offered in terms of economic theory, was basically ideological and political—the regime's unspoken apology to the hard-pressed consumer. It is clear (see lower half of the table) that during the initial industrialization period, the bias toward producer goods in the Soviet Union equaled or exceeded that of the largest exporters of such goods who were able to compensate for this by the corresponding imports of consumer goods (as the Soviet Union is not). As the transformative phase of Soviet development drew to a close and a friendlier policy toward the consumer became necessary, the bias gradually lessened, though not without periodic, and immediately damaging, relapses into the hard line. One of the most conspicuous policy aims of the 1971–75 Five-Year Plan was to reverse the traditional priority of producer goods production. In practice, as Table 1 shows, nothing of the kind happened. Since 1981 there has been a real shift in the main sectoral priorities of Soviet industry, though not yet to such an extent as to significantly modify a pattern that has been consolidated over a number of decades.

Table 2 shows how trends in main sectoral priorities have been reflected at the level of industrial branches. The reader should bear in mind that these figures do not include production by the nine defense ministries of the Soviet Union—which do, of course, produce substantial amounts of goods for civilian use. The shares of light industry and the food industry have fallen inexorably, although the rate of decline eased considerably in the 1970s. The predominance of engineering, in terms of both share and rate of growth of share, is clear-cut over the period 1950–70. By 1980 it had suffered a slight decline in share, reflecting both a moderation in the rate of growth of aggregate investment and an increasingly high proportion of imported equipment to total machinery installed in the Soviet economy. By around 1980 that proportion may have been as high as one-third. Growth in the relative importance of the chemicals industry has reflected the increasing technical sophistication of the economy and the specific sectoral needs of agriculture.

It is largely the development of industry that has permitted the Soviet Union to reach a level of national income of about 60 percent of the U.S. level—around 65 percent of the EC level—as of 1980. Yet while the Soviet defense industry impresses qualitatively as well as quantitatively, industry as a whole at the present time is affected by a number of striking weaknesses. There is a steel shortage; whether that stems primarily from bottlenecks in the steel industry or from excessive utilization of steel in a system still plagued by a tendency to excessive heaviness is not clear. Insufficient high-quality silicon is produced to supply the needs of the fledgling microchip industry. The Soviet Union still has to import large-diameter pipes for its trunk gas pipelines. As overall growth rates have fallen, the Soviet authorities have tended to allow rates of growth of investment to fall also; but as the capital stock ages, the leadership may now be pondering whether the ratio of investment to national income should not be pushed up, with all that that implies for consumption levels. Alternative scenarios in which industrial lags are obviated without recourse to belt-tightening exercises would have to be based on significant improvements in efficiency trends, and that brings us right back to the issue of planning reform.

THE SITUATION IN EASTERN EUROPE

When Eastern Europe passed under Soviet influence it was at first so tightly clasped in the Stalinist embrace that few manifestations of genuine independence, or even local differentiation, could be expected in any field. For close onto a decade (except in the case of Yugoslavia) there was no significant departure from the Soviet model in economic policy or openly expressed economic thought. When the heavy hand was finally lifted in the early or mid-1950s, it was to liberate a considerable potential in pent-up criticism and original thought. In contrast to their Russian predecessors, the Marxist intellectuals of Poland or Yugoslavia had no need to justify or instigate the movement away from capitalism in their countries; nor did they need to consolidate their position in an isolated stronghold. Instead, they were able and anxious to concentrate on operational blueprints and models designed

Table 1

ANNUAL GROWTH RATES OF INDUSTRIAL PRODUCTION
(%)

Industry:	Total (A)	Producer goods (B)	Consumer goods (C)	Lead of producer goods* (D)
1928–37	14.1[a] (18.2)[c]	(23.1)[c]	(13.4)[c]	(8.6)[c]
1951–55	9.4[b] (13.2)[c]	(13.8)[c]	(12.0)[c]	(1.6)[c]
1956–60	10.4	11.3	8.5	2.6
1961–65	8.6	9.6	6.3	3.1
1966	8.6	9.0	7.0	1.9
1967	10.0	10.2	9.0	1.1
1968	8.2	8.4	8.4	0.0
1969	7.1	7.0	7.4	−0.4
1970	8.5	8.3	8.9	−0.6
1971	8.0	8.0	8.0	0.0
1972	6.5	6.5	5.6	0.8
1973	7.0	8.7	5.3	3.2
1974	8.1	8.0	7.5	0.5
1975	7.5	8.1	6.2	1.8
1976	4.9	5.5	2.9	2.5
1977	6.0	5.8	5.7	0.1
1978	4.4	4.9	4.0	0.9
1979	3.6	3.5	3.2	0.3
1980	3.6	3.6	3.4	0.2
1981	3.4	3.3	3.6	−0.3
1982	2.8	2.8	2.9	−0.1
1983	4.0	3.9	4.3	−0.4

Manufacturing:	Total	Main producer goods[e]	Main consumer goods[f]	Lead of main producer goods*
U.S.S.R 1928–37[d]	16.0	21.8	11.1	9.7
1951–55[d]	10.7	16.6	11.4	4.7
United States 1949–56	4.6	6.7	1.0	5.0
Britain 1949–56	4.0	5.3	1.3	3.9
West Germany 1949–56	14.5	16.8	12.1	4.2
EC 1949–56	9.7	11.6	7.6	3.7

* Computed as $1 + \dfrac{D}{100} = \left(1 + \dfrac{B}{100}\right) \div \left(1 + \dfrac{C}{100}\right)$.

[a] Average of three Western estimates (National Bureau of Economic Research 10.7, D. Hodgman 15.7, F. Seton 16.0).

[b] Average of three Western estimates (National Bureau of Economic Research 7.7, D. Hodgman 9.9, F. Seton 10.5).

[c] Official claims.

[d] Estimates by F. Seton.

[e] Basic metals, engineering and metal working, chemicals.

[f] Light industry, textiles, footwear and food industry.

Source: From official Soviet data unless otherwise stated.

Table 2
GROSS OUTPUT BY INDUSTRIAL BRANCHES
(PERCENTAGE DISTRIBUTION, TOTAL INDUSTRY = 100)

	Electricity	Fuel	Ferrous metallurgy	Engineering	Chemicals	Construction materials	Light industry	Food
1950	1.7	6.5	8.6	14.2	3.5	2.0	32.0	26.1
1960	2.2	5.4	8.6	21.3	4.4	3.6	26.9	21.7
1970	2.8	4.2	8.2	29.8	6.4	3.6	20.9	18.4
1980	3.1	6.0	6.5*	27.4	7.6	3.8	20.5	18.1

* Estimate by D. A. Dyker.
Sources: Official Soviet and U.N. statistics.

to promote the material progress of the postcapitalist economy in their own surroundings of time and space.

These surroundings differed from Soviet experience in three main respects: (a) the longer tradition of personal land ownership among the peasantry; (b) the smaller size of the national unit and its consequent dependence on international trade; and (c) the closer acquaintance of sizable groups in the population with Western modes of life and thought. Each of these factors served in its own way to accelerate the reductio ad absurdum of the cruder Stalinist impositions and to sharpen the reaction against them.

Peasant resistance to collectivization and the government's enforced retreat in Yugoslavia, Poland and Hungary necessitated genuine incentive prices in agriculture, followed by a drift toward incentive wages in alternative urban occupations. The resulting cost inflation in industry, sometimes reinforced by demand inflation originating from the peasant sector, played havoc with the centrally administered price structure. Production units intended as a source of profit for central investment found themselves in need of state subsidies a short time after every new price reform. This produced disincentive effects on management, calling for fresh adjustments and revisions. In proportions varying with the labor intensity (i.e. proneness to inflation) of different industries, official selling prices ceased to reflect current costs almost as soon as they had been centrally determined, and as a consequence the planners' resource allocation and investment choices went widely and demonstrably astray.

Apart from agriculture, the classic instance of an economic sector resistant to central planning and control is foreign trade. Its decisive importance in the people's democracies injected further elements of uncertainty and confusion. Owing to rapid changes in foreign markets and political relations within the bloc, imported raw materials soon came to enter the domestic price structure at purely historic valuations, deviating both from the terms of trade at which they had been obtained and the relative costs at which they could be produced at home. It became increasingly difficult, if not impossible, to decide which goods should be exported and which retained for internal use.

The many instances of glaring and prolonged wastefulness that resulted provoked responsible intellectuals to turn to their own, often very extensive, knowledge of Western economics in search of analytic tools and operational practices that might be suitable for adaptation to the new environment. It was clear, however, that the resulting recommendations could not hope to avoid dangerous ideological overtones and might be identified as an open or implied protest against the Soviet impositions of the recent past.

The Yugoslav defection of the late 1940s and the Polish defection of October 1956 had a strong influence on economic thinking in Eastern Europe. In Poland a prolonged debate culminated in the famous *Theses* of the Economic Council (published in 1957), which laid down the desirable principles of price formation to be pursued. In the nature of things, the debate could only touch the behavioral rules to be followed by the price commissions of the center and could not advocate any devolution of price-forming functions to lower organs, let alone enterprise managers; still less could it abolish the output target, which tended to distort resource allocation even when prices were right. But the debate was an important first move back to the scientific marginalism in economics that the Marxist orthodoxy had rejected for so long. It was in Poland also that the contribution of productive resources other than labor was first readmitted to a semblance of its right place in the formation of social value.

While the political overtones of the Prague Spring provoked brutal Soviet suppression of reform trends in Czechoslovakia, the Hungarians, with a discretion born, perhaps, of the tragedy of Budapest in 1956, managed to introduce in 1968 a New Economic Mechanism (NEM) that carried Hungary most of the way to market socialism, short of the establishment of workers' councils of the Yugoslavian type. In terms of both growth rates and the quality of goods, the Hungarian NEM quickly produced impressive results, and Hungarian agriculture has been one of the great Eastern European success stories of the last two decades. But a continued failure to subject the investment sphere to the discipline of the market, coupled with the destabilizing effects of oil crises and world recession in the decade after 1973, reduced Hungary's national income growth rate for 1980–83 to just one percent. Undismayed, the Hungarian authorities have sought since 1980 to inject new impetus into the economic reform movement and to cut away some of the bureaucracy that had crept back in in the 1970s. But while the Soviets profess admiration for Hungarian agriculture, they are inclined, not surprisingly perhaps, to read their Eastern European lessons on industrial planning from Bulgaria and East Germany, the two countries of Eastern Europe whose growth rates have stood up best to the world recession. These loyal Soviet allies have displayed a striking capacity to retain the formal structure of central planning, while modifying it at the operational level in such a way as to introduce a good deal of the flexibility and quality consciousness of a market economy.

The dominating problem at the present time for most Eastern European countries, whether centrally planned or market-socialist, is the burden of international debt inherited from the strategy of "import-led growth," itself a reflection of the inappropriate application of Soviet principles of development. There seems little prospect of that problem being solved through deepening cooperation with the Soviet Union. For Eastern Europe and the

Soviet Union alike, the ultimate basis of the "intensification" so crucial for contemporary development plans must be high technology, which they can get only from the West, not from each other. It is these factors that are likely to determine trends in economic organization in Eastern Europe over the next few years.

FURTHER READING

van Brabant, J. M. *Socialist Economic Integration: Aspects of Contemporary Economic Problems in Eastern Europe.* Cambridge: Cambridge University Press, 1980.

Cave, M. and Hare, P. *Alternative Approaches to Economic Planning.* London: Macmillan, 1981.

Clarke, R. A., and Matko, D. J. I. *Soviet Economic Facts, 1917–81.* London: Macmillan, 1983.

Dyker, D. A. *The Future of the Soviet Economic Planning System.* London: Croom Helm, 1985.

Ellman, M. *Socialist Planning.* Cambridge: Cambridge University Press, 1979.

Gregory, P. R., and Stuart, R. C. *Soviet Economic Structure and Performance.* 2nd ed. New York: Harper and Row, 1981.

Hanson, P. *Trade and Technology in Soviet-Western Relations.* London: Macmillan, 1981.

Nove, A. *An Economic History of the U.S.S.R.* Rev. ed. Harmondsworth: Penguin, 1982.

——. *The Soviet Economic System.* 2nd ed. London: Allen and Unwin, 1980.

Smith, A. *The Planned Economies of Eastern Europe.* London: Croom Helm, 1983.

EAST-WEST TRADE AND TECHNOLOGY TRANSFER

PHILIP HANSON

INTRODUCTION

THE economic significance of East-West trade to the West is small. If by "East" we mean the USSR and its six Warsaw Pact allies,[1] and by "West" the member-nations of the Organization for Economic Cooperation and Development (OECD), the East-West trade in recent years has been about three to four percent of the West's total trade. This means that less than one percent of total Western output is for export to the European Council for Mutual Economic Assistance (COMECON) countries, and less than one percent of total final domestic spending in the West is on goods imported from those countries.[2]

The chief economic interest of East-West trade, therefore, arises from its importance to the Eastern economies.

DIMENSIONS IN THE EARLY 1980S

Between them, Tables 1, 2 and 3 show how much larger East-West trade looms in the total trade of European COMECON countries than it does in that of their Western partners. Table 1 shows that in the early 1980s the Soviet Union's trade with the West was somewhat larger than that of the Eastern European Six. Table 2 shows that trade with the Soviet Union was around two percent of the total trade of the larger Western European

---

[1] Bulgaria, Czechoslovakia, the German Democratic Republic (GDR), Hungary, Poland and Romania. These will be referred to here as the "Eastern European Six." Together with the Soviet Union, these countries are the European members of the Council for Mutual Economic Assistance (COMECON). The COMECON members outside Europe are Mòngolia, Cuba and Vietnam.

[2] More precisely, on goods imported from the Soviet Union and Eastern Europe for final consumption and investment, and on the value of imported Soviet and Eastern European raw materials, components, etc., incorporated in other finished goods. The fact that individual Soviet (but not Eastern European) import orders are sometimes huge, attracts more publicity for Soviet-Western trade than its total size would warrant. This can also make it very important for particular Western firms and regions.

404

Table 1
SOVIET AND EASTERN EUROPEAN TRADE WITH THE
DEVELOPED WEST (U.S.$ MILLION, CURRENT PRICES) IN 1975, 1980,
1982 AND 1983

	1975	1980	1982	1983
Bulgaria				
Imports	1,289	1,657	1,909	1,673
Exports	474	1,638	1,257	1,278
Czechoslovakia				
Imports	2,244	3,691	2,931	2,708
Exports	1,673	3,242	2,785	2,680
GDR*				
Imports	3,704	6,332	5,366	6,378
Exports	2,631	4,542	6,325	6,766
Hungary				
Imports	1,966	3,719	3,110	2,893
Exports	1,327	3,040	2,593	2,825
Poland				
Imports	6,199	6,699	3,022	2,857
Exports	3,278	5,857	3,597	3,621
Romania				
Imports	2,285	4,073	1,933	1,500
Exports	1,899	4,292	3,408	3,200
Eastern European Six				
Imports	17,687	26,171	18,271	18,009
Exports	11,282	22,611	19,965	20,370
USSR				
Imports	13,566	24,386	26,204	26,364
Exports	8,588	24,934	26,224	26,610

* Including trade with West Germany.
Source: CIA, *Handbook of Economic Statistics* [hereafter *HES*] *1983* and *1984*,
Washington, D.C., 1983 and 1984. Based on Soviet and Eastern European trade
returns, converted to $ at official ruble exchange rate.

countries. Trade with the Soviet Union and the Eastern European Six combined, therefore, was typically of the order of four percent of all trade, for
these countries, and the equivalent to around one percent of gross national
product (GNP). For the West as a whole these ratios would be slightly
lower because Japan and the United States, which bulk large in the total
Western world economy, trade proportionately less with the European
COMECON countries.

The Eastern side of the picture is less clear. Domestic prices in the Eastern
economies differ substantially from foreign trade prices, so that trade/GNP
ratios can not be calculated straightforwardly. Moreover, Eastern countries'
prices in trade with the West differ from their prices in trade among themselves, so that the percentage shares of East-West in total trade of COM-

Table 2
IMPORTANCE OF SOVIET-WESTERN TRADE TO SELECTED WESTERN COUNTRIES, 1981–1982

| | Exports to USSR | | | | Imports from USSR | | | |
| | As a % of total exports | | As a % of GNP | | As a % of total imports | | As a % of GNP | |
	1981	1982	1981	1982	1981	1982	1981	1982
Britain	0.9	0.6	0.2	0.1	1.0	1.1	0.2	0.1
France	1.8	1.6	0.3	0.1	2.8	2.5	0.6	0.9
West Germany	1.9	2.2	0.5	0.6	2.5	3.0	0.6	0.7
Italy	1.7	2.0	0.4	0.1	3.4	4.1	0.9	1.1
Japan	2.2	2.8	0.3	0.7	1.4	1.3	0.2	0.1
United States	1.0	1.2	0.1	0.5	0.1	0.1	neg.*	neg.*
Austria	3.1	3.5	0.6	0.6	6.2	5.1	0.7	0.5

* neg. = Negligible.
Source: CIA, *HES 1983* and *HES 1984*, Washington, D.C., 1983 and 1984.

ECON countries (Table 3) have no clear meaning.[3] On the other hand, the impression given by Table 3 is grossly misleading. In relation to total

Table 3
TRADE WITH THE WEST AS A PERCENTAGE OF TOTAL TRADE* OF THE USSR AND EASTERN EUROPE, 1982

	Imports	Exports
Bulgaria	16.7	11.4
Czechoslovakia	19.0	17.7
GDR	27.3	29.0
Hungary	36.1	29.6
Poland	30.9	32.6
Romania	19.8	29.5
USSR	33.5	29.9

* The differences in pricing between East-West and intra-COMECON trade (see text) make these percentage shares only very rough-and-ready guides to the importance of the former in COMECON countries' trade.
Source: *Statisticheskii ezhegodnik stran-chlenov SEV 1983*, Moscow, 1983; CIA, *HES 1983*, Washington, D.C., 1983.

[3] They cannot, moreover, all be adjusted by a single coefficient that would make the dollar and ruble prices comparable. The reason for this is that the degree of departure from Western world market prices in intra-COMECON trade varies between categories. Marvin Jackson has calculated that in 1983, if one used the official ruble-dollar exchange rate, the average ratio of intra-COMECON to world prices would be 2.45:1 for machinery; 2.22:1 for manufactured consumer goods; 1.71:1 for food; 1.19:1 for raw materials, and 1.01:1 for fuels. See his "When Is a Price a Price? The Level and Patterns of Prices in the CMEA," *Radio Free Europe Background Report* BR/155, August 24, 1984.

national economic activity, this means that East-West trade is very important for the smaller Eastern European countries. The extreme case would be Hungary, whose total imports of goods and services may account for as much as half of total final domestic spending. At the opposite extreme is the Soviet Union itself, where some assessments put total imports at over 20 percent of Soviet national income, although most estimates are rather lower. Even for the Soviet Union, however, imports from the West in the early 1980s might well amount, in comparable prices, to over five percent of total final domestic expenditure.

LIMITS TO EAST-WEST TRADE

From the 1920s onward, there have been periodic announcements by Western politicians and businesspeople that commerce between East and West was about to blossom. It has persistently not blossomed, and for good reasons.

First, the Soviet Union and parts of Eastern Europe are on a substantially lower level of economic development than North America, Japan and Western Europe, and trade has tended to expand most strongly—at any rate since World War II—among the most highly developed nations.

Second, political hostility and suspicion between nations hinder, though they do not preclude, trade between them. This is a factor operating most strongly in the case of the Soviet Union, where xenophobia is officially prescribed. It is also particularly important in the United States, where Russophobia alternates with less well-founded obsessions. Western strategic trade controls and Soviet reluctance to part with economic information are the sort of phenomena that give East-West trade its peculiar character.

Third, the difference in economic systems creates fundamental difficulties in expanding trade. For example, domestic prices in Soviet-type economies do not reliably reflect production costs and are insulated from, and not systematically related to, world prices. The currencies of these countries are not convertible into other currencies on international currency markets; the official exchange rates need not reflect the "purchasing power parity" of the domestic currency in terms of internationally tradeable goods; and both the flows of imports and the supplies offered for export are determined by administrative fiat and not necessarily by the pursuit of real cost and price advantages. So whether a Soviet or Eastern European export offer constitutes "fair competition" is extremely hard to establish. For the same reason, it is hard for the planners in a centrally administered economy to know which items it is really cost-effective to export and import.

An even more basic systematic problem is the lack of East-West movements of risk capital and labor. Commodity trade among capitalist nations is accompanied by international equity investment and by labor migration on a large scale. These movements of labor and capital upset old-fashioned nationalists, and are often impeded by legislation. But they tend on the whole to narrow the gaps in development levels within the capitalist world. Both capital and labor tend to move from countries where they are relatively abundant to countries where they are relatively scarce. Possibly more important in the long run is the way in which such flows carry technical knowhow with them across national boundaries.

The European COMECON countries are insulated from these factor movements. They borrow from the West, but mostly in the form of medium-term loans to finance the purchase of capital goods. Their "arm's-length" acquisition of technology through these capital-goods purchases and by the buying of licenses and know how entails much less intimate contact with the providers of advanced technology than occurs through the operations of multinational companies. It is true that the European COMECON countries themselves set up wholly owned companies in the West—over 400 of them by the end of 1981—but they are overwhelmingly concerned with the marketing of Soviet and Eastern European products.[4] Movements of labor across national boundaries are extremely limited even within COMECON. Between East and West such movements are minuscule.[5]

There is a sense, therefore, in which the Soviet Union and Eastern Europe are outside the normal traffic of people and ideas that occurs for commercial reasons within the Western world and between the West and many of the developing countries. It may be this factor, as much as the deficiencies of the centrally administered economic system, which has led to a fall in the European COMECON countries' already small share in Western countries' imports of manufactures between the mid-1960s and the early 1980s. The countries whose share of Western imports of manufactures has risen are the small group of newly industrializing Third World countries: Brazil,

---

[4] Importing, marketing, retailing and servicing were the principal activities of 280 of the 403 Soviet and Eastern European companies identified as active in the West at end-1981. See Carl H. McMillan, "Soviet and East European Participation in Business Firms and Banks Established in the West: Policy Issues," in NATO Economics Directorate, *External Economic Relations of CMEA Countries: Their Significance and Impact in a Global Perspective*, Brussels, NATO, 1984, pp. 287–301, Table 2. About one-third of the identified COMECON investment in the West for which equity structure was known was in the form of minority or 50–50 ownership, but information structures were not known for a considerable number of the 403 companies. *Ibid.*, Table 3.

[5] Small numbers of workers move between COMECON countries on a temporary basis, usually for particular construction projects such as the laying of gas pipelines. One of the larger recent flows of this kind has been the use of Vietnamese workers in the Soviet Union, East Germany, Bulgaria and Czechoslovakia: 50,000 of them, according to a deputy premier of Vietnam in 1984 (Reuters dispatch from Hanoi, May 18, 1984). The flows from East to West have an odd history: an emigration of around 200,000 persons a year from East to West Germany from 1945 to 1961, when the Berlin Wall was built to stop it; large emigrations from Hungary in 1956 and Czechoslovakia in 1968–69; a total of about 250,000 Soviet Jews and smaller numbers of Armenians and ethnic Germans from the Soviet Union in 1972–82, on what were officially "family reunification" grounds; and a sprinkling of escapees and political exiles. Emigration from West to East is confined, by and large, to "busted" spies.

Singapore, Taiwan, Hong Kong and South Korea. This group of countries has been open to multinational investment.[6]

STRUCTURE AND DYNAMICS

We have so far emphasized the severe limitations within which East and West trade with one another. It would be wrong, however, to suggest that East-West trade is doomed to stagnate. For most of the 1970s it grew faster than world trade as a whole. There are sizable advantages in it for Western firms and Soviet and Eastern European planners, and there is room for considerable further growth of East-West trade in the long run. The limitation is that East-West trade cannot become a large part of Western economic activity so long as the political divisions and systemic incompatibilities remain.

Nonetheless, the geographical proximity of Eastern and Western Europe and the complementarities between Eastern and Western resources create opportunities for mutually advantageous trade. These opportunities are greatly underexploited, but the trade flows that are actually attained indicate their nature.

The USSR has a rich natural endowment of hydrocarbons,[7] minerals, metals and timber. It also has an economic system that handicaps its agriculture and its development of new technologies. In these respects it is a trading partner whose economic strengths and weaknesses make it highly complementary to the Western world. Thus about four-fifths of Soviet exports to the developed West consist of oil, oil products, natural gas and a very small amount of coal. And in 1982 and 1983 together, almost 75 percent of Soviet imports from the developed West consisted of capital goods and food.[8]

The Eastern European situation vis-à-vis the West is different. Apart from Poland's traditional coal exports, the Eastern European countries have not been able to rely on net energy exports. In total they are substantial net importers of energy, chiefly from the Soviet Union. They have therefore

[6] The share of the Eastern European Six (plus Albania) in total OECD imports of manufactures was 1.56 percent in 1965 and 1.46 in 1981; the Soviet share was 0.82 and 0.51, respectively; the combined share of 14 "newly industrializing countries" was 2.74 and 6.95. (U.N. Economic Commission for Europe, *Economic Bulletin for Europe*, Vol. 35, 1983, p. 3.18. This U.N. study provides an extended analysis of these changing shares.)

[7] These include 40 percent of proved and probable world reserves of natural gas, and a smaller but still substantial share of world oil reserves; also 40 percent of world coal reserves (Edward Hewett, reported by VPI from Washington, September 17, 1984. For thorough discussion, see Hewett's *Energy, Economics and Foreign Policy in the Soviet Union*, Washington, D.C., Brookings Institution, 1984, Chapter 2).

[8] Derived from the Soviet trade returns, *Vneshnyaya torgovlya SSSR v 1983 g.*, Moscow; Finansy i statistika, 1984. "Capital goods" here means machinery and equipment (ETN 1 in the Soviet trade classification) plus pipe (ETN 266). "Food" is food, drink and tobacco, including food materials and animal fodder (ETN 7 and 8).

depended much more, in their trade with the West, on the export of agricultural products and manufactures. Here the systemic weaknesses of the centrally administered economy have tended to handicap them, though in Hungary and Bulgaria, in particular, agricultural performance has been better than in the Soviet Union.

The development of East-West trade during the 1970s and early 1980s has, as a result, been quite different for the Soviet Union and for Eastern Europe. In 1971–80, the current value of Soviet hard-currency exports rose tenfold, but most of this increase consisted of price increases—chiefly for oil and gas in the wake of the two major oil-price rises. Export volume (the amount exported, when measured in constant prices) grew only 45 percent over the period. The prices of Soviet imports from the West also rose considerably, but much less than export prices. The terms of trade for the Soviet Union improved, in fact, by an average of eight percent a year, facilitating a much larger volume increase for imports than for exports: about 100 percent, against 45 percent.[9]

In addition, Soviet capacity to import from the West was greatly enhanced by two other developments not allowed for in these terms-of-trade calculations. The gold price in 1982 was 10 times higher than in 1970, and had been 20 times higher on some occasions between those years;[10] Soviet gold sales in 1980 netted about $1.6 billion from some 80 metric tons, compared with $0.3 billion from 158 tons in 1972. And Soviet arms sales to less-developed countries (LDCs) for hard currency rose from about $400 million in 1970 to about $4.2 billion in 1981.[11] (See also Table 4.)

The Eastern European countries benefited from no such windfall gains in the terms of trade as the Soviets derived from the oil, gas and gold price explosions. Indeed, several Eastern European countries suffered severely from deteriorating terms of trade in the 1970s. The terms of Hungary's "dollar" trade deteriorated by 20 percent in 1974–75.[12] Nor did the Eastern European countries have the commercial advantage of a burgeoning arms trade—not, at any rate, on anything like the Soviet scale. Thus the Eastern European Six were badly hurt by the OPEC price rises and the Western stagflation of most of the past decade. The early 1980s cutbacks in their trade with the West, discussed in the next section, are attributable in large part to this circumstance.

FINANCING

Not all East-West trade is "hard-currency" trade. And not all the European COMECON countries' hard-currency trade is East-West trade. But the

[9] See Joan Parpart Zoeter, "USSR: Hard Currency Trade and Payments" in U.S. Congress Joint Economic Committee, *Soviet Economy in the 1980s: Problems and Prospects*, Part 2, Washington, D.C.; U.S. Government Printing Office, 1983, pp. 479–507. The meaning and importance of hard-currency trade are discussed in the next section.

[10] CIA, *Handbook of Economic Statistics, 1983*, Washington, D.C., 1983, p. 48.

[11] Zoeter, *op. cit.*, pp. 503, 504.

[12] U.N., *Economic Survey of Europe in 1983*, Chapter 4.

Table 4

ESTIMATED SOVIET HARD-CURRENCY ACCOUNT BALANCE IN 1983
($ MILLION)

Soviet merchandise		Soviet merchandise	
exports	32,529	imports	−27,630
of which:		of which:	
arms to LDCs	6,000	capital goods	−13,338
	approx.	food	−8,328
other exports to LDCs	3,420	(and of which from Western	
to Western Europe	21,492	Europe	−14,024)
to other West	1,617	Net interest payments	−1,300
Invisibles other than interest,			
net	1,100		
Gold sales	750		
Current account balance			
(+)	5,499		

Source: CIA, *HES 1984*, Washington, D.C., p. 72, modified and amplified by author's calculations from *Vneshnyaya torgovlya SSSR v 1983g.* as detailed in Hanson, "The Soviet Stake in European Détente," paper presented at a conference at the Stiftung Wissenschaft und Politik, Ebenhausen, October 1984.

two flows overlap to a great extent, and the Eastern countries' hard-currency balance of payments is a crucial influence on their trade with the West.

COMECON hard-currency, or convertible-currency, trade is that part of the COMECON countries' foreign trade for which settlement is in convertible currencies: dollars, Deutschmarks, pounds sterling, yen, and so on. The national currencies of the Soviet Union and Eastern Europe are themselves purely domestic currencies, not freely convertible into other currencies or even into one another. They are therefore not acceptable as a means of international payment, either outside or inside COMECON. In most intra-COMECON trade and in Soviet and Eastern European trade with some LDCs, the method of bilateral settlement is used: roughly speaking, a bartering of goods and services exchanged, avoiding currency settlement. In trade with the developed West,[13] with many LDCs and to a modest extent within COMECON, balances between trading partners are settled in Western convertible currencies. This is hard-currency trade. Since convertible currencies are freely convertible into one another, the major financial constraint on, say, Soviet trade with the United States, is the state of the Soviet hard-currency balance as a whole, and not of the bilateral Soviet-American balance.

Official balance-of-payments data are not published by the Soviet Union and most of the Eastern European countries, and their payments position is estimated by Western specialists from a variety of banking and other sources. Earnings from and payments for shipping, tourism and other services, as well as interest payments and receipts, affect the current account

[13] Though not in all cases. E.g., Soviet-Finnish trade is subject to bilateral settlement.

(see Table 4). Lending, borrowing and repayments of principal determine the capital account. Soviet borrowing has been cautious and the debt-service ratio (the proportion of all merchandise and services earnings of hard currency that is required, in a given year, to pay interest and repay principal on outstanding debt) has consistently been kept low.

The external financial position of the Eastern European countries has recently been much weaker than that of the Soviet Union. Of the approximately $78 billion total gross hard-currency debt owed by European COMECON countries in mid-1984, the Soviet portion was only about $21 billion. Poland's debt was about $27 billion, East Germany's $10 billion and Romania's $9 billion.[14] The rise of Eastern European debt to the West in the late 1970s led to the drastic import reductions in the early 1980s, as indicated in Table 1. With the exception of Poland, it has been shown that Western bankers were right in their traditional belief in the ability of Soviet and Eastern European policy makers to cure balance-of-payments problems, if necessary, by cutting import bills through direct administrative decision. To that extent, the high credit ratings of these nations in the 1960s and early 1970s have been shown to have had some foundation. After a dip, those credit ratings have tended to improve again, while those of the major LDC debtor nations have stayed on the floor.[15] But the costs of this adjustment to the domestic economies of Eastern Europe have been high, with cutbacks in investment and—most markedly in Poland—reductions in consumption levels.

TECHNOLOGY TRANSFER AND EAST-WEST TRADE

Two reasons why indebtedness to the West became a problem have already been indicated. One is the reduced volume of Western demand for imports combined with the rapid inflation of Western export prices following the oil-price shocks. Another is the generally mediocre export performance of Eastern European countries on competitive markets.

The other major influence was the pursuit in the 1970s by most of the COMECON countries of a strategy of "import-led growth." The idea behind this strategy was that a rapid expansion of imports of Western machinery, licenses and knowhow would modernize domestic production, updating the product range, improving quality and introducing new and more cost-effective production processes. This would allow domestic growth to accelerate, at least for a time, export performance on competitive markets to improve and major existing categories of imports to be replaced by domestic production. In view of the latter expected consequences, it was reasonable to finance the initial acceleration of technology imports by increased borrowing; this could be repaid later, and the whole process could become self-sustaining.

[14] *Journal of Commerce*, August 1, 1984.
[15] The magazine *Institutional Investor* publishes twice yearly a ranking of the "sovereign risk assessments" of a large number of countries. Here the fall and rise of the USSR and Eastern Europe in the "fashion-conscious" minds of bankers can be traced.

This strategy was pursued extravagantly and chaotically by Poland under Gierek; scarcely at all by Bulgaria and Czechoslovakia; and to some intermediate extent by the other countries of the region. It failed, in the sense that the growth did not become self-sustaining and the technology imports had to be cut back. This was partly because of developments in world markets that were unforseeable in the early 1970s. The Soviet Union alone experienced no serious difficulties, but this was because world price changes greatly boosted the earnings of its traditional exports, not because its economic performance and export market shares were perceptibly improved. Indeed, Soviet economic growth declined sharply in the late 1970s. The other main reason why the strategy failed was that the extra inflows of Western technology did not improve domestic production as much as was hoped.

The impact of technology imports has been most closely studied in the Soviet case.[16] The share of imported Western capital goods in Soviet equipment investment has generally remained below 10 percent. It may have been close to that level in the mid-1970s and have returned to it—probably only temporarily—in 1983–84. Studies of particular Soviet industries show that personnel levels in imported plant are generally higher than they would be in the same plant in the West, and that diffusion of the imported technology to domestically built plant has been extremely limited. The Western technology acquired in this way is unlikely to have added more than half a percentage point to the annual growth rate of Soviet industrial output.

In general, the technological sluggishness of the economic systems inhibits the use made of commercially imported technology. This is not surprising, since Soviet development has always relied heavily on the acquisition and assimilation of foreign technology. The main change over the past 30 years has been toward a greater emphasis on direct, commercial acquisition of that technology, rather than more roundabout and costly copying.

In the smaller Eastern European countries, the share of imported Western machinery in equipment investment was capable of rising to much higher levels. Hungary may have done better in using imported technology than other Eastern European countries, though this is hard to demonstrate firmly. What seem to be Hungarian advantages are a fairly cautious policy at the macroeconomic level and, at the level of the individual farm or industrial enterprises, the greater scope given by the Hungarian semidecentralized system for initiative and for close working relationships with Western firms.

CONCLUSION

In the early 1980s, East-West trade was more inhibited by East-West political antagonism than it had been a decade earlier. But Western recession and the incompatibilities of Western and Eastern economic systems produce

[16] This and the next paragraph draw on the author's *Trade and Technology in Soviet-Western Relations*, London, Macmillan, 1981; "The End of Import-Led Growth? Some observations on Soviet, Polish and Hungarian Experience in the 1980s," *Journal of Comparative Economics*, Vol. 6, no. 2, June 1982, pp. 130–47; and "The Soviet State in European Détente," conference paper, Stiftung Wissenschaft und Politik, Ebenhausen, October 1984.

financial and organizational limits to East-West trade that would be apparent even in a less tense political setting. On the other hand, the COMECON countries cannot do much to help one another, in the long run, in remedying their weaknesses in food production and technological innovation. Their interest in doing business with the West is therefore built into their present economic system, even though that system simultaneously hinders trade.

COMECON

VLADIMIR SOBELL

THE EVOLUTION OF COMECON INSTITUTIONS

THE Council for Mutual Economic Assistance (CMEA, also known by its acronym COMECON) was founded in January 1949 in Moscow during an economic conference held by the founding member countries—Bulgaria, Czechoslovakia, Hungary, Poland, Romania and the USSR.[1] Although the precise reasons that prompted Stalin to establish COMECON are not clear, there is a consensus that his motives were more political than purely economic. The move enabled the Soviet Union to offer the Eastern European countries an alternative international economic authority as a substitute for the Marshall Plan in which, after Soviet pressure, these countries refused to participate. The CMEA also proved an effective tool for isolating Tito's Yugoslavia from the rest of the socialist community headed by the Soviet Union. By the same stroke, it frustrated plans to create the Balkan customs union then contemplated by Dimitrov and Tito. Finally, it ensured the cohesion of the emerging Eastern bloc at a time of rising East-West tensions and economic warfare. Having satisfied these geopolitical aims, Stalin lost interest in the CMEA and the organization was largely moribund for the first five years of its existence.

In the meantime, the member countries began rapid Soviet-type industrialization accompanied by a drastic reorientation of the member countries' trade away from their traditional Western partners and toward the Soviet Union. Amid this process the CMEA gradually became a useful bloc-level forum for at least some measure of trade coordination, mutual consultation and the diffusion of technology. Its institutional structure in this early period was rudimentary, consisting mainly of a system of ad hoc working parties and subdivisions of the permanent Moscow-based CMEA Bureau (later the CMEA Secretariat).

As industrialization passed through its initial stage, the objective pressures

[1] The German Democratic Republic joined the grouping in 1950; Albania was a member in 1949–62; and Mongolia became a full member in 1962, Cuba in 1972 and Vietnam in 1978. Other countries participate as observers. These have included the People's Republic of Korea, the People's Republic of China (1956–66) and, more recently, Afghanistan, Angola, Ethiopia and Laos. Finland and Yugoslavia have enjoyed a loose associate status with the CMEA since the mid-1960s.

415

for managing intrabloc trade and cooperation more effectively grew more and more intense. Specifically, the central European countries did not possess sufficient energy and raw materials to sustain the strategy of industrialization, and more and more primary commodities had to be imported from the Soviet Union. Secondly, since all the countries embarked upon an identical autarkic pattern of industrialization with scant regard for intrabloc specialization, there soon arose severe problems with marketing their goods. After Stalin's death in 1953 it became possible to place CMEA on an institutionally firmer footing and to seek solutions to these fundamental problems. This led to the creation in 1956 of the first standing commissions dealing with cooperation in various industries and sectors. More standing commissions were added in the late 1950s and early 1960s; three more were established in the early 1970s.[2]

Other important measures included the creation in 1962 of the executive committee, composed of deputy prime ministers of the member countries (see Figure 1), and the opening in 1964 of the International Bank for Economic Cooperation (IBEC), based in Moscow and operating with its own unit of account—the Transferable Ruble (TR).

The standing commissions' main tasks were the drawing up of projections using information provided by the national planning offices, and the formulation of cooperation and specialization recommendations. Although their recommendations were produced on a relatively high level, they remained inadequate as tools for overcoming the structurally inherent production parallelism and industrial nationalism strongly entrenched in COMECON. Founding the executive committee was part of Khrushchev's efforts to equip the CMEA with some measure of supranational planning authority to combat these forces. This strategy failed largely due to conflict between Romania and the "northern tier" of membership supported by the Soviet Union, and no fresh moves were made until the end of the decade.

The system that evolved under Khrushchev may have failed to turn COMECON into an effective supranational planning agency, but the experience gained during its formation was valuable for future development. In particular, it became clear that the increased authority of the CMEA, derived from its ability to enforce more rational cooperation and specialization, required abandoning an implicit veto (whereby the opponent of any integration project, most frequently Romania, was in a position to block its acceptance) in favor of the "interested-party" principle. Eventually this led to the evolu-

---

[2]There are now 22 standing commissions. They include: Electrical Energy (established in 1956, located in Moscow), Ferrous Metallurgy (1956, Moscow), Foreign Trade (1956, Moscow), Nonferrous Metallurgy (1956, Budapest), Machine Building (1956, Prague), Chemical Industry (1956, Berlin), Gas and Oil (1956, Bucharest), Agriculture (1956, Sofia), Coal Industry (1956, Warsaw), Light Industry (1958, Prague), Transport (1958, Warsaw), Construction (1958, Berlin), Peaceful Utilization of Nuclear Energy (1960, Moscow), Standardization (1962, Berlin), Statistics (1962, Moscow), Currency and Finance (1962, Moscow), Geology (1963, Ulan Bator), Food Industry (1963, Sofia), Radio Technology and Electronics (1963, Budapest), Post and Telecommunications (1971, Moscow), Civil Aviation (1975, Moscow), and Public Health (1975, Moscow).

tion of new institutional forms—the international economic organizations (IEOs) established by the interested parties outside the CMEA proper but having strong legal and operational links with it. The first IEO—the Organization for Cooperation in the Ball Bearing Industry (OSPP or *Interpodshipnik*) created in April 1964—and the best-known IEOs (*Intermetall* and *Interkhim*) were all founded without Romanian participation.

With Brezhnev's consolidation of power in the early 1970s, it became possible to commence new initiatives in CMEA integration. This was expressed in the adoption in June 1971 of the *Complex Program for the Further Extension and Improvement of Cooperation and the Development of Socialist Economic Integration* (henceforth, *Complex Program*). This document committed member countries to a schedule of cooperation projects in key industrial branches, projects that could be implemented according to the interested-party principle. At the same time, Khrushchev's notion of supranational planning was replaced by Brezhnev's spirit of pragmatism, stability, piecemeal reform and technocratization. The reforms of the CMEA structure and the evolution of new institutional forms reflected this new spirit. In 1971, the bureau of the executive committee, consisting of the deputy chairmen of the national planning agencies, was upgraded to form the committee for cooperation in planning, whose members are the chairmen of these agencies. The creation of such an international planning board resulted in the formation of direct links between the executive committee and the national planning agencies. This reform considerably strengthened the effectiveness of CMEA-wide planning but eschewed full-fledged supranational planning, since the recommendations generated by the new system continue to be subjected to member-government approval in the spirit of the interested-party principle. Similar reform occurred in the organization of joint research; in 1971 the former standing commission for coordination of scientific and technical research was upgraded to become the committee for scientific and technical cooperation and was charged with the supervision of research coordinating centers that were subsequently established throughout COMECON. In 1974, another such committee was added—the committee for cooperation in material and technical supplies. Finally, to assist the financing of the planned joint projects, the International Investment Bank (IIB) was established in Moscow in 1971.

Pragmatism was apparent also at the lower levels of intra-CMEA relations. While in the 1970s only three new standing commissions were added, there occurred a proliferation of less formal and more operative and flexible forms of institutional arrangement. These were the IEOs and IEO-like organizations, interstate commissions to implement specific tasks, such as construction of the Soyuz natural gas pipeline, international laboratories and coordinating centers. At present there are over 50 multilateral and bilateral organizations of this type, as well as over 60 centers. In addition to the IEOs mentioned above, the most important include *Interatomenergo* (cooperation in nuclear-reactor production), *Interatominstrument* (nuclear-industry instrumentation), *Interkhimvolokno* (chemical fibers), *Intertekstilmash* (textile machinery), *Interelektro* (electrotechnical equipment), *Agromash* (fruit- and vegetable-cultivation machinery) and *Intersputnik* (satellite communication). Apart from these multilateral IEOs, there are also similar organizations on a bilateral basis, such as the East German–Soviet *Assofoto* (photographic materials) or the Polish–Hungarian *Interkomponent* (electro-technical and electronics equipment). Finally, special mention must be made of the International Commission for Cooperation in Computer Technology, which is playing a central part in stimulating the production of electronic components, including microprocessors, for the much-needed computerization of COMECON industries and final products.

These COMECON-related organizations have several advantages not shared by the system of standing commissions. First, they are able to effect cooperation among the interested parties without having to dwell on the niceties of their precise legal position; being an expression of a pragmatic spirit, they tend to be concerned with getting *some* tangible results, rather than with the official "COMECON building" prevalent in the Khrushchev era. Second, whereas the standing commissions organize cooperation on the level of industrial ministries, the IEOs and IEO-type organizations usually operate at the middle or microeconomic levels, establishing direct links among Eastern European industrial associations and individual enterprises. (In this respect, the IEOs have a role similar to that of Western multinational companies, now in the process of economic integration.) Third, they are better placed to promote industrial cooperation and specialization on the microeconomic level, within individual industrial branches and sub-branches. Here much progress can be made without certain nonspecializing countries having to give up the development of entire industrial sectors. The precise organizational structure and legal position of individual IEOs vary and are largely determined by the function they perform; they are denoted in Figure 1 under their generic heading of functional organizations.

Soon after the adoption of the *Complex Program* the reinvigorated institutions of COMECON began to translate their commitment to intensified cooperation into action. In 1973, the 27th session of the council (meeting annually, composed of prime ministers and permanent representatives to the CMEA; see Figure 1) resolved that a special section for "integration measures" be introduced in member countries' annual, five-year and long-term plans, and harmonized into a coherent plan by the committee for co-operation in planning. In 1975, the 29th session approved the first plan for multilateral integration measures for 1976–80; another such plan was prepared for the 1981–85 period. The 1976–80 plan included some very large projects, such as the construction of the Soyuz natural-gas pipeline. In the course of this plan's preparation it became clear that enlarged joint planning made little sense unless it was accompanied by a still more complex and comprehensive "systems" approach. The 30th session, held in 1976, resolved to prepare five major integration programs, referred to as "long-term target programs" (LTTPs), plotting the course of cooperation up to the year 2000. The LTTPs were prepared and adopted in the course of the 1976–80 plan in the following sectors: energy and raw materials, engineering, agriculture and the food industry, transport and the consumer-goods industries. The LTTPs are modeled on Soviet experience with target planning. Essentially they amount to a broad multilateral agreement on desirable long-term object-

Figure 1

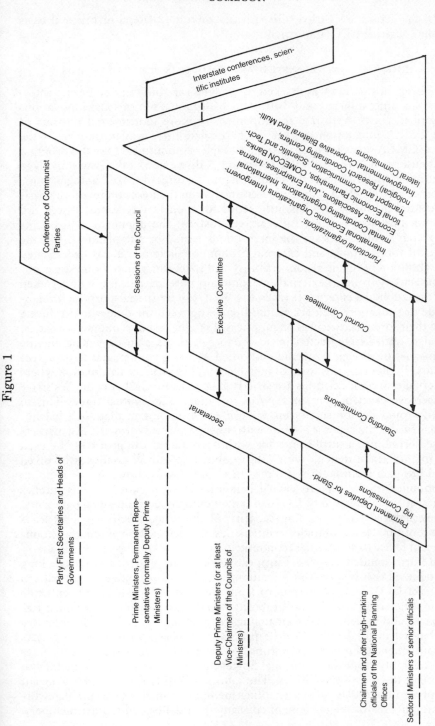

THE STRUCTURE OF COMECON INSTITUTIONS

Conference of Communist Parties

Party First Secretaries and Heads of Governments

Sessions of the Council

Prime Ministers, Permanent Representatives (normally Deputy Prime Ministers)

Executive Committee

Deputy Prime Ministers (or at least Vice-Chairmen of the Councils of Ministers)

Secretariat

Council Committees

Standing Commissions

Chairmen and other high-ranking officials of the National Planning Offices

Permanent Deputies for Standing Commissions

Sectoral Ministers or senior officials

Interstate conferences, scientific institutes

Functional organizations: International Economic Organizations (Intergovernmental Coordinating Organizations, International Economic Associations, Joint Enterprises, International Economic Partnerships, COMECON Banks, Transport and Communication, Scientific and Technological) Research Coordinating Centers, Intergovernmental Cooperative Bilateral and Multilateral Commissions

419

ives; the details are settled subsequently on a multilateral or bilateral basis in the course of LTTP implementation.

The Brezhnev period was marked by pragmatism, but can also be characterized as a time of inertia and drift. The institutional reforms and innovations described above were not accompanied by more fundamental reforms of the CMEA integration system. In particular, there was no reform of the intra-CMEA financial mechanism, although a commitment to such a program was enshrined in the *Complex Program*. A discussion of the issues involved requires a brief outline of the main systemic features of CMEA integration.

Since all COMECON member countries run their economies on the basis of central planning, there is little scope for monetary relations, prices and market forces to become fully active. Instead, the dominant instruments of resource allocation are the instructions issued by the planners. On the level of foreign trade and external economic relations this has necessitated the abolition of financial convertibility and strict isolation of domestic economic activity from the external environment. Foreign trade is not undertaken by the individual enterprises (as in the West) but by special-purpose foreign-trade organizations that act as middlemen between the domestic producers and their foreign customers or suppliers. Like the rest of economic activities, foreign trade is conducted in accordance with its plan drawn up by the ministries of foreign trade and embodied in intergovernmental trade agreements. In practice, this form of management has produced a situation where external economic relations are strictly bilateral: the CMEA countries strive to achieve exact balance of exports and imports in mutual trade. This in itself would not be significant were it not for the fact that such balance is achieved at the expense of trade with other partners. Normally, in a market-based economy, a surplus in trade with one country can profitably be used to finance trade deficits with other countries, and all countries involved stand to gain from increased trade. In COMECON, however, all member economies try to achieve virtual balance with one another. This implies that trade flows tend to be less than they would under multilateral payments, being reduced to the earning capacity of the weakest partner. This leads to suboptimal levels of trade, to intensities of specialization within the grouping and hence to substantial economic losses.

Reform-minded Eastern European economists and officials have long recognized that bilateralism is a stumbling block to a more efficient pattern of intra-COMECON division of labor. Several proposals have been made to multilateralize payments. In recent years, these pressures have most frequently and forcefully been emanating from Hungary, because that country embarked in the late 1960s on a program of market-oriented reforms. As a consequence, Hungary now runs a system that in some respects diverges considerably from the traditional Soviet model and at points conflicts with those of the rest of the CMEA. The foundation of IBEC in 1964 was meant to promote multilateralism, enabling member countries to accumulate surpluses in TRs for the purpose of covering their deficits with other members.

However, member countries have continued to adhere to bilateral practices and have been reluctant to accumulate assets in TRs. (Reformers and Western observers do not consider that the TR performs the functions of genuine money; in their view it merely serves as a unit of account.) More fundamental reforms are obviously necessary. Genuine multilateralism could be achieved with a Hungarian-like reform in most of the member countries. Apart from adopting measures designed to reactivate money and prices (both internally and externally), such reforms must introduce some measure of commodity convertibility. Individual enterprises should be able to engage in direct trade with their partners in other member countries without having to secure approval of each such transaction from industrial ministries and ministries of foreign trade. Reforms of this nature unfortunately face formidable political obstacles, for they involve a significant devolution of decision making power from the central organs to the enterprise managers. All CMEA countries, including the Soviet Union, have experimented with market-oriented reforms, but only Hungary has succeeded in implementing some of the features of a market economy.

As noted, the *Complex Program* contained a commitment to reform, due largely to Hungarian insistence. This part of the *Complex Program* has been completely disregarded, although some minor changes in IBEC regulations have been introduced. The only reform of the intra-CMEA financial system of any significance was the introduction in 1975 of a new principle for the formation of intra-COMECON prices. These prices are not market related, but are fixed in the course of trade agreement negotiations—the world market price for the commodity in question being only one of the factors. Since 1975, prices have been fixed on the basis of a five-year moving average, instead of the previous system under which prices were fixed each five years. This reform aimed at forcing the CMEA economies to be more responsive to the world markets' inflation, particularly with regard to energy and raw-materials prices. It also enabled the Soviet Union to charge more for its exports of oil to COMECON; the 1974 energy-price rise would have placed an unacceptable burden on the Soviets if proceeds from exports of energy to COMECON were not allowed to increase in line, after a time lag, with Western inflation. Though it has been significant, the reform did not address those more fundamental issues that would have made the CMEA's integration more efficient.

As is indicated in Figure 1, the entire structure of COMECON and its related institutions is presided over by meetings of the Communist party leaders and heads of governments of the member countries. Gatherings of top leaders and officials, devoted specifically to COMECON affairs, are rare, although COMECON issues are discussed during other such occasions, and top leaders also meet prior to the formal annual sessions of the CMEA council. The most important COMECON summits were those of May 1958, which formulated the principles of cooperation prevalent in the Khrushchev era; June 1971, which adopted the *Complex Program*; and, more recently, the summit of June 1984. The need for this latest summit was first announced by Brezhnev in early 1981. It was to consider the many problems and changed circumstances since 1971. In particular, it was to deal with the planning

421

and implementation of the LTTPs, with the COMECON economies' unprecedented slowing of growth rates and their severe balance-of-payments problems, and with disruption of intra-CMEA trade caused by the collapsing Polish economy. The preparations for this summit took place amid the hopes that the new Soviet leader, Yuri Andropov, would put an end to the drift of the Brezhnev era. There was also speculation that the summit would deal with the long-neglected, much-needed reforms of the COMECON integration system. In the event, the gathering, which Andropov did not live to see, merely reiterated the need for greater cohesion in the face of the increasingly hostile West and for more effective alignment of entire strategies of development to prevent a recurrence of the errors of the 1970s (such as excessive dependence on imports of Western technology and on Western loans). The issue of systemic reform was hardly touched on at all. Yet most observers now accept that there is at least some chance of meaningful moves on this front with the accession to power of a new generation of Soviet leaders under Mikhail Gorbachev.

THE CHANGING FOCUS OF COMECON INTEGRATION

Discussion of the intra-CMEA financial mechanism cannot be separated from larger aspects of economic development in Eastern Europe. The CMEA was established during a period of rapid industrialization of the predominantly agrarian Eastern European economies. There was then plenty of scope for fast growth as industrialization (in particular, industrialization according to the Soviet model) ensured speedy mobilization of unemployed or underemployed resources. By the late 1960s and early 1970s, however, this extensive strategy of growth had largely run out of factors of production; the planners had to work more and more on efficiency and productivity rather than relying on the sheer addition to the existing factors of production as before. In other words, the COMECON economies entered the age of intensive growth.

These fundamental shifts were reflected in the realm of intra-COMECON trade and cooperation. As the member countries embarked on rapid industrialization, they needed to import ever-growing quantities of energy and raw materials. The Soviet Union, which by 1965 was the only net exporter of such commodities, was prepared to satisfy the bulk of their needs. The supplies of primary commodities from the Soviet Union to the rest of the group came therefore to constitute the core of the COMECON's integration system; the joint erection of energy infrastructure (oil and natural gas pipelines, electricity grids) is a dramatic manifestation of this development. The transition to the intensive mode of growth implies that the center of gravity of CMEA integration must shift away from energy to cooperation in intensification of the member economies. Instead of serving as a vehicle for securing ever-increasing supplies of primary commodities, CMEA must be turned into a tool for making more out of the available resources by means of joint research, production specialization and joint investment in plants supplying advanced technology.

One of the primary causes of inefficient production, waste of primary

materials, low technical standards of final products and poor export performance is the lack of computerization. There has been insufficient application
of electronics, especially microprocessor technology, at all stages of production and in the final products. The progress of computerization in COM-
ECON has been hampered by the relatively low development level of
electronics components, and especially by the slow transition to use of microprocessors. In order to help eliminate this bottleneck, the Council's 25th
session in 1981 concluded a general agreement to cooperate in creating a
unified range of electronic components. A similar agreement was signed
in 1982 to cooperate in the production of microprocessors. These agreements
should rapidly increase the production and mutual intra-CMEA exchanges
of these strategically important items. Their assimilation should also make
an appreciable impact on productivity. The fact that these agreements coincided with the imposition of ceilings on exports of Soviet oil to
COMECON is a sign that the above-noted shifts in the purpose of the
CMEA will be gradually implemented in the 1980s and beyond. COM-
ECON's computerization, however, is bound to be a long-drawn-out affair,
and will not be possible without the cooperation of Western companies.
Such a massive transition requires a more flexible institutional and financial
mechanism, capable of promoting direct interenterprise links. The present
lack of political will suggests that most CMEA governments are prepared
to tolerate losses due to suboptimal specialization. Yet there is the possibility
that sufficient progress will be made by means of incremental, piecemeal
improvements—such as the further expansion and improvement of IEOs
and IEO-type organizations.

AGRICULTURE

EVERETT M. JACOBS

INTRODUCTION

THE Soviet Union and the countries of Eastern Europe (except for Czechoslovakia and East Germany) were backward and overwhelmingly agricultural
before the communists seized power. The major part of the labor force in
these countries was engaged in farming, and exports consisted mainly of
large shipments of grain to Western Europe. Little had been done, however,
to modernize the agricultural sector of these countries. As a result, farming
methods remained generally primitive, rural areas suffered from acute overpopulation and most peasants lacked sufficient land to provide an adequate
standard of living for their families.

Once in power, the communists' goal was to apply Marxist principles
to transform these backward countries into advanced industrial societies.
In effect this doomed independent small-scale peasant farming, since Marxist
ideology demanded the collective ownership and large-scale use of the means
of production. The new system of collectivized farming was first developed
in the Soviet Union and was later adopted with some modification by most
of the communist countries of Eastern Europe.

THE SOVIET EXAMPLE

The Bolsheviks responded to the peasants' seizure and division of the land-
lords' estates by decreeing a land reform as soon as they took power in
the Soviet Union. The New Economic Policy (NEP), adopted after the civil
war, succeeded in restoring industrial and agricultural production to prerevolutionary levels by about 1927. However, agricultural production and deliveries were not rising fast enough to meet the economy's needs. The regime
wanted to carry out rapid industrialization with major emphasis on heavy
industry; under the conditions then prevailing, this required large quantities
of cheap grain to feed the growing urban population and provide goods
for export. At the same time, agricultural investments had to be kept to
a minimum. Stalin's solution was to force the peasants to join collective
farms where their production activities could be more closely controlled
by the state.

Almost 60 percent of the peasant households were enrolled in collective
farms by March 1930, at which time strong peasant opposition forced a

temporary decollectivization. Recollectivization began less than a year later, and by the end of 1936, more than 90 percent of the peasant households and almost all of the country's sown area had been collectivized.

Three types of collective farms had been organized during the NEP period, but the simplest form, called the cooperative tillage association (TOZ) and the most radical form, called the commune, were eliminated during mass collectivization in favor of the artel form of collective. In the artel (commonly called the *kolkhoz* after 1936), the peasants' land, machinery and most of their animals became the collective property of the farms' members, though the peasants were allowed to keep small garden plots and limited numbers of animals for their own use. Instead of receiving fixed wages, each peasant earned "labor days" computed on the basis of job classification and the number of days worked. After all of the farm's obligations, excluding wages, had been met, the remaining income in cash and kind was distributed to the peasants in accordance with the number of labor days they had accumulated. The value of a labor day, therefore, varied from farm to farm and, if a farm did poorly, the peasants received little or no remuneration for their work. Because labor day payments were usually very low, minimum labor day quotas were established to force the peasants to work on the collectives.

The collective farm's first duty was to fulfill burdensome state production plans. In order to ensure this, a state-run system of machine-tractor stations (MTSs) was given responsibility for economic and political control over the farms. The MTSs had a monopoly on farm machinery and carried out all mechanized work in return for a payment in kind. Political surveillance was maintained by the MTS political departments.

A number of state farms, termed *sovkhozes*, were also set up. *Sovkhozes* were much larger than *kolkhozes*, were financed by the state and received the most modern machinery and equipment. In contrast to collective farms, *sovkhoz* workers were state employees and therefore received fixed wages (mainly in cash) and state pensions, and also belonged to a trade union. A *sovkhoz* worker's income was often several times higher than a collective farmer's, though lower than an industrial worker's. *Sovkhozes* were considered the highest form of socialist agriculture and were supposed to serve as models for the *kolkhozes*. However, they were expensive to run, and the government decided to concentrate on the expansion of the *kolkhoz* system in the prewar years.

Soviet agriculture has been reorganized several times since the war, but only some of the changes have been of lasting importance. Among them, a campaign to create giant collectives by amalgamating smaller farms caused the number of *kolkhozes* to drop by more than 252,000 in mid-1950, to 36,276 in 1965 and to only 26,039 at the end of 1983, at which time each averaged an agricultural area of 6,650 hectares (ha.)[1] and a work force in the communal economy of 496. By contrast, the number of *sovkhozes* has increased steadily since 1954, first as a result of the development of the Virgin Lands and then as a result of the conversion of many weak

[1]One hectare equals 2.471 acres.

kolkhozes into *sovkhozes*. The number of state farms rose from 5,134 in 1955 to 11,681 in 1965 and to 22,313 at the end of 1983, when each had an average agricultural area of 16,900 ha. and a work force of 534 (including those working in *sovkhoz* factories and ancillary enterprises). An experiment to end most state subsidies to selected *sovkhozes* and make them fully responsible for their own profits and losses (as *kolkhozes* always have been) was introduced in 1967. By 1975, all *sovkhozes* had been transferred to this system of "full economic responsibility." In 1983, *sovkhozes* accounted for 62.3 percent of the USSR's agricultural land, while *kolkhozes* accounted for 28.7 percent.

Another major change was the abolition of the MTSs and the sale of their machinery to the *kolkhozes* in 1958. A declared aim of this move was to give the farms more say in their production activities. In practice, however, neither the abolition of the MTSs nor the adoption of new model statutes for *kolkhozes* in 1969 has made the collective farms the masters of their own fate. State and Communist party agencies still maintain close control over both *kolkhozes* and *sovkhozes*. Moreover, strict central planning of agricultural production and deliveries to the state for all farms has meant that little real independence has been granted to the agricultural sector.

Since the mid-1970s, Soviet agricultural policy has stressed the specialization and concentration of agricultural production on the basis of interfarm cooperation and agro-industrial integration. The decision to move in this direction was based on an assessment of foreign (particularly U.S., but also Bulgarian) experience, and the operation of large-scale specialized farms and inter*kolkhoz* associations in the USSR. Horizontal integration, involving greater financial and economic cooperation and coordination among farms in large-scale production work and production specialization, was to be achieved through the creation of interfarm enterprises uniting *kolkhozes*, *sovkhozes*, or both *kolkhozes* and *sovkhozes*, with or without the participation of nonagricultural enterprises. The number of interfarm associations rose from 6,330 in 1975 to 9,638 in 1980 and 9,897 in 1983, with farms (especially *kolkhozes*) typically belonging to two or more interfarm associations. Activities include the production of meat, poultry, eggs, milk, and mixed and other feeds, as well as electrification, construction work and the manufacture of building materials. Vertical integration, involving the integration of the agricultural sector with the industrial sector relating to it, was to occur through establishing agro-industrial enterprises. These could involve *kolkhozes*, *sovkhozes*, interfarm enterprises, processing enterprises, and transport and other enterprises that, besides producing agricultural products, would also process, pack, store and even market them. The scant data on these agro-industrial enterprises suggest that vertical integration of Soviet agriculture has, in practice, a very low priority; there were "more than 500" agro-industrial enterprises of various types at the end of 1980, and only 475 at the end of 1983.

In spite of, or perhaps because of, slow progress towards agro-industrial integration, Brezhnev's May 1982 reforms (as part of the so-called Food Program) called for the creation of district-level agro-industrial associations (RAPOs) throughout the country. Each RAPO was to incorporate *kolkhozes, sovkhozes,* interfarm formations and other agricultural enter-prises, as well as enterprises and organizations providing services to them and connected with agricultural production and the processing of produce. The aims were to strengthen the district level of agricultural management, rationalize and improve the coordination of agricultural production within and between districts, and foster agro-industrial integration. Agro-industrial associations at the province, republic and national level were created to over-see the operations of the RAPOs. By mid-1983, RAPOs had been established in 3,105 of the country's 3,213 districts. Because so many bodies (including Communist party organizations, local government, various ministries and departments, and various industrial and other enterprises) have retained cer-tain responsibilities for aspects of local agricultural production, the RAPOs have found it difficult to achieve their aims and have been accused of duplica-tion of work and attempts at petty tutelage.

COLLECTIVIZATION IN EASTERN EUROPE

The Eastern European communist regimes have in general based their agricul-tural policies on the Soviet example, beginning with land reform and ending, except in Yugoslavia and Poland, with full collectivization. One important difference is that in Eastern Europe the communists, not the peasants, initiated the postwar land reforms. The most radical reforms occurred in Czechoslovakia, Poland, Hungary and East Germany, countries in which there were large concentrations of land in private ownership. On the other hand, communist land reform had almost no effect in Bulgaria, was of minimal importance in Yugoslavia and had only moderate impact in Romania, since prewar reforms had eliminated most inequalities in land ownership in these countries.

Collectivization followed land reform much sooner in Eastern Europe than in the Soviet Union, though the pace and extent of collectivization varied from country to country. In countries where land reform had little effect, collectivization began almost immediately. Bulgaria started first, followed by Yugoslavia in 1945. Most of the other countries began collectivi-zation in the early and mid-1950s in connection with programs for rapid industrial development.

Collectivization speeded up in Yugoslavia after the break with the Comin-form, but a reversal of policy in 1953 brought with it the permanent dissolu-tion of Yugoslavia's collectives. Meanwhile, Bulgaria, Czechoslovakia, Hungary and Romania accelerated their collectivization drives between 1950 and 1953, though the movement failed to make much progress during this period in Poland and East Germany.

Collectivization came to a temporary halt in Eastern Europe during the "new course" adopted after Stalin's death. The area collectivized actually decreased by one-third in Hungary and Czechoslovakia in 1953; but by 1955 the process had resumed on a moderate scale in most places except Bulgaria, which had begun rapid collectivization. The disturbances in Hun-gary and Poland in 1956 caused a short-lived decollectivization in the former, and the permanent breakup of the fledgling collective farm system in the latter. Czechoslovakia, Hungary and Romania began mass collectivization again after 1958, followed by East Germany in 1960. Collectivization was completed by Bulgaria in 1958, by Czechoslovakia, East Germany and Hungary in 1961, and by Romania in 1962. Yugoslavia has remained uncollectivized, and only about 4.5 percent of Poland's agricultural land was farmed collectively in 1982 (as opposed to about one percent in 1967).

Although the Soviet Union eliminated all other types of collective farms in favor of the *kolkhozes* during the period of mass collectivization, most Eastern European countries found it necessary to maintain from two to four different types of collective farms with varying degrees of collective ownership. The lower types resembled the Soviet TOZ, while the highest type was similar to the *kolkhoz*. Only Bulgaria adopted a *kolkhoz*-type farm as the sole form of collective. By the mid-1960s, most Eastern European countries had begun to eliminate the lower types of collectives by upgrading them until they reached the highest type. East Germany, the last country in which the lower-type collectives were of economic significance, completed its upgrading program in 1976. The lower types of collectives that still exist in Eastern Europe, e.g., commercial garden cooperatives in East Germany and specialized production cooperatives in Hungary and Czechoslovakia, are negligible in number and in economic importance.

The process of upgrading collective farms took a unique turn in Bulgaria in the early 1970s when collective and state farms ceased to exist as separate entities and were reorganized into a system of giant agro-industrial complexes (APKs), each covering an average of 30,000 ha. of agricultural land in 1975. Since 1978, there has been a tendency to divide the APKs into smaller, more manageable, units. At the end of 1982, there were 296 APKs in Bulgaria, each averaging 12,400 ha. of agricultural land and about 2,660 full-time farmers. Bulgarian APKs are thus by far the largest socialist farms of any type outside the Soviet Union. In the other Eastern European countries, collective farms are still considerably smaller than state farms, in spite of periodic campaigns to amalgamate collective farms. In 1982, Romanian collectives were the smallest in collectivized Eastern Europe, averaging about 2,100 ha. of agricultural land. However, the ongoing merger campaign promises to make Romanian collectives larger in the near future. In Czechoslovakia, collective farms averaged about 2,600 ha. of agricultural land, and in Hungary, 4,375 ha. of cultivated land. In East Germany, the reorganization of farms into highly specialized crop or livestock enterprises, beginning in 1975, has led to the creation of the largest collective farms in Eastern Europe (collective crop farms averaged 4,725 ha. of agricultural land in 1982, with a number of them ranging from 15,000 to 30,000 ha.).

Poland's tiny collective-farm sector, in 1982 comprising only about 2,400 farms, each averaging 335 ha. of agricultural land and 55 member households, is complemented by a network of cooperative organizations called agricultural circles. The circles, established with the collapse of collectivization in 1956, originally acquired farm machinery and equipment for the collective use of the individual peasant farms. Since 1964 they have also engaged in the collective cultivation of land, milk processing, livestock breeding, drainage, etc. In the early 1970s, cooperative associations of agricultural circles were formed, uniting the circles of several villages. The number of circles and cooperative associations has remained relatively stable over the past 10 years, amounting to about 35,000 circles and 19,000 cooperative associations in 1982. However, the membership in the circles has declined gradually since the end of the 1970s, to 2,337,000 in 1982 (still about half of all Polish peasants)—reflecting the fall in the peasant population and the diminishing importance of the circles thanks to the greater availability of individually owned tractors and farm machinery to the peasants.

Each Eastern European country at one time set up a state farm system based on the Soviet model, though on a far less extensive scale. As mentioned above, Bulgaria no longer has state farms per se, having merged them with collective farms in the early 1970s to form APKs. In 1982, state farms (excluding other state agricultural enterprises) occupied almost 20 percent of agricultural land in Czechoslovakia and Poland, 12 to 15 percent in Yugoslavia, Romania and Hungary, and only about seven percent in East Germany. In terms of average size, Eastern European state farms fell into three general groups in 1982: relatively small (1,000–1,250 ha. of agricultural land), in Poland and Yugoslavia; relatively medium-sized (about 5,200 ha.), in East Germany (crop-growing state farms) and Romania; and relatively large, in Czechoslovakia (6,400 ha.) and Hungary (7,200 ha.).

For the most part, the Eastern European countries have followed the Soviet example of abolishing the MTSs and selling their machinery to the collectives. Certain exceptions are still to be found in Czechoslovakia, Bulgaria and Romania. In Czechoslovakia, most MTSs were abolished by 1961. About 100 were retained in agriculturally poorly endowed regions and were renamed construction and tractors stations. They currently provide certain construction, mechanization, land melioration and related services for collective farms. In Bulgaria, the APKs as a rule each formed an agrochemical center and a machinery enterprise of their own by the mid-1970s. However, MTSs have been retained in certain badly off regions to provide mechanization services. Bulgaria had 34 MTSs in 1980, reorganized into 68 by 1982. In both Czechoslovakia and Bulgaria, however, the vast bulk of farm machinery is now in the hands of the collective farms or APKs. In Romania, the MTSs were converted into Stations for the Mechanization of Agriculture (SMAs), which were originally responsible for controlling all the major machinery used on collective farms. In 1979, the machinery parks of the state farms were combined with those of the SMAs so that the SMAs became responsible for allocating machinery to all Romanian farms and also took over the transport tasks for the agricultural section. Since 1981, all SMA machines and their operators have been hired on long-term contracts to individual enterprises, although the SMAs retain machinery ownership, perform maintenance and repair, provide fuel and lubricants, oversee general machinery use and purchase new machinery.

In terms of agro-industrial integration, Bulgaria was the first, and so far the only, communist country to introduce horizontal integration on a national scale, through the APKs. The APKs originally were hindered by excessive size, overspecialization and planning inflexibility, but measures to alleviate these faults have been introduced since the late 1970s. Bulgarian policy is

429

for each of its counties to achieve self-sufficiency in crop and livestock production. Since 1981, only "surplus" production is to be transported out of a county, thus saving the cost of transporting goods that will have to be returned later. Each APK normally concentrates production on four or five main crops and usually only one branch of livestock production. Planning flexibility has been increased by limiting an APK's compulsory indicators to four main items: obligatory sales to the state of no more than eight products; tax payments to the state budget on the basis of total agricultural land; import and export targets; and limits on the supply of basic kinds of machinery, raw materials, fuel and power.

Bulgaria has also moved forward with vertical integration, though rather slowly and in only a few spheres. A small number of Industrial-Agricultural Complexes (PAKs), distinguished by the predominance of an industrial enterprise in their organization, have specialized in the production and processing of sugar beets since the early 1970s. They have apparently accounted for about half the sugar beet area since the late 1970s, but their production results have been disappointing. Scientific Production Associations (NPOs), combining research establishments with large-scale production and processing enterprises, have functioned with some success in seed production and the production and processing of poultry and pork since the mid-1970s. At the end of 1982, the poultry NPO controlled 21 meat and egg combines housing 22.6 million fowl, and the pork production NPO had 18 production establishments with 965,000 pigs.

East Germany's attempt at horizontal integration through the creation of large-scale specialized crop and livestock farms in the mid-1970s has encountered many difficulties. The rigid separation of the two sectors has hampered the necessary transfer of labor and resources and has made intersector coordination difficult. Moreover, the large size of the crop-growing farms, often covering five or six villages, has led to considerable additional costs in transport and labor in order to get workers, produce, materials and machinery from place to place. Also, the weakening of village links through the creation of large, specialized farms has led many farm workers, especially the young, to treat farming more as purely a job rather than as a way of life. The resultant lack of motivation and the drift of young specialists from the land have hindered moves to raise labor productivity and have contributed to the rural labor shortage. In an effort to remedy some of these problems, 1,170 so-called cooperation councils were given the task, in 1981, of achieving economic coordination between the 1,119 crop and 2,830 livestock collective farms. Having had little success under present arrangements, the cooperation councils are scheduled to take over handling both supplies and finance for the two sectors as of 1986. However, little has been achieved to improve the coordination between the 73 crop and 319 livestock state farms.

Horizontal integration schemes for crop production, livestock production and the provision of joint production services have been introduced fairly extensively in Romanian agriculture since the early 1970s. However, their operation has been somewhat unsatisfactory, and the system has been reformed several times. Integration schemes typically have involved four or five farms (usually, but not necessarily exclusively, collective farms), but some schemes have involved 50, 60, or even 100 farms, sometimes 100 to 150 kilometers apart. In February 1979, 709 "unitary state and cooperative agro-industrial councils," covering an average of 15,000 to 20,000 ha. of agricultural land, were created. One of their tasks was to achieve "even fuller integration" in the production activities of the state and collective farms, SMAs and integration associations they were to oversee. However, little was achieved in practice. In November 1982, new emphasis was given to links between collective farms and state enterprises for the production, purchase and sale of agricultural commodities. In June 1983, old-style inter-cooperative associations linking several collective farms (accused by party leader Ceauşescu of disorganizing production and operating worse than the basic units) were replaced by almost identical intercooperative economic associations. However, such regular administrative tinkering is no substitute for genuine economic and management reform, and further changes can be expected.

The only other Eastern European country to have undertaken significant measures for concentration and specialization of production (except through farm amalgamations) is Hungary. In the early 1970s, Hungary began to introduce advanced technology and industrial methods largely imported from the West to create Closed Production Systems (CPSs) for the production, and sometimes also the processing, of such products as wheat, maize, sunflower seed, sugar beets, milk and poultry. The organizer of the CPS is as a rule a larger, leading specialist producer, which through contracts unites a number of farms providing land, production facilities and labor. The chief enterprise provides participating farms with equipment, machinery, spare parts, seeds, fertilizers, herbicides, breeding stock, etc. The organizing farm also works out the technology of production, organizes training of personnel, sees to technical services, and so on. In return, the beneficiary farms pay the chief enterprise a defined percentage commission from the additional production received by the farm after the introduction of the system. The dramatic improvement in Hungarian productivity in recent years is to a large extent attributable to the countrywide adoption of CPS methods.

PRODUCTION RESULTS

The essence of collectivization has been to take the most possible out of agriculture while putting the least possible into it. Because industrial development has traditionally received higher priority than agricultural development in the communist countries, the tendency has been to keep agricultural investment to minimum levels, resulting in relatively low mechanical and technical standards and also poor performance. However, the increasing realization that the slow rate of growth in the agricultural sector was retarding overall economic development led a number of countries to step up agricultural investment in the 1970s (see Table 1). However, by the start of the 1980s, serious economic problems in Bulgaria, East Germany, Yugoslavia and Romania led to reductions in agriculture's share of national investment as part of a general belt-tightening. By contrast, the Soviet Food Program

Table 1

CAPITAL INVESTMENT IN AGRICULTURE, AND TRACTOR AND FERTILIZER USE

Country	Agriculture's share[a] of total productive capital investments in the economy (%)			Tractor horsepower per 100 hectares of arable land and perennial plantations			Mineral fertilizer consumption per hectare of arable land and perennial plantations (kilograms of active ingredients)		
	1960	1970	1981–1983[b]	1960	1970	1983	1960	1970	1983
Soviet Union	13.2	17.9	19.6	22	51	97	12	47	103
Bulgaria	29.7	15.7	10.7	21	54	97	36	159	248
Czechoslovakia	16.8	10.7	12.9	43	109	176	95	230	344
East Germany	11.7	12.8	8.9	49	143	206	188	319	290
Hungary	14.7	21.7	16.3	24	56	86	29	150	300
Poland	12.6	16.3	19.7	12	51	219	49	162	215
Romania	19.6	16.4	15.9	17	59	107	8	67	134[c]
Yugoslavia	22.8	11.7	6.0[c]	16	37	145[c]	34	77	122[c]

[a] Including investments in forestry; prices of corresponding years.
[b] Average annual share.
[c] 1982.

Sources: *Statisticheskii ezhegodnik stran-chlenov Soveta Ekonomicheskoi Vzaimopomoschchi, 1980*, Moscow, 1980, pp. 143, 147, 239, 242; *Statisticheskii ezhegodnik...1984*, Moscow, 1984, pp. 131, 135, 201, 204; *Statistički Godisnjak Jugoslavije, 1980*, Belgrade, 1980, pp. 182–83, 186; *Statistički Godisnjak...1983*, Belgrade, 1983, pp. 186, 202, 229, 238.

envisaged spending the country out of its agricultural problems. It called for agriculturally related investments (including those for land improvement, rural housing and roads, and development of related manufacturing and processing industries) to climb to approximately one-third of all productive and nonproductive capital investments in 1986–90, as against around 27 percent in 1981–85. Czechoslovakia and Poland likewise began gradually to increase agriculture's share of investments at the start of the 1980s. Meanwhile Hungary, having invested heavily in agriculture in the 1970s, cut back noticeably at the start of the 1980s and, at least in the short term, reaped the rewards of previous investment policy.

The level of mechanization has improved in all communist countries in recent years, most especially in Poland and Yugoslavia, where tractors have been made available in increasing numbers for the private sector. However, throughout the communist countries, spare parts remain in short supply, maintenance costs are high and, as in the past, large numbers of tractors remain out of operation for long periods because of inadequate maintenance and repair facilities. It is interesting to note that Hungary now has the lowest amount of tractor horsepower per 100 ha. of arable land and perennial plantations; but for the most part it has still been able to achieve yields high by Soviet and Eastern European (and sometimes Western European) standards (see Tables 1 and 2). This is partly due to Hungary's high level of fertilizer consumption, the application of Western production systems and the fact that Hungary has the highest share of arable land in proportion to total agricultural land (that is, there is little other land on which tractors or fertilizers would be wastefully used). Although Romania still uses less fertilizer than almost any other communist country (in part accounting for Romania's relatively low yields), consumption of fertilizers has risen very quickly (in part accounting for the rapid growth of yields). In spite of much attention given to the fertilizer industry, the Soviet Union is still inadequately supplied, resulting in its very low and relatively stagnant yields.

Most of the communist countries have made great strides in recent years to improve their yields (Table 2). Notable successes in the past 20 or so years include the doubling of wheat yields in Bulgaria and Hungary; the doubling of maize yields in Bulgaria, Hungary, Yugoslavia and Romania; a doubling of sunflower yield and a rise of more than 90 percent in milk yields in Hungary. The rate of growth of yields in the Soviet Union has been comparatively slow (no official grain yields or production figures have been released since 1980, seemingly underlining this), and more often than not, the USSR now has the lowest yields of the communist countries. The poor Soviet performance, having so great a weight in the average figures for the communist countries taken as a group, tends to mask often quite good results from Eastern Europe.

Of course, the figures in Table 2 can tell only part of the story, shedding no light on sizable harvest losses (typically 15 to 35 percent) due to poor transport and storage, declining sugar content in sugar beets, the large proportion of underweight animals sent for slaughter, the usually poor quality and insufficient supply of livestock feed, etc. Overcoming such problems has an important place in the agricultural programs of the area. Especially

Table 2
AVERAGE ANNUAL YIELDS OF SELECTED AGRICULTURAL PRODUCTS (quintals* per hectare)

	Wheat		Maize for grain		Sunflower seed		Sugar beets		Potatoes		Milk (kilograms per cow)		
	1961–1965	1981–1983	1961–1965	1981–1983	1961–1965	1981–1983	1961–1965	1981–1983	1961–1965	1981–1983	1960	1970	1983
Soviet Union	9.7	16.1[a]	22.8	27.0[a]	11.2	11.8	165	201	94	113	1,779	2,110	2,258
Bulgaria	18.1	40.2	25.1	49.9	13.4	18.2	205	245	86	109	1,444	2,211	3,132
Czechoslovakia	24.1	44.0	26.3	46.6	9.9	17.3	270	329	114	181	1,862	2,565	3,488
East Germany	31.5	45.7	19.8	37.9	—	—	243	276	166	177	2,669	3,160	3,463
Hungary	18.6	42.8	26.1	61.3	9.6	20.2	246	389	79	172	1,863	2,252	4,310
Poland	19.7	31.4	23.5	41.8	—	—	267	327	154	164	2,122	2,456	2,806
Romania	14.6	23.3[a]	17.7	35.0[a]	11.1	15.6[c]	149	247[d]	85	165	1,368	1,607	1,952
Yugoslavia	18.0	34.4[b]	22.7	47.1[b]	16.5	17.8[b]	279	407[b]	87	94[b]	1,141	1,223	1,658
	1961–1965	1983	1961–1965	1983	1961–1965	1983	1961–1965	1983	1961–1965	1983	1965	1970	1983
Eastern Europe and Soviet Union	10.6	18.7	21.4	35.6	11.3	13.3	185	247	111	134	1,805	2,137	2,372
Western Europe	21.7	39.3	24.9	55.7	15.6	12.1	350	432	181	208	3,018	3,210	3,967

* One metric ton equals 10 quintals.

Note: Eastern Europe and Soviet Union includes Albania but excludes Yugoslavia; Western Europe includes Yugoslavia, Ireland and Great Britain.

[a] 1983; FAO estimate.   [b] 1983.   [c] Including rapeseed.   [d] 1982.

Sources: *Statisticheskii ezhegodnik...1980*, pp. 217–21, 236. *Statisticheskii ezhegodnik...1984*, pp. 181–85, 197. U.N. Food and Agriculture Organization, *FAO Production Yearbook, 1972*, Rome, 1973, pp. 209–10; 1975, pp. 61, 67, 80, 107, 192; 1983, pp. 108–09, 145; 1970, pp. 129–30; 1975, p. 164. *Statistički Godišnjak Jugoslavije 1966*, p. 145; 1970, p. ...

where yields are presently very low, the potential exists in principle for further significant improvements in the coming years. Whether this sort of development will be posssible in practice is another question, depending not only on investments, materials inputs and weather, but also on the incentives offered to the farmers to improve labor productivity and overall production results.

The data in Table 3 put agricultural production results into greater perspec-

Table 3
INDEX NUMBERS OF PER CAPITA GROSS AGRICULTURAL
PRODUCTION (1974–76 = 100)

Country	1972	1976	1980	1981	1982	1983
Soviet Union	92	102	96	95	98	101
Bulgaria	102	107	104	109	117	107
Czechoslovakia	93	98	106	104	112	112
East Germany	91	96	106	113	102	103
Hungary	95	97	113	111	124	124
Poland	95	100	89	87	91	90
Romania	97	114	112	109	116	110
Yugoslavia	87	103	103	103	112	109
Eastern Europe and Soviet Union	93	101	97	97	100	102
Western Europe	94	98	109	108	111	110

Source: *FAO Production Yearbook, 1983*, p. 88.

tive by revealing by how much the growth in production has exceeded the growth in population. Between 1974 and 1983, the rate of population growth in East Germany, Hungary and Bulgaria was lower than the average for Western Europe (from −2.5 percent to 3.2 percent, as against 3.6 percent); in Czechoslovakia it was somewhat higher (4.8 percent); and in Romania, the Soviet Union, Yugoslavia and Poland, it was higher still (from 7.6 percent to 8.6 percent). In most of the communist countries, increases in agricultural production have largely only kept pace with population growth. Only in Hungary and Romania, and recently in Czechoslovakia, has the rate of growth of per capita gross agricultural production exceeded the Western European average. This is in spite of the fact that a constant task in Western Europe since the 1960s has been to cut back production of many items (milk, butter, cheese, meat, eggs, etc.) in order to reduce mounting surpluses. In stark contrast, these items have remained in short supply in the communist countries, where strenuous efforts are being made to increase their production.

The livestock sectors in most communist countries have developed at faster rates than the crop sectors in recent years (Table 4). This is in keeping

Table 4

RATES OF GROWTH OF CROP AND LIVESTOCK PRODUCTION, AND THE STRUCTURE OF GROSS
AGRICULTURAL PRODUCTION, 1960–83[a]

| | Rate of growth of production (1970 = 100) | | | | | | | | | Structure of gross agricultural production (%) | | | | | |
| | Gross agricultural production | | | Crop production | | | Livestock production | | | Crop sector | | | Livestock sector | | |
Country	1960	1975	1983	1960	1975	1983	1960	1975	1983	1960	1975	1983	1960	1975	1983
Soviet Union	72	103	123	72	93	118	73	112	129	47.1	47.3	45.6	52.9	52.7	54.4
Bulgaria	72	116	134	75	108	102	67	128	159	67.3	64.7	44.7	32.7	35.3	55.3
Czechoslovakia	81	114	130	91	112	128	74	115	132	50.6	45.3	43.7	49.4	54.7	56.3
East Germany	88	114	124	100	102	114	79	124	131	48.3	42.4	38.3	51.7	57.6	61.7
Hungary	82	126	150	90	132	145	73	119	156	60.8	50.2	47.3	39.2	49.8	52.7
Poland	80	120	113	78	112	113	83	130	117	58.2	58.4	57.9	41.8	41.6	42.1
Romania	81	137	173	87	132	174[b]	72	143	177[b]	65.3	58.8	60.6[b]	34.7	41.2	39.4[b]
Yugoslavia	74	116	131[b]	79[c]	121[c]	121[b,c]	75	124	147[b]	—	57.8[d]	—	—	36.1[d]	—

[a] In "comparable prices," except for the structure of production in Hungary and Romania.
[b] 1982.
[c] Arable farming only, excluding fruit, vine and green land production.
[d] The residuum (6.1 percent) is the value of on-farm processing in private peasant households.
Sources: *Statisticheskii ezhegodnik stran-chlenov Soveta Ekonomicheskoi Vzaimopomoschi, 1980*, Moscow, 1980, pp. 191–95; *Statisticheskii ezhegodnik ... 1984*, pp. 157–59; *Statistički Prikaz poljoprivrede 1950–1971*, Belgrade, 1973, p. 46; *Statistical Pocket Book of Yugoslavia, 1983*, Belgrade, 1983, p. 74.

with the desire to provide more meat for domestic consumption and, in some cases, also for export. However, several countries experienced serious food shortages (especially of livestock products) at the start of the 1980s—the Soviet Union in 1981, East Germany in 1982 and 1983, and Poland and Romania in 1981–85. The shortages reflect excess demand at given prices since in these countries retail food prices on the whole have been highly subsidized at a time when incomes have been increasing and sufficient alternative consumer goods have been unavailable. Retail prices in Hungary and Czechoslovakia have been raised in recent years so that they more closely reflect production costs and at the same time bring supply and demand into closer balance. However, food prices remain heavily subsidized in most countries (particularly the USSR, Bulgaria, Czechoslovakia, East Germany and Poland).

The low productivity and output of the livestock sector is in part related to the problems of the crop sector. The most persistent shortcoming has been the inability of most countries except Hungary to provide their animals with sufficient quantities of high-grade feed. For example, the Soviet Union has failed in its attempt to overcome its feed shortage by expanding maize production. Similarly, some Eastern European countries have increased the area devoted to feed and industrial crops at the expense of grain crops. However, this has not solved their feed problem, while it has created further deficits in grain production. The low productivity of the livestock sector can also be attributed to inadequate development of livestock breeding, especially in the Soviet Union where the bogus genetic theories of Lysenko hampered scientific research until the mid-1960s. Since then, most countries have been active in improving the quality of their livestock, especially through breeding with Western European and North American strains.

The tendency in the communist countries has been to blame the disappointing results of recent years on natural calamities such as droughts, floods, poor weather at sowing or harvest, etc. Such an explanation overlooks the innate shortcomings of socialist agriculture as it is practiced in most countries. For one thing, the enormous size of most collective and state farms makes them very difficult to manage. For another, the farm directors' freedom of action has been seriously hampered by constant interference from central and local authorities responsible for seeing that the farms conform to centrally established plans. The main exception here is in Hungary, where farms have been accorded a large degree of operational autonomy.

Another factor inhibiting output is that financial incentives to the farms to increase production often are lacking or are insufficient. On the whole, rises in procurement prices have tended to lag behind increases in costs for fuel, energy, fertilizer, machinery, labor and other inputs. This has caused socialist farms in many countries to lose money or produce at low profitability in many spheres, especially livestock. To counter this, one of the keys to Hungary's agricultural success in recent years has been the use of economic "levers," mainly in the form of state-controlled prices, to encourage the more efficient and rational use of inputs and to stimulate (or discourage) production of certain agricultural products. In the absence of obligatory output or procurement plans, farms base their major production decisions on expected profitability, given state-controlled prices for procurements and most inputs (except labor) and the obligation to pay taxes and contribute to enterprise funds. Moreover, Hungarian farms have wide scope for developing agricultural and nonagricultural subsidiary enterprises, including those linked with the private sector, to provide income for the farms and employment for their members.

While the level of fertilizer consumption is on the whole no longer a major factor holding back production, serious problems remain in the sphere of mechanization. It has been reported in the Soviet Union that twice the 1984 machinery output would be necessary to equip farms adequately, and that more than 45 percent of tractor deliveries are simply for replacement. Moreover, because of high-price, low-quality spare parts, repairs during the lifetime of a tractor typically cost twice the original purchase price. Repairs are expensive also in East Germany, but for a different reason. Centralization of farm machinery repairs and the supply of spare parts in the hands of Farm Machinery Associations has led to an exaggeration of the work necessary and its cost, which amounted to more than 10 percent of the gross agricultural production of the socialist sector in 1983. Other common problems in the communist countries are slow deliveries of machinery, the continued use of low-productivity, obsolete equipment and a lack of trained operators.

Some of the shortcomings of socialist agriculture have also affected Poland and Yugoslavia, where most of the farms remain in private hands. In particular, both countries display a certain ambivalence toward private farming, having to rely on it for the bulk of agricultural production at present but planning to supplant it by socialist agriculture in the long term. This is reflected in investment policy; in 1982, Poland's small socialist sector (about 24 percent of arable land and 19 percent of gross farm output) received about 43 percent of capital investments, and Yugoslavia's somewhat more important socialist sector (18 percent of arable land and 33 percent of gross farm output) received 48 percent. At the same time, the especially low level of investment for all sectors of agriculture in Yugoslavia seriously hampers productivity gains and the overall modernization of agriculture there. In general, both countries have tried to foster integration between the private and socialist sectors by linking the supply of certain inputs (especially fertilizers, machinery, feed and coal) to peasant cooperation with the socialist sector, e.g., through the contract sale of produce. However, the peasants have tended to be suspicious of such dealings, fearing government control and disadvantageous terms. As a result, the private sector has not contributed as much as it might to overall production in Poland and Yugoslavia. Restrictions on private production have also adversely affected production results in most of the other communist countries (see below).

The failure of socialist agriculture has been such that most of the countries are no longer net exporters of grain, and many have been forced to import part of their supplies. Between 1980 and 1983, the USSR was a net importer of an average 34.4 million tons of grain a year (about half of it wheat), Poland of 5.7 million tons, East Germany of 3.0 million tons, Czechoslovakia of 1.0 million tons, Romania of 0.7 million tons and Yugoslavia of 0.3 million tons. Bulgaria had a slight net export of 0.1 million tons of grain a year, while Hungary was the only country to have net grain exports each year, averaging 1.3 million tons (about 70 to 80 percent wheat and the rest mainly maize). Most importing countries would undoubtedly have liked to import more grain, especially to boost their livestock production, but were restrained by a high level of foreign indebtedness and the consequent need to curtail hard-currency imports.

THE PRIVATE SECTOR

Small-scale peasant farming has continued to make an important contribution to Soviet and Eastern European agriculture despite the numerous offical restrictions placed on the peasants' private plots (officially termed "personal" or "subsidiary" plots). Although the regimes claim that the private plots draw the peasants away from collective work and also encourage capitalism, they have hesitated to abolish them for fear of mass peasant opposition on the one hand, and a decline in overall production on the other. In fact, in recent years a number of countries (particularly the Soviet Union, Bulgaria and East Germany) have encouraged state farm workers and also members of the general public to take on private plots in an effort to improve the overall supply of food.

In the collectivized countries, the size of the plot is usually limited to half a hectare. Restrictions are typically placed on the kinds of machinery and the amount of livestock that a peasant can own, although Bulgaria and Romania lifted livestock limitations in the early 1980s. In uncollectivized Poland, the maximum size of a private farm is 30 to 50 ha., but in actuality farms average about 5 ha. and usually consist of a number of separate plots. In Yugoslavia, the maximum size of a private farm is 10 ha., except in hilly, less fertile regions where it is 100 ha. However, as in Poland, the average farm is quite small (3.2 ha.) and is usually fragmented.

Because they lack sufficient means to compete with the socialist sector in the production of industrial or extensively farmed crops, the private plot users have tended to concentrate on those items that the socialist sector is unable to supply in quantity or quality. Private plot farming has thus centered around producing potatoes, vegetables, fruits, eggs, milk and meat. The plot farmers consume part of their output themselves, and sell their surpluses either in the local market (usually at free market prices) or else to a cooperative or government agency. The plots thus provide those using them with a vital source of income as well as food.

Private farming is naturally most important in Poland and Yugoslavia, where in 1982 it accounted for, respectively, 81 percent and 67 percent of gross farm output. In both countries, the private sector owns the majority of the livestock and grows considerably more than half the crops. In Poland, only maize and rapeseed production are concentrated in the socialist sector, while in Yugoslavia, the socialist sector dominates only in the production of sugar beets and oil seeds. The efforts by the governments to promote integration between the private and socialist sectors have not yet proved popular with the peasants, as mentioned earlier. However, new incentives to enter into contract arrangements (for example, the provision of feed supplies, credit on favorable terms and, in Yugoslavia, the chance to purchase additional land) may help to break down resistance. In Poland, long-standing peasant grievances include difficulties in buying land and getting titles of ownership recognized, insufficient availability of agricultural inputs, price manipulations, pressure to enter into contracts and arbitrary authority by local leaders.

Among the collectivized countries, Hungary has led the way in positively encouraging the private sector and at the same time fostering its integration with socialized production. The supply of pesticides, chemical fertilizers and small machinery and tools for the private sector has improved considerably. Also, preferential loans are given for the purchase of livestock, small machinery and cloches for early crops, for renovation of farm buildings and for planting vines and fruit trees. Cooperation contracts between the peasants and socialist farms or cooperative enterprises are now common. These commit private producers to deliver a given quantity of products in return for a price set in advance and improved access to essential inputs. With livestock fattening contracts, the socialist enterprise usually supplies the farmers with young animals and either provides feed or allots them additional land to grow their own feed. With contracts for vegetable (or fruit) growing, socialist enterprises typically provide seeds, fertilizers and plant protection agents, and sometimes help in cultivating the land and providing transport. Such cooperation is beneficial to both sides and has contributed to the obvious prosperity of the Hungarian countryside. In 1983, private production in Hungary covered about 14 percent of arable land but accounted for about 33 percent of gross agricultural output (and 49 percent of net agricultural output), and moreover contributed 25 percent of all agricultural exports to the dollar sector.

Bulgaria has also been successful in encouraging the integration of private and socialized production through cooperation contracts. For example, in 1983 the private sector provided 27 percent of the meat and eggs marketed by the socialized sector, and 12 percent of the milk. Even though most plots are located on poor or mountainous land, in 1982 they covered about 13 percent of the country's arable area but still accounted for 25 percent of gross agricultural production (33 percent of all vegetable, 51 percent of all potatoes and 37 percent of all fruit).

Over the years, the private sector in the Soviet Union has remained crucial in feeding the country in the face of indifferent production results in many areas of the socialist sector. In 1982, private plots covered about 2.7 percent of the country's arable area (1.4 percent farmed by *kolkhoz* peasants and 1.3 percent by other users). Yet private plots accounted for about 25 percent of gross agricultural production (including 63 percent of the country's potatoes, about 30 percent of the vegetables, meat, milk and eggs, and 24 percent of the wool) and 13 percent of gross marketed output. In 1979, the value of private plot produce either sold by the farmers or consumed by them amounted to more than 33 percent of a *kolkhoz* family's average total income and to 18.5 percent of a *sovkhoz* worker's average total income.[2] In 1985, one of Chairman Gorbachev's most important decisions was to increase the permissible size of private plots. This is sure to make a large and rapid difference in food supplies for Soviet cities.

In Romania, widespread food shortages and the state's simultaneous demand for more agricultural exports in recent years have led to the regime to move from merely controlling private production to effectively directing its operations as a way of forcing the peasants to deliver more to the state. Since 1983, peasants have had to devote their plots to crops specified in the farm's production plan (which in turn must conform to the local state plan for sowing) and to make obligatory minimum "contract" deliveries of crops and livestock products at low prices to the socialized sector. Likewise, peasants are required to raise specific minimum numbers of animals, depending on plot size and number of family members. A typical minimum livestock holding includes one cow or two to three goats, 10 sheep, one pig, 15 laying hens and 15 chickens for consumption. Private slaughtering of animals is forbidden. Compliance with delivery quotas leads to certain benefits—access to fertilizers, the use of state-owned grazing land or of land to grow fodder as a second crop, and/or the chance to purchase feed concentrates. Failure either to cultivate land according to instructions or to meet any obligatory delivery quotas can lead to confiscation of the plot and/or to a prison term of up to five years. Furthermore, in a so far unsuccessful effort to stamp out the black market in food, peasants wanting to sell surpluses from their plots in local markets are supposed to obtain certificates from the local authority and then charge no more than the unrealistically low official posted prices. These and other restrictions on the Romanian private sector are reminiscent of those imposed by Stalin, to the great detriment of Soviet agriculture. They will most likely have the effect of curtailing private production (14 percent of gross agricultural production on 13 percent of the country's arable area in 1982), thereby worsening the Romanian agricultural situation.

Until recently, efforts were made to eliminate private agricultural production in Czechoslovakia, particularly through encouraging collective farmers to give up their plots in return for certain quantities of produce as compensation in kind. By 1982, private plots of all kinds covered only three percent of arable land (most of it outside the collective farms). Most families that had been to a large degree self-sufficient in food had become consumers, satisfying their requirements, particularly for meat, from commercial outlets. Because of the need to increase domestic meat production while at the same time reducing feed imports, measures were adopted in the early 1980s to develop contractual animal fattening on private plots. However, managers in the socialist sector have given such contracts little priority, so this type of farming has been slow to develop.

In East Germany also, private plots have been discouraged by the government.

---

[2] M. S. Gudzenko and M. V. Shulga, *Podsobnoe khozyaistvo grazhdan*, Moscow, 1983, pp. 5, 7, and *Narodnoe khozyaistvo SSSR v 1982g.*, Moscow, 1983, pp. 192, 198.

In 1984, they accounted for about five percent of arable land, and concentrated mainly on livestock production (producing 40 percent of the material output of eggs and 60 percent of beef and pork in the first half of the year).

PROSPECTS

One should not be too optimistic about the future of Soviet and Eastern European agriculture. In spite of advances made in the 1970s, agriculture was still the Achilles' heel of the Soviet and Eastern European economies (except for Hungary) in mid-1985. Any significant improvements in the rates of growth of agricultural production and in the ability of these countries to feed themselves and improve the diets of their populations will depend very much on qualitative rather than quantitative developments in farming. If history is any guide, progress will be slow in improving the efficiency of investments and of material and labor inputs. Similarly, the recent emphasis in most countries on ever-larger production units and on more rigid central planning in the absence of sufficient incentives to farms and farmers is likely to exacerbate the current problems.

Although farming could benefit from increased levels of investment in some countries, a major problem over the years has been that what investments have been made have not always been used effectively or efficiently. The policy in Poland and Yugoslavia to concentrate investment in the tiny socialist sector, neglecting the private sector, has already been mentioned. Moreover, in many countries, excessive concentration on large-scale projects and pet programs (e.g., the Soviet Virgin Lands, farm amalgamations and reorganizations, construction schemes, or agro-industrial integration) has diverted resources from more mundane but extremely important tasks, such as improvements in collection, storage and processing facilities, and in rural transport and roads. Relative inattention to such basic tasks has led to significant production losses over the years.

In the sphere of irrigation, huge sums have been spent by various countries with disappointing results. For example, Bulgaria's irrigation network, covering 28 percent of arable land, has been criticized there for producing yields below expectations. In Romania, where 20 percent of arable area is classified as irrigated, much of the irrigation equipment is in disrepair, much of the capacity is unused because of silting and the system was incapable of preventing large losses in the 1983 and 1984 droughts. Romania's inability to correct erosion and excessive fertilization, currently affecting an estimated 40 percent of its agricultural land, has not prevented it from embarking on a grandiose scheme to dam, drain and irrigate some 84,000 ha. of the Danube delta by 1990. The Soviet land melioration system, encompassing 19.1 million ha. of irrigated land (including eight percent of arable area) and 18.1 million ha. of drained land in 1983, was criticized by Soviet Communist party leaders in October 1984 for mismanagement, slow introduction of new technology and hybrids, poor water distribution on irrigated land, poor use and distribution of fertilizers, defects in equipment, failure to inaugurate schemes on schedule, etc. Nevertheless, the decision was taken to create a large "guaranteed farming zone," immune to the effects of weather, by expanding the irrigated area to 30 to 32 million ha. and drained land to 19 to 20 million ha. by the year 2000. The guaranteed farming zone then is to account for 50 percent of crop output, in contrast to 33 percent in 1984. Economically, it is doubtful whether the hoped-for improvement can justify the huge planned expenditures (50 billion rubles in 1986–90 alone, or 1.7 times the level of all productive capital investments in agriculture in 1983). Politically, however, it appears that the Soviet Union is finally trying to rid itself of agricultural dependence on the West.

Because wages and living conditions are for the most part better in the urban areas than in the villages, many farmers, particularly the younger ones, have left the farms. As a result, the size of the agricultural labor force in the Soviet Union, Bulgaria, Czechoslovakia, East Germany and Hungary has declined to the point that there are now labor shortages, particularly of trained personnel. At the same time, the average age of the remaining farmers has risen steadily, creating problems for the future. The rates of decline of the agricultural populations of Poland and Yugoslavia have indeed been high in recent years (about 17 percent and 25 percent, respectively, between 1970 and 1984), and labor shortages are now beginning to be felt there too. Only in Romania, where about 43 percent of the population works in agriculture, are there still evident labor surpluses on the farms, mainly because industry is not sufficiently developed to absorb the rural overpopulation.

Labor shortages have focused increasing attention on the need to raise labor productivity. Most of the collectivized countries have introduced schemes to train more tractor drivers and machinery operators. However, shortages of such workers remain because farmers are deterred by the long hours, shift work, and relatively low (by urban standards) wages at the end of training.

Another approach has been to introduce work incentive schemes, usually involving an individual or collective norm-piecework system (i.e., payment based on fulfillment of work norms), or else a piecework-bonus system (also called a collective contract system). Typically, under the piecework-bonus system, a relatively small group of farmers is put in charge of an area of land, the materials to plant it and equipment to work it for one or more seasons. The group enters into binding delivery contracts at mutually agreed upon prices with the farm, receives bonuses for exceeding contract delivery norms and underspending production cost norms, and distributes wages and bonuses independently. Most collectivized countries use a form of the norm-piecework system, and Bulgaria has also introduced a number of variants on the piecework-bonus system. Soviet farms were told to "show more concern" for introducing the piecework-bonus (collective contract) system in mid-1982 and again in October 1984. However, progress toward its adoption has been slow, in part because the production teams, having worked hard and made a lot of money, reportedly tend to break up after only a few seasons. The normless variant of the contract system, in the form of a normless "link" or team (with six to 10 workers) or normless brigade (with 50 to 100), establishes only an aggregate sales plan, and members share in the profit from above-plan sales. Brezhnev rejected the normless link as being too individualistic, but it might possibly be revived under Gorbachev, one of its most ardent supporters in the mid-1970s. Variants of the normless system are common in Hungarian agriculture.

The greatest weakness of most current incentive schemes is that they concentrate on providing farmers with more money, whereas the farmers are concerned more with what that money can buy. Therefore, providing more and better consumer goods in rural areas will be crucial in making the incentive schemes more effective.

Qualitative improvements in farm management will also be necessary to overcome many of the current problems of agriculture. Control of socialist farms through economic levels rather than administrative orders and rigid central planning is the rule only in Hungary, whose production achievements are admired by the other countries. The trend to end or reduce subsidies on inputs, and simultaneously to increase purchase prices and also retail prices to levels more closely reflecting production costs, suggests that part of the Hungarian model has been accepted by other communist countries. However, other aspects of the model, such as greater farm management autonomy and the important role given to private plots, are a long way from being applied elsewhere. The Hungarian model, which after all requires reforming the entire economy and not merely the agricultural sector, may not be the answer to every other country's problems, but it does suggest a promising way forward within the context of socialist agriculture. While the Yugoslav and Polish attempts to improve farming techniques and more closely integrate the private and socialist sectors may prove beneficial in the long run, these countries must proceed cautiously with the socialization of agriculture if they are to avoid renewed peasant opposition and a consequent decline in production.

FURTHER READING

Davies, R. W. *The Industrialization of Soviet Russia.* Vol. 1: *The Socialist Offensive: the Collectivization of Soviet Agriculture, 1929–1930.* Vol. 2: *The Soviet Collective Farm, 1929–1930.* Cambridge, Massachusetts: Harvard University Press, 1980.

Francisco, Ronald D., et al., eds. *Agricultural Policies in the USSR and Eastern Europe.* Boulder, Colorado: Westview Press, 1980.

Mitray, David. *Marx against the Peasant: A Study in Social Dogmatism.* New York: Collier, 1962.

Organisation for Economic Cooperation and Development. *Prospects for Agricultural Production and Trade in Eastern Europe.* 2 vols. Paris: OECD, 1981–82.

Sanders, Irwin, T., ed. *Collectivization of Agriculture in Eastern Europe.* Lexington: University of Kentucky Press, 1958.

Stuart, Robert C., ed. *The Soviet Rural Economy.* Totowa, New Jersey: Rowman and Allanheld, 1984.

Volin, Lazar. *A Century of Soviet Agriculture: From Alexander II to Khrushchev.* Cambridge, Massachusetts: Harvard University Press, 1970.

Wadekin, Karl-Eugen. *Agrarian Policies in Communist Europe: A Critical Introduction.* Totowa, New Jersey: Allanheld, Osmun; The Hague: Martinus Nijhoff, 1982.

———. *Current Trends in the Soviet and East European Food Economy.* West Berlin: Dunker & Humbolt, 1982.

TOURISM IN THE SOVIET UNION AND EASTERN EUROPE

GARY MEAD

In its attitude toward the West, the Soviet Union today can be described as a political chameleon, simultaneously entertaining two apparently contradictory notions: that the West poses a real threat and remains the old ideological enemy; but that it is also a rich financial fruit, ripe for the picking. Depending on the context, Soviet officials can happily move from one view to the other with consummate ease. This blend of declared hostility and cash calculation can most easily be understood and seen when we consider the Soviet bloc's view of tourism.

For the leading officials in the Soviet Union, and their surrogates in the rest of the Warsaw Pact and the Council for Mutual Economic Assistance (COMECON), Western tourists are unofficially regarded as something of a gamble: a definite risk, but so tempting that it would be folly to refuse their presence. The benefits are obvious, for tourism in the Soviet bloc is a multibillion dollar business. The risk is less tangible, but no less worrying to the authorities for that. By permitting Western tourists to enter and view otherwise closed communist systems, it is possible that the visitors may take away with them a rather dim view of the achievements of those systems. Besides, such tourists bring with them the untidy mental and social baggage of their own very different societies. Soviet officials want to ensure that none of that baggage falls into the eager hands of ordinary Soviet citizens.

Soviet-bloc tourism is therefore somewhat schizophrenic. Officially, Western tourists are welcomed, because this promotes "international goodwill and understanding." Unofficially, the pleasure is less philanthropic, and more a matter of delight at seeing the billions of dollars, yen, francs, and other hard currencies flow into the coffers of the state. Unofficially, too, one of the major concerns for the Soviet-bloc tourist industries is to isolate, as far as possible, the Western visitor from the local populations. The communist system in the Warsaw Pact countries already has but a tenuous grip on the hearts and minds of its subjects—everything possible is done to guarantee that the regular visits by millions of Westerners do not further undermine that system.

As a general rule, Western visitors to the Soviet-bloc nations will find themselves under extremely close supervision, usually at the hands of officially appointed couriers rather than the secret police or intelligence services. It has to be said, though, that very often there is little difference between couriers and secret police—the jobs often go together. Visitors are required, usually, to register with the police on arrival, and to set out before arrival what exactly they intend to do during their visit. They will be expected in some countries to follow a precise itinerary, no deviation from which is allowed. In general, the closer tourists are to the ideological heart of Soviet-style communism, the more restricted they will be in movements and contacts with local people. In the few countries where resistance to Soviet domination has been not wholly unsuccessful, particularly Hungary and Poland, tourists benefit by having a greater chance to mingle with the local life, if they so choose. Although the authorities will do everything possible to ensure that Western tourists' impressions of a two-week package tour to Moscow, Warsaw, Budapest or any other large city in the Soviet bloc are as favorable as possible, this is, for several reasons, becoming less easy for them. The Soviet system is creating its own internal strains and tensions, notably in the economy, and this has been filtering through to the otherwise well-catered-for tourist from the West, who in some countries has inevitably been struck by the lines outside shops, the emptiness of those shops, the absence of basic food items, the shortages of gasoline and the lack of other basic requisites for well-satisfied vacationers. Up to a point, the Soviet system can still conceal its own internal difficulties, particularly those in the political sphere, but the problems are now such that even the most myopic tourist will notice that the system is not working as smoothly as the courier will proclaim. In fact, Western tourists on short package vacations will most likely be struck by a series of paradoxes. On the one hand the museums, theaters, ballet performances, hotels and restaurants they are shown will seem exemplary. The carefully selected industrial sites may well appear to be models of efficient production. But against that, why should the waiter during the evening meal back at the hotel offer to exchange local currency at dramatically better rates than those offered in the state banks? Why should the taxi driver ask if you have anything you want to sell? Why should the hotel maid try to persuade you to sell her your rather old pair of shoes? And, unusually perhaps, why should a furtive individual you meet casually in a bar stammeringly ask you to carry a letter to the West, for a relative or friend?

TRAVEL DIFFICULTIES

As soon as a frontier anywhere is crossed, problems arise concerning language, culture and outlook, let alone the mundane difficulties of hotel reservations and visa regulations. All such common difficulties are exaggerated when traveling to the Soviet bloc, unless the traveler happens to be on a package tour, when most of the problems will have been ironed out before arrival. There are four main types of tourists to the Soviet bloc: business or diplomatic officials; independent travelers; package-deal tourists; and people visiting relatives (these travelers may even once have been citizens of the country being visited). Only the independent traveler faces the possibility of major problems, partly an accidental byproduct of systemic inefficiencies, partly by design to deter such travelers from repeating the venture. Independent travelers in many Soviet-bloc nations are regarded with suspicion from start to finish—after all, they have to be up to no good somehow, otherwise why on earth would they go to the bother of arranging their own hotel rooms, train tickets, visas and currency exchanges? All these things, which can be simply arranged on a package tour, can for individuals under their own steam be inordinately time-consuming and frustrating. They will also have to deal face to face with obstinate officials whose one passion often seems to be to present yet another form to be filled in. Dealing with state officials inside the Soviet bloc can be one of the most unpleasant and trying experiences of the whole journey, and it will not usually confront the package-deal tourist. Independent traveling inside the Soviet bloc is perhaps one of the last remaining genuine challenges to the spirit of human adventure and patience.

Not that the package tourist is guaranteed total satisfaction. All too often hotels and restaurants are awesomely indifferent to the needs and comforts of the Western tourist, and it is small comfort to watch citizens from other Soviet-bloc countries receiving even worse treatment. Things can and do go wrong on any vacation or excursion, and not only in the Soviet bloc. But because of the usual centralized planning in Soviet tourism, when things go wrong they do so on a mammoth scale.

TRAVEL TO THE WEST

Tourism is normally a two-way, or even a multiway, process, but not for citizens of the Soviet bloc, most of whom experience insuperable difficulties in traveling outside the bloc. Nor are they permitted easy access to other Warsaw Pact countries, several of which still bar tourists from Poland, for example, unless they are in an organized group. Foreign travel inevitably encourages the traveler to make comparisons. The Soviet authorities are distinctly hostile to the possibility that their subjects may go to the West and make comparisons to the disadvantage of communism. For most Soviet-bloc citizens, travel to the West is an unimaginable luxury, far beyond their pockets and politically quite sensitive. In part, economic matters require the Soviet authorities to discourage travel to the West: with a multibillion-dollar debt to the West, every Eastern-bloc citizen going there aggravates the imbalance. Soviet-bloc citizens who make the attempt deserve considerable admiration. For Westerners, it is simply a matter of making travel arrangements and reservations, getting passports and visas, and venturing forth. For ordinary Soviet citizens, the hurdles are almost endless. They will first need a clean political record and then must begin filling in forms; getting the right stamps on certain documents; facing close questioning by officials, including the police; lining up for this and that vital piece of paper; and eventually they must be scrutinized closely by the embassy of the Western country they want to visit, in case they are planning defection. People traveling to the West are usually, therefore, trusted party members or other state officials, or people who will be leaving behind them something of great value, either property or family, as an inducement to return and to return without having rocked the boat while abroad.

The same ambivalence felt toward tourists from the West is shown toward Soviet-bloc citizens who wish to go to the West. Both directions of travel carry a degree of unspecifiable political risk, but travel to the West is sometimes outweighed by benefits to the state. People going to the West will usually bring back something: technological or educational benefits; hard currency through illegal work (which will eventually find its way back into the state's coffers through the black market or hard-currency shops); or at the very least material goods that are scarce in state shops, thus easing to some extent the strains on the domestic consumer market.

TRAVEL TO THE SOVIET UNION

All foreign visitors require visas, usually obtainable in advance. Applications for individual visas must be submitted at least six weeks before the journey, but Western travel firms cooperating with the Soviet state tourist agency, Intourist (which has a monopoly), can generally get group visas in less than two weeks. Visitors must stay strictly within the itinerary and the areas designated—fewer than 150 of the Soviet Union's 2,000 cities are open to foreign tourists, either from the West or the Warsaw Pact nations. Whole republics are barred in several cases. Motorists have the choice of 16 different routes and must stick closely to departure and arrival times, which are arranged beforehand. Since June 1984, Soviet citizens have been required to notify the police prior to having foreign guests stay overnight.

According to official Soviet figures, over 5 million people went to the Soviet Union as tourists in 1983, and they were able to choose from 600 different Intourist schedules. In that year, no figures on Western tourists were made available, but in 1977 tourists from the West comprised 40 percent of the total, or approximately 1.75 million, with almost 1 million of those coming from one country, Finland. It is probable that the same balance, 40 percent from the West and 60 percent from other socialist countries, still holds true.

Soviet tourism is a massive industry, with about 200,000 people employed directly by the state. It is believed that the Soviet Union now earns from it more than $1 billion annually. How much of that is profit is a matter of speculation, since the exchange rates are artificially constructed to reflect a stronger ruble than is actually the case in market terms.

As is the case in the majority of Soviet-bloc nations, the Western tourist in the Soviet Union is required daily to exchange a certain sum of hard currency into rubles, over and above any hotel bills and traveling expenses. At the time of writing, this sum is roughly the equivalent of $20. There are hard-currency shops exclusively for Western visitors' use: officially, Soviet citizens are not allowed to possess hard currency. Inevitably, however, there is a black market, dealing not only in goods and services but also in currency exchange at rates more favorable to the Western visitor than the officially stated rate. Dealing in currency is illegal, and is a serious offense

448

both for visitors and Soviet citizens. There are no restrictions on the amount of currency that may be brought into the country, but it must all be declared on entry, and a certificate is provided to ensure that visitors cannot take out more hard currency than was brought in. This regulation is standard practice in most Soviet-bloc countries, as is that which prohibits the import or export of rubles and other "soft" currencies.

The cost of a stay in the Soviet Union, and most Soviet-bloc nations, can be rather high for a Western visitor. While the package tourist will generally find that a two-week stay in Moscow is somewhat cheaper than a similar stay in most Western capitals, this is primarily due to the fact that the tourist is paying hard currency (desperately needed by the Soviet bloc), while all the people providing services, and all the costs of the stay, are calculated in soft currency paid by the state. The state controls wages, prices and the cost of all official services, and can therefore afford to charge considerably less than might be the case in the West. Profits are therefore smaller than might be for Western tourism, but in relative terms the Soviet-bloc tourist industry can afford to make smaller profits in order to encourage Western tourists. A two-week holiday in the Soviet Union can seem even more attractive, when it is half the price for a similar stay in, for example, Paris. But independent travelers will discover that a night in a Moscow hotel can easily cost more than $100, while the services are often less welcoming and efficient than in an equivalent Western capital. Western tourists are anyway paying about five times more for their rooms than Soviet citizens; in a Warsaw hotel, a room costing 250 zlotys for Polish citizens may go for 1,500 zlotys or more for Western visitors, and they will have to pay for it in hard currency at the completely unrealistic official exchange rate. In other words, they will on the whole pay Western prices without getting the quality of Western accommodations.

As is the case with most Soviet-bloc countries, tourists in the Soviet Union are prohibited from taking out of the country all sorts of objects, particularly anything made before 1945, and most especially items regarded as part of the national cultural heritage. The list is very comprehensive, and it is undoubtedly sensible to get official permission to export anything unusual before arriving at the airport for the flight home. Once again, official permission is useless without a much-stamped piece of paper, the precise document for the job.

Western tourists will soon discover that their movements are severely restricted. Westerners resident in Moscow must get official approval before leaving Moscow to travel beyond a radius of 40 kilometers. Inside Moscow, or inside the other designated tourist areas, movement is relatively free. The KGB is, in any case, well aware of the Soviet citizens who need watching, and of Western visitors who might be more risky than normal; long before arrival, the Western tourist will have been officially scrutinized and approved, at least on paper. The ordinary Western tourist may therefore be surprised at the unobtrusive manner with which he is observed. This does not reflect a more liberal attitude, merely a more efficient secret police, which no longer wastes time following the obviously innocuous tourist. Nevertheless, Soviet citizens are encouraged from childhood to regard all Westerners (and occasionally even citizens from other Warsaw Pact nations) as suspect. In recent years, Soviet authorities have stepped up their harassment of U.S. officials resident in the Soviet Union, but in general this is official action, not indicative of a naturally hostile attitude toward the West. Most Western visitors leave with a sense of the natural hospitality of the Soviet people, although people in Moscow have a reputation for being sullen. That has probably as much to do with the stress of living in a large city anywhere, as with any resentment specifically aimed at Western tourists.

The limited activities available to the Western tourist will provide entertainment of a kind, rather straitlaced but nevertheless unusual. This entertainment may or may not outweigh frustrations occurring in both petty and important matters, ranging from poor hotel service to unforeseen cancellations of reservations. Perhaps the most difficult eventuality to confront the first-time Western visitor is the double-think endemic to Soviet society. There is almost always an official and an unofficial way of doing anything, and the only difference is that the former is legal, cheap but inordinately difficult, while the latter is usually illegal, expensive and smooth. This social schizophrenia may well pass unnoticed by the package tourist, whose stay is carefully preplanned. But for anyone visiting regularly it makes itself felt very quickly. It is a reality firmly denied by official Soviet statements, but at the same time it works to the advantage of the state in the short term. In the long term, however, it operates to the moral and social detriment of all concerned.

TRAVEL TO BULGARIA

According to official figures released in October 1984, over 6 million foreigners visit Bulgaria every year. That month, the country set up the Bulgarian Association for Tourism and Recreation, which is responsible for all foreign and domestic tourism, and which directly supervises the state-owned foreign tourist agency, Balkantourist. Bulgaria's main tourist spots have been developed over the last 20 years, the majority of them on the Black Sea coast. Profits from Western tourism are not officially given, but are probably far less than the Soviet Union's, since the bulk of tourists come from the rest of the Soviet bloc; perhaps as few as 200,000 annually come from the West. Many of the Soviet-bloc visits are also very brief: the visitors are on transit visas through the country. Until October 1984, Bulgaria had very relaxed visa requirements, but several terrorist incidents encouraged the authorities to reimpose stricter regulations. Independent travelers are now required to have officially approved invitations from a Bulgarian family before they can obtain a visa. It is now no longer possible to automatically extend visas after crossing into the country, and a transit visa is valid for 30 hours only. Foreigners must stay at designated camping sites and hotels. Tourists on package vacations for which everything is arranged by the tour operator, are unaffected by these changes.

In 1977, Bulgaria abolished the regulation requiring Western tourists to exchange each day a fixed sum of hard currency into Bulgarian leva at the official rate, and at an official bank. The authorities claimed then that this demonstrated Bulgaria's liberal policy toward tourists. The unofficial explanation, however, is that Bulgaria had been experiencing falling numbers of Western visitors, adversely affecting its hard-currency income. The exchange regulation was dropped in order to attract more Western tourists, who would keep the hard-currency income at reasonable levels. Various reports, however, suggest that independent tourists still find themselves required to make the daily exchange, despite its no longer being official policy. Movement within Bulgaria, as within the Soviet Union, is rather restricted, an understandable situation given the close ideological support Bulgaria gives its largest ally.

TRAVEL TO EAST GERMANY

East Germany is not a particularly attractive country for tourists, with its extreme suspicion of the West and dominating police-state atmosphere. Few Soviet-bloc tourists would consider going there, except to purchase consumer goods scarce in their own countries. In fact, East Germany is widely regarded as the shopping center for the bloc as a whole.

Most visitors from the West come from West Germany, and the bulk of those are in transit to Berlin. Over 3 million West Germans went there in 1983, an increase of almost five percent over 1982. The total annual number of visitors is around 16 million, the bulk of them being short-stay shoppers from Poland, the Soviet Union and Czechoslovakia. In October 1980, East German authorities introduced regulations suspending passport- and visa-free travel from Poland. The East German–Polish border was opened for free tourist exchange only in 1972, but the relationship has been uneasy ever since. East Germans resent seeing hordes of Polish shoppers cross the border, causing chaos on trains and in shops, and Poles traditionally have little love for East Germans.

East Germany's image—a combination of Prussian authoritarianism and Soviet ruthlessness—makes it somewhat forbidding for Western tourists. Added to that, the East German economy is rather successful in Soviet-bloc terms, so the country does not need to encourage Western tourism. As with motorists in the Soviet Union, those on transit through East Germany are required to follow the transit route closely. East German traffic police are not the most affable of people, and crossing the East German border by car can be one of the most intimidating of touring experiences.

TRAVEL TO AND FROM CZECHOSLOVAKIA

Czechoslovakia permits visitors from all socialist states except Albania to enter without visas. Only Finland, however, among Western countries, has an arrangement with Czechoslovakia permitting visa-free travel. As with most other Soviet-bloc nations, no distinction is made between tourists and people visiting on official business. A daily exchange of hard currency is also applicable, as it is in the Soviet Union, East Germany, Poland and Romania. Foreigners may choose their own accommodations, but must register their stay with the police.

Over 14 million people visited the country in 1983, 15 percent more than in 1982, and just over 1 million of these came from the West. This is, however, a considerable drop from the 1981 total of 18 million, and is largely explained by Czechoslovakia adopting restrictive regulations against other Soviet-bloc visitors, the "shoppers." In December 1981, Czechoslovakia made individual tourism from Poland dependent on the production of an officially approved invitation from a family. At the same time, it also banned the export from Czechoslovakia of a comprehensive list of goods. As in the other, more "sovietized," countries in the bloc, Western visitors can be subjected to a high degree of official scrutiny and suspicion, and movements are rather restricted. Hard-currency profits from tourism are not officially revealed, but it is certainly not a negligible facet of the economy.

Restrictions on Czechoslovaks traveling to the West are extreme; of more than 9 million going abroad in 1982, less than 0.5 million went to the West. It is estimated that as many as 3,000 Czechoslovaks annually emigrate to the West, mainly by taking package tours to Yugoslavia, then slipping across the borders to neighboring Western countries.

TRAVEL TO AND FROM ROMANIA

In 1982, 6 million foreigners visited Romania, an increase of 1 million over 1981. Most Western tourists come from West Germany. The decline of Western tourism has much to do with the dismal condition of the economy, which has affected all levels of society, and even affects the normally well-cared for Western tourist. Poor hotel service, inadequate food supplies, fuel shortages and an underdeveloped tourist infrastructure have all meant that standards have been dropping.

All Western tourists require visas, ranging from three to 30 days, with a possible maximum extension of up to 90 days. All foreign visitors must stay in state-owned hotels. Travelers returning to the West report that, in recent years, official discourtesy has abounded and basic provisions for tourists have been very bad. One much-repeated complaint is that official couriers are of poor quality; this has much to do with the fact that they are appointed for their political reliability rather than their grasp of foreign languages. Since November 1981, many basic food items have been rationed, and certainly Romania is one of the Soviet bloc's most strictly controlled police states. Contacts between Western visitors and Romanian citizens are kept to a minimum, and the secret police are not as unobtrusive as their Soviet counterparts.

Romania is desperately short of hard currency, and in recent years has tried to attract more Western tourists back to the country. Several measures were introduced in 1983 to tighten up standards, and the undercutting of Western travel agencies began. For example, in 1983 a round-trip-flight on Lufthansa to Bucharest from Munich would cost 1,500 marks, but the Romanian state-owned airline, Tarom, was offering the same deal for 500 marks, with full board and hotel room for two weeks thrown in. Reportedly, 70,000 tourism employees are being trained to higher standards. Once again, there is an enormous difference between being a package tourist to Romania and traveling there independently—in terms of cost, freedom of movement and general treatment. Romania is also far more interested in receiving tourists than sending them out; in 1981, out of a population of 22 million, fewer than 1 million traveled abroad, and only 300,000 of those went to the West.

TRAVEL TO POLAND

The events since August 1980 have had a major impact on the Polish tourist industry, on every imaginable level. Visitors, except those from Finland, Sweden and the Soviet bloc, must have visas. There are theoretically no restrictions on movement, and no restriction on where visitors stay, although they must register with the local police. The daily exchange of hard currency is required and again, there exists a flourishing black market, on which the unofficial currency exchange rates are dramatically different from the official. Poland had, in 1981, just over 2 million foreign visitors—70 percent fewer than in 1980, which in turn was 30 percent down from the 1979 figure. This is extremely worrying for the Polish authorities, who, with a hard-currency debt of about $25 billion, desperately need Western tourist levels to regain their pre-1980 state. Poland now discourages independent Western travelers, although it is once again possible for people to travel through the country by car, fuel being paid for with hard-currency vouchers obtainable at hotels and banks. Hotel prices for independent visitors can be exorbitant, but the ubiquitous black market can make life cheaper, if the traveler is willing to risk either being caught by the police or defrauded by the dealer. Western visitors are generally warmly welcome, for altruistic reasons, both by ordinary citizens and officials, although the familiar Soviet-bloc surliness is to be found in some situations. Extremes of generosity and rudeness may be experienced, and a mercenary instinct may lie behind the welcome extended by some Poles.

There are many social problems faced every day by Poles that can blight a short visit by a Westerner. Among them are the bureaucratic difficulties in simply buying a train ticket, or the almost endless delays everywhere, in shops, bars and hotels. Such things obtain throughout the bloc, however. What makes up for them in Poland is the relative ease of close contact with the local population and the much less unpleasant police-state atmosphere than in most of the rest of the Soviet bloc.

TRAVEL TO AND FROM HUNGARY

The relative freedom of Hungary within the Soviet bloc is apparent in its view of Western tourists. Western tourists from anywhere but Finland or Austria need visas, but there is no compulsory exchange of hard currency and no restrictions on movement or place of stay. Western tourism is Hungary's second-largest earner of hard currency (after agriculture), and according to official figures, Hungary had a surplus of $165 million in 1983 from its tourist industry. Western visitors may obtain multientry visas, and are required to register with the police within 48 hours of entry. In 1980, Hungary received a $300 million loan from Austria to build new hotels in Budapest and to expand the Budapest airport. The official exchange rate for the forint is virtually the same as that available unofficially, and the economy, from the Western tourist's point of view, is therefore rather stable, with no noticeable shortages in shops or hotels. It is illegal, however, for Hungarians to receive hard currency as payment. Western visitors, on the whole, will find a relaxed and informal atmosphere. Yet not only is this an exception in the Soviet bloc, it is also a superficial impression, concealing a range of political problems that are deeply built into the fabric of Hungarian society.

Unlike the rest of the Soviet bloc, travel to the West is regarded by Hungarians as a really normal activity, and Hungarians who defect on trips to the West are actually rather rare.

TRAVEL TO YUGOSLAVIA

Yugoslavia is not a part of the Soviet bloc, and its very status as a communist country is, to some, open to question. What is beyond doubt is the extremely important role tourism plays in its economy. In 1983, it earned somewhat more than $750 million from tourism. But with a hard-currency debt of around $20 billion, it needs to keep tourist levels high. In 1982, 18 million people visited Yugoslavia, a third of them from the West. As do many nations in the Soviet bloc, Yugoslavia offers various incentives to Western tourists, encouraging them to use hard currency instead of local by means of various discounts in shops, hotels and bars. In 1982, many visitors reported difficulty in finding basic goods such as meat and milk, and fuel was scarce. As long as tourists pay for fuel in hard currency, however, they are now supposedly guaranteed enough for their needs, and the government claims to have solved food-shortage problems. But the increasingly high costs of vacations in Yugoslavia have had their effect, in 1983, there was a three percent drop in the number of people traveling there. Tourists find that movement is largely unrestricted; the majority of Western citizens do not need visas; and the quality of service is generally higher than that found in other communist nations.

TRAVEL TO ALBANIA

Albania is certainly the most repressive country in Europe, and the regime is fiercely isolationist and hostile to both West and East. Very few people travel there, and the only way for an Albanian to leave is either to flee across the border or by an official visit. The only way to enter Albania is on a package tour; and before crossing the border visas must be in order, the tourist must be dressed and attired in a manner deemed satisfactory by the border guards, and until recently bearded men could be asked to shave. Once inside Albania visitors are chaperoned virtually every moment, and the local population will shun contact for fear the secret police will accuse them of attempted espionage. The country is still extremely backward, cars are rare and tourist provisions minimal. While it can be revealing to visit a country still living in the early decades of the 20th century, the atmosphere is one of extreme paranoia.

TRANSPORT IN THE SOVIET UNION AND EASTERN EUROPE

DAVID TURNOCK

TRANSPORT is obviously of particular importance in developed economies where raw materials and manufactured goods must be moved to and from centers of manufacturing, with major flows of certain commodities occurring between regions and countries according to the level of specialization achieved. Transport is also of the greatest importance for the movement of labor, although on the passenger side there is a social as well as an economic function. Finally, strategic considerations make it imperative that all parts of a country be immediately accessible. So central planning in the Soviet Union and Eastern Europe inevitably gives a high priority to transport in order to ensure that these various demands can be met. This is especially important in the Soviet Union, given the need for a comprehensive infrastructure despite a very low density of population in many areas and the presence of a whole range of environmental constraints. Yet transport is not considered to be "productive" in the material sense, hence planners aim at a "unified transport system," with the fullest coordination between the different transport media. There is very little duplication, seen as actually or potentially wasteful, so that any lengthy journey, for goods or passengers, usually involves a mix of modes of transportation. The railway is fundamental for both goods and passengers, but short journeys of less than 50 kilometers are increasingly being made by road, while very long journeys are often accomplished by air, at least for passengers. Long freight hauls still use rail, but shipping by sea, river, or canal is an option in some cases, while bulk transfers of oil and natural gas are frequently made by pipeline. Where the terrain is extremely difficult or where traffic is too small to justify a railway, even long hauls by road may be allowed, as in the case of minerals from remote areas of Siberia; and even air freight may be employed in a few exceptional cases.

It is interesting to note the changing relative importance of the various prime haulers, particularly in the Soviet Union, where data is available for a 50-year period from 1928 to 1979 (see Table 1). Railways are still fundamental for the movement of freight, although the share is falling due to the increased importance of the pipelines, roads and shipping lines. The railway

455

Table 1
FREIGHT AND PASSENGER TRAFFIC IN THE SOVIET UNION,
ALLOCATED TO PRIME HAULERS, 1928–78 (Percent)

	Freight:				Passengers:			
	1928	1940	1965	1978	1928	1940	1965	1978
Railway	78.2	85.2	70.6	56.0	90.4	92.4	55.0	38.5
Road	0.2	1.8	5.2	6.8	0.7	3.1	32.9	43.2
Sea	7.8	5.0	14.1	14.2	1.1	0.8	0.4	0.3
Waterway (Inland)	13.3	7.3	4.8	3.9	7.7	3.5	1.3	0.7
Air	0.0	[1]	[1]	0.1	0.0	0.2	10.4	17.3
Pipeline	0.6	0.8	5.3	19.1	0.0	0.0	0.0	0.0
Total[2]	119.5	494.4	2764.0	5984.6	27.1	108.7	366.6	870.6

[1] Indicates less than 0.1 percent.

[2] Total figures give the actual traffic: billion tons per kilometer of freight and billion passengers per kilometer.

Source: Official Soviet statistics quoted by J. C. Dewdney, *U.S.S.R. in Maps*, London, Hodder & Stoughton, 1982, p. 78 and R. E. H. Mellor, *The Soviet Union and Its Geographical Problems*, London, Macmillan, 1982, p. 148.

lobby has always been very strong, and although there is more interest now in road transport for short freight hauls, the importance of the railway for long-distance movements is unlikely to diminish very significantly. For passengers, however, the fall in the railway share has been much more marked. This is due to a rapid increase of commuting by bus, and to the availability of air services for longer journeys. Air and road transport together accounted for only 3.3 percent of passenger-kilometers in 1940, but had climbed to 43.3 percent in 1965 and to 60.5 percent in 1979. The position varies from country to country within the Eastern bloc, however, and for this reason, as well as because of the integrated nature of transport services, it would be appropriate to examine the unified system in each region.

RAIL TRANSPORT

Growth of the System
Construction was generally delayed until the second half of the 19th century, when lines were built to serve the needs of the three great empires, Austria-Hungary, Germany and Russia. In the case of Austria-Hungary, lines were built from Vienna through the Moravian Gate to Southern Poland (1841–47) and also to Budapest and Prague (1845–50), while the *Südbahn* to Trieste afforded an important maritime outlet to the southwest. From Budapest, construction was extended to the Adriatic coast at Rijeka and also to the Banat, Slovakia and Transylvania. The Germans attached great importance to links between the capital and the eastern provinces, and completed railways from Berlin to Breslau (Wrocław) in 1846, to Danzig (Gdańsk) in 1852 and to Königsberg (Kaliningrad) in 1853. In Russia, the first trunk lines were from Leningrad to Moscow (1851) and Warsaw (1861), with routes

to the Black Sea opened during the following decade. The Trans-Siberian route, running entirely over Russian territory, was developed from 1892 but not fully opened until 1916. In Russia, after the 1914–18 war, further "supertrunk" lines were built, including the Turkestan-Siberian ("Turksib") with important links to the Vorkuta coalfield in the Soviet Arctic and to Sovetskaya Gavan on the Pacific coast, in anticipation of German and Japanese war action.

The territorial upheavals in Eastern Europe posed great problems for the emerging successor states. The new state of Poland inherited parts of the Austrian, German and Russian systems. It had to adapt the latter's broad-gage lines to accommodate standard-gage traffic and construct new lines in the center between Warsaw and Poznań and Warsaw and Cracow, as well as the coal line from Silesia through the corridor to the Baltic. Elsewhere, large developments were required to link the Czech lands more effectively with Slovakia; Transylvania with the Danube provinces of Romania; and Serbia with Yugoslavia's Croatian and Dalmatian regions. Very often the completion of these programs was delayed until after 1945, when further territorial changes had to be taken into account. Even now, however, there are few areas where a really dense system exists. The historical legacy is still very considerable; while the *Südbahn* and the Cracow-Bucharest routes now run rather illogically through corners of Yugoslavia and the Soviet Union respectively, former frontier cities like Lódź in Poland and Braşov in Romania still lack the importance for rail traffic that their central positions would now suggest.

At present, there are some 227,200 kilometers of railway in the Soviet Union and Eastern Europe, 9.59 kilometers for every thousand square kilometers of area and 5.72 kilometers for every 100,000 people (see Table 2). But these values vary greatly between the Soviet Union and Eastern Europe with regard to area: 6.37 in the case of the former, and 66.19 in the latter. Allowance must be made in the Soviet case for the vast areas of desert and Arctic waste, where settlement is too sparse to justify railway building. Even in the more settled areas, railways have often been expensive to build and maintain. Much of the topography is flat or undulating, yet gullies, swamps and floodplains frequently intervene; and the winters bring problems of frost heaving and drifting snow, and constrain efficient operation through serious loss of heat in steam locomotives, high viscosity of fuel in diesel locomotives, and icing on the catenary in the case of electrified lines. There are variations again throughout Eastern Europe. In relation to both area and population, East Germany and Czechoslovakia come out very prominently compared with the Balkan states. The historical legacy is important here, for there was rapid development of the rail network in the German and Habsburg empires before 1941. In spite of recent development (still continuing in Albania), the importance of road transport for local movement has restricted the scope for new railways.

Operation
Table 3 shows that in 1980, railway traffic amounted to 3,839.9 million tons per kilometer of freight and 480.6 million passengers per kilometer,

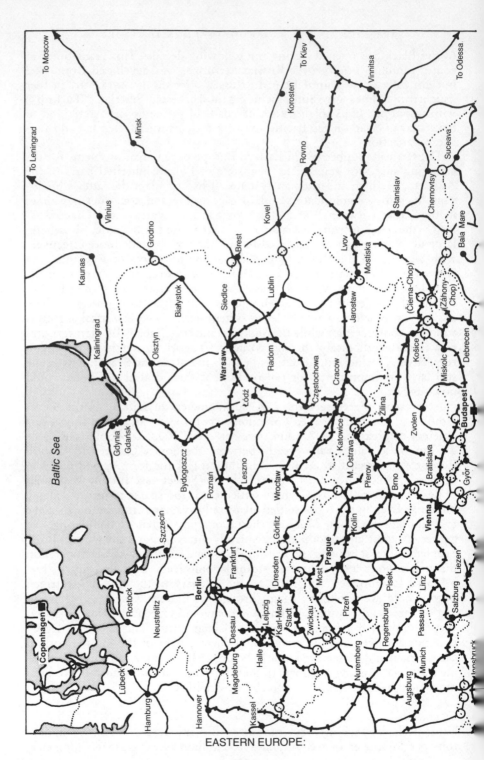

EASTERN EUROPE:

RAILWAYS

Table 2
RAILWAY NETWORKS IN THE SOVIET UNION AND EASTERN EUROPE, 1980

	A	B	C	D	E
Soviet Union	142.80	44.80	31.4	6.37	5.44
Eastern Europe	84.37	20.69	24.5	66.19	6.26
Albania	0.50	0.00	0.0	17.64	1.96
Bulgaria	4.04	1.65	40.8	36.47	4.55
Czechoslovakia	13.13	3.03	23.1	102.67	8.59
East Germany	14.22	1.68	11.8	131.43	8.50
Hungary	7.62	1.55	20.3	81.89	7.11
Poland	24.36	7.09	29.1	77.89	6.78
Romania	11.11	2.37	21.3	46.78	5.00
Yugoslavia	9.39	3.32	35.4	36.72	4.19
Total	227.17	65.49	28.8	9.59	5.72

A = Total route length (thousand kilometers).
B = Route length electrified (thousand kilometers).
C = Percentage of total route length electrified.
D = Kilometers of railway route per thousand square kilometers of total area.
E = Kilometers of railway route per 10,000 of total population.
Source: *CMEA Statistics Yearbook*, 1984.

Table 3
RAILWAY TRAFFIC IN THE SOVIET UNION AND EASTERN EUROPE, 1980[1]

	Freight (billion tons per kilometer)				Passengers (billion passengers per kilometer)			
	A	B	C	D	A	B	C	D
Soviet Union	3440.0	37.9	24.69	13.11	332.0	25.1	2.32	1.26
Eastern Europe[1]	399.9	34.3	4.75	2.97	148.6	18.1	1.77	1.10
Bulgaria	17.7	27.3	4.37	1.99	8.0	9.6	1.99	0.90
Czechoslovakia	66.2	18.4	5.04	4.33	18.0	−4.8	1.37	1.18
East Germany	56.4	35.9	3.97	3.37	23.1	30.5	1.62	1.38
Hungary	24.4	23.3	3.20	2.28	14.7	−9.8	1.92	1.37
Poland	134.7	35.6	5.53	3.75	51.3	39.0	2.11	1.43
Romania	75.5	57.3	6.80	3.40	23.2	30.3	2.09	1.05
Yugoslavia	25.0	29.5	2.66	1.11	10.3	−5.5	1.09	0.46
Total[1]	3839.9	37.5	16.92	9.67	480.6	22.9	2.12	1.21

[1] Excluding Albania, for which no data are available.
A = Total freight/passenger movement, 1980.
B = Percentage of change over 1970.
C = Traffic per kilometers of railway: million tons per kilometer or million passengers per kilometer.
D = Traffic per capita: thousand tons per kilometer or thousand passengers per kilometer.
Source: *CMEA Statistics Yearbook*, 1984.

increases of 37.5 percent and 22.9 percent, respectively, over 1970. It is evident, however, that the growth has been rather more rapid in the Soviet Union than in Eastern Europe, where road transport is becoming more important. But the picture in Eastern Europe is not uniform, because East Germany, Poland and, especially, Romania, have registered a rapid growth of railway traffic during the 1970s, while Czechoslovakia, Hungary and Yugoslavia have recorded relatively modest increases in freight and decreases in passenger traffic. Significant differences in policy therefore emerge. It is also useful to relate the amount of traffic to the size of the network and the population in each country. Passenger traffic in the Soviet Union is relatively heavy according to both criteria, although the contrast with Eastern Europe is more marked for freight than passenger traffic. Whereas Eastern Europe's railway freight works out at 4.75 million tons per kilometer of railway, the Soviet Union scores 24.09. And while each kilometer of railway in Eastern Europe carries 2.97 million passengers, the matching Soviet figure is 13.11 million. Contrasts certainly exist within Eastern Europe, with Poland and Romania making particularly heavy use of their railways (also Czechoslovakia for freight and both Bulgaria and Hungary for passengers), but it is the contrast over freight that impresses most, reflecting the mammoth scale of long-distance transfers in the Soviet case. Exchanges take place between the main industrial bases of the Center, Donbas, Ural and Kuzbas; the strain that such traffic has placed on the system has been a factor influencing the choice between regional policies of specialization and self-sufficiency.

Long-distance hauls link the Soviet Union with Eastern Europe. Here the differences in gage have demanded the provision of elaborate facilities at Chop (for Czechoslovakia and Hungary) and at Brest and Mostiska (for Poland), where freight car loads can be readily transferred. Movements by rail within Eastern Europe encompass timber, fruit and other raw materials from the Balkans in exchange for manufactured goods; Czechoslovakia and Hungary both play a key role in this international traffic by virtue of their central positions. Freight traffic to and from Western Europe is increasing, and a number of lines formerly cut by the Iron Curtain have been reopened. An important development of the last 15 years has been the growth of container traffic, not only between the Soviet Union and its Eastern European neighbors but between Western Europe and Japan using the Siberian Rail Bridge of roughly 10,000 kilometers between the frontier points of Brest (for France and West Germany), Chop (for Austria, Switzerland, France and the Iberian Peninsula), Luzhaika (for Finland) and the Pacific ports of Nakhodka and Vostochny neara Vladivostok. This transit traffic began in a modest way in 1967, under an agreement between Russian and Swiss forwarding companies, but has now developed into whole trainloads sent from various Western European countries. The land route is quicker (one month rather than the two required for the sea voyage) and also cheaper (because of competitive freight rates and savings on insurance and packaging). With expanded port facilities now available on the Soviet Union's Pacific coast, there seems no reason why other Asian countries should not use the Siberian transit route. The Soviet Union stands to gain from this considerable amount of foreign exchange at the expense of Far Eastern shipping lines.

Passenger traffic by rail is still very heavy, although road and air transport are carrying increasing proportions of short-distance and long-distance passengers respectively. Through trains from the Soviet Union are again affected by changes in gage, and here special arrangements are made to change the bogies of sleeping and restaurant cars at the frontier using systems and equipment developed in East Germany. Important routes link the Eastern European capitals by way of Berlin and Prague through Budapest to Belgrade, Bucharest and Sofia, or from Warsaw to the Balkans through Lvov (Soviet Union) to Bucharest and Constanţa, where a sea link with Istanbul enables this route to be used as an alternative to the direct routes from Western Europe to Turkey. Tourist traffic to the Black Sea resorts from Czechoslovakia, Germany and Poland is heavy, and along with travel to the Adriatic coast of Yugoslavia justifies augmented services from Western Europe, as do the routes through Vienna and Trieste.

Recent developments
In some countries, the postwar program of new railway construction has been considerable. In the Soviet Union, numerous new branch lines have been opened to tap new raw material sources, and additional "supertrunks" are being provided in Western and Central Siberia; these include the South Siberian ("*Yuzhib*") and the Central Siberian ("*Sredsib*"). A most ambitious railway project is now under way to duplicate the Trans-Siberian Railroad east of Tayshet. A branch from Tayshet to Ust Kut near Bratsk on the Lena was completed in 1954, and the easternmost section from Komsomolsk to Sovetskaya Gavan, linked with the Trans-Siberian at Khabarovsk, was opened in 1947. But now the intervening section between Ust Kut and Komsomolsk is being built through sparsely populated countryside. The new construction, now approaching completion, covers a distance of 3,145 kilometers through an area affected by permafrost and subject to winter temperatures as low as −60 degrees Celsius. This Baykal-Amur Mainline will provide a shorter route to Vladivostok and also a more secure route well to the north of the Chinese border. Its main purpose, however, is to open up mineral resources: asbestos, coal, copper and nickel. Very high grade timber stands will also be made accessible. Much of this timber will be felled and exported as roundwood through Nakhodka. It is possible that in the future the railway will reach the Arctic mining outpost of Norilsk—only an extension east from Urengoye to the Yenisei is needed—but lines projected to run along the Okhotsk coast to the Bering Strait and through Yakutsk to the Lena seem much less likely.

Apart from the new railway built by East Germany to avoid transit through West Berlin, practically all postwar construction in Eastern Europe has been restricted to the Balkans. Romania has improved its links from Bucharest to Oltenia, Moldavia and Maramureş. Yugoslavia has completed the broadening of the narrow-gage line from Sarajevo to Ploče (Kardeljevo) and a new link from Valjevo to Titograd (which gives direct access from Belgrade to the Montenegrin port of Bar); both projects were financed by the World Bank. The main emphasis has recently switched from new construction to increasing the capacity of overloaded main lines. The volume of traffic has increased much more rapidly than the route length. There is a whole range of improvements to existing lines: modern signaling, new stations, provision of a second track on single-line railways, programs for building coaches and freight cars. We must also emphasize the changes in traction because of the demise of the steam locomotive, now seldom seen outside East Germany and Poland. Dieselization has reached an advanced stage, and electrification is also making rapid progress.

Provided that power is available, electrification of heavily used lines is considered preferable to either the construction of more powerful steam locomotives (with attendant weight problems) or dieselization. The Soviet Union had only 3,000 kilometers of electrified line in 1950, but the total is now over 40,000 kilometers. Electrification of the Kizel-Chusovaya-Sverdlovsk line in the Urals was based on thermal power, but hydropower was subsequently used on mountainous stretches of railway in the Caucasus and Kola Peninsula. The whole of the Trans-Siberian is now electrified. Progress in Eastern Europe has been of a similar order; most countries had only insignificant amounts of electrified sections at the end of World War II. Overall, one-quarter of the Eastern European railways are now electrified, compared to nearly one-third in the Soviet Union, but the proportions are relatively high in Bulgaria (40.8 percent) and Yugoslavia (35.4). The number of underground railways is increasing. They are operating, or are under construction, in 16 Soviet cities and in a number of Eastern European capitals.

ROAD TRANSPORT

Outside Eastern Europe and European Russia, modern road systems have been very slow to develop, because of limited demands and high construction costs in areas of permafrost. Russian military requirements were an important stimulus, and the Georgian, Osetian and Sukhumi military roads are fine examples of road building in the Caucasus. The Pamir and Uzbek roads in Central Asia, and the Aldan and Ussuri roads in eastern Siberia are other important examples of "routes without rails". The construction of such secondary roads is increasing as part of a new Soviet leap forward in road transport in places where initial costs are cheaper than those for rail construction. Roads are already taking a substantial proportion of the total passenger traffic in the Soviet Union, and it is intended that eventually all short-distance freight traffic (shorter than 50 kilometers) will be handled by roads as well. There is, however, still no major road straight across the Soviet Union, and quite apart from imposed restricted access (a particularly serious constraint for foreign motorists in the Soviet Union), there is still no possibility of traveling by road right across Siberia to the Pacific coast. Roads play an important part in most countries of Eastern Europe, especially in the industrial regions of Bohemia, Halle-Leipzig and Silesia. Some new roads have been built, notably the Dalmatian highway in Yugoslavia and sections of highway on the principal routes out of most capital cities in the region. But there is little evidence of any international highway scheme. Indeed, the reverse is more demonstrable, since the interwar German autobahns from Berlin toward Stettin (Szczecin) and Breslau (Wrocław) now peter out short of the present frontier with Poland, and the former autobahn in East Prussia is abandoned. Most improvements are concerned with upgrading existing roads—surfacing, with some widening and realignment.

Road traffic in the past has consisted largely of trucks, an increasing number of which are of the modern articulated type, able to make long journeys to Western Europe as well as international movements within the region. Bus services have developed to complement rail services, and operate principally between towns and cites lacking a direct or speedy rail connection. In Poland, the density of such services is very high in the eastern, formerly Soviet-administered territory, where railway network remains sparse, whereas in the former German and Austrian lands, railways are much more important. Bus services in Romania operate on the several Carpathian routes that, because of the old frontier with Austria-Hungary along the crest of the mountains, have never been followed by railways; the eastern Carpathians demonstrate the point especially well, with one bus service operating from the railhead at Vatra Dornei along the Bistriţa Valley to Bacău and thence across Moldavia to Iaşi.

The private car, however, is becoming very prominent, especially in the more developed states of Eastern Europe. Several countries have a car assembly industry, in addition to bus, truck and tractor capacities. The result is that a considerable amount of road traffic is geared to recreation, supported by a growing number of motels and other tourist facilities. Levels of car ownership lag far behind those of North America and Western Europe, but there are significant variations within the region. In 1973, 21 percent of households in Czechoslovakia and East Germany owned a car, compared with 14 percent in Yugoslavia, 12 percent in Bulgaria and Hungary, eight percent in Poland, and only four percent in Romania and the Soviet Union. There is some concern among Soviet authorities that the individual freedom provided by car ownership will weaken concern for collective achievements and thus foster "bourgeois" attitudes, such as a desire for consumption as an end in itself, which conflict with the ideals of the "new Soviet person." Difficulties for motorists arise through poor garaging facilities, high fuel costs and even some restrictions on the use of cars designed to reduce demand for fuel. Motoring by foreign visitors has become very prominent now that virtually all main roads are modernized, but all tourism in Albania is very strictly controlled, and in the Soviet Union visitors may travel only on a small number of approved roads.

INLAND WATERWAYS

There are many navigable inland waterways in the Soviet Union and Eastern Europe, and the low terrain of the North European Plain reduces the cost of building link canals in places where the natural river systems do not coincide with the main lines of trading movements. During the 18th and 19th centuries, therefore, canals were built to link the Rhine with the Elbe, Oder, Vistula and Dnieper, but except in the case of the larger Mittelland canal in Germany, their capacity is too small for them to be valuable today. To accommodate larger vessels, much higher levels of capital investment are

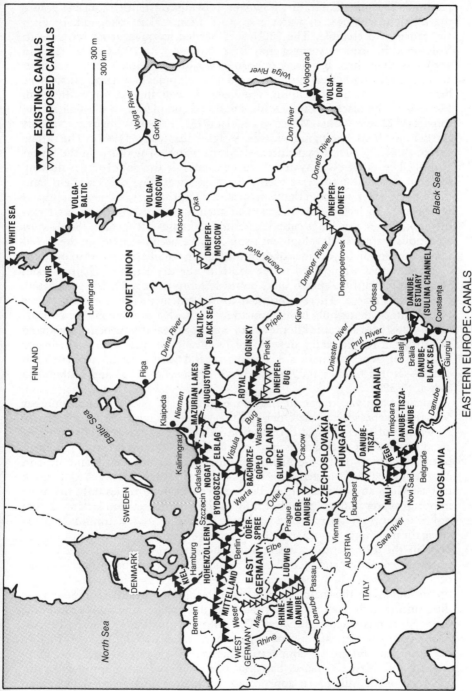

EASTERN EUROPE: CANALS

required. The potential traffic, however, is being constantly reduced because the inherent slowness of water transport often makes road, rail, or even air transport preferable. The 180 hours needed to travel from Moscow to Volgograd by express steamer may be compared with 20 hours by rail and with less than three by air. Consequently, although many canal schemes are attractive on physical grounds, actual developments of large canals have been few. In the Soviet Union, the Volga is well aligned for traffic from Moscow to the Black Sea and Donbas with the completion of the Volga-Don canal (1952) and Volga-Moscow canal (1973), and movement is possible further north to Leningrad via the Volga-Baltic canal (1967). The Volga system, in fact, carries two-thirds of all the waterborne traffic in the Soviet Union. The other river systems are less helpful; the south-north-flowing Siberian rivers lie transverse to the main east-west line of movement, and these rivers enter an ocean that is frozen most of the year, so their usefulness is restricted to feeding the railways at such main crossing points as Krasnoyarsk, where the Trans-Siberian Railroad crosses the Yenisei. Some very ambitious waterway development projects have been discussed in the Soviet Union, most notably the idea of damming the great Siberian rivers to produce a vast lake that would feed water south to the dry lands of Central Asia. Water from the Ob, specifically, could feasibly be taken 2,500 kilometers to the Amu Darya. There is no plan to implement this scheme in the near future, although it would have importance for navigation. However, a north-south transfer of six cubic kilometers of water per year is now being organized in European Russia, and a new Volga-Don canal features among the major engineering works. There are already several very long Soviet irrigation canals—North Crimea (400 kilometers), Kara-Kum (850) and Golodnaya Steppe (1,300).

Inland waterway traffic in Eastern Europe highlights a limited number of major rivers, such as the Oder and the Vistula. Navigation often requires a measure of international cooperation. The Elbe was formerly important as an outlet for Czech goods moving northward for export via Hamburg, but the situation of the German interzonal frontier between Hamburg and Magdeburg has encouraged some transfer of traffic to the railways to Rostock in East Germany or Szczecin in Poland. The Danube is certainly the most important river in the region, but limited traffic potential and lack of unified political control in the past often discouraged the necessary stimulus to overcome the main physical hazards. The removal of the Turkish economic monopoly in the 19th century, along with the expansion of grain and timber traffic, eventually prompted the navigation scheme at the critical sections of the Iron Gates where the Sip canal was built (through which vessels moved upstream against the strong current with the aid of a steam locomotive running on the Serb-Yugoslav bank) and the delta where the Sulina river was dredged, straightened and dyked. The political situation in Central Europe in the interwar and early postwar periods was hardly conducive to further development, but greater cooperation between the riparian states, including Austria and West Germany, has now been achieved and improvements to the river made still more appropriate by a combination of navigational requirements with hydromelioration schemes.

A new canal is being built to link the Rhine and Danube and to open a waterway extending across Europe from Rotterdam to Sulina on the Black Sea. But for the waterway to operate efficiently, it will be necessary to complete the regularization of the Danube. A major achievement here has been the Iron Gates dam, built jointly by Romania and Yugoslavia, to provide electricity and improve navigation facilities and flood-control systems. Further dams may be built downstream at Gruia, Turnu Măgurele and Cernavodă. Hungary plans locks and power stations on the Adony-Mohács section, and is also collaborating with Czechoslovakia over the canalization of the river through a lateral canal taking off at Dunakiliti with major installations, including locks and power stations, at Gabčikovo and Nagymaros. With the benefit of such works, it will be possible to navigate day and night and to use vessels of 1,600 tons, pushed or towed by a new generation of motorboats.

The Europa canal should exert a strong influence on individual Eastern European countries served directly by the Rhine-Danube axis. Certain categories of freight may be transferred from rail to water, and it may become feasible to build linking canals so that more industrial centers can be integrated with the water highway. In Hungary, the Danube-Tisza canal (from the Danube at Dunaharaszti, between Budapest and Adony, to the Tisza at Csongrád) will provide a link with northeast Hungary extending as far as the Soviet frontier at Záhony. Quite apart from the benefit to Hungary, there is an opportunity for the Soviet Union to channel freight to the Rhine-Danube system by this route, in preference to the use of Ismail on the Danube delta. Once again, however, there will have to be a further program of hydro-power navigation complexes, but there will be an important by-product in the provision of more irrigation water. Yugoslavia has shown considerable interest in developing other Danube tributaries in order to reach the Adriatic coast (by the Sava) and gain access to the Greek port of Thessaloniki through the Morava-Vardar corridor. In Romania, the Danube-Black Sea canal, running across the Dobrogea from Cernavodă to Constanța, opened in 1984. It will allow goods coming into Constanța by sea to be transferred directly onto barges, whereas before the railway haul to Cernavodă meant an additional dividing up of bulk. The canal will be useful to Romania for the movement of bulky raw materials destined for factories situated along the Danube (and also for firms in the capital city, if the proposed Bucharest-Danube canal is built). Other countries may use the canal, but there is no question of the canal replacing the shipping route through the Danube delta. Ocean-going ships will continue to sail upstream from Sulina to the Romanian ports of Brăila and Galați and the Russian ports of Ismail and Reni, with transfer of cargo to river barges in many cases. In this connection, it is interesting to note the activities of the Interlighter international shipping enterprise jointly created by the Soviet Union, Bulgaria, Czechoslovakia and Hungary. The idea is to integrate river and sea transport by introducing container barges (of 1,100 tons) that can be transfered bodily to sea-going vessels (of 36,000 tons) at the river mouth, presumably Ismail or Reni. The company is expected to handle about 1.5 million tons of goods annually.

It is possible that in the future an Oder-Danube canal from Bratislava to Raciborz, and branch canals to the Elbe and Vistula, will finally integrate the major rivers of Eastern Europe into a unified navigation system. For the present, however, progress seems to be geared largely to domestic projects in the various countries. Poland is working on an ambitious Vistula plan (sanctioned in 1978), with thoughts of a Silesian canal to link the Oder and Vistula through the expanding Rybnik coalfield; East Germany may decide to connect Berlin with the port of Rostock.

SEA TRANSPORT

Although the Soviet Union and its Eastern European neighbors have a very lengthy coastline, the scope for transport by sea is much reduced by ice, which poses major problems in the north beyond the port of Riga. Although reliable bases exist at Murmansk and Petropavlovsk-Kamchatsky, the northern sea route carries little traffic, since it is affected by ice from seven to 10 months of the year and suffers from the additional liability of fogs during the short open season. The introduction of icebreakers, including the atomic-powered *Lenin* and *Arktika*, has increased reliability, but the capacity is still very limited. Much of the sea traffic, is, therefore, limited to those individual seas where the problem of freezing is less severe. On the Black Sea, Odessa and Sebastopol can normally be kept open throughout the year, as can the entry to the Sea of Azov, and a vigorous coasting trade has developed, embracing Bulgarian and Romanian ports (Burgas, Varna, Constanţa, Galaţi, and Brăila). The train-ferry service operating between Ilyichovsk, near Odessa, and Varna is particularly important. Ice affects all ports in the Baltic, including those of East Germany and Poland, although most of them can be kept open if icebreakers are available. Riga suffers particularly from pack ice, which accumulates during onshore winds. Leningrad is the most important port, but it has suffered from the difficulty of guaranteeing the security of the Gulf of Finland as well as from the problem of ice; the acquisition of the former German port of Königsberg (Kaliningrad) with its outport of Pilau (Baltiysk) has improved the strategic situation in the Baltic from the Soviet standpoint, while Tallinn and Murmansk are now well placed to act as winter ports for Leningrad.

East Germany and Poland have developed their Baltic ports partly for their own requirements but also to attract traffic from Czechoslovakia and Hungary. The East German development of Rostock under difficult conditions complements the Polish effort at Szczecin and Gdańsk-Gdynia. Yugoslavia's principal Adriatic ports are Rijeka and Split; along with Trieste in Italy, they handle some of the transit traffic to and from the landlocked states. Additional capacity is being installed at Ploče (now Kardeljevo) and Bar, backed up by the plans for better rail links across the Dinaric Alps.

There has been a big expansion of shipping in Eastern Europe. The Soviet Union moved some 229 million tons of freight by sea in 1978, compared with only 54 million in 1955. By 1980, the Soviet fleet had grown to 21.9 million gross tons (7,495 vessels), making it the sixth largest in the world. The growth has arisen out of the widening scope of commercial contacts across the world geared to the support of allied states, such as Cuba and Vietnam, and the growing trade in certain key commodities, such as cereals, oil and wool, with capitalist states. Ships have become much larger, following developments in the rest of the world, and maximum utilization of these vessels has led to opening up various "triangular" shipping routes. Further flexibility has come from the construction of vessels that can carry both dry and liquid cargoes. It is an interesting question how far the largest Soviet ships can be used to full capacity in domestic waters, in view of 100,000-ton limits on both the Danish Sound and the Bosphorus, as well as reported problems over shallow water at many Russian ports. Several new deep-water berths and harbors are under construction: Arkhangelsk and Murmansk in the Arctic; Grigorevsky on the Black Sea; Ventspils on the Baltic and Vostochny (Wrangel Bay) in the Far East. The Eastern European countries—even the landlocked states of Czechoslovakia and Hungary—also possess modern fleets. A number of vessels are available for international charter.

PIPELINES

The total extent of the pipeline network is difficult to measure, but there must now be more than 200,000 kilometers of pipelines for gas or oil in the Soviet Union alone. Much of the development has been recent, because there was very little building before World War I, apart from the 800-kilometer Baku-Batumi project; the total length was still little more than 5,000 kilometers in 1950. Oil pipelines have been important in Romania since the late 19th century, when oil was exported from Ploieşti through the Danube port of Giurgiu upstream to Hungary and Austria. The Romanian network has been extended following the extension of drilling into Oltenia, but the Soviet system is now much more important, carrying crude oil from the Caspian and Middle Volga oil fields to the refineries located at the ports and major centers of consumption, including Leningrad and eastern Siberia (Irkutsk).

After some initial postwar dependence on imported oil, the Soviet Union has become an important exporter of oil. Japan is importing considerable quantities from Moskalvo in Sakhalin, and a depot has been built at Ventspils on the Baltic for export to the West. Most important, however, is the "Friendship" pipeline system to Eastern Europe; this takes the form of two arms, one of which runs through Poland to the East German frontier at Schwedt an der Oder, while the other extends to Százhalombatta near Budapest in Hungary and also to Bratislava and Záluží-Most in Czechoslovakia. Following this impressive symbol of COMECON integration, new refining and petrochemical complexes have emerged at Płock in Poland, Schwedt in East Germany and Bratislava in Czechoslovakia, areas removed from the older concentrations of industry. Bulgaria, Yugoslavia and Romania import oil now by sea, but not necessarily from the Soviet Union; this is partly for political reasons, but also because the Soviet Union cannot be relied upon indefinitely to meet Eastern Europe's requirements from its own resources. Pipelines also run from the Adriatic (near Rijeka) to Sisak, Belgrade and Budapest, also from Burgas on the Black Sea to Sofia.

469

The Soviet Union and Romania possess rich resources of natural gas, which pipelines are also used to transport. Soviet pipelines have been built from Stavropol, Saratov and the western Ukraine to Moscow, Gorky and Leningrad, and further extensions will serve the Center and Donbas industrial regions as well as the Black Sea ports. The opening up of new gas fields in remote areas like northwestern Siberia has brought about a rapid increase in the pipeline system, and this now extends into Eastern Europe where there is a serious energy deficit. The "Union" pipeline runs from the Orenburg gas field in the Urals for some 2,750 kilometers to the frontier, and is then continued through Czechoslovakia. Soviet gas is also exported through Romania to Bulgaria and through Czechoslovakia to various Western European countries. Romania has built a comprehensive distribution system from its Transylvanian fields, first to the main towns of that province (Braşov, Cluj, Sibiu), and more recently to Bucharest and the peripheral provinces as well. In the Banat, the gas is used to increase the efficiency of the blast furnaces, while in Moldavia and Oltenia large chemical plants based on gas supplies are helping to build new industrial nodes in formerly backward areas. Romania exports gas to the Hungarian chemical-manufacturing town of Tiszapalkonya, but this is unlikely to increase because of Romanian requirements that its resources be used to support its own industrialization program rather than to benefit its more highly industrialized neighbors.

AIR TRANSPORT

An air service linked Moscow with Gorky in 1923. But before World War II, there were shortcomings both in the design and the construction of aircraft. U.S. and German expertise has now been assimilated, and several distinguished Soviet designers have made their mark. While domestic routes have multiplied, however, the potential for international traffic in the Soviet Union is largely unexploited because of reluctance to tolerate flights of foreign aircraft over most parts of the country. The Soviet Union and each Eastern European country now have their own airlines linking capital cities with their respective provincial centers and with each other. In the Soviet Union, however, air transport plays a particularly important role in view of the greater distances involved. Moreover, in remote areas with a harsh environment, providing air service may be only one-tenth as expensive as opening a road or rail link, so air transport is seen as the initial prime hauler. Services operate to such centers as Magadan and Norilsk, and serve the scientific and military bases in the Arctic. Yakutsk is an important center for air services in northeastern Siberia.

ELECTRICITY TRANSMISSION

Although not considered as one of the prime haulers, the electricity grid has become a crucially important transporter of energy, enabling power generated at the main fuel bases to be supplied to consumers across the region. As long as distribution systems were limited to the immediate vicinity of each power station, it was necessary to transport coal or oil by rail in order to supply power stations situated in each area of demand. Such transport costs made electricity relatively expensive in certain areas and discouraged industrial development. The development of electrical engineering has enabled rapid progress to be made during the postwar period, and each country now has its national transmission system, with high voltage lines (often 500 kilovolts or above) crossing frontiers in several places to provide a unified "Peace" system, allowing surpluses and deficits among member states to be ironed out. Because of the vast distances involved in the Soviet Union, there have been serious technical problems concerned with energy losses in the grid; very high voltages are needed to reduce these to acceptable levels. The Far East is still isolated from the rest of the country, but Central Asia and central and western Siberia, formerly independent regions, are now being drawn into the network embracing European Russia and the Urals. Thus power can be pumped westward from the coalfields of Kansk-Achinsk and Kazakhstan, and from the hydroelectric stations on the great Siberian rivers.

CONCLUSION

Transport is often considered as an integrated set of systems designed by national and regional planners, yet there is a chronically insufficient allocation of funds, so provision lags seriously behind demand. The identification and removal of bottlenecks is a continuing problem for transport managers throughout the region. Despite recent improvements, movement tends to be rather slow by Western standards, and the uncomfortable journeys to work on heavily congested buses and trains constitute a major irritant of life for Soviet and Eastern European commuters. Only limited progress has been made in creating unified international transport systems, despite the coordinating role of COMECON. Crossing points are few in number, particularly on the frontier between Eastern Europe and the Soviet Union, and formalities are very protracted by Western standards. Coordination sufficient to meet Soviet strategic and economic interests is certainly maintained, and the various countries are linked together through the centrally controlled "Peace" electricity grid and the railway freight car pool system known as OPW (*Obszczy Park Wagonow*). Albania's electricity and railway systems are, however, still isolated, and although the decision has been taken, in principle, to connect Shkodër with Titograd by rail, the small amount of traffic likely to flow means there is little determination to complete this link. Yet throughout the region, the scale of international (as opposed to domestic) traffic is small; progress with highway construction and railway electrification reveals the emphasis on domestic circulation. The dependence of Eastern Europe on Soviet hydrocarbon fuels has given rise to international pipeline systems for both oil and gas, but the scale of other transfers is limited enough for existing rail and road services to handle without any pressing need for international waterways where potential economies could only be won by very large increases in traffic. The commitment shown on national projects, such as the Danube-Black Sea canal, is rarely found at the international level.

FURTHER READING

Armstrong, T. *The Northern Sea Route.* Cambridge: Cambridge University Press, 1952.

Banister, C. E. "Transport in Romania: A British Perspective." *Transport Review.* Vol. 1, 1981, pp. 251–70.

Fuchs, R. J., et al. "Commuting in the U.S.S.R." *Soviet Geography.* Vol. 19, 1978, pp. 363–425.

Fuchs, R. J., and Demko, G. J. "Commuting in the U.S.S.R. and Eastern Europe: Causes, Characteristics, Consequences." *Eastern European Quarterly.* Vol. 11, 1977, pp. 463–75.

Hunter, H. *Soviet Transportation Policy.* Cambridge, Massachusetts: Harvard University Press, 1957.

———. *Soviet Transport Experience: The Lessons for Other Countries.* Washington, D.C.: Brookings Institution, 1968.

Kramer, J. M. "Soviet Policy towards the Automobile." *Journal of East and West Studies.* Vol. 22, no. 2, 1976, pp. 16–35.

Krivoruchko, O. N. "Maritime Economic Systems of the U.S.S.R." *Soviet Geography.* Vol. 17, 1976, pp. 153–59.

MacDonald, H. *Aeroflot: Soviet Air Transport since 1923.* London: Putnam, 1975.

Mellor, R. E. H. "Transport: Holding the Soviet Economy Together," in Mellor, R. E. H., *The Soviet Union and Its Geographical Problems.* London: Macmillan, 1982, pp. 146–69.

Micklin, P. P. "Recent Developments in Large-scale Water Transfers in the U.S.S.R." *Soviet Geography.* Vol. 25, 1984, pp. 261–63.

Sigalov, M. R. "Railroads as a Base for the Economic Development of Sparsely Populated Regions." *Soviet Geography.* Vol. 21, 1980, pp. 1–14.

Symons, L., and White, C., eds. *Russian Transport: An Historical and Geographical Survey.* London: G. Bell & Sons, 1975.

Taylor, Z. "Seaport Development and the Role of the State: The Case of Poland," in Hoyle, B. S., and Hilling, D., eds., *Seaport Systems and Spatial Change*, Chichester, Sussex: Chichester & Sons, 1984, pp. 217–38.

Williams, E. W., et al. *Freight Transportation in the Soviet Union.* Princeton: Princeton University Press, 1962.

Wilson, O. "The Belgrade-Bar Railway: An Essay in Economic and Political Geography," in Hoffman, G. W., ed., *Eastern Europe: Essays on Geographical Problems.* London: Macmillan, 1971, pp. 365–93.

ENERGY

IAIN ELLIOT

USSR

The Soviet Union has vast energy resources that should allow Moscow and its Eastern European allies to plan their industrial growth on a secure basis well into the 21st century. Most of these unexploited reserves of oil, natural gas and coal, however, lie in remote, underdeveloped areas beyond the Ural mountains, and efforts to tap them must overcome problems presented by the harsh Siberian climate and lack of infrastructure. To maintain the USSR's remarkable expansion of fuel and power production attained over recent decades, economic planners have invested in workers and materials on a huge scale, but by the 1980s the exhaustion of many major sources of energy in the European territories, along with difficulties encountered in tapping new Siberian fields, meant that total coal and oil output no longer showed a regular annual increase. Natural gas, however, maintained an impressive growth rate, and the contribution of nuclear power expanded in the main industrial regions.

The ratio of energy consumption to gross national product (GNP) has not improved sufficiently for energy savings to compensate for the slowdown in fuel consumption rates, and by the 1980s the inefficient use of power resources was having a severely deleterious effect on industrial growth. The capital investment required to ensure supplies of fuel and power to Eastern Europe in 1976–80 was double the cost in the previous five years and continued to rise sharply in the 11th Five-Year Plan for 1981–85. Yet the Council for Mutual Economic Assistance (CMEA, or COMECON) member countries required two to three times more energy for each unit of GNP than Japan or West Germany. The need to save energy is a major theme in media exhortations, but demand in Eastern Europe was expected to rise from 580 million standard fuel tons in 1975 to over 1,000 million tons by 1990.

The Soviet Union is by far the most important energy producer of the CMEA countries (see Table 1). With a sixth of the earth's inhabitable area, it can claim more than half the earth's resources of coal and peat, more than 40 percent of natural gas and oil shale and more than a third of the known oil bearing areas. The Soviet Union has some 97 percent of CMEA energy resources, of which about 90 percent lie east of the Urals. In 1968, later than for most industrialized countries, coal was surpassed by oil in

Table 1
POWER AND FUEL PRODUCTION IN THE SOVIET UNION AND EASTERN EUROPE

	Electricity (million MWh)	Oil (million tons)	Natural gas (billion cubic meters)	Hard coal (million tons)	Brown coal (million tons)
Bulgaria					
1960	4.7	—	—	0.6	15.4
1970	19.5	—	0.5	0.4	28.9
1980	34.8	—	0.2	0.3	29.9
1983	43	—	0.1	0.3	31.3
Czechoslovakia					
1960	24.5	0.1	1.4	26.4	57.9
1970	45.2	0.2	1.2	28.2	81.3
1980	72.7	0.1	0.6	28.2	94.9
1983	76	0.1	0.6	27	100
East Germany					
1960	40.3	—	—	2.7	225.5
1970	67.7	—	—	1.1	261.5
1980	98.8	—	—	—	258.1
1983	105	—	—	—	278
Hungary					
1960	7.6	1.2	0.3	2.8	23.7
1970	14.5	1.9	3.5	4.2	23.7
1980	23.9	2.0	6.1	3.1	22.6
1983	26	2.0	6.5	2.8	22.4
Poland					
1960	29.3	0.2	0.5	104.4	9.3
1970	64.5	0.4	5.0	140.1	32.8
1980	121.9	0.3	6.0	193.1	36.9
1983	126	0.2	5.1	191	43
Romania					
1960	7.7	11.5	10.0	3.4	3.4
1970	35.1	13.4	24.0	6.4	14.1
1980	67.5	11.5	33.3	8.1	27.1
1983	70	12	35	7.8	36.7
Soviet Union					
1960	292.3	147.9	42.2	355.9	134.2
1970	740.9	353	184.5	432.7	144.7
1980	1,293.9	603.2	405.6	492.9	159.9
1983	1,416	616	499	487	155
Britain (1983)	276	110	40	116	—
United States (1983)	2,480	427	530	680	50

Sources: *Statisticheskii ezhegodnik stran-chlenov Soveta ekonomicheskoi vzaimopomoshchi, 1981*, Moscow, 1981; *SSSR v tsifrakh v 1983 godu*, Moscow, 1984.

its share of the Soviet energy balance; and in 1980 coal was surpassed by natural gas also (see Table 2). By the year 2000, natural gas is expected to supply more energy than oil or coal, and nuclear energy will provide the main alternative to fossil fuels (see Figures 1 and 2).

The expansion of the Soviet fuel industries after the devastation of World War II was phenomenal, and has only recently shown signs of faltering

Table 2
COMPARATIVE FUEL PRODUCTION IN THE SOVIET UNION
(IN PERCENTAGE OF TOTAL OUTPUT)

	Oil	Gas	Coal	Peat	Shales	Wood	Total (in million standard fuel tons)
1950	17.4	2.3	66.1	4.8	0.4	9.0	311.2
1960	30.5	7.9	53.9	2.9	0.7	4.1	692.8
1970	41.1	19.1	35.4	1.5	0.7	2.2	1,221.8
1975	44.7	21.8	30.0	1.2	0.7	1.6	1,571.3
1980	45.5	27.1	25.2	0.4	0.6	1.2	1,895.6
1981	44.9	28.4	24.3	0.6	0.6	1.2	1,938.2
1982	44.0	29.7	24.1	0.4	0.6	1.2	1,990.2
1983	43.3	31.1	23.6	0.4	0.5	1.1	2,036.2

Sources: *Narodnoe khozyaistvo SSSR v 1983 g.*, Moscow, 1984, p. 152; *Pravda*, January 26, 1985.

Table 3
FUEL PRODUCTION IN THE SOVIET UNION

	Oil (million tons)	Gas (billion cubic meters)	Opencut coal (million tons)	Total (in million standard fuel tons)
1950	37.9	5.8	27.1	261.1
1960	147.9	45.3	102.0	509.6
1970	353	197.9	166.6	624.1
1975	490.8	289.3	225.8	701.3
1980	603.2	435.2	270.9	716.4
1981	608.8	465.3	275.5	704.0
1982	612.6	500.7	286.1	718.1
1983	616.3	535.7	291.4	716.1
1984	613	587	n.a.	712

Sources: *Narodnoe khozyaistvo SSSR v 1983 g.*, Moscow, 1984, p. 152; *Pravda*, January 26, 1985.

(see Table 3). Output almost doubled every decade; the Soviet Union surpassed the United States as the world's major oil producer and almost matched U.S. coal and natural gas output. This was achieved despite ever-greater dependence on fields among the frozen wastes in the northern Tyumen region of western Siberia, which by 1985 accounted for 62 percent of Soviet oil output and over 55 percent of gas production. This rapid growth, however, is unlikely to continue, since it has been dependent on the uniquely rich Samotlor oil field and Urengoi gas field, and no similar discoveries

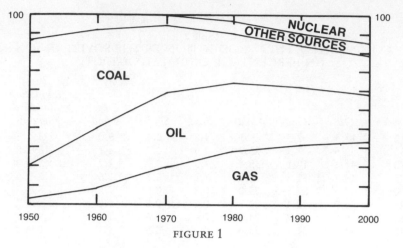

FIGURE 1

SOVIET ENERGY BALANCE, 1950–2000

Sources: *Narodnoe khozyaistvo SSSR v 1970 godu*, Moscow, 1971, p. 183; *Narodnoe khozyaistvo SSSR 1922–1972*, Moscow, 1972, p. 162; and Melnikov, N. V., *Toplivno-energeticheskie resursy SSSR*, Moscow, 1971, p. 7.

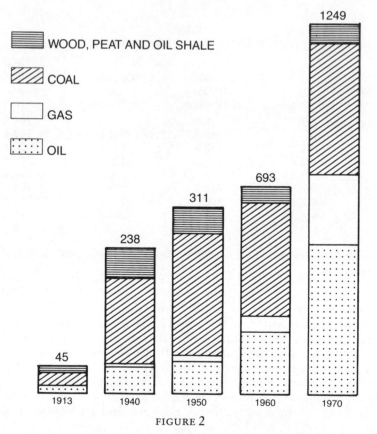

FIGURE 2

COMPARATIVE GROWTH IN SOVIET OUTPUT OF FUELS, 1913–1970

Sources: As for Figure 1.

EASTERN EUROPE: NATURAL RESOURCES AND ENERGY

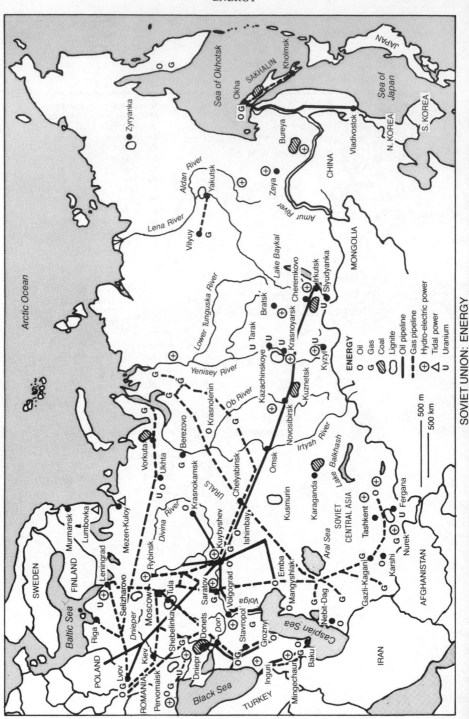

SOVIET UNION: ENERGY

ENERGY

O Oil
G Gas
⬮ Coal
⬭ Lignite
– – – Oil pipeline
· · · Gas pipeline
⊕ Hydro-electric power
△ Tidal power
U Uranium

500 m
500 km

have been made recently. Future expansion will require exploiting many smaller fields, which will be much more costly to commission.

Oil

Until 1984, the impressive rise in western Siberian output (from 31 million tons in 1970 to 312 million tons in 1980) more than compensated for the falling production of the older fields in the Volga-Ural basin and the Baku region of Azerbaidzhan. The smaller deposits in the Komi ASSR, at Mangyshlak in Kazakhstan, and near Orenburg, also increased production satisfactorily throughout the 1970s. In 1984, with total oil output registering a decline for the first time, considerable concern was voiced about inefficient management and poor oil-recovery rates, as oil ceased flowing under natural pressure. In February 1985, Nikolai Maltsev, the minister for the oil industry, was replaced by the more successful minister for the gas industry, Vasily Dinkov. Although workers and materials have been poured into western Siberia, labor productivity and the ratio of oil produced per meter drilled have fallen so sharply that the cost of raising output by one ton and transporting it to the consumer was estimated at three times what it should cost to save a ton by instituting economy measures.

Natural gas

The gas industry is one of the most successful sectors of the Soviet economy. From a share of less than three percent in the Soviet fuel balance in 1950, it expanded to account for more than 31 percent in 1983. The main producing republics are the Russian SFSR (with western Siberia alone accounting for over half the total Soviet output), Turkmenia, the Ukraine, Uzbekistan and Azerbaidzhan. Production in the Ukraine fell from 61 billion cubic meters (bcm) to 51 bcm in 1980 and in the North Caucasus from 47 to 11 bcm; but during the 1970s, new discoveries at Orenburg were brought rapidly on stream, increasing output from one to more than 50 bcm. The Vuktyl field in Komi ASSR began production in the 1960s and produced 18 bcm in 1980. Output in Turkmenia rose sharply from 13 bcm in 1970 to about 70 bcm by 1985, while production in Azerbaidzhan was less spectacular, rising from 6 bcm in 1970 to 15 bcm in 1980.

The reserve base for increased extraction of natural gas was not in doubt; the major difficulties were the lack of infrastructure in Siberia and the need for further rapid construction of pipelines. Working and living conditions were appalling, and some 1.3 million square meters of housing, hospitals, canteens, shops and schools were planned for 1981–85 in the towns of Nadym and Novy Urengoi; but the population of the latter was to grow from 18,000 to 70,000 in the same period. The costs of expanding output in the northern Tyumen region of western Siberia rose steeply; construction projects for Urengoi alone in 1981–85 demanded as much investment as for the whole of the western Siberian gas industry in the previous five years. Urengoi, however, was to compensate for falling output in the European territories, producing by 1985 five times the 1980 figure of 50 bcm. By 1985, pipelines from Urengoi to the European center and the Urals had helped add almost 50,000 kilometers to the 131,000 kilometers of gas pipeline already existing in 1980 (Table 4). Problems with the construction of compressor stations and importing turbines kept the pipeline network below capacity, however.

Table 4
COMPARATIVE *PER CAPITA* FUEL AND POWER PRODUCTION, 1983

	Electricity (kilowatt-hours)	Oil (kilos)	Gas (cubic meters)	Coal* (kilos)
Bulgaria	4,770	—	6	3,620
Czechoslovakia	4,948	6	38	8,263
East Germany	6,284	—	—	16,646
Hungary	2,404	187	608	2,359
Poland	3,440	6	140	6,388
Romania	3,114	514	1,596	1,973
Soviet Union	5,203	2,261	1,832	2,354
Britain	4,918	1,960	713	2,075
United States	10,589	1,823	2,071	3,040

Source: *Narodnoe khozyaistvo SSSR v 1983 g.*, Moscow, 1984, pp. 72, 73.
* The figures for coal are somewhat misleading since they mix high-quality hard coal with brown coal, which has a much lower calorific value.

Coal

Although coal production increased rapidly from 261 million tons in 1950 to 716 million tons in 1980, the momentum was faltering by the 1980s, and had neither kept pace with the rise in oil and gas output nor achieved its targets. The accessible deposits in European areas were approaching exhaustion, and the vast reserves beyond the Urals were difficult to tap and transport to consumers.

The Donets Basin peaked at 224 million tons in 1976, but by mining deeper and narrower seams the Ukrainian miners tried to stabilize output at around 200 million tons in the 1980s. However, the Donets Basin continued to be criticized for lagging behind in opening new mines. The Moscow basin peaked in 1958 at 47 million tons, and was producing under 25 million tons in the 1980s.

High-grade steam and coking coals are supplied mainly by the Donets, Kuznetsk, Karaganda and Pechora basins. With the decline of the Donets Basin, the rail transport costs are rising as more coal is hauled from the outlying fields. The Kutznetsk Basin increased output from 111 million tons in 1970 to about 150 million tons by the 1980s; its reserves could support annual production of 500 million tons, but again construction of new mines suffered from a lack of investment.

Output at Ekibastuz, Karaganda and Pechora has expanded, but consumption is limited by the saturation of the rail transport network. Power stations were planned to make use of the extra capacity at Ekibastuz—which could rise from 67 million tons in 1980 to 150 million in the 1990s—and at Kansk-Achinsk in southern Siberia, where output of poor-quality lignite could be increased from 30 million tons to 350–500 million tons, if the problems of transmitting electricity by high voltage lines thousands of miles from the mineside power stations to European consumers can be solved. In 1981, Academician Sheindlin urged that the program for producing synthetic liquid fuels from Kansk-Achinsk coal should press ahead from the pilot plant in Krasnoyarsk, since synthetic fuels would be needed as oil output dropped; and in 1985 it was reported that an industrial plant was under construction.

Electricity
Plans to reverse trends and restore coal as the main fuel base for power generation have been delayed by lack of investment and the remoteness of the vast Siberian reserves. In the Soviet Union, the share of thermal power stations dropped from 86 percent in 1975 to 80 percent in 1980, while hydroelectric and nuclear power expanded to 14 and six percent respectively in 1980.

Output has grown more rapidly than in most industrial countries, but is still lower than in the United States in per capita terms (see Table 4). In 1960, the Soviet Union produced only 33 percent as much electricity as the United States; by 1983, it achieved 57 percent of U.S. production. The average American still enjoyed a far higher living standard and consumed a far greater proportion of electricity output for private domestic appliances. By 1982, the Soviet Union increased the amount of electricity consumed by industry to 96 percent of the U.S. figure. The USSR has concentrated construction efforts on more efficient plants of 1,000-megawatts (MW) capacity or higher; by 1980, almost 60 per cent of power production was from just 76 of these giant plants, including 57 thermal, 14 hydroelectric and five nuclear stations. Combined heat and power (CHP) plants are widely used to supply heating in nearby housing blocks. By 1985, there were about 1,000 such stations in 800 Soviet cities, and nuclear CHP plants were under construction in Gorky, Voronezh, Odessa, Minsk and Volgograd. No protest movements were reported.

The Soviet regions are linked by a unified power grid, which is of considerable advantage in coping with peak demands in a territory so vast that when it is noon in Moscow it is 5 p.m. in Irkutsk and 7 p.m. in Khabarovsk. A high-tension AC line of 1,150 kilovolts (kV) will bring the Urals an additional 5,000 MW annually from Ekibastuz power stations, which will also supply power by a high-voltage DC line of 1,500 kV over 2,400 kilometers to the industrial center. An even more ambitious scheme to use Kansk-Achinsk coal (building as many as 10 stations of 6,400-MW capacity) to transmit power over 3,000 kilometers to the center was modified in early 1985 to a plan for just two or three stations.

Efforts to boost the share of nuclear energy to above 14 percent in 1985 fell behind schedule because of difficulties at the Atommash plant at Volgodonsk, which was built to produce up to 10 reactors of 1,000 MW a year. By 1985, there were 14 major nuclear plants in the Soviet unified grid, with a total capacity of 23,000 MW; the Leningrad and Chernobyl plants each had a capacity of 4,000 MW. The country has some 12 percent of total world hydropower potential, and Siberia has some of the world's largest hydroelectric stations: at Krasnoyarsk (6,000 MW), Bratsk (4,500 MW), Ust-Ilimsk

(3,600 MW) and Sayan-Shushensk (3,200 MW, with planned capacity of 6,400 MW). Of a total Soviet capacity in 1983 of 294,000 MW, hydropower stations accounted for 57,000 MW. The great Siberian rivers and rushing streams of Central Asia are still underused; only a tiny proportion of total potential has as yet been tapped.

EASTERN EUROPE

Oil

Only Romania and Hungary have significant reserves and production of oil, but discoveries on the Baltic coast have allowed Poland to hope for a small rise in annual output by the late 1980s. Hungary's reserves are thought sufficient to maintain yearly production at two million tons to the end of the century. Romanian output peaked in 1976 at 14.7 million tons and fell to 11.5 million tons in 1980. Reserves and recovery rates were low, and despite discoveries in the Black Sea shelf in 1979, exploration did not greatly improve prospects of maintaining output.

Natural gas

Romania is the major producer of natural gas among the Eastern European CMEA members, but unless further reserves are found in the Black Sea shelf, output is likely to fall from the 35 bcm annual rate of the early 1980s. Hungarian production peaked in 1978 at 7.35 bcm. Poland and East Germany joined the Soviet Union in exploring the Baltic shelf, but Soviet imports remained the main source for increasing Eastern European consumption.

Coal

Poland is a major coal exporting country, with hard coal output, mainly in the Upper Silesian basin, reaching 201 million tons in 1979 before political unrest reduced production. Strip mining at Turoszow, Konin-Turek and Belchatow provides brown coal for power generation. Provisional plans for 1990 projected hard coal output at 260 million tons and brown coal at 115 million tons, but by 1985 that seemed unrealistic.

East Germany mines more brown coal than any other country, but no longer extracts any hard coal. Brown coal output, mainly from the Leipzig-Halle and Lower Lusatian basins, reached 278 million tons in 1983 and was used mostly in mineside power stations or made into briquets.

Czechoslovakia mines both hard coal (in the Ostrava–Karvina region) and brown coal (in the North Bohemian basin and the Sokolov region), the latter mainly for power generation.

Hungary produced in 1983 some 3 million tons of hard coal near Pécs and some 22 million tons of brown coal at various small mines.

Romania mines brown coal in the Oltenian region for power generation, expanding output from 3 million tons in 1960 to 37 million tons in 1983. The Petroşeni region accounts for most hard coal, output rising from 3 million tons in 1960 to a peak of 8.1 million tons in 1979.

Bulgaria has conformed to general CMEA energy policy by exploiting its brown coal deposits for power generation, using mainly poor-quality

East Maritsa lignite with some better brown coal from the Pernik and Bobov-dal basins.

Electricity
The expansion of nuclear power continued into the 1980s at the Greifswald and Rheinsberg plants in East Germany and the Jaslovske Bohunice and Kozlodui plants in Czechoslovakia. It was planned to build further nuclear power stations by 1990: at Magdeburg-Stendahl (East Germany); Dukovany, Mahovce and Milovice (Czechoslovakia); Zarnowiec in Poland; Paks in Hungary; Cernovodă in Romania. Brown coal, however, remained the main basis for power generation, except for Romania with its domestic oil and gas and its Iron Gates hydroelectric scheme built jointly with Yugoslavia.

Yugoslavia has widely distributed reserves of brown coal and lignite, oil and natural gas; hydroelectric schemes are of considerable significance (see Table 5). In the 1980s, new coal mines were commissioned to supply fuel

Table 5
YUGOSLAV FUEL AND POWER PRODUCTION

	Hydroelectricity total (million megawatt hours)	Brown coal	Lignite (million tons)	Oil	Natural gas (billion cubic meters)
1975	40.0 (19.3)	9.4	25.5	3.7	1,554
1980	59.4 (28.2)	9.7	36.9	4.2	1,820
1982	62.1 (24.0)	10.7	43.5	4.3	2,286

to mineside heat and power plants, and an oil refinery was opened in Skopje with a projected annual capacity of 2.5 million tons. Despite growing dom-estic energy production, however, the rising cost of fuel imports remained a major problem for the Yugoslav economy.

Albania left COMECON in 1961 and is sparing with its economic statis-tics. Its mineral resources are underdeveloped; production of brown coal grew from 0.6 million tons in 1970 to 1.4 million tons in 1979; oil output rose from 1.5 million tons in 1970 to 2.2 in 1978. Hydroelectric power is important, providing 1.2 out of 1.6 million megawatt hours (MWh) in 1973. In 1978, some 2.1 million MWh were produced. Small quantities of natural gas are also extracted.

EXPORTS

Energy exports are of crucial importance to the Soviet Union. They add to the Eastern European dependence on Moscow and they earn hard currency to buy grain and technology from the West and to pay off hard currency debts. Oil exports will continue to fall in the 1980s, but natural gas may actually permit an increase in total fuel exports. The political element is evident in the names given to the main energy transmission systems to Eastern Europe: the Friendship oil pipeline, the Fraternity and Union gas pipelines and the Peace electricity grid.

Soviet exports of oil and oil products grew from 33 million tons in 1960 to 163 million tons in 1978, then declined to 159 million tons in 1980. Apart from falling output, the growing number of Soviet private motorists (12 million by 1985) put rising demands on already overstrained refineries. Gas exports, however, increased sharply from 2.2 bcm in 1970 to 57.3 bcm in 1980. Solid fuel exports rose from 15 million tons in 1960 to over 30 million tons in the mid-1970s and dropped to 26 million tons in 1980. Electricity was transmitted to neighboring countries in rising quantities—from 5.2 million MWh in 1970 to 23.7 million MWh in 1983. The relative importance of Soviet energy exports to Eastern Europe is shown in Table 6. Romania remained the least dependent on the Soviet Union.

Table 6
SOVIET ENERGY EXPORTS TO EASTERN EUROPE, 1983

	Coal and coke	Oil and oil products (million rubles)	Natural gas	Electricity (million megawatt hours)
Bulgaria	347	1,785	540	4.5
Czechoslovakia	139	2,434	951	2.4
East Germany	216	2,749	712	1.8
Hungary	74	1,157	438	8.2
Poland	55	2,185	664	0.3
Romania	94	—	—	—
Yugoslavia	95	1,196	—	—

Source: *Vneshnyaya torgovlya SSR v 1983 g.*, Moscow, 1984.

The Eastern European countries have been diversifying their sources for oil imports, buying oil from the Middle East, Algeria, Libya and elsewhere. This means much less-favorable pricing, because Moscow sold oil to COMECON countries at the average world market price for the previous five years, cushioning them from the immediate impact of price increases. In 1980, the Soviet Union sold about 80 million tons to Eastern European countries and 57 million tons to Organization for Economic Cooperation and Development members; the best capitalist customers were Finland, France, Italy, West Germany and the Netherlands.

The Eastern European countries have obtained Soviet natural gas also at cheaper prices, in return for participating in its extraction and transportation. For example, the Soyuz (Union) gas pipeline from Orenburg to Uzhgorod was built as a cooperative project, the Eastern Europeans receiving gas at reduced prices in return for their efforts. They are participating also in the enormous pipeline project to deliver Urengoi gas to CMEA countries and Western Europe, a project that plans eventually to carry 40 bcm a year (Table 7).

CONCLUSION

Despite failures to attain plan targets, wasteful consumption of energy and an actual decline in oil output, the Soviet Union has such vast energy reserves

Table 7
SHARE OF SOVIET-BLOC COUNTRIES IN WORLD ENERGY
PRODUCTION (IN PERCENTAGES)

	Electricity	Oil	Gas	Coal
1950	15	8	5	34
1960	21	16	12	54
1970	23	18	21	55
1980	26	25	31	56
1983	27	29	38	57

Source: *Narodnoe khozyaistvo v 1983 g.*, Moscow, 1984.

that by substituting coal, gas and nuclear power for oil in domestic consumption, it should be possible to meet the demands of Soviet and Eastern European industry, while continuing to earn hard currency by expanding natural gas exports. This will require the construction of several additional pipelines from Siberia, which makes the participation of Western countries a factor of critical importance. Although Soviet industry has the skills to produce compressors and large-diameter pipes, their quality and quantity cannot match what is available in the West and Japan; delays in completing the new pipelines would severely damage the prospects for CMEA economic development.

THE SOVIET NORTH

TERENCE ARMSTRONG

THE northern land areas of this planet are climatically uninviting, sparsely inhabited and economically underdeveloped. They have long been thought to conceal riches, both mineral and biological, on plausible grounds of probability; more recently this has been demonstrated to be the case. The pressure to make use of these territories is therefore bound to increase as the number of human beings in the world grows. In the Soviet Union, particular interest has been taken in this, because the government, motivated by the desire for a strong and self-sufficient economy, has made strenuous efforts to locate and exploit domestic sources of supply.

EXTENT AND CHARACTER OF THE NORTHLANDS

First, it is necessary to delimit, at least in broad terms, the territory to be considered. This is essentially the area north of all the major industrial and agricultural regions of the country. Soviet planners distinguish such an area, which they call "the Soviet North." It embraces both the Arctic and sub-Arctic as climatologists define them, and its southern boundary runs not far from latitude 60 in Europe, dropping to latitude 50 as it approaches the Pacific seaboard. Over half the country lies north of this line, but the population is only 8.2 million.

The territory is largely forested, broken by mountains in the east and giving place to tundra in the north. Permanent ice caps are found only on some of the offshore islands in the Arctic Ocean. The climate everywhere is severe, in the sense that temperature extremes are great and the summers, though short, are often hot. There is abundant animal life. Virtually the whole area, apart from the offshore islands in the Arctic Ocean, was inhabited, if sparsely, before the Russians moved in from the south and west over the last 10 centuries.

TRANSPORT

In the last 50 years, the major concern of the Soviet Union has been the mineral resources, and the main prerequisite for gaining access to these (or anything else in the area) was a transport system. Historically, the waterways had been the highways, usable even if frozen. It was the waterways that were selected first again—the rivers and the seas. Nature has provided a good network of rivers, remarkably free of rapids, and their mouths are

486

joined by the offshore waters of the Arctic Ocean. The first major project, therefore, was to organize a northern sea route that would permit access to the Siberian rivers from either the Pacific or the Atlantic. With the aid of icebreakers and a highly developed system of weather and ice reporting and forecasting, traffic built up to the present level of some hundreds of ships operating in these waters each season. Dramatic improvements have been made in the last 10 years in lengthening the navigation season. In the southwest Kara Sea, access to the Yenisei River has been extended from about four months to almost year-round as a result of the roles played by both nuclear and shallow-draft icebreakers. On other parts of the route, the navigation season remains from about three to four months, but there is an intention to lengthen that too. Serious difficulties with the ice in the Chukchi and east Siberian seas in the autumn of 1983, however, led to the loss of one ship and the temporary immobilization of 50 others, so the task will not be easy.

The sea route has never been of any significant economic use as a link between Atlantic and Pacific, although this is the role commonly ascribed to it. Only in 1967 did this aspect receive any prominence, when the Soviet Union invited foreign shippers to make use of Soviet navigational aids, for a fee, and to save perhaps 13 days sailing time between, say, Hamburg and Yokohama. None accepted the offer during the first season it was open, and nothing more has been heard of it since.

A spectacular excursion into the central Arctic Ocean was successfully undertaken in August 1977, when the nuclear icebreaker *Arktika* (later renamed the *Leonid Brezhnev*) attained the North Pole itself—the first time a surface vessel had ever done so. The voyage was officially stated to be a preliminary to more trans-Arctic navigation, but apart from another, less spectacular voyage by two ships in 1978, there has been no follow-up. The Soviets apparently wanted to demonstrate a superior capacity, and this has not been challenged so far by any other country.

On the rivers large fleets of powered craft and barges have been assembled. Hydrofoils have been extensively used, bringing travel time down from days to hours. The sea-river combination does provide a solution to at least some of the freighting problems, but the time factor is a serious drawback. The possibility of sidestepping this by use of submarine freighters—suggested in other Arctic areas—has apparently been considered but not taken up. Certainly the very wide continental shelf would cause difficulty.

A fortunate coincidence has been the advance in aircraft technology at just this period. Air transport has made all projects very much easier, and in some cases has been the decisive factor. A town such as Yakutsk, 8,000 kilometers from Moscow, with a population of 170,000, has five flights daily direct to the capital. At the other end of the scale, a farming village of 500 people on the Yana River has two single-engined aircraft calling every day. Aeroflot also lets out aircraft on charter at very reasonable rates, so prospectors and scientists are well served. The helicopter has helped enormously, though distances are often too great for its economic operation. Hovercraft, curiously, are not in use, nor even, it would seem (despite protestations to the contrary), under very serious consideration.

SOVIET UNION: NATURAL RESOURCES

On land, the winter track has been the most widespread medium of communication and there is still little of greater sophistication. Very few all-weather roads exist and these are chiefly in the northeast; and a few spurs of railway line reach the southern fringe of the area. One from Tyumen in western Siberia to Surgut and Urengoi in the country's major oil field should be mentioned. But the most notable advance in the 1970s and 1980s is the construction—started in 1974 and initially completed in 1985—of the Baikal-Amur Magistral (BAM) line. This is 3,150 kilometers long, traverses extremely difficult terrain and parallels the existing Trans-Siberian line two to three hundred kilometers to the north. The object is both to improve communications with the Far East and to open up large new areas for mineral and other exploitation. A small spur reaches into Yakutia, in order to serve the coal deposits of Neryungri; it is due one day to lead on to Aldan and Yakutsk itself (or more likely the right bank of the Lena opposite it). There has been mention also of a longer "northern Trans-Siberian." This is a line that may ultimately parallel the existing line 300 kilometers or so to the north; its route will be Tobolsk-Surgut-Kolpashevo-Maklakovo-Boguchany-Ust Ilim, and then along the line of the BAM.

DRILLING AND MINING

The transport system, despite its shortcomings, is a remarkable achievement in its context and it has permitted the growth of many major operations. Much the biggest is the development of the oil and gas field in northwestern Siberia. A vast area between the lower reaches of the Ob and the Yenisei has been found to be one of the great hydrocarbon provinces of the world. Production in the early 1980s was in the order of 350 million tons (seven million barrels a day) of oil and gas condensate and 200 billion cubic meters of gas; these were, respectively, a little over half and somewhat under half of total Soviet production, and in each case approximated 12 percent of world production. On a much smaller scale, but still important, is gas production at two other northern centers, in Komi ASSR and Yakutskaya ASSR. An extensive network of pipelines takes the oil and gas to consumers in Siberia, Soviet Europe and beyond.

There is also coal production in the north. Besides several relatively small operations, serving local needs, the most important is the Pechora coalfield, centered on Vorkuta in Komi ASSR, from which the annual output of nearly 300 million tons goes mainly to Leningrad. The Neryungri field, served by the BAM, is growing fast and produced four million tons in 1982.

As far as other minerals are concerned, the emphasis has always been, naturally, on those of exceptional value. If we take these in order of their importance to the country today, diamonds should come first. The country had virtually none until the spectacular discovery of not only alluvial but reef diamonds in the basin of the Vilyuy, a tributary of the Lena, in the 1950s. The mining center, Mirny, today has over 26,000 inhabitants. Then there is gold, which historically was the first important mineral to be worked in the north, in the Yenisei valley. Now the workings are further east, around the Aldan, another tributary of the Lena, and in the far northeast, near

Bilibino in Chukotka. Tin is probably the third most important, with workings also in Chukotka, at Iultin, and at Deputatsky and Ege-Khaya, both between the Yana and Indigirka rivers. The ore at Deputatsky is so rich and accessible that the capital investment required was many times less than that at two major producing areas in the central regions. Next in order of importance comes nickel, which is mined at Pechenga, in what used to be Finland until 1944, and at Norilsk, close to the Yenisei estuary. This last is the most striking example of mineral-based development in the wilderness, for the town of Norilsk, founded in 1935, today has over 180,000 inhabitants, although it stands 2,080 kilometers from the nearest mainline railway station. Of almost equal importance is apatite, a source of mineral fertilizer; one of the major deposits in the world is 100 kilometers south of Murmansk.

Production and reserve figures are not released with respect to these mining developments, apart from the fuels. We can only be guided by such comments as this by V. Uvachan, a regional party secretary, writing in 1967: "The north contains virtually all the diamond resources of the country, nearly half the gold and tin, and a large part of the nickel, mica, and apatites."

This alone justifies, in the past and in the future, heavy investment in northern development. It has given rise to ancillary industries. Local food production has been stimulated and now makes a significant contribution to supplying these northern settlements, though it will never, of course, free them from the need to import much from the south. The reindeer industry, with over two million domesticated animals in the north, is prominent in this respect. Local sources of fuel are also tapped. A hydroelectric station on the Vilyuy serving the diamond industry is attracting special attention as the first of its kind in this environment.

BIOLOGICAL RESOURCES

The obvious primacy of mineral extraction must not obscure the existence of other important northern industries that exploit renewable resources. Fur, the original stimulus to Russian occupation of almost the whole of this area, is still hunted and ranch-produced, and the annual Leningrad auction remains a highly significant event in the world fur trade. Timber is cut and processed in very large quantities. Much of this is done in the most southerly parts of the country, but the European north and part of central Siberia provide lumber of high quality and are the main sources of exports. Mention should also be made of the very large and fast-growing sea fishery that, though not an exclusively northern undertaking, has two major bases in the north: Murmansk and Petropavlovsk-na-Kamchatke. Murmansk is probably the busiest fishing port in the world.

TECHNICAL PROBLEMS

The two main kinds of problem that may be distinguished in the development of the area are technical—how to build and operate the necessary plant—and human—how to get people to work there.

Examples of major technical problems are those posed by the existence of frozen subsoil (permafrost) in almost the whole of the area and by the presence of floating ice on the waterways. The permafrost problem is simply described. Any major structure, whether building, road, bridge or runway, will, unless precautions are taken, cause the soil temperature to change, with consequent differential settling of foundations; damage, up to and including the collapse of the structure, may result. The necessary precautions, therefore, have been studied in some detail. Geologists, geophysicists and soil mechanics specialists, working chiefly in the Institute of Permafrost Studies, whose headquarters are now at Yakutsk, have evolved solutions in principle to most of the problems. This is a successful example of directing effective scientific enquiry to a practical field where results are urgently needed. The Soviet Union is, understandably, the world leader in permafrost studies. The emphasis now is on finding quicker, cheaper solutions and on paring down the safety margin.

The floating-ice problem was attacked in a similar way. A group of oceanographers and meteorologists was assembled at the Arctic Institute in Leningrad in the early 1930s, and they have developed forecasting techniques that have given very real assistance to shipping. At the same time, the construction of icebreakers has been pressed forward, often with use of Finnish yards and designers. Several new classes of diesel-electric icebreakers have been introduced. The application of nuclear power to icebreakers has been pioneered, and up to now carried out, in Soviet yards, with the introduction of the *Lenin* in 1959 and of the *Arktika* and *Sibir* in 1975 and 1977. Two more are currently under construction, and a third, combining nuclear power with shallow draft, is at the design stage in Finland. There has never been, as far as one can tell, any attempt to relate the cost of the scientific program in an exact way to the income to be derived from the activities thus assisted. If there had been, it is doubtful support would have been so generous.

These are two technical problems among many. The effective way in which they have been handled is repeated in some of the other cases, but not in all. A complaint loudly voiced over many years is that too much mechanical equipment used in the north was not specifically designed for that environment. It has been used because it was all there was, and the breakdown rate has been high. Work could be done in spite of this; after all, conditions, both natural and manmade, are severe in much of the rest of the country. But it was and is demonstrably wasteful.

LABOR

Human problems are generally more intractable than technical ones, and this is probably true of the Soviet north, even though people have at times been treated as if they were machines. Attracting labor into an area that in undeniably less comfortable than other possible places of work has been attempted in various ways. From the 1930s to the early 1950s, forced labor was widely used. This was inefficient as well as cruel, and is not likely to be repeated for any economic reasons. Contemporaneously, but rising to a peak after the forced-labor period, appeals to patriotism, sense of

491

adventure and Bolshevik endurance were tried, and seem to have had a certain success. But ever since the early 1930s, and underpinning the other methods, there has been an elaborate system of incentive payments and privileges. These "northern increments," as they are called, are scaled to vary with locality and length of stay. Every few years the law in which they are embodied has been amended, and new rates introduced. This happened in 1945, 1960, 1967, 1972 and 1974, and the changes were generally in an upward direction. In addition, there is another set of wage differentials called "regional coefficients," which are essentially cost-of-living allowances. These are paid as percentage increases on basic pay, and vary in the north between 30 and 100 percent, depending on locality. The northern increments and regional coefficients, taken together, have ensured that workers who volunteer for northern service and stay on the job for, say, five years, are between two and three times better off in various ways than they would have been had they continued to work in a central region.

There is another possible source of labor in the indigenous peoples. The north, in this sense, contains about 950,000 "natives," belonging to some 25 different national groups. This is only about 15 percent of the total population (1979 figures), but it is the fraction with the greatest ability to live in this environment. The most numerous groups—Karelian, Komi and Yakut, who between them account for all but 160,000 of the 950,000—are to some extent integrated in the industrial economy, which has come in from the south, and some of their number are employed in mining, transport and administration. The remaining peoples, in general less technologically advanced, have continued to follow their traditional pursuits of hunting, fishing and reindeer herding. This has been Soviet policy, on the grounds that as long as food and fur are required, these peoples are the most skilled at producing them. The standard of living of the pastoral groups is below that of the industrial workers, so perhaps, it is argued, young people in the former group should be attracted into industry. An important factor is that since 1960, the native inhabitants of these regions have been eligible for the northern increments, and this has tended to reduce the disparity (*sovkhoz* workers therefore receive them while *kolkhoz* workers do not).

Despite these measures, there is a labor shortage in places, and the turnover of labor remains much higher in some regions than is consistent with efficient and economic running of the enterprises. The upward revision of the increments was of course designed to ease these problems, but they still persist.

THE FUTURE

What is quite clear is that solutions to all these problems are being energetically sought. The approval of the wage increments must involve many millions of rubles, and so makes unlikely any abandonment or cutting down of the northern investment program as a whole. It is true, however, that more and more is being written about the need to reduce costs. Furthermore, an idea novel to the Soviet context is being advanced: that northern development should be strictly limited to necessities; that big cities, like Norilsk, arose at least partly from prestige considerations and are not economically justifiable; and that settlement in the north should be planned for the expected period of exploitation of the resource and no longer. Much is written about the shift method (*vakhtennyy metod*) and expedition method of working, whereby the work force is flown in from the south on relatively short shifts, and the need to build elaborate facilities in the north is avoided. The economies resulting would more than offset the cost of transportation, and would become especially apparent if account were taken of the indirect as well as the direct costs of the enterprise. The reason that these simple and logical views were not advanced long before seems to be that the motives for northern development had previously always been more than just economic. Confirming sovereignty over the area, sovietizing the northern peoples, making strategic dispositions—all these undoubtedly played a part. If serious thought is now being given to a policy of comparatively short-term settlement in the area, this must indicate diminishing relative importance of the other motives. At least it can no longer be considered grossly unpatriotic to suggest that the population of these remote areas might be permitted to stop rising. If this is to be the trend (and one should emphasize that these views are not yet dominant), then it will accord with the latest thinking on the North American north. For there, too, the accepted idea that a continuously growing population is essential to economic development is being questioned. New transport media may be making it unnecessary, and the rising value of wilderness and open space in an urbanized society may be making it undesirable. In the Soviet case, economic activities will still be at a high level, because the known resources happen to be very valuable, and continuing geological exploration will undoubtedly produce more of value. Development will thus proceed in any case, but its motivation may be more exclusively economic.

FURTHER READING

Armstrong, T. E., et al. *The Circumpolar North*. London: Methuen, 1978.
Conolly, V. *Siberia Today and Tomorrow*. London: Collins, 1975.
Howe, G. M. *The Soviet Union*. 2nd ed. Plymouth, Devon: Macdonald and Evans, 1983.
Slavin, S. V. *The Soviet North*. Moscow: Progress, 1972.
Whiting, A. S. *Siberian Development and East Asia*. Stanford, California: Stanford University Press, 1981.

PART FOUR

SOCIAL

CHANGING SOCIAL STRUCTURE

GEORGE KOLANKIEWICZ

THERE are stereotypic views of class and social structure in Soviet and Eastern European societies, yet the reality is far more complex, intellectually variegated and ultimately confusing than the various official pictures of the situation. Not the least of the reasons for this highly unsatisfactory state of affairs has been the absence, until recently, of politically independent sociological thought emanating from these societies. Lately, however, émigré analysis, partly inspired by the Polish experience and partly by the Hungarian economic "success story," has brought some coherence and credibility to the study of the sources of social inequality in Soviet-type societies. This, in turn, has made the study of class and related phenomena within the Soviet Union itself that much more meaningful.

For some considerable time, the "socialized" ownership of the means of production and distribution in these societies nonplussed Marxist and non-Marxist sociologists alike. Modernization imposed by the government, with its attendant social mobility, had radically altered the social structure of these societies in the postwar period, or so it seemed. During this period of social disorganization, it was difficult to identify the emerging centers of class formation, if any, or the basis for an order for social status that might stabilize the position of such classes.

For these and other reasons, most sociologists tended to accept more or less implicitly the Marxist-Leninist orthodoxy with its appropriate variations: namely, that there existed two major classes, the proletariat and the collective-farm peasantry (in Poland, a private landowning peasantry). These in turn were served by a stratum of intelligentsia and routine white-collar employees. The residual existence of these classes and strata could provide the bases for "noncontradictory class conflicts"—those whose resolution was positive in outcome and did not subvert the existing order of things. This perspective was not deemed to be very useful by those regime sociologists who were concerned with highlighting the extent and nature of social inequality. They thus turned to Western stratification theory and its multidimensional analysis of prestige, income, education and authority/position. In their empirical studies they were able to indicate the coalescence of certain attributes of social position, which were being generated by the socialist system itself and could become the basis of the new stratification order.

497

Class, class conflict, exploitative class relations and class domination (except by the proletariat over itself), however, were concepts not applicable to "real socialism," whatever the societal tensions that broke through from time to time.

SOCIETIES IN SEARCH OF A THEORY?

Western-based neo-Marxist sociologists, for their part, were caught up in a sterile "ownership v. control" debate, but as applied to the Soviet bloc. Was collective ownership or control of the means of production exercised by a bureaucratic-collectivist class? How were these relationships of ownership or control exercised? State capitalism, a degenerate workers' state, state socialism, etatism, all these labels were applied in the hope that they would reveal the "secret" of understanding workers' food riots in Poland, the passivity of the Soviet working class or the essence of "market socialism" in Hungary. Were these class societies of a different genus from their capitalist counterparts or were they, indeed, despite their internal contradictions, on the way toward classless socialism? All the empirical data pointed toward increasing income inequality and worker discontent expressed through absenteeism, work indiscipline, sabotage and pilfering. Extensive poverty was officially admitted. Bureaucratic corruption was compounded by inertia in the face of mounting crises of the system. Social-welfare policy did not mitigate social inequalities; indeed housing, health and educational provision appeared to foster a cumulative inequality between various sections of the population. Trade unionism, workers' self-management and participation in mass organizations, whether political, social or cultural, were officially criticized as "passive" even before the advent of Solidarity in Poland. Yet during the 1960s and 1970s, membership in the indigenous Communist parties grew apace. Officially fostered consumerism together with a burgeoning second economy were seen as part of the "social contract" arrived at between the party-state on the one hand and society, the population, on the other. Its other components were high job security, low productivity and work intensity, no official unemployment, wages unrelated to effort and a safety net that, though admittedly of low quality, nevertheless provided fairly extensive welfare benefit. Despite the publicly stated exhortations for systemic reform, particularly within the economy, it became increasingly clear during these decades that the formal irrationalities of Soviet-style socialism clearly served the interests of some sections of society better than others. Why else should these societies gravitate back to, and never break free from, what was officially labeled the "directive-distributive," centrally planned, command economy? Whether dubbed "elite immobilism," "bureaucratic inertia," or "conservative modernization," the evidence pointed increasingly to some axial principles that could explain the emerging social structure.

In the early 1970s the Hungarians seemed to provide an answer that would be intelligible, if not acceptable, to Marxists and non-Marxists, alike. They switched emphasis away from ownership and control of production means to the actual processes involved in the generation and appropriation of the surplus product. If the direct producers, the peasants and workers, did not control the production and distribution of this surplus, as they clearly did not, then who did? Put thus, the question of who appropriated the surplus could in part be answered by examining which sections of society gained most from its centralized redistribution and the manner in which this redistribution was effected. The previously mentioned stratification research was able to show who benefited most from housing subsidies, from socialized medicine, from free higher education, etc.

The picture that emerged was that of a corporate quasi-bureaucratic apparatus encompassing all the bodies of social decision making, execution and control. Integrated through the omnipresent Communist party, they sought to maximize the surplus product extracted from the producers under the guise of taut plan fulfillment. The party ideologues elaborated theories equating planning with socialism, the command principle with efficiency and social justice. From their perspective, employee self-management, autonomous trade unionism, wage bargaining, or democratic enterprise-based planning could only limit managerial and therefore central control. Economic reform in the shape of decentralization and the introduction of market mechanisms, unless carefully monitored, would likewise allow key sections of the economy to move out from under the control of the so-called "redistributors."

Presented in this way, otherwise apparently meaningless activity took on new significance. Absenteeism (one in 12 state employees absent each working day) and high labor turnover (25–30 percent a year for some enterprises) were seen as forms of resistance to managerial dominance in the absence of effective trade unions. The "second economy," which was estimated to provide additional income for some 70 percent of state employees in Hungary and was as high as 10–12 percent of personal incomes in Poland, also falls outside the effective control of the state apparatus.

The impact of the second economy is a major factor distorting the analysis of inequality under state socialism, particularly in its effect upon official wage differentials. It is impossible to ascertain whether its functioning is egalitarian in outcome or not. "Surrogate queuers" in Poland enhance their meager state pensions by reselling scarce consumer durables at a considerable markup. Polish and Hungarian skilled workers can earn several times their official wage by private contract work. The chronic shortage of quality goods and services allows the market to operate throughout most of the so-called planned economy. The intertwining of market and nonmarket mechanisms of allocation of goods and services makes it more understandable why some sociologists have preferred to apply Max Weber's model of social stratification. The coming together of class (i.e., one's chance of betterment in the market place) and formal status is exemplified by the ability of government bureaucrats to translate official position into material gain. Likewise, those with key positions in the market for goods and services (highly skilled surgeons, specialist fruit and vegetable growers, actors, among others) can evade and manipulate the directives and regulations that are the basis of bureaucratic power. The *nomenklatura*, or the authority of the Communist party to nominate, recommend, or veto the personnel of key administrative positions, is the instrument of power defining the sphere of officialdom. Standing opposed to this is an increasingly overt labor and commodity market, with its emphasis upon skill, conscientious effort and professional qualification, generating in its wake competing bases of social stratification. Officialdom is increasingly dependent upon the market to assuage consumer demand and to satisfy career aspirations. For their part, those who inhabit the market come to feel ever more vulnerable and subject to the fiat of the official the more that market expands (after all, the market is formally unacceptable to socialist ideologues). Hence those belonging to each of these official and unofficial hierarchies seek to take on the visible attributes of the other in order to ease this tension and legitimate the right of both to exist. Bureaucrats and apparatchiks strive for credentials and formal qualifications, and display consumerist life-styles. Socialist entrepreneurs and professionals, for their part, take out party membership, accept posts in administration or local government, and do not flaunt their wealth. Very often the tension is resolved in the second generation, with sons and daughters providing powerful integrative factors.

It is in this symbiotic interchange between producer and redistributor and between class (or market power) and officialdom that it is possible to identify the sources of social inequality in Soviet-type societies.

TOWARDS A SOCIALIST INEQUALITY

What then are the major dimensions of social inequality characterizing the stratification systems of Soviet-type societies? Given that most of these, save possibly East Germany and Czechoslovakia, were rural agrarian societies when the present regimes came to power, the urban-rural divide provides a suitable starting point.

State, collective and private landholding are the usual forms of land ownership. In Hungary, the success of the cooperative sector under "market socialism" has undermined the central role played by the previously highly profitable private plot, which had provided considerable cash incomes for collective-farm peasants. Conversely, in the Soviet Union the success of the private plot, the one-third hectare of land used by peasant families with relative market freedom has underlined the failure of collective and state-run agriculture. In both cases, the income derived by peasant families has made rural life tolerable and often a source of ill-placed but officially sponsored envy. In particular, some peasant families have been able to straddle the agriculture-industry, peasant-employee divide and to exploit market shortages by means of the collective-farm market. The "peasant-worker" phenomenon is most obvious in Poland, where highly fragmented land-tenure structures compel one or more members from more than a million peasant families to combine agricultural activity with full-time work outside agriculture. However, the hidden costs of commuting in an "underurbanized" society with gross shortfalls in all forms of societal infrastructure are enormous, biting deeply into cultural and family life as well as leisure time.

Despite constitutional guarantees of private ownership for those who farm over 70 percent of Poland's arable land, state control is formidable. A developed system of "contract purchase," restrictive conditions for obtaining state pension benefits, as well as the state's monopoly position as purchaser of crops produced in bulk, severely circumscribe peasant autonomy. No easy conclusions can therefore be drawn from closer examination of private and socialized landholding if official labels are not taken at face value.

Similarly, while agricultural and industrial incomes may have edged closer together, the urban-rural divide in terms of those factors determining the so-called quality of life are still enormous. The Soviet internal passport system and the existence of virtually closed cities, when placed alongside other features of "underurbanization," serve to maintain the "idiocy of rural life." Urban residence has been shown to act as a safety net against downward social mobility for the less able and as a barrier against upward social mobility for those living outside the large urban conglomerations. Indeed, the Polish system of positive discrimination, intended to assist children from peasant and manual worker backgrounds to gain access to higher education, is currently under severe attack. Its critics have argued that favor should be shown to those from rural small town milieus regardless of social background, since cultural deprivation cuts across traditional class-stratum boundaries. Cynics may argue, of course, that this only reflects chagrin on the part of some manual workers, successfully promoted into the ranks of the new intelligentsia and state apparatus, who feel that their children are now being penalized unjustly for their parents' success.

There can be little doubt that the ideological prominence given to upward social mobility, one of the few planks upon which communist regimes can build their legitimacy, has created a multitude of problems. An overproduction of white-collar positions and formally educated cadres now stands in stark contrast to the need for skilled and even unskilled industrial manual workers. This need is magnified by the fact that Soviet-bloc countries are finding it increasingly difficult to make the much publicized jump from "extensive" to "intensive" growth. Demographic shortfalls compound the problems, and traditional sources of reserve labor supply are fast drying up. These factors, more than any related to ideology, have served to lift some manual workers' wages above those of the white-collar workers and technical intelligentsia—as happened, for example, in Poland in 1983. This is perhaps just as well, since blocked opportunities for upward mobility, associated with some downward social mobility, can serve only to harden the outlines of social stratification. Unless propaganda imperatives change and the circulation of cadres and personnel across generational, class and stratum divides becomes more accepted and fluid, then the Polish experience of 1980–81 stands to be repeated elsewhere, if in different forms.

SOCIALIST MOBILITY

The residual private sector and secondary economy currently provide alternative outlets for blocked aspirations or disillusioned achievement. Unless major economic and political reform, with an attendant diversification of social roles, is forthcoming, the bureaucratic apparatus of party-state power will be rocked by various internal contradictions working through the system. Chief among these is how a political order, basing most of its legitimacy on the incorporation through social mobility of key sections of the population into the Communist party and other hierarchies, can continue to operate within an essentially stagnant sociopolitical system. An analysis of patterns of social mobility in Soviet-type societies points up most of the social fissures and tensions within them. As always, it is the manual-nonmanual interface that attracts most attention.

The inherent inefficiency of most of the economies discussed here serves to diminish the manual-nonmanual divide by putting a premium on the exchange of goods and services in a face-to-face, quasi-barter system. Similarly, intelligentsia status is difficult to maintain when styles of life become uniform and homogenized through lack of variety and the constant scarcity of consumer durables. The prestige of nonmanual work comes under increasingly severe pressure when not buttressed by political or administrative authority. Higher education recruitment, while still a focus of intense competition, is producing uncharacteristic shortfalls in certain technical and scientific subjects, a development more in line with Western experience. This is a reflection of the gradual devaluation of qualifications for higher education in the face of both increased graduate production, reduced pay differentials and the declining influence of the scientific and cultural establishment. The Communist party, the military, government agencies and the security apparatus all recruit directly into their own ranks or produce their own "in-house" intelligentsia. Only a major shift, reemphasizing broad-based scientific and technological innovation, genuine managerial and entrepreneurial skills, and high-level academic research and scholarship, can reestablish the position of the "intelligentsia" proper vis-à-vis the bureaucratic apparatus of state power.

Paradoxically, although Poland abolished the use of the manual-nonmanual job descriptions from official usage and the work code, political debates still continue in these terms. They often conceal issues having little to do with either, but referring to critiques, for example, of the wages systems and the role of incentives; of managerial power vis-à-vis the party, trade unions, or self-management bodies; of party loyalty and professional integrity.

The constant debate about the role of the intelligentsia under socialism is one of the most difficult to decipher. The concept of the intelligentsia is a slippery one for Western sociologists to handle. It should, however, be remembered that even the apparently simple question of who or what constitutes the working class under state socialism taxes the collective minds of entire Marxist-Leninist research institutes. Higher education has generally been accepted as essential for membership in the intelligentsia, but the term also carries with it connotations of creative, independent thought, anti-bureaucratic sentiments, freedom of conscience and a politically autonomous world view. These attributes do not square easily with the status quo in Eastern Europe. Nor does this definition have much in common with the official view of the intelligentsia as a social stratum, situated alongside the basic classes of the proletariat and the peasantry, which can be internally differentiated according to its members' roles in the social and technical division of labor—technical or cultural intelligentsia, managers, bureaucrats, and so on. But the crucial fact remains that these people are, in the main, state employees; they provide cultural and scientific products; and they must satisfy censors, political leaders and an increasingly discerning public, as well as industrial managers being forced to search for higher productivity. They lack the potential industrial or political muscle of the working class, as well as the obviously critical position of the peasantry as suppliers of food. Added to this is the inherent suspicion of the intelligentsia and intellectuals in general held by communist leaders rooted in Marxist-Leninist political culture. What price, then, to become a member of this social stratum?

Earning at best twice the average manual workers' wage (in East Germany, the Soviet Union and Czechoslovakia) or at worst less than the manual worker (in Poland), the intelligentsia still have an autonomy in the organization of their working and nonworking lives far superior to that of their manual counterparts. They may enjoy urban residence, subsidized books, theater and films, an unexacting work discipline, and the ability to pile up part-time ad hoc jobs and a network of useful friends. These provide a relatively attractive life-style for members of the socialist intelligentsia, always provided they do not engage in political dissent of an overt nature. It was noted long ago by Max Weber that where the basis of acquisition and distribution of goods are relatively stable, stratification by status is favored. Emphasis on style of life, occupational status, antimarket sentiment, restriction on social mixing and a tendency to closure (the prevention of others from attaining coveted status) all serve to maintain the concept of the intelligentsia —pertinent today as it was a hundred years ago.

A SOCIALIST UNDERCLASS

At the other end of the social spectrum are found those persons with the least personal or collective autonomy. Women represent 51.2 percent of the labor force in the Soviet Union, and the figure is approximately the same for the other socialist states. On average, they earn two-thirds of the male wage; are to be found in traditional, low-paid industries; and at best represent one in 10 of managers, or those with authority over others. They are a token 20 per cent of the ruling Communist party, rarely if ever attaining the seats of power. While preschool, child-care and maternity facilities appear to be generously provided, this is clearly motivated by the pronatal concerns of party leaders. These leaders are extremely concerned with the drop in the birthrate (often to a point below the reproduction rate), and the rise in fertility rates among lower-class workers or ethnic minorities (unskilled workers, collective-farm peasants, the Muslims of the Central Asian republics). The low birthrates, plus the extraordinarily high rates of abortion and of infant mortality, are a reflection of, and a response to, housing shortages, a poor diet, a time-budget stretched between work and the interminable shopping lines and an almost total absence of leisure. Even apparently high-status but feminized occupations, such as medicine, reveal internal structures in which men hold the most prestigious and powerful positions, thus re-emphasizing the socially subordinate position of women. While East Germany and Hungary appear to be rectifying this situation, changes are

503

often quantitative rather than qualitative, and reflect the relative economic affluence of these societies.

THE NEW DIVIDE: GRANDPARENTS—GRANDCHILDREN

An allied problem taxing party policy makers concerns pension provision and the changing demography of these societies. Pensions, along with most other cash transfers and such payments as sickness benefits, are inegalitarian and regressive, being tied to earned income. While the picture of aged cohorts moving collectively up to the apex of power and authority in communist systems is largely accurate, it ignores the inherent inequality visited upon the aged who don't make it. The huge loss of life in World War II tended to defer the problem during the immediate postwar years, but age as a source of inequality is now a major issue. It is compounded by the inability of the system to absorb or incorporate sufficient sections of the young and ambitious managers, politicians and apparatchiks. This is largely due to the role played by informal personal relations in career mobility: experience in the system is critical when few indicators of successful achievement exist other than the opprobrium or praise bestowed by supervisors on subordinates. Solidarity was often described as a movement of the young. The description was only partially correct, but it reflected a desire to overcome the constraints on life imposed by an ageing hierarchy. It was an attempt to divide social stratification into political generations.

CONCLUSION

There can be little doubt that the communist states of Eastern Europe are generating social structures that are unchanging, even inimical to their own pattern of development. Forced modernization, underurbanization, command and centralized economies with monolithic ruling Communist parties —these are some of the systemic properties creating new patterns of social stratification. Officially sponsored theories have no power to deal with these emerging properties, which often diverge from the communist ideal. There is a need, on the one hand, for incentives, material and nonmaterial rewards, consumer satisfaction, productivity and efficiency, and participation in the public sphere, to coexist with privacy and family life. On the other hand, the type of society aimed for has a blueprint drawn up more than a century ago. The resulting tension is creating cracks in the edifice of these societies.

FURTHER READING

Feher, F., et al. *Dictatorship over Needs: An Analysis of Soviet Societies*. London: Blackwell, 1983.

Kerblay, Basile. *Modern Soviet Society*. London: Methuen, 1983.

Kolosi, T., and Wnuk-Lipinski, E., eds. *Equality and Inequality under Socialism*. London: Sage, 1983.

Lane, David. *The End of Social Inequality? Class Status and Power under State Socialism*. London: Allen and Unwin, 1982.

Littlejohn, G. *A Sociology of the Soviet Union*. London: Macmillan, 1984.

Matthews, M. *Privilege in the Soviet Union: A Study of Elite Life-Styles Under Communism*. London: Allen and Unwin, 1978.
Pankhurst, J. G., and Sacks, M. P., eds. *Contemporary Soviet Society Sociological Perspectives*. New York: Praeger, 1980.

THE WORKING CLASS

ALEX PRAVDA

SIZE, economic muscle and ideological status make the working class the most important social group in the Soviet Union and Eastern Europe. Manual workers are generally the largest group in these societies, outstripping white-collar workers by a far greater margin than in the West. Economically, workers are important, because production in the region remains heavily dependent on physical labor.

The working class figures prominently in the political calculus for practical and symbolic reasons. Though less interested in politics than the intelligentsia, workers are less easily controlled. Once roused to protest, even small groups can seriously disrupt political stability. And the use of force against working-class dissidents is particularly embarrassing for regimes whose legitimacy rests largely on proletarian myths and symbols.

WORKERS AND SOCIALISM

To a greater extent than other social groups, workers tend to favor "real existing socialism" inasmuch as they support nationalized industry and a strong welfare state. Of course the degree of support varies between countries; while a majority of Czechoslovak, Bulgarian, East German or Soviet workers may endorse the system, such views are shared by only a minority of Polish workers. Working-class attitudes stem not from any commitment to Marxism-Leninism but from an attachment to the "cradle-to-grave" welfare dimensions of the socialist system, which workers have come to see as their rights. These include full employment, a welfare wage rather than one based strictly on productivity, stable prices and low pay differentials (Soviet and Eastern European workers are strong egalitarians).

Because they are so attached to these features of "real existing socialism," workers are prepared to accept a fairly authoritarian state and to tolerate considerable constraints on civil liberties and pluralism. For the most part workers seem politically quiescent, asserting their interests through action within the factory. In many ways they have a parochial outlook, assessing national politics according to conditions in the workplace and local community. Where deterioration in these conditions coincides with the failure of the state to safeguard working-class "rights," however, workers are ready to challenge the system by leading protests and even by establishing independent organizations.

WORKERS IN SOCIETY

The working classes of the region vary in size and social age. In East Germany and Czechoslovakia the working class forms a majority of the population and consists largely of hereditary blue-collar workers. In the Soviet Union these form a minority, while in Hungary and Poland every second worker is only one generation away from the farm. Bulgaria, Romania, Yugoslavia and Albania have the largest proportions of first-generation workers and the smallest working classes, amounting to between a third and a fifth of the population.

Over the last two decades social mobility has slowed; fewer workers come from villages and fewer make it through the barrier of college into the professions. As the social contours surrounding the working class have become clearer, so workers have become increasingly aware of belonging to a class of "ordinary working people," including some white-collar workers, but distinct from the intelligentsia and political elites whose privileges they often resent. For while workers do relatively well in terms of nominal pay, they are far behind the professions in overall living standards and social prestige.

Any stronger working-class awareness or cohesiveness is weakened by divisions that run along economic-sector, skill, gender, age and ethnic-group lines. Although rising levels of education are blurring some of these divisions, their very multiplicity makes working-class solidarity a rare phenomenon that appears only under exceptional conditions, usually associated with a general crisis.

AT WORK

In the best East German, Czechoslovak, Soviet and Yugoslav factories, conditions compare favorably with those in Western Europe; elsewhere they are generally inferior. All enterprises provide a wide range of welfare services, including some housing, and this may contribute to the strong sense of community that seems to underpin many workers' satisfaction with their situation. Among the labor force in general, a lack of commitment is more widespread than discontent; it surfaces in the form of absenteeism, pilfering and low work effort.

Managers tolerate rather than combat such laxness because they are reluctant to sour relations with workers they can ill afford to lose (labor is in short supply) and on whom they rely for extra effort when rushing ("storming") to meet plan targets. Labor relations vary considerably over the region; Soviet workers seem happier on this score than Eastern Europeans, though this may be due to lower expectations.

Of course, tensions exist and disputes arise, usually over management arbitrariness, work conditions, piecework rates and bonuses. Many disputes are settled directly between workers and managers at shop level. More serious conflicts are supposedly prevented by representative organizations within the factory: production conferences or councils, trade unions and the Communist party.

REPRESENTATIVE ORGANIZATIONS

Participative bodies. To point up the socialist nature of industrial relations, a variety of production committees, conferences and councils exists to involve workers in enterprise management. Only in Yugoslavia, where a decentralized economy makes self-management viable, are workers' councils effective vehicles for participation, commanding widespread worker confidence. Elsewhere, participative bodies offer workers little more than the opportunity to hear management reports and ask a few questions.

Trade unions. Because they are charged specifically with defending their members' interests, unions potentially offer more effective channels for the working class. But the framework within which they operate severely limits this role. The axiomatic unity of labor and management interests under socialism excludes collective bargaining, and means that unions serve workers' "real interests" by helping management to increase production. Even where unions are empowered to protect workers' legal rights—as in the case of dismissals—they find themselves strapped by dependence on management, whose decisions they seldom challenge. Unions generally concentrate on administering welfare benefits; some of the more energetic unions, particularly in the Soviet Union and East Germany, press for better safety or housing. Workers therefore see unions as weak rather than totally useless, as personnel departments rather than as representative organizations defending working-class interests.

Union performance outside the factory confirms this verdict. Occasionally unions use their consultative rights on all policies affecting labor to modify party and government proposals on wages and prices. But there is no question of unions challenging the party, because they accept its "leading role" and are often headed by former party or government officials. That is why serious efforts at union reform (Hungary and Poland in 1956, Czechoslovakia in 1968 and Poland in 1970–71 and 1980–81) have sought greater independence of party as well as of management.

The Communist party. The party undoubtedly has the power at factory and national level to be an effective channel for workers' interests. While workers typically make up between 40 and 50 percent of total membership, they remain far less well represented than white-collar groups. Whereas every second or third professional is a party member, only one in five to eight skilled workers and one in 15 to 20 laborers belong to the party. These discrepancies grow as one looks higher up the organizational pyramid.

To most workers, the party represents the interests of the bosses rather than the working class. Generally the secretary of the party committee works hand in glove with management, and together with the union chairperson forms the enterprise "establishment." Not that workers ignore the party altogether as a forum for their demands. Some skilled worker-communists—

notably in Hungary, Czechoslovakia, East Germany and the Soviet Union—manage to use the party organization as a vehicle to press their demands; such behavior helps link the party to the shop floor. Yet even where workers manage to have some say at the grassroots level of the party, they find it difficult to be heard at the national level, let alone to affect policy. Attempts to improve communications encounter strong bureaucratic resistance and the party leaders' basic unwillingness to allow workers an independent organization to voice worker interests.

WORKING-CLASS ASSERTIVENESS AND UNREST

Outside these inadequate institutional channels, workers assert themselves in a variety of ways—from individual job-related actions to mass protests and organized political movements.

1. *Individual assertiveness.* This is most apparent when workers change jobs and reduce their work effort. Neither action is directly political, of course, but their economic consequences and their spontaneous, uncontrolled nature lends them political significance. Labor turnover is high by Western standards, running at around 20 percent per year. (Poland is on the high side and East Germany well below.) Workers find it easy to move because, with the exception of Yugoslavia, these economies suffer from a labor shortage created by overstaffing, heavy demand for manual labor and falling birthrates. The intensity of work is probably lower in Soviet and Eastern European factories than in the West. Absenteeism and drunkenness are commonplace, with one in 10 workers actually disciplined every year for these and other misdemeanors. Many invest most of their energy in second-economy jobs, using factory property. Perhaps as much as 20 percent of working time is lost through lack of discipline, poor work organization and supply shortages.

Measures to combat such individual assertiveness founder on the reluctance of managers to apply sanctions. Schemes like the Schekino experiment to reduce overstaffing have been used cautiously; politicians are wary of infringing too openly on what workers see as their "socialist right" to secure employment.

2. *Small-group action.* Workers often use their ability to slow down production in order to force better conditions from management. Such informal pressure-group action further reduces, in one way, the authority of the unions and party. In another sense it may help to defuse tensions and to explain the rarity of overt industrial conflict, particularly in East Germany, Hungary, Czechoslovakia and the Soviet Union.

3. *Strikes.* The number of strike reports reaching the West every year can be counted in tens rather than hundreds. East Germany, Hungary and Bulgaria seem to have the fewest; Poland has the most. The exception is Yugoslavia, with an annual average of 250 strikes through the 1960s and larger, if perhaps fewer, stoppages since then. Official toleration of strikes as a last resort, coupled with the decentralized nature of the economic system—

which makes it possible to extract improvements from enterprise management—help to account for this relatively high level of industrial action. Neither condition obtains elsewhere in the region, making striking a risky business. The right to strike hangs in a kind of limbo, neither explicitly prohibited nor sufficiently safeguarded to secure strikers against dismissal and prosecution. Workers therefore go on strike only when attempts to use other means have failed.

Strikes tend to follow a long period of mounting tension. They break out in response to the introduction of unpopular changes, such as the adjustment of piece rates. Most take place in large industrial plants, particularly in the metallurgical and mining sectors, which have a strong sense of community and large numbers of skilled workers with the confidence and organizational ability to take action even when they are opposed, as is almost invariably the case, by unions and party. Strikers typically demand withdrawal of specific innovations plus modest improvements in pay and conditions. Because strikes are politically embarrassing, management and local officials usually make quick concessions, bringing a return to work within hours or within one or two days at most.

4. *Strike-led protests.* In exceptional circumstances, strikes spread to several factories and escalate into mass demonstrations that come close to being real working-class protests. Such escalation is triggered by national policy changes, most commonly by price increases, that affect workers as consumers as well as producers, turning their protests away from the enterprise management towards the local and national governments. What often drives workers into the streets is anger at government duplicity, because changes frequently follow official assurances of stability. Strike-led protests, therefore, are usually the result of the mismanagement of relations rather than of purely economic factors, even if many outbursts are preceded by stagnating living standards (as in the 1950s) or by severe discontinuity (as in Poland in the 1970s).

The following summaries give some idea of the course and scope of the major strike-led protests.

East Germany, June 1953. Unrest began on June 15 with stoppages and demonstrations by building workers in East Berlin against rises in piecework norms. News spread quickly and sparked off strikes in 250 industrial centers that involved 300,000 workers, many of whom were driven to protest by low living standards and the slight relaxation in control in the country following Stalin's death. They called for lower work norms, better food supplies and, at the height of the demonstrations, free elections. Demonstrators ransacked party buildings; at least 19 were killed (some Western estimates go as high as 267), and 200 were injured in clashes with security forces and Soviet troops.

Czechoslovakia, June 1953. A sudden currency devaluation, which broke government promises, triggered strikes and demonstrations in several industrial centers. The largest protest took place in Plzeň where 5,000 workers from the huge Škoda plant led a large crowd in demanding pay raises and chanting antigovernment slogans. Seventy were injured in the security operation that ended the protest.

The Soviet Union, 1959–62. The uncertainty created by policy changes, particularly in the economic field, shaped the context for the most serious period of working-class unrest the Soviet Union has seen since World War II. The first large strike-led protest occurred in 1959 in Temir-Tau, Kazakhstan, where 20,000 young construction workers took to the streets in protest against poor living conditions and food supplies. There were smaller demonstrations in Kemerovo in 1960. In June 1962, increases in the price of meat and butter provoked a wave of protests, the largest of which took place in the Donbas and centered on Novocherkassk. Here a lowering of piecework rates at the Budenny locomotive factory brought workers out on strike, heading a mass demonstration against the price rises. Action by KGB troops left 70 to 80 dead and more than a thousand injured. The whole area was placed under martial law for several weeks.

Poland, 1970–71. The announcement on December 12, 1970, of 15 to 30 percent increases in the prices of food and fuel set off a strike centering on the Baltic cities of Gdańsk, Gdynia, Elbląg, Sopot and Szczecin. Clashes between demonstrators and the security police resulted in 45 dead and over a thousand injured. The events led to the replacement of Gomułka by Gierek as party first secretary on December 19. Little else changed; and January 1971 saw renewed strike action, notably at the Warski shipyard in Szczecin. Demands there included not just a withdrawal of the price increases, but free elections to local party and union committees and the establishment of independent unions. In a face-to-face discussion with strikers, Gierek promised reforms, but it took another strike in February by the Łódź textile workers for price rises to be rescinded. None of the promised reforms materialized although an economic boom, funded largely by Western credits, delayed further working-class response until 1976.

Poland, 1976. Mounting economic pressures induced Gierek to attempt to raise food prices by an average of 39 percent. Angered by this renewed attempt at surprise price increases, workers went on strike in 10 industrial centers, including the Baltic ports, Łódź, Płock and Warsaw. The largest and most violent demonstration took place in Radom, where protesters ransacked the party headquarters; clashes with the security police caused at least two deaths and hundreds of injuries. The price rises were quickly rescinded but reprisals followed, with thousands attacked and harassed by the police. Such persecution brought the Roman Catholic church to the aid of strikers' families, many of whom were also helped by the Workers' Self-Defense Committee (KOR) formed in 1976 by a small group of intellectuals. This was the first firm link between working-class and intellectual dissidence.

Romania, 1977. Throughout the early 1970s, miners in the Jiu valley in southwest Romania, had taken sporadic strike action for better pay and conditions. In August 1977, most of the 90,000 miners came out on strike to protest a new law entailing lower preretirement pay and fewer pension benefits. Ceauşescu promised a meeting of 35,000 miners that their demands would be met and no reprisals taken. Nonetheless, 4,000 miners lost their jobs and many of them were harassed by the police; the whole valley was sealed off until early 1978.

Comparing the unrest of the 1950s and early 1960s with more recent strike-led protests, one can see shifts symptomatic of a more sophisticated and ambitious working class. Angry protests against material shortages have been succeeded by better-organized and more purposeful actions that advance wider-ranging demands, most notably institutional change.

5. *Independent trade union movements.* Two indications of the salience of institutional demands outside Poland are the small Soviet and Romanian independent union groups that emerged in 1978–79. In January 1978, a group of 200 workers from 42 cities, who had met while petitioning the authorities in Moscow, formed the Association of Free Trade Unions of Workers in the Soviet Union. In October 1978, soon after Klebanov and other leaders had been rounded up by the police, another group, including both workers and professionals, established the Free Interprofessional Association of Workers. Despite police action, the latter group was reported in 1982 to have 300 members organized in 21 groups monitoring abuses of labor rights and extending aid to victims. Similar activities were envisaged by the group of 14 workers and five professionals who set up the Free Trade Union of the Workers of Romania in February 1979. Police action apparently prevented the group from pursuing its objectives.

By contrast, the three free trade union committees established in Poland in 1978 (at Gdańsk, Szczecin and Katowice) were highly successful in preparing the organizational and strategic ground for Solidarity. They also provided a bridge between shop-floor activism and dissident intellectuals around the KOR, which encouraged the free trade union movement and influenced its thinking through the samizdat bulletin *Robotnik*.

6. *Working-class involvement in political crises.* The working class has played an important role in all four major Eastern European crises—Poland and Hungary in 1956, Czechoslovakia in 1968 and Poland in 1980–81.

In the first three crises, workers were slow to become involved. During the first months of political ferment they remained skeptical about intellectual debates and wary of proposals for economic reform that might threaten their established "rights." Workers' action was limited to strikes for material gain. Only when the situation became polarized with pressure from Moscow did the working class actively support democratic change. Nationalism clearly played a part in mobilizing Polish workers behind Gomułka in October 1956; it also sustained Hungarian workers in fighting Soviet troops from November 1956 to January 1957.

In this respect, Poland in 1980–81 seemed to break the mold. The working class, rather than students or intellectuals, sustained the political momentum. In other ways, though, the events of 1980–81 confirmed and extended features of working-class involvement evident in previous crises. These events illustrated how very difficult it is for the organized working class to shape policy, rather than exact concessions through confrontation and the use of the general strike.

512

Solidarity also embodied many of the strengths and weaknesses of previous forms of working-class organization. In 1956 and 1968, trade unions came a poor second to workers' councils as vehicles for working-class action. Formed in most large factories, these councils hardly had the time to set up any national organization and were uncertain, especially in the Polish and Czechoslovak crises, about pursuing an overtly political role. Only the Greater Budapest General Workers' Council came close, in November–December 1956, to being a political voice for the working class and acting in the syndicalist style of the Soviets of 1917. Although a trade union in name, Solidarity followed in this tradition.

Perhaps because it had a relatively long life and a very large membership (9.4 million of the 12.5 million in the state sector) organized in 39 regional bodies, Solidarity was troubled by internal splits over strategy and objectives more acute than those evident in previous crises. As in 1956 and 1968, some favored concentrating on controlling factory management; others wanted to play a purely adversary role in national politics. Wałesa and the moderates envisaged working closely with party and government in a corporative arrangement. Few if any wanted Solidarity to establish a political party. In contrast to the multiparty parliamentary system envisaged by the Greater Budapest council in 1956, Solidarity advanced the rather vague notion of a self-governing republic based on social control from below. Not even the 16 months of life Solidarity was allowed proved sufficient to resolve the basic problem of defining a role for an independent working-class organization within a system ruled by a Communist party.

OUTLOOK

Another Solidarity is unlikely to emerge elsewhere in Eastern Europe. Many of the factors aiding its growth were specific to Poland, including a long record of successful working-class protest, strong links between workers and the church and a regime that lacked unity or legitimacy. Yet some of the roots of 1980–81 extend throughout the region: economic discontinuity, poor institutional representation of working-class interests and pressure on workers' traditional "rights."

In 1980–81, the attention of all party leaders focused on the need for new ways to placate the working class, as the maintenance of traditional "rights" became more costly and less effective. The experience of Hungary has shown that better public relations, plus a semilegitimate second economy, can help to tide the working class over large price increases. Still, the East German and Soviet authorities continue to subsidize rather than raise prices, and all governments proceed warily on reducing overstaffing. Even the disciplinary drives launched by Moscow have been half-hearted. More important, they are unlikely to bring an economic upturn. All these regimes are caught in a vicious spiral of low labor productivity and stagnating living standards, both of which undermine labor incentives.

Unable to extricate themselves by the use of coercion or imported goods, the authorities are turning their attention to increasing workers' representation and involvement. Solidarity prompted widespread measures to revitalize trade unions, but these have been purely cosmetic.

Given the dangers of real union reform producing demands for autonomy, the politicians seem now to have pinned their hopes on harnessing small-group loyalties and energies. Hence the current stress on low-level participation, typified by the 1983 Soviet law on workers' collectives and the campaign to make labor brigades—groups of 10 to 20 workers—more self-reliant. The Romanians have upgraded existing workers' councils, while the Bulgarians are following Hungary in giving the unions more say in participation.

The small-group participation strategy may seem a safe way of raising productivity, yet the strengthening of such groups could place additional stress on already weak institutional machinery. If, as seems likely, living standards continue to stagnate, workers throughout the region will begin to press the institutions more forcefully, not just for a better economic deal but for a greater say for the working class in how the factories and the state are run.

FURTHER READING

Kahan, A., and Ruble, B., eds. *Industrial Labor in the U.S.S.R.* New York: Pergamon, 1979.

Pravda, A., and Ruble, B., eds. *Trade Unions in Communist States.* London: Allen and Unwin, 1985.

Ruble, B. *Soviet Trade Unions: Their Development in the 1970s.* Cambridge: Cambridge University Press, 1981.

Schapiro, L., and Godson, L., eds. *The Soviet Workers—Illusions and Realities.* London: Macmillan, 1981.

Triska, J. F., and Gati, C., eds. *Blue-Collar Workers in Eastern Europe.* London: Allen and Unwin, 1981.

SOVIET SOCIAL POLICIES

MERVYN MATTHEWS

THE PROBLEM OF EGALITARIANISM

THE central aims of Soviet social policies are said to be the furtherance of equality and the molding of the new Soviet person.[1] In his article "The State and Revolution" (1917), Lenin predicted that the withering away of the state, which he regarded as the main instrument of inequality, would begin immediately after the proletariat (or rather, its "vanguard," the Communist party) had seized power. He emphasized that the first act of the socialist state would be to give "workingmen's wages ... [to all] technicians, foremen, accountants ... indeed, to *all* state officials." This was intended to bring Russia into line with Marx's well-known proposition on the "lower" stage of communism, commonly called socialism, when each toiler would be paid according to his or her *labor*. It was only in the highest stage, after the state had disappeared, that each toiler would be paid according to his or her *needs*. Lenin, of course, subscribed to the widespread but erroneous belief that the first stage would usher in relative, and the second complete, egalitarianism.[2] He envisaged the new Soviet person as a selfless being, devoted to socialist society, living under an economically and socially egalitarian system, enjoying no personal privileges, yet being conscientious enough to give the utmost for moral, rather than material, incentives.

Lenin tried to implement these simplistic egalitarian ideas during the years 1918–21, when the land was torn by civil and military strife. The result was the impoverishment not only of former exploiters, but of most Soviet citizens. There was hyperinflation, money all but ceased to function, enterprises run or controlled by workers' committees produced but a fraction of their former output and famine gripped the land. Foodstuffs were acquired from the peasants by force, the former bourgeoisie was dispossessed and social order, as it had existed under the czars, was completely undermined.

The new Soviet society may indeed have been more egalitarian than its

---

[1] Professor Dimitry Pospielovsky, who wrote an article with this title for the first edition of the Handbook, has kindly permitted me to retain its framework and some historical references.

[2] This formula must surely have caused some of the most widespread delusions in modern political philosophy. Any effective equalization of human "need" would demand intervention of a truly magical nature.

predecessor to begin with, but it was also much poorer and more oppressive. Moreover, such egalitarianism as was introduced began to recede soon after its advent was proclaimed. In conditions of hunger, poverty and hyper-inflation, the people on whom the Bolsheviks relied most—party and state officials, bourgeois engineers, administrators and specialists—had to be rewarded at rates far above the average. Systems of controlled access to deficit goods and services, together with considerable wage differentiation and other types of state privilege, appeared long before Lenin died in January 1924.

Stalin was primarily interested in the consolidation of his own power, the centralization of the state and rapid industrialization. He saw Leninist egalitarian principles as a hindrance to these policies and even—in a speech made in 1931—spoke disparagingly of them. His rule, lasting until March 1953, was characterized by deliberate, long-term social differentiation of a peculiar Soviet variety. The degree of social differentiation became ever more a matter of state policy, as the private sector was finally suppressed and wage control became more meticulous. Party and state functionaries enjoyed good salaries and living conditions, together with access to special stores selling imported goods at nominal prices, and restaurants offering food unobtainable elsewhere. By 1937, the basic wage differentiation between the highest- and lowest-paid workers in the key metalworking industry, for example, was raised to a ratio of 1:3.6. Bonuses and premiums were introduced for fulfilling and overfulfilling production norms.[3] Improved housing and the use of special rest homes and sanatoriums were granted to norm-exceeders. Collectivization meant that the peasantry lost many of its civil rights, and was by and large reduced to a state of penury.

Khrushchev, whose years of power extended from approximately September 1953 to October 1964, tried to move back to greater egalitarianism, while retaining something of the later Leninist framework. Starting in the mid-1950s he caused wage differentials to be narrowed: the maximum basic wage differential in industry, in fact, fell to a ratio of 1:2.42 in 1962. A modest minimum wage was reintroduced (it had lapsed under Stalin), the state pension system was revised and improved, several steps were taken to improve the income and legal status of the peasant (without, however, abolishing the collective farm), more emphasis was placed on consumption (at the expense of investment) and some of the elite benefits (less necessary under easier economic conditions) were abolished. Living standards rose markedly, helping the poor. By the time Khrushchev fell, however, the rate of economic advance had slowed considerably.

Brezhnev, who wielded effective power from the time of Khrushchev's

[3]The best known of the norm-exceeding movements in industry was the *Stakhanovsh-china*, named after a Donets Basin coalminer, Stakhanov, who was reputed to have cut 102 tons of coal in one shift in 1935. This was to some extent a fraud, for Stakha-nov's pneumatic pick was assured of a constant supply of compressed air, and two timberers were attached to him exclusively to do the pit-propping. At regular intervals Stakhanov was served hot food not provided to ordinary miners. All these facts were concealed from Soviet workers, who were encouraged to emulate Stakhanov's production rate under normal conditions.

dismissal until his own death in November 1982, was suspicious of his predecessor's social policies. Yet he was anxious to satisfy, as far as militarization would allow, consumer needs, and also to improve the lot of the peasantry. During his secretaryship, more emphasis was placed on output; the industrial differential fell to 1.86 by 1975, but evidently began to increase again soon after. Minimum wage rates were raised to 70 rubles a month, and there were various piecemeal improvements in the social security system, which Khrushchev had extended to the peasantry in January 1965. In 1976 peasants were finally granted internal passports, a right that had been acquired by state workers and employees when the system was inaugurated in December 1932. Possession of a passport somewhat facilitated movement throughout the country.

The 15 months of Andropov's tenure of office, November 1982–February 1984, were notable in the social sphere mainly for a tightening of labor discipline, the preparation of yet another reform of the educational system and a continuing concern with the supply of consumer goods. The Chernenko leadership did not effect any major changes of direction in this respect, but Gorbachev has begun to reemphasize labor discipline.

It is generally believed that at the beginning of the 1980s, after all the policy changes of previous decades, Soviet society was still very differentiated but nevertheless more "egalitarian" than capitalist society. The main reason for this was the absence of extremely wealthy landowners and of people owning companies or other valuable objects—individuals frequently encountered in capitalist societies. A Soviet elite could easily be perceived, while up to a third of the population was still living under a poverty threshold described by Soviet scholars in the mid-1960s. An authoritative U.S. estimate put Soviet per capita consumption at 34.4 percent of that of the average U.S. citizen in 1976. It is noteworthy that the Soviet income tax system, with a maximum rate (for state earnings) of 13 percent, has never been used for purposes of income redistribution.

SOCIAL SECURITY PROVISIONS

The basis of the present Soviet pension system was established shortly after the Bolsheviks came to power. It was designed primarily to help state workers and members of the armed forces who were unable to work. Old-age pensions, now the dominant type, were introduced only in the late 1920s, and the peasantry was altogether outside state social security until January 1965.

The technical details are, of course, intricate, and only the most important of them can be reviewed here. The system is unitary in the sense that it now covers, in one form or another, all Soviet citizens; it leaves no place for private or independent schemes, such as exist in the West. Since it is also noncontributory and (when possible) service-linked, the individual employee cannot easily influence the size of his or her entitlement other than through the work record. The recipients of benefits fall into four broad and sometimes overlapping categories: the aged, the disabled, minors and surviving dependents, and women who are pregnant or need help with their children. The number of people covered has grown greatly in recent years and by 1981, 18.8 percent of the Soviet population received pensions of some kind (see Table 1).

Table 1
SOVIET PENSIONERS (*millions, by year*)

Year	All pensioners	All old-age pensioners	All peasant pensioners	All pensioners as % of total population
1960*	21	5	—	10.0
1965*	27	9	—	11.7
1970*	40	24	12	16.5
1975	44.4	28.8	12.1	17.5
1981	50.2	34.0	11.2	18.8

* Fractions of a million not available for the first three years.

The "Khrushchev" pension law of July 1956 is a good starting point for analysis. It revised and improved regulations that went back to 1928, while retaining their central principles. Old-age pensions were payable as a right to workers, employees, and servicemen until the time of death. Eligibility for a full pension normally started at the age of 60 for men, providing they had not less than 25 years of service behind them, and at 55 for women with 20 years of service. These starting ages were low by international standards. A minimum of five years service, three of them uninterrupted, immediately before retirement was a condition of eligibility for a full pension. Any shortfall in the regulatory 20 or 25 years of service brought a partial pension with a proportionate reduction in the rates payable. People formerly receiving other types of pension sometimes had the right to switch to old-age pensions if they thought it advantageous to do so.

The rate of full pensions varied, with some exceptions, from 100 percent of the lowest wage bracket to 50 percent of the highest. When applying for their pensions, employees were allowed to propose the years of maximum earnings, so as to obtain the most advantageous rate. No Soviet pension, incidentally, was subject to income tax. Lower starting ages, or augmentations, were available in certain deserving cases. There were supplements of 10 percent for one dependent and 15 percent for two or more. Rates for workers and employees living in rural areas and employed in agriculture were 15 percent below the urban norms. A separate but similar system of "long-service" pensions was retained for military, academic, teaching and medical personnel.

The tie between pension rights and regular employment in a state or co-operative organization naturally posed a problem for people (especially housewives) whose work record was interrupted or incomplete. The pension then payable was commensurate with the years of service, subject to a minimum pension of one-quarter of the full rate. The Soviet authorities have never recognized the concept of national assistance—maintenance payments based solely on assessed need—so inadequate pensions could not be supplemented in this manner.

The main changes in these provisions up to the present have contained both positive and negative elements, but there has hardly been any departure from the principles outlined above. The minimum full old-age pension was raised to 50 rubles a month in January 1981.[4] The restriction on pension recipients working, imposed in 1956, has gradually been eased; a decree of September 1979, for instance, directed that overaged workers in production, trade and service industries could draw between 50 percent and 100 percent of their normal pensions on top of their salary. Most pensions payable to them subsequently, on cessation of employment also became subject to an exceptionally high ceiling of 150 rubles a month. The scheme proved exceedingly popular and was taken up by several million people.

Peasants' pensions require a separate discussion. For three decades after the establishment of the collective-farm system, they had nowhere to turn for sustenance in old age. The fact that they were expected to feed—by means of taxation and obligatory farm deliveries—the state-insured worker was one of the greatest ironies of the Soviet system. In general, elderly farm members either had to live off their private plots or to rely on the generosity of relatives and friends. The 1965 system of state pensions, though a great step forward, was still inferior to that enjoyed by workers and employees. Although the length-of-service requirements were the same, men became eligible only at 64, women at 60, and the range of payments was much lower. There is little doubt that the modest income of most collective-farm members and their well-known reluctance to work in the communal sector, kept the majority of peasants' pensions close to the bottom of the scale.

The Brezhnev years brought a series of improvements to this system. In 1967, the ages of eligibility for peasants were lowered to match those of workers and employees. Mainly as a result of this, and the aging of the collective-farm population, the number of pensioners rose from seven million in 1966 to a peak of 11.2 million by 1981. More flexibility was introduced into the provisions for determining individual rates. In July 1978, the peasants' minimum monthly pension was raised to 28 rubles. Such improvements certainly alleviated the financial difficulties faced by the elderly on the farms, but still left them worse off than workers.

Disability and survivor pensions bear many similarities to old-age pensions, although the complexity of the rules for issuance and the lack of detailed figures again make summarization difficult. Under the terms of the 1956 legislation, disability was categorized according to severity (from "total" in group 1 to "partial" in group 3) and also according to rank (professional

---

[4] The sums mentioned in this section are more meaningful if compared with the following average monthly wage rates for workers and employees: 1955—71.5 rubles; 1970—122 rubles; 1981—172.5 rubles. Minimum rates rose from 26 rubles in 1956 to 70 rubles in 1981.

or nonprofessional). The highest rate, 100 percent of earnings, was payable to "professional" invalids in group 1, while the nonprofessionals in group 3 could receive as little as 16 rubles a month.

As the years passed, principles of eligibility remained largely unchanged, but significant increases were authorized in the amounts payable. By 1981, the minima stood at 70 rubles for group 1, 45 rubles for group 2 (both work-related and otherwise) and 25 or 21 rubles, work-related or not, respectively, for group 3. The "best" minimum therefore equaled the state minimum wage. Among the minor modifications was the payment of 15 rubles a month to group 1 recipients for home help.

Peasants were also brought into this scheme in 1965 but on disadvantageous terms. In September 1967, however, pensions were introduced for the hitherto unrecognized peasant group 3 invalids, and in 1978 the minima were raised to 45, 28 and 16 rubles for peasant groups 1, 2 and 3, respectively. The maxima matched those enjoyed by workers and employees.

Between 1966 and 1982, the number of persons receiving nonretirement pensions throughout the country remained remarkably stable at about 16 million. In 1979, to judge from a comment in the census returns, some 7.6 million of these still derived their main income from other sources, presumably full or part-time employment.

The 1956 pension law for workers and employees defined survivors as persons immediately related to, and entirely dependent upon, a deceased and pensionable individual, the definition of "death" being supplemented by "proven disappearance." The three main categories of survivors covered minors, surviving spouses or parents when they became of pensionable age or had a child under the age of eight to look after, and grandparents without other means of sustenance. It will be evident that this categorization left adult survivors who had not reached pensionable age, and who had no young children to look after, without coverage. Clearly, such adults—among them many housebound mothers with children older than eight—were expected to find employment expeditiously.

The size of these pensions depended on many factors: the cause of death of the person originally providing support—whether it was work-related or not; if the cause of death was work-related, the wage formerly received; the nature of the work performed; the number of years of service; and the number of dependents (one, two, three or more). The low minimum payments (16, 23 and 30 rubles per respective group in 1956), plus the "three or more" formulation, clearly meant great difficulty for larger families. Survivors reaching retirement age had a strong incentive to switch to an old-age pension, if their work record entitled them to do so.

This system also remained relatively stable, with only two important modifications. Rates by 1981 reached 26, 50 and 75 rubles per group, although the normal maximum of 120 rubles remained unchanged. The rates for survivors of military personnel were a few rubles higher.

The other modification was the extension of pensions of this type to cover the peasantry. The categorization of survivors was the same as for workers and employees, and the rates were likewise dependent on former earnings. The minima were, however, only about half of those enjoyed by workers and employees. Such small sums suggest that the authorities wished to introduce the principle of payment without facing the financial implications of practice. Improvements did, however, follow, and by July 1978 the peasant minima were 20, 28 and 45 rubles per group. The maximum rates were again the same as for survivors of workers and employees resident in rural areas. On the whole, the minimum rates of survivor pensions were raised more than those of disability pensions, but most recipients in both town and country must still have lived far below the poverty threshold.

The best-known payments of a family-allowance type are those made to mothers with large families—defined as four or more offspring. The system has apparently remained unchanged in form and content since its establishment in November 1947. The allowance is first payable when eligible children reach their first birthday, and ceases on their fifth. Rates are extremely low, ranging from four rubles a month for the fourth child to 15 rubles for the 11th and any others. However, mothers of five or more children who rear them to the age of eight may also claim earlier eligibility for an old-age pension. The production and successful rearing of 10 children brings the honored title of Heroine Mother. Instituted in 1944, this award has always entitled its recipient to extra pension, accommodation and other benefits. Lesser degrees of motherhood (from the fifth child up) are marked by the Order of Maternal Glory (with three degrees) and the Maternity Medal (with two). All large-family payments are made regardless of income.

The long-standing policy of strengthening family bonds has not precluded help for unmarried mothers. Under the 1947 law, unmarried mothers were entitled to monthly grants for each child up the the age of 12. The payments were again low, five rubles a month for one child, seven rubles 50 kopecks for two and 10 rubles for three or more. Single mothers, however, were entitled to have their children maintained free in a state home, if they so desired, and got a 50 percent reduction in kindergarten charges if their monthly income was below 60 rubles. These provisions were still in force in the early 1980s.

It was perhaps the nominal character of these payments that prompted the introduction, in September 1974, of a system of child allowances specifically for low-income families. Families whose average monthly income was 50 rubles per person or less, regardless of social category, gained the right to draw 12 rubles a month for each child up to the age of eight. Entitlement to the benefit was interpreted in a relatively broad way, provided that at least one adult was already eligible for social security. It has been calculated that by 1980 about 14.9 percent of Soviet children were receiving it.

A long-standing system of maternity benefits and "birth grants" also underwent some development. A law of March 1956 envisaged, basically, 112 days of maternity leave for mothers employed in the state sector, including 56 days before the anticipated birth and 56 days after. Limits were placed on the nature of the work that the mother could undertake in this period. The rate of payment depended principally on her work record, but requirements were lax and apparently allowed a majority to claim full pay. In July 1973, full pay was extended to virtually all working mothers, regardless of their length of service. Peasant women were first included in the scheme in November 1964, and the 1973 law extended the equivalent of full pay to them as well.

SOVIET FAMILY POLICY

Official Soviet attitudes toward the family have shown some remarkable shifts over time. Free love was advocated at the time of the Bolshevik Revolution by Aleksandra Kollantai, a leader of the (Marxist) Social Democratic Party, and Inessa Armand, Lenin's close friend and translator. After the Bolsheviks came to power, it was actually permitted by decree in some localities. An extreme case was that of the Vladimir Regional Council, which proclaimed:

> After 18 years of age every (unmarried) girl becomes state property ... and must ... register at the office of "free love" attached to the Commissariat of [Social] Care. The registered girl is given the right to select for herself a cohabitant/husband in the 19 to 50 age group ... the right to select from the girls of 18 years or older is also given to males. Males aged 19 to 50 themselves have the right to select women registered with the office, in the interest of the state, even if the latter do not agree. Children born as the result of such cohabitation become the property of the state.

Lenin opposed these extreme views, but wrote nothing substantial on sexual relations, nor on the family and marriage under communism. The most likely explanation is that, though opposed to the disintegration of the family as such, he never considered the issue important enough to merit serious thought.

The new leaders, so ready to undermine the traditional and religious values of family life, were unable to replace these values by anything positive. Other forces were also having a directly disintegrative effect. The civil war, war communism and a serious famine not only disrupted family life and played havoc with sex habits, but also resulted in massive shortages of males.

The first Soviet laws on marriage appeared in 1918. The people's commissar of justice, N. Krylenko, stated that the main purpose of the legislation was to undermine religion-sanctified marriage, and registration procedures were indeed simplified. Although common-law cohabitation of man and woman was not given the status of legal marriage, children born out of wedlock were given equal rights with those born in it. Many "cohabitations" were in fact church marriages of couples who did not want to undergo "atheist" registration, particularly as the Russian Orthodox church had expressed its "negative attitude" to the new form of civil marriage. The divorce procedure was also made easier. If one partner wanted a divorce, his or her petition had to go through the local courts, but if both partners agreed on it, all they had to do was send a joint statement to the local registry office, and their union was dissolved automatically. Marriage was declared free from interference by parents, relatives or any other interested group. Fatherhood was established on the basis of a simple statement at the registry office by the mother or guardian of the child, or by the child itself. On November 18, 1920, abortions were made legal and free of charge if performed in the state hospitals.

The mid-1920s saw the consolidation of much social legislation, including laws pertaining to marriage. The major 1926 law on marriage and divorce largely reiterated earlier enactments, but broadened the concept of legal marriage to include "factual marriages"—unregistered cohabitations in which "man and woman live together, and consider their union as wedlock, rather than living in lewdness." This innovation was prompted by the many cases of husbands, married in church, later abandoning their wives and children without incurring any legal responsibility for their actions. The 1926 law, however, also facilitated the procedure for divorce. Now, only one partner had to submit a written petition to the registry office for the courts to refrain from participation in the divorce procedure.

Naturally, these laws, given the social, economic and political instability of the new order, resulted in a tremendous growth both of divorces and of abortions. In Leningrad alone the divorce rate rose from 1.9 per 1,000 inhabitants in 1920 to 11.3 in 1929; in Moscow, by 1934, there were three abortions for each live birth, and in the countryside (which is normally much more conservative) the ratio was approximately 1:3.

The rapid industrialization, urbanization and collectivization of agriculture that characterized the worst years of Stalinism introduced new pressures on family well-being. The purges, deportations and annihilation of entire social groups resulted in millions of fatherless families and homeless orphans, the *besprizorniki*. The authorities further undermined parental authority by teaching schoolchildren to report on their elders if the latter were in any way opposed to the regime. There was the infamous case of Pavlik Morozov, who denounced his parents for counterrevolutionary activity, for which they were executed. Concern for the family as a desirable social unit reappeared, ironically, as part of Stalin's relative conservatism. After the establishment of "socialism in one country," the "Soviet family," like so many aspects of Soviet reality, was declared an ideal type. Since then, there has been a constant reaffirmation of the importance of the family unit, though the legislation bearing upon it has been subject to much detailed change.

The first major laws to reflect Stalin's more protective attitude was the ban on abortions in June 1936. Doctors performing abortions were sent to prison, as were men who encouraged women to undergo them. A decree in April 1945 substantially limited divorce rights. Divorce could thenceforth be effected only through the courts, whose first responsibility was to reconcile the parties. Costs were raised considerably, and the court hearings (on two levels, the lower being concerned with reconciliation, and the upper with the actual divorce) were made public. Witnesses had to be called and advance notice given in the local press. As a result of this legislation, it was said that the rate of divorces, which had reached almost one in every five marriages in 1939, fell by a factor of over 14. An unwanted consequence of this legislation was, however, "a great discrepancy between divorces registered and the number of factual disruptions of marriages" (*Izvestia*, July 12, 1936). The practice of unregistered couples living together as man and wife became more widespread.

The 1945 legislation also freed the father of all responsibility for illegitimate children, i.e., those born out of registered wedlock. Furthermore, such

523

children could be registered only under their mother's name, even if another man was available for the purpose. This practice was particularly distressing because of the common use of the Russian patronymic, which a child born out of wedlock could not properly claim. Soviet sociologists justified the abolition of legal abortion and the legislation freeing fathers from responsibility for illegitimate offspring on the grounds that it was necessary to increase the birthrate, and to make up for war losses. It may, however, have had a stabilizing influence on the sexual activity of young women.

The more permissive attitude toward family relations that followed Stalin's demise was first reflected in the law of November 1955, which again legalized abortion. A decree of December 1965 confined divorce procedures to the low-level local court, abolished the necessity to announce forthcoming hearings, limited the number of written certificates that had to be presented and permitted the courts to use their discretion in establishing fees.

The present basic law on the Soviet family was implemented (at the Russian SFSR level) on July, 30 1969, and has not since been subject to any major change. Its primary aim is declared to be "the strengthening of the Soviet family, based on the principles of communist morality." It is moderately protective of the marriage state, and of the interests of the children. The law emphasizes the equality of rights of the marriage partners; a husband cannot alone initiate divorce procedure during his wife's pregnancy, nor for one year after the birth of a child; divorce normally involves court proceedings; illegitimate children enjoy rights similar to those born in wedlock; parents bear maintenance responsibility for their offspring (in the absence of other obligations, one quarter of income for one child, one third for two and one half for three or more); and the material obligations of family members, other than parents, are also specified.

The existing legislation on the Soviet family needs, of course, to be viewed in the context of current problems. Although the massive disruption of the war and prewar years is receding, measures are needed to counter the fall in the birthrate. The employment of women (who now comprise 51 percent of the labor force) must be better compensated. Furthermore, the growing divorce problem must be countered. In 1960, for example, there were 12.1 marriages and 1.3 divorces per 1,000 of the population; but by 1980, the number of marriages was down to 10.3, against 3.5 divorces. The abortion rate was also very high. It was estimated in 1981 that the average Soviet woman had six abortions in her lifetime. A desire to protect the family and the younger generation lies behind the various state payments to large families or low-income families, pregnant women and mothers.

HEALTH AND MEDICAL CARE

The Bolsheviks early decided that control of the nation's medical services, like education, should be firmly in their hands. In July 1918, Lenin formally created a People's Commissariat of Health to "unify" all medical and public health work in the Russian SFSR. The new organization had a virtual monopoly of all medical facilities, and power to register and draft all technical personnel. The medical profession was thus, in effect, turned into a body of state employees, and most private practice disappeared. The attention of the service was directed, in the first years of its existence, to countering the appalling epidemics promoted by civil war and famine. But as the situation improved, the training of medical personnel and the establishment of a nation-wide system of medical facilities became preeminent. By the outbreak of World War II, the number of physicians was said to have reached 155,300, while hospital beds numbered 790,900, as against some 14,000 and 149,000 respectively in 1917. The USSR Constitution of 1936 granted Soviet citizens the right to free medical attention, while the current (1977) document declares that all Soviet citizens have the right to protection of health through free, qualified medical help in state institutions; use of a growing network of sanatoria; safety precautions at work; and healthy surroundings (Article 42).

Soviet achievements in medicine have undoubtedly been considerable over past decades, and the authorities now claim to have 1 million doctors, or over one-third of the total world supply. In 1981, there were said to be 38.5 doctors per 10,000 of the population, as against 22.6 in the United States and 18.3 in Great Britain. The ratios for hospital beds were on the same basis: 126 (USSR), 60.1 (United States), 81.8 (Britain).

Medical services cannot, however, be assessed merely in terms of numbers. Soviet medicine is still thought to lag well behind that of advanced capitalist states in terms of quality, equipment and general provision. Poor housing conditions among the people encourage hospitalization rather than home care. The great expanses of land and sparsity of population, combined with poor transportation and communication facilities, require a considerably higher number of physicians than in Central or Western Europe. However, life is so difficult in the Soviet countryside and in the smaller towns that medical personnel often avoid these locales. Further discrepancies of provision exist between the republics. In Georgia, which enjoys a good climate and one of the highest standards of living in the Union, there were 49.6 doctors per 10,000 inhabitants in 1981. Tadzhikistan, at the other extreme, had only 24.2 doctors per 10,000.

The average Soviet doctors have poorer educations than their Western colleagues. Their training lasts only five and a half years, with a 10-year primary and secondary school education preceding it. As most of the new graduates are sent by the state administration to work for three years in a specified job, rural and small-town clinics tend to be staffed by young, inexperienced graduates who move on to bigger towns as soon as their postings are over. It is not surprising, therefore, that medical standards in the countryside are lower than those in the towns. The practice of medicine also suffers from the low pay of most personnel. In the early 1980s, doctors' basic rates varied between 100 and 170 rubles, against an average workers' salary of 173 rubles.

Although medical care is basically free of charge in the Soviet Union, there are important exceptions. Besides working as employees in the state hospitals and clinics, physicians may, and do, run private practices after hours. The going rate for ordinary consultations is around 10 rubles, but senior doctors may charge much more. Large towns have public, state-run clinics where fees are legally charged (presumably for better service). Nine such institutions were listed in Moscow in 1977. Apart from this, a few high-quality hospitals and wards are retained for elite usage. All out-patients have to buy their own medicines, the more modern and sophisticated of which are frequently in short supply.

The overall state of the nation's health is difficult to judge, because many common statistics are withheld. Moreover, analysis is further inhibited by the failure of the authorities to publish more than a few pages of results from the January 1979 population census. The overall rates for births, deaths and natural growth in 1981 for the Soviet Union, the United States and Britain (together with the People's Republic of Mongolia, to illustrate demographic movement in an underdeveloped land) are shown in Table 2. They

Table 2
BIRTHS, DEATHS AND NATURAL GROWTH, 1981

	Birthrate*	Death rate*	Natural growth*
Soviet Union	18.5[1]	10.2	8.3
United States	16.2	8.9	7.3
Britain	13.5	11.8	1.7
Mongolia	36.7	9.2	27.5

* All figures are per 1,000 of the population.
[1] The Soviet birthrate rose to 20.1 in 1983, a 40-year high.

indicate that the USSR on the whole now follows the pattern of advanced industrial states. The sociodemographic problems that lie behind these figures include a high rate of natural growth of Muslim and non-Slav peoples, compared to those of Russians and Slavs (e.g., 35.7 percent between 1970 and 1979 for Tadzhiks, as compared to 6.5 percent for the Russians); a sharply rising death rate, and a fall in life expectancy (reaching, by 1980, 67 years at birth for males and 73 for females); and a disturbing increase in infant mortality, which is thought to have risen to 35.6 per 1,000 by 1976. The incidence of six of the seven diseases for which the Soviet authorities regularly publish figures (typhus, scarlet fever, diphtheria, whooping cough, tetanus, acute poliomyelitis and measles) was between three and 30 times higher than in the United States.

The reluctance of the authorities to provide more detailed data on the nation's health (in stark contrast to data with respect to educational achievement) suggests that many basic indexes are unsatisfactory, which in turn implies unsolved social problems and/or poor performance on the part of the medical services.

FURTHER READING

Dunn, S. P., and Dunn, E. *The Study of the Soviet Family in the USSR and in the West.* Columbus, Ohio: AAASS, 1977.
Field, M. G. *Doctor and Patient in Soviet Russia.* Cambridge, Massachusetts: Harvard University Press, 1957.
———. *Soviet Socialized Medicine.* New York: Free Press, 1967.

von Frank, A. *Family Policy in the USSR since 1944*. R. & E. Research Associates, 1979.

Geiger, K. *The Family in Soviet Russia*. Cambridge, Massachusetts: Harvard University Press, 1968.

Knaus, W. A. *Inside Russian Medicine*. New York: Everest House, 1981.

EDUCATION IN THE SOVIET UNION

MERVYN MATTHEWS

BACKGROUND AND PRINCIPAL CHARACTERISTICS

OVER the decades since the revolution, the Soviet Union has made impressive progress in extending the coverage of its educational facilities and in adapting the content of the courses to its overriding economic and ideological needs. The all-union population census of January 1979 showed that the illiteracy rate for persons aged between nine and 49 was down to less than 0.2 percent, as compared with 44 percent in 1926. According to the 1981–82 estimates, some 103 million people, over a third of the entire population, were engaged in full- or part-time study or training of some kind (see Table 1).

Table 1
NUMBER OF PERSONS STUDYING IN THE SOVIET UNION*
(At the beginning of the academic year, in 000s)

	1914–15	1940–41	1945–46	1960–61	1970–71	1981–2
All persons studying	10,588	47,547	37,385	52,600	79,634	102,822
Full-time general schools	9,656	34,784	26,094	33,417	45,448	39,656
Part-time general schools	—	768	714	2,770	3,745	4,600
Vocational and technical schools	106	717	945	1,113	2,591	3,998
Secondary special educational institutions	54	975	1,008	2,060	4,388	4,557
Higher educational institutions	127	812	730	2,396	4,581	5,284
Training of all kinds directly at the workplace	645	9,491	7,894	10,844	18,881	44,727

* Covering all types of institutions.
Sources: *Strana Sovetov za 50 Let*, Moscow, 1967, p. 273; *Narodnoe khozyaistvo SSSR, 1922–1982*, Moscow, 1983, p. 499.

The Soviet educational system differs in many important respects from those of most noncommunist states. Its aim is not so much to develop the

528

capabilities of individuals, or help them compensate for shortcomings, as to train them in a manner most useful to the state. Administratively, the institutional network is highly centralized, and although the Soviet Union is by no means unique in this respect, the Soviet authorities probably take the principle further than most. Major policy decisions lie with the Central Committee of the party, but day-to-day control over all aspects of education is exercized through the union-republican Ministry of Higher and Middle Special Education, the union-republican Ministry of Public Education (for the general schools), and the union-republican committees for vocational and technical training. The ministries and committees operate through their representatives in the local soviets.

Pedagogical science maintains a rather conservative position. Intelligence tests are in principle disallowed, in deference to the Marxist principle that the circumstances of an individual's existence are more important than hereditary factors in determining his or her consciousness. Teaching is imbued whenever possible with Marxist-Leninist philosophy, as currently interpreted. Careful attention is paid to nurturing patriotic responses and to the fundamentals of military training. The general school seems to aim at imparting as much factual material as possible, rather than developing the pupils' critical faculties. Indeed, there have been frequent complaints that school courses are overloaded and demand too much of the pupils' time. In the upper classes of the general school, for example, classwork alone takes up to 32 hours a week, and homework may be onerous. Compulsory lectures at establishments of higher education may be just as time-consuming. In the post-Stalin period, attempts have been made to deal with this problem, but with little success; a long school year and bulky textbooks remain characteristic of the system. Science subjects tend to be emphasized at the expense of the arts, and there is also a tendency to underline the practical application of what is taught. Examinations are frequent and mostly oral; academic standards on the whole appear to be reasonably high. Part-time study is something of an exception in this respect, but is nevertheless widely encouraged.

Since June 1956, education has been free at all levels above the nursery school, while certain categories of pupils and students have long been able to claim maintenance allowances. The provisions made for leisure activities are highly standardized. Students' clubs (especially sports clubs) tend to be large and somewhat impersonal. The small, ephemeral student societies typical of Western European universities are absent. The great majority of youngsters now belong to one of the country's political youth organizations—the Young Pioneers or the Communist Youth League (Komsomol)— and many teachers are members of the party.

None of these features has changed fundamentally since Stalin's death, although successive leaderships have introduced numerous modifications. Khrushchev took a keen interest in education, and his main contribution (apart from partially de-Stalinizing the curriculum) was a massive "polytechnization" drive that reached its peak in the educational reform of December 1958. By this means, the Soviet leader tried to change the nature of the school, making theoretical subjects more practical, introducing manual labor into the curriculum and even teaching the pupils trades. At the same time, he abandoned the aim of 10-year education for all in favor of an eight-year school for most children, with an 11-year course for a minority. Pupils from the polytechnized general schools would thus possess manual skills, be more fit to start work immediately and possibly less anxious to get into the country's crowded universities and institutes (VUZy, in the Russian abbreviation). Another benefit envisaged by Khrushchev would be a blurring of class distinctions, which until then had been actually fostered by the Soviet school system. His policy was reinforced by the reorganization and expansion of the vocational school network, attempts to introduce "sandwich" courses at VUZ level, changes in VUZ intake rules so as to favor workers and peasants (as against children from more favored social groups) and an extension of part-time education.

Khrushchev's ideas were extremely unpopular and administratively difficult to implement. From August 1964, if not before, there was a steady retreat from them. The plan for an 11th class was rejected; and soon after, the principle of a 10-year general education for all was reestablished. Polytechnization schemes were watered down, then actually abandoned in many schools. A subsidiary scheme for a rapid development of boarding schools was also quietly dropped. In a decree passed in November 1966, the authorities announced the toleration of some specialization, outside the general core curriculum, in the form of a few optional hours. At the same time, a general revision of the curriculum was started, and a new drive was launched to improve facilities in the most backward sector of Soviet education, the village schools. As far as the VUZy were concerned, entrance rules approved in 1965 practically abolished privileges for "proletarian" candidates in full-time jobs, and little more was heard about the sandwich courses. New interdisciplinary subjects of study were introduced, and part-time education at the higher levels was encouraged somewhat.

The Brezhnev era (October 1964–November 1982) saw renewed concern with manual training in the general schools, although by more sophisticated means than hitherto (using "intraschool production training centers"), and furtherance of some academic specialization, particularly in the form of schools with certain subjects taught in a foreign language. The elementary-grade vocational sector was expanded, so as to ease the transfer of schoolchildren into manual jobs; part-time higher education, despite its recognized drawbacks, also increased. However, the functioning of the general school, particularly as a provider of manual labor for the economy, continued to be a cause of concern, and a new set of proposals was published in January 1984. These envisaged a massive exercise in polytechnization (which strongly recalled the Khrushchev reform), convergence between the general and the vocational sectors, and earlier school entrance (at six years, rather than seven). The impact of these measures remains to be seen.

GENERAL EDUCATION

The first rung of the Soviet educational ladder takes the form of crèches for children aged from two months to three years, and kindergartens, which admit children aged three to seven. Together, in 1981, they cared for nearly

15 million children, though another 5 million attended temporary institutions in the summer. Altogether something like one-half of the corresponding age groups were taken care of by the permanent institutions.

This is important in view of the fact that about four-fifths of all able-bodied women in the Soviet Union are in full-time employment. Attendance at these institutions must be paid for, at rates that vary depending on the type of school and the parents' income.

The Soviet complete general school (or general labor polytechnical school, to give it its full title) still consists basically of 10 classes, with an 11th added in non-Russian areas where Russian is taught as a foreign language. The school is split into three parts: classes 1 to 3, classes 4 to 8 and classes 9 and 10. By 1962, Soviet educational authorities were claiming that eight years of schooling (that is, for youngsters from the age of seven to 15) had been introduced for everyone; by 1977, 10 years of general education, or its equivalent, had evidently been extended to some 91 percent of the relevant age groups on a full- or part-time basis. Implementation proved most difficult in the countryside, where settlements are scattered, schools small and teaching staff relatively scarce. The standardization of courses mentioned above means that children finishing eight classes in any "incomplete" school may continue their studies without academic disruption at another. The teaching is apparently fairly efficient, the examination failure rate in the Russian SFSR averaging, in the late 1970s, only three to seven percent.

The curriculum of the eight-year school begins by concentrating on Russian language and literature and on mathematics, with some music, physical training and manual work, but by the seventh class most of the subjects familiar to Westerners have crept in. The school week consists of 24 hours of obligatory classes in the first year, rising to 32 by the ninth class, distributed over six days a week. The school year lasts from September 1 to June 30.

The last two classes of the general school, which in 1982 enrolled 9.5 million pupils, deserve separate mention. They are still considered to be the high road to a university education because a general school-leaving certificate, or *attestat zrelosti*, is an essential VUZ entry requirement. Recent sociological studies have revealed that these classes tend to be filled by children of the intelligentsia.

The curriculum at this stage contains a number of new features. Social studies (of a Marxist-Leninist variety) and astronomy find a place in the 10th class, at the expense of hours earlier devoted to Russian language and geography. Five hours of physics and the same of mathematics are supplemented by three hours of chemistry and two of biology. Two to four hours extra may be allotted for optional classes, as stipulated in the November 1966 decree. Two types of option are permitted. First, many schools provide optional courses from the seventh class on, as the local authorities think expedient. Second, there is, for a limited number of schools only, intensive study of arts or science subjects in the ninth and 10th classes. Before the present arrangement, the only special schools were those catering to musically or artistically gifted children, together with a few hundred schools with instruction in a foreign language, and schools for the handicapped. (See Table 2 for a summary of the standard general curriculum.)

Table 2
STANDARD CURRICULUM FOR PRIMARY, EIGHT-YEAR AND
COMPLETE GENERAL SCHOOLS, 1979–80
(Russian Schools of the Russian SFSR)

Subject	Number of hours per week in classes									
	1	2	3	4	5	6	7	8	9	10
1 Russian language*	12	11	10	6	6	4	3	2	—	—
2 Russian literature	—	—	—	2	2	2	2	3	4	3
3 Mathematics	6	6	6	6	6	6	6	6	5	5
4 History	—	—	—	2	2	2	2	3	4	3
5 Fundamentals of Soviet state and law	—	—	—	—	—	—	—	1	—	—
6 Social studies	—	—	—	—	—	—	—	—	—	2
7 Nature studies	—	1	2	2	—	—	—	—	—	—
8 Geography	—	—	—	—	2	3	2	2	2	—
9 Biology	—	—	—	—	2	2	2	2	1	2
10 Physics	—	—	—	—	—	2	2	3	4	5
11 Astronomy	—	—	—	—	—	—	—	—	—	1
12 Technical drawing	—	—	—	—	—	—	1	1	1	—
13 Chemistry	—	—	—	—	—	—	2	2	3	3
14 Foreign language	—	—	—	—	4	3	3	2	2	2
15 Art	1	1	1	1	1	1	—	—	—	—
16 Music	1	1	1	1	1	1	1	—	—	—
17 Physical education	2	2	2	2	2	2	2	2	2	2
18 Labor	2	2	2	2	2	2	2	2	2	2
19 Primary military training	—	—	—	—	—	—	—	—	2	2
TOTALS (weekly)	24	24	24	24	30	30	30	31	32	32
20 Practical work (in days)	—	—	—	—	5	5	5	—	22	—
21 Options	—	—	—	—	—	—	2	3	4	4

* In schools for ethnic minorities, where there is a need to perfect the senior pupils' knowledge of the Russian language, the Russian SFSR Ministry of Enlightenment recommends the introduction, for the ninth and 10th classes, of optional lessons based on the program published in *Optional Lessons in the Humanities*, and the allocation of one hour [of Russian] a week in the classes indicated. (From original source.)
Source: Approved by A. I. Danilov, Russian SFSR Minister of Education, on January 9, 1979. Order No. 13-M, in *Sbornik prikazov i instruktsii ministerstva prosveshchenia*, Russian SFSR.

In 1982, some 4.4 million persons were studying at the country's part-time general schools (known as "evening" or "shift" schools). Nearly all of these pupils were in the part-time equivalent of classes 8 to 10, many of them aiming specifically at secondary special or higher education, despite the fact that they were already in full-time employment. These schools offer basically the same curriculum as is taught during the day, and the courses require a rigorous 20 to 24 hours of study a week. Students who attend them may claim limited day-release from their jobs, but even so the demands on their time are great. This, combined with often inadequate facilities, causes a dropout rate of about 16 percent per year, along with generally poor attendance and weak academic performance. The authorities, nevertheless, see an important place for the system as a benefit for people who do not finish the full-time school.

The increasing employment of women has encouraged the growth, since the early 1960s, of "extended day schools" where children may be left under proper supervision until parents return home from work in the late afternoon or evening. Attendance at such institutions rose from 600,000 in 1961 to 11.3 million in 1982.

VOCATIONAL AND MIDDLE-GRADE SPECIALIST TRAINING

Vocational training in manual skills is provided, in the case of about one-quarter of all new entrants to the nonpeasant labor market, by the 7,378 schools of the state committees of vocational and technical training. Other youngsters learn their jobs in groups (brigades) directly at their place of work, although some tuition in such skills as dressmaking or typing may be available in informal, part-time courses in the towns. Figures for trainees in factory, farm or office are not readily available; they are usually combined with those for persons acquiring further skills.

The vocational school system contained many different types of institutions until the reform of December 1958. They were then turned into "vocational-technical schools" (PTUs, in the Russian abbreviation) with training periods of from 10 months to three years, designed primarily to take pupils from classes 8 to 10 of the general school without an entry examination. Most of the common industrial and agricultural trades are taught in them. During the 1970s, some 70 percent of the pupils were men, and 60 percent came from rural areas. On finishing, the pupils are directed to a job, which they are not supposed to leave for four years. This requirement more or less precludes them from proceeding immediately to a full-time VUZ education and this, together with the elementary nature of the training, means that the vocational schools have remained one of the less attractive options in the system. During the Brezhnev era, however, much was done to increase intakes, and to merge the PTUs with the general schools. By 1982, 58 percent of pupils were doing combined general courses (which led to a school certificate), and 10 percent were in part-time or evening PTUs. The sector is evidently set for considerable expansion.

General school-leavers who wish to set their sights a little higher may take the examinations for one of the country's secondary special educational institutions, where they may do a two- to four-year course depending on their educational status and choice of subject. These institutions are run on the same lines as the VUZy, offering much the same assortment of courses, although at a lower level, with a similar procedure for the planned placement of graduates. They tend to be regarded as a last resource, and complaints about the relative shortage of middle-grade specialists (whom they are designed to train) are commonplace.

THE UNIVERSITIES AND INSTITUTES

The Soviet authorities are justly proud of the development of higher education in their country. In 1981, the country's 891 VUZy provided the economy with some 831,200 graduates, which was close to overall national needs. According to Soviet estimates, the Soviet Union has twice as many students per 10,000 of the population as Britain, but still lags far behind the United States (the respective ratios being 197:98:261). Such claims must be treated with caution, of course, because in 1982, 43 percent of all Soviet VUZ students were taking part-time and correspondence courses, which, like other courses of this type, are demanding and suffer from a heavy dropout rate. Nevertheless, the national achievement is considerable.

VUZy fall into two main types, universities and institutes. Each of the country's 66 universities offer training in a wide variety of specialities, as in the West; the institutes, however, usually much smaller establishments, are limited to a few closely allied faculties. There are, as might be expected, considerable differences in the standing of different VUZy. Although in 1981, about one 10-year school-leaver in four had a chance of a VUZ place, the competition varied enormously between institutions.

The VUZy provide courses in a total of 449 officially approved specialities (as of 1979), with arts subjects taking about four years, engineering and science five and medicine six. The academic year is divided into two semesters, and students attend obligatory two-hour lectures and seminars for up to 36 hours a week. These include theoretical and practical work in their subject, up to four hours a week of sociopolitical studies (Marxist dialectical and historical materialism, political economy, history of the Communist party, and so on) and, for men, one afternoon a week of military training. In their last year, students write a short dissertation, choosing the topic from a list compiled by the faculty board. Most men also finish their military training at this point and are commissioned as officers.

Soviet VUZ courses (except for their political bias—primarily in history, economics, literature and the arts) are as demanding as those of Western institutions. Centralism is also here in evidence, in that all subjects and textbooks are approved by one of the ministries and entered on a central register. Faculties or departments may plan and offer a limited number of subspecializations or experiment with combinations of different subjects, with the approval of the VUZ rector or learned council. Soviet students have much less choice of subjects than their counterparts in Britain or the United States, once they have picked their main field of concentration.

Higher education is free, and over 70 percent of the full-time students were recently said to be receiving modest maintenance grants; family circumstances are the deciding factor in their allotment.

On graduating, students receive a diploma (possibly "with excellence"), and under the terms of regulations that have been in force in one form or another since 1928, they are obliged to spend three years at a job offered to them by the VUZ "personal placement commission," which interviews

534

them a few months before graduation. In this way the state endeavors to get the best value for its investment. Although students in full-time VUZy do some practical work at local enterprises during their senior years, when graduates arrive at their place of work, they usually have much to learn, for management training schemes as such are unknown in the Soviet Union. Part-time students, however, usually already have some practical experience.

From the point of view of social origins, the Soviet student body is in many respects similar to that in the West, especially because most university students are drawn from the more privileged social groups. But the nature of Soviet education, and Soviet reality itself, inevitably leave a distinctive imprint. The inability to travel abroad, restrictions on information about the outside world and an ignorance of the past make many, though not all, of these students rather limited in their outlook.

Two research degrees are granted in the Soviet Union. The first is the candidate's degree, which is roughly the equivalent of an M.A. and takes three years to complete, two on specialized study for an examination, and one on a thesis. The Soviet doctorate is rather more difficult to achieve than a British or U.S. Ph.D., and requires a minimum of three years after the candidate's degree.

The award of higher degrees is ultimately controlled by the prestigious Soviet Academy of Sciences, which in 1976 had 241 full members, 437 corresponding members and over 250 affiliated research institutes. Figures on the award of higher degrees are not published regularly, but 26,021 *aspiranty* completed candidates' courses in 1975. In the same year, 326,800 candidates and 32,300 doctors were said to be employed in the economy. Soviet scholarship is generally recognized to be of very good quality (when not limited by state censorship). The authorities have been particularly concerned to promote research in science and technology, and it is here that the most impressive gains have been made.

FURTHER READING

De Witt, N. *Education and Professional Employment in the USSR*. New York: National Science Foundation, 1962.

Grant, Nigel. *Soviet Education*. 4th ed. London: University of London Press; Gloucester, Massachusetts: Peter Smith, 1979.

Matthews, Mervyn. *Education in the Soviet Union*. London: Allen and Unwin, 1982.

Rudman, Herbert. *The School and State in the USSR*. New York: Macmillan, 1967.

Soviet Education (translations of selected Soviet articles on education). New York: International Arts and Sciences Press, 1958ff. Monthly.

Tomiak, J. J., ed. *Soviet Education in the 1980s*. London: Croom Helm, 1984.

LEGAL SYSTEM

W. E. BUTLER

ALTHOUGH their presocialist legal tradition is based, directly or indirectly, upon Romano-Germanic civil law, the Soviet and Eastern European legal systems, together with those of China, Mongolia, North Korea, Vietnam and Cuba, comprise a family of socialist legal systems distinct from Anglo-American common law and continental European civil law systems. The common core that, for analytical purposes, unites socialist legal systems into a distinctive grouping, notwithstanding differences within the grouping, is much debated by comparatists. Most, however, would give weight to such factors as a shared ideology; national economic planning; state ownership of the instruments and means of production; the relationship between the ruling parties and the legal systems; the educational role of law; novel legal institutions such as state *arbitrazh*, (tribunals), the procuracy and comrades' courts; and attitudes toward the role of law in society.

The 1917 October Revolution, in the exuberance of its triumph, proclaimed a complete break with the past; and in 1918, imperial legislation was formally repealed. But law is not merely the body of legislation at any given moment; it represents an accumulation of historical experiences, values, terminology and attitudes constructed in the course of human affairs over many centuries, elements that do not simply disappear overnight when revolution occurs. Eastern European countries did not even attempt so sharp a break with their former legal order. Laws of the old regimes were repealed or amended piecemeal, as required, and new laws and legal institutions based on the Soviet model were introduced. Poland, for example, continues to use portions of the 1934 Commercial Code, and in 1984 reinstated certain repealed provisions of that code regarding business associations; nor has Poland nationalized land as most other socialist legal systems have done.

SOURCES OF LAW

Socialist legal doctrine distinguishes between two types of "sources of law." In their fundamental sense, the sources of law are the socioeconomic order of a particular society that gives birth to and shapes a distinctive political, economic and legal superstructure. Sources of law in their technical meaning encompass the rules of law erected or sanctioned by state agencies in a duly established procedure. In all socialist legal systems, the paramount source of law is legislation enacted by the legislative and executive organs "on the

536

basis of and in execution of" normative legislative acts. Under certain circumstances, nonstate social or cooperative organizations are empowered to create rules of law either in collaboration with state organs (for example, trade unions and collective farms) or by themselves (consumer cooperatives). Binding rules of law governing economic contracts operate in the instructive regulations and general or special conditions adopted by state *arbitrazh* agencies. In wartime conditions, military commands have been granted law-making authority. And many socialist jurists believe that the "guiding explanations" issued by the plenums of supreme courts in socialist legal systems are sometimes a source of law; there are examples of such enactments transcending the normal bounds of interpretation and application of the code. Doctrinal writings of jurists are not a formal source of law, but in specially designated circumstances, custom may be. International treaties are regarded as a source of law, provided they have been ratified and appropriate action taken, if required, to transform or incorporate their provisions into the domestic law.

LEGAL PERSONNEL

Judges
In Soviet and Eastern European legal systems the judges are commonly elected, for a five-year term, either by the populace at large in electoral districts for the lowest level courts, or by the respective legislative organ of government for courts at the intermediate and highest levels. In some countries, such as Poland, the judiciary is a career service; in others, notably the Soviet Union, it is not. The modern practice is to elect only persons with a university degree in law or equivalent legal experience, although not all socialist legal systems impose this as a statutory requirement.

People's assessors
The principle of collegiality is well established in socialist legal systems; this requires that when sitting at first instance, the courts be composed of a judge and two lay persons, each having equal rights. The lay assessors are elected at large by collectives of working people, and they commonly serve two weeks per year with paid leave from their normal employment.

Advocates
Nearly all socialist legal systems have retained the profession of advocate for the representation of parties in civil cases and of the accused in administrative or criminal proceedings. Advocates are organized into self-governing professional bodies that admit members and establish the canons for practice—commonly under the general supervision of the Ministry of Justice or the courts. Fee schedules are fixed or confirmed by the state. Clients pay the requisite fees to the law office to which the advocate is attached. Free legal assistance for indigent clients is available, and the fees, in any case, are quite nominal. Despite the apparent anachronism of a fee-based profession in a socialist society, the advocates are now widely accepted as performing an essential service in a socialist legal system.

537

Jurisconsults

This segment of the legal profession has enjoyed massive expansion during the 1970s, their numbers doubling in the USSR alone during that period. Jurisconsults are legal advisers employed by ministries, state enterprises, local organs of government, collective and state farms, and large social organizations to advise on economic contracts and other legal matters. They are protected against dismissal by management and must certify the conformity to law of all legal transactions entered into by their employers. Jurisconsults commonly represent their organizations in state *arbitrazh* proceedings and may advise employees on a wide range of legal questions.

Procurators

The Soviet model of the procuracy has been adopted throughout Eastern Europe. A highly centralized institution, immune from local governmental influence and perhaps the most prestigious component of the legal profession, the procuracy has a number of functions. It prosecutes criminal cases on behalf of the state; supervises the principal organs of preliminary investigation; exercises supervision over correctional-labor institutions; and, most significantly, exercises powers of "general supervision" over the legality of actions of state officials, organizations and institutions, and the courts. In the latter instance, the procuracy issues a reasoned "protest" against illegal actions and requires compliance or a refusal to comply within stipulated periods. A refusal to comply will be protested by the procuracy to the agency superior to the noncomplying organ or official.

State arbitrazh

Economic disputes between state enterprises are within the jurisdiction of a specialized network of tribunals called state *arbitrazh*. The disputes are decided by a single arbitrator, who is a full-time employee of the state *arbitrazh* and expert in both civil and economic law and in the technical engineering side of industry. Jurisdiction is compulsory and binding upon the parties.

Notaries

Employees of the state *notariat* are responsible for certifying or authenticating legal transactions as required by law, including contracts, wills, leases, gifts, translations, signatures, and the like. They also open and administer estates, and in certain instances may issue writs of execution without judicial proceedings for the collection of minor debts.

ZAGS

The registries for civil affairs register births, deaths, marriages, divorces, paternity and changes of name. Secular marriage or registration thereof is required in socialist legal systems if the union is to have legal validity; religious ceremonies are permitted but have no legal effect.

Other legal personnel

The term "jurist" in socialist legal systems is widely used to denote either individuals who possess a university degree in law or individuals employed

538

in some type of legal institution. In addition to the categories of legal person-nel already mentioned, the term would encompass law teachers and legal research personnel, preliminary investigators and police agencies; the term is frequently used more loosely for quasi-legal personnel, such as the members of administrative commissions who deal with administrative penalties, or the members of people's control commissions and even those who staff non-state social bodies linked to law enforcement, such as members of comrades' courts, people's guards and social centers for the protection of order.

COURT ORGANIZATION

Soviet and Eastern European legal systems organize their judicial systems in basically similar ways, although the names of the courts and other details may vary. The lowest court, usually called a people's court, hears the great majority of civil and criminal cases at first instance. The judges of these courts are usually elected directly by the populace of a given locality. When acting as a trial court, just as all higher courts that hear cases at first instance, the people's court functions as a collegial body; that is, the judge sits with two people's assessors, all having equal rights, and a majority vote decides the case. In minor cases, some Eastern European countries allow the judge to hear the case alone.

The numbers and appellations of intermediate courts will depend on the administrative-territorial subdivisions of the country. Intermediate courts normally hear difficult, complex or serious cases at first instance, again acting collegially, and decide appeals from inferior courts. In federated socialist legal systems, such as the USSR and Yugoslavia, there is a supreme court for each constituent republic; these supreme courts hear exceedingly complex or serious cases at first instance and either consider appeals from inferior courts or review judicial practice upon protests from duly authorized officials or of their own volition. The power of review is widely used and may ordinar-ily be invoked at any time after a judgment has entered into force. Supreme courts in Soviet and Eastern European legal systems have very limited powers of judicial review over the constitutionality of legislation, and only over subordinate acts. Yugoslavia has experimented with a constitutional court to ensure that the constituent republics do not stray from federal rules.

The supreme courts enjoy the power to issue "guiding explanations" bind-ing upon all inferior courts. Although intended to facilitate the interpretation and application of law, some of these explanations have been lawcreating and may be sources of law. The supreme courts often publish bulletins con-taining the texts of leading decisions that, although they do not have the force of precedent, are considered an authoritative guide to future decisions and are taken into account by lawyers when advising clients or pleading in court.

COURT PROCEDURE

Soviet and Eastern European legal systems have all adapted their earlier continental civil law tradition in court procedure to modern conditions.

539

In a criminal proceeding, the court will have available beforehand the full record of the inquiry or preliminary investigation carried out by a state official or organ specially given that responsibility, and the opinion of the procuracy endorsing the findings of the investigation. In a civil proceeding, the court will have all the documentation relevant to the case submitted by the parties. The court examines these materials in a closed administrative session and will defer trial if material defects are discovered. During trial, the court follows the order and stages laid down in the detailed codes of civil and criminal procedure. The judge and the people's assessors actively question all trial participants and take the lead in carrying on the proceedings. When the trial is completed, the bench retires to a separate room to come to their decision. Dissenting opinions are not disclosed in open court but are attached to the file of the case and come to the notice of appeal or review panels. The rules of evidence laid down in the procedure codes are far less stringent than in Anglo-American law because the court is entitled to hear and weigh all relevant evidence and, since there is no jury system, need not preclude hearing extraneous matters. In its judgment, the court must indicate what evidence it relied upon and why. A plea of guilty has no evidentiary value in a criminal case; the prosecution must prove guilt conclusively without reliance upon confession. Once proved, however, acknowledgment of guilt may affect the sentence. The court judgment encompasses both verdict and sentence, and both elements may be appealed by any trial participant. In civil cases, the settlement of a dispute pending trial may require the permission or approval of the court. Even though a civil dispute is between two parties, the state may intervene on either side if a matter of state interest is involved or if third-party interests require protection.

CONSTITUTIONAL FOUNDATIONS

The Soviet and Eastern European legal systems all have a written constitution and, indeed, all have adopted several constitutions coincident with their transition from one level of societal development to another. They are in every instance the fundamental law of the country concerned. Nevertheless, a combination of constitutional doctrine and one-party rule has in fact meant that the constitution does not represent a perpetual constraint upon the state itself. Modern Soviet and Eastern European constitutions have a similar structure of provisions: the sociopolitical and economic system of society; the state and the individual; citizenship and equality of citizens; the basic rights, freedoms and duties of citizens; the state structure; the electoral system; the powers and functions of legislative and executive agencies; the state arms, flag and anthem; and the procedures for amendment.

THE SUBSTANTIVE LAW

Law in socialist legal systems is regarded as one of the social sciences and consequently is divided into a number of branches, each of which governs a designated sphere of legal relations. These branches of law do not necessarily coincide with branches of legislation and in any event often overlap with

540

one another. The theory of law in socialist legal systems devotes much time to the proper classification of law into branches, and theoretical debates regarding the proper objects or subjects of legal regulation have on occasion profoundly affected patterns of legislation.

In the Soviet Union, the branches of law include constitutional, administrative, civil, family, labor, economic, collective farm, natural resource or nature conservation, criminal, criminal procedure, civil procedure, transport, and financial law. Some of these categories are disputed. Soviet doctrine is debating whether civil and criminal procedure and court organization should not be combined into "justice law." Economic law is now, after years of controversy, widely accepted as a branch of legal science and a branch of legislation but, it is conceded, overlaps appreciably with civil, administrative and planning law. Transport law is a contested category, for many jurists doubt whether the kinds of transport (air, sea, river, rail, road and perhaps pipeline) and their domestic and international aspects can be unified within a single branch of law. Many Soviet jurists would subdivide natural resources law into land, water, forest and mining law as distinct branches. In Eastern Europe, several countries retain branches of law inherited from the pre-socialist period or recreated to cope with the private sector—for example, in Poland, company law and restrictive practices law.

Economic law is perhaps the most significant recent conceptual development in socialist legal theory and substantive law. Eastern Europe has in some respects led the way, especially Czechoslovakia and the German Democratic Republic, which have actually enacted an economic code. In all socialist legal systems, economic legislation comprises by far the greatest body of law whether measured in numbers of words or enactments. The dilemma for policymakers in the socialist planned economy has been to find an effective way to combine the traditional horizontal civil law relationships between state enterprises governed by contract and legislation, with the vertical administrative and planning relationships between a state enterprise and its superior agencies. Economic law undertakes to regulate both types of relationship, but many socialist jurists fear that in doing so the civil law authority of the enterprise retained in Soviet civil law since national economic planning began will be irreparably compromised.

Economic reforms in the USSR and Eastern Europe since the 1960s have stressed the value of enterprise autonomy. Planning controls have been loosened, especially in light industry, and powers of enterprises to make many of their own production decisions, sometimes requiring the confirmation of planning authorities, have been broadened. Broader discretion in horizontal relations and reduced vertical restrictions have led to an enhancement of the role of law. Economic legislation, economic contracts, professional legal assistance in the form of staff jurisconsults, and a larger role for state *arbitrazh* are the principal devices and institutions used to discipline the exercise of enterprise autonomy in the USSR and Eastern Europe; most Eastern European legal systems have extended enterprise autonomy to the realm of foreign trade in selected large enterprises by allowing them to handle their foreign transactions directly and to enter into joint ventures. This approach to enterprise autonomy has also required greater stress upon the role of economic accountability in enterprise management and the development of economic-legal indicators appropriate for guiding enterprise operations along optional lines. The vertical relationships are less satisfactorily dealt with. Administrative restrictions requiring superior agencies not to interfere arbitrarily in enterprise operations are almost impossible to enforce, although the law does require administrative bodies, when altering planning obligations, to make compensatory adjustments all along the line so as to minimize distortions of economic accountability.

Economic accountability has been the core element of the civil law personality of the state enterprise. An enterprise is allocated state property and land to commence operations and is granted a state charter defining its powers and functions. It is responsible for its liabilities out of its assets, is not responsible for state obligations and vice versa, and can sue and be sued. So useful has the concept been as a means of assessing economic performance, that in the Soviet Union some ministries are being trasferred in part to economic accountability on an experimental basis.

LEGALITY

In the post-Stalin era, the expression "socialist legality" has come to embrace both conformity with existing legislation and the concept of due process, whereunder the legal system must contain adequate safeguards against abuse of state power and persons acting illegally, whether citizens or officials. Legal reforms in the Soviet Union and Eastern Europe have been directed, on the whole, toward refining and raising the standard of both types of legality without, however, abandoning the principles of Communist party rule. Reformist and dissident movements in nearly all the countries concerned have urged the following reforms: a more tolerant attitude in the Soviet and Eastern European legal systems toward diversity of views; a relaxation of censorship; and social pluralism within the existing framework. Although repressive legal measures have been employed by the various regimes to suppress these movements, formal legality in the sense of conformity to law has been preferred, often on both sides, with views differing as to what proper observance of formal legality requires. The pressures for tolerance and pluralism are enormously varied, ranging from religious observance; ethnic identity and use of native language; freedom of the press, speech and assembly; the formation of trade unions; emigration; artistic expression; and access to juridical proceedings, up to approaches to economic policy. Although by both Western and Eastern standards the guarantees of legality still require improvement, there has undoubtedly been progress in all the legal systems concerned in both law and practice since the Stalin era.

PENOLOGY

Marxism has always emphasized the social context of the individual. The ills of society are to be found in the iniquities of class relations, oppression, exploitation, the concentration of ownership of the instruments and means of production in the hands of the capitalist class, the use of law and state to pursue narrow class interests, and the economic basis of society. Socialist revolution promised to redress these economic and social causes of societal dysfunction; by doing so, the objective reasons for crime would disappear. One consequence of this approach was the emergence after the 1917 October Revolution of an approach to criminology in the USSR that dispensed with the concept of moral guilt in criminal law and investigated the economic and sociological factors contributing to criminal behavior. Although not wholly compatible with the class approach to dispensing justice, as laid down in the 1926 Russian SFSR criminal code, this explanation of the causes of crime led to an emphasis upon the reeducation and reform of offenders rather than retaliation and punishment. During the early 1930s criminal codes were drafted that did away completely with the special part of the criminal code. That pattern was reversed in 1935–36 and punishment was stressed as an appropriate weapon against class enemies. Criminology was severely curtailed both in the Soviet Union and Eastern Europe until Stalin's death. To this day in the USSR, criminal statistics remain a state secret; some Eastern European countries, however, regularly publish their statistics.

Soviet criminology was resuscitated in the early 1960s and has empirically explored the causes of crime. The individual element in criminal behavior is no longer wholly discounted, but social factors are still considered to be primary. Urbanization, industrialization, low incomes, inadequate housing, excessive drinking and lack of education are among the social factors identified as contributing to criminal behavior, and it follows that state resources directed toward ameliorating these conditions should in time produce a lower crime rate. Several Eastern European countries, especially Poland, have pioneered interesting sociological studies of crime.

Post-Stalin criminal law reforms in the Soviet Union and Eastern Europe have reinstated reeducation and reform as the principal objects of the criminal law. A broad range of punishments is provided for by the criminal codes, and, as in Western countries, criminologists differ over whether a severe or a lenient application of punishment is most likely to produce the desired educational result. During the past quarter century penal policy in all these legal systems has vacillated somewhat between both schools of thought. The 1960 Russian SFSR criminal code was markedly less severe than its predecessor. The maximum term of deprivation of freedom was reduced in most cases from 25 to 15 years. Suspended sentences were encouraged, especially for minor crimes and first offenders. Apparently, the code was felt to be too lenient, for in 1961–62 the punishments for a broad range of offenses were increased. In 1982, the first comprehensive amendment of the 1960 code, affecting about two-thirds of all the articles, introduced more flexible measures for treating first offenders and raised penalties for serious crimes and second offenses. Recidivists are dealt with especially severely, apparently on the premise that they have deliberately resisted education and reform measures. Correctional-labor measures likewise are being reevaluated, for apparently they have often not lived up to the expectations of those who devised them.

The punishments that can be imposed by Soviet and Eastern European courts are normally divided into basic and supplementary. All these legal systems apply the death penalty as an exceptional measure of punishment for certain crimes; it is never mandatory. Deprivation of freedom is served in the correctional-labor institutions of the various regimes, depending on the gravity of the crime committed and the personality of the offender. Reform through labor is the basic premise of these institutions, and all inmates are expected to learn a trade and apply their skills constructively to national production requirements. Prisons are normally only used when a prisoner is dangerous to others and requires complete isolation from society. A correctional measure such as the withholding of up to 20 percent of a convicted person's salary at his or her normal place of work for a term of up to two years is widely employed as a criminal punishment. Social censure may be applied for less serious offenses. Exile and banishment may be imposed for certain crimes, although the reeducational purpose of these measures is far from self-evident. Fines, dismissal from office, making amends for harm caused and prohibitions against holding specified posts or engaging in specified activities may be assigned in some situations. Confiscation of property or deprivation of title or rank are supplementary punishments when the special part of the criminal codes so provides; certain property, however, is not subject to confiscation.

In Eastern Europe, exile and banishment are little used. Poland uses ordinary prisons more than correctional-labor colonies and gives sentences of life imprisonment for some offenses.

Penology in the Soviet and Eastern European legal systems cannot be understood, however, without reference to what technically is a nonpenal matter: administrative offenses. These have no counterpart in the Anglo-American legal tradition. All the legal systems concerned take administrative offenses into account, but the most comprehensive modern law is the 1984 Russian SFSR Code on Administrative Violations. An administrative offense is an "unlawful, guilty (intentional or negligent) action or failure to act that infringes the state or social order, socialist ownership, the rights and freedoms of citizens, or the established administrative order," for which administrative responsibility is provided by legislation. There are literally hundreds of such offenses under Soviet law, mostly petty violations of traffic, safety, trade, energy, finance, public order and administrative rules. The penalties are usually imposed on the spot when an offender is apprehended in the act by a duly authorized official or inspector. Fines are perhaps the most common penalty imposed, but other penalties include seizure or confiscation of property, deprivation of a right (to drive, for example), correctional tasks and, for certain offenses, even administrative arrest for a term of up to 15 days. The Russian SFSR code introduces procedural uniformity and due process to a greater extent than existed previously, including a right to counsel when cases or appeals are heard by administrative commissions or administrative sessions of people's courts. None of these offenses is regarded as a crime; the codes of criminal procedure do not apply to administrative proceedings and, of course, the incidence of such offenses is excluded from criminal statistics. Ordinary citizens in the course of their daily affairs are far more apt to encounter administrative penalties than the criminal law.

LAW OF SOCIALIST ECONOMIC INTEGRATION

In its widest sense, the law of socialist economic integration might be stretched to include not only the legal institutions and rules developed by Council for Mutual Economic Assistance (COMECON) members to further economic integration, but also to the network of multilateral and bilateral arrangements among the USSR and nations of Eastern Europe that unify, harmonize or facilitate legal relations. Family, succession, pension, remittance, consular and other matters are regulated by networks of bilateral conventions, whereas planning and other economic links are being standardized within COMECON institutions. Increasingly, the recommendations of COMECON institutions are being transformed or incorporated into municipal legislation at all levels, creating unusual problems regarding precedence in the hierarchy of normative acts. One COMECON institution, the Meeting of Representatives of COMECON Member Countries on Legal Questions, devotes its activities exclusively to the unification of law. The 1971 comprehensive program, for the first time in any major COMECON document, acknowledged law to be a significant force in achieving socialist integration.

FOREIGN RELATIONS LAW

Although not treated as a separate branch of law, foreign relations legislation in the USSR and Eastern Europe is distinctive in several respects. Some legal systems, such as that of the USSR, have adopted special laws defining the legal status of foreigners. All organize the conduct of foreign trade so as to give either the state an exclusive monopoly (as in the Soviet Union) or a substantial monopoly and regulatory role (as in Eastern Europe). During the 1970s, Eastern European countries pioneered joint ventures and other schemes to attract foreign investment, up to and including foreign ownership of part of the venture. Czechoslovakia, the German Democratic Republic and Hungary are among the countries that have authorized certain large enterprises to trade directly abroad without going through specially created foreign trade organizations. The latter are normally established as independent corporate entities to exercise the state foreign trade monopoly in specified goods and services. They have their own charters, capital assets, boards of directors and legal personality. In most countries, the foreign trade organizations act as the principals in contracts with foreign partners and conclude wholly separate and distinct transactions with domestic partners. In the Soviet Union and Eastern Europe, disputes arising out of foreign trade transactions are nearly always referred to a designated foreign trade or maritime arbitration commission within one of the socialist countries. In some Western and Third World countries, the Soviet Union and Eastern Europe have established foreign trade representations having full or partial diplomatic status in order to represent foreign trade interests. All the countries concerned have chambers of commerce to promote trade, organize exhibitions and give certain certifications.

Under Soviet law, foreign trade transactions require mandatory signature formalities in order to be legally valid.

FURTHER READING

Berman, H. J. *Justice in the U.S.S.R.* Rev. ed. Cambridge, Massachusetts: Harvard University Press, 1963.

———, and Spindler, J. *Soviet Criminal Law and Procedure: The RSFSR Codes.* 2nd ed. Cambridge, Massachusetts: Harvard University Press, 1972.

Butler, W. E. *Basic Documents on the Soviet Legal System.* Dobbs Ferry, New York: Oceana, 1983.

———. *Soviet Law.* London: Butterworth, 1983.

Hazard, J. N. et al. *The Soviet Legal System.* 4th ed. Dobbs Ferry, New York: Oceana, 1984.

THE POLITICAL AND SOCIAL SETTING OF THE CONTEMPORARY ARTS

GEORGE GÖMÖRI

THE ROLE OF THE INTELLECTUAL

SOCIETY creates culture; culture reflects, expresses and shapes society. Considering the political and social factors that influence the character of the arts, especially literature, in European communist countries, this survey should perhaps begin with the thesis that in the Soviet Union and Eastern Europe intellectuals, and writers in particular, have always played a much more important role than in other societies. This peculiarity is the consequence of the uneven, distorted and often interrupted course of development in the history of these countries. It is bound up with such facts as the nonexistence of a proper middle class and the search for an independent nationhood or national survival. Traditionally, the artist was a client of a rich patron, a town or a select social group, commissioned to serve and delight patrons. There were, of course, always artists and writers who criticized the social institutions of their age, but the scope of their criticism was on the whole limited. Only after the French Revolution and the ensuing social turmoil did the writer appear in the new role of a social "prophet" and political leader. The great Romantics were the first to raise the banner of revolt against society, with different consequences in the East and West. While Shelley's, and even Victor Hugo's, revolt was of little significance in the context of English or French politics, the Russians Pushkin and Lermontov, the Poles Mickiewicz and Słowacki, the Hungarian Petőfi or the Bulgarian Botev left an indelible imprint on the collective national consciousness of their respective peoples. All these poets were alienated from the center of power in their countries, were opposed to the status quo for national or social or, as in the case of Eastern Europe, both reasons. Byron's or Shelley's hatred of tyranny expressed in their poetry was shared by many liberals and radicals in England who were free to voice their opinions through democratic channels. Literature in Russia and Eastern Europe has been able to play such a significant role in the past 150 years because writers, alienated from the assumptions upon which power rested, both expressed and intensified the

547

frustrations felt, but *not expressed*, by the educated majority of their society. This majority was either disenfranchised or intimidated by feudal tradition, religious obscurantism or political terror. The poet or writer became, in fact, the voice of a whole nation. Since no proper institutions existed, the writer became an institution. The intellectuals acted as substitutes for a nonexistent or very weak middle class and at certain moments poets volunteered as political leaders. The classic example of the prophetic poet-leader is the Polish poet, Adam Mickiewicz, who twice within a decade left his civilian occupation and family to organize Polish military units to fight against Austria and Russia—enemies of his partitioned country.

The Soviet Union

Here it is necessary to distinguish between the Soviet Union proper, on the one hand, and Eastern Europe on the other, though even the countries of Eastern Europe differ among themselves. The source of these differences lies above all in national tradition. Russia's past weighs heavily upon the present; its religious, Byzantine and autocratic traditions are still very much alive under the veil of communism. "Cosmopolitanism" is one of the most pejorative words in the Soviet vocabulary—meaning treason to the homeland. In this respect, Soviet communism under Stalin successfully incorporated certain emotional elements of traditional Great Russian nationalism. Non-Russian nationalities and national minorities do not, of course, feel the same attachment to "Mother Russia"; this partly explains why Lithuanians, Ukrainians, Armenians and Jews played such an important role in democratic movements of the 1966–83 period.

Another outstanding feature of Soviet communist ideology is the uncompromising nature of its demand for "truth." For the sake of the peasant masses everything had to be simplified to basic truths, to "either-ors." Petru Dumitriu, the émigré Romanian author, sardonically suggested that, for the ordinary Russian, literature is a ritual "where virtue triumphs and evil is exorcised" and that the Stalinist demand for a "positive hero" (a salient feature of socialist realism) in the contemporary novel is the outcome of the traditional reading habits of the Russian peasantry; its chief reading matter was the *Lives of the Saints*. Writers and readers alike expect everyone to be loyal to the state and not to be in collusion with foreigners in revealing the real state of affairs in the Soviet Union. Those Soviet writers who step out of line and criticize their society abroad ignore this Russian tradition at their own peril; they are branded as "traitors," and not only by their Stalinist colleagues. Pasternak's experience is the perfect example; the publication of *Doctor Zhivago* in the West was denounced in vitriolic terms by many of his fellow writers (including some anti-Stalinists), and none of his friends had the courage to make a public statement in his defense. This attitude, though, changed during the 1960s decade—there were far more people willing to support Solzhenitsyn as long as he lived in the Soviet Union.

The growth of civic courage in the post-Stalin period and, in particular, in the 1960s was interconnected with the development of a new "critical intelligentsia" in the USSR. Although this group is still relatively small (it can be counted in thousands against the millions of conformist intellectuals) and is concentrated in big cities, it is enhanced by the large-scale growth of the new "specialist" class. An interesting feature of the democratic (or dissident) movement in the Soviet Union is the involvement of a sizable number of scientists and mathematicians in its activities, indeed, after the enforced departure of Solzhenitsyn in 1974, Andrei Sakharov, a distinguished nuclear physicist took his place as the leading spirit of the movement. Ever since 1966, the critical intelligentsia has been fighting against the Soviet state monopoly on information. An important milestone in this struggle was the publication of an information bulletin (*Chronicle of Current Events*, 1968–72), while a constant flow of samizdat books and pamphlets kept alive the spirit of free inquiry under Brezhnev, Andropov and Chernenko.

The first event that galvanized the critical intelligentsia into open action was the Sinyavsky-Daniel trial in 1966. Since then, a continuous pattern of dissident activism and policy retaliation has characterized Soviet society, a pattern that culminated in the major crackdown on dissidents in 1979–80 and the internal exile of Dr. Sakharov to Gorky. During these years, the Soviet authorities diversified their methods of suppressing dissent; apart from jailing and exiling dissidents, they encouraged, and sometimes enforced, emigration to the West. Solzhenitsyn and Joseph Brodsky had no choice but to leave the Soviet Union; but apart from them, new émigrés have included Andrei Amalrik, Vladimir Bukovsky, Anatoly Kuznetsov, Vladimir Maksimov, Viktor Nekrasov, Andrei Sinyavsky, Aleksandr Zinoviev and recently Vasily Aksionov. They were joined in the West by such eminent artists as the ballet dancer Baryshnikov, the cellist Rostropovich, the theatrical director Yuri Lyubimov and the filmmaker Andrei Tarkovsky (probably the best living Soviet film director). During the same period, most of the "angry young men" of the early 1960s, such as Yevtushenko and Voznesensky, eschewed social criticism and became prosperous conformists in a regime which in recent years has used intellectual bribes and friendly persuasion as much as naked force in its efforts to keep down the level of dissent in the Soviet Union.

Poland and Hungary

In Poland and Hungary the position of the writer has been historically different. The Polish state was wiped out of existence at the end of the 18th century and there seemed little or no hope that this situation could be reversed. After the failure of the Polish uprising and war of independence of 1830–31 when Poland's best statesmen, writers and scholars emigrated to the West, the importance of the written word increased enormously—it became the last refuge of those who could not accept foreign domination. The Polish obsession with national independence evident in the works of Mickiewicz, Słowacki and Krasinski is an outcome of the loss of independent statehood. The emphasis on the value of language in part explains the exalted position of the poet—the maker of words, the bard, the spiritual leader. The position of the poet, by and large, survived even after 1918 when Poland regained its independence. It was dramatically enhanced during the World War II years of German occupation, when all Polish schools and institutes of higher education were closed and publishing in the Polish language was disrupted by the Germans. Twenty-three years after, the official ban imposed on Mickiewicz's drama *The Forefathers' Eve* galvanized the Warsaw students into protests that ended in street fighting with the police.

The Hungarian national model for writers is also based on opposition to unrepresentative government and rule. Hungary was more fortunate than Poland; even if it was for centuries ruled from Vienna, most traditional Hungarian institutions were (not without recurring struggles) preserved and in the first half of the 19th century were able to evolve toward complete self-determination for the nation. Hungary's main problem before the 1848 revolution was that its social grievances were inseparable from its lack of independence, since dependence on Austria perpetuated the country's agrarian structure and anachronistic feudal customs. The best thinkers and writers demanded both social reforms and national self-determination. This is why Sándor Petőfi, the most popular and one of the best poets of the age could be both an ardent Magyar patriot and a radical revolutionary. His dream was the realization of the threefold slogan of the French Revolution—he was all for brotherhood and could not imagine freedom without equality or equality without freedom. His vision of "Heaven on Earth" is certainly utopian, but the spirit of dedicated revolt that emanates from his work exerted a powerful influence on future generations. He saw the poet as a "pillar of fire," a spiritual leader of the people toward a Canaan to be won by revolution. Petőfi was admired and his rebellion was kept alive by such outstanding Hungarian poets of our century as Endre Ady, and after Ady, Attila József and Gyula Illyés. Between the two wars, Petőfi's demands—the demands of democratic revolution—were shared by the group of Populist "village explorers" and by the socialists, in fact by the entire Hungarian left; even the communists when making a bid for power would pose as "Petőfi's heirs," as his name (and that of Lajos Kossuth) meant the *authentic revolution* for many Hungarians who had never read a line of Marx or Lenin. But no dictatorship can contain the spirit of real revolution. Petőfi appeared once again in 1956 as the patron saint of the famous Petőfi Circle (a debating society of the young intelligentsia) that, together with the Hungarian Writers' Association, led the first attacks against the bastions of Stalinism in Hungary. The important thing about Petőfi, and for that matter Ady and the entire "revolutionary line" in Hungarian literature, was that in his case national aspirations could only strengthen social revolt (unlike the Russian experience) and that by trying to be more European, the Hungarian writer or artist would only become more, and not less, Hungarian. Whereas the conservative-radical split existed in Hungarian society as much as anywhere else, only the peculiar inter-war social and political situation actually produced conflicts between "Hungarophiles" and "Westernizers." Since 1945 (when the democratic revolution was at long last carried out in Hungary) the "national poetic model" has lost some of its relevance.

This pattern, traditional for Poland and Hungary, began to undergo a change in the 1960s and even more in the 1970s. With the development of autonomous social sciences and a renewed interest in national history, the center of gravity of intellectual investigations noticeably shifted away from literature. The rapid development of television and a new wave of documentary filmmaking also acted as agents of diversification. Literature has lost some of its traditional positions (and readership); as for poetry, it has definitely lost its predominance within literature. It is symptomatic that in an "advanced" socialist country such as Hungary, debates about the falling birthrate, the situation of the underprivileged in society and the obstacles to innovation, although mostly conducted in literary weeklies and periodicals, involves far more social scientists and members of the technical intelligentsia than writers. Also, one of the major events in the history of the contemporary Hungarian cinema was Ferenc Kósa's film about the outstanding athlete András Balczó (*Vocation*), which asked pertinent questions about the opportunities for excellence in a society that, both for social and political reasons, favored the mediocre.

While in most Eastern European countries literature seems to have lost its predominance first to the filmmakers and then to the social scientists, there still exists a possibility of a reversal of this situation. The widespread boycott of the media by Polish actors during the imposition of martial law in Poland (between 1981 and 1984), just as the noncollaboration of Czech writers with the authorities after 1969, created peculiar situations in which clandestine literature gained in importance almost to the point of restoring the primacy of the printed word over centrally controlled images. It is another matter that the conditions of samizdat impose a limit on the availability of truthful or qualitatively superior literature. While millions watch TV, whether good or bad, and tens of thousands read books available in bookshops, readers of samizdat literature (with the possible exception of those in Poland) never exceed a few thousand. Moreover, even publications available in samizdat differ in their subject matter; the Polish and Hungarian samizdat of recent years consisted of far more historical and sociological books than of belles lettres.

Czechoslovakia

In the case of Czechoslovakia, national tradition produced another, perhaps more sophisticated, model. Whereas in Poland and Hungary (and to a certain extent in Bulgaria) poets were in the vanguard of national awareness, in the Czech and Moravian lands poetry did not play such a distinctive role. The Czech national character has changed much since the Hussite wars when the Czechs were regarded as the best soldiers in Europe; it has both been hardened and mellowed by circumstances, changing from being romantic, poetic and revolutionary to rational, matter-of-fact and evolutionist. Nonetheless, intellectuals have been an important force in Czech history—people like the historian Palacký whose part in the new rise of Czech national consciousness cannot be exaggerated. The greatest Czechs were traditionally preachers, thinkers or educators: Jan Hus, Chelčický and Komenský, Palacký and Masarýk. The independent Czechoslovak state that came into being after World War I was an achievement of the intellectuals in which, however, the contribution of journalists, philosophers and historians was decisive. This is not to underestimate the influence of such figures as Čapek or Halas. But the specific cultural traditions of the Czech nation made it more receptive to an objective mode of discourse, while in its scale of values, time and again, priority was given to seeking the absolute truth as opposed to seeking one's own truth or own right. (This does not apply to the Slovak lands where historical tradition influenced cultural impulses similar to those in Poland or Hungary.) At the same time, the fact that Czech intellectuals fought for specific national rights as well enhanced their position and standing in the eyes of the nation. So in the Czech context, once again, there was little contradiction between universal and national ideals. Whereas in Poland and Hungary sharp conflicts developed after 1918 between the ideals of the progressive intelligentsia and the realities of actual power, this was not so in Czechoslovakia, the questions of national minorities excepted. The socialist and communist movements in Czechoslovakia enjoyed the support of the majority of the Czech and Slovak intellectuals, who were the most willing supporters of radical social reform. This is why the "humanization" of socialism in Czechoslovakia was (and still is) a test case. If we accept the thesis that the full collaboration and support of the intelligentsia is indispensable to the success of socialism and if no humanist form of socialism can be created in this small Central European country with its strong left-wing traditions, then socialism has no real future in Europe.

MARXIST-LENINIST IDEOLOGY AND SOCIALIST REALISM

Apart from national tradition and Western influences, the third factor that shapes the thinking of writers and artists in the Soviet Union and Eastern Europe is Marxist-Leninist ideology. Neither Marx nor Engels had worked out a coherent system of aesthetics. This accounts for the fact that behind Marxist aesthetics one usually finds Hegelian or positivistic views. From various notes and hints, however, one can see the nature of the demands that Marx made of artists; they should be progressive in their politics and realists in art, and if one of the two requirements had to be sacrificed, realism was the one to remain. In other words, writers should try and grasp the essence of human and social relations and it is the truthfulness of their work that should impress the reader not the loftiness of their political ideas. Lenin's fateful addition to this rather sane theory was his much-quoted article of 1905, "Party Organization and Party Literature" in which he formulated the demand that literature should become "party literature," "part of the Social Democratic ... party work." This article is fateful because it was the base upon which the entire Stalinist-Zhdanovist superstructure of literary control was later erected. Significantly, such an eminent anti-Stalinist Marxist thinker as Georg Lukács has never ceased to oppose the theory of *partiynost* (party-mindedness) derived from Lenin's article. For "party literature" in Stalinist terms meant not only administrative control over funds, publishing houses and art galleries but also literature and art geared to the immediate political aims of the Communist party. What the enforcement of *partiynost* meant was the total subordination of the arts to the interests of political power and their constant manipulation and inevitable debasement in the serving of the ruling bureaucracy, even though the furtherance of long-term political aims or ideals might detract from the authenticity of the work of art.

Socialist realism in the arts is simply the "best" (and in the long run the only approved) method that ensures the realization of Lenin's claim for literature. In the dogmatic Stalinist interpretation of socialist realism, which is still dominant though by no means omnipotent in the Soviet Union, the writer's task is to depict society truthfully, on a high artistic level *and* in a party spirit. The latter demand stipulates optimism and simplicity as well. All this is possible only if the party's interest is in every case compatible with the objective (social) truth or the writer's subjective truth. In fact, these coincide only by chance, so socialist realism (a blend of revolutionary romanticism and critical realism) is a contradiction in terms. Writers can choose between following their own taste and convictions, in which case they will "deviate" towards "bourgeois" realism or some other artistic ism, or following the party line and thereby inevitably committing the sin of "embellishing" reality.

This short description explains the dilemma of the artist both in the Soviet Union and in Eastern Europe during the period that is now regarded as the heyday of Zhdanovism (in the Soviet Union 1946–53, in Eastern Europe 1948–53). That socialist realism should reign supreme above all other methods of writing, painting or composing music is a constant desideratum of the cultural policy of communist regimes. Whereas in the 1950s, socialist realism was discredited in Eastern Europe as a Soviet-inspired method of ruthless artistic regimentation, lately there has been less insistence on its exclusive merits. This reflects, of course, the political concessions that had to be made to the people after the crisis of de-Stalinization in the Soviet Union, Poland and Hungary in 1956, in Czechoslovakia and, to some extent, in Romania after 1963. As soon as the fiction of complete unity within the ranks of the ruling party was exposed and the "unflinching support" of the population for party policy disappeared, a period of uneasy tolerance was ushered in. Standards for creative activity other than socialist realism began to be accepted as temporary alternatives. In recent years, the whole issue of socialist realism has been conveniently sidetracked (if not completely buried) in most Eastern European countries, not unlike the issue of the Holy Trinity in the period of the Enlightenment. Even in the Soviet Union, attempts were made to redefine and, to some extent, refine the concept itself. A. Ovcharenko in his book on *Socialist Realism and the Contemporary Literary Process* (1968) and in his later essays on the same subject, suggests that although *partiynost* should remain the guiding principle of Soviet literature, socialist realism should incorporate any literary techniques or devices that further its main purpose. In other words, simplicity of style and accessibility to a wide readership are no longer regarded as basic requirements to official acceptance even in present-day Soviet literature.

POLITICS AND CULTURE

Policy affecting cultural activities fluctuates in countries with communist regimes. The extent to which writers or composers are free depends on the overall political situation, the exigencies of the moment and the party officials in charge of cultural affairs. There is a direct and obvious connection between "hard" and "soft" periods in politics and a "freeze" or "thaw" in the arts. Although the Soviet leaders regard literature merely as a super-structure, they are in fact well aware of the impact that writers can make on a nation in moments of crisis. Khrushchev is reputed to have stated to a group of Soviet writers in 1957 that had the Hungarians shot a few of their "troublemakers" (i.e., rebellious writers) in time, there would never have been an uprising in Hungary. It is also significant that before and after the military intervention of the five Warsaw Pact countries in Czechoslo-vakia, the Soviet press reserved its special wrath and invective for those writers and journalists who wanted "to undermine socialist achievements" in that country.

All this does not mean that in Eastern Europe *every* writer has to be politically committed. Post-Stalinist communism is by definition more flex-ible and less coercive in matters of secondary importance than its monolithic predecessor; composers, painters and even writers can now afford to be apolitical in most Eastern European countries. Although formal experiments are not necessarily encouraged, they are no longer banned by the party overseers of culture. The emergence of a neo-avant-garde trend in the fine arts, in the theater and in literature was a feature of Poland in the 1960s but also in Hungary in the late 1970s (and in Yugoslavia throughout both decades). It is symptomatic that the editor of the Hungarian cultural review *Mozgó Világ* was sacked in 1983, not because of the paper's neo-avant-garde literary tendencies but because of the unorthodox sociological and historical essays it contained. As for apolitical (social or psychological) realism, one could argue that in 1984 this was regarded as "safe" literature by most Eastern European regimes. That is why Vladimir Páral is published in large editions in Czechoslovakia, why Kuśniewicz and Kuncewiczowa in Poland, Magda Szabó or Iván Mándy in Hungary are constantly on the list of publishing houses. While 10 to 15 years ago the growth of apolitical writing seemed to worry the ideological watchdogs, today it seems that in spite of ritual exhortations to produce literature of an edifying socialist kind, "apolitical attitudes ... are preferred to any genuine artistic, philosophical or indeed political commitment," according to the writer Jan Hrachor.

We have mentioned the demand for the supremacy of socialist realism as a constant factor in communist cultural policy. An equally important principle is the organizational control exercised by the state and party over artists. No wholly independent artistic union is tolerated, for such an organi-zation would sooner or later represent an ideological challenge to the ruling bureaucracy. For example, the revolt of Hungarian intellectuals, which pre-pared the ground for the 1956 revolution, began in the Writers' Association; the struggle to overthrow Novotný gained strength in 1967 when Czech and Slovak writers took a stand against him at the Fourth Congress of their Writers' Union. The role played by the Warsaw branch of the Polish Writers' Union in the student protest movement of February–March 1968 is also well known. The Communist party must retain control over these potentially dangerous organizations even if in certain transitional periods it is willing to make compromises. In times of political crisis the professional association can be suspended or closed down, as for example in 1957 in Hungary, or during Husák's "normalization" campaign in Czechoslovakia during 1969–70. In Poland, after the 16 heady months of the Solidarity period and the longer and more depressing period of martial law, all artistic associations were asked to purge their leadership and those refusing to comply were disbanded. The new Writers' Union in Poland is at present a pale imitation of the old one; approximately one-fifth of the old membership joined, and among those there are few genuine writers. On the other hand, there are signs that the pliant and for a long time strictly controlled Hungarian Writers' Association has now begun to play a more active role in society. The new leadership voted in at the 1981 congress reflects the resolve of the Hungarian writers to strengthen their autonomy in a situation, when in other Eastern European countries the margin of freedom enjoyed by their colleagues is getting dangerously narrow.

CENSORSHIP

Censorship is the most important method of negative control exercised by communist governments. The severity of censorship varies from country to country, and from one period to another; some Eastern European countries (e.g. Romania and Hungary) claim not to have formal censorship at all. In any case, censorship operates on two levels: external and internal. The external forms of censorship are not the same in every communist country—for instance, in Czechoslovakia each editorial office has its own censor, whereas in Poland censorship is centralized, and a copy of each newspaper or periodical has to be sent to the censor's office for approval before publication. In all communist countries, the editor of a literary review as well as the editor of a publishing house is a part-time political censor—this is, so to speak, written into the responsibilities of the job. In countries that have no formal censorship, like Hungary, editors are even more cautious and circumspect than elsewhere because they are liable to be reprimanded or sacked following the publication of an objectionable article. While in Poland, Hungary or Czechoslovakia there is no law to forbid publication abroad, in the Soviet Union this is immediately interpreted as anti-Soviet and is punished by severe reprimand (as in the case of Yevtushenko), officially organized campaigns of vilification (Pasternak) or sentencing to jail or labor camp (Sinyavsky, Daniel).

Apart from the external machinery of censorship, the "internal censor" has been very active in communist regimes. An artist who has lived in a society that for decades has had so little regular contact with foreigners as the Soviet Union, must find it hard not to conform. It became second nature for many to question inspiration in terms of whether it was "correct" or "incorrect" from the party point of view. No one likes writing a poem or painting a canvas that will never reach its public. Yet the extraordinary resilience of those Soviet writers who survived the purges of the 1930s and the partial breakdown of censorship after the 20th Congress of the Soviet Communist party is a hopeful sign in itself. Akhmatova wrote her moving cycle of poems *Requiem*, Bulgakov *The Master and Margarita* and Pasternak

Doctor Zhivago in the worst years of oppression. It could be argued that they all belonged to the older generation of intellectuals born before the Bolshevik revolution, so they were less prone to hypocrisy and servile opportunism. The rise of a new and more daring generation (that of Yevtushenko and Voznesensky) and a slow but steady erosion of "internal censorship" occurred in the late 1950s. However, the unprecedented flow of samizdat, of self-printed mimeographed periodicals and novels, from the Soviet Union in the course of the last 15 years indicates that if the Soviet government wishes to contain the wave of legitimate criticism from its young intellectuals, it will once again have to resort to traditional autocratic methods of control, since the functioning of the internal censor is becoming less and less reliable.

PARTY CONTROL IN EASTERN EUROPE

Poland

This is particularly true of Eastern Europe, especially Poland and Czechoslovakia. In these countries, socialist realism left less of an impression on literature than it did in the Soviet Union. Nevertheless, before 1953 the system of external and internal checks worked quite well and it was only in the permissive atmosphere of the post-1953 thaw that important books critical of the system came to be published. Between 1954 and 1957, Poland enjoyed the greatest artistic freedom (with the exception of Yugoslavia). Apart from the politically charged works of Andrzejewski, Brandys, Marek Hłasko and Adam Ważyk, abstract painting, modern music and the experimental theater flourished in Warsaw and Cracow. Polish films, especially the works of Wajda, Munk and Polański, won the acclaim of Western juries and audiences. Gomułka's increasingly dogmatic rule, however, put an end to these developments: first, by curbing intellectual freedom and exuberance, later by strengthening the censor's hand to the point of the absurd.

This process, which can perhaps be defined as the rollback of intellectual freedom, culminated in 1968 when the official ban imposed on Dejmek's production of Mickiewicz's classic *The Forefathers' Eve* (*Dziady*) Part III sparked off student demonstrations and a vicious campaign of the government against "antisocialist" and "Zionist" intellectuals. When Gierek came to power in the wake of the workers' riots of December 1970, the party's control of culture relaxed, but by 1976 most of the old grievances (narrow-minded and senseless censorship, lack of information in the media, bans on politically controversial books) reappeared. New riots in Radom and the Ursus factory near Warsaw took place in 1976, the year of the emergence of the Workers' Self-Defense Committee (KOR) that, for the first time since 1956, bridged the gap between workers and intellectuals and in a sense was a prelude to the near-miraculous birth of Solidarity, the first autonomous trade union movement in postwar communist history. During the Solidarity period there was a new relaxation of central controls that, although it led to an unprecedented flourishing of the cultural press and a pluralistic cultural life, did not include the radio and the television, tightly controlled by the government. In July 1981, a new and less restrictive censorship law was pased by the

Sejm. It was during these months that Andrej Wajda made his film *Man of Iron*, for all its rhetoric a lasting memorial to the struggle for autonomy of the Polish working class.

The military takeover of December 1981 created a new situation. Censorship, including widespread telephone tapping, was imposed on a society that by now had got used to free speech and open debate; the reactivization of underground structures became inevitable, including a samizdat press and publishing network. While a number of Polish writers did not return to Poland from abroad, or left the country as a reaction to Jaruzelski's coup (Jacek Bierezin, Janusz Głowacki, Wojciech Karpiński and Adam Zagajewski), others were interned and only released in 1983. The lifting of military rule did not lead to a real normalization; most artistic associations were disbanded or their democratically elected leadership was forced to resign. The new, "loyal" Writers' Association, though it has large sums of money at its disposal, hardly represents the Polish literary community. As for the Polish PEN Club, it was suspended by the military in December 1981 and has been left in a curious limbo ever since. Many Polish writers who are not members of their new union write mainly for the underground press or for Catholic cultural periodicals (*Tygodnik Powszechny*, *Znak*, *Więź*), which enjoy certain privileges, or in some cases for both. Publishing of books in the West has also become a common practice, and although on occasion writers such as Marek Nowakowski were persecuted for publishing their work abroad, there are others who so far have not suffered for their "double life." The worst effect of the suppression of Solidarity, and of military rule, according to Czesław Miłosz, was "a politicization of the imagination," the obsession of writers with their "moral duty" to write against the regime. In fact, the present level of repression is still far less severe than in post-1968 Czechoslovakia; a considerable amount of cultural diversity is tolerated and the Jaruzelski regime is trying to win back the intelligentsia more with bribes and selective concessions than with threats and degrading treatment.

Czechoslovakia

In Czechoslovakia, apart from a short-lived glimmer of hope in 1956, artistic freedom began to expand about 1963. This ushered in a few good years for Czech filmmakers, but the publication of such politically explosive books as Mňačko's *Delayed Reports* and *The Taste of Power* were fought by Novotný to the last moment of his unimaginative rule. After January 1968, censorship was first relaxed, then lifted completely; there were two or three months in Czechoslovakia during which practically any literary work of merit could be published. In this short-lived "Dubček Era," literary weeklies like *Literární Listý* in Prague and *Kultúrny Život* in Bratislava were important rallying points for progressive writers and journalists, though the Slovak writers, concerned with Slovak autonomy, were not so united in their insistence on radical reforms as their Czech colleagues. The purge following the military intervention of Warsaw Pact countries also hit Czechs far worse than Slovaks; out of the 500,000 party members dismissed, about 90 percent were Czechs. Consequently, the anti-intellectual and repressive policies of the Husák regime wrought much more damage on Czech culture than on the Slovaks—the only outstanding Slovak writer to have become a nonperson after 1970 was the novelist Dominik Tatarka, while in the Czech lands the list is too long to enumerate. Some Czechoslovak writers of distinction (Milan Kundera, A. J. Liehm, E. Goldstücker, J. Škvorecký and Jan Vladislav) chose emigration, the playwright Václav Havel was imprisoned and others, not necessarily active during the Prague Spring, chose noncollaboration with the Husák regime. Since 1973 the samizdat publisher Petlice (Padlock) has brought out more than 200 titles. Its authors include well-known prose writers such as Ivan Klima, Pavel Kohout and Ludvik Vaculik and poets such as Jiři Kolář and Jan Skácel. Nobel Prize-winner Jaroslav Seifert's cycle of poems *Plague Column* was also first published by Padlock.

In 1977, Husák's so-called normalization efforts suffered a setback—the Charter 77 movement emerged. A charter for human rights was issued, initially signed by around 250 intellectuals whose number later grew to over a thousand. Nonetheless, the charter signers were unable to mobilize the working class, whose attitudes remained, by and large, apathetic. It looked as if the main success of dissenting Czech intellectuals during the past 15 years was the preservation of their integrity (and their sanity) against enormous odds. Although the recent economic difficulties of the Husák regime may ease matters in culture, no liberalization is expected in the near future, and the Prague Spring of 1968 will remain as a distant beacon, a reminder of the historic chance for modernization that was lost because of the boundless opportunism of the present masters of Czechoslovakia.

Hungary

The spell of artistic freedom that Hungary enjoyed between 1954 and 1957 was reduced to a minimum in the first years of Kádár's rule; many writers chose silence or employed their talents exclusively as translators. In the early 1960s, however, when all the writers imprisoned after the 1956 revolution were released, a new cultural deal was struck and a more liberal cultural policy emerged that culminated in the publication of Tibor Déry's work, of Sándor Weöres's poetry (philosophically alien to the ruling ideology) and of József Lengyel's dramatic account of his experience in Soviet labor camps. The younger generation made its successful debut with such works of social and psychological realism as Endre Fejes's *A Generation of Rust* (1962), Akos Kertész's *Makra* (1971) and György Konrád's *The Case Worker* (1969, English translation 1974). The New Economic Mechanism introduced in 1968 was supposed to create a more relaxed cultural climate, and while a number of exciting and probing Hungarian films were made in the 1970s (by Gothár, Makk, I. Szabó and Sándor, to mention only a few names), the long-expected "new wave" in prose materialized only in the second half of the decade (with writers such as Esterházy, Nádas and Hajnóczy). The early 1970s were peppered by such incidents as the ban on the publication of József Lengyel's last novel *Confrontation*, the arrest of Konrád and his sociologist friend Iván Szelényi (Szelényi later emigrated to the West while Konrád was allowed out of Hungary on long study-trips to West Berlin and the United States) and unsuccessful attempts by some writers to unseat György Aczél, the key man responsible for the selectively liberal cultural policies of the regime. The period between 1976 and 1983 has been character-ized by two parallel developments: an opening to Hungarian émigré writers, including opportunities to publish in Hungary, and to the experimentations of the young modernists; and, at the same time, the appearance of a substantial number of samizdat publications. These had their origins in the warm res-ponse of Hungarian intellectuals to the Czech Charter 77 movement; by 1981 the Hungarian opposition published mimeographed journals and even founded an underground publishing house AB. Samizdat publications include a new novel by György Konrád, otherwise unavailable in Hungary, a book of poems by György Petri, a Hungarian translation of Bill Lomax's book on the Hungarian Revolution of 1956, and many others. While people active in the samizdat movement are often harassed and occasionally beaten up by the police (as happened in 1983 to Gábor Demszky), there have been no serious attempts on the part of the Hungarian authorities to stamp out all manifestations of unauthorized dissent. At present, Hungary is still "the most liberal" country of the communist bloc, with a vivid intellectual life and a fairly pluralistic literary production. The recent case of the Budapest periodical *Mozgó Világ* and the press campaign against Sándor Csoóri (a distinguished poet who spoke up forcefully in defense of the Hungarian minority in Czechoslovakia) indicated however, the existence of a strong group in the higher party echelons that had grown weary of the pragmatic and cautious practices of the regime vis-à-vis its recalcitrant intellectuals and wanted to see more repressive measures against them.

Yugoslavia
After Tito's break with Stalin in 1948, the Yugoslav cultural scene was domi-nated by a permissiveness unimaginable in other Communist countries at the time and wistfully admired by them well into the 1960s. The first major split that divided Yugoslav literature into rival camps of realists and moder-nists was followed by others. Now there exists a multitude of groups and periodicals, each complete with its own artistic method and theory, most of them subsidized by state or local government funds. Socialist realism has long been buried and forgotten, and for many years artists not defying or attacking the basic assumption of Yugoslav socialism were more or less safe from official interference. Nevertheless, in 1975, the Zagreb-based philo-sophical review *Praxis*, for well over a decade an important forum for revision-ist Marxism was banned by the Yugoslav government; at the same time a number of Marxist professors were dismissed from the Philosophical Faculty at Belgrade University. There were also instances of jailing intellec-tuals for political dissent—the well-known cases of Milovan Djilas and Mihajlo Mihajlov were soon followed by others.

Since Tito's death, the Yugoslav leadership has been unable to solve the economic crisis affecting Yugoslavia and it was partly this impotence that has led to restrictions in cultural matters. In 1980, Dobrica Ćosić and Ljubomir Tadić tried to launch an independent journal *Javnost* that, though it enjoyed the support of Serbian intellectuals, was sharply attacked and rejected by the Yugoslav party leaders. In 1981, the Serbian poet Gojko Djogo was arrested and his collection of verse, *Woolen Times*, confiscated by the authorities for having represented "falsely, and with ill intent, social and political circumstances in Yugoslavia," including an alleged slander on the late President Tito. Although a number of distinguished Yugoslav writers protested against his imprisonment, Djogo was sentenced to two years in prison and was released only in May 1983. Other writers jailed in recent years include the Croatian poet Vlado Gotovac and several Albanian writers involved in the Kosovo unrest, the best known of whom was probably Adem Demaci. These cases show that fear of nationalist (and by implication, "secessionist") agitation remains one of the main concerns of the ruling elite, some members of which nevertheless sympathize with the dissident movement pressing for democratic reforms. At any rate, the recent reprisals against Yugoslav intellectuals (which include the suppression or the purge of journals and publishing houses as well as trials for organizing "illegal discussion groups") contribute to the skepticism with which other Eastern Europeans now view the Yugoslav model in cultural policy.

Romania

The most striking thing about Romania is how its ruling ideology has evolved (or regressed) from an enforced internationalism in the wake of the end of World War II to a thinly-veiled ultranationalism since the 1960s. Various stages in this process were the elimination of the group of "internationalist" communists in 1952 (Pauker, Luka, Georgescu), the withdrawal of Soviet troops from Romania (1958), Ceauşescu's rise to power as secretary general of the Romanian Communist party (1965) and his election as president of the Romanian Socialist Republic (1974). There were periods in Romanian intellectual life when party controls momentarily slackened—in 1956–57 just as in 1968–70, when the leadership needed every support it could get. While in these periods a few courageous writers stood up for the autonomy of literature, subsequent events (which in 1958–59 included imprisonment of a large number of intellectuals) showed that the communist leadership could use and manipulate them almost at will. Ceauşescu returned from China in 1971 with his own ideas of a "cultural revolution," and Romanian literature has been suffering the effects of his theories and despotic practices ever since. Institutionalized nepotism, inefficient management, widespread corruption and chronic shortages of goods (including paper for the press and for book publishing) make Romania one of the most oppressive countries in the Eastern bloc. The ultranationalist and self-congratulatory rhetoric of Ceauşescu cannot hide the fact that Romania is the only communist country apart from the USSR where dissidents are confined to psychiatric clinics, where the security police regularly beats up political opponents and where, since April 1983, all private citizens have to register their typewriters with the police.

Although the work of Marin Preda, M. Constantinescu, D. R. Popescu, Ivasiuc and Buzura show the vigor and possibilities of contemporary Romanian literature, the publishing houses are inundated with sycophantic poetry praising Ceauşescu and the party, and with pseudohistorical novels glorifying carefully selected episodes and personalities of Romanian history, including the sadistic madman Vlad Ţepes (better known as Vlad the Impaler), the

15th-century Prince of Wallachia. A typical case of an aggressively nationalistic piece of writing was Ioan Lăcrănjan's *Discourse on Transylvania* (1982), the factual falsifications and intolerant tone of which provoked a response from Hungary, including a well-argued essay by György Száraz. Resistance against the Ceauşescu regime has so far been sporadic and isolated. While some Romanian writers defected to the West (Virgil Tanase, Petru Popescu, Ion Caraion) and a number of writers belonging to Romania's two-million strong Hungarian ethnic minority emigrated to Hungary, the most celebrated case of a Romanian writer opposing the regime was that of Paul Goma. Goma, who now lives in Paris, has pointed out that although there is no formal censorship in Romania, actual censorship is stronger than ever; as to the possibility of change, his views are pessimistic; if it comes, it will not be initiated by Romanian intellectuals who, whatever their inner conviction, have in recent history been pliant and obedient servants of authority.

Bulgaria

In Bulgaria, where conservative dogmatism had strong native roots, the Soviet model of socialist realism was on the whole faithfully emulated until the 20th Congress of the Soviet Communist party. Nonetheless, the appearance of the "new critics" (Zdavko Petrov, Tsvetan Stoyanov, Vlado Svintilla) between 1952 and 1956 may have prepared the ground for the literary renewal of the 1960s. The young poets of this period, Konstantin Pavlov, Lyubomir Levchev and Stefan Tsanev, wrote about their experiences in a more dynamic, rebellious and subjective tone than their predecessors and were hailed by readers not unlike Yevtushenko's generation in the USSR. Following in their footsteps, a number of prose writers also jettisoned the antiquated tenets of Zhdanovian socialist realism, initiating a complex critical view of reality and the human personality. These included Vasil Popov, Nikolai Khaytov and Pavel Vezhinov; an interesting newcomer is Ivan Arnaudov whose 1980 novel was praised as a fascinating work, innovative in technique and style. Bulgaria also had its homebred structuralist critics of whom at least two, Julia Kristeva and Tsvetan Todorov, emigrated and are working in Paris.

A recent broadening of creative possibilities does not mean that the Communist party has renounced its prerogative to supervise literature and the arts; it only shows that the Zhivkov regime is pragmatic in its treatment of intellectuals. The Bulgarian pattern seems to be short periods of cultural liberalization (1956–57, 1961–63, 1976) followed by longer periods of mildly repressive equilibrium. In fact, all periods of "rebellion" ended in a compromise; the rebels were either integrated into the system or politically neutralized. In 1963, for example, the outspoken journal *Literarni Novini* was suppressed and other cultural papers purged, but at the same time Zhivkov made sure that some leading writers of the previous thaw were given posts in the cultural establishment. This did not entirely stave off dissent. When several Bulgarian writers, among them Hristo Ganev and Valeri Petrov, refused to sign an official Bulgarian letter condemning Solzhenitsyn, they were expelled from the Bulgarian Communist party; the writer Lazar Tsvetkov was jailed for his involvement in samizdat publication; and a number of writers were quietly allowed to emigrate to the West. The latter included novelist Georgi Markov whose attacks broadcast by the BBC incensed the Bulgarian leadership and who consequently was assassinated by agents of the Bulgarian security police in London in 1978. Nevertheless, the integration of some "rebel writers" of the 1960s into the establishment means that, for all the innate conservatism of that body, perhaps those Bulgarian intellectuals who in Blaga Dimitrova's words "work quietly away within the system" have a chance of creating a more tolerant and liberal atmosphere in the future.

East Germany

The German Democratic Republic (GDR) is an economically prosperous but culturally impoverished state. This has nothing to do with attendance at concerts of classical music or numbers of copies of works by Lessing or Goethe printed. What makes the GDR "impoverished" is the ideological rigidity and strict controls imposed upon society by the Communist party (SED). Although a cautious economic reform was introduced in 1963 (to be dropped finally in 1970), neither Ulbricht who retired in 1971, nor his successor Erich Honecker could accept the pluralistic principle inherent in the free development of culture. In other words, while segments of the technological intelligentsia may have been reconciled to *Abgrenzung* (demarcation) and the concomitant material benefits of technological progress controlled by the party, intellectuals in the humanities keep asking awkward questions, at the same time pointing out the gap between the ideals and the reality of their avowedly socialist state—an attitude that inevitably leads to confrontation. At any rate, the GDR has incomplete control over the channels of information; according to recent estimates, between 80 and 90 percent of the East German population listens to West German radio and TV programs.

At the Eighth Congress of the SED in 1971 Honecker claimed that if artists proceeded from a firm socialist basis, there would be no taboos for them in art and literature. Events in the second half of the 1970s, however, showed the hollowness of this statement. Neither Robert Havemann, Professor of Physical Chemistry in East Berlin, nor Rudolf Bahro, for many years a state functionary in the GDR, could publish their Marxist critique of East German socialism in East Germany; moreover, the exodus of writers and intellectuals that had started in the 1950s gained new momentum. In 1976, Wolf Biermann, a popular poet and balladeer, critical of conditions in both parts of Germany, was stripped of his East German citizenship while on a concert tour in West Germany. This move provoked a wave of protests among East German artists and writers, but the GDR authorities, instead of relenting, forced even more of their critics to emigrate to the German Federal Republic. Sarah Kirsch, Günter Kunert and Rainer Kunze all left the GDR; the veteran Communist writer Stefan Heym did not leave, but became the target of furious press attacks. In the meantime, a law was passed enabling the East German authorities to jail writers for the publication of their work in West Germany. It was invoked in December 1980 when a young writer, Lutz Rathenow, was briefly detained for having published his short stories in West Germany; others arrested and harassed on similar grounds include Frank-Wolf Matthies (who after his release emigrated to the West) and philosopher Lutz Hesse (in jail in Dresden in 1984). What must have worried the authorities was the fact that the level of opposition did not seem to have declined among the young; although no serious samizdat network exists in East Germany, readings of nonconformist work have taken place in recent years in private homes and churches. The unofficial peace movement also activated for dissent a group of so far apolitical young workers and intellectuals. While valuable artistic work has been produced by writers not in open disagreement with the regime (Volker Braun, Christa Wolf), the bureaucratic conformism of the party and state apparat forces underground or diverts to the West any serious social criticism or artistic innovation deemed to be dangerous for the present status quo.

INCENTIVES

Until now only the *negative controls* of the Communist party over writers and artists have been discussed. There are, of course, positive ones as well—incentives can be enlisted into the service of communism not only by attractive ideas or veiled threats but by rewards as well. In countries where the state is the only employer, the artists enjoy the same benefits as other state employees. These are special funds established for them; for example, the Literary Fund gives loans and grants to writers, maintains "creative homes" (retreats for creative work) at secluded places of beauty in and around the country and supports writers' families in cases of need. Besides these altogether admirable funds (which support even artists who are not members of the professional association in their field of activity), the annual awards given by the state to outstanding artists represent a very strong incentive. In the Soviet Union, the Lenin Prize (up to 1956, the Stalin Prize) is awarded to writers and artists; in Poland the State Prize, in Hungary the Kossuth Prize and some minor artistic and literary prizes serve the same purpose. In some communist countries the heavily subsidized system of royalties is designed to make the writer's occupation socially desirable and at the same time rather privileged. The fact that what the state gives to artists in appreciation of their work can be, if political circumstances warrant it, easily withheld, undoubtedly helps to cement the solidarity of some artists behind the regime.

THE ARTIST'S POSITION IN COMMUNIST SOCIETIES

Socially and also materially, the artist is a privileged citizen in communist society, successful artists being more privileged than average party functionaries because, for one thing, they have less to worry about. On the other hand, some artists may feel that the price of a good life—conformity and political "good manners" in Eastern Europe, active political engagement in the Soviet Union—is too high for them. The more nonconformist the artists are by nature, the more rebellious they become when that authority that first seemed to encourage their search for truth, frustrates their creativity under a different political situation. This is when the force of national tradition, the psychologically binding "posture" of the writer or poet usually reasserts itself—for example, in Poland and Hungary in 1956 when even seasoned communist writers took an anti-Soviet stand, and in Czechoslovakia in 1968.

An artist's loyalty toward the communist regime can be swayed for one or more of the following reasons: revolutionary, national or aesthetic-individualistic discontent. When all three are mobilized together on a wide front, the intellectual movement is capable of changing, if not the whole structure of the regime, at least its ugliest features. This is what removed Rákosi and Novotný from power and it could happen to others. Perhaps the Soviet leaders are aware of this danger and this is why they keep such a close watch on rebellious writers and intellectuals in Kiev and Vilnius as well as in Moscow. For apart from "charismatic" politicians (at present nonexistent in the Soviet Union), only intellectuals and, above all, writers can influence public opinion effectively and prepare the painful transition of the Soviet Union from Stalinism to the pluralism of modern 20th-century society.

FURTHER READING

Birnbaum, Henrik, and Eekman, Thomas, eds. *Fiction and Drama in Eastern and Southeastern Europe*. Columbus, Ohio: Slavica, 1980.

Gömöri, George, and Newman, Charles, eds. *New Writing of East Europe*. Chicago: Quadrangle, 1968.

Hayward, Max. *Writers in Russia 1917–1978*. London: Harvill, 1983.

Kołakowski, Leszek. "The Intelligentsia" in Brumberg, Abraham, ed. *Poland: Genesis of a Revolution*. New York: Random House, 1983.

Liehm, Antonín, and Kussi, Peter, eds. *The Writing on the Wall: An Anthology of Contemporary Czech Literature*. New York: Karz-Cohl, 1983.

Ludz, Peter. *The Changing Elite in East Germany*. Cambridge, Massachusetts: MIT Press, 1972.

Silnitsky, Frantisek, et al., eds. *Communism and Eastern Europe*. Brighton, Sussex: Harvester, 1979.

Slavov, Atanas. *The "Thaw" in Bulgarian Literature*. Boulder Colorado: East European Monographs, 1981.

Tőkés, Rudolf L., ed. *Dissent in the U.S.S.R. Politics, Ideology, and People*. Baltimore, London: The John Hopkins University Press, 1975.

RELIGION IN THE SOVIET UNION AND EASTERN EUROPE

JUDY DEMPSEY

ROMAN CATHOLICS AND UNIATES IN EASTERN EUROPE AND THE SOVIET UNION

AFTER the communist takeover of Eastern Europe, it was relatively easy to speak of a uniform communist policy toward religion throughout the region. Under Stalin, religious orders and communities, churches, schools and religious institutions were closed. The policy appeared straightforward; the aim was to secularize society, and in the process weaken if not destroy those areas of autonomy, such as religion, that would have effectively challenged the monopoly of power exercised by the ruling Communist parties. The attitude and policy of the Communist party toward religion over the past 35 years reflect the fact that Eastern Europe is by no means a monolithic entity, and shares neither similar political cultures or similar belief systems. The policy changes fall into three main categories:

1. The immediate impact of the post-1948 communist takeovers on religious life.
2. The *Ostpolitik* initiated by Pope John XXIII and continued by his successor, Pope Paul VI.
3. The reappraisal by the Polish Pope, John Paul II, of church-state relations in Eastern Europe and the Soviet Union.

Within these contexts, each country in Eastern Europe will be briefly considered in the text following.

ALBANIA

Only 10 percent of Albanians are Roman Catholics. The majority of the population (70 percent) is Muslim and 20 percent is Orthodox. In the 19th century, during the Turkish occupation, Catholicism played a role in protecting Albanian national culture. During the period of national awakening (1878–1912), the Catholic nationalist leader, Vasa Pasha, closely identified Catholicism with Albanian nationalism. After the communist takeover in

565

1944, Enver Hoxha did not completely suppress the churches, but did supress the teaching of religion in schools. Gradually the religious media and press were censored, the churches forbidden to undertake any form of social work and their lands confiscated. The state very soon gained complete control over all church appointments, that is, the appointment of bishops and archbishops, editors of religious newspapers and other prominent figures affiliated with the church. (This was the case in most of Eastern Europe.) By the end of the 1940s in Albania, however, the Catholic church, as well as the Muslims and the Orthodox church, was completely deprived of any independent income and became dependent on the state. Many church leaders were sent to prison camps. In 1951, the Catholic church was forced to sever its links with the Vatican. A campaign discrediting religion and describing religion as inherently irreconcilable with the communist outlook lasted throughout the 1950s and the 1960s.

Unlike those countries in Eastern Europe that responded to a new Vatican initiative begun in the 1960s, which attempted to redefine the relationship between church and state under communism, no such change took place in Albania. In 1966, an "ideological and cultural revolution" designed to suppress all religious practices intensified. In 1967, the statutes stipulating the relationship between church and state were annulled. This paved the way for the announcement by Enver Hoxha himself that Albania had become the "first atheistic state." All buildings used for public worship were closed. Catholic and Orthodox libraries or churches, if not closed, were turned into museums. Organized religion was virtually destroyed. Vatican Radio reported in 1973 that "only vague and rare traces of the Catholic church remained." As a rule, those who have been caught praying or carrying out their religious duties face imprisonment or even execution. One recent case was that of Bishop Ernesto Coba, the apostolic administrator of the archdiocese of Shkodër who was beaten to death in 1979 by camp guards for celebrating Easter.

Nevertheless, and despite the intensive propaganda campaign against religious ritual and activities, there are repeated reports coming out of Albania suggesting that certain religious practices are still being observed. For instance, the Muslim population regularly observes the one-month fasting period of Ramadan. Muslim graves still face Mecca in some districts. The graves of Muslim women are said still to be dug deeper than those of Muslim men, in keeping with tradition. In the case of Christians, an Albanian newspaper report (*Bashkimi*, September 18, 1973) complained that at one agricultural cooperative, nobody, including Communist party cadres, reported for work on Easter Day, even though, as the paper reported, they were still in the middle of the spring sowing. To combat such activities, the Albanian media launched a wide campaign during the mid-1970s to "increase the struggle against religion." To demonstrate its success, a church in Shkodër was opened as the "Museum of Atheism." Here visitors are shown "the inhuman acts committed by those who have worn cassocks or carried the Koran."

Against this background of almost relentless religious persecution and propaganda, the Vatican under John Paul II has attempted to provide some moral support to believers in Albania. In his inaugural address in 1978, the Pope spoke in Albanian—a reminder to believers there that he is concerned with their situation. In September 1980, in response to the news that a priest had been sentenced to death in Albania for fulfilling his religious duties, the Pope sharply criticized religious persecution by the authorities in Tirana. In November 1983, Vatican Radio denounced the "very harsh and systematic" religious persecution and asked all Catholics to pray for believers in Albania. And during a visit to the burial place in southern Italy of St. Nicholas of Myra, one of the patron saints of the Russian Orthodox church, John Paul said that he was "thinking of our brothers and sisters of Albania who cannot openly express their religious faith, a fundamental right of the human person."

BULGARIA

As in Albania, Roman Catholics in Bulgaria constitute a very small minority of some 50,000. After the communist takeover, religious instruction was banned in schools. In 1949, relations between the Vatican and Sofia were broken. In 1952, the Catholic bishop of Nikopolis, Monsignor Eugene Bossilkov, was arrested and executed. Some degree of liberalization took place after Stalin's death in 1953. Latin and Uniate Catholics and Orthodox delegates, for example, were allowed to attend sessions of the Vatican Council. But the Catholic Church has no seminary, and in 1960 it was reported that the Catholic Church consisted of only 30 churches, one bishop and some 40 priests.

In the mid 1970s, there were signs that a thaw was taking place between the Vatican and the Bulgarian authorities. Communist party leader and head of state Todor Zhivkov held a private meeting with Pope Paul VI. The pope expressed hope that Catholics would continue to be permitted religious freedom in Bulgaria, and that though few in number, they would contribute to meeting the needs of Bulgarian society. The visit to the Vatican by the Bulgarian leader was primarily prompted by the need of the authorities to gain access to those Bulgarian archives held in the Vatican library. Bulgaria was preparing to celebrate the 1,300th anniversary of the nation. The talks were important from the Vatican's point of view also. Zhivkov approved the appointment by the papacy of new bishops for the two vacant Latin-rite dioceses. Bogdan Dobranov (who was secretly consecrated as its apostolic administrator in 1959) became apostolic vicar of Sofia-Plovdiv. Vasco Seirekov was appointed bishop of Nikopolis but died soon afterward, in 1977. Relations between Sofia and Rome were stepped up after Zhivkov's visit. In November 1975, Bulgarian pilgrims were allowed to visit Rome for the Holy Year. And in the same month, Cardinal Agostino Casaroli, the Vatican secretary of state, met Bulgarian Foreign Minister Petr Mladenov in Sofia.

In practical terms, the situation did not improve markedly for priests, the majority of whom were in their 70s. But when John Paul II met Mladenov in December 1978 in Rome, the pope stressed that the church "was not seeking any privileges but needs a little *Lebensraum* to fulfill its religious mission." Six months later, Sofia-Plovdiv, hitherto an apostolic vicarate, was raised to the status of a bishopric. Bogdan Dobranov became a full diocesan bishop and Samuel Dzhundrin was named bishop of Nikopolis. (In 1952, the latter had been sentenced to 12 years' imprisonment on charges of spying.) The appointment, initiated by the Vatican and accepted by the Bulgarian authorities marked a positive change in relations between church and state. Small but significant other changes took place. During the anniversary in 1981 of the apostles to the Slavs, Cyril and Methodius, the Bulgarian authorities celebrated the occasion and Catholic delegates visited the Vatican for some of the celebrations. The authorities also allowed two young priests— a Uniate and a Latin rite—to study in Rome for two years. Talks are taking place concerning the possibility of reopening a Catholic seminary in Bulgaria.

CZECHOSLOVAKIA

Czechoslovakia is probably unique in Eastern Europe in its conduct of church-state relations. Repression against believers has continued almost unabated since 1948. There was a brief liberalization in the mid-1960s and during the Prague Spring. Yet paradoxically, of all the countries in Eastern Europe, with the exception of Poland, the religious revival has been strongest. That revival began not when the Polish pope ascended St. Peter's throne in 1978; it occurred some years previously, in the early 1970s, due partly to the repression, partly in reaction to the passivity of the Catholic church hierarchy in Czechoslovakia, perceived by believers. Catholicism in Slovakia, where religion is closely identified with nationhood and nationalism, has in recent years provided an important focus for believers. The religious revival is strongest there where nearly 80 percent of the population is Catholic.

The Stalinist Era
Following the communist takeover, two laws were passed, both related to church-state relations. The first, concerning agrarian reform, led to the confiscation of nearly all church lands (about 320,000 hectares). The second law, concerning education, nationalized all schools and prohibited religious teaching in schools. In 1948, most of the Catholic publications were suppressed. Catholic charity organizations, Catholic hospitals and Caritas, the welfare organization, were brought under the aegis of the government. In 1949, the authorities stepped up their campaign against the Catholic church. All meetings, retreats and clerical congresses were prohibited, in order to weaken the institutional and social links between bishops and priests. This also meant that priests would be increasingly separated from the laity since the prohibitions on church meetings denied regular contact with practicing Catholics—an essential element of Catholicism. Church property was liquidated, thus depriving the clergy of economic independence.

In May 1949, the Czech bishops issued a major pastoral letter criticizing the antireligion policies. In an attempt to divide the clergy, the authorities then arrested a splinter group of the Catholic Action Association. The main function of this group was to seek some support from Catholics for the communist regime. The group was, however, allowed to publish a journal —*Katolické Noviný*—which continues to this day. On June 15, 1949, the archbishop of Prague, Joseph Beran, was harassed by the authorities. Four days later he was arrested. The following October, a State Office for Ecclesiastical Affairs was set up; government officials were now responsible for all religious affairs. All clergy received a state salary, appointments had to be approved by the state, and priests had to swear an oath of loyalty to the state. By the end of 1949, the state controlled the episcopal administration. Pastoral letters and all ecclesiastical statements were censored. In April 1950, the remaining monasteries and convents were closed down. In 1951, the Vatican estimated that some 2,000 out of 7,000 secular and regular clerics had been deported, imprisoned, or subjected to forced labor. Two out of the original six seminaries remained open, with considerable restrictions. Before the communist takeover, Czechoslovakia had had 13 Latin-rite dioceses and one Uniate-rite diocese; by 1955, 13 bishops had been removed from their sees. Some were imprisoned; others were prevented from exercising their administrative and religious duties. The state-sponsored *Pacem in Terris*, founded in September 1951, served as a propaganda organization the main function of which was to publicize the healthy state of relations between the regime and the Catholic church. Priests were forced to join. It was only under Pope John Paul II that *Pacem in Terris* became publicly discredited, at least from the Vatican's point of view and from that of some of the Czech bishops.

Czechoslovakia and Ostpolitik

After Pius XII died in 1958, a gradual shift began to take place in the Vatican's approach toward the Soviet Union and Eastern Europe. The new pope, John XXIII, who had considerable experience in the Balkans, argued that if the institutional and hierarchical structures of the Catholic churches were to be preserved, then the Vatican would have to begin negotiating with the communist authorities. There was a practical consideration as well. Priests were needed, especially in Hungary and Czechoslovakia. And the only way to allow priests to carry out their religious duties was to negotiate with the communist authorities, who were in a strong position, having effectively stifled the church through persistent repression. The church was demoralized, which to some extent placed the Vatican in a weaker bargaining position vis-à-vis the communist regimes. Nevertheless, the Vatican was primarily concerned with preserving the church hierarchies and was therefore prepared to negotiate with the authorities.

One of the first overtures made by the Vatican to Czechoslovakia took place in July 1963 when Cardinal Franz Koenig, Archbishop of Vienna, then President of the Secretariat for Dialogue with Unbelievers, went to Prague. The meeting led to the release of three bishops, and later five more, including the much respected primate of Czechoslovakia, Bishop František Tomášek, who became apostolic administrator of Prague. In 1968, the liberalizing spirit of the Prague Spring extended to religious activities. Many clergy and laity were allowed to resume their practices. *Pacem in Terris* fell apart. But the liberalization was shortlived; in 1969, religion was again suppressed. The Vatican, still pursuing its *Ostpolitik* toward Eastern Europe did not openly condemn the new wave of persecution. Indeed, it did not categorically denounce the Soviet-led invasion of Czechoslovakia in August 1968.

In November 1969, a new, revamped *Pacem in Terris* was founded. The early 1970s in some ways replicated the 1950s. Priests were restricted to particular geographical regions; pastoral duties were monitored by the state. Young children and believers were intimidated. In Trnovo, the St. Adelbert Society (the Slovak counterpart of the publishing department of the Czech Catholic clergy) was reduced and censored. Retreats and conferences, and training courses for priests, nuns and monks, were restricted. *Numerus clausus* was reintroduced, limiting entry into the seminaries.

Throughout the 1970s, religious activities were closely monitored by the state. The Vatican continued its policy of *Ostpolitik*. Negotiations between President Husák and the Vatican took place between 1970 and 1975, but led to few improvements for believers and priests. In 1972, because of deaths and government interference, only one of Czechoslovakia's 13 Catholic dioceses (including one Uniate diocese) had a resident bishop with full powers. In April 1974, Cardinal Stefan Trochta, bishop of Litomerice (Bohemia) died soon after an hour-long interrogation by a communist official.

The Vatican, however, gained some concessions. In 1974, four new bishops —Josef Feranec, Jan Pasztor, Julius Gabriš and Josef Vrana—were appointed. All four bishops were associated in some way with *Pacem in Terris*. No progress was made concerning religious instruction in schools. Nevertheless, however much the Vatican was criticized for its apparent policy of détente toward the Czechoslovak regime at a time when the regime showed no signs of reducing its pressure against dissidents and religious activists, Monsignor Casaroli, the Vatican secretary of state and the pope's envoy in Eastern Europe, succeeded in having Cardinal Tomášek installed as archbishop of Prague on Easter Sunday, 1978. That appointment established Archbishop Tomášek as a leading figure of the Catholic hierarchy in Czechoslovakia and gave considerable encouragement to the Czech faithful. There were some other important changes. A new Slovak ecclesiastical province was created, with Trnovo as its see. Since the days of the Austro-Hungarian Empire, most Slovak dioceses (for example, Nitra, Banská Bystrica and Spiš) had been formally at least dependent on the Hungarian archdiocese of Esztergom, while other dioceses, Košice and Rožňava, were until the late 1970s attached to the Hungarian archdiocese of Eger. In practice, however, the Slovak dioceses were directly dependent on the Vatican. Now, in 1978, after decades of formal Hungarian dependence, but de facto Vatican administration, the Slovak Catholic church was granted administrative independence —important in a country where Catholicism and national identity are closely tied.

Pope John Paul II and Czechoslovakia

Soon after Cardinal Wojtyła became pope in 1978. Ivan Medek, a Charter 77 signatory, wrote a letter to the Vatican in which he sharply criticized the *Ostpolitik* policies pursued by the Vatican. "We all know," Medek wrote, "that nothing will be solved merely by filling vacant diocesan posts, especially when any such appointments are certain to be the result of a compromise in which the Holy See will be asked to make most of the concessions...." Matters had already been made complicated when the independent human rights movement, Charter 77, started in January 1977. The Catholic bishops declined to give their support to the movement. And Cardinal Tomášek, because the Vatican was still at that time being conciliatory toward the Czechoslovak regime, declared in the Catholic newspaper, *Katolické Noviný*, that the bishops were not signatories of the Charter. The underground, or secret, churches were already spreading, partly because of the passivity of the church hierarchy, and because the church itself was providing little spiritual or moral leadership to the country's believers. Father Josef Zverina, a signer of Charter 77 and a well-known and respected theologian, wrote to Cardinal Tomášek insisting that the church hierarchy take a stand against the continuing repression exercised by the authorities. Thus, the growing strength of the secret churches, Charter 77 and individual priests led to a more outspoken criticism of the Vatican's *Ostpolitik*.

Pope John Paul II responded to these pressures, and a noticeable change took place within the Czech hierarchy itself. In an interview in the Italian publication *Il Regno* (April 15, 1980) Cardinal Tomášek openly condemned *Pacem in Terris*. He said that the organization "depends totally on the state. Its program is inspired by slogans of brotherhood and cooperation but in reality it does nothing for the church . . . it has no dialogue with the hierarchy. I am in total disagreement with it because it does not have the approval of the Vatican." The Vatican's disapproval was confirmed in March, 1982, when the Roman Sacred Congregation for the Clergy, in its decree, *Quidam episcopi*, forbade all priests, worldwide, to become members of political organizations. The decree prompted a number of priests, among them two capitular vicars, to leave this state-controlled organization. A continuing movement to resign from the organization was partially blocked by the state with threats against those leaving and against the Czechoslovakian Catholic church as a whole.

The pope's more forthright attitude and criticism had undoubtedly given greater encouragement to believers and priests alike. But the persecution continued almost unabated, particularly in the early 1980s. In early 1983, dozens of Franciscans were detained and some were arrested; many believers and many religious activists were imprisoned; children attending religious instruction classes were intimidated. In spite of the continuous harassment, religious samizdat, both in the Czech lands and in Slovakia, has increased. At the same time however, the administrative and institutional structure of the Catholic church is far from satisfactory. Of the six dioceses in the Bohemian and Moravian church provinces, only one, the archdiocese of Prague has a diocesan bishop, Cardinal Tomášek; and one, the archbishopric of Olomouc has an apostolic administrator appointed by the pope. The four remaining bishoprics are headed by capitular vicars, that is, priests not appointed by the pope but by the respective cathedral chapters, generally upon instruction by the state. The situation is somewhat better in Slovakia. Of the seven bishoprics there, two have a diocesan bishop—Banská Bystrica and Nitra.

It was precisely these issues and the pope's outspoken attacks on *Pacem in Terris* that led to an unprecedented meeting between Czechoslovak foreign minister Bohusláv Chňoupek and the pope in December 1983. So far, there has been little improvement concerning the filling of the vacant bishoprics. So far, too, the authorities have continued to harass religious activists and believers.

EAST GERMANY

The Catholic church in East Germany is in a very different position from the one it holds in Czechoslovakia, Hungary and Poland. For one thing, only eight percent of the population belongs to the Catholic church. Also, after communist power was gradually established in East Berlin and later throughout East Germany, the communist authorities did not repress the churches. It is in a different position from the rest of Eastern Europe for another reason, too. Because prewar Germany was more industrialized, religion played a less significant role, except perhaps among the small agrarian population.

During the 1950s, no show trials of churchmen were held and no bishops were prevented from carrying out their religious duties (except Bishop Doepfner of Berlin, who in the 1950s was resident in West Berlin and who from 1958 onward was allowed to visit East Berlin only). Neither were monasteries closed down. The Vatican, however, had to inform the East German authorities of episcopal appointments before officially announcing the nominations.

In contrast to the Protestant churches (see below), the Catholic church has refused to be drawn into any kind of dialogue between Christians and Marxists; until the early 1970s, it avoided any political activities. This policy was actively supported and promoted by the late Cardinal Bengsch. As chairman of the Berlin Episcopal Conference—an international organization of Catholic clergy and laity, mainly from the Soviet bloc—he had a post that confers on the holder the status of primate of East Germany, and he was primarily concerned with maintaining a complete church hierarchy and a united church. In his relations with the authorities, he never formally met with the East German Communist party leaders, Walter Ulbricht or Erich Honecker. In short, Cardinal Bengsch guided the Catholic church on the principle that the purity of the faith and the unity of Catholics was of primary importance.

Relations between the Vatican and the authorities posed few problems. After a series of meetings between officials from both sides during the early 1970s, the Holy See in July 1973 reorganized the ecclesiastical units that had been under the jurisdiction of West German bishops into three new dioceses—Erfurt, Meiningen and Magdeburg-Schwerin. The Vatican also named three East German apostolic administrators to these dioceses. In August 1975, the Vatican, when it named a new papal nuncio to West Germany, changed his title from "Nuncio to Germany" to "Papal Nuncio in the Federal Republic of West Germany," an implicit recognition of the existence of a separate East German state.

Although relations between church and state throughout the 1960s and 1970s remained untroubled, on some matters the Catholic church spoke out. The first time it did so was in 1972, when the church issued a pastoral letter objecting to the legalization of abortion. Though the church failed to prevent the passage of the bill, it did influence dissent within the People's Chamber—the first time since 1945 that votes of abstention and opposition were recorded. In 1974, another pastoral letter drawn up by the Catholic bishops was read throughout East German churches. It criticized the disadvantages suffered by Christian youths under the East German educational system. And in 1978, the Berlin Episcopal Conference sent a letter to the government protesting against the introduction of military instruction in schools. But the Catholic church did not join with the Lutheran church in supporting sections of the independent peace movement until 1983.

The new assertiveness on the part of the Catholic church in the early 1980s stemmed partly from the appointment by Pope John Paul II of Joachim Meisner as cardinal in January 1983. Before Meisner was appointed, Catholics, as individuals, had been involved in the unofficial peace movement along with Protestants; no representative of the Catholic church hierarchy, however, had made a public statement on the church's overall attitude toward the peace question, which had assumed greater importance because the Soviet Union was preparing to site missiles on East German soil after the Bonn Parliament had voted to accept U.S. missiles on West German soil. In January 1983, a pastoral letter issued by the bishops represented a change in attitude. It advocated controlled disarmament and an official alternative to army service for conscientious objectors, and objected also to military training in schools. In November 1983, Catholic priests joined with Lutheran pastors in condemning government petitions calling on factory and office workers to welcome the stationing of new Soviet missiles in the country by working on certain free days to meet the costs of the deployment. This new confidence by the Catholic church—though not especially effective in applying pressure on the state to revise its policy on the education system and the disarmament issue—suggested that the younger generation of Catholic churchmen were attempting to redefine the church's role and identity in East German society.

HUNGARY

Traditionally, the Catholic church in Hungary played a prominent political and social role. The church controlled half of the educational institutions. It published several newspapers and journals. Political parties, charitable organizations and social groups had close ties with the church, especially during the 19th century. Catholic bishops were ex officio members of the Upper House of parliament. To a large extent, the Catholic church was closely linked with, if not indeed, one of the mainstays of the Hungarian ruling elite. It also had substantial landholding interests commensurate with its social and political status in pre-World War II Hungary. And unlike Father Tiso of Slovakia or the Ustaša of Croatia, the Hungarian Catholic church was not tainted by any pro-Nazi sympathies during the war. When the Nazis set up the pro-German Arrow Cross government in Hungary in October 1944, the church refused to cooperate. After the war, the communists, trying to consolidate their power, did not interfere to any great extent into ecclesiastical affairs.

When Cardinal Justinian Serédi, the Hungarian primate, died in March 1945, he was succeeded by József Mindszenty. There was no interference by the authorities. This was not to last, however. In March 1945, the apostolic nuncio was expelled, as were all foreign delegates. The communist authorities introduced agrarian reforms, which included confiscating church lands. By the end of 1948 nearly 4,000 Catholic associations, including the influential Catholic youth organization, had been dissolved. In June 1948, the Hungarian Parliament, now controlled by the Communist party, nationalized denominational and private schools. The church lost all its 1,216 primary schools, 1,669 general schools and 32 teacher training schools. Cardinal Mindszenty tolled the bells throughout the country in protest; those Catholics who supported the nationalization program were excommunicated. From then on, church-state relations deteriorated rapidly. Mindszenty was arrested on December 27, 1948. The following February he was tortured, tried for "high treason" and sentenced to life imprisonment. The Vatican openly condemned the sentence. With Mindszenty effectively silenced, the bishops, under pressure from the authorities, reached an agreement with the regime, accepting the status quo in return for assurances of financial support and freedom of religious worship. This took place on August 29, 1950. Shortly afterward, eight secondary schools were returned to the church. But, with a similar pattern developing throughout the rest of Eastern Europe, a State Office for Church Affairs was created in Hungary in May 1951, giving the government full powers over church appointments and institutions. Pressure on the church and repression continued until after Stalin's death.

After the 1956 Revolution in Hungary was quashed, clerics and ministers were detained and many were charged with "counterrevolutionary" activities. In September 1957, Pope Pius XII ordered all clerics, under the threat of excommunication, to desist from political activity. Peace priests, that is those who supported the regime, were given seats in the parliament.

The Kádár regime, set up immediately after Soviet tanks rolled into Budapest, owed its existence to the Red Army. In an attempt to seek a measure of acceptance from Hungarian society, Kádár pursued what could be described as a centrist position, coopting intellectuals, giving them a measure of freedom in return for passive acceptance of the new regime. The authorities began to woo the church too, by approaching the Vatican. In October 1962, with these policies in mind and supported by Nikita Khrushchev's interest in détente and controlled liberalization, the Hungarian authorities allowed two Hungarian bishops, five priests and two lay Catholics to attend the first session of the Second Vatican Council. The Vatican and the Hungarian regime had common interests in improving relations. One aim was the need for improved church-state relations in Hungary, to be achieved by removing Cardinal Mindszenty who, since 1956 had sought asylum in the U.S. legation in Budapest. Since that time, Mindszenty had been openly criticizing the regime and had adopted a courageous but uncompromising attitude toward the communists. Going over the head of Mindszenty, Monsignor Casaroli and József Prantner, chairman of the State Office for Church Affairs, signed a church-state agreement that included an act and a document. It named five bishops to administer vacant dioceses (Hungary had three Roman Catholic archdioceses and seven dioceses and one Uniate diocese); stipulated that the oath of allegiance to the constitution and the laws of Hungary had to be taken by people holding certain church offices, and that the oath was to be considered binding by the church but only in so far as those laws did not contradict the principles of Christian faith; and decreed that the Hungarian Papal Institute in Rome was to be administered by priests acceptable to the Hungarian government. In return, the authorities guaranteed that the institute's activities would not be obstructed and that each year every Hungarian diocese would be allowed to send a priest there.

The accord, as it was called, was signed in 1964 by the Vatican and the Hungarian regime and paved the way for further negotiations. During the mid-1960s, however, priests were still being imprisoned and harassed for activities against the state. Only in 1971 did relations between church and state begin to improve markedly. Cardinal Mindszenty, a broken man, left the American Embassy for Vienna on September 28, on the instructions of the pope. In 1974, Pope Paul VI dismissed the cardinal from the see at Esztergom. In May 1975, Mindszenty died.

Mindszenty's death gave the primate, Cardinal Lászlo Lékai, more leeway in terms of improving church-state relations. Throughout the 1970s, the government did not interfere with the Vatican's appointment of bishops and the filling of archbishoprics. And in contrast to neighboring Czechoslovakia, all the bishoprics were filled. This was one of the main intentions of the *Ostpolitik* pursued by the Vatican to which Lékai adhered absolutely. The marked improvement in church-state relations was shown in two important events. In April 1977, Hungarian archbishops and bishops were received by the pope in Rome. Secondly, János Kádár, party leader since 1956, visited Rome on June 9, 1977, at which time Vatican Radio commented:

> The Holy See is guided not by considerations of the advantage of the popularity of the moment, but by the profound demands of its religious mission and by its vocation to be at the service of man. .... Experience confirms the validity of the path undertaken: the path of dialogue on various matters, attentive to the safeguarding of the rights and legitimate interests of the church and of believers but at the same time open to an understanding of the state's preoccupation with and action in fields that lie within its proper competence.

Relations between church and state continued to improve. There were signs however that the Vatican under John Paul II was anxious to give the Catholic church in Hungary a more prominent position. Some indications of these sentiments were revealed in a series of articles published in the Hungarian Catholic weekly *Új Ember* (January 2, 23 and 30, 1983), which stated that the church in Hungary was now ready to assume a more active role in Hungarian society. One of the articles was written by the bishop of Pécs, Monsignor József Cserháti. He hinted that the gradual step-by-step approach adopted by the Hungarian Catholic church could no longer serve the needs of today's society nor satisfy the spiritual and moral demands of the younger generation. And he stated: "After many variants of rhetoric, we consider freedom of action indispensable in carrying out our actual pastoral work with regard to the family, basic religious education, the youth and social care." (*Uj Ember*, January 30, 1983). Cserháti may well have been reflecting some of Pope John Paul II's views on church-state relations in Hungary. While Cardinal Lékai considerably eased the tension between the two bodies, a carefully worded letter by the pope to Lékai, published in a Hungarian Catholic publication *Magyar Kurier* (December 12, 1978) looked at the long-term consequences of such a dialogue. The pope pointed out that the Catholic church in both Poland and Hungary, from its beginning, had been identified with the national tradition. Hinting that the Hungarian church was perhaps too passive, the pope wrote: "You should strive toward bearing your apostolic witness in such a way that it would be effective and that it would honor your national tradition." And in September 1980, Radio Vatican criticized a statement made by the Hungarian episcopate marking the 30th anniversary of the first agreement between the communist authorities and the Catholic Church, saying that current cooperation should not ignore past persecution of believers in Hungary. Given Hungary's social problems, particularly among the younger generation, the Vatican considered that the church in Hungary could play a more active role, specifically in setting down guidelines and support for the country's youth.

Indeed, this was precisely the theme taken up by Bishop Cserháti during 1983 and 1984. He pointed out that in the past three years, over a third of all marriages had ended in divorce, resulting in 100,000 children from broken homes. And on the basis of a 1981 survey, not a single school in Budapest was free of drugs or alcohol—a fact that concerns church and state alike (*Uj Ember*, January 30, 1983).

In the late 1970s and particularly during the early 1980s, the Basic Communities were a considerable source of tension within the church. The Basic Communities, led by a Piarist father, György Bulányi, follow the teaching of the Bible, often literally, and are pacifists. Over the years, they have attracted several thousand followers, some of whom openly object to military conscription and advocate the right not to bear arms. The Hungarian authorities in the past have responded by giving prison sentences to those who refused to be conscripted. The growing religious samizdat prompted the authorities in the early 1980s to confiscate material, impose fines and put pressure on the episcopate to discipline Bulányi and his supporters. The authorities were particularly concerned with the potential support for Bulányi's pacifist views. The dispute involved the Vatican, which supported the Hungarian Bench of Bishops who ruled that Bulányi's teachings consisted of doctrinal errors. The pope, however, urged reconciliation and understanding from both the church and the Basic Communities.

POLAND

In contrast to neighboring East Germany, Poland is predominantly Roman Catholic with over 80 percent of the population of 35 million actively belonging to the church. In contrast, too, to Hungary and Czechoslovakia, the church in Poland has never formed part of the ruling elite or establishment. The church has traditionally retained its autonomy and independence. And throughout Poland's checkered history—the three partitions in the late 18th century, the period between 1795 and 1918 when Poland was effectively divided under three empires—the Catholic church played a major role in protecting the nation's identity, guarding the country's language and preserving its culture. During the late 19th century, the Catholic church opposed forcible Germanization. During the interwar period, the church's influence was greatest among the country's large peasant population and weakest among the intelligentsia. But throughout this period, it refused to be drawn into the political establishment, preferring instead to protect its autonomy. It is precisely this autonomy that the communist authorities after 1945 attempted to exploit and eventually weaken; this has been one of the main sources of conflict between church and state in Poland ever since.

Postwar period and Stalinism
The first attempts to weaken church autonomy occurred in September 1945 when the Polish government repudiated the 1925 Concordat with Rome, which had given the church full freedom to conduct its affairs. The Vatican had refused to recognize the new Polish government and refused to appoint permanent bishops for the Oder-Neisse region until a German peace treaty was concluded. The Vatican also continued to recognize the jurisdiction of the Polish bishops in those lands annexed to the Soviet Union. The Polish government set about forming a group of lay Catholics led by the extreme right-wing politician Bolesław Piasecki. The group, called Pax, sought with government backing to promote cooperation between communists and Catholics in "building socialism." Pax was also intended to weaken the unity of the church and challenge the authority of the bishops.

In a further campaign against the church, church hospitals were nationalized in 1945. In 1950, the church's welfare organization, Caritas, was brought under the direct supervision of the state. Most of the church's lands were confiscated. However, on April 14, 1950, the archbishop of Gniezno and Warsaw, Monsignor Stefan Wyszyński, signed a 19-part agreement with the state. The Polish episcopate acknowledged the authority of the government in all secular matters. In return, freedom of worship was guaranteed; the church's autonomy was legalized and it could teach religion in school, run a Catholic press and also involve itself in welfare organizations. The independence of the Catholic University at Lublin was also acknowledged. By signing the agreement, the church hoped to prevent any further repression. The authorities had their own interests to consider too. They were about to launch a collectivization program and wanted a reasonably silenced church. Relations soon deteriorated, however. On July 22, 1952, a new constitution was passed, making all church appointments subject to government approval. Censorship of the church press and the media in general was increased; the Catholic weekly *Tygodnik Powszechny*, respected for its integrity, was silenced in March 1953. In September, Cardinal Wyszyński was confined to a monastery. Subsequently, the Polish bishops took an oath of loyalty to the regime on December 17. By the end of 1955, the teaching of the catechism was banned in all schools.

Post-Stalinism

Some improvement between church and state took place soon after Włady-sław Gomułka took over in 1956. Cardinal Wyszyński was released; a new, revised version of the 1950 agreement was drawn up and signed; religious instruction in schools was allowed; and generally, a more pragmatic attitude evolved between church and state. A Catholic group, called Znak, consisting of intellectuals, writers, journalists and academics, was set up to represent the church's interests. Znak formed the Clubs of Catholic Intellectuals (KIK). But the relationship with the authorities was continually under strain. By 1958, the short burst of liberalization had almost come to an end; and Gomułka attempted to assert government control over the appointment of Catholic bishops. In the meantime, the Vatican continued to refuse to recognize the Polish communist government. Nor did the Vatican change the episcopal administration boundaries of the Oder-Neisse territories, which greatly displeased the Warsaw government. The authorities applied increasing pressure on the church, refusing to grant it building permits, especially for new churches in the rapidly growing industrial centers; the printing of missals was restricted; and in 1961, religious instruction in schools was once again outlawed. Throughout this period, communist ideology competed with Catholic ritual and fervor. An example of this competition occurred in 1966, the millennium of Polish Christianity. In Poznań, separate (but unrelated) celebrations took place on the same day.

It was not only ritual and the strength of religious feeling that exacerbated relations between the Polish communists and the Polish bishops. During the anti-Semitic campaign in March 1968 in Warsaw, Polish cardinals wrote to the authorities demanding the release of those students arrested and warned that a "truncheon is never an argument in a free society." With the collapse of Gomułka's rule in 1970, his successor, Edward Gierek, sought a "full normalization of relations between the church and the authorities". This announcement came shortly after the recognition by Willi Brandt, West German chancellor and leader of the Social Democrats, of the Oder-Neisse borders. This was important since the Vatican was put in a position whereby it had to reconsider its own ecclesiastical boundaries in Poland. But it could not do so without the consent of the Polish bishops. For many years, the bishops were reluctant to allow the Vatican to negotiate with the Polish regime directly and over the heads of the Polish episcopate. Finally, Monsignor Casaroli, with the consent of Wyszyński, reached an agreement with the Polish authorities. In January 1971, the Vatican's yearbook, *Annuario Pontificio*, excluded the names of the former German bishops in the Oder-Neisse region. This indicated that the Vatican was ready to recognize the region as Polish territory. It was a sign, too, for the Polish authorities to make concessions, which it did. In June, the government gave over to the Catholic church its full titles to nearly 7,000 former church buildings, and 2,000 acres of land in the Oder-Neisse territories. Relations continued to improve. In February 1972, the government—about to embark on a pro-Western, money-borrowing campaign—conceded that the Catholic church would no longer have to submit reports on income and expenditure. But Cardinal Wyszyński kept up the pressure, demanding more building permits for churches. On June 28, 1972 the Vatican named permanent bishops to the Oder-Neisse region.

The Catholic church and the opposition
Administrative concessions and the recognition of the Catholic church's autonomy were not the sole preoccupations of Cardinal Wyszyński and the episcopate. The latter was very closely involved with the needs of Polish society, not only in terms of maintaining a specific Polish national identity but also of maintaining the independent activities of the society. Poland, during the 1970s may be characterized by a number of major developments. The first saw the end of the "revisionist" era. The opposition movement of the 1960s and individuals including Jacek Kuroń had clung to the idea that reform was in fact possible within the ruling communist party. Such revisionist ideas were destroyed not only by the failure of the Prague Spring but by the events taking place in Poland itself. The campaign against intellectuals in the late 1960s, the shooting of workers in Gdańsk in 1970 and the food riots in 1976 confirmed the impossibility of major reforms within the Communist party.

The second development was the founding of various independent groups, the most important of which were KOR (Workers' Self-Defense Committee) and ROPCiO (Movement for the Defense of Human and Civil Rights). KOR, founded by Kuroń, Michnik, Lytiński and others, initially set about helping those families who were victimized after the 1976 riots, in general providing material and legal assistance to them. The movement, however, soon expanded, publishing its own newspaper *Robotnik*. Essentially, it tried to forge an alliance between workers and intellectuals, an alliance hitherto entirely absent ever since the imposition of communist rule in Poland after the war. KOR's main strategy, however, was to publicize the cases of unjust prosecution and the infringement of human rights.

On the human rights issue, the church adopted an increasingly active role. One of the first opportunities to express its attitude toward human rights came in 1975–76 when the authorities drew up a number of amendments to the 1952 constitution. One of the amendments stipulated that "the leading role of the party" be written into the constitution. The proposed amendment also referred to Poland's "unshakable bond" with the Soviet Union; citizens' rights were conditional on the "honest fulfillment of duties"—a term flexible and ambiguous enough to allow a number of interpretations to a number of different interest groups.

In January 1976, the church sent two memorandums to the Polish government, and Cardinal Wyszyński and Cardinal Wojtyła of Cracow, in separate sermons attacked the constitutional amendments. On February 10, 1976, the Sejm (the Polish Parliament) adopted the amendments; but the leader of the Znak group, Stanisław Stomma abstained. Znak divided on the amendment debate. And after Stomma's resignation, the group became largely controlled by the proregime deputies.

Following the Radom riots and strikes in June 1976, Cardinal Wyszyński spoke out in September against repression and victimization of workers. He spoke out again the following April, criticizing the authorities for their policy toward workers, who, the cardinal said, "under pressure from propaganda machinery, have hardly one Sunday free in a month; since three consecutive Sundays have been used for mining, might the fourth be free?" The church also took tacit interest in the Flying University, an unofficial grouping of intellectuals who gave seminars and lectures throughout the country on a number of subjects and topics normally banned from the colleges and universities.

Pope John Paul II and Poland

The elevation of the archbishop of Cracow, Karol Wojtyła, to the papacy on October 16, 1978 created an entirely new situation in Poland. In the past, popes John XXIII and Paul VI had not given their full backing to the Polish bishops in their relations with the government. Soon after his election, Polish bishops, along with opposition intellectuals, campaigned against censorship. In September 1978, the bishops had already issued a pastoral letter that was read at masses throughout Poland. It stated that it was "imperative to abolish the intervention of censorship." Uncertain about the consequences of a Polish pope in the Vatican, the Polish authorities, for the first time since the war, broadcast mass on Polish radio during the installation of Pope John Paul II. That Christmas, the authorities—counterproductively as it turned out—censored the first message of the Polish pope to his countrymen. The censored passages referred to the role of the church in Poland: "As bishop of the Cracow church, St. Stanisław, Poland's patron saint, defended his contemporary society from the evil that threatened it and he did not hesitate to confront the rulers, which the defense of the moral order called for. ..." And in a revealing censored passage, the pope referred to St. Stanisław as an "advocate of the most essential human rights on which man's dignity, his morality and true freedom depends. ..." The editor of *Tygodnik Powszechny* refused to publish the censored text. In a state of confusion and weakness, the authorities apologized to the Vatican, blaming the incident on an "over-zealous" official. The planned papal visit to Poland the following June reflected equal confusion and uncertainty among the authorities, who were unsure about the security, the censorship and the pope's itinerary. In the event, the visit was made, and it demonstrated the extremely close links between Polish nationalism and Catholicism, besides, of course, providing a deep sense of the fervor and solidarity among Polish society.

The experience was not repeated when the pope returned to Poland in the summer of 1983. Church-state relations had become complicated and difficult after the imposition of martial law on December 13, 1981. Initially, the church, or at least, its primate, Cardinal Józef Glemp (who succeeded Wyszyński in the summer of 1981) appealed for calm and understanding; this was difficult given the circumstances: widespread repression and imprisonment, and a full-scale attempt at normalizing Polish society. The main question within the church episcopate was the extent to which the church could now play the role of a mediator between the authorities and the society. Such a role for the church was one of the main features during the 1970s. But with an outlawed Solidarity movement, and with the government reluctant, indeed refusing, to consider negotiating with independent groups, the church found itself in an increasingly difficult position. On the one hand, it sought to gain some concessions from the authorities: the release of prisoners, amnesty and the end to martial law. In return, the church would appeal for realism and even at times dissuade Solidarity sympathizers from demonstrating.

The delicate relationship established between the authorities and the church proved to be somewhat successful, but only within certain limits. For instance, when the pope finally returned to Poland in the summer of 1983 Polish society was exhausted. And whereas the pope in 1979 could promise hope for the future, it was clear from his 1983 messages that the only kind of hope now possible was a spiritual hope cut off from the unanimous public articulation of that feeling just four years earlier. Some of the church's demands were met: prisoners were released, an amnesty was declared and martial law was lifted, though the restrictions built into the legal system only served to tighten the authorities' control over people's activities.

Among the grassroots of the clergy, there was noticeable dissent vis-à-vis the Polish episcopate. Several Solidarity supporters openly preached sermons and said masses that criticized martial law and the way in which society was being denied not only basic human rights but the opportunity to express judgments based on truth and justice. Priests, including Jerzy Popiełuszko and Stanisław Malkowski to name but two, refused to remain silent even though they were indirectly disciplined by the Polish bishops and by the primate. One priest, Father Nowak was sent away from his parish near Ursus because of his outspoken support for Solidarity. And in an extraordinary incident, Father Popiełuszko was murdered by the internal security forces in October 1984. For months, this young priest had preached in Warsaw, openly supporting the need for a society based on human rights, truth and justice. His funeral, held in Warsaw on November 3, was attended by over a quarter of a million people. The Polish authorities under Gen. Wojciech Jaruzelski had created a new Polish martyr.

In practical terms, the church was negotiating two important things with the Polish authorities. The first concerns classifying the precise legal position of the church in Poland today; negotiations took place throughout late 1983 and early 1984 in an attempt to formalize the relationship between the church, the Vatican and the regime in Poland. The second matter for negotiation concerns church buildings. The authorities, for a number of reasons, have been granting more building permits to the church.

ROMANIA

The Uniate church in Romania was completely destroyed as an institution after the communist takeover. In 1948, three of its four dioceses were dissolved and the authorities forcibly merged the 1,500,000 members, most of whom were Romanians from Transylvania, with the Romanian Orthodox Church, the country's largest denomination. Uniate monasteries and seminaries were closed. Priests were imprisoned, executed or simply disappeared. The Catholic church, though not persecuted to the same extent, was made administratively impotent by the end of the 1940s. The authorities refused to allow the appointment of bishops to all the five dioceses. Not only was Catholicism seen as incompatible with communist doctrine but, especially in the late 1950s and throughout the 1960s, the communist regime under President Nicolae Ceauşescu regarded Romanian nationalism as an exclusive ideology, whose basic tenet focused on loyalty to the Romanian government and nation; within that definition there was practically no room for any expressions of autonomy, which would include religion.

Romanian Catholics amount to only eight percent of the total population of 20 million, and most of the Catholics in Romania belong to the Hungarian or German minorities, mainly located in Transylvania. In 1950, Catholic monasteries and convents were closed, and Catholic welfare organizations and hospitals run by nuns were either closed or nationalized. The state supervised church appointments—similar to what was already taking place in Hungary and Czechoslovakia.

The *Ostpolitik* pursued by the Vatican led to the opening up of relations between Rome and Bucharest in 1965 when Cardinal Koenig of Vienna visited the country. In December 1965, it was agreed that the Romanian authorities would recognize the appointment of Petru Plesca of Fico as titular bishop of Fico. In late 1967, the bishop of Alba Julia, Aaron Márton, who had been arrested in 1949 and had been under house arrest from 1955, was released. In January 1968, Prime Minister Ion Gheorghe Maurer and Foreign Minister Corneliu Mănescu visited the Vatican. The continuing papal *Ostpolitik* led to the appointment by the Vatican of Bishop Anton Jakab, an ethnic Hungarian, as coadjutor, with right to succeed Bishop Márton.

During the 1970s and 1980s, the dioceses of Timişoara, Oradea and Iaşi, though dissolved by the authorities, had vacant episcopal seats. After 1976, Iaşi was administered by an ordinary—who did not hold the rank of a bishop. The same situation arose in Timişoara and Oradea. In October 1983, Pope John Paul II appointed Father Sebastien Krauter, an ethnic German, to the diocese of Timişoara and Father Stefan Daszka, an ethnic Hungarian, to Oradea. These two appointments hold the rank of ordinary. They have been given charge of a diocese by the pope but without formal episcopal status and have only informal consent of the state. In other words, they can be removed at any time. The Romanian media did not report the appointments.

The appointment of priests to these two dioceses followed shortly after a Romanian pilgrimage to Rome—the first since 1945. The occasion was the beatification of Jeremiah of Wallachia (1556–1625) the first Romanian Catholic to be included in the calendar of saints. These concessions by the Romanian authorities suggested some improvement in relations between church and state. On the practical level, however, books, Bibles, missals and other materials of religious instruction are in very short supply, and there is a shortage of church buildings. Among the outstanding issues between the Vatican and Bucharest is the fate of the Uniate church. In 1983, the Vatican created a bishopric for Uniate Romanians resident in the United States. And a year earlier, the Vatican appointed a Uniate Romanian, Monsignor Drian Crişan, as secretary of the Vatican's Sacred Congregation for the Cause of Saints. This clearly suggested to many observers that the Vatican was unwilling to accept the continuing suppression of the Romanian Uniate church. The Uniates themselves have tried to present their case to a wider audience. At the follow-up conference on Security and Cooperation in Europe in Madrid, three Romanian Uniate priests, Alexandru Todea, Ion Dragomir and Ion Ploscaru, sent a message demanding the Uniate church be recognized as an official church. The statement called for the restitution of buildings and property seized from the church, the official recognition of Uniate bishops and the right to have seminaries to train new priests.

In a separate development, Pope John Paul II on October 30, 1984 named a bishop to Bucharest—the first time since 1954 that a bishop was to administer the city. Since 1978, Monsignor Ion Robu, the bishop named by the pope, had headed the diocese as an ordinary—that is, as a cleric who was given charge of the dioceses by the pope with the consent of the authorities. The Vatican named Robu as apostolic administrator in Bucharest. In the Catholic hierarchy, an apostolic administrator manages a diocese but must report directly to Rome, whereas a resident bishop has more autonomy. With the appointment of Robu, two of Romania's 12 dioceses—six Roman Catholic, five Byzantine rite and one Armenian—are now headed by bishops. Three others are headed by ordinaries. The appointment was seen as a sign of an improvement in the Vatican's relations with Romania. Most of the negotiations have been carried out by Archbishop Luigi Poggi, the pope's special envoy to Eastern Europe.

YUGOSLAVIA

Nationality and religious affiliation in Yugoslavia are closely identified with each other. Generally speaking, the republics of Serbia and Montenegro come under the Serbian Orthodox church. Macedonia has had its own Orthodox church since 1967. The republics of Croatia and Slovenia are overwhelmingly Catholic, though there are some important Orthodox settlements in these areas. Bosnia-Hercegovina contains a mixture of Catholic Croats, Serbian Orthodox and Slav Muslims. The autonomous province of Vojvodina, which is constitutionally linked to the Republic of Serbia, is Catholic and Orthodox. The second autonomous province, Kosovo, also linked constitutionally with the Republic of Serbia is overwhelmingly Muslim, though a small minority, mostly Serbs, are Orthodox.

Postwar Yugoslavia and church-state relations
The history of postwar church-state relations in Yugoslavia is markedly different from that of its Eastern European neighbors. Under the late Marshal Tito, it was extremely divisive to outlaw religious practices, since nationalism and religious identity were too closely linked. And because Tito based Yugoslavia on a federal structure, with each republic enjoying equal rights in terms of culture, politics and social life, it was impossible to separate republican identity from religious outlook. Nevertheless, there are certain religious (and by implication, nationalist) tensions that go back to the early years of World War II and that, in some ways, have shaped the outlook of the Croatian and Serbian Communist party leadership today.

In 1941, when German, Hungarian, Bulgarian and Italian armies invaded Yugoslavia, an indepedent state of Croatia was created. A pro-German government was set up and the rest of Yugoslavia was partitioned. The leader of the new Croatian state, Ante Pavelić, set up an extreme nationalist group that carried out massacres against Serbs and Jews, which accounts for some of the animosity existing between Serbs and Croats today. The Pavelić regime—identifying itself with Catholicism—campaigned against Orthodox Christians and, by implication, Serbs. The archbishop of Zagreb (capital of Croatia), Aloysius Stepinac, objected to the massacres. He personally wanted an independent Croatian state and like other Croats did not want Serbia to rule over Croatia if and when a Yugoslav state was formed. But he objected to the methods deployed by the Ustaša. The fact that other Catholics, Archbishop Sarić of Sarajevo, for example, had collaborated with the Nazis, may partially explain Tito's campaign against the Catholic church after 1944. That year, an agrarian law was passed, which in effect led to the confiscation of church lands. Schools were nationalized, religious instruction in schools was denounced and many priests were shot, imprisoned, or tortured. Between 1945 and 1952, more than half the entire Catholic clergy was in prison at any one time.

In 1946, Stepinac was tried and charged with supporting the Pavelić regime; in December 1951, he was released from prison. By the end of 1953, the Vatican made Stepinac a cardinal, which Tito regarded as an affront to his own authority. Nevertheless, relations between church and state began to improve. One of the reasons for a greater relaxation of tensions stemmed from the fact that Tito had broken with Stalin in 1948 and needed as much support as possible from within Yugoslavia itself, and this included the Catholic church.

During the 1950s, the church was allowed greater freedom. And when Cardinal Stepinac died in 1960, Tito permitted him to be buried in Zagreb cathedral, the capital of Yugoslav Catholicism. Negotiations between the Vatican and Belgrade in an attempt to normalize relations were started in 1963, and when antireligious laws were relaxed in 1964–65, Pope Paul VI received Yugoslavia's ambassador to Italy, Ivo Vejvoda. In 1966, a protocol was agreed upon by Belgrade and Rome and diplomats (not with ambassadorial status) were exchanged. The agreement recognized Rome's jurisdiction over the Catholic church in Yugoslavia in ecclesiastical and spiritual matters. The agreement included the separation of church and state and rights of freedom of conscience and religious toleration. The Vatican also agreed that priests should not involve themselves in politics, and condemned all acts of terrorism. In August 1971, Belgrade and the Vatican formally restored full diplomatic relations.

In practical terms, the Catholic church in Yugoslavia has gained considerable concessions from its improved relations with the communist authorities. Each of the 23 dioceses, for instance, is not only filled with residential bishops, appointed by the pope, but each diocese has its own newspapers, the most important of which are *Glas Koncila* (published in Zagreb) and *Družina* (published in Ljubljana, Slovenia).

THE CATHOLIC CHURCH IN THE SOVIET UNION

The Catholic church is a minority church in the Soviet Union. Most of the country's Roman Catholics are in Lithuania, Latvia and in the western part of Belorussia and the Ukraine. Unlike the Russian Orthodox church, the Catholic church has not been allowed to create a central ecclesiastical authority, although, with numerous restrictions, the church in Lithuania and Latvia has been allowed to organize itself into a diocesan structure. Catholics in Belorussia and the Ukraine are under the jurisdiction of the archdiocese of Riga or Kaunas.

Lithuania

The Catholic church in Lithuania is probably the most important and influential of all the Catholic communities in the Soviet Union. After Lithuania was absorbed into the Russian empire in 1794 (along with neighboring Poland), the church became increasingly identified with Lithuanian nationalism. In the 19th century it acted as the guardian of Lithuanian culture, preserving the language and literature by publishing, where possible, dictionaries and missals, underground journals and newspapers in Lithuanian. The 19th century was a period of considerable repression for Lithuanians and Catholics. Church lands were confiscated. Nevertheless, the Lithuanian clergy resisted the widespread attempts at Russification—attempts resisted by Poland too. After the 1917 revolution, the Lithuanian church maintained contacts with the Vatican. But in June 1940 the communist authorities expelled the papal nuncio from the country. The concordat between the Vatican and Lithuania was abrogated on July 3, 1940.

In 1944, the diocesan administration was paralyzed and four of the six dioceses were deprived of bishops, several of whom were imprisoned or shot, including Bishop V. Borisevicius of Telsiai in 1947. By 1953, the Catholic church administration hardly functioned. There was a slight thaw after Stalin's death. Many priests returned from the camps. Some bishops returned too, including Bishop P. Paltarokas of Panevezys. In September 1955, he consecreated in secret Julijonas Stepanovicius as bishop of Panevezys and Petras Mazelis as bishop of Telsiai. Only Bishop Mazelis was allowed to exercise his office. The thaw was brief. Khrushchev launched an antireligion campaign in 1959.

The church responded to the pressure by sending petitions and letters directly to the government and also abroad. These petitions began circulating in the 1960s. They criticized the Kremlin's persistent campaign against religious practices and the continuing repression against the Uniate church, and they even critized the *Ostpolitik* of the Vatican. Because of a united church, close links between clergy and laity and the close identification between Lithuanian nationalism and Catholicism, a huge petition, the Memorandum, was circulated at the end of 1971 and was signed by thousands of Lithuanians. The Memorandum was sent to the Soviet leadership. It protested against the restrictions on religious education, the imprisonment of priests for instructing children and the enforced exile of bishops Stepanovicius and Sladkevicius. The Memorandum was also sent to the United Nations.

585

At about the same time, the first issue of *Chronicle of the Catholic Church in Lithuania* (CCCL) appeared. The publication was printed and distributed in samizdat. It had two aims: to provide accurate information about the state of religion in Lithuania; and by publicizing accurate, verifiable details of unlawful persecution, the editors hoped to exert pressure on the Soviet authorities. The reaction by the authorities was swift. In April 1972, Juozas Rugienis, head of Lithuania's branch of the Council for Religious Affairs, summoned all the bishops in office and the administrators of the dioceses. The bishops were told to instruct the priests to read out a pastoral letter, drawn up by the state, in all churches on April 30. In the event, some priests omitted certain passages that criticized those who had signed the Memorandum; other priests simply refused to read the letter. The following May, a group of Lithuanian priests issued a declaration expressing their disapproval of the letter. The authorities continued to apply pressure. From November 1973 through 1975, priests and laity, and anyone suspected of being connected with the CCCL were arrested. Several were imprisoned. At the same time, the authorities tried to implement a divide-and-rule policy, promoting those proregime priests within the church. Thus, when Cardinal Alfred Bengsch of Berlin visited Lithuania in August 1975, he was prevented from meeting any of the independent-minded clergy. His visit was generally concealed from Lithuanian Catholics. The aim of the authorities was to present to those outside the Soviet Union an image of a reasonably relaxed state of affairs between the Catholic church in Lithuania and the authorities.

The editors of the CCCL dented that image. They directed their criticism not only against the Soviet authorities but also against the Vatican's continuing *Ostpolitik* and its apparent lack of support of Lithuanian Catholic dissidents. In one issue, for instance, the editors challenged the Vatican:

> While defending victims of discrimination all over the world [the Holy See] barely recalls the "Church of Silence and Suffering," does not bring up and does not condemn covert and overt persecution of the faithful in the Soviet Union ... dialogue, it seems, is useful [to the communist regime] only so that the Vatican will keep silent about the persecution of Catholics in the Soviet Union ...."

In the late 1970s, the Lithuanian clergy continued their open support of religious rights. Five Lithuanian priests founded the Committee for the Defense of Believers, which had wide support from the clergy and considerable support from the laity. When the church drew up a petition addressed to the authorities, demanding that an illegally confiscated church in Klaipėda be restored to its original function, about five percent of the population signed this petition—an indication of the mutual trust and support of clergy and laity.

Pope John Paul II and Lithuania: Pope John Paul II has taken a keen interest in Lithuanian church affairs. In a sermon in March 1984, the pope called on all Catholics in Europe to remember their brothers and sisters in Lithuania. The occasion was the 500th anniversary of the death of St. Casimir, a Polish prince and grand duke of Lithuania who was patron saint of both countries. Previously, in 1978, the pope had written a long letter to Bishop Stepanovicius. It is thought that he was the secret cardinal created by the pope. The following year, on January 23, the pope met with Soviet Foreign

Minister Andrei Gromyko and proposed that the Vatican was in fact willing to revise the diocesan boundaries in Lithuania and Poland so as to make them correspond to the postwar Polish-Soviet borders, something which the Soviet authorities welcomed. At the moment, Vilnius is formally under two apostolic administrators; one is in Poland, the other has been banished by the Soviet authorities. The pope apparently asked that in return for recognition of the borders, vacant bishoprics in Lithuania should be filled, particularly in Vilnius; this city would, if recognized., become the seat of the metropolitan, which at present is Kaunas. So far, the boundary changes have not taken place. And today, two out of the six dioceses remain vacant. Four of the dioceses are under the jurisdiction of apostolic administrators.

On other matters relating to the situation of Catholics in Lithuania, the Vatican has gained some important concessions from the Soviet authorities. In 1983, for example, Bishop Antanas Vaicius was appointed to the diocese of Telsiai—vacant since 1975. And Archbishop Sladkevicius was allowed to return to the diocese of Kaisiadorys after spending 23 years in exile. Eighteen seminarians were ordained in 1982—the largest numbers since 1963 but hardly sufficient for Lithuania's 3 million Catholics. And for the first time since 1938, four Lithuanian bishops were officially allowed to pay an *ad limina apostolarum* visit to Rome. These visits, during which bishops consult with the pope on diocesan matters, normally take place every five years. In the past, the bishops were not given permission to leave the country *and* return. In November 1984, the Vatican elevated one of the four bishops to the rank of archbishop. Archbishop Liudas Povilonis, president of the Lithuanian Bishops' Conference, will be assisted by a new auxiliary bishop, Juozas Preikshas. That most recent development raised the number of bishops in Lithuania to six, including the archbishop.

Such concessions were not coupled with any improvement for Lithuanian Catholics in terms of greater religious tolerance. In 1983, for example, two priests, fathers Tamkevicius and Svarinskas were sentenced to between seven and 10 years imprisonment. Father Tamkevicius was cofounder of the Catholic Committee for the Defense of Believers. The motive for the arrests and sentences was the fear of the authorities that a large opposition would rally behind the church.

There were no concessions on the question of providing new church buildings. Since 1939, the number of churches has fallen from 717 to 628 and there are more than 98 parishes without priests. The seminaries have been reduced in number from four to one.

Nevertheless, the presence of a Polish/Slav pope in the Vatican has provided considerable moral and spiritual leadership to Lithuanian Catholics, many of whom during the 1960s and 1970s had believed that the Vatican was misinformed about the situation in Lithuania. In the words of the Catholic Committee for the Defense of Believers, the pope provided the inspiration for a "living church" in the region.

Belorussia

The position of the Catholic church is far weaker in Belorussia than in Lithuania. For one thing, only 25 percent of the population is

Catholic, mostly of Polish extraction. Few Russians belong to the Catholic church.

By 1939, all the Catholic churches in eastern Belorussia were closed. This region was part of the Soviet Union between 1917 and 1939. Eventually, in 1981, a church was opened in Minsk. Western Belorussia, in contrast, had 154 churches in 1959 but was reduced to 112 churches by 1981—one church to every 20,000 believers. The number of priests is even lower. In 1979, there were 45, many of whom were over 60 years of age. The Vatican and the Soviet authorities were apparently on the verge of agreeing to the consecration of a Belorussian bishop in the early 1970s, but the late Cardinal Wyszyński preferred a Polish bishop.

Some concessions were made to the Vatican. After 1944, there was no seminary in Belorussia. The Soviet authorities refused to allow any candidate from Belorussia to study either at Kaunas seminary—the only seminary in Lithuania—or at Riga, the only other seminary in the Soviet Union. A secret seminary was founded on papal instructions. Some priests were secretly ordained. The Soviet authorities, possibly preferring a more open church and therefore one that could be brought under its direct scrutiny, allowed a Belorussian, Antoni Chanko, to study at Riga seminary. In 1978 he was ordained and made assistant pastor in Zoludek parish. His first mass was attended by almost all the priests in Belorussia and thousands of believers.

Even today, however, there are no bishops in Belorussia. The last two bishops died (in Poland) in the late 1950s. Until 1970, the two Belorussian dioceses were administered from Poland, by apostolic administrators. In 1970, three vicars-general were created in Belorussia. With powers somewhat similar to bishops they can, for instance, ordain priests.

Unofficially, there are between 60 and 70 nuns working in Belorussia. Because so many of the priests are old, the nuns carry out some of the pastoral duties and also instruct children, and they are reported even to have copied out the catechism by hand. They also work, unofficially, in hospitals and schools and because monks and nuns are banned from Belorussia, they live in secret convents.

There is little evidence of any samizdat activities. However, because all books and religious material needed by priests in Belorussia are in Polish, and since most of the younger generation are no longer fluent in Polish and cannot read Latin script, a samizdat catechism has been produced in Polish but in Cyrillic lettering. There are no genuine samizdat publications, nor is there any movement for religious rights such as exists in Lithuania. The Lithuanian samizdat journal *Ausra*, however, publishes reports from Belorussian parishes.

Ukraine

The Catholic church in the Ukraine is small, and details concerning its activities are restricted. Most of the Catholics in the Ukraine are Poles. In 1961, 132 Catholic churches are known to have existed. Some 40 remain today. The other denomination in the Ukraine is the Uniate church, which was forcibly merged with the Russian Orthodox church in 1946. One of the main opponents of this policy was the late Cardinal Slipyj who, because of his continuing opposition to the authorities, was imprisoned in 1946, allegedly for collaborating with the Nazis. On his release in 1953, he refused to accept the new status of the Ukrainian Uniate church and was again imprisoned until 1962. In the meantime, a catacomb, or underground, Uniate church was formed. And Cardinal Slipyj, though resident in Rome since 1963, spoke out in its defense, demanding that the church be granted its individual status. He organized a Permanent Synod of Ukrainian Catholic Bishops in November 1971 and adopted the title of patriarch.

It was not until Cardinal Wojtyła became pope in 1978 that some Catholics in the Ukraine could hope that their case for a separate church would be heard in Rome. In 1980, the pope sent a letter to Slipyj in which he defended the right of the Ukrainian Catholic church to exist. In March, the pope convened a synod of the Catholic hierarchy. One of the main tasks was to elect a candidate to be metropolitan of Lvov. The pope named Archbishop Myroslav Lubachivsky as successor to Cardinal Slipyj. This ensured the continuity of the Lvov metropolitate, canonically the highest institution in the Ukrainian Catholic church, which the Soviet authorities had condemned. In spite of the continuing repression, an Initiative Group for the Defense of the Rights of Believers was set up in September 1982. One of the organizers was Josef Terelya, a human rights activist. The authorities reacted in much the same way as they responded to the Lithuanian human rights groups. They arrested and imprisoned several of the organizers.

FURTHER READING

Indispensable for information on all religions in the Soviet Union and Eastern Europe is *Religion in Communist Lands*, a quarterly journal published in Kent, England.
Beeson, Trevor. *Discretion and Valour*. London: Collins Fontana, 1974.
Bociurkiw, Bohdan R., and Strong, John W., eds. *Religion and Atheism in the USSR and Eastern Europe*. London: Macmillan, 1975.
Catholicism in Eastern Europe:
Alexander, Stella. *Church and State in Yugoslavia since 1945*. Cambridge: Cambridge University Press, 1979.
Dunn, Dennis J. *Détente and Papal-Communist Relations, 1962–1978*. London: Westview, 1979.
Michnik, Adam. *L'Eglise et la gauche: Le Dialogue polonais*. Paris: Seuil, 1979.
Pomian-Srzednicki, Maciej. *Religious Change in Contemporary Poland: Secularisation and Politics*. London: Routledge and Kegan Paul, 1982.

THE ORTHODOX CHURCH IN EASTERN EUROPE AND THE SOVIET UNION

The Orthodox church consists of about 70 million believers; the majority of these (some 30 million in the Soviet Union and another 30 million in Eastern Europe) live under communist rule, that is under a government policy of militant atheism, antireligious legislation and sometimes open persecution. Since 1917, the Orthodox hierarchy of the Soviet Union has gradually evolved a compromise relationship with the state that has also been followed by Orthodox churches in Eastern Europe.

ROMANIA

The Romanian Orthodox church is the largest church in the country, with over 12 million believers. The church has been largely dependent on the Moscow patriarchate and has cooperated with the state. Because of the patriarchate's cooperation with the Communist party, the Orthodox church remained the national church after 1945. There was no official separation of church and state. This gave the Orthodox church certain privileges: salaries for the clergy and eight church publications. A large number of churches are open, but since 1958 over half of Romania's monks and nuns have been forced to leave their religious houses, and the orders have been forbidden to accept novices. The largely Uniate region of Transylvania was forced to unite with the Orthodox church under government pressure.

The monasteries have become something of a showcase, at least for tourists. But as the Romanian human rights activist Paul Goma reported in March 1978, Elena Ceauşescu, the wife of the president and Communist party leader Nicolae Ceauşescu, ordered the demolition of the Ene church—an historical Orthodox structure in Bucharest—and removed all publications on the monasteries from the shops. This last she had done because nuns in the Agapia monastery had apparently refused to stop the liturgy when Mrs. Ceauşescu entered the monastery during a visit in the autumn of 1977. During the 1970s, there was a move to halve the number of Orthodox clergy by insisting on the retirement of those over 65 years of age. However, Patriarch Justinian postponed such a decision.

Documentation reaching the West during this period reported on the insufficient number of parish churches, especially in the new industrial towns. For example, Father Costica Maftei, a young priest who was appointed to the modern complex of Titan in Bucharest, found that his parish of 300,000 believers had no suitable church. He brought this to the attention of the inspectorate in the patriarchate, which reported that it was not Maftei's affair. He was soon sent back to his village. Other priests who have questioned the relationship between the church and the authorities have been subjected to pressure and psychiatric abuse. Father Samisnicu, one of several, was put in a psychiatric institution in 1974. He had organized religious cells.

There have been other incidents of dissent within the Romanian Orthodox church. The most notable case so far has been that of Father Gheorghe Calciu-Dumitreasa. He is important for a number of reasons. In autumn 1977, he protested against the demolition of the Ene church in Bucharest. In early 1978, in the patriarchal cathedral in Bucharest, he described atheism as a philosophy of despair. Many students attended his Lenten sermons given at the seminary in Bucharest in March and April, 1978. He was removed by the church authorities from his teaching post at the theological faculty to an administrative post in the patriarchate. In June 1978, a "Committee for the Defense of Priest Gheorghe Calciu" was formed. More troubling, from the point of view of the authorities, was when, in February 1979, a free trade union was formed. The leaders of the Committee for the Defense a of Religious Freedom and Freedom of Conscience, Pavel Niculescu and Father Calciu, established relations with the independent trade union. The authorities reacted swiftly. The members of the trade union disappeared, and on March 10, 1979, Father Calciu was arrested along with the founders of the trade union, Dr. Ion Cana and Gheorghe Braşoveanu. After considerable publicity from Western politicians and human rights organizations, Father Calciu was released in August 1984. He is reported to be under 24-hour house surveillance.

YUGOSLAVIA

The Orthodox church of Serbia, with its 9 million believers, has never been influenced by the Moscow patriarchate to the same extent as the other Eastern European Orthodox churches. It underwent considerable persecution by the Yugoslav communist government after 1945, but retained considerable prestige because of its sufferings under the Nazis. Relations between church and state improved during the 1960s. A number of churches were built and the training of priests was expanded.

In 1958, a church council decided to restore the bishopric of Ohrida with its seat in Skopje, capital of the Republic of Macedonia. The Serbian Orthodox church regarded this as an attempt by the Yugoslav authorities to fragment the church. Three Macedonian dioceses became independent of the Serbian church in 1967, with the support of the federal government. The authorities considered that an independent Macedonian church would help to strengthen Macedonian national identity.

Over the years, the Serbian Orthodox church has continued to retain much of its independence from the state; it has relative freedom to publish; and its priests are allowed travel abroad. It does not recognize the independence of the Macedonian church.

BULGARIA

The 600,000-strong Bulgarian Orthodox church cooperates fully with the state. The church has one seminary and a large number of monasteries. Antireligious legislation is severe. The Bulgarian church has some prestige because of its position as a symbol of national sovereignty and Slav culture. On May 24, 1969, there was a national holiday in memory of Cyril and Methodius, the founders of the Bulgarian church and originators of the Cyrillic alphabet. The occasion was marked by an Orthodox conference under the aegis of the Moscow patriarchate.

HUNGARY

The small Hungarian Orthodox church has a membership of 40,000. It has no ecclesiastical jurisdiction. The Orthodox believers are divided between the four patriarchates of Serbia, Romania, the Soviet Union and Bulgaria. Each section is governed by the appropriate episcopal representative. Religious instruction for children is permitted in schools.

POLAND

Poland's Orthodox church consists of 460,000 members, of whom 200,000 are Uniates who were absorbed into the Orthodox church in 1945. The Polish Orthodox church conforms to the policies of the Moscow patriarchate. Children are allowed—on a voluntary basis—religious instruction in schools.

CZECHOSLOVAKIA

Before 1968, the Czechoslovak Orthodox church was in a position similar to that of Poland's, with Moscow-oriented policies. The church was subject to severe pressure from Antonín Novotný's government, and a large number of Uniates were forcibly incorporated into the Orthodox church. The reforms initiated by Alexander Dubček in January 1968 marked a new church-state relationship that persisted even after the Soviet-led invasion of Czechoslovakia in August 1968. Today, the church press is restricted.

The Uniate church has been rehabilitated and its 250,000 members have left the Orthodox church. The Czechoslovak Orthodox church was the only church in Eastern Europe to support the intervention in 1968.

ALBANIA

In 1945, about 20 percent of the country's population of under 2 million belonged to the Orthodox church. There is little current information available on the Orthodox church, and since in 1967, Albania was declared, officially, the first atheistic state, presumably Orthodox believers are persecuted as much as Catholics and Muslims for practicing religion.

THE SOVIET UNION

Three events crucial to the future position of the Orthodox church under communism took place between 1917 and 1918. First, the patriarchate was restored in 1917, transferring influence from the six-man holy synod to the one man elected as patriarch. (Policy toward the state depends largely on the personality of the incumbent patriarch.) Second, in 1918 the Soviet constitution guaranteed "freedom of religious and antireligious propaganda"; and third, the decree on the separation of church and state deprived the church of its property, allowing churches to be used for worship at the discretion of local authorities; convents, monasteries, seminaries and theological academies were closed.

Violent persecution of believers took place during 1918–1926. Patriarch Tikhon tried to remain politically impartial. After his death and the imprisonment of his nominated successors, the metropolitan, Sergei, took over the leadership, though he was elected patriarch only in 1943. In 1927, Sergei made a declaration avowing the Orthodox church's absolute loyalty to the Soviet state—a declaration that forms the basis of the Orthodox hierarchy's relations with the state to the present. Statements were and are issued by the church in support of state foreign policy and claiming, against all evidence to the contrary, the existence of "religious freedom" in the Soviet Union. In 1929, the constitution was amended to guarantee "freedom of religious belief and antireligious propaganda"; in 1936 "belief" was changed to "worship," which has been retained to the present. The church exists in Soviet law solely for the purpose of worship. It is forbidden to organize charitable or social work, to give children religious instruction or to conduct classes for adults. Priests must receive special permission from the local deputy of the Council for Religious Affairs to conduct services even where believers are allowed to use a church for worship.

During World War II, the Orthodox church supported the government. This won it a measure of greater toleration. The number of churches increased from 4,255 in 1941 to 22,000 in 1947. The number of priests increased from 5,665 to 33,000. Eight seminaries and two theological academies were permitted to open. The church's legal position, however, has been little improved. The atheist campaign has continued, almost unabated; churches have been often closed down illegally and priests are still imprisoned. The Orthodox church's regular (and only) publication, *Journal of the Moscow Patriarchate*, is strictly censored. There is a shortage of Bibles and prayer books, and these are not obtainable in the official bookshops.

The Soviet authorities publish an official atheist magazine, *Science and Religion*, which frequently castigates party members and the Komsomol for taking part in baptism, marriage and funeral services. Indeed, in October 1984, the Soviet media spoke out strongly against the interest being taken by young people in religion. A number of earlier articles had appeared in the Soviet press that suggested that in spite of an almost unremitting antireligion campaign, there is considerable interest in religion among the younger generation. But such campaigns against religious activities are a regular feature of *Science and Religion* and other publications. In 1954–58, for example, a more ideologically oriented campaign against religion was attempted; there was a lessening of direct pressure on believers and an intensification of atheist education programs. But 1958 marked the beginning of a more direct attack against religious activities. The pressure took various forms. *Science and Religion* has often openly encouraged both the dismissal of believers from their jobs and direct interference with the legal right of parents to instruct their children in religion. In some districts, children have been forcibly prevented from entering churches and even removed from the custody of their parents; priests have also been forbidden to give communion to children.

The policy of the hierarchy toward the state
Generally, the Orthodox hierarchy has accepted such pressure with silence. However, there have been signs that a considerable section of Orthodox opinion no longer agrees with the patriarchate's submissive policy toward the government. In 1965, for example, two priests of the Moscow diocese, Nikolai Eshliman and Gleb Yakunin, sent open letters to President Podgorny, the patriarch and all bishops, protesting against the state infringements on the right to religious worship guaranteed in the Soviet constitution. They charged the church authorities with submitting to secret dictates from the authorities. Both priests were barred by the patriarch in 1966 from their activities "for disrupting the internal peace of the church." That incident sparked off many other protests and petitions, the main argument being

that the state acted illegally with regard to its relationship with the church. This insistence on legality, citing the Soviet constitution and church canon law was also the main thrust of the debate Archbishop Yermogen initiated with the patriarchate. Yermogen was removed from his see at Kaluga after disputes with the local authorities. In his letters to the patriarch (1956–66) protesting his enforced retirement, he accused the Council of Religious Affairs of acting unconstitutionally against the church and implied that the Orthodox hierarchy, far from defending the church's legal rights, acquiesced in state illegalities, such as the closing of churches in 1961–64. Yermogen also accused the hierarchy of breaking their own canon law in electing bishops without the participation of all existing bishops. He was supported by eight bishops in 1965.

The writings of two Orthodox laymen, Anatoly Levitin and Boris Talantov, which were illegally circulated in the Soviet Union in the late 1960s, also reflected dissatisfaction with the policy of the hierarchy in its relations with the authorities. Both men criticized the passivity of the church and its unwillingness to protect its spiritual and moral interests.

During the 1970s, Father Yakunin continued his campaign for believers' rights. In 1975, the Soviet authorities declared Easter Sunday a working day. Yakunin wrote a sharp letter of protest to the Politburo. Shortly afterward, he was dismissed from his job as watchman in a Moscow church. Along with Lev Regelson, a layman, he wrote a long appeal to the World Council of Churches (WCC) Assembly in Nairobi. Father Yakunin was dismissed from yet another job, but the appeal was taken up by the WCC to the extent that for the first time a debate on the repression of religion in the Soviet Union took place at the Assembly. At the end of 1976, Yakunin was one of the three founder-members of the Christian Committee for the Defense of Believers' Rights in the Soviet Union, which, among other things, monitored the violations of religious rights in the country. In August 1979, Yakunin was arrested and sentenced to 10 years' imprisonment.

There were other signs of dissent during the 1970s. Father Dimitri Dudko, a Moscow priest, held a series of unprecedented question-and-answer sessions after Saturday evening service in his church during the winter of 1973–74. Crowds flocked to hear him. The response of the patriarchate (headed by Patriarch Pimen, elected in 1971) was predictable. Father Dudko was forbidden to continue these sessions. He continued to give sermons, however, and his example was followed by other Christians who formed the Christian Seminars, as they were known in the West, which were broken up by the KGB in 1976. Pressure was increased against those campaigning for religious freedoms. The Seminars' founders, Aleksandr Ogorodnikov and Vladimir Poresh, were sentenced to 11 and eight years in prison, respectively. Arrests continued throughout the late 1970s. Under considerable intimidation and pressure, Father Dudko appeared on Soviet television on June 20, 1980 and made a public "confession" and "recantation" of his former activities. He was released.

Other groups were set up in the early 1980s. Zoya Krakhmalnikova was arrested in August 1982. She had compiled a collection of Christian religious reading entitled *Nadezhda*. She was charged with a political offense, although the material had no political content. She was given a one-year prison sentence and five years of internal exile.

The campaign against any dissent was complemented by church closures, in Belorussia, Gorky and other places. Yakunin, in the early 1960s, reported that some 10,000 churches—roughly half of all those that existed in the mid-1950s—were closed. Official Soviet publications stated that the number of churches in 1971 was 7,500. The Council for Religious Affairs reported in 1974 that there were 7,062 registered churches, but it was reported at a closed meeting in 1976 that "about 1,000 were formally listed but were not in use."

Regional churches of the Soviet Union

The Orthodox churches of Trans-Carpathian Ukraine and Galicia, which was annexed in 1945 from Poland and Czechoslovakia, contains a large number of former Uniates, whose church was declared illegal in 1945. The number of churches in this region has been significantly reduced because of the allegedly nationalist Ukrainian character of its priests.

The other Orthodox church of the Soviet Union—the Georgian church—is completely subject to the Moscow patriarchate. It has been much persecuted and is said to have only 100 churches and their priests left. The Georgian church has no seminary of its own; candidates for the priesthood have to study at seminaries where they receive little instruction in Georgian religious literature.

The Armenian Monophysites are in a better position, with 3,500,000 believers, one seminary and discreet aid from Armenians abroad. The Armenian patriarch is elected by the laity, which includes all Armenians, believers and unbelievers alike. The government is, as a result, able to exercise considerable direct pressure on the patriarchal elections.

FURTHER READING

Conquest, Robert, ed. *Religion in the USSR*. London: Bodley Head, 1968.

THE PROSTESTANT CHURCHES IN EASTERN EUROPE AND THE SOVIET UNION

After the communist takeover, Protestants suffered just as much as Catholics. Whereas the Catholic church is essentially hierarchical in structure and depends greatly on an ecclesiastical structure and administration that guarantees its continuity, Protestants are in a somewhat different position, relying more on Bible readings and preaching than on power structures.

In some Eastern European countries, the Protestant churches, though repressed in the immediate postwar years, have sought an accommodation with the communist authorities.

EAST GERMANY

The Protestant church is the largest church in East Germany, consisting of nearly 14 million members out of a population of 17 million. It has suffered little of the repression experienced by the churches in Czechoslovakia or Hungary. During the 1950s, a number of pastors were imprisoned for opposing atheistic propaganda. After the building of the Berlin Wall in 1961, East German pastors continued to share some of their activities with the West German Protestant church. The separation of both churches took place in 1969 when a Federation of Protestant Churches in East Germany was established. Although the state has reached a modus vivendi with the church, it has sought to diminish church influence, particularly in education. A secular youth confirmation ceremony designed to replace the church's confirmation ceremony was denounced by the Protestant church. At a synod in April 1976, the late Bishop Albrecht Schönherr of Berlin said that children were being pressured at schools to prepare for the *Jugendweihe*, as the secular ceremony was called. And in protest against this state interference, Pastor Brusewitz committed suicide by self-immolation in August 1976.

There have been other protests too. When the draft party program of the Socialist Workers' party was published in 1976, just before the Ninth Party Congress in May, the draft omitted guaranteeing equal rights to all citizens irrespective of ideology, religious belief or social status. The church protested against the omission and the clause was eventually included in the final version. The church also protested against the introduction of premilitary training in the schools in 1978. Thus, while the Protestant church agreed with the authorities that it was a church within socialism, this did not mean that it was subservient to the state on certain moral and social issues that involved the church.

In many ways, the state has incorporated the church, without resorting to repressive measures. East German Communist party leader, Erich Honecker, held talks with Protestant church leaders on March 6, 1978. Both sides agreed that Christians had a role to play in East German society, and that the state should recognize the Protestant community as an indispensable group within that society. Concessions soon followed this meeting. The church was given greater access to television and radio; they were allowed to choose their own speakers for the religious broadcasts; permission was granted to build a large number of new churches, especially in new housing estates; and promises were made that Christians would not be discriminated against in education and at work.

The concessions did not weaken the Protestant church in terms of its independent stance on some issues. Indeed, throughout the late 1970s and early 1980s, the younger generation became increasingly attracted to the church, primarily because of its role in the independent peace movement. For one thing, the church not only spoke out against the militarization of East Germany society but criticized the arms race and the increasing tension between the United States and the Soviet Union. In one of its most outspoken statements in many years, the Protestant church demanded that no new short-range missiles should be deployed by the Soviet Union in East Germany. The church also asked the state to allow young people to express their views freely. These statements were made by the Federation of Protestants at a synod in Potsdam in September 1983. The chairman of the federation, Bishop Johannes Hempel, argued that the socialist, centralized control of the economy, together with the world economic crisis, had created disillusionment among East German youth. The bishop criticized the authorities in 1982 when they banned the biblical symbol "Swords into Ploughshares," which had become a symbol of the unofficial peace movement. Earlier, in February 1982, a petition known as the "Berlin Appeal" was circulated. It was drawn up by a group of pacifists led by Pastor Rainer Eppelman. It called for the withdrawal of foreign troops and nuclear weapons from both East and West Germany. It also called for the abolition of military training in East Germany. This newly formed alliance—however informal—between the independent peace movement and members of the Protestant church (especially from among the grass roots) stemmed partly from the fact that the postwar generation of churchmen had become considerably disillusioned with the apparent passivity of the church, and openly challenged the view of the church's role held by the prewar generation of churchmen. And when a Peace Forum was held in Dresden in February 1982 and 1983, Rainer Eppelman's views received considerable support. The authorities reacted with some restraint; at that time the state was preparing for the Luther anniversary celebrations.

The 500th anniversary of the birth of Martin Luther was celebrated with enormous ceremony throughout East Germany. The state joined with the Protestant churches in preparing for the event. Indeed, Erich Honecker himself chaired the steering committee that supervised the Luther celebration arrangements. The occasion was marked by lectures, tours and meetings; and the East German authorities invited leading Protestant theologians from the West to attend the celebrations. The anniversary was important for two reasons. First of all, it demonstrated that church-state relations were indeed satisfactory. More importantly, however, it demonstrated the state's ability and willingness to rewrite history. Whereas, after the communist takeover, Martin Luther had been labeled a bourgeois thinker, with little real regard for the masses, in 1983 he was hailed as a kind of populist thinker and theologian who spoke out against injustices directed against the peasants. It was a considerable turnabout in the rewriting of history, and suggested that the East German authorities were capable of using history in order to legitimate the East German state.

HUNGARY

The two most important Protestant groups in Hungary are the Reformed (Calvinist) church, with a membership of nearly 2 million, and the Lutheran church, which has over 500,000 members. In 1948, both churches signed an agreement with the state authorities, accepting government control over church life in return for legally recognized status. The agreement was renewed in January 1969 and included a provision that the state would guarantee subsidies to cover salaries, maintenance costs and the general upkeep of church buildings. The Calvinist Bishop Lajos Ordass, in contrast, spoke out against any state interference in church affairs. He was charged in 1948 with illegal currency deals, sentenced to two and a half years' imprisonment and was removed in 1950. His rehabilitation and reinstatement in 1956 were shortlived, for he was not allowed to resume his duties and remained in office only until 1958; he died in Budapest, isolated, in 1978. Bishop Ordass was not the only individual to suffer and to be denied support from the church leadership. During the 1960s, a number of pastors were imprisoned and Methodist ministers in particular were harassed by the authorities. During the early 1980s, the Methodists, especially in parts of Eastern Hungary, began taking an active interest in Hungary's poor, especially among the gypsy community.

In September 1968, the Hungarian Communist party's ideological journal *Pártélet* (September) promised the churches continued existence and "lasting cooperation," provided they adhered strictly to the church-state agreements and dissociated themselves from "reactionary elements" among the clergy. Indeed, it is the apparent passivity of the Hungarian Lutheran church, particularly on the part of the leadership, that provided the basis of a significant debate in Hungary among church members. The gist of the debate, which began in the mid-1970s and became more vocal in the early 1980s, focused on the long-term implications of the theology of "diaconia," or service. The main exponent of diaconia was and continues to be Bishop Zoltán Káldy, who in August 1984 was chosen as president of the Lutheran World Federation. Basically, Káldy has argued that one of the aims of the Lutheran church is to offer service to humanity in a socialist society without formally adopting the principles of Marxism-Leninism. The church, he argues, can fulfill its confessional needs. It should not be driven into a ghetto. It can cooperate with the authorities and avoid a confrontation. In Káldy's words:

> We have often said that the dialogue between Christian and Marxist is conducted in political life. That is by our cooperation. This has proved correct and fruitful. We have thereby avoided the temptation of the *Kulturkampf*. Such a struggle would have set members of our family against one another, not alongside one another. And that cooperation has stood the test; however, it becomes important to advance the Marxist-Christian dialogue by presenting some basic questions so that we may be able to achieve a broader and more courageous cooperation. . . .

Some members of the Lutheran church in Hungary and in the West have questioned the degree to which the Lutheran church should cooperate with the state. Indeed, the Lutheran and Catholic churches in Hungary were the only churches in Eastern Europe to remain silent when Hungarian troops, as part of the Warsaw Pact army, marched into Czechoslovakia in August 1968. Nor did the churches speak out during the Polish crisis of 1980–81.

CZECHOSLOVAKIA

The Protestant denominations in Czechoslovakia include the Czech Brethren (Calvinists and Lutherans united after 1918; the membership is 260,000); the Lutheran church (50,000 Silesian Evangelical Lutherans, mainly Poles, and the Slovak Evangelical church with 400,000 members); the Reformed church in Slovakia (150,000 members, mainly Hungarians); the Moravian church (10,000 members); and the Seventh-Day Adventists (18,233 members). There are smaller groups of Baptists, Unitarians and the Assemblies of God. The Czechoslovak National church, which was formed in 1920 as a breakaway movement from Roman Catholicism, has 500,000 members. The Protestant leaders in Czechoslovakia gave their full support to the state legislation on churches in 1949, which for some time provided a relatively relaxed atmosphere. The clergy have to swear an oath of allegiance to the government and their stipends are paid by the state. Since 1968 the publications of the clergy have been subjected to considerable censorship. At the same time, a theological faculty is maintained at the Charles University in Prague.

The Protestants in Czechoslovakia have been among the most zealous supporters of the communist-controlled peace movements, and since 1958 Prague has been the center of the Christian Peace Conference founded by the Protestant theologian Josef Hromádka. The Peace Conference has consistently supported Soviet policies and advocated the necessity of a Christian-Marxist dialogue. After the invasion of Czechoslovakia by Warsaw Pact forces in August 1968, Professor Hromádka, together with other Protestant leaders, declared his loyalty to the Czechoslovak government and addressed a bitter protest to the Soviet authorities.

The situation deteriorated rapidly after 1968. In the early 1970s, many pastors were refused permission to carry out their duties. When the human rights movement, Charter 77, was founded in January 1977, the Communist party daily *Rudé Právo* published an article stating that no official of the synod of the Evangelical church of Czech Brethren had signed the "defamatory document." The Evangelical Council reacted by distributing the text of its statement, issued to pastors in Bohemia and Moravia, to the effect that it did not even know about the contents of the document. Some leaders of the church were interrogated and were asked to expel from the church those who had signed the statement. Dr. Keyr, the synod elder, had to explain to the authorities (apparently with difficulty) that excommunication was not possible within the Evangelical church. Pressure was put on the Czech Hussite church, along with representatives of the Church of Seventh-Day Adventists and members of other Protestant sects to criticize Charter 77 openly.

It was during 1977–78 that the West got a clearer insight into the situation of the churches in Czechoslovakia, in particular, the Czech Brethren. An analysis of life in that church was drawn up by 11 Czech Brethren. They addressed their complaints to the Federal Assembly of the church. Among conditions of which they complained were the restrictions placed by the authorities on the freedom of movement of the Czech Brethren. They could not move outside their own parishes and were therefore prevented from communicating with other Brethren; special permission was needed for lectures and discussions, cultural activities and concerts; any relations with foreign churches and the WCC had to be conducted through "official intermediaries"; ecumenical meetings on a parish level were suppressed. There were restrictions on pastoral work, administration and general spiritual and religious duties. The document cited a number of individuals who were deprived of approval by the State to preach. It stated too, that 13 students at the Comenius Theological Faculty were dismissed or else could not receive state permission to carry out their pastoral duties after graduation. In 1969–70, there were 800 students of theology (all denominations); now there were 400, despite the growing number of applicants. Thirty parishes (of Czech Brethren) were without pastors. The document complained of continuing state interference in other areas. In 1974, for example, the interior ministry dissolved the Association of Pastors of the Evangelical Czech Brethren who in the past held a theological course twice a year. The Czech Brethren were discriminated against in jobs, the civil service and the state administration. In education, the document argued, Czech Brethren children and those wanting to attend university were intimidated. The Czech Brethren's publications, *Ceský Brato* and *Kostnické Jiskrý*, are censored and are restricted in size and distribution.

Other Protestant churches have suffered similar repressive measures. During 1983, for example, the authorities arrested several members of the Seventh-Day Adventist Church.

BULGARIA

The Bulgarian Protestants—Methodists, Baptists, Congregationalists and Pentecostals—number about 33,000. The Protestant churches were almost destroyed as organized bodies in 1949 when 15 Protestant leaders were put on trial on charges of illegal currency deals and espionage. The WCC was named as the "foreign agency" responsible for collecting the secret information. The accused were sentenced to life or long-term imprisonment. The trial paralyzed normal church activities and led to an almost complete severance of ties with the Protestant churches in the West.

The Pentecostals are the largest Protestant community, with some 10,000 members and 120 churches. The largest congregation is at Burgas on the Black Sea. The church is organized by the state. There is a Pentecostal Union in Sofia. Organized evangelical activity is forbidden. There is a shortage of prayer books. Most Pentecostal pastors are untrained, and there is no theological training college. The only way that Protestants can receive theological training is by attending the Sofia Theological Academy, an Orthodox institution. Although information is very limited, during the 1970s there were signs of a revival in the Pentecostal church, with large numbers of converts attending services. The authorities responded accordingly; a wave of house arrests took place in March 1979.

POLAND

The Polish Protestant churches—the Evangelical-Augsburg church, or Lutheran church (200,000 members); the Evangelical Reformed church, or Calvinist church (only a few thousand); the Polish Baptist church (6,000 members); the Methodist church (4,500); the United Evangelical church (a few thousand)—are recognized by the state. Most of the churches have their own publications and are not subjected to harassment. Most of the Protestant churches belong to the Polish Ecumenical Council, founded in 1946, with the aim of reconstructing the Protestant churches that were practically destroyed during the war. The council finally stabilized its relations with the state in 1967 when its status was legally ratified. A Christian Theological

Academy was founded in 1954. Since 1982, member churches of the Polish Ecumenical Council along with the Seventh-Day Adventists can broadcast religious services on Polish radio.

ROMANIA

The total membership of the Romanian Protestant churches is about 1.2 million and their adherents are largely members of the Hungarian and German minorities. This figure includes 780,000 Reformed, 218,000 Lutherans, 160,000 Baptists, 50,000 Pentecostals and 70,000 Seventh-Day Adventists. The Romanian constitution of 1965 provides for the citizen's right to "profess or not to profess a religious faith," but the government's campaign of antireligious propaganda is extremely intense. The churches receive no state subsidies. They had few contacts with Western Protestants until 1961 when active association with the WCC was resumed.

The Baptist church is the most active in terms of campaigning for greater religious freedoms and human rights. In 1973, a Baptist pastor, Josif Ţon, then a teacher at the Baptist seminary in Bucharest, described the restrictions placed on the church by the state. He pointed out that pastors could not be appointed without state approval and that the church leadership and membership were subjected to government control; and he called all Baptist leaders to stand up for their religious and civil rights. Other protests followed. A joint protest by Baptist and Pentecostal believers was signed in May 1974 in response to the arrest and imprisonment of Vasile Rascol. He had distributed Bibles and other religious material. The authorities interrogated Ţon and Pavel Niculescu, and later questioned hundreds of others.

The protests grew into a small movement demanding religious rights. After the 27th Congress of the Baptist churches, held in February 1977 in Romania, a document, drawn up by Ţon, Niculescu and Avril Popescu, criticized the discrimination against believers in education and employment, and called for the right of free association. The document formed part of the United States' Helsinki Commission report on Romania presented in Belgrade in 1977. The authorities put pressure on the leadership of the Baptists to silence the protesters. In February 1978, Niculescu and Popescu were banned from preaching. In April, Niculescu along with Dimitru Ianculovici, formed the Committee for the Defense of Religious Freedom and Freedom of Conscience. They demanded, among other things, "free religion in a free state" and redress for Greek Catholics in Romania, and they highlighted the discrimination against believers. Membership on the committee grew in spite of the harassment by the authorities. Two members of the Orthodox church reported on the repression felt by their own church, an unusual occurrence since the Orthodox church in Romania has traditionally been too closely identified with the state to speak out against religious discrimination and issues concerning human rights. In September 1978, Niculescu and Popescu were expelled from the Baptist church, along with other members of the committee. Arrests of Baptists continued for some months.

The Baptist church

The Baptist church is the second largest Christian community in the Soviet Union after the Russian Orthodox church. In 1966, an official Baptist report stated that there were a quarter of a million adult baptised members and another quarter of a million nonadults and adherents. Twelve years earlier, in 1954, the official Soviet Baptist magazine, *Bratsky Vesnik*, gave a considerably larger figure—half a million baptised believers, with another three million adherents, including believers' families. The discrepancy between the two figures is probably due to the fact that many Baptist communities have been denied registration over the past several years. This, in turn, is connected with an inner schism within the Baptist church, which goes back to 1961 when a "reform" or "initiative" movement began to develop.

The Baptist reformers accused the official church leadership (the All Union Council of Evangelical Christians and Baptists) of having betrayed the true faith by allowing the state authorities to exercise full control over the church and its activities. They demanded an end of state interference in church affairs and a strict application of the constitutional decree concerning the separation of church and state.

The activities of the Baptist reformers and their demand for a spiritual revival within the church were denounced by the Soviet authorities as antisocial and illegal. The "initiative" communities have been subjected to considerable pressure and persecution, in the form of hundreds of long prison sentences. The reform movement continues, however, and has even provided the impetus for similar tendencies among the Orthodox clergy, as well as for considerable conversion to Baptism among the younger generation.

Equally, the Soviet authorities have continued to imprison and intimidate those Baptists who carry out "unofficial" activities. In June 1971, the reform Baptists announced the setting up of a printing agency called The Christian. By August of the same year, they declared that they had printed 40,000 copies of the New Testament, hymnbooks and other religious materials. The police discovered one of the printing presses in October 1974 in Latvia. Seven people were arrested and then sentenced to prison terms of up to four years.

One publication that appeared frequently was the *Bulletin of the Council of Prisoners' Relatives*, founded in 1971. The aim of the *Bulletin* was to provide accurate information concerning those people who were persecuted for their religious beliefs or activities. One of these included a prominent leader of the reform Baptists, Georgi Vins. He was imprisoned from 1966 to 1969 for his religious activities. On his release, he resumed the leadership of the reform Baptists. In March 1974 he was again arrested, and in January 1975 he was sentenced to five years in a prison camp followed by five years in exile in Yakutia (Siberia).

The Lutheran church

The Lutheran church is the other large church of the Protestant communities. It is estimated that there are some 500,000 members in Latvia and some 350,000 in Estonia. Small Lutheran communities exist in other parts of the Soviet Union, but since they have no clergy, they have little hope of survival.

The Calvinist church in the Transcarpathian Ukraine has about 90,000 members, all Hungarians. Other Protestant communities include the Seventh-Day Adventists, a much harassed community with a membership of 40,000, and the Mennonites and the Molokans—the former combining characteristics of the Baptists and Friends, the latter being strict fundamentalists and pacifists who live in Transcaucasia. The two sects have an estimated combined membership of 25,000. Soviet Pentecostals (17,000), who have close links with the Baptist communities, were banned under the *Instruction on the Application of the Law on Cults* (March 16, 1961). However, during the late 1960s, a few Pentecostal churches were registered as individual congregations not belonging to the Union of Evangelical Christians and Baptists, a body supervised by the state. Some of the Pentecostal congregations registered, but most prefered an existence outside the Union. The unregistered Pentecostal congregations flourished during the 1970s; at the same time, the emigration movement among Pentecostals, which began in 1976, had grown to some 20,000 applicants by May 1978. The Soviet authorities have stepped up their campaign to register the Pentecostal congregations, which would in effect deny them their autonomy. Members of the congregations have been threatened with arrest. Indeed, many of the leaders of the Pentecostal movement have been imprisoned and denied emigration, which in part accounted for a Pentecostal family taking refuge in the U.S. Embassy in Moscow in 1978.

FURTHER READING

de George, Richard T. and Scanlon, James P. *Marxism and Religion in Eastern Europe.* Boston: Reidel, 1976.
Kolarz, Walter, *Religion in the Soviet Union.* London: Macmillan, 1961.

ISLAM IN THE SOVIET UNION AND EASTERN EUROPE

THE SOVIET UNION

The Soviet Muslim community is located in three main areas: Central Asia, where 75 percent of the Muslim population lives; the Northern Caucasus and Eastern Transcaucasia with 12 percent of the total Muslim population; and the Middle Volga region and the Southern Urals with 13 percent. Small Muslim groups exist in Western Siberia (Siberian Tatars), in Central Russia (Kasimov Tatars) and in Lithuanian Belorussia (Lithuanian Tatars). Seventy-five percent of the Soviet Muslims are Turks; the rest are divided equally between Iranians and Ibero-Caucasians. There are a small number of Muslim Semites: the Arabs of Samarkand (less than 20,000) and the Chalas, Bukharan Jews who converted to Islam but remain crypto-Jewish (less than 1,000). There are also between 40,000 and 50,000 Chinese Muslims (Dungans); 100,000 gypsies in Central Asia; and two North Caucasian nationalities, the Abkhazians (83,000 in 1970) and the Ossetians (489,000 in 1978) who are divided between Islam and Christianity.

Two features of the Muslim community distinguish them from other nationalities/minorities in the Soviet Union today. First, Muslims have lived under Russian domination since the mid-16th century, and they have been one of the most successful of the nationalities in preserving their culture, traditions and identity in spite of continuing pressure from the Soviet authorities to stamp out religious belief. Second, between 45 and 50 million Muslims live in the Soviet Union. That makes them the largest minority (after the ethnic Russians). One in every five Soviet citizens is a Muslim. By the year 2000, based on current demographic trends, the Muslim population will have risen to 100 million and the total Soviet population to 310 to 320 million; one in every three Soviet citizens will then be a Muslim.

These two trends—the persistence of an identity that inhibits assimilation and an extremely high birthrate—raises some interesting questions for the Soviet authorities. Since 1945, the Muslim community, as a result of often extreme repression, has been politically passive, raising no persistent demands for autonomy and self-determination. With the growing influence of Islamic fundamentalism outside the Soviet Union—in Iran and other parts of the Middle East—and with the continuing war in Afghanistan (the majority of whose population is Muslim), the Soviet authorities cannot ignore the impact Islamic fundamentalism might have on the Muslim population at home. It should be said, however, that the majority of Soviet Muslims are Sunnis (the orthodox branch of Islam), whereas Iranian Muslims are Shiites (followers of Mohammad's son-in-law, Ali); and Iran is unique in the Muslim world, in that Shiism is very closely identified with nationalism. To a large extent, the fervor of Islamic fundamentalism has been confined to Iran.

The demographic trends are equally important. Not only do they raise the question of the Russian-Muslim relationship, but the pattern of recruitment, command and structure of the Red Army poses some long-term problems for the Soviet authorities. The Muslim recruits do not speak Russian, and if they do, it is not fluent.

Soviet Policy toward the Muslims

After 1917, the Soviet authorities tolerated few Muslim customs. Most of the 25,000 mosques were closed. Shariat courts were closed, along with madrasalis (religious schools). The institution of *waqf* (charitable endowments) was ended and the *hajj* (pilgrimage to Mecca) was prohibited. Other practices were proscribed, including the giving of the *zakat* (prescribed tithe) and *sadaqah* (voluntary alms). The printing and distributing of religious material was also banned. The new antireligous laws introduced in 1928 increased the pressure on the Muslims. Arabic script, in which the Koran is written, was abolished. The traditional Islamic way of life was completely disrupted.

After World War II, Soviet attitudes toward the Muslims changed. The nationalities policy drawn up by the authorities involved the classification of the larger Muslim nationalities, defining those living in Bukhara and Khiva, as "nations" and constituting those bordering on foreign countries—Kazakhs, Uzbeks, Kirghiz, Tadzhiks, Turkmenis and Azerbaidzhanis—as "union republics." An essential aim of the Soviet nationalities policy has been the breaking up of the old tribal and extended-family society, prevalent among all the Muslim communities of the Soviet Union. This policy aimed at the "drawing closer" (*sblizhenie*) of Muslims and other Soviet nationalities, to be followed later by the "merging" (*sliyanie*) with the Russian nation. All the evidence shows that there has been no drawing together either culturally, linguistically or socially among Muslims and Russians. There is little evidence, for example, of intermarriage. More importantly, the Muslims have persistently refused to migrate, even though many millions were forcibly resettled before and after World War II. Those Russians who settled in the more eastern parts of the Soviet Union often migrate back to the Russian-dominated regions. And in spite of the intense antireligious campaigns, there is little evidence to suggest that Muslim ritual and belief is diminishing. On the contrary, articles in the Soviet press report on the persistence of belief and religious practices among the Muslim community.

In an effort to break up traditional Muslim communities and to supervise the religious life of Muslims, the Soviet authorities set up four spiritual directorates, which are located in four Muslim areas. There is a Spiritual Directorate of Central Asia and Kazakhstan; a Spiritual Directorate of the European SSR and Siberia; a Spiritual Directorate of Northern Caucausia and Daghestan; and a Spiritual Directorate of Transcaucasia. The directorates are concerned with every aspect of Islam in the Soviet Union and it is through them that the Soviet authorities exercise considerable control over the lives of the Muslim community. The directorates come under the control of the Council for Religious Affairs of the Council of Ministers, and their headquarters is at Tashkent. The only major Islamic library is located in Tashkent, which is an important center of Islamic publications and writings as well as a seat of learning. In Tashkent the Soviet authorities have allowed the opening of two madrasalis, which produce about 20 mullahs (Muslim schoolteachers) and imams (leaders of Muslim communities) a year, hardly adequate for the country's large Muslim community, of which 80 percent are practicing believers. Some of those graduating from the madrasalis are permitted to continue their education abroad. Those who graduate join the 1,900 officially registered clergy, again an insufficient number for the entire community. The Koran is in short supply, along with other religious publications. The Muslims' only magazine, *Muslims of the Soviet East*, which is not printed in Arabic characters, is primarily used for propaganda purposes abroad.

Nevertheless, mosques have been opened over the years, and the Soviet authorities are allowing more communication between Soviet Muslims and Muslims from other countries. But such visits and the conferences held in Tashkent are under considerable Soviet control. Through the official clerics, the Soviet authorities exercise influence.

In the past, the official clerics have neither protested against the antireligious propaganda nor the atheistic character of the Soviet state. They appear completely loyal to the regime, even accepting that believers can become members of the communist party. But the acceptance of dogma and the actual belief in dogma/ideology are two separate things for the Muslim community. Muslims can often adopt the practice of *taquiya* (dissimulation of one's beliefs in certain circumstances), which raises an interesting question concerning the degree of loyalty the Muslims have for the Soviet regime and to what extent the Soviet authorities, in a major crisis (for example, a greater reception by Soviet Muslims of the more fundamentalist aspects of Islam), could rely on the political subservience of the Muslim population. At the moment, despite access to a limited number of mosques—only 400 to 450 mosques officially operate—and limited opportunities for education and employment, the Muslim population has gained considerably from the communist regime. The cost has been high, however. The Crimean Tatars, in particular, have continued to suffer, with arrests and sentences meted out to those who continue to carry on their religious practices. The chairman of the directorates, Mufti Babakhanov, acting as a kind of unofficial Muslim ambassador of the Soviet authorities, plays an important role in publicizing to other Muslim countries the apparently good relationship between the authorities and its Muslim community.

There is however an "unofficial" side to Soviet Islam. This facet has evolved because the official Muslim clergy cannot satisfy the needs of believers. As Alexandre Bennigsen recently pointed out, "official" Islam would rapidly have lost its prestige and ascendancy were it not supported by a parallel unofficial, clandestine Islam, represented by the Sufi fraternities (or *tariqas*). These fraternities are well organized, and are much more active in intellectual and cultural matters and in many aspects of religious life than the official Muslim hierarchy; they are also hostile to the Soviet regime. The Sufi fraternities are located mostly in the northern Caucasus (Daghestan and Chechen-Ingush ASSR) and in parts of Central Asia, particularly in those territories where the population has preserved its tribal structures—for example, in Turkmenistan, Kirghizia and Kazakhstan.

The fraternities maintain a number of clandestine Koranic schools. Figures are unobtainable, and even if available could not be verified, precisely because of the clandestine organization. But it is thought that the fraternities maintain a number of unofficial "houses of prayer" sited near holy places, and that they engage in "intense, violent, antisecularist, anti-Soviet propaganda." These two trends, the offical liberal wing and the unofficial conservative wing have served to preserve Islam in the Soviet Union. The presence of the clandestine fraternities also limits the maneuverability of the Soviet authorities. If an antireligious campaign became unbearable for official Muslims, many could conceivably move across to the Sufi fraternities; if the attitude of the official Muslims becomes too submissive, it is equally conceivable that some believers would move over to the conservatism and intellectual and religious rigor of the fraternities.

The international dimension
For a considerable period, Soviet propaganda perceived that the main threat to the existence of Soviet communism and Marxism-Leninism came from the West, that the "imperialist" and "antisocialist" forces were doing everything in their power to defeat socialism. This view has not changed; what has changed in the past 10 years is the introduction into Soviet propaganda of the Islamic dimension.

This is an important development. The Soviet Union has close ties with some countries in the Middle East. Inevitably, Soviet attitudes—both ideological and political—toward Islam have undergone considerable reappraisal.

The 1979 invasion of Afghanistan, a Muslim-dominated country, clearly suggested to certain Islamic groups in the Middle East that communism and Islam were in fact irreconcilable; or, if not irreconcilable, that communism had little tolerance for Islamic belief—a belief that challenges the monopoly of power (and therefore ideology) as practiced under Soviet-type systems. Even before the invasion, the impact of Islamic fundamentalism was asserting itself in Iran. And although, so far, the Soviet Union has had few problems with containing the impact of this phenomenon, it has to project an image abroad that Islam and communism can in fact be compatible.

When the Shah was overthrown in 1979, the Soviet media supported those forces that overthrew his corrupt administration. The Soviet argument was that modernization had broken down, a modernization that was supported by the capitalist West. It was argued, too, that the Islamic revival in Iran was itself proof of the failure of the Western model of development, a development that led to the weakening of traditional values but not the erosion of religion, because in those countries experiencing a religious revival some significant parts of the religious hierearchy were excluded from the political process. E. M. Primakov, head of the Institute of Eastern Studies of the Academy of Science, wrote that the Western model was being discredited, which would lead to a move away from capitalist development. Primakov went on to argue that the religious elements cannot rule alone and that the more "progressive" elements should try and fill this void. From the Soviet point of view, that would demand a much greater toleration of religion and Islamic practices if such elements were to fill that void. Islamic communities abroad need evidence that Soviet communism is not antagonistic toward religion. This is why, over the past five years, the Soviet authorities have given great emphasis to conferences on Islam (held in Tashkent) and have sent their roving Muslim leader, Mufti Zia ed-Din Babakhanov, on frequent trips abroad to lecture on the compatibility between Soviet communism and the Islamic faith.

At home, it is clear that the authorities are concerned with the impact the Pan-Islamic movement might have on its Muslim population. Reports in the Soviet press suggest that the authorities have fostered a kind of Muslim nationalism—which is potentially risky.

EASTERN EUROPE
Yugoslavia
Eastern Europe's largest Muslim population lives in Yugoslavia. Over 4 million Muslims are scattered throughout the country, of whom nearly half live in the republic of Bosnia-Hercegovina. Bosnian Muslims are descended from the inhabitants of the old kingdom of Bosnia, which was conquered by the Turks in 1463. Many Catholics also embraced Islam. Ethnically, the Bosnian Muslims are Slavs. Under a law of 1971, the Muslims in Bosnia were given the status of a nationality, putting them on an equal footing with other ethnic groups, such as Serbs and Croats who live in Bosnia. But by recognizing the Muslims as a third major national group, the authorities released a potentially dangerous nationalism: Islamic nationalism.

Traditionally, Yugoslav communist officials treated the Muslim community delicately. After World War II, the Muslims were persecuted, since many had cooperated with those forces opposed to the partisans led by the late Marshal Tito. Over the years, however, Tito pampered the Muslims, building mosques, allowing several Muslim publications and financing trips abroad for those who wanted to visit Mecca. Many students studied abroad, too, in the main Islamic centers. Tito openly encouraged this. He was in need of cheap oil supplies and one of the ways in which he could get them was by demonstrating to countries in the Middle East, most notably Libya, that Yugoslavia treated its Muslim community very well indeed.

However, those students returning to Yugoslavia came back with ideas of a fundamentalist nature. Some were influenced by the writings of the Iranian revolutionaries. And in the late 1970s, with the overthrow of the Shah and the spread of Islamic fundamental thinking in the Middle East, the Yugoslav authorities became increasingly concerned with the impact such ideas might have on the Muslim community in Bosnia.

Signs of this concern were revealed in late 1970 when President Tito gave his backing to a campaign to prevent the spread of "Pan-Islamic revolutionary ideas." Several Muslim leaders, including the Mufti of Belgrade, were singled out for severe and repeated warnings for allegedly seeking to disrupt the atmosphere of "brotherhood and unity" among Yugoslavia's multinational population. Other Muslim clerics were accused of using religious rites, such as burial services, as occasions for making political statements opposed to Communist party policies. At the time, it was thought that the media campaign directed against the Muslims in Bosnia was intended as a warning against those who might adopt certain Islamic nationalist beliefs.

Warnings against "Islamic fanatics" continued. And in September 1983, the authorities put on trial 12 Yugoslav Muslim intellectuals accused of plotting to establish an "ethnically pure" Muslim republic within Yugoslavia. The court indictment said the group had links with an unnamed third country; it was thought at the time that the authorities were referring to Iran. One of the pieces of evidence produced during the trial was a declaration said to have been written by one of the leaders of the Islamic group that, according to the indictment, urged Muslims to follow Islam as a way of life, regardless of state norms. If that were true, then such sentiments posed a serious challenge to the Yugoslav Communist party.

Other trials took place in 1984. Professor Vojislav Šešelj was charged with spreading hostile propaganda and sentenced to eight years imprisonment, later halved. The Yugoslav media said that Šešelj had suggested, among other things, the "de-Titoization of the whole system" and declared that the concept of a separate "Muslim nation" should be quashed. Bosnia's party leader, Hamdija Pozderac, complained earlier that Muslim intellectuals had too much influence in the press in Bosnia, and also in the universities and publishing houses. He accused the Islamic community's official authorities of "passivity" toward the militant Muslims. In Zavidovici, a town in central Bosnia, for example, local Muslims refused to accept the imams appointed by their official leaders and elected their own.

The threat of an Islamic revival poses a number of problems for the Yugoslav authorities. Islamic fundamentalism conflicts with the basic tenets of Marxism-Leninism. And although the Yugoslav authorities may not actually believe in the ideology, the exercise of power and the structure of the political process make it impossible for them to face challenges from any other political or social groupings. If the authorities resort to force or crack down on the press, then their image will be hurt abroad.

More important is that Islamic fundamentalism within a Yugoslav context challenges the whole basis upon which the Yugoslav federal system operates, with the various nationalities granted equal rights. That Tito created a Muslim nationality in 1971, in an attempt to solve the age-old struggle between Serbs and Croats for control of Bosnia, only unleashed, in the process, a revival of Islam. And in a country where religious belief is so tied up with ethnic identity, the Islamic revival taking place in Bosnia poses a serious political challenge to the Yugoslav state.

Other Eastern European Muslim communities

Elsewhere in Eastern Europe, the Muslim communities are small. In Albania, the country's 1.5 million Muslims have no opportunities to practice their religious duties, openly, though there is evidence of clandestine observance. In Bulgaria, two-thirds of the Muslims are Turks, some of whom have already emigrated to Turkey. The remainder are Pomaks, Bulgarian-speaking Muslims, known to have few opportunities or freedom to practice their religious beliefs. The majority of the Albanian population living in Kosovo, one of the two autonomous provinces in Yugoslavia, is Muslim; there are few signs that Islamic fundamentalism has had any impact on the Muslim community there. Elsewhere in Eastern Europe, there are some 100,000 Muslims in Poland and Romania.

FURTHER READING

The *Central Asia Review*, a quarterly journal, published in Oxford, England, provides important information and analysis on Islam in the Soviet Union.

Akiner, Shirin. *Islamic Peoples of the Soviet Union.* London: Routledge and Kegan Paul, 1983.

Bennigsen, Alexandre, "Islam in the Soviet Union." *Soviet Jewish Affairs*, No. 2, 1979, pp 3–14.

Bennigsen, Alexandre, and Enders Wimbush, S. *Muslim National Communism in the Soviet Union.* Chicago: University of Chicago Press, 1979.

Bennigsen, Alexandre, and Lemercier-Quelquejay, Chantal. *Islam in the Soviet Union.* London: Pall Mall, 1967.

Ruthven, Malise. *Islam in the World.* Harmondsworth: Penguin, 1984.

JEWS IN EASTERN EUROPE AND THE SOVIET UNION

Before 1939, there were nearly 7.5 million Jews in Eastern Europe and the Soviet Union. Some 5.5 million perished under the Nazis. After 1945, thousands of Jews left for Israel diminishing the number even further. Today, just under 2.5 million Jews live in the Soviet bloc. Yet in spite of the small, almost insignificant number, anti-Semitism is not uncommon.

JEWS IN EASTERN EUROPE

Between 1948 and 1953, Stalin encouraged anti-Semitism, often equating Jewishness with "cosmopolitanism," which was regarded as irreconcilable with the goals of communist ideology and internationalism. Poland probably represents the most vivid case of persistent anti-Semitic activity. Pogroms took place at Kielce in 1946–47, when rumors of ritual murders sparked off anti-Semitic riots. Such events were not only confined to Poland. In Topolčany, Slovakia and in Kunmadaras in Hungary, pogroms took place in the late 1940s.

At the height of the Stalinist period latent anti-Semitic feelings were ventilated in some countries in Eastern Europe. Jews in Hungary, Czechoslovakia and Poland especially tended to hold fairly senior posts in the ruling Communist parties and other important official positions. This to some extent singled them out and made them easy scapegoats during the early 1950s when there took place in Eastern Europe a number of trials of alleged counterrevolutionary elements. The trial and execution of Rudolf Slánský in December 1952 demolished the myth that the Czech Jews had become assimilated. Hungary's trials took place in the late 1940s when Lászlo Rajk, former minister of the interior and at that time foreign minister, was tried. Anti-Semitism was officially fostered in the early 1950s when party secretary Mátyás Rákosi deported "capitalist" and other "unproductive" elements from Budapest to distant villages. It is estimated that Jews accounted for about one-third of the tens of thousands who were deported during this period.

In Romania, the hard core of the Romanian Communist party was made up of Soviet-trained Jewish activists. It was this faction that was ousted by party leader Gheorghiu-Dej in 1952, not because they were Jewish but because they were not "home" communists and had pro-Soviet inclinations. The aim of the Romanian Communist party leadership was to "Romanianize" the party, both in the leadership and at the grassroots level. By 1957, all the leading Jewish party officials had been purged. In 1959, the Romanian authorities issued a statement accusing "Israel and imperialist circles of unleashing a diversionist campaign trumpeting abroad the crude invention that there was a mass emigration of Jews to Israel. ..." By 1951, a third of Romania's Jewish community had emigrated, but no exit visas were allowed until 1959. Jews were often deported; many were imprisoned. And in 1959, dozens of Jews were tried on charges of treason. During the 1960s, there was some relaxation. Visas were granted to Jews wishing to emigrate. During the 1970s, there has been some evidence of anti-Semitism, expressed generally in the journals.

The Six-Day War sparked off a wave of anti-Semitism throughout Eastern Europe; the communist regimes had supported the Arabs in June 1967. In Poland it is known that public opinion was pro-Israel. After the Arab defeat, anti-Semitism was expressed quite openly by the Polish authorities, or at least among some factions within the leadership. There were anti-Semitic demonstrations in Warsaw in March 1968. And anti-Semitism became so intense that over half of Poland's Jewish community of 25,000 left the country. These included journalists and academics, writers and economists. Jewishness and Jewish identity remain a sensitive issue in Poland today (but not as sensitive as in Hungary), not only in terms of Poland's history but in terms of the relationship between the Jews and the country's large Catholic church, and between the Jews and the Communist party (at least immediately after World War II), and in terms of the reaction by the Polish authorities toward KOR (the Workers' Self-Defense Committee founded in 1976) and Solidarity.

If Poland's Jewish community is small, Czechoslovakia's community hardly exists. Yet the Six-Day War brought to the surface latent anti-Semitism. It was the Soviet-led invasion of Czechoslovakia in August 1968 that articulated these sentiments more forcibly. An anti-Zionist propaganda campaign, instigated by Moscow and disseminated by both East German and the Polish media, branded members of Alexander Dubček's presidium as Zionists. Those accused of Zionism included František Kriegel and Eduard Goldstücker. As the writer Pavel Kohout pointed out at the time, the Jewish population hardly exceeded 12,000.

Hungary's reaction to the Six-Day War was far more restrained. Diplomatic relations were broken off with Israel on June 12, 1967. The official controlled media in Hungary spelled out the Hungarian position vis-à-vis the Arabs. Kádár, at a speech given to a communist youth congress in June said that "we always reject racial theories and fought without reservation and with all our might during World War II against racial discrimination, persecution of Jews and the barbarism of Hitler fascism ... during past decades many Jewish people emigrated to Israel, also from Hungary; it is understandable that one's political attitude is disturbed if a brother ... of his lives in the country that committed the aggression ... but the stance on foreign policy must be based on principle." The Soviet Union permits practically no deviance on foreign policy matters within the bloc.

If Hungary has adopted a more pragmatic foreign policy, at least in terms of language, it has also given Hungary's Jewish community (80,000 to 100,000) access to synagogues, of which there are 30 in Budapest. Hungary has the only rabbinical seminary in Eastern Europe. There is also a Jewish senior secondary school in Budapest, a Jewish museum and a library. All these institutions are maintained by state funds, supplemented by voluntary contributions. Nevertheless, in spite of reasonable facilities for the country's small Jewish community, the whole question of what constitutes "Jewish identity," "Hungarian Jewry" and "Hungarian nationalism" has remained an extremely sensitive subject since World War II. Indeed, it was only in the early to mid-1970s that the question of Jewish identity was mooted. In the summer of 1975, the Hungarian politico-sociological monthly Valóság published a long article by György Száraz, entitled "On the Trail of a Prejudice," which dealt with anti-Semitism. Part of the reason for the sensitivity goes back to the Holocaust, when, toward the end of the war, in 1944, over 200,000 Jews were sent to the camps. The consequences were in many ways traumatic for the Jewish community. For one thing they could not regard Hungary as their homeland, since although during the 19th century Jews had adapted, within certain contexts, to Hungarian social life, the myth that they had in fact been successfully assimilated had now been destroyed.

It is precisely the problem of assimilation and identity that has formed part of the debate taking place in Hungary today. The debate is by no means open. Not only does it inevitably involve the relationship between Hungarian

Jews and ethnic Hungarians, but it also implicitly involves the question of Hungarian nationalism itself, a highly sensitive and complex topic addressed in contemporary Hungarian writing.

In contrast, Bulgaria seems almost exemplary in its treatment of the Jewish community. Bulgarians and Jews (mostly Sephardic) have coexisted for many centuries. The Jewish population has always been small—not exceeding one percent of the total population of 8,800,000. Although Bulgaria had close links with Germany during the 1930s, the Jews were protected. There were anti-Jewish laws in Bulgaria during this period, concentration camps, compulsory wearing of the Star of David, but few Bulgarian Jews lost their lives because of anti-Semitism. After the communist takeover, many thousands of Jews emigrated from Bulgaria, fearing a backlash arising from the Yugoslav-Soviet split. In 1948 alone, some 13,681 Jews left Bulgaria. Between 1918 and 1948 a total of only 7,057 Jews had left Bulgaria for Palestine. Between 1948 and 1956 nearly 90 percent of the Jewish community left Bulgaria. During the 1950s, several Jewish schools, banks, cultural centers and vocational training schools were closed. And in 1957, the Jewish communities were replaced by a new organization, the Social, Cultural and Educational Organization of Jews in the People's Republic of Bulgaria. Nevertheless, there is an Ecclesiastical Israelite Religious Council in Bulgaria that "fulfills religious functions." Three synagogues exist in the country—at Sofia, Samokov and Vidin. Religious rituals are observed. The remaining Jews who live in Bulgaria are integrated, prosperous and almost completely assimilated.

JEWS IN THE SOVIET UNION

A large-scale campaign directed against Jewish festivals began in the Soviet Union after 1917. The Jews were also deprived (like the Catholics) of any central organization. A widescale persecution of rabbis took place at the end of the 1920s. The Jewish community was subjected to far less persecution during the war, but between 1946 and 1953, the cultural policies introduced by Zhdanov were both chauvinist and anti-Semitic, attacking in particular Jewish traditions and customs.

The repression eased somewhat after Stalin's death in 1953. A seminary was legally opened in Moscow in 1956, the first time since the revolution; registration was, however, both limited and difficult. But during the 1960s, the Jewish religious communities were subjected to violent atheist attacks. Synagogues continued to be closed. For example, in 1917 there were about 5,000 functioning synagogues. By 1941 this figure had dropped to 1,011. There were 92 synagogues in 1964. Today, according to a Western publication, there are 69, 23 of which are located in the Caucasus and the Asiatic part of the Soviet Union.

Inevitably, many thousands of Jews have tried to emigrate. During the 1970s, between 2,000 and 4,000 Jews were emigrating every month. The figures reached a peak in 1979 when a monthly average of 4,000 was recorded. Since then, however, the Soviet authorities have refused visas to many wishing to leave. The "Refusniks"—those who do not receive permission to emigrate—are often intimidated or lose their jobs precisely because they want to leave the Soviet Union. In fact, two trends became noticeable in the late 1970s: not only was the number of emigrants decreasing, but the authorities adopted a tougher policy with respect to the activities of those who remained. For example, members of unofficial Jewish seminars, people such as Alexander Paritsky, have been interrogated or arrested. Jews who have given private lessons in Hebrew have been interviewed by the KGB and warned. It seemed, certainly during the late 1970s, that the authorities wanted not only to reduce the emigration but also to weaken if not stamp out the impulse behind Jewish emigration.

The lessening of Jewish emigration continued into the early 1980s. Indeed, figures published by Jewish organizations in the West showed, in December 1983, that the total number of Jews allowed to emigrate from the Soviet Union was the lowest for the 14 years since records for emigration figures were set up. During 1982, only 1,300 Soviet Jews were given permission to leave the country. The official Soviet explanation was that virtually all the Jews who wished to emigrate had in fact already done so. However, it is known that there are some 20,000 Jews who have applied for visas but have been refused. The other explanation is that in 1980 new regulations were introduced by the Soviet authorities, under the terms of which those wishing to emigrate had to have an invitation to Israel from a parent or a child. Hitherto, it had been simply enough to have a distant relative living in Israel. The new regulations obviously made it easier for the Soviet authorities to reject many applications. The 1980 regulations may have indicated, too, that the Soviet Union was gaining little in terms of international prestige by allowing so many Jews to emigrate during the 1970s; and that with the breakdown of détente, there was equally little to be gained by allowing more Jews to leave the country.

Restrictions on Jewish activities and reductions of the number of those allowed to emigrate continued throughout the Andropov period (November 1982–February 1984) and in the early stages of the Chernenko period. Figures released by the Intergovernmental Committee for Migration (ICM) reported in November 1984 that Jewish emigration from the Soviet Union fell to an all-time monthly low of just 29 people in October 1984. In the first 10 months of 1984 the Soviet Union had allowed 709 Jewish citizens to leave the country. The record number of departures had been set in 1979 when some 51,330 Jews were allowed to leave the country. The latest figures (November 1984) are the lowest since 1971.

The restrictions on emigration have been coupled with increasing propaganda against the Jews. In March 1983, an Anti-Zionist Committee was set up. The leaders of the committee nevertheless insisted at the time that the struggle against Zionism in the Soviet press was not anti-Semitic and that the "Jewish question" was not an issue in the Soviet Union today.

FURTHER READING

Judaism:
Soviet Jewish Affairs, a quarterly journal published in London, is indispensable.

It covers both the Soviet Union and Eastern Europe, providing information, history and analysis. See also:

Lendvai, Paul. *Anti-Semitism in Eastern Europe*. London: Macdonald, 1971.

Shafir, Michael. "The Men of the Archangel Revisited: Anti-Semitic Formations among Communist Romania's Intellectuals." *Studies in Comparative Communism*, Vol. XVI, no. 3, 1983, pp. 223–43.

Szafar, Tadeusz. "Anti-Semitism, a Trusty Weapon," in A. Brumberg, ed., *Poland: Genesis of a Revolution*. New York: Vintage, 1983.

Vago, Bela, ed. *Jewish Assimilation in Modern Times*. London: Westview, 1981.

CONCLUSION: THE FAILURE OF SECULARIZATION?

The communist takeover of Eastern Europe after World War II set out to destroy those areas of autonomy—education, the legal system, the judiciary and religion as well—that had existed in the region before the war. In destroying those autonomous or semiautonomous social structures, the communist regimes set out to exercise power based largely on coercion, motivated in part by the ideological demands of Marxism-Leninism.

Those Marxist-Leninist demands also necessitated the destruction of religious *belief*, because, in political terms, religion challenged the monopoly of power held by the ruling communist parties. Religious belief posed a threat in ideological terms as well, for within the framework of Marxism-Leninism, it blocked the way to the successful unfolding of the revolution. Religion was regarded as a "pseudoscience," a set of beliefs that were false; the perpetuation of that kind of false consciousness only inhibited the progress of the revolution, and of course inhibited the realization of true consciousness.

One of the ways in which the communist regimes sought to stamp out religious belief was through coercion, the eventual aim being to secularize society. That proved rather difficult. For one thing, the role of religion in Eastern Europe, was, in varying degrees, part of the region's political culture; for another, although the communist regimes attempted to destroy these autonomous values and structures, they did not replace them in any substantial way. The language of Marxism-Leninism was to a large part based on rhetoric, backed by a strong repressive apparatus. True, in the 1960s and 1970s, the rhetoric had been replaced in a number of ways. Increasingly, the communist regimes have appealed to the individual/national characteristics of their respective countries in an attempt to gain some measure of legitimacy.

The complex program of modernization and industrialization did not, contrary to expectations, destroy religious belief—a trend characteristic of Western European societies. Nor did rapid urbanization, indoctrination, propaganda, censorship, or communist-controlled mass media weaken adherence to religious belief in such a way that the communists could claim that society had been successfully secularized. Indeed, it is precisely the persistence of religious belief and adherence to ritual and ceremony that must baffle some Western and indeed Eastern European observers as well.

The explanations for this persistence of belief are too complex to be dealt with in detail here. Briefly, however, two points are worth mentioning.

First, because the communist regimes destroyed all other means by which people could articulate their needs, religion, or at least the churches (what remained of them in terms of structures), served to fill that gap; and forced into a not entirely suitable role, religion assumed a place in society that has brought it into the political domain. Poland is a classic example; here, the Catholic church not only became closely identified with Polish nationalism, but assumed the role of mediator between state and society, the one invested with almost absolute power, the other denied all access to the political process. As a mediator, the Polish Catholic church has gained certain concessions: permission to build churches, access to the media. But this also meant that the state could to some extent influence the church, as happened during the post-Solidarity period. Society has leaned greatly on the church as mediator, not only because the church, however indirectly, could articulate society's needs, but because the church, particularly under the late Cardinal Wyszyński, commanded considerable moral and spiritual respect from society. It has become a focus for Polish society and a force within Polish politics that delays the process of secularization. In effect, the church in Poland has become an institutionalized alternative to communist rule.

The other churches in Eastern Europe, for various political and social reasons, have not assumed the role or power of Poland's Catholic church. Nevertheless, religious belief has persisted. Religion as a set of values has come to play an increasing role especially for the younger generation, some of whom have rejected the materialism, the atheistic propaganda and the rhetoric of the communist regimes. And it is precisely because the rhetoric has lost all meaning that the religious revival taking place in Czechoslovakia today is motivated by a desire for an inner spiritualism—an inner set of values based on human dignity and personal religious experiences. Indeed, several Czechoslovak publications have reported on the attraction of the country's youth toward religion.

Clearly the persistence of religious belief has weakened the communists' claim to complete monopoly over people's lives. Equally, the way in which power has been exercised and industrialization carried out, the way in which civil society has been repressed and propaganda organized have only served to "desecularize" society. The revival of religion in Eastern Europe over the past 10 years seems to confirm this view.

INDEX

ABM (antiballistic missiles), 219; Treaty (1972), 219
Abortions, 523, 524
Abramov, F., 237
Abrasimov, Pyotr, 342
Absenteeism, 499, 500
Aczél, György, 74, 559
Aden, used by Soviet Navy, 283
Adventist churches, see Seventh Day Adventists
Advocates, 537
Ady, Endre, 550
Afghanistan: Muslims, 258, 604; Soviet invasion and War, 96, 114, 136, 216, 256, 284, 372–73, 604, 606
Ağca, Mehmet Ali, 26
Agrarian Union (Bulgaria), 191
Agriculture, 180, 181, 424–44; agro-industrial integration, 426–27; capital investment, table, 432; collectivization, 424–25, 427–31; crop production and growth, table, 436; drift to the towns, 181, 443, 501; Eastern Europe, 427–31; fertilizers, table, 432; Kolkhozes, 425–28; labor shortages, 443; livestock, 435–37; mechanization, 433, 438; private sector, 438–42; production results, 431–39; RAPOS, 426–27; shortages, 437–39; Sovkhozes, 425, 426; tractors, table, 432; yields, 433–35
Air defense (Soviet Union), 221
Air transport, 470; in Soviet north, 487
Akhamatova, Anna, 555
Akhromeyev, Marshal, 224
Aksyonov, Vasily, 213, 545
Albania, 14–23; Albanian people, 288; break with Soviet Union, 293, 294; and China, 16, 17, 197; Communism, 16; constitution, 22–23; defense, 17; degree of autonomy, 250; economy, 17–19; education, 20–21; electricity, 471; geography, 14; Great Revolutionary Action campaign (1966), 17; and Greece, 16–17, 200, 295; high birthrate, 307; and Italy, 17, 200; leaves

COMECON, 484; map, 15; mass media, 21–22; mineral resources, 484; minority in Yugoslavia, 306–08, 352, 361–62; National Front, 248; nationalism, 295; party state linkage, 299; People's Republic, 16; population, 14, 16; railways, 460, 471; recent history, 16–17; religion, 565–67, 592; and Romania, 198; single-party system, 248; social welfare, 19–20; and Soviet Union, 16, 17, 189, 190, 197, 293, 294; Stalinism, 8, 16, 17; travel in, 454; Warsaw Pact, withdrawal from 16, 200; working class, 507; and Yugoslavia, 136, 200, 295–96
Alexander II, Tsar, 233
Alexander III, Tsar, 233
Alexandrov, Chudomir, 33
Alfa class submarines, 225
Algeria, oil from, 485
Alia, Ramiz, 17, 23
Aliyev, Geidar A., 129
All-Russian Christian Social Union for the Liberation of the People (VSKhSON), 239
All-Russian Society for the Conservation of Nature, 238
All-Russian Society for the Preservation of Historical and Cultural Monuments, 238
All Union Council of Evangelical Christians and Baptists (Soviet Union), 602
Alma-Ata, 110
Amalrik, Andrei, 259, 549
Andrei, Stefan, 103
Andropov, Yuri, 113, 130, 131, 181, 186, 211, 239, 242, 246, 249, 256, 342, 389, 422, 517, 549, 613; and industrial planning, 398, 399
Angola, Soviet Union and, 284
Anti-Semitism, see Jews
Antonessu, Ion, 94
Apatite, production in Soviet North, 490
APKs (agro-industrial complexes) (Bulgaria), 428–30
Arctic Institute, Leningrad, 491
Arctic Ocean area, 487; offshore islands, 486